Lecture Notes in Computer Science 8489

Commenced Publication in 1973
Founding and Former Series Editors:
Gerhard Goos, Juris Hartmanis, and Jan van Leeuwen

Gianfranco Ciardo   Ekkart Kindler (Eds.)

Application and Theory of Petri Nets and Concurrency

35th International Conference, PETRI NETS 2014
Tunis, Tunisia, June 23-27, 2014
Proceedings

 Springer

Volume Editors

Gianfranco Ciardo
Iowa State University
Department of Computer Science
226 Atanasoff Hall, Ames, IA 50011, USA
E-mail: ciardo@iastate.edu

Ekkart Kindler
Technical University of Denmark
DTU Compute
Richard Pedersens Plads, 2800 Kgs. Lyngby, Denmark
E-mail: ekki@dtu.dk

ISSN 0302-9743   e-ISSN 1611-3349
ISBN 978-3-319-07733-8   e-ISBN 978-3-319-07734-5
DOI 10.1007/978-3-319-07734-5
Springer Cham Heidelberg New York Dordrecht London

Library of Congress Control Number: 2014939850

LNCS Sublibrary: SL 1 – Theoretical Computer Science and General Issues

Typesetting: Camera-ready by author, data conversion by Scientific Publishing Services, Chennai, India

Printed on acid-free paper

Springer is part of Springer Science+Business Media (www.springer.com)

Preface

This volume constitutes the proceedings of the 35th International Conference on Application and Theory of Petri Nets and Concurrency (Petri Nets 2014). This series of conferences serves as an annual meeting place to discuss progress in the field of Petri nets and related models of concurrency. They provide a forum for researchers to present and discuss both applications and theoretical developments in this area. Novel tools and substantial enhancements to existing tools can also be presented. This year, the satellite program of the conference comprised four workshops, a Petri net course, some advanced tutorials, and a doctoral symposium.

Petri Nets 2014 was co-located with the Application of Concurrency Theory to System Design Conference (ACSD 2014). Both were organized by the Computer Science and Communication Departments of Tunis El Manar University (ENIT), Manouba University (ENSI), and Carthage University (INSAT) and took place in Tunis, Tunisia, June 23–27, 2014. We would like to express our deepest thanks to the Organizing Committee chaired by Kamel Barkaoui for the time and effort invested in the local organization of the conference.

This year, 48 papers were submitted to Petri Nets 2014, including 39 full papers and nine tool papers. The authors of the submitted papers represented 25 different countries. We thank all the authors who submitted papers. Each paper was reviewed by at least four referees. The Program Committee (PC) meeting took place electronically, using the EasyChair conference system for the paper selection process. The PC selected 19 papers (15 regular papers and four tool papers) for presentation. After the conference, some authors were invited to publish an extended version of their contribution in the *Fundamenta Informaticae* journal.

We thank the PC members and other reviewers for their careful and timely evaluation of the submissions before the meeting, and the fruitful discussions during the electronic meeting. The Springer LNCS team and the EasyChair system provided excellent support in the preparation of this volume. We are also grateful to the invited speakers for their contribution: Christel Baier (Energy-Utility Analysis Using Probabilistic Model Checking), Matthieu Latapy (Complex Networks and Link Streams for the Empirical Analysis of Large Software), Kurt Lautenbach (Propagation Nets), and W. Murray Wonham, who delivered the Distinguished Carl Adam Petri Lecture (Supervisory Control Synthesis for Discrete-Event Systems).

June 2014

Gianfranco Ciardo
Ekkart Kindler

Organization

Steering Committee

W. van der Aalst, The Netherlands
J. Billington, Australia
G. Ciardo, USA
J. Desel, Germany
S. Donatelli, Italy
S. Haddad, France
K. Hiraishi, Japan
K. Jensen, Denmark
J. Kleijn, The Netherlands
F. Kordon, France

M. Koutny, UK (Chair)
L.M. Kristensen, Norway
C. Lin, China
W. Penczek, Poland
L. Pomello, Italy
W. Reisig, Germany
G. Rozenberg, The Netherlands
M. Silva, Spain
A. Valmari, Finland
A. Yakovlev, UK

Program Committee

Hassane Alla	Université de Grenoble, France
Kamel Barkaoui	Conservatoire National des Arts et Métiers, France
Marco Beccuti	Università degli Studi di Torino, Italy
Luca Bernardinello	Università di Milano-Bicocca, Italy
Didier Buchs	University of Geneva, Switzerland
Piotr Chrzastowski-Wachtel	Warsaw University, Poland
Gianfranco Ciardo	Iowa State University, USA
José-Manuel Colom	Universidad de Zaragoza, Spain
Jörg Desel	Fernuniversität in Hagen, Germany
Raymond Devillers	Université Libre de Bruxelles, Belgium
Maria Pia Fanti	Politecnico di Bari, Italy
João M. Fernandes	Universidade do Minho, Portugal
Henri Hansen	Tampere University of Technology, Finland
Monika Heiner	Brandenburg University of Technology, Germany
Joost-Pieter Katoen	RWTH Aachen University, Germany
Victor Khomenko	Newcastle University, UK
Ekkart Kindler	Technical University of Denmark, Denmark
Hanna Klaudel	Université d'Evry-Val d'Essonne, France
Jetty Kleijn	Leiden University, The Netherlands
Ranko Lazic	University of Warwick, UK
Niels Lohmann	University of Rostock, Germany
Irina Lomazova	Higher School of Economics, Moscow, Russia
Andrew Miner	Iowa State University, USA

Madhavan Mukund	Chennai Mathematical Institute, India
Artem Polyvyanyy	Queensland University of Technology, Australia
Wolfgang Reisig	Humboldt-Universität zu Berlin, Germany
Riadh Robbana	Carthage University, Tunisia
Stefan Schwoon	ENS Cachan and Inria, France
Carla Seatzu	Università di Cagliari, Italy
Antti Valmari	Tampere University of Technology, Finland
Michael Westergaard	Technische Universiteit Eindhoven, The Netherlands

Organizing Committee

Kamel Barkaoui (Chair), France

Workshops and Tutorials Chairs

Jörg Desel, Germany   Serge Haddad, France

Tools Exhibition Chair

Mohamed Khalgui, Tunisia

Publicity Chair

Kaïs Klai, France

Additional Reviewers

Akshay, S.
Balbo, Gianfranco
Barros, Joao Paulo
Bashkin, Vladimir
Ben Hfaiedh, Imen
Bergenthum, Robin
Blätke, Mary-Ann
Bonsangue, Marcello
Bruintjes, Harold
Cabasino, Maria Paola
Carmona, Josep
Chatain, Thomas
Colange, Maximilien
Cordero, Francesca

Costa, Aniko
Dehnert, Christian
Di Giusto, Cinzia
Dojer, Norbert
Dzikowski, Raffael
Ferigato, Carlo
Geeraerts, Gilles
Geldenhuys, Jaco
Gierds, Christian
Golubcovs, Stanislavs
Gomes, Luis
Haddad, Serge
Herajy, Mostafa
Hoogeboom, Hendrik Jan

Distinguished Carl Adam Petri Lecture

Supervisory Control Synthesis
for Discrete-Event Systems

W.M. Wonham

Systems Control Group
ECE Department
University of Toronto

Abstract. In this lecture we first introduce supervisory control theory for discrete-event systems (DES) in a framework of finite automata and regular languages, with emphasis on the criteria of nonblocking and maximal permissiveness. Also stressed is the importance of control modularity and transparency. Turning to Petri Nets (PN), we indicate how the counterpart control design problem can be posed and (in many but not all cases) solved using integer linear programming. Finally we discuss the feasibility of a "DES transform" approach by which the PN problem is first converted to a DES problem, and the DES solution converted back to a PN implementation. Here we point out several interesting issues for further research.

Table of Contents

Tool Papers

Erratum

Propagation Nets

Kurt Lautenbach

University of Koblenz-Landau, Universitätsstr. 1, 56070 Koblenz, Germany
laut@uni-koblenz.de
http://www.uni-koblenz.de/~ag-pn

Abstract. This paper is to introduce *Propagation nets* as a kind of Petri nets whose flowing objects are uncertain values. The approach is influenced by Bayesian networks (J. Pearl [10]) and probabilistic Horn abduction (D. Pool [12]). In contrast to Bayesian networks, the algorithms are not "hidden" but part of the nets. The net structure together with a simple firing rule allows uncertain reasoning in backward and forward direction, where backward and forward direction are dual to each other in terms of a Petri net duality. Propagation nets allow to deal with several kinds of uncertainties. This is shown for probabilities, intervals and fuzzy numbers.

1 Introduction

This paper is to introduce *propagation nets* which are intended for transporting (row) tuples of uncertain elements as for example probabilities, intervals, fuzzy numbers. Propagation nets (*PNs* for short) have a transition boundary. The input boundary transitions put a-priori-tuples on the net which is initially empty; the output boundary transitions take a-posteriori-tuples from the net which is finally empty again. So, the empty marking is going to be reproduced which points to t-invariants [1,2].

Except for the output boundary transitions all transitions have exactly one output place; i.e. logically speaking, every transition represents a *Horn clause* [4]. This relation to propositional logic will play an important part in the following.

To all inner (*non-boundary*) transitions matrices are assigned. When a transition fires, the cartesian product of the row tuples on the input places is multiplied from the left by its matrix. The resulting tuple is put on *the* output place and the input places are emptied.

So, the firing rule is a very simple one which is entirely in agreement to the linear nature of Petri nets.

A running example from the *maritime risk analysis* will be used to introduce the essential concepts and to show the way PNs are used.

When working with PNs forward and backward reasoning is possible. Forward reasoning takes place in so-called *dependency nets* (*DNs for short*) which will be defined as "overlays" of overlapping *Horn nets* [4]. Backward reasoning takes place in a dual form of the DNs [2,8].

G. Ciardo and E. Kindler (Eds.): PETRI NETS 2014, LNCS 8489, pp. 1–19, 2014.

The main concepts arising in the course of dualizing are *transition tokens* and *non-events*. A PN, finally, is a combination of a DN and its dual.

This paper is organized as follows.

A short introduction into the *main example* is given in chapter 2. The 3rd chapter is dedicated to *dependency nets* (DNs). They are the part in the propagation nets (PNs) that describes the dependency structure of the uncertain variables and operates the forward calculations. Compared to *Bayesian networks* (BNs) they perform, for the special case of probabilities, the calculations in arc direction. In contrast to BNs the algorithms are not hidden but follow the simple firing rule mentioned above. The *duality of Petri nets with markings* is introduced in chapter 4. Finally, in chapter 5 *propagation nets* (PNs) are defined as a combination of DNs and their dualization - and that for probabilities, intervals, and fuzzy numbers.

I am greatly indebted to Andreas Schmidt for his excellent assistance.

2   Running Example

The example outlines a modern scenario of offshore installations for oil production [14,15,13]. This technique brings three sorts of ships into operation, in particular to avoid building fixed pipelines if this is not profitable. It concerns

- FPSO-units (Floating, Production, Storage, Offloading)
- support vessels for the FPSO-units, and
- shuttle tankers.

The FPSO-units (for example rebuilt tankers) are anchoring near some oil well (e.g. a platform) to which they are connected by flexible pipelines. They take in the mixture of crude oil, gas, water, and sand. They separate these ingredients and store crude oil and gas.

The support vessels serve to supply and maintain the FPSO-units, and the shuttle tankers take crude oil and gas to the nearest docks.

The pipe connection between FPSO-unit and shuttle tanker is established by means of the so-called *bow loading*. First, a hawser is shut from the FPSO-unit to the shuttle. Then a flexible pipeline is dragged by the hawser from the FPSO-unit to the shuttle.

To master the bow loading, a specific training in simulators is essential. The maritime risk with the offshore production is due to the danger of collisions between FPSO-units and support vessels or shuttle tankers. Consequences of such collisions are often personnel losses, disastrous environmental pollutions, and major damages of the ships. The technique of tandem (off-)loading involves considerable risks because of the close proximity of two big ships. Whatever the collision reasons are, 80% are due to human errors (according to reliable estimates).

Non-predictable and uncertain events play a part within maritime risk analysis. Uncertainty is differentiated in *vagueness* and *randomness*. Vagueness results from inaccurate observations. In maritime analysis this is mainly due to inaccurate and unreliable measuring instruments. To deal formally with problems like that, one makes use of fuzzy reasoning approaches. Randomness arises by reason of non-predictable events and is above all represented by probability theory.

In our example, there are six crucial points: *human errors* (X), *adverse weather* (Y), *shuttle tanker position* (Z), *malfunction of support vessel* (V), *collision with FPSO-unit* (U), and *personnel injury/loss* (W). Their dependency structure is shown by the Bayesian network of Figure 1.

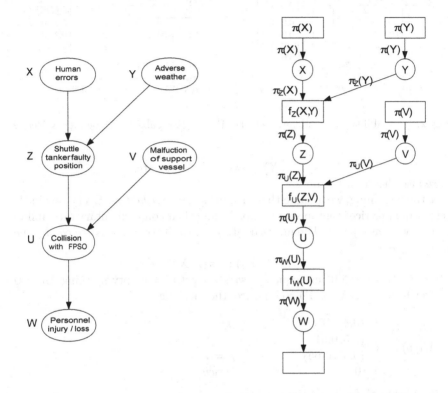

Fig. 1. The Bayesian network (on the left) and the corresponding dependency net

A Petri net version of the example will be used for probabilistic and fuzzy logic analyses. It supports the *forward calculation* of the uncertain variable W given the a-priori values of X, Y, V, as well as the *backward calculations* from W to X, Y, V to see the tendential change of the input values given a desired value of W.

3 Dependency Nets

3.1 The Example

Figure 2 shows the quantities which correspond to the dependency structure of Figure 1. The matrices corresponding to the inner transitions *with the same names* and the prior values of the vectors

$f_Z(X,Y)$		Z	
X	Y	1	2
1	1	0.65	0.35
1	2	0.2	0.8
2	1	0.2	0.8
2	2	0.05	0.95

$\pi(X) = (0.4, 0.6)$
$\pi(Y) = (0.5, 0.5)$
$\pi(V) = (0.35, 0.65)$

$f_Z(X,Y)$		Z	
X	Y	1	2
1	1	0.65	0.35
1	2	0.2	0.8
2	1	0.2	0.8
2	2	0.05	0.95

$\pi(X) = (0.4, 0.0)$
$\pi(Y) = (0.5, 0.5)$
$\pi(V) = (0.35, 0.65)$

$f_W(U)$	W	
U	1	2
1	0.75	0.25
2	0.002	0.998

$f_U(Z,V)$		U	
Z	V	1	2
1	1	0.25	0.75
1	2	0.2	0.8
2	1	0.2	0.8
2	2	0.05	0.95

$f_W(U)$	W	
U	1	2
1	0.75	0.25
2	0.002	0.998

$f_U(Z,V)$		U	
Z	V	1	2
1	1	0.25	0.75
1	2	0.2	0.8
2	1	0.2	0.8
2	2	0.05	0.95

$\pi(Z) = (0.245, 0.755)$
$\pi(U) = (0.1307, 0.8693)$
$\pi(W) = (0.0997, 0.9003)$

$\pi(X_1 Z) = (0.17, 0.23)$
$\pi(X_1 U) = (0.06055, 0.33945)$
$\pi(X_1 W) = (0.0460914, 0.3539086)$

Fig. 2. (Probability) Dependency Nets 1   **Fig. 3.** (Probability) Dependency Nets 2

$$\pi(X) = (\pi(X_1), \pi(X_2)), \text{ etc.}$$

are also shown in Figure 2.

At the beginning, we assume that all values are *probabilities*. Every row in the vectors and matrices contains a probability and their complementary probability. So, all row sums equal 1. The matrices attached to the transitions are *conditional probability tables*:

$$f_Z(X,Y)) := \pi(Z|XY), \text{ etc.}$$

In order to show a firing sequence, we start with the empty marking $M_0 = \mathbf{0}$. After firing of $\pi(X), \pi(Y), \pi(V)$ once, the marking is

$$M_1(p) := \begin{cases} (0.4, 0, 6) & \text{if } p = X \\ (0.5, 0.5) & \text{if } p = Y \\ (0.35, 0.65) & \text{if } p = V \\ 0 & \text{otherwise} \end{cases}$$

After firing of $f_Z(X,Y)$ the marking is

$$M_2(p) := \begin{cases} (0.245, 0.755) & \text{if } p = Z \\ (0.35, 0.65) & \text{if } p = V \\ 0 & \text{otherwise} \end{cases}$$

In detail: according to the firing rule,

the cartesian product $\pi(X) \times \pi(Y)$ of the vectors on the input places X and Y multiplied by the corresponding matrix $f_Z(X,Y)$ is put on the output place Z, and the input places are emptied.

$$\pi(X) \times \pi(Y) = (\pi(X_1), \pi(X_2)) \times (\pi(Y_1), \pi(Y_2)) = (0.4, 0.6) \times (0.5, 0.5)$$
$$= (0.4 \cdot 0.5, 0.4 \cdot 0.5, 0.6 \cdot 0.5, 0.6 \cdot 0.5) = (0.2, 0.2, 0.3, 0.3)$$

$$M_2(Z) = (\pi(X) \times \pi(Y)) \cdot f_Z(X,Y)$$

$$= (0.2, 0.2, 0.3, 0.3) \cdot \begin{pmatrix} 0.65 & 0.35 \\ 0.2 & 0.8 \\ 0.2 & 0.8 \\ 0.05 & 0.95 \end{pmatrix}$$

$$= (0.245, 0.755)$$

Similarly:

$$M_3(p) := \begin{cases} (0.1307, 0.8693) & \text{if } p = U \\ 0 & \text{otherwise} \end{cases}$$

$$M_4(p) := \begin{cases} (0.0997, 0.9003) & \text{if } p = W \\ 0 & \text{otherwise} \end{cases}$$

$$M_5(p) := M_0 = \mathbf{0}.$$

The last translation (without a name) is not really necessary for the calculation of $\pi(W)$. But it completes the net to a t-invariant which simplifies the search for DNs and firing sequences in large nets.

In the following we will need the probability $\pi(X_1|W_1)$. The calculation by means of the DN is nearly the same, apart from the fact that we have to start with $\pi(X) = (0.4, 0.0)$ and that now

$$(\pi(X) \times \pi(Y)) \cdot f_Z(X, Y) \text{ equals } \pi(X_1 Z) \text{ etc.}$$

Finally, we get $\pi(X_1|W_1) = \frac{\pi(X_1 W_1)}{\pi(W_1)} = \frac{0.0460914}{0.09974864} = 0.4621$

For details see figure 3. The value of $\pi(W_1)$ is somewhat more precise than in figure 2.

3.2   Preliminaries

In this section, I want to briefly repeat own approaches to combine Petri nets with linear algebra and propositional logic in order to prepare the general definition of DNs.

Definition 1. (invariants [1,2])
Let i be a place vector and j a column vector of a p/t-net $N=(S,T,F,W)$;
    i is a place invariant (p-invariant)   *iff $i \neq \mathbf{0}$ and $i^t \cdot [N] = \mathbf{0}^t$*
j is a transition invariant (t-invariant) *iff $j \neq \mathbf{0}$ and $[N] \cdot j = \mathbf{0}$.*   □

Proposition 1. ([1,2])
If σ is a firing sequence which reproduces a marking M, then the firing vector $\overline{\sigma}$ is a t-invariant;

for all follower markings M of the initial marking M_0 and all p-invariants i
$i^t \cdot M = i^t \cdot M_0$ *holds.*   □

Definition 2. (net forms of invariants)
The net form $N_i = (P_i, T_i, F_i, W_i)$ of a p-invariant i *is defined by*

$$P_i := \|i\|$$
$$T_i := {}^\bullet P_i \cup P_i^\bullet$$
$$F_i := F \cap ((P_i \times T_i) \cup (T_i \times P_i))$$
$$W_i \text{ is the restriction of } W \text{ to } F_i.$$

The net form $N_j = (P_j, T_j, F_j, W_j)$ of a t-invariant j *is defined by*

$$T_j := \|j\|$$
$$P_j := {}^\bullet T_j \cup T_j^\bullet$$
$$F_j := F \cap ((P_j \times T_j) \cup (T_j \times P_j))$$
$$W_j \text{ is the restriction of } W \text{ to } F_j.$$

$\|i\|$ *is the set* $\{p | i(p) \neq 0\}$, $\|j\|$ *is the set* $\{t | j(t) \neq 0\}$ □

The following approach of combining p/t-nets and *propositional logic* originates from [4].

Definition 3. (canonical p/t-net representation)
Let α be a proposition logical formula in conjunctive normal form (CNF-formula)
and let $N_\alpha = (P_\alpha, T_\alpha, F_\alpha)$ be a p/t-net whose arc labels are equal to 1;
N_α *is the* canonical p/t-net representation of α *iff*
$$S_\alpha = \mathbf{A}(\alpha) \text{ (set of atoms of } \alpha) \text{ and}$$
$$T_\alpha = \mathbf{C}(\alpha) \text{ (set of clauses of } \alpha)$$
$$\text{for all } \tau = \neg a_1 \vee ... \vee \neg a_m \vee b_1 \vee ... \vee b_n \in \mathbf{C}(\alpha)$$
$$where\{a_1, ..., a_m, b_1, ..., b_n\} \subseteq \mathbf{A}(\alpha)$$
$$F_\alpha \text{ is determined by } {}^\bullet\tau \{a_1, ..., a_m\}, \tau^\bullet \{b_1, ..., b_n\}   □$$

Example 1. The DN of figure 1 can be considered the net representation of the formula
$$\alpha = X \wedge Y \wedge V \wedge (\neg X \vee \neg Y \vee Z) \wedge (\neg Z \vee \neg V \vee U) \wedge (\neg U \vee W) \wedge \neg W$$

□

The p/t-net representations are called *canonical* because all names of the places are atoms, i.e. the are non-negated.

Definition 4. (non-canonical p/t-net representation)
Let $N_\alpha = (S_\alpha, T_\alpha, F_\alpha)$ be the canonical p/t-net representation of a CNF-formula;
$N_\alpha^* = (S_\alpha^*, T_\alpha^*, F_\alpha^*)$ *is a* non-canonical p/t-net representation *of α iff*
$$\text{for at least one place } a \in S_\alpha$$
$$(\neg a) \in S_\alpha^* \text{ with } {}^\bullet(\neg a) = a^\bullet \text{ and } (\neg a)^\bullet = {}^\bullet a \text{ holds in } N_\alpha^*.$$

□

Example 2. (canonical and non-canonical p/t-net representation)   □

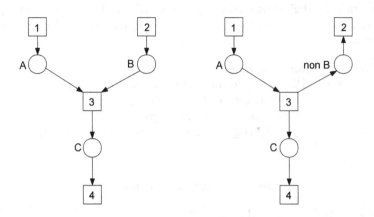

Fig. 4. A canonical and a non-canonical p/t-net representation of the formula
$\alpha = A \wedge B \wedge (\neg A \vee \neg B \vee C) \wedge (\neg C)$

Definition 5. (Horn nets)

A clause κ is a Horn clause iff it contains at most one non-negated literal (atom);
A CNF-formula is a Horn formula iff its clauses are Horn clauses;
The canonical p/t-net representation of a Horn formula α is a Horn net.

□

Lemma 1. *A Horn formula α is contradictory iff in its canonical p/t-net representation N_α the empty marking is reproducible.*   □

The reproducibility of the empty marking implies that N_α is transition bounded.

Example 3. (continued)
The CNF formula α in example 2 is contradictory, and the empty marking is reproducible in N_α. The reproducing firing sequence can be interpreted as a proof for C.   □

Theorem 1. (reproduction theorem)
Let $N = (S, T, F)$ be a p/t-net whose arc labels equal 1;
the empty marking is reproducible in N iff there exists a non-negative t-invariant R whose net form N_R neither contains a trap nor a co-trap.

Proof: see [3]. □

At the end of this section, we come to the definition of the *dependency net (DN)*. Even though in the following the inscriptions of DNs will be rather varying, they don't play a role concerning the structure. So, we may define DNs on the level of p/t-nets.

Definition 6. (dependency net)

A dependency net (DN) *is a p/t-net N=(S,T,F) where the following holds:*

N has a transition boundary

N is connected and circle free

$$\sum_{k\in(P\cup T)} ((|{}^{\bullet}k| \geq 2 \Rightarrow k \in T) \wedge (|k^{\bullet}| \geq 2 \Rightarrow k \in S))$$

□

DNs are *overlays* of Horn nets with transition boundary.

Example 4. (Overlay of two Horn nets, figure 5)

The two Horn formulas and Horn nets are

$a\wedge b\wedge(\neg a\vee\neg b\vee d)\wedge(\neg d\vee g)\wedge\neg g,$ the corresponding net has the transitions P,Q,U,V,X

$a\wedge b\wedge(\neg a\vee\neg b\vee d)\wedge(\neg d\vee h)\wedge\neg h,$ the corresponding net has the transitions P,Q,U,W,Y.

□

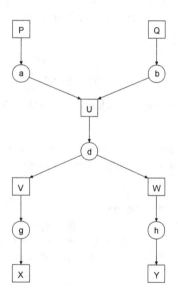

Fig. 5. Overlay of two Horn nets

Remarks

(1) It is easy to realize that Horn nets with transition boundary are net forms of t-invariants and so they are simple DNs.

(2) If it is necessary to distinguish the DNs from the versions defined below, we will call them *probability dependency nets*.

3.3 Interval Dependency Nets

The next objects we want to observe on their run through the DNs are *intervals*. They are used if a value is not exactly known (e.g. a probability), but an interval is known which definitely contains this value. We will approach the intervals by *exchanging the number calculations by the interval arithmetic* operation by operation.

Definition 7. (interval arithmetic)
If in definition 8 (arithmetic of triangular numbers)
  the marks "appr." are omitted, and
  in all triangular numbers $[a, b, c]$ *the middle entries are omitted,*
then the reduced elements $[a, c]$ *can be interpreted as* closed real intervals *and the rules remain correct.*

□

Figures 7 and 8 are the interval DNs corresponding to the DNs in figures 2 and 3. Of course the calculations are more extensive in the case of intervals, but the idea is elementary: *numbers have to be exchanged by intervals and number operations by the corresponding interval operations.*

Remarks

(1) If necessary, we will speak of *interval dependency nets*.

(2) We will realize that the probability values $\pi(Z), \pi(U), \pi(W), \pi(XZ_1)$, $\pi(XU_1), \pi(XW_1)$ are contained in the intervals with the same names.

3.4 Fuzzy Number Dependency Nets

Next, we want to deal with *triangular* (fuzzy) numbers. For space reasons we will skip *trapezoidal* (fuzzy) numbers (also called *fuzzy intervals*) to deal with which is very similar to handle triangular numbers.

Definition 8. (arithmetic of triangular numbers)
Let $[a_1, b_1, c_1]$ *and* $[a_2, b_2, c_2]$ *be two triangular numbers where* $a_i \leq b_i \leq c_i$ *are non-negative reals,* $i \in \{1, 2\}$;
$$[a_1, b_1, c_1] + [a_2, b_2, c_2] := [a_1 + a_2, b_1 + b_2, c_1 + c_2]$$

for reals $\alpha \geq 0$ *and* $\beta \leq 0$:
$$\alpha[a_1, b_1, c_1] := [\alpha a_1, \alpha b_1, \alpha c_1]$$
$$\beta[a_1, b_1, c_1] := [\beta c_1 \beta b_1, \beta a_1] \text{ hold;}$$
particularly for $\beta = -1$:
$$-[a_1, b_1, c_1] := [-c_1, -b_1, -a_1];$$

$$[a_1, b_1, c_1] - [a_2, b_2, c_2] := [a_1, b_1, c_1] + (-[a_2, b_2, c_2])$$
$$= [a_1, b_1, c_1] + [-c_2, -b_2, -a_2] = [a_1 - c_2, b_1 - b_2, c_1 - a_2]$$

particularly for non-negative reals:

$$[a_1, b_1, c_1] \cdot [a_2, b_2, c_2] \underbrace{=}_{appr.} [a_1 \cdot a_2, b_1 \cdot b_2, c_1 \cdot c_2]$$

particularly for $a_1, b_1, c_1 \geq 0$ and $a_2, b_2, c_2 > 0$:

$$[a_1, b_1, c_1] : [a_2, b_2, c_2] \underbrace{:=}_{appr.} [a_1/c_2, b_1/b_2, c_1/a_2].$$

$\square$

Example 5. (triangular numbers, figure 6)

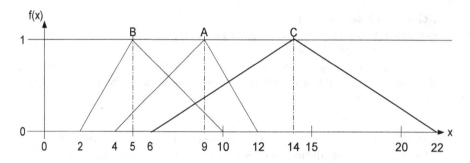

Fig. 6. Sum of two triangular numbers

$$[2, 5, 10] + [4, 9, 12] = [6, 14, 22] \text{ or for intervals } [2, 10] + [4, 12] = [6, 22] \qquad \square$$

$$\pi(X) = ([0.39, 0.41], [0.59, 0.61])$$
$$\pi(Y) = ([0.49, 0.51], [0.49, 0.51])$$
$$\pi(V) = ([0.34, 0.36], [0.64, 0.66])$$

$$f_Z(X, Y) = \begin{bmatrix} [0.64, 0.66] & [0.34, 0.36] \\ [0.19, 0.21] & [0.79, 0.81] \\ [0.19, 0.21] & [0.79, 0.81] \\ [0.04, 0.06] & [0.94, 0.96] \end{bmatrix}$$

$$\pi(Z) = (\pi(X) \times \pi(Y)) \cdot f_Z(X, Y)$$
$$= ([0.2251, 0.2659], [0.7161, 0.7953])$$

$$f_U(Z, V) = \begin{bmatrix} [0.24, 0.26] & [0.74, 0.76] \\ [0.19, 0.21] & [0.79, 0.81] \\ [0.19, 0.21] & [0.79, 0.81] \\ [0.04, 0.06] & [0.94, 0.96] \end{bmatrix}$$

$$\pi(U) = (\pi(Z) \times \pi(V)) \cdot f_U(Z, V)$$
$$= ([0.1103, 0.1534], [0.7936, 0.9507])$$

$$f_W(U) = \begin{bmatrix} [0.74, 0.76] & [0.24, 0.26] \\ [0.001, 0.003] & [0.997, 0.999] \end{bmatrix}$$

$$\pi(W) = \pi(U) \cdot f_W(U)$$
$$= ([0.0824, 0.1194], [0.8177, 0.9896])$$

Fig. 7. Interval Dependency Nets 1

$$\pi(X) = ([0.39, 0.41], [0.0, 0.0])$$
$$\pi(Y) = ([0.49, 0.51], [0.49, 0.51])$$
$$\pi(V) = ([0.34, 0.36], [0.64, 0.66])$$

$$f_Z(X,Y) = \begin{bmatrix} [0.64, 0.66] & [0.34, 0.36] \\ [0.19, 0.21] & [0.79, 0.81] \\ [0.19, 0.21] & [0.79, 0.81] \\ [0.04, 0.06] & [0.94, 0.96] \end{bmatrix}$$

$$\pi(X_1 Z) = (\pi(X) \times \pi(Y)) \cdot f_Z(X,Y)$$
$$= ([0.1586, 0.1819], [0.2159, 0.2446])$$

$$f_U(Z,V) = \begin{bmatrix} [0.24, 0.26] & [0.74, 0.76] \\ [0.19, 0.21] & [0.79, 0.81] \\ [0.19, 0.21] & [0.79, 0.81] \\ [0.04, 0.06] & [0.94, 0.96] \end{bmatrix}$$

$$\pi(X_1 U) = (\pi(X_1 Z) \times \pi(V)) \cdot f_U(Z,V)$$
$$= ([0.0517, 0.0704], [0.3080, 0.3734])$$

$$f_W(U) = \begin{bmatrix} [0.74, 0.76] & [0.24, 0.26] \\ [0.001, 0.003] & [0.997, 0.999] \end{bmatrix}$$

$$\pi(X_1 W) = \pi(X_1 U) \cdot f_W(U)$$
$$= ([0.0386, 0.0546], [0.3195, 0.3913])$$

Fig. 8. Interval Dependency Nets 2

$$\pi(X) = ([0.39, 0.4, 0.41], [0.59, 0.6, 0.61])$$
$$\pi(Y) = ([0.49, 0.5, 0.51], [0.49, 0.5, 0.51])$$
$$\pi(V) = ([0.34, 0.35, 0.36], [0.64, 0.65, 0.66])$$

$$f_Z(X,Y) = \begin{bmatrix} [0.64, 0.65, 0.66] & [0.34, 0.35, 0.36] \\ [0.19, 0.2, 0.21] & [0.79, 0.8, 0.81] \\ [0.19, 0.2, 0.21] & [0.79, 0.8, 0.81] \\ [0.04, 0.05, 0.06] & [0.94, 0.95, 0.96] \end{bmatrix}$$

$$\pi(Z) = (\pi(X) \times \pi(Y)) \cdot f_Z(X,Y)$$
$$= ([0.2251, 0.245, 0.2659],$$
$$[0.7161, 0.755, 0.7953])$$

$$f_U(Z,V) = \begin{bmatrix} [0.24, 0.25, 0.26] & [0.74, 0.75, 0.76] \\ [0.19, 0.2, 0.21] & [0.79, 0.8, 0.81] \\ [0.19, 0.2, 0.21] & [0.79, 0.8, 0.81] \\ [0.04, 0.05, 0.06] & [0.94, 0.95, 0.96] \end{bmatrix}$$

$$\pi(U) = (\pi(Z) \times \pi(V)) \cdot f_U(Z,V)$$
$$= ([0.1103, 0.1307, 0.1534],$$
$$[0.7936, 0.8693, 0.9507])$$

$$f_W(U) = \begin{bmatrix} [0.74, 0.75, 0.76] & [0.24, 0.25, 0.26] \\ [0.001, 0.002, 0.003] & [0.997, 0.998, 0.999] \end{bmatrix}$$

$$\pi(W) = \pi(U) \cdot f_W(U)$$
$$= ([0.0824, 0.0997, 0.1194],$$
$$[0.8177, 0.9003, 0.9896])$$

Fig. 9. Fuzzy Number Dependency Nets 1

$$\pi(X) = ([0.39, 0.4, 0.41], [0.0, 0.0, 0.0])$$
$$\pi(Y) = ([0.49, 0.5, 0.51], [0.49, 0.5, 0.51])$$
$$\pi(V) = ([0.34, 0.35, 0.36], [0.64, 0.65, 0.66])$$

$$f_Z(X,Y) = \begin{bmatrix} [0.64, 0.65, 0.66] & [0.34, 0.35, 0.36] \\ [0.19, 0.2, 0.21] & [0.79, 0.8, 0.81] \\ [0.19, 0.2, 0.21] & [0.79, 0.8, 0.81] \\ [0.04, 0.05, 0.06] & [0.94, 0.95, 0.96] \end{bmatrix}$$

$$\pi(X_1 Z) = (\pi(X) \times \pi(Y)) \cdot f_Z(X,Y)$$
$$= ([0.1586, 0.1700, 0.1819],$$
$$[0.2159, 0.2300, 0.2446])$$

$$f_U(Z,V) = \begin{bmatrix} [0.24, 0.25, 0.26] &][0.74, 0.75, 0.76] \\ [0.19, 0.2, 0.21] & [0.79, 0.8, 0.81] \\ [0.19, 0.2, 0.21] & [0.79, 0.8, 0.81] \\ [0.04, 0.05, 0.06] & [0.94, 0.95, 0.96] \end{bmatrix}$$

$$\pi(X_1 U) = (\pi(X_1 Z) \times \pi(V)) \cdot f_U(Z,V)$$
$$= ([0.0517, 0.0606, 0.0704],$$
$$[0.3080, 0.3395, 0.3734])$$

$$f_W(U) = \begin{bmatrix} [0.74, 0.75, 0.76] & [0.24, 0.25, 0.26] \\ [0.001, 0.002, 0.003] & [0.997, 0.998, 0.999] \end{bmatrix}$$

$$\pi(X_1 W) = \pi(X_1 U) \cdot f_W(U)$$
$$= ([0.0386, 0.0461, 0.0546],$$
$$[0.3195, 0.3539, 0.3913])$$

Fig. 10. Fuzzy Number Dependency Nets 2

Figure 9 and figure 10 correspond to figure 2, figure 7 and figure 3, figure 8 w.r.t. the values of $\pi(X_2)$. All triangles in figures 10 and 16 are isosceles.

4   Duality

To approach propagation nets (PNs), we need the concept of a dual marked net.

Definition 9. (dual of a marked p/t-net [2])
Let $N = (P, T, F)$ be a p/t-net, M a marking of N, and $[N]$ its incidence matrix;
the dual net $N_d = (P_d, T_d, F_d)$ is defined by $[N_d] := [N]^t$.

So, for N_d the following holds:

$$P_d = T, T_d = P, F_d = F^{-1};$$
$$M_d = M, i.e. \forall x \in T_d = P : M_d(x) = M(x).$$

The tokens in N_d are **transition tokens** *which are drawn as little squares.*

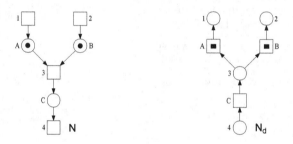

Fig. 11. A p/t-net with marking and its dual net

Example 6. Figure 11 shows a net N with a marking M and the dual net N_d with their respective markings M and M_d. In figure 12 one can see that there are good reasons to define **place firing against the arc direction** as the *dual operation to transition firing.*

Dualizing only does not produce any profit. One gains nothing but a strange and bizarre version of the original net. However, combining elements of both, the original and the dual net, can augment the modeling power.

Example 7. If one interprets (in the left hand net of figure 13) the transition token on transition 4 as the fact, that this transition did not (or must not) fire, then we can assume that transition 3 did not (must not) fire, and furthermore transition 1 did not (must not) fire, because transition 2 might have fired according to the place token on place B.

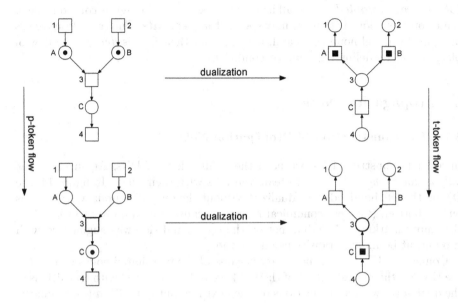

Fig. 12. P- and t-token flow

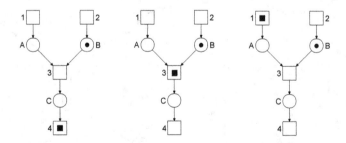

Fig. 13. P- and t-tokens block each other

This shows that **place tokens block transition tokens and vice versa** because of duality reasons, and in addition that **a transition with a token is not enabled** even all its input places are marked. Similarly, **a place with a token is not enabled** even if all its output tokens are marked. A consequence of these considerations is that we may speak of **non-events**. The transition tokens in figure 13 model non-events and, beyond, that their flow is *dual* to the flow of place tokens modeling e.g. fulfilled conditions.

5   Propagation Nets

5.1   The Construction of Propagation Nets

In order to construct PNs, we need the dualizations of DNs. Again, *dualizing only is not enough*. We have to team the DNs with their duals. In figure 14, the DN on the left hand side was dualized without the output boundary transitions on the bottom (for net-economical reasons because they are only to reproduce the empty marking). The dual net on the right hand side was augmented with two output boundary transitions on the top.

Connecting both nets is necessary because of the two shared nodes U and d in the DN. So, the places a and b of the DN have to be connected with transitions of the dual: a (b) with all transitions on the next row but not with a (b). Similarly, the places V and W of the dual have to be connected with transitions of the DN: V (W) with all transitions of the next row above but not with V (W) (see [5,6,11,7]).

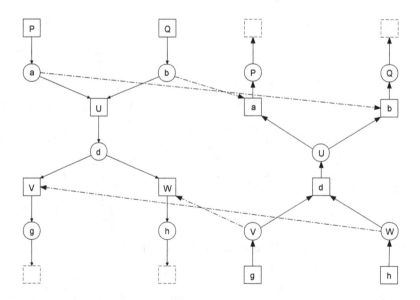

Fig. 14. The complete propagation net structure corresponding to the DN of figure 5

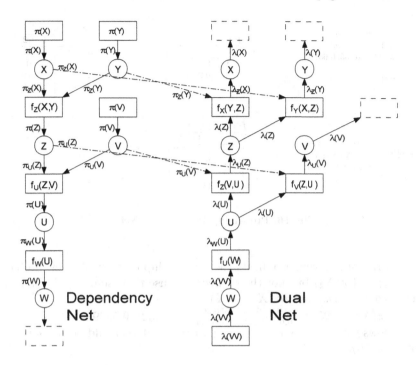

Fig. 15. The complete PN belonging to the DN of figure 1

Figure 15 shows the augmented DN of the offshore example. Names beginning with λ refer to *likelihoods*. The matrices in the dual part, which are associated to the to the non-boundary transitions, are *generalized transposes* of the corresponding matrices in the dependency part. For example, the values $1, 1, 2$ for the variables X, Y, Z (in that order) have the value 0.35 in the matrix $f_Z(X,Y)$ of figure 2 and as well in its transpose w.r.t. X $f_X(Y,Z)$ of figure 16. The matrix $f_U(W)$ is the usual transpose of $f_W(U)$, $f_U(W) = f_W(U)^t$ (the same figures).

5.2 Probability Propagation Nets

Let us assume now that an accident had happened with personnel injury/loss, which will be represented by $\lambda(W) = (1.0, 0.0)$. We want to know whether we should reassess $\pi(X)$, the probability of human errors. In figures 15 and 16, the result of the firing squence

$$\pi(X), \pi(Y), \pi(V), \lambda(W), f_U(W), f_Z(V,U), f_X(Y,Z) \text{ yields the value}$$
$$\lambda(X) = (0.1152285, 0.0894225).$$

The new value of $\pi(X)$ (following Pearl: the *belief of X*, see [10,9]) is calculated as follows:

$$\pi(X) \circ \lambda(X) := (0.4 \cdot 0.1152285, 0.6 \cdot 0.0894225) = (0.046091, 0.0536535)$$

($\circ$ denotes the *componentwise multiplication*).

$\pi(X) = (0.4, 0.6)$
$\pi(Y) = (0.5, 0.5)$
$\pi(V) = (0.35, 0.65)$

$\lambda(W) = (1, 0)$

$f_U(W)$		U	
W		1	2
1		0.75	0.002
2		0.25	0.998

$f_Z(V,U)$		Z	
V	U	1	2
1	1	0.25	0.2
1	2	0.75	0.8
2	1	0.2	0.05
2	2	0.8	0.95

$\lambda(X) = (0.1152, 0.0894)$
$\pi(X|W1) = \pi(X) \circ \lambda(X)$
$\quad = (0.4621, 0.5379)$

$f_X(Y,Z)$		X	
Y	Z	1	2
1	1	0.65	0.2
1	2	0.35	0.8
2	1	0.2	0.05
2	2	0.8	0.95

Fig. 16. Probability Propagation Nets

The entries of this vector indicate the relationship between the new probabilities $\pi(X_1)$ and $\pi(X_2)$ but not their values because their sum is $\neq 1$. That will be achieved by *normalizing* $\pi(X) \circ \lambda(X)$:
$$\pi(X) \circ \lambda(X) \approx \frac{(0.0460914, 0.0536535)}{0.0460914 + 0.0536535} = (0.4621, 0.5379).$$
This shows that the original vector $\pi(X) = (0.4, 0.6)$ should be *reassessed* by $(0.4621, 0.5379)$.

It should be noted that $\pi(X) \circ \lambda(X)$ was partly calculated in the *dual part* of the net,

whereas $\pi(X_1|W_1) = \frac{\pi(X_1 W_1)}{\pi(W_1)} = 0.4621$ (at the end of subsection 3.1) was completely calculated in the *dependency part*. Moreover, the last calculation consists of a division of probabilities.

5.3   Interval Propagation Nets

In a similar way we will deal with *intervals*. All relevant vectors and matrices are given in figure 17. The same firing sequence
$$\pi(X), \pi(Y), \pi(V), \lambda(W), f_U(W), f_Z(V,U), f_X(Y,Z) \text{ yields for intervals}$$
$$\lambda(X) = ([0.0989, 0.1333], [0.0744, 0.1062]) \text{ (not normalized) and then}$$
$$\pi(X|W_1) = \pi(X) \circ \lambda(X) = ([0.038571, 0.054653], [0.043896, 0.064782])$$
$$\text{(also not normalized).}$$
Now the question is how to normalize $\pi(X|W_1)$. To normalize intervals like numbers is not very reasonable: $\frac{([a,b],[c,d])}{[a,b]+[c,d]} = \frac{([a,b],[c,d])}{[a+c,b+d]} = ([\frac{a}{b+d}, \frac{b}{a+c}], [\frac{c}{b+d}, \frac{d}{a+c}])$.

The sum of these two intervals is $[\frac{a+c}{b+d}, \frac{b+d}{a+c}]$ which is not comparable to the value 1 for numbers.

Normalizing on the central points of both intervals of $\pi(X|W_1)$ seems to be a useful idea. The central points are 0.046612 and 0.054339 and their sum equals $0.100951 \approx 0.1$. So we get
$$\pi(X|W_1) = (1/0.1) \cdot ([0.038571, 0.054653], [0.043896, 0.064782])$$
$$= ([0.38571, 0.54653], [0.43896, 0.64782]).$$

The sum of the central points of these two intervals equals 1. In doing so, we give preference to pairs $\pi^*(X_1|W_1), \pi^*(X_2|W_1)$ whose sum equals 1. That is acceptable because the unknown values are complementary to each other.

Since we are mainly interested in $\pi(X_1|W_1) = [0.38571, 0.54653]$, the length of this interval should be *as small as possible*; the length is $0.54653 - 0.38571 = 0.16082$. The result of the interval length calculated by forward calculation is

$$\pi(X_1|W_1) = \frac{\pi(X_1W_1)}{\pi(W_1)} = \frac{[0.0386,0.0546]}{[0.0824,0.1194]} = [\frac{0.0386}{0.1194}, \frac{0.0546}{0.0824}] = [0.3233, 0.6626].$$

The length of this interval is $0.3393 > 0.16082$. So we have good reasons to reassess

$$\pi(X) = ([0.39, 0.41], [0.59, 0.61]) \text{ by } ([0.38571, 0.54653], [0.43896, 0.64782]).$$

$\pi(X) = ([0.39, 0.41], [0.59, 0.61])$
$\pi(Y) = ([0.49, 0.51], [0.49, 0.51])$
$\pi(V) = ([0.34, 0.36], [0.64, 0.66])$
$\lambda(W) = ([1, 1], [0, 0]) = [1, 0]$

$\pi(X) = ([0.39, 0.4, 0.41], [0.59, 0.6, 0.61])$
$\pi(Y) = ([0.49, 0.5, 0.51], [0.49, 0.5, 0.51])$
$\pi(V) = ([0.34, 0.35, 0.36], [0.64, 0.65, 0.66])$
$\lambda(W) = ([1, 1, 1], [0, 0, 0])$

$f_U(W)$	U	
W	1	2
1	$[0.74, 0.76]$	$[0.001, 0.003]$
2	$[0.24, 0.26]$	$[0.997, 0.999]$

$f_U(W)$	U	
W	1	2
1	$[0.74, 0.75, 0.76]$	$[0.001, 0.002, 0.003]$
2	$[0.24, 0.25, 0.26]$	$[0.997, 0.998, 0.999]$

$f_Z(V,U)$		Z	
V	U	1	2
1	1	$[0.24, 0.26]$	$[0.19, 0.21]$
1	2	$[0.74, 0.76]$	$[0.79, 0.81]$
2	1	$[0.19, 0.21]$	$[0.04, 0.06]$
2	2	$[0.79, 0.81]$	$[0.94, 0.96]$

$f_Z(V,U)$		Z	
V	U	1	2
1	1	$[0.24, 0.25, 0.26]$	$[0.19, 0.20, 0.21]$
1	2	$[0.74, 0.75, 0.76]$	$[0.79, 0.80, 0.81]$
2	1	$[0.19, 0.20, 0.21]$	$[0.04, 0.05, 0.06]$
2	2	$[0.79, 0.80, 0.81]$	$[0.94, 0.95, 0.96]$

$f_X(Y,Z)$		X	
Y	Z	1	2
1	1	$[0.64, 0.66]$	$[0.19, 0.21]$
1	2	$[0.34, 0.36]$	$[0.79, 0.81]$
2	1	$[0.19, 0.21]$	$[0.04, 0.06]$
2	2	$[0.79, 0.81]$	$[0.94, 0.96]$

$f_X(Y,Z)$		X	
Y	Z	1	2
1	1	$[0.64, 0.65, 0.66]$	$[0.19, 0.20, 0.21]$
1	2	$[0.34, 0.35, 0.36]$	$[0.79, 0.80, 0.81]$
2	1	$[0.19, 0.20, 0.21]$	$[0.04, 0.05, 0.06]$
2	2	$[0.79, 0.80, 0.81]$	$[0.94, 0.95, 0.96]$

$\lambda(X) = ([0.0989, 0.1333],$
$\qquad [0.0744, 0.1062])$
$\pi(X|W1) = \pi(X) \circ \lambda(X)$
$\qquad = ([0.3857, 0.5465],$
$\qquad [0.4390, 0.6478])$

$\lambda(X) = ([0.0989, 0.1152, 0.1333],$
$\qquad [0.0744, 0.0894, 0.1062])$
$\pi(X|W1) = \pi(X) \circ \lambda(X)$
$\qquad = ([0.3867, 0.4621, 0.5479],$
$\qquad [0.4401, 0.5379, 0.6495])$

Fig. 17. Interval Propagation Nets   **Fig. 18.** Fuzzy Number Propagation Nets

5.4   Fuzzy Number Propagation Nets

The last kind of PNs in the offshore example deals with *triangular fuzzy numbers*. With the data of figure 18 the firing sequence $\pi(X), \pi(Y), \pi(V), \lambda(W), f_U(W), f_Z(V,U), f_X(Y,Z)$ leads to

$$\lambda(X) = ([0.0989, 0.1152, 0.1333], [0.0744, 0.0894, 1062]).$$

18   K. Lautenbach

Then we have
$$\pi(X|W_1) = \pi(X) \circ \lambda(X) = (\pi(X_1) \cdot \lambda(X_1), \pi(X_2) \cdot \lambda(X_2))$$
$$= ([0.39 \cdot 0.0989, 0.4 \cdot 0.1152, 0.41 \cdot 0.1333],$$
$$[0.59 \cdot 0.0744, 0.6 \cdot 0.0894, 0.61 \cdot 0.1062])$$
$$= ([0.0386, 0.0461, 0.0547], [0.0439, 0.0537, 0.0648]).$$

We will normalize on the middle values (which in general are not the central values of the intervals given by the outer values).

The middle values are 0.0461 and 0.0537 and their sum equals 0.0998. So we get
$$\pi(X|W_1) = (1/0.0998) \cdot ([0.0368, 0.0461, 0.0547], [0.0439, 0.0537, 0.0648])$$
$$= ([0.3867, 0.4621, 0.5479], [0.4401, 0.5379, 0.6495]).$$

The length of the interesting left "interval" is $0.5497 - 0.3867 = 0.1630$. The calculation by dividing fuzzy numbers yields a similarly bad value as in the case of intervals. In order to update $\pi(X)$ we replace
$$\pi(X_1) = [0.39, 0.4, 0.41] \text{ by } [0.3867, 0.4621, 0.5479]$$
$$\pi(X_2) = [0.59, 0.6, 0.61] \text{ by } [0.4401, 0.5379, 0.6495]$$

In summary, we have seen, that reasoning in the dual part of propagation nets leads to smaller intervals. Dividing intervals can result in intervals with absurd lengths, which is a well known problem in interval arithmetic.

The values of this example are from [13].

6 Conclusion

In this paper, a class of Petri nets (*propagation nets*) is introduced for working with uncertain quantities. These nets are a mixture of two main parts, the structurally simple *dependency nets* for representing the relations between the uncertain quantities and the *dualized dependency nets*. In the probabilistic case, *probabilities* are flowing through the dependency nets and *likelihoods* through their dualization. Propagation nets have a simple firing rule which is generalizable for more complicated uncertain quantities as intervals and fuzzy numbers.

References

1. Lautenbach, K.: Exakte Bedingungen der Lebendigkeit für eine Klasse von Petri-Netzen. Gesellschaft für Mathematik und Datenverarbeitung Bonn, Bericht Nr. 82 (1973)
2. Lautenbach, K.: Simple Marked-graph-like Predicate/Transition Nets. Arbeitspapiere der GMD Nr. 41. In: Informatik Fachberichte 66, Bonn (1983)
3. Lautenbach, K.: Reproducibility of the empty marking. In: Esparza, J., Lakos, C.A. (eds.) ICATPN 2002. LNCS, vol. 2360, pp. 237–253. Springer, Heidelberg (2002)
4. Lautenbach, K.: Logical Reasoning and Petri Nets. In: van der Aalst, W.M.P., Best, E. (eds.) ICATPN 2003. LNCS, vol. 2679, pp. 276–295. Springer, Heidelberg (2003)
5. Lautenbach, K., Pinl, A.: Probability Propagation in Petri Nets. Fachberichte Informatik 16–2005, Universität Koblenz-Landau, Institut für Informatik, Universitätsstr. 1, D-56070 Koblenz (2005)

6. Lautenbach, K., Pinl, A.: Probability Propagation Nets. Arbeitsberichte aus dem Fachbereich Informatik 20–2007, Universität Koblenz-Landau, Institut für Informatik, Universitätsstr. 1, D-56070 Koblenz (2007)

7. Lautenbach, K., Pinl, A.: A Petri net representation of Bayesian message flows: importance of Bayesian networks for biological applications. Natural Computing 10, 683–709 (2011)

8. Lautenbach, K., Susewind, K.: Probability Propagation nets and Duality. Fachberichte Informatik 11–2012, Universität Koblenz-Landau, Institut für Informatik, Universitätsstr. 1, D-56070 Koblenz (2012)

9. Neapolitan, R.E.: Probabilistic Reasoning in Expert Systems – Theory and Algorithms. Wiley (1990)

10. Pearl, J.: Probabilistic Reasoning in Intelligent Systems: Networks of Plausible Inference. Morgan Kaufmann Publishers Inc., San Francisco (1988)

11. Pinl, A.: Probability Propagation Nets – Unveiling Structure and Propagations of Bayesian Networks by means of Petri Nets. Ph.D. thesis, Universität Koblenz-Landau, Campus Koblenz (2007)

12. Poole, D.: Probabilistic horn abduction and bayesian networks. Artificial Intelligence 64, 81–129 (1993)

13. Ren, J., Xu, D.L., Yang, J.B., Jenkinson, I., Wang, J.: An offshore risk analysis method using fuzzy bayesian network. J. Offshore Mech. Arct. Eng. 131(4), 12 (2009)

14. Ren, J., Wang, J., Jenkinson, I.: Fuzzy bayesian modelling in maritime risk analysis. In: GERI Annual Research Symposium, Liverpool John Moores University, UK (2005)

15. Ren, J., Wang, J., Jenkinson, I., Xu, D., Yang, J.B.: A methodology to model human and organisational errors on offshore risk analysis. In: IEEE International Conference on Automation Science and Engineering, October 8-10, pp. 144–149 (2006) ISBN 1-4244-0310-3

Energy-Utility Analysis for Resilient Systems Using Probabilistic Model Checking*

Christel Baier, Clemens Dubslaff, Sascha Klüppelholz, and Linda Leuschner

Institute for Theoretical Computer Science
Technische Universität Dresden, Germany
{baier,dubslaff,klueppel,leuschner}@tcs.inf.tu-dresden.de

Abstract. The automated quantitative system analysis in terms of probabilistic model checking (PMC) is nowadays well-established and has been applied successfully in various areas. Recently, we showed how PMC can be applied for the trade-off analysis between several cost and reward functions, such as energy and utility. Besides utility, also the resilience of a system, i.e., the systems capability to operate successfully even in unfavorable conditions, crucially depends on costs invested: It is well-known that better resilience can be achieved, e.g., through introducing redundant components, which however may yield higher energy consumption.

In this paper, we focus on the interplay energy, utility and resilience. The formalization of the resulting trade-offs requires several concepts like quantiles, conditional probabilities and expectations and ratios of cost or reward functions. We present an overview how these quantitative measures for resilience mechanisms can be computed when the resilient systems are modeled either as discrete or continuous-time Markov chains. All the presented concepts of multi-objective reasoning are not supported by state-of-the-art probabilistic model checkers yet. By means of a small case study following the modular redundancy principle, we exemplify a resilience analysis within our prototype implementations.

1 Introduction

Nowadays, computer systems also have to face non-functional requirements which need to be guaranteed for the system to operate successfully. Typical examples for such systems contain unreliable or only partially known components, where stochastic distributions can be used to model the system load or the frequency of failures (e.g. message losses, bit flips in hardware components). Verification of non-functional requirements especially for critical components of the system is highly desirable. Various formal models and methods for the analysis of probabilistic systems have been proposed in the literature. We focus here

---

* The authors are supported by the DFG through the collaborative research centre HAEC (SFB 912), the cluster of excellence cfAED, Deutsche Telekom Stiftung, the ESF young researcher groups IMData (100098198) and SREX (100111037), the Graduiertenkolleg QuantLA (1763) the DFG/NWO-project ROCKS, and the EU-FP-7 grant MEALS (295261).

G. Ciardo and E. Kindler (Eds.): PETRI NETS 2014, LNCS 8489, pp. 20–39, 2014.

on *probabilistic model checking* (PMC) on Markovian system models, which can be seen as automata annotated with probabilistic distributions and cost or reward functions modeling stochastic phenomena or resource requirements. The Markovian property that the future system behavior only depends on the current state but not on the history makes these models best-suited for algorithmic quantitative analysis. We mainly consider Markovian models in terms of discrete Markov chains and its time-sensitive counterpart, continuous-time Markov chains. Markov chains can be seen as transition systems where probabilities are attached to the outgoing transitions of each state. In the case of continuous-time Markov chains, exit-rates are furthermore assigned to the states, formalizing also mean sojourn times in the state as reciprocal of the exit-rate. Usually, the task of PMC on a given discrete Markov chain is to compute the probability of path properties specified by some formula of linear temporal logic (LTL) [35,15], the path-formula fragment of probabilistic computation tree logic (PCTL) or its variant PRCTL with reward-bounded temporal modalities [23,12,16,2]. For continuous-time Markov chains, the time-aware counterpart of PRCTL, continuous stochastic reward logic (CSRL) [4], also allows for reasoning over properties and rewards depending on the sojourn times. Algorithms for Markovian models and LTL-, PRCTL- or CSRL-specifications were implemented in various model checkers, such as PRISM [25] and MRMC [27]. They provide several engines with sophisticated techniques to tackle the state-explosion problem, have been continuously extended by new features and were successfully applied in many areas, such as randomized distributed systems, multimedia, security protocols and systems biology.

Energy-Utility Trade-off. In current inter-disciplinary research projects, where we apply (among others) PMC for the analysis of low-level resource-management algorithms, we made a series of interesting observations concerning the strengths and limitations of state-of-the-art PMC-techniques. Within these projects, the PMC-based approach is complementary to the measurement- and simulation-based analysis conducted by project partners to provide insights in the energy-utility, reliability and other performance characteristics from a global and long-run perspective. The evaluation results obtained by a probabilistic model checker guide the optimization of resource-management algorithms. They can be useful to predict the performance of management algorithms on future hardware or low-level protocols that have not been implemented yet, making measurements impossible. We successfully applied PMC, e.g., for the analysis of a spinlock protocol [6], a lock-free synchronization protocol for read-write problems [8], a bonding network device [20] and an energy-aware job scheduling scenario [5]. The application of PMC was, however, not straightforward. Besides the expected state-explosion problem, difficulties arose to find appropriate probabilistic distributions to model cache-effects and other hardware details [6]. To our surprise, our case studies revealed the lack of performance measures that have been identified as most significant by our cooperation partners, but were not supported by existing probabilistic model checkers. This mainly concerns the calculation of measures that provide insights in the trade-off between multiple cost and reward functions, such as energy and utility. For example, the performance of a CPU measured, e.g., in the maximal number of instructions per second, crucially depends on its frequency, but so does its energy consumption. Network activity (as the opposite of latency) and throughput are further examples for utility measures taken from the network systems domain depending on the energy invested. Usually, it can be expected that the gained utility increases with the energy budget invested and the general aim is to maximize the performance, while minimizing the energy consumption.

Resilience. In this paper, we focus on resilient systems, i.e., systems which include mechanisms to enable the system to operate even under the influence of negative and unforeseen impacts. It is well-known that the resilience of a system can be increased following the three principles of *redundancy, diversity* and *adaptability* (see, e.g., [29,30]). In redundant systems, the tasks of crucial system parts are solved through multiple equivalent components. Thus, a failing component does not hamper the whole system to operate, since its task can be also solved by another redundant component. If these redundant components are conceptional different within the approach for solving their tasks, i.e., the system diversity is high, the reasons for component failures are also different. A higher diversity usually yields also a better overall resilience of the system. Resilience can furthermore be increased by implementing strategies to adapt to the impact of unfavorable situations, e.g., following different execution strategies depending on the environmental conditions or launching repair mechanisms turning failed components into functioning ones.

As a running example of this paper, we consider a simple resilient system which makes use of the *multi modular redundancy* (MMR) concept [37] and follows the principles for increasing resilience mentioned above. Within this concept, multiple versions of system components are maintained and operate redundantly in parallel (redundancy). The components may differ in their reliability characteristics, e.g., have a different probability that failures occur (diversity). Computed results of the components are periodically compared by a trustworthy module, called *master*, and the result most of the components returned is taken as granted. We extend the basic MMR model by allowing faulty components, i.e., all components with a result differing from this majority, to be scheduled for repair. Then, each component has three possible states: either it is stable (not faulty), within a failure state, or the repair mechanism is currently taking place. Assume our MMR model consists of N components that run in parallel and their results are evaluated by a master component. This leads to the abstract operational behavior of component $i \in \{1, ..., N\}$ and the master component as illustrated by the following transition system.

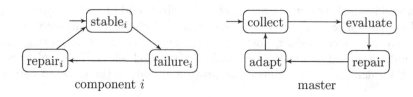

component i master

The composed system is in a stable state if all its components are, and in a failure state if there exists a component in which a failure occurred.

Furthermore, our model allows for various strategies to adapt the system after failures occurred, e.g., by spawning more replicas or deactivate existing ones (adaptivity). The smallest instance of MMR consists of tripling components – this concept is also called *triple modular redundancy (TMR)*. TMR is well-suited for binary decisions and has been proven to be feasible in practice even with this low degree of redundancy, e.g., within error correction algorithms, or space satellite, aerospace and automotive systems. However, if non-binary results are computed by the components or the failure probability is comparatively high, TMR is not sufficient.

Energy-utility Analysis for Resilient Systems. Introducing resilience mechanisms, e.g., following the principles stated above, clearly influences the energy consumption of the system as well as its performance. Especially in the case these mechanisms take effect, e.g., after a component becomes faulty or an overall failure occurred, non-functional properties such as the *mean time to recover (MTTR)* or the amount of energy required for recovery are of utter interest to estimate their efficiency. Our methods developed for the quantitative analysis of the trade-off between energy and utility can also be used for analyzing resilient systems, a possibility we merely considered yet. Assuming a given cost function for the energy consumption and a reward function for the achieved degree of utility, we consider the design of algorithms answering multi-objective queries for resilient systems. The system models are discrete and continuous-time Markov chains over some state space S. In particular, we exemplify the benefits of this approach by the following queries and tasks

(P) What is the worst-case probability that the system recovers from a failure (i.e., reaching a stable state) within at most t time steps?

(Q) Minimize the energy budget sufficient to guarantee recovery from a failure with probability at least 90% while still gaining at least u utility?

(Qe) What is the maximal utility that is gained when the expected energy needed to recover from a failure is at most e?

(C) Does the system almost surely recover from any failure within an MTTR of at most t under the assumption that the system never breaks completely?

(Ce) Under the assumption that it is always possible to recover from a failure, what is the maximal amount of energy which has to be expected for the recovering mechanism?

(R) Given an MMR network system, what is the probability that always at most 1% of the time, requests cannot be served and that the probability to recover from a failure is greater than 90%?

The first task **(P)** can be answered using standard methods of PMC. However, rather new techniques for multi-objective reasoning which we summarize in this paper can be used to answer the other tasks: **(Q)** can be formalized as a *quantile*, **(C)** as an instance of *conditional probabilities* and **(Ce)** as a *conditional expectation*. Although quantiles and conditional probabilities and expectations are standard concepts in mathematics and statistics, they have drawn very few attention in the context of PMC. Our recent work [34,5] shows how quantiles can be derived from computation schemes for the probabilities or expectations of reward-bounded path properties. A brief summary will be provided in Section 3. Explanations on the computation of conditional probabilities are provided in Section 4, based on our recent work [10]. Tasks **(R)** refers to the quotient of two cost or reward functions, e.g., one for the energy and one for the utility. There has been some work on such ratios, e.g., by [1,36] for expected ratios or [17] for long-run ratios when the denominator has the purpose of a counter. This work does not seem to be adequate for solving the tasks stated above. Instead, we show in Section 5 that instances of **(R)** are reducible to problems that have been studied for probabilistic push-down systems [13]. Within a small case study concerning our MMR example, we illustrate in Section 6 how parts of the exemplified queries stated above can be used for analyzing resilient systems.

2   Theoretical Foundations

We provide a brief summary of our notation for discrete and continuous-time Markov chains and their quantitative analysis. For further details we refer to textbooks on model checking [14,9] and on probability theory and Markovian models [32,28,24,31].

The reader is assumed to be familiar with ω-automata and temporal logics, surveyed for instance in [14,22,9]. We often use notation of linear temporal logic (LTL) and computation tree logic (CTL), where $\Diamond$, U and $\Box$ stand for the temporal modalities "eventually", "until" and "always", while $\exists$ and $\forall$ are used as CTL-like path quantifiers to state that there exists or for all paths a temporal state formula holds. The notion *path property* is used for any language consisting of infinite words over 2^{AP}, where AP is the underlying set of atomic propositions. LTL-formulas are often identified with the path property of infinite words over the alphabet 2^{AP} that are models for the formulas. Having in mind temporal logical specifications, we use the logical operators $\vee$, $\wedge$, $\neg$ for union, intersection and complementation of path properties.

2.1   Probabilistic Models

A *distribution* on a nonempty, countable set S is a function $\mu : S \to [0,1]$ such that $\sum_{s \in S} \mu(s) = 1$. For $U \subseteq S$, $\mu(U)$ denotes $\sum_{s \in U} \mu(s)$. We consider two models for probabilistic resilient systems, discrete and continuous-time Markov chains. If statements in this paper hold for both types of models, we simply refer to *Markov chains*.

Discrete Markov Chains.   A discrete Markov chain is a pair $\mathcal{M} = (S, P)$ where S is a finite, nonempty set of states and $P : S \times S \to [0,1]$ a function, called the transition probability function, such that $\sum_{s' \in S} P(s, s') = 1$ for each state s. A path π in $\mathcal{M}$ is a finite or infinite sequence $\pi = s_0\, s_1\, s_2 \dots$ of states built by transitions, i.e., $P(s_i, s_{i+1}) > 0$ for all $i \geqslant 0$. The length $|\pi|$ denotes the number of transitions taken in π. We refer to the value

$$\text{prob}(\pi) \;=\; \prod_{0 \leqslant i < n} P(s_i, s_{i+1})$$

as the probability for π. We write $FinPaths(s)$ for the set of all finite paths π starting in the state s. Similarly, $InfPaths(s)$ stands for the set of infinite paths starting in s. We use $FinPaths$ and $InfPaths$ to denote the sets of all finite paths, respectively infinite paths.

The *probability space* induced by a discrete Markov chain is defined using classical concepts of measure and probability theory. The basic elements of the underlying sigma-algebra are the cylinder sets spanned by the finite paths, i.e., the sets $Cyl(\pi)$ consisting of all infinite paths ζ such that π is a prefix of ζ. Elements of this sigma-algebra are called *(measurable) path events*. The probability measure $\mathbb{P}_s^{\mathcal{M}}$ is defined on the basis of standard measure-extension theorems stating the existence of a unique probability measure $\mathbb{P}_s^{\mathcal{M}}$ with $\mathbb{P}_s^{\mathcal{M}}\big(\,Cyl(\pi)\,\big) = \text{prob}(\pi)$ for all $\pi \in FinPaths(s)$, whereas cylinder sets of paths not starting in s have measure 0 under $\mathbb{P}_s^{\mathcal{M}}$. The probability measures $\mathbb{P}_s^{\mathcal{M}}$ rely on the assumption that s is the initial state. If μ is a distribution, viewed as an initial distribution, then $\mathbb{P}_\mu^{\mathcal{M}} = \sum_{s \in S} \mu(s) \cdot \mathbb{P}_s^{\mathcal{M}}$.

Continuous-time Markov Chains. A continuous-time Markov chain is a pair $\mathcal{C} = (\mathcal{M}, E)$, where $\mathcal{M} = (S, P)$ is a discrete Markov chain and $E : S \to \mathbb{R}_{\geqslant 0}$ a function that specifies an exit-rate for each state s. $\mathcal{M}$ is called the *embedded discrete Markov chain* that describes the time-abstract operational behavior of $\mathcal{C}$. Intuitively, $E(s)$ stands for the frequency of taking a transition from s. More formally, $E(s)$ is the rate of an exponential distribution and the probability to take some transitions from s within t time units is given by $1 - e^{-E(s)\cdot t}$, where e is Euler's number. A *trajectory* (or *timed path*) of $\mathcal{C}$ is a path in $\mathcal{M}$ augmented with the sojourn times in the states. Formally, a trajectory in $\mathcal{C}$ is an alternating sequence $s_0 \, t_0 \, s_1 \, t_1 \, s_2 \, t_2 \ldots$ of states s_i such that $P(s_i, s_{i+1}) > 0$ and the t_i's are non-negative real numbers. An infinite trajectory $\tilde{\vartheta}$ is said to be *time-divergent* if $\sum_{i \geqslant 0} t_i = \infty$. In this case, $\tilde{\vartheta}@t$ denotes the state s_i, where i is the greatest index such that $t_0 + t_1 + \ldots + t_i \leqslant t$ for $t \in \mathbb{R}_{\geqslant 0}$. For finite trajectories we require that they end in a state. We write $FinTraj(s)$ for the set of finite trajectories starting in state s and $InfTraj(s)$ for the infinite time-divergent trajectories from s. If the starting state s is irrelevant, we omit s and write $FinTraj$ and $InfTraj$.

To reason about probabilities for conditions on trajectories, one can again rely on standard concepts of measure and probability theory to define a sigma-algebra where the events are infinite trajectories. Let $s_0 \, s_1 \ldots s_n$ be a finite path in the embedded discrete Markov chain $\mathcal{M}$ and let $I_0, I_1, \ldots, I_{n-1}$ be bounded real intervals in $[0, \infty[$. We write $\mathcal{T} = s_0 \, I_0 \, s_1 \, I_1 \ldots I_{n-1} \, s_n$ for the set of all finite trajectories $s_0 \, t_0 \, s_1 \, t_1 \ldots t_{n-1} \, s_n$ with $t_i \in I_i$ for $0 \leqslant i < n$ and refer to $\mathcal{T}$ as a *symbolic finite trajectory*. The infinite trajectories $\tilde{\vartheta}$ that have a prefix in $\mathcal{T}$ constitute the cylinder set $Cyl(\mathcal{T})$. For state s, $\mathbb{P}_s^{\mathcal{C}}$ is the unique probability measure on the smallest sigma-algebra containing the sets $Cyl(\mathcal{T})$ for all symbolic finite trajectories $\mathcal{T}$ such that

$$\mathbb{P}_s^{\mathcal{C}}\big(\,Cyl(\mathcal{T})\,\big) \;=\; \prod_{0 \leqslant i < n} P(s_i, I_i, s_{i+1}),$$

where for s, $s' \in S$ and real numbers t_1, t_2 with $t_1 \leqslant t_2$ we have:

$$P(s, [t_1, t_2], s') \;=\; P(s, s') \cdot \left(e^{-E(s)t_1} - e^{-E(s)t_2} \right)$$

It is well-known that under $\mathbb{P}_s^{\mathcal{C}}$ almost all trajectories are time-divergent [19]. As in the case of discrete Markov chains, we define $\mathbb{P}_\mu^{\mathcal{C}} = \sum_{s \in S} \mu(s) \cdot \mathbb{P}_s^{\mathcal{C}}$ for an initial distribution μ.

2.2   Weights and Rewards

For modeling, e.g., resource requirements and performance, we enrich the presented probabilistic models within weight functions. A weight function for a Markov chain $\mathcal{M} = (S, P)$ is a function of the form $wgt : S \cup S \times S \to \mathbb{Z}$ that assigns an integer to all states and transitions, where $wgt(s, s') = 0$ if $P(s, s') = 0$. If wgt is non-negative, i.e., $wgt(s) \geqslant 0$ for all states s and $wgt(s, s') \geqslant 0$ for all state pairs (s, s'), we refer to wgt as a *reward function*. We say that a non-negative wgt is positive if $wgt(s, s') > 0$ or $wgt(s) > 0$ for all state pairs (s, s') where s' is a successor of s. Occasionally, we also consider weight functions with rational values and refer to them as *rational-valued* weight functions.

Discrete Markov Chains. When $\mathcal{M}$ is a discrete Markov chain, the *accumulated weight* of finite paths in $\mathcal{M}$ is defined as

$$wgt(s_0 s_1 \dots s_n) \;=\; \sum_{i=0}^{n-1} wgt(s_i) + wgt(s_i, s_{i+1})$$

For defining expectations over a reward function rew for $\mathcal{M}$, let χ be a predicate for finite paths in $\mathcal{M}$. The random variable $rew_\chi : \mathit{InfPaths} \to \mathbb{Z} \cup \{\infty\}$ assigns to each infinite path $\zeta = s_0 s_1 \dots$ the accumulated reward of the longest prefix of ζ where χ does not hold till the last transition. That is:

$$rew_\chi(s_0 s_1 \dots) \;\overset{\text{def}}{=}\; \max\{ rew(s_0 s_1 \dots s_k s_{k+1}) \,:\, k \in \mathbb{N}, \, s_0 s_1 \dots s_k \not\models \chi \}$$

The supremum over the empty set is defined to be 0. We will use two types of predicates for finite paths: reachability constraints $\chi = \mathrm{Reach}(goal)$ where $goal$ is a state predicate (i.e., Boolean combination of atomic propositions defining a set of states) and reward constraints $\chi = (rew \trianglelefteq r)$ imposing a lower bound on the accumulated reward (where $\trianglelefteq \in \{\geqslant, >\}$ and $r \in \mathbb{N}$). When $\pi = s_0 s_1 \dots s_n$ is a finite path, $\pi \models \mathrm{Reach}(goal)$ if $s_k \models goal$ for some $k \in \{0, 1, \dots, n\}$ and $\pi \models (rew > r)$ if $rew(\pi) > r$. For these types of predicates, the set $\Diamond \chi$ of infinite paths $\zeta = s_0 s_1 \dots$ with $s_0 s_1 \dots s_k \models \chi$ for some position $k \in \mathbb{N}$ is measurable. Obviously, reachability predicates $\mathrm{Reach}(goal)$ can be mimicked by the predicate $\chi = (rew \geqslant 1)$ where rew is a fresh reward function with $rew(s) = 0$ for all s and $rew(s, t) = 1$ if $t \models goal$ and $rew(s, t) = 0$ otherwise.

   Given state s of $\mathcal{M}$ with $\mathbb{P}_s^{\mathcal{M}}(\Diamond \chi) = 1$, the *expected accumulated reward* until χ, denoted $\mathbb{E}_s^{\mathcal{M}}[rew](\Diamond \chi) = \sum_\pi \mathrm{prob}(\pi) \cdot rew(\pi)$ is the expectation of the random variable rew_χ. Here, π ranges over all finite paths with $\pi \models \chi$.

Continuous-time Markov Chains. In case the considered probabilistic system is a continuous-time Markov chain $\mathcal{C} = (\mathcal{M}, E)$, the *accumulated weight* of finite trajectories in $\mathcal{C}$ is defined as

$$wgt(s_0t_0s_1t_1\ldots s_n) \;=\; \sum_{i=0}^{n-1} t_i \cdot wgt(s_i) + wgt(s_i, s_{i+1})$$

Then, the accumulated reward of a trajectory and the expectation until a predicate χ take over from discrete Markov chains by only replacing paths by trajectories and the maximum by supremum in the formal definitions.

2.3   Analysis of Probabilistic Systems

The analysis of probabilistic systems requires methods for computing the probabilities and expectations of measurable path events. All the properties we investigate in this paper defining measurable sets of path events rely on unbounded and reward-bounded reachability of a fixed set of states. We only sketch the approaches and refer to the literature for further details (e.g., [9]). In the unbounded reachability case, graph algorithms in combination with solving linear equation systems are sufficient for Markov chains. An iterative matrix/vector-multiplication yields the probability of reaching a set of states in a discrete Markov chain within generating only a certain amount of reward if the reward function is positive. In case the associated reward function is non-negative, i.e., some transitions may have a reward of zero, further iteratively solving a linear equation system is required [5]. The probability of a time- or reward-bounded reachability event in continuous-time Markov chains can be obtained via a transient system analysis and uniformization [4]. Expected accumulated rewards are computable using linear-programming techniques [32,18].

With these methods we are able to solve the task **(P)** analyzing the resilience mechanism of repairing faulty components as mentioned in the introduction. Formally, **(P)** amounts of computing the minimal value p_s over all states $s \in S$, where

$$p_s \;=\; \mathbb{P}_s\big(\Diamond^{\leqslant t}\text{stable}\big)$$

denotes the probability of fulfilling a time-bounded reachability property in s. Whenever we exemplify such tasks, we identify atomic propositions (or Boolean combinations thereof) with the sets of states where the atomic proposition is fulfilled. For instance, $\Diamond^{\leqslant t}\text{stable}$ denotes the set of paths reaching stable states within a time of at most t.

3   Probabilistic and Expectation Quantiles

Quantiles are well-established in statistics (see, e.g., [33]), where they are used to reason about the cumulative distribution function of a random variable R. If $p \in \,]0, 1[$, then the p-quantile is the maximal value r such that the probability for the event $R > r$ is at least p. Although quantiles can provide very useful insights in the interplay of various cost functions and other system properties, they have barely obtained attention in the model-checking community. We provide here a brief summary of the concepts presented in [34,5]. The formula

$$\phi_{e,u} = \Diamond\big(\ goal \wedge (energy \leqslant e) \wedge (utility \geqslant u)\ \big)$$

states that eventually a goal state will be reached along some finite path where
the accumulated energy is at most e and the accumulated utility value is at
least u. Path properties $\varphi[e]$ (and $\psi[u]$) parametrizing only over the energy costs
(utility reward, respectively) are obtained from $\phi_{e,u}$ by fixing the maximal energy
costs e (minimal utility u, respectively). Whereas $\varphi[e]$ is *increasing* with the
available energy budged e, $\psi[u]$ is *decreasing* with the requested utility u.

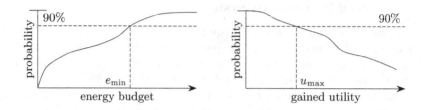

Fig. 1. Quantiles for increasing (left) and decreasing (right) properties

Quantiles now ask for the minimal amount of energy e (maximal utility u) such
that the probability of all paths starting in a designated state and fulfilling $\varphi[e]$
($\psi[u]$, respectively) exceed a given probability threshold p. The arising quantile
values are illustrated in Figure 1 for $p = 0.9$.

In order to formally define quantiles more formally in the context of this paper,
let us fix a discrete Markov chain $\mathcal{M}$ and a reward function $rew : S \cup S{\times}S \to \mathbb{N}$
as in Section 2. Given an increasing path property $\varphi[r]$, where parameter $r \in \mathbb{N}$
stands for some bound on the accumulated reward, we can define the following
types quantiles, where decreasing path properties are denoted by $\psi[r] = \neg\varphi[r]$,
$\unrhd \in \{\geqslant, >\}$, $s \in S$ and $p \in [0,1] \cap \mathbb{Q}$:

$$\min\big\{\, r \in \mathbb{N} \ :\ \mathbb{P}_s^{\mathcal{M}}\big(\varphi[r]\big) \unrhd p \,\big\} \quad \text{and} \quad \max\big\{\, r \in \mathbb{N} \ :\ \mathbb{P}_s^{\mathcal{M}}\big(\psi[r]\big) \unrhd p \,\big\}$$

If the extrema are taken over the empty set, they are defined to be ∞ in the case
of minima and as undefined in the case of maxima. We illustrate how reward-
bounded reachability properties can be used to serve as increasing or decreasing
path properties. For instance, when a is an atomic proposition or a Boolean
combination thereof, the path properties $\Diamond^{\leqslant r} a$ and $\Box^{\geqslant r} a$ are increasing, while
their duals $\Diamond^{\geqslant r} a$ and $\Box^{\leqslant r} a$ are decreasing.[1] Within these notations, the formula
$\phi_{e,u}$ above can be reformulated as $\Diamond^{\leqslant e}(goal \wedge (utility \geqslant u))$ when the consumed
energy is modeled by a reward function and the accumulated utility is assumed
to be encoded in the states, or as $\Diamond^{\geqslant u}(goal \wedge (energy \leqslant e))$ when utility is
represented by a reward function and the consumed energy is augmented to
states. Thus, query **(Q)** as mentioned in the introduction for analyzing resilience

---

[1] The semantics of the reward-bounded eventually and always operator is as follows.
If ζ is an infinite path, then $\zeta \models \Diamond^{\bowtie r} a$ where $\bowtie \in \{\leqslant, \geqslant\}$ if there exists a position
$k \in \mathbb{N}$ with $rew(pref(\zeta, k)) \bowtie r$ and $\zeta[k] \models a$. Similarly, $\Box^{\bowtie r} a \equiv \neg(\Diamond^{\bowtie r}\neg a)$.

mechanisms of a system corresponds to the task of computing the maximal value over all the quantiles e_s, $s \in S$ expressed by

$$e_s = \min\{e \in \mathbb{N} : \mathbb{P}_s^{\mathcal{M}}(\lozenge^{\leqslant e}(\text{stable} \wedge (\textit{utility} \geqslant u))) \geqslant 0.9\}$$

Note that the reward-bounded reachability property inside the quantile expression is equivalent to $\phi_{e,u}$ when *goal* is the set of stable states. Similar to the already mentioned quantiles, we can define expectation quantiles, where the probability bound is replaced by a bound on an expected accumulated reward. For resilient systems, such quantiles can be exemplified by the query (**Qe**) defined informally in the introduction. Answering (**Qe**) then amounts to compute the minimal value over all the quantiles u_s, $s \in S$ where

$$u_s = \max\{u \in \mathbb{N} : \mathbb{E}_s^{\mathcal{M}}[\textit{energy}](\lozenge^{\geqslant u}\text{stable}) \leqslant e\}$$

We now sketch how quantiles can be computed in discrete and continuous-time Markov chains for analyzing resilience mechanisms.

Computing of Quantiles. For qualitative quantiles with upper-bounded eventually properties, i.e., quantiles with the probability bounds $=1$, <1, $=0$ or >0, the quantile values can be computed in polynomial time using a greedy method that shares some ideas of Dijkstra's shortest-path algorithm [34].

For other probability bounds, the schema for computing the quantile is as follows. We explain here the case $e_s = \min\{e \in \mathbb{N} : \mathbb{P}_s^{\mathcal{M}}(\lozenge^{\leqslant e}\textit{goal}) \geqslant p\}$ for answering (**Q**) with $goal = \text{stable} \wedge (\textit{utility} \geqslant u)$. The treatment of other probability quantiles of the above types is analogous [34,5].

1. Compute $p_s = \mathbb{P}_s^{\mathcal{M}}(\lozenge goal)$ for all states s using standard methods. Then, with $X = \{s \in S : p_s < p\}$ we have $e_s = \infty$ iff $s \in X$.
2. If $S \neq X$ then for $r = 0, 1, 2, \ldots$ compute the values $p_{s,r} = \mathbb{P}_s^{\mathcal{M}}(\lozenge^{\leqslant r}\textit{goal})$ for all $s \in S$. Proceed with step 3, as soon as $p_{s,r} \geqslant p$ for all states $s \in S \setminus X$.
3. For each $s \in S \setminus X$, return $e_s = \min\{r \in \mathbb{N} : p_{s,r} \geqslant p\}$.

The computation of the values $p_{s,r}$ in step 2 can be carried out using linear-programming techniques and reusing the values $p_{t,i}$ for $i < r$ computed in previous iterations.

The computation of expectation quantiles as u_s required for answering (**Qe**) follows an analogous approach as for probability quantiles. The idea is to identify the states where the expectation quantile is infinite first. Then, we iteratively compute the values $e_{s,r} = \mathbb{E}_s^{\mathcal{M}}[\textit{energy}](\lozenge^{\geqslant r}\text{stable})$ for $r = 0, 1, \ldots$ solving linear programs until $e_{s,r} > e$. Then, for all $s \in S$ we have $u_s = \max\{r \in \mathbb{N} : e_{s,r} \leqslant e\}$. The minimal value over all u_s provides the answer to query (**Qe**).

Quantiles in Continuous-time Markov Chains. Quantiles in continuous-time Markov chains can be defined in a similar way as for discrete Markov chains. However, since paths have to be replaced by trajectories, the quantile can be a real number rather than an integer. Thus, every maximum in the definition of the discrete case needs to be replaced by a supremum (respectively, minimum replaced by infimum): Let $\mathcal{C} = (\mathcal{M}, E)$ be a continuous-time Markov chain and *rew* a reward function. Then, quantiles are

$$\inf\{\, r \in \mathbb{R} \,:\, \mathbb{P}_s^{\mathcal{C}}(\varphi[r]) \trianglerighteq p \,\} \quad \text{and} \quad \sup\{\, r \in \mathbb{R} \,:\, \mathbb{P}_s^{\mathcal{C}}(\psi[r]) \trianglerighteq p \,\},$$

where $\trianglerighteq \,\in\, \{\geqslant, >\}$ and $\varphi[r]$ ($\psi[r]$) is an increasing (respectively decreasing) path property. As in the discrete case, the quantiles are ∞ if the infimum is taken over the empty set and and undefined for the supremum over the empty set.

We exemplify the approximative computation of quantiles in $\mathcal{C}$ for minimizing quantiles over CSRL-like [4] reward-bounded reachability properties of the form $\varphi[e] = \Diamond^{\leqslant e}\, goal$. With $goal = \text{stable} \wedge (utility \geqslant u)$, computing this quantile for all states s in $\mathcal{C}$ solves task (Q). An infinite trajectory $\vartheta = s_0\, t_0\, s_1\, t_1\, s_2\, t_2\, \dots$ satisfies $\varphi[r]$ if there is some $n \in \mathbb{N}$ such that $rew(s_0\, t_0 \dots t_{n-1}\, s_n) \leqslant e$ and s_n is a stable state. Given some probability bound p and a non-stable state s in $\mathcal{C}$ with $\mathbb{P}_s^{\mathcal{C}}(\Diamond goal) > p$, a simple approximation scheme can be applied to compute $e_s = \inf\{\, e \in \mathbb{R} : \mathbb{P}_s^{\mathcal{C}}(\Diamond^{\leqslant e}\, goal) \geqslant p \,\}$ [7]. The first step is an *exponential search* to determine the smallest $i \in \mathbb{N}$ such that $\mathbb{P}_s^{\mathcal{C}}(\Diamond^{\leqslant 2^i}\, goal) \geqslant p$. For this, we might use known algorithms for computing reward-bounded reachability probabilities in continuous-time Markov chains [4]. The existence of such an index i is guaranteed by the assumption $\mathbb{P}_s^{\mathcal{C}}(\Diamond goal) > p$. If $i \geqslant 1$, we then perform a *binary search* to determine some value $e \in [2^{i-1}, 2^i]$ such that

$$\mathbb{P}_s^{\mathcal{C}}\left(\Diamond^{\leqslant e - \frac{\varepsilon}{2}}\, goal\right) < p \quad \text{and} \quad \mathbb{P}_s^{\mathcal{C}}\left(\Diamond^{\leqslant e + \frac{\varepsilon}{2}}\, goal\right) \geqslant p$$

for some user-defined $\varepsilon > 0$. Then, e is indeed an ε-approximation of the quantile e_s. In the case where the exponential search aborts immediately with $i = 0$, we proceed in the first step by an exponential search to the left (by considering the reward-bounds $2^0 = 1, \frac{1}{2}, \frac{1}{4}, \frac{1}{8}, \dots$) and determine the smallest $i \in \mathbb{N}$ with $\mathbb{P}_s^{\mathcal{C}}\left(\Diamond^{\leqslant 2^{-i}}\, goal\right) < p$. The second step then corresponds to a binary search in the interval $[2^{-i}, 2^{-i+1}]$.

4 Conditional Probabilities and Expectations

Probabilities and expectations under the assumption that some additional temporal condition holds are often needed within the quantitative analysis of protocols. Also within resilient systems they provide interesting insights when analyzing the resilience mechanisms with respect to multi-objective properties. For instance, in the context of energy-utility analysis, conditional probabilities and expectations are useful to analyze the energy-efficiency of the resilience mechanisms, while assuming that a certain condition on the achieved utility is still guaranteed. In some cases, conditions are even required to enable analysis methods, e.g., for computing reachability expectations where the target set of states is not reached almost surely and hence, expectations are undefined.

Let φ and ψ are path properties, called *objective* and *condition*, respectively. If for a given Markov chain $\mathcal{M}$ we have $\mathbb{P}_s^{\mathcal{M}}(\psi) > 0$, the conditional probability of the objective can be computed simply by the definition of conditional probabilities as the quotient of ordinary probabilities:

$$\mathbb{P}_s^{\mathcal{M}}(\varphi \mid \psi) = \frac{\mathbb{P}_s^{\mathcal{M}}(\varphi \wedge \psi)}{\mathbb{P}_s^{\mathcal{M}}(\psi)}$$

This approach has been taken in [3], where the condition and the objective are specified as PCTL path properties. The quotient method has been extended recently [21,26] for discrete and continuous-time Markov chains and patterns of path properties with multiple time- and cost-bounds. An alternative approach relies on a polynomial transformation $\mathcal{M} \rightsquigarrow \mathcal{M}_\psi$ such that for all measurable path properties φ the conditional probability for φ of $\mathcal{M}$ under condition ψ agrees with the standard (unconditional) probability for φ in $\mathcal{M}_\psi$. Besides this approach turns out to outperform other approaches, this approach also has the advantage that the transformed $\mathcal{M}_\psi$ only depends on the condition ψ and can hence be used within different objectives. We sketch this transformation in the following and refer to [10] and [7] for further details.

Computing Conditionals. Let $\mathcal{M} = (S, P)$ be a discrete Markov chain and condition $\psi = \Diamond F$ with $F \subseteq S$. The new Markov chain $\mathcal{M}_\psi = (S_\psi, P_\psi)$ arises from $\mathcal{M}$ by doubling the state space of $\mathcal{M}$ by $S_\psi = S^{bef} \cup S^{nor}$, where:

$$S^{bef} = \left\{ s^{bef} : s \in S, s \models \exists \Diamond F \right\} \qquad S^{nor} = \left\{ s^{nor} : s \in S \right\}.$$

We refer to states $s^{nor} \in S^{nor}$ as states s in "normal mode". Analogously, we refer to states $s^{bef} \in S^{bef}$ as states s in "before mode". For the states in before mode we only consider states that can satisfy condition $\psi = \Diamond F$, i.e., states that can indeed reach F. The states in normal mode $\mathcal{M}_\psi$ behave exactly as in $\mathcal{M}$ as for those states we preserve the transition probabilities appearing in $\mathcal{M}$, whereas the probabilities for states in before mode are normalized with respect to the reachability probability of F. If $s \in S \backslash F$, $v \in S$ and from s and v the set F can be reached in $\mathcal{M}$, then

$$P_\psi(s^{bef}, v^{bef}) \;=\; P(s, v) \cdot \frac{\mathbb{P}_v^{\mathcal{M}}(\Diamond F)}{\mathbb{P}_s^{\mathcal{M}}(\Diamond F)}$$

For $s \in F$, we define $P_\psi(s^{bef}, v^{nor}) = P(s, v)$, modeling the switch from before to normal mode. Obviously, all states in the before mode can reach $F^{bef} = \{v^{bef} : v \in F\}$. This yields $\mathbb{P}_{s^{bef}}^{\mathcal{M}_\psi}(\Diamond F^{bef}) = 1$ for all states s of $\mathcal{M}$ with $s \models \exists \Diamond F$. Then, if $\psi = \Diamond F$ is a condition and φ is an arbitrary path property measurable in $\mathcal{M}$, then labeling the states s^{bef} and s^{nor} in $\mathcal{M}_\psi$ as s in $\mathcal{M}$ yields

$$\mathbb{P}_s^{\mathcal{M}}(\varphi \mid \Diamond F) \;=\; \mathbb{P}_{s^{bef}}^{\mathcal{M}_\psi}(\varphi)$$

This statement can be generalized for the case of ω-regular conditions ψ used instead of a reachability condition $\psi = \Diamond F$. Hence, this approach can be used to answer the task **(C)** for analyzing resilient systems mentioned in the introduction, which is formalized as the question whether

$$\mathbb{P}_{s_{init}}^{\mathcal{M}} \left(\Box(\text{failure} \implies \text{MTTR}_{\leqslant t}) \mid \Box \Diamond \text{stable} \right) = 1?$$

Here, s_{init} stands for an initial state of $\mathcal{M}$ and $\text{MTTR}_{\leqslant t}$ denotes the set of states where the mean time to recover is bounded by t, i.e.,

$$\text{MTTR}_{\leqslant t} = \left\{ s \in S : \mathbb{E}_s^{\mathcal{M}}[time](\Diamond \text{stable}) \leqslant t \right\}.$$

Note that assuming the condition in the above expression is a fairness condition which is sufficient for guaranteeing that the inner expectation is defined, since it implies $\mathbb{P}_s^{\mathcal{M}}(\Diamond\text{stable} \mid \Box\Diamond\text{stable}) = 1$ for all $s \in S$.

The results about conditional probabilities can be also extended to reason over expectations of some reward function $rew : S \cup S{\times}S \to \mathbb{N}$ using the conditional probability measure induced by $\mathcal{M}_\psi$ instead of the standard probability measure of $\mathcal{M}$. Hence, also the conditional expectation for reaching F can be computed using the same transformation as for conditional probabilities:

$$\mathbb{E}_s^{\mathcal{M}}[rew](\Diamond F \mid \Diamond F) \;=\; \mathbb{E}_{s^{bef}}^{\mathcal{M}_\psi}[rew_\psi](\Diamond F_\psi),$$

where $F_\psi = \{s^{bef} : s \in S, s \models \exists\Diamond F\} \cup \{s^{nor} : s \in S\}$ and rew_ψ arises from rew by annotating bef and nor, except for all states s, t in $\mathcal{M}$ with $P(s,t) > 0$ and $t \not\models \exists\Diamond F$, where $rew_\psi(s^{bef}, t^{bef}) = 0$. This approach yields a method for computing (**Ce**) from the introduction: First, compute for all $s \in S$ the expectation

$$e_s \;=\; \mathbb{E}_s^{\mathcal{M}}[energy](\Diamond\text{stable} \mid \Diamond\text{stable})$$

Then, the maximum of all e_s provides the answer to the resilience property (**Ce**). As in the case for conditional probabilities, we can extend this approach towards goal and reward reachability predicates as objectives and ω-regular conditions ψ using an automata-theoretic product construction.

Conditionals in Continuous-time Markov Chains. The transformation presented above can be done similarly for continuous-time Markov chains. Let $\mathcal{C} = (\mathcal{M}, E)$ where $\mathcal{M}$ is as before, $E : S \to \mathbb{R}$ an exit-rate function and $\psi = \Diamond F$ with $F \subseteq S$ a condition. We define $\mathcal{C}_\psi = (\mathcal{M}_\psi, E_\psi)$, where $E_\psi(s^{bef}) = E_\psi(s^{nor}) = E(s)$ for all states s in $\mathcal{C}$. The mentioned one-to-one correspondence between paths in $\mathcal{M}$ and paths in $\mathcal{M}_\psi$ carries over to trajectories in the continuous-time Markov chains $\mathcal{C}$ and $\mathcal{C}_\psi$. This allows to use the same approaches for computing conditional probabilities and expectations with respect to (untimed) ω-regular conditions as in the discrete case, allowing among others to compute the answers for (**C**) and (**Ce**) also for continuous-time Markov chains.

Conditional Quantiles. Since the presented transformation is independent from the objective, this also enables to combine the approaches of computing quantiles and conditionals towards algorithms for *conditional quantiles*

$$\min\{r \in \mathbb{N} : \mathbb{P}_s^{\mathcal{M}}(\varphi[r] \mid \psi) \geqslant p\} \;=\; \min\{r \in \mathbb{N} : \mathbb{P}_s^{\mathcal{M}_\psi}(\varphi[r]) \geqslant p\},$$

where $\varphi[r]$ is an increasing path property such as $\Diamond^{\leqslant r}\text{stable}$ (see also Section 3).

5   Reasoning about the Cost-reward Ratios

Another important type of non-standard multi-objective requirements on resilient systems is provided by reasoning over properties containing the quotient of two accumulated reward functions. For instance, the task (**R**) mentioned in the introduction relies on the relative availability time of a network system, which can be formalized as the quotient

$$rel\_avail = \frac{total\_time - outage\_time}{total\_time}$$

of the two accumulated rewards $outage\_time$ and $total\_time$. For a resilient system modeled by a discrete Markov chain $\mathcal{M} = (S, P)$ with starting state s_{init}, (**R**) then can be answered by calculating

$$\mathbb{P}^{\mathcal{M}}_{s_{init}} \left(\square \left(rel\_avail > 0.99 \right) \wedge \square(\text{failure} \implies \text{stable}_{\geqslant 0.9}) \right),$$

where $\text{stable}_{\geqslant 0.9}$ stands for the set of states from which within at least 90% probability, a stable state is reached, i.e.,

$$\text{stable}_{\geqslant 0.9} = \{s \in S : \mathbb{P}^{\mathcal{M}}_{s} \left(\lozenge \text{stable} \right) \geqslant 0.9\}$$

In order to provide algorithms for computing the above probability, we discuss some generalized patterns of probabilities depending on such ratios for probabilistic systems modeled by discrete Markov chains. We assume two weight functions, say $cost$ and $reward$, where the cost weight function is supposed to be positive. Let $ratio = \frac{reward}{cost} : FinPaths \to \mathbb{Q}$ given by $ratio(\pi) = reward(\pi)/cost(\pi)$ if $|\pi| \geqslant 1$, $\alpha, \beta \in \mathbb{Z}$ and $\theta = \alpha/\beta$ the *quality threshold*. Using an LTL-like syntax, we define the path property $\psi_\theta = \square(ratio > \theta)$, where $\zeta \models \psi_\theta$ iff $ratio(pref(\zeta, k)) > \theta$ for all positions $k \in \mathbb{N}$ with $k \geqslant 1$. We are now interested in algorithms for computing $\mathbb{P}^{\mathcal{M}}_{s_{init}} (\psi_\theta \wedge \varphi)$, where φ is an ω-regular path property for $\mathcal{M}$. Using a simple transformation $(cost, reward) \mapsto wgt$ permits to replace the ratio-constraint ψ_θ with a constraint $\square(wgt > 0)$ for a single weight function $wgt : S \cup S \times S \to \mathbb{Z}$ defined by

$$wgt(s) = \beta \cdot reward(s) - \alpha \cdot cost(s)$$
$$wgt(s, t) = \beta \cdot reward(s, t) - \alpha \cdot cost(s, t)$$

for all $s, t \in S$. It is clear that for all finite paths π, we have that $ratio(\pi) > \theta$ iff $wgt(\pi) > 0$, such that for all infinite paths ζ holds $\zeta \models \psi_\theta \wedge \varphi$ iff $\zeta \models \square(wgt > 0) \wedge \varphi$. Before we turn to quantitative questions, we are first interested in solving the qualitative questions whether

$$\textbf{(1)} \quad \mathbb{P}^{\mathcal{M}}_{s_{init}} (\psi_\theta \wedge \varphi) = 1 \qquad \textbf{(0)} \quad \mathbb{P}^{\mathcal{M}}_{s_{init}} (\psi_\theta \wedge \varphi) > 0$$

Almost-sure Problem. Obviously, for the almost-sure problem **(1)** we have

$$\mathbb{P}^{\mathcal{M}}_{s_{init}} (\square(wgt > 0) \wedge \varphi) = 1 \quad \text{iff} \quad \mathbb{P}^{\mathcal{M}}_{s_{init}} (\square(wgt > 0)) = 1 \text{ and } \mathbb{P}^{\mathcal{M}}_{s_{init}} (\varphi) = 1.$$

The condition $\mathbb{P}^{\mathcal{M}}_{s_{init}} (\varphi) = 1$ can be checked in time polynomial in the size of $\mathcal{M}$ using standard techniques. The condition $\mathbb{P}^{\mathcal{M}}_{s_{init}} (\square(wgt > 0)) = 1$ is equivalent to $s \not\models \exists\lozenge(wgt < 0)$ and can be checked in polynomial time using standard shortest-path algorithms.

Positive Probability Problem. Let us now turn to **(0)**, where the task is to check whether $\mathbb{P}^{\mathcal{M}}_{s_{init}} (\psi_\theta \wedge \varphi) > 0$. The challenge in providing algorithms for this problem becomes clear as they depend on the concrete transition probabilities of $\mathcal{M}$. Consider the discrete Markov chain $\mathcal{M}_p$ in the following picture, where $p \in {]}0,1{[}$ is a probability parameter and all transition rewards are zero:

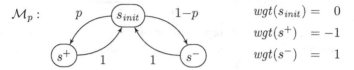

$$wgt(s_{init}) = 0$$
$$wgt(s^+) = -1$$
$$wgt(s^-) = 1$$

Finite paths in $\mathcal{M}_p$ starting and ending in s_{init} constitute a biased random walk which drifts to the right and never reaches position s^- with positive probability if $p > \frac{1}{2}$, whereas for $0 < p \leqslant \frac{1}{2}$, position s^- will be visited almost surely. Thus, $\mathbb{P}^{\mathcal{M}_p}_{s_{init}}\big(\Box(wgt \geqslant 0)\big) > 0$ iff $p > \frac{1}{2}$. As a consequence, the answer for **(0)** may depend on the concrete transition probabilities. This observation rules out simple algorithms relying on shortest-path arguments as for **(1)**. Nevertheless, the problem **(0)** turns out to be decidable, as shown in the next paragraph.

Quantitative Problems. The *quantitative task* to check whether $\mathbb{P}^{\mathcal{M}}_{s_{init}}(\psi_\theta \wedge \varphi) \bowtie p$ for some given $p \in [0,1] \cap \mathbb{Q}$ and $\bowtie \in \{\leqslant, <, \geqslant, >\}$ can be shown to be decidable. We rely here on a reduction to the quantitative model-checking problem for probabilistic push-down automata (pPDA) and apply the techniques presented, e.g., in [13]. The idea is simply to consider the states of $\mathcal{M}$ as control states of a pPDA and to mimic each transition $s \to s'$ in $\mathcal{M}$ of weight $k > 0$ by k push operations and each transition $s \to s'$ with weight $-k$ by k pop operations. This reduction yields a pPDA which is of size exponential in the size of $\mathcal{M}$. Solving the quantitative model-checking problem for this pPDA and ω-regular properties is doable within space polynomial in the size of the pPDA. This yields also a method for answering task **(R)** for analyzing resilient systems. Better upper complexity bounds including for task **(0)** are left for future work.

6   Quantitative Analysis of an MMR Protocol

In this section, we present a model for a variant of the resiliency concept MMR, which we analyzed with respect to various kinds of quantitative measures and (non-standard) multi-objective properties as illustrated in the previous sections. For presentation purposes, we focus on results for selected quantiles [5] and conditional probabilities and expectations [10] that have been achieved with our extensions of the explicit engine of the probabilistic model checker PRISM. The MMR model used for our analysis is based on a discrete Markov chain that is equipped with reward functions for different cost and utility measures.

6.1   Protocol and Model Description

Our model consists of N replicated components, a master, a repairing module, and a controller, each modeled as separate modules in PRISM. Furthermore, we introduced an extra module for characterizing the error probabilities of the components. As illustrated in the introduction, our variant of an MMR protocol operates in rounds managed by the master and consisting of four phases:

(1) The master *collects* the (possibly faulty) result of each component,
(2) and *evaluates* for majority among the provided results. If a majority cannot be found the protocol repeats phase (1).
(3) Broken components are disabled and enqueued for *repair*.
(4) The controller makes *adaptations* on the system by switching components on and off (e.g. for saving energy or to increase the resilience of the system).

Operational Behavior of the Model. In the first phase, we only consider binary results provided by the components, i.e., "correct" or "faulty". The probability to fail for a component is provided by an error model, differing between the components and depending on the age of them. Aging of the components is modeled by counting the time steps starting when a component is new till a maximal aging time is reached. The longer a component is in operation, the higher is its probability to fail: starting within a minimal probability p_a increasing linearly towards p_z, reached at the maximal aging time. If the outcome of the majority is the wrong result, i.e., more than half of the components are faulty, the components that produced an output different from the majority are considered to be broken and scheduled for repair. Broken components cannot be used in successive rounds unless they are repaired by the repair module. At most one component can be repaired in each round, i.e., if more than one component is broken, then some of the components can only be used again with a certain delay. Based on a reliability measure, components can be switched off or additional components are switched on in the step before a new round starts. If the current reliability exceeds some bound, active components are switched off. In case that the reliability is too low, the controller tries to activate additional components that are currently switched off.

Reward Structures. We implemented several reward structures to describe quantitative behavior of the system. First, there is a reward structure for counting the number of rounds. Second, we count the number of correct majority decisions. On the cost side, we introduced a reward structure for the energy consumption of the components. Each component consumes one energy unit while operating and no energy if it is switched off or broken, whereas each repair step consumes 10 units of energy.

6.2   Quantitative Analysis

For our experiments, we analyzed an instance of our MMR model with three and five components and different individual error probabilities. Each error model of a component is formalized as a pair $(p_a, p_z) \in [0,1]^2$, where p_a stands for the initial error probability when the component is freshly replicated and spawn or just repaired and p_z is the error probability when the maximum age of the component ($= 4$) has been reached. The following five different error models E1 - E5 for the five component used in our case study: Note that the first component's

error model	component 1	component 2	component 3	component 4	component 5
E1	(0.2, 0.2)	0.19, 0.25)	(0.18, 0.3)	(0.17, 0.35)	(0.16, 0.4)
E2	(0.3, 0.3)	(0.29, 0.35)	(0.28, 0.4)	(0.27, 0.45)	(0.17, 0.5)
E3	(0.4, 0.4)	(0.39, 0.45)	(0.38, 0.5)	(0.37, 0.55)	(0.18, 0.6)
E4	(0.5, 0.5)	(0.49, 0.55)	(0.48, 0.6)	(0.47, 0.65)	(0.19, 0.7)
E5	(0.6, 0.6)	(0.59, 0.65)	(0.58, 0.7)	(0.57, 0.75)	(0.20, 0.8)

Fig. 2. Error models of the used components

error probability is not influenced by aging, whereas it is for all the others. The calculations for this paper were carried out on a computer with 2 Intel E5-2680 8-core CPUs at 2.70 GHz with 384Gb of RAM.

Quantile Experiments. First, we considered the query **(Q)**, formalized as

(Q) $\max\{e_s \mid e_s = \min\{e \in \mathbb{N} : \mathbb{P}_s^{\mathcal{M}}(\lozenge^{\leq e}(\mathit{correct\_decisions} \geq c \wedge \mathrm{stable})) \geq 0.9\}\}$,

where e is the amount of energy consumed to reach a stable state with correct decisions used as utility measure. Furthermore, we had to implement the number of correct decisions in the model instead of using a reward, following the approach as detailed in Section 3. We considered the instance with the first $N = 3$ components, which yield a model consisting of 44,074 states. The model checking computations for values $c = 10, 20, \ldots, 100$ and each error model E1 - E5 required in total 3,375 seconds. The results depicted in Figure 3 show that

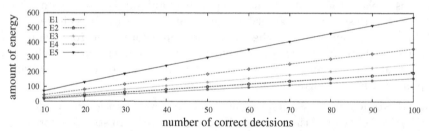

Fig. 3. Quantile values for query **(Q)**

the correlation of total number of rounds and the number of correct decisions is almost proportional, although broken or inactive components highly increase the probability of building wrong majority decisions.

Conditional Expectation Experiments. We also investigated a variant of the the conditional query **(Ce)**

(Ce') $\max\{e_s \mid e_s = \mathbb{E}_s^{\mathcal{M}}[\mathit{energy}](\lozenge\mathrm{stable} \mid (\mathit{num\_broken} < 2) \: \mathrm{U} \: \mathrm{stable})\}$,

where $\mathit{num\_broken}$ denotes the number of components the master marked as broken. This query asks for the maximal amount of energy that can be expected until the system reaches a stable state, assuming that not more than one component remains broken in each step. We analyzed a model with $N = 5$ components, which yield a model with 82,712 states. The whole experiment took 80 seconds of computation time. Figure 4 shows the result for each of the error models E1 - E5, where the energy consumption decreases with error models E4 and E5. This is as expected, since the probability to fail within these error models and hence the probability to mark wrong components as broken is higher than the probability to make the right decision, which yield lower energy costs but also lowers resilience.

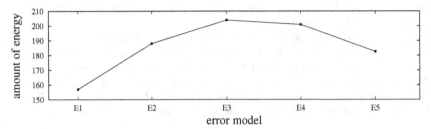

Fig. 4. Conditional expectation value for query **(Ce')**

7   Conclusions

Based on several exemplary tasks, we showed how recently emerging approaches for multi-objective reasoning can be used for the quantitative analysis of resilient systems. We mainly put the focus on the inspirations that we got for theoretical work on quantitative measures to reason about the duality of two weight functions, such as energy and utility. As we restricted ourselves on resilient systems modeled by either discrete or continuous-time Markov chains, we could provide algorithms for solving quantiles, conditional probabilities and expectations, as well as properties depending on a ratio of accumulated reward functions. Also for resilient systems modeled by Markov decision processes, where besides probabilistic choices, non-deterministic decisions can be modeled in the system, algorithms exist [7,5,10,11]. However, whereas the picture for Markov chains is almost complete, there are several gaps for approaches within Markov decision processes. Filling these gaps and providing more efficient algorithms especially for the positive probability problem for ratios is left for further work. Unfortunately, the effort with respect to the ratio framework is rather limited, e.g., by recent undecidability results [11]. We also plan to investigate further application areas such as analyzing resilient systems specified in a probabilistic product line using our recent probabilistic framework [20] and to analyze long-run properties within our MMR case study.

References

1. Aggarwal, V., Chandrasekaran, R., Nair, K.: Markov ratio decision processes. Journal of Optimization Theory and Application 21(1) (1977)
2. Andova, S., Hermanns, H., Katoen, J.-P.: Discrete-time rewards model-checked. In: Larsen, K.G., Niebert, P. (eds.) FORMATS 2003. LNCS, vol. 2791, pp. 88–104. Springer, Heidelberg (2004)

3. Andrés, M.E., van Rossum, P.: Conditional probabilities over probabilistic and nondeterministic systems. In: Ramakrishnan, C.R., Rehof, J. (eds.) TACAS 2008. LNCS, vol. 4963, pp. 157–172. Springer, Heidelberg (2008)
4. Baier, C., Cloth, L., Haverkort, B.R., Hermanns, H., Katoen, J.-P.: Performability assessment by model checking of Markov reward models. Formal Methods in System Design 36(1), 1–36 (2010)
5. Baier, C., Daum, M., Dubslaff, C., Klein, J., Klüppelholz, S.: Energy-utility quantiles. In: Badger, J.M., Rozier, K.Y. (eds.) NFM 2014. LNCS, vol. 8430, pp. 285–299. Springer, Heidelberg (2014)
6. Baier, C., Daum, M., Engel, B., Härtig, H., Klein, J., Klüppelholz, S., Märcker, S., Tews, H., Völp, M.: Locks: Picking key methods for a scalable quantitative analysis. Journal of Computer and System Sciences (to appear, 2014)
7. Baier, C., Dubslaff, C., Klein, J., Klüppelholz, S., Wunderlich, S.: Probabilistic model checking for energy-utility analysis. In: Kashefi, E., Palamidessi, C., Rutten, J. (eds.) Panangaden Festschrift. LNCS, vol. 8464, pp. 96–123. Springer, Heidelberg (2014)
8. Baier, C., Engel, B., Klüppelholz, S., Märcker, S., Tews, H., Völp, M.: A probabilistic quantitative analysis of probabilistic-write/Copy-select. In: Brat, G., Rungta, N., Venet, A. (eds.) NFM 2013. LNCS, vol. 7871, pp. 307–321. Springer, Heidelberg (2013)
9. Baier, C., Katoen, J.-P.: Principles of Model Checking. MIT Press (2008)
10. Baier, C., Klein, J., Klüppelholz, S., Märcker, S.: Computing conditional probabilities in markovian models efficiently. In: Ábrahám, E., Havelund, K. (eds.) TACAS 2014. LNCS, vol. 8413, pp. 515–530. Springer, Heidelberg (2014)
11. Baier, C., Klein, J., Klüppelholz, S., Wunderlich, S.: Weight monitoring with linear temporal logic: Complexity and decidability. In: 29th ACM/IEEE Symposium on Logic in Computer Science, LICS 2014 (2014) (accepted for publication)
12. Bianco, A., de Alfaro, L.: Model checking of probabilistic and non-deterministic systems. In: Thiagarajan, P.S. (ed.) FSTTCS 1995. LNCS, vol. 1026, pp. 499–513. Springer, Heidelberg (1995)
13. Brázdil, T., Kučera, A., Stražovský, O.: On the Decidability of Temporal Properties of Probabilistic Pushdown Automata. In: Diekert, V., Durand, B. (eds.) STACS 2005. LNCS, vol. 3404, pp. 145–157. Springer, Heidelberg (2005)
14. Clarke, E., Grumberg, O., Peled, D.: Model Checking. MIT Press (2000)
15. Courcoubetis, C., Yannakakis, M.: The complexity of probabilistic verification. Journal of the ACM 42(4), 857–907 (1995)
16. de Alfaro, L.: Formal Verification of Probabilistic Systems. PhD thesis, Stanford University, Department of Computer Science (1997)
17. de Alfaro, L.: How to specify and verify the long-run average behavior of probabilistic systems. In: 13th Annual IEEE Symposium on Logic in Computer Science (LICS), pp. 454–465. IEEE Computer Society (1998)
18. de Alfaro, L.: Computing minimum and maximum reachability times in probabilistic systems. In: Baeten, J.C.M., Mauw, S. (eds.) CONCUR 1999. LNCS, vol. 1664, pp. 66–81. Springer, Heidelberg (1999)
19. Desharnais, J., Panangaden, P.: Continuous stochastic logic characterizes bisimulation of continuous-time Markov processes. Journal of Logic and Algebraic Programming 56(1-2), 99–115 (2003)
20. Dubslaff, C., Klüppelholz, S., Baier, C.: Probabilistic model checking for energy analysis in software product lines. In: 13th International Conference on Modularity (MODULARITY). ACM Press (to appear, 2014)

21. Gao, Y., Xu, M., Zhan, N., Zhang, L.: Model checking conditional CSL for continuous-time Markov chains. IPL 113(1-2), 44–50 (2013)
22. Grädel, E., Thomas, W., Wilke, T. (eds.): Automata, Logics, and Infinite Games. LNCS, vol. 2500. Springer, Heidelberg (2002)
23. Hansson, H., Jonsson, B.: A logic for reasoning about time and reliability. Formal Aspects of Computing 6, 512–535 (1994)
24. Haverkort, B.: Performance of Computer Communication Systems: A Model-Based Approach. Wiley (1998)
25. Hinton, A., Kwiatkowska, M., Norman, G., Parker, D.: PRISM: A tool for automatic verification of probabilistic systems. In: Hermanns, H., Palsberg, J. (eds.) TACAS 2006. LNCS, vol. 3920, pp. 441–444. Springer, Heidelberg (2006)
26. Ji, M., Wu, D., Chen, Z.: Verification method of conditional probability based on automaton. Journal of Networks 8(6), 1329–1335 (2013)
27. Katoen, J.-P., Zapreev, I., Hahn, E., Hermanns, H., Jansen, D.: The ins and outs of the probabilistic model checker MRMC. Performance Evaluation 68(2) (2011)
28. Kulkarni, V.: Modeling and Analysis of Stochastic Systems. Chapman and Hall (1995)
29. Laprie, J.-C.: From dependability to resilience. In: 38th Annual IEEE/IFIP International Conference on Dependable Systems and Networks(DSN), Page Fast Abstracts, Abstracts, Anchorage, AK (June 2008)
30. Maruyama, H., Minami, K.: Towards systems resilience. Innovation and Supply Chain Management 7(3) (2013)
31. Panangaden, P.: Measure and probability for concurrency theorists. Theoretical Computer Science 253(2), 287–309 (2001)
32. Puterman, M.: Markov Decision Processes: Discrete Stochastic Dynamic Programming. John Wiley & Sons (1994)
33. Serfling, R.J.: Approximation Theorems of Mathematical Statistics. John Wiley & Sons (1980)
34. Ummels, M., Baier, C.: Computing quantiles in Markov reward models. In: Pfenning, F. (ed.) FOSSACS 2013. LNCS, vol. 7794, pp. 353–368. Springer, Heidelberg (2013)
35. Vardi, M.: Automatic verification of probabilistic concurrent finite-state programs. In: 26th IEEE Symposium on Foundations of Computer Science (FOCS), pp. 327–338. IEEE Computer Society (1985)
36. von Essen, C., Jobstmann, B.: Synthesizing systems with optimal average-case behavior for ratio objectives. In: International Workshop on Interactions, Games and Protocols (iWIGP). EPTCS, vol. 50, pp. 17–32 (2011)
37. von Neumann, J.: Probabilistic logics and the synthesis of reliable organisms from unreliable components. In: Automata Studies. Annals of Mathematics Studies, vol. 34, pp. 43–98. Princeton University Press, Princeton (1956)

Complex Networks and Link Streams for the Empirical Analysis of Large Software

Matthieu Latapy[1,2] and Tiphaine Viard[1,2]

[1] Sorbonne Universités, UPMC Univ Paris 06, UMR 7606, LIP6, Paris, France
[2] CNRS, UMR 7606, LIP6, Paris, France
`FirstName.LastName@lip6.fr`

Abstract. Large software may be modeled as graphs in several ways. For instance, nodes may represent modules, objects or functions, and links may encode dependencies between them, calls, heritage, etc. One may then study a large software through such graphs, called complex networks because they have no strong mathematical properties. Studying them sheds much light on the structure of the considered software. If one turns to the analysis of the dynamics of large software, like execution traces, then the considered graphs evolve over time. This raises challenging issues, as there is currently no clear way to study such objects. We develop a new approach consisting in modeling traces as link streams, i.e. series of triplets (t, a, b) meaning that a and b interacted at time t. For instance, such a triplet may model a call between two modules at run time. Analyzing such streams directly turns out to be much easier and powerful than transforming them into dynamic graphs that poorly capture their dynamics. We present our work on this topic, with directions for applications in software analysis.

Keywords: complex networks, dynamic graphs, link streams, software traces.

1 Introduction

With typically millions of lines of code, large software are among the most complex human-designed objects ever built, and they play a key role in all aspects of modern life. As a consequence, they are at the core of an intense research and engineering activity, and much work is devoted to understanding them better. They are the focus of several, complementary scientific areas like software engineering, complexity, or proof systems; basically most computer science researches are related to them. Despite this, our current understanding of large real-world software remains very limited. Typically, ensuring their reliability, efficiency and robustness remains out of reach although this is crucial.

Because software are human-crafted objects, the classical approach for studying them is design-oriented: one relies on an accurate knowledge of their building blocks and the study focuses on the way they are combined to form larger blocks, ultimately leading to entire software. By carefully controlling these building steps, one is able to ensure wanted properties for the whole object and/or to

---

The original version of this chapter was revised: The second author name was changed. The erratum to this chapter is available at 10.1007/978-3-319-07734-5_23

G. Ciardo and E. Kindler (Eds.): PETRI NETS 2014, LNCS 8489, pp. 40–50, 2014.

explain its actual properties. This approach is of course sound and promising. Nowadays, it makes it possible to improve software quality and dependability at an ever-growing scale. And yet, most real-world software remain out of reach of these approaches because of their size, their empirical design process, and they sheer complexity. As a consequence, software are still subject to various kinds of failures, as we all experience in everyday life.

In parallel, an approach inspired from natural sciences has been developed. It consists in viewing software as complex systems which may be studied from the outside, without relying on an accurate knowledge of their design and components. This is similar to the way biologists study living organisms or physicists study the universe. This approach is data-oriented: it relies on data regarding various features of the software under concern, obtained through observations and measurements of various kinds. Surely, this approach seems counter-intuitive for studying systems designed by humans as one may expect that the design-oriented approach has access to much more information. However, it turns out that the data-oriented approach captures well the complexity of real-world large software, and sheds lights on several important questions.

2   Contribution

In this paper, we focus on a key element of software seen as complex systems: the networks representing their structure at various scales. More precisely, we consider a software artifact (like its source code or an execution trace) and we model it as a graph. Nodes of this graph represent entities like functions, variables, objects, etc, and links between these entities represent relations like function calls, dependencies, inheritance, etc (we will be more specific below). Such graphs are called *complex networks* because they have *a priori* no simple mathematical structure. They are at the center of a very active field, called network science, born in the end of the 90s. This paper presents and discusses connections between network science and software science, with a focus on dynamical aspects. We propose in particular a new approach for modeling such dynamics, using an formalism called *link streams*.

The paper is organized as follows. First, we explain how software may be modeled as complex networks at various levels, and we introduce a concrete example that we use all along the paper to illustrate our presentation. Then we shortly present the main areas of application of network science to software engineering and the insights obtained this way. We turn to the network science contributions to the study of the dynamics of large software, be it the time evolution of their source code or the analysis of execution traces. Finally, we introduce the approach based on link streams for the study of execution traces and show how it captures the both temporal and structural nature of these objects.

Before entering in the core of this paper, let us insist on the fact that it does *not* aim at at reviewing all the literature dealing with complex networks and software, which contains a wide variety of works. Instead, it aims at giving some insight on what is done and what *could* be done in the context of empirical software studies with network science, with an emphasis on dynamical aspects.

Similarly, although we will use a guiding example all along the paper, our aim is *not* to obtain new results on this specific example. We use it for illustrative purpose only, in order to make our discussion more concrete. Applying the techniques we present remains case-dependent, and a significant piece of work has to be done for interpretating the obtained results. Such applications and interpretations are out of the scope of this paper.

Finally, let us insist on the fact that we are aware of the fact that there is already much work devoted to the analysis of software structures and their execution traces. For instance, some authors model traces with grammar-oriented languages [26,25]. We take here a much more descriptive and empirical perspective, which is complementary to these work. Indeed, given a large network representing the structure of a software (for instance, function calls in its source code), network science describes it through a set of coarse-grained statistics able to capture the structure of the network. Similarly, the link streams approach we propose aims at giving an empirical description of real-world traces, in terms of their dynamics and structure. Hopefully, the next sections will make clearer the (potential) contribution of network science and link streams to the field, and its complementarity with existing approaches.

3   From Software to Complex Networks

Many complex networks may be defined from software artifacts, at various levels. If one starts with the source code of the software, the most classical network probably is the call graph: nodes are functions or methods, and there is a link from node a to node b if there is a call to function b in the source code of function a. One may also focus on dependencies between modules, inheritance between object classes, or even relations between variables.

One may also define complex networks from execution traces, capturing for instance memory transfers, run-time calls, scheduling of tasks, etc. In this situation, for instance, nodes may represent memory cells and there is a link from node a to node b if data was copied from memory location a to memory location b. Going further, some authors model bugs in software systems by graphs where nodes are bugs and a link exists between two bugs if they have similar features [15]. Others model how developers interact [22] or how they are involved in the edition of source code [5]. Examples are as numerous and diverse as the questions on software artifacts.

The choice of an appropriate network modeling of a software depends of the target application and on available artifacts. Obtained graphs may have between a few dozens and millions (or even more) of nodes and links. Network science, because of its statistical nature, is best suited for the study of large-scale structures. In all cases where statistics make sense, though, the obtained graph may be studied through network science principles with much benefit.

In order to illustrate the notions and discussions presented in this paper, we consider a simple illustrative example. It consists in the source code of a small program dedicated to the computation of the number of triangles (*i.e.* three nodes with three links between them) in a graph [9]. This program is written in C and has approximately 700 lines of code. It contains the definition of 28 functions, and slightly more than 100 variable declarations. It contains implementations of four distinct algorithms for computing triangles (for comparison purposes), as well as an implementation of quick-sort and binary search.

We model this program as a graph in two different but closely related ways. First, we consider variable affectations in the source code, and build a graph in which nodes are variable names and there is a link between two variable names a and b if the result of a computation involving variable b is affected to variable a. The obtained graph has around 100 nodes and links. The other graph we build is obtained from a running of the program on a medium-sized input which we do not detail here. The nodes of this second graph are the addresses of variables used during the execution of the code, and there is a link between two addresses a and b if a computation involving a variable at address b is affected to a variable at address a. The obtained graph has almost 30 000 nodes and 300 000 links.

The two considered graphs are very different in nature. First, although both capture data transfers between variables, they represent very different objects: a static one obtained from source code and a dynamic one obtained at run time. For instance, a line like a = b+c; in the source code leads to two links in the first graph: one between variables names a and b, and one between a and c. At run time, this line may be executed many times with different addresses for variables a, b, and c (if they are local variables in particular). It may therefore lead to many links in the second graph we consider. Notice that the two graphs indeed have very different sizes.

Although it is rather small and the graphs we consider are quite arbitrary, this example has several key advantages. First, its small size allows to get some insight from visualization, as we will see below. Moreover, the program implements several algorithms performing the same computation (but in a different way). Therefore, one may compare the different algorithms from the complex network perspective, as well as the whole code. Another advantage is that the first graph may be observed only from source code, but the second one may be observed even without access to the source code. This illustrates two very different but equally interesting situations. Notice also that these objects capture important information on the considered program, like its structure, locality of memory usage, propagation of computation errors and imprecision, etc.

4   Insights from Network Science

A first way to gain insight on a complex network is to draw a picture of it, see Figures 1 and 2. However, graph drawing is a challenging task and results are often disappointing. Getting insight from such a drawing requires more work, often done manually. In addition, there are many possible drawings of a same network, and so interpretating drawings may be misleading. As a consequence, although a drawing of a complex network is a natural entry point for describing it, it is far from sufficient in general.

Fig. 1. A graphical representation of the complex network modeling affectation in the source code of our guiding example. Heterogeneous degrees are clearly observable, as well as some local structures and a global tree-like shape. The small component at the top of the drawing is composed of the variables used for monitoring time performance of the different algorithms in the code; they do not interact with other variables.

Network science provides a wide set of notions that are now classically used to describe a complex network. Among them, the degree distribution, *i.e.* the fraction of nodes with k links, for all k, probably is the most famous. Another key property is the density, *i.e.* the probability that any two randomly chosen nodes in the network are linked together. This global property has its local counterpart, known as the *clustering coefficient*, which is the probability that two neighbors of any node in the network are linked together. Finally, a classical topic in the field is community detection [6]. Intuitively, a community is a set of densely connected nodes with only few connections to nodes outside the group, see Figure 3. Many variant and extensions of these notions exist and are used at various places in the literature.

The key point here is that the vast majority of real-world complex networks have similar features regarding these properties: they have a low density, a very heterogeneous degree distribution (sometimes well fitted by a power-law), a high clustering coefficient, and community structures at several scales. This makes them very similar to each other, and very different from random graphs, in contradiction with most previous assumptions.

Complex networks modeling software are no exceptions to this regard: it was shown in a wide variety of cases that they have the same properties as other real-world complex networks, see for instance [18,21,7]. As a consequence, a large stream of studies were devoted to the characterization and description of software networks with the tools of network science. Some of these works go further: they use network statistics to estimate the complexity of software source codes, their level of modularity, their robustness, or even to detect pieces of codes that should be separate modules [14,23,16,11,19,10,13,7,24].

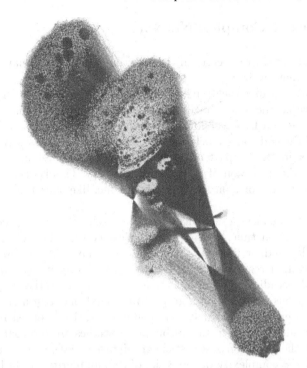

Fig. 2. A graphical representation of the complex network modeling affectation (memory transfers) in a running of our guiding example. Although visualization at such scales are difficult to interpret and often misleading, one may observe different component and sub-components, as well as nodes connecting them like bridges.

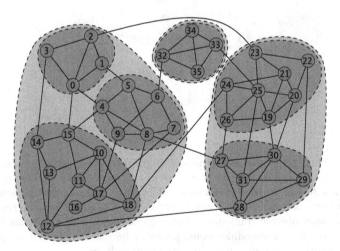

Fig. 3. Communities in complex networks: the graph contains dense sub-graphs with only few links between them. Often, these sub-graphs themselves contain denser sub-sub-graphs with much less connections between them, and so on. This is called a hierarchical community structure.

5   Dynamics of Complex Networks

A key feature of large software certainly is their time evolution. It may be studied at two very different levels.

First, one may consider successive versions of a source code. Each version is modeled by a graph (the function call network for instance), and one studies the evolution of this graph from version to version. This captures the evolution of the structure of the code, and much insight may be obtained this way. One may for instance describe the impact of decisions on the code design, the addition of new features, the evolution of code complexity, etc. This is crucial for large software systems that evolve on long periods of time, like operating systems for instance.

In this context, one faces a sequence of graphs, each representing the software source code at a given time. The dynamics then consists in addition and/or removals of nodes and/or links. For instance, one may write a new function, add a function call, or remove some code. We call such objects *dynamic graphs*. They are generally studied by observing the evolution of the statistical properties presented in previous section from a graph to the next one, and more generally their evolution over time. One may also compute statistics on each dynamic event (each link addition, for instance) but most studies are too coarse grained for this. Instead, the evolution of statistical graph properties over time represents the evolution of the complexity of the code, of its modularity, etc [3,12,19]. We illustrate this in Figure 4, where dynamic communities are used to represent the changes in the structure of a source code.

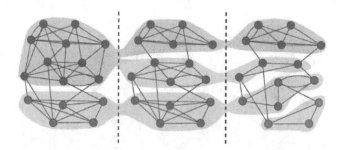

Fig. 4. A dynamic graph seen as a sequence of graphs with dynamic communities: we display the graphs representing the structure of the source code of three consecutive versions of a software. Shaded areas with colors show communities in each of these graphs, and how communities of a given version are related to communities of other versions. One may observe community splits, which indicate that splitting the corresponding module into two modules would probably be relevant, as well as appearance of new communities which may indicate new functionalities.

Dynamics of a software may also be studied at a much finer grain, through execution traces. Then, the software itself does not change, but one studies its dynamics at run-time. This is illustrated by the trace of variable affectations in our guiding example: the graph actually consists in a large sequence of links between different memory addresses. One may then study the dynamic graph defined by considering the graph obtained during the beginning of the execution, then the graph obtained during the next period of time, and so on. Studying the time evolution of these graphs certainly leads to relevant insight [4,1], but it is clear that this approach induces important losses of information. This is why we propose the link stream approach in the next section, which models such objects much better than sequences of graphs.

6   Link Streams

A link stream is a sequence of triplets (t, a, b) meaning that an interaction between a and b occurred at time t. Many real-world data may be modeled like this, including email exchanges, network traffic, phone calls, contacts between individuals, etc. In the software context, examples include function calls at run time as well as memory transfers. Figure 5 displays an example.

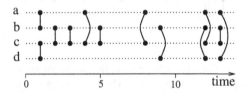

Fig. 5. **An example of link stream:** $L = (l_i)_{i=1..12}$ with $l_1 = (1, a, b)$, $l_2 = (1, c, d)$, $l_3 = (2, b, c)$, $l_4 = (3, b, c)$, $l_5 = (4, a, c)$, $l_6 = (5, a, c)$, $l_7 = (8, a, c)$, $l_8 = (9, b, d)$, $l_9 = (12, a, c)$, $l_{10} = (12, b, d)$, $l_{11} = (13, b, c)$, and $l_{12} = (13, a, d)$. Notice that the set of all links appearing until time 5 form a both structurally and temporally dense sub-stream. and so does the set of links appearing after time 10. This does not hold for the two links in between as they involve different nodes and so are not structurally dense. One may also notice patterns like repeated interactions between b and c within short periods of time.

As explained above, link streams are generally studied in network science by building series of graphs G_t, for $t = 1, 2, \cdots$, where the links in G_t are the interactions occurring between times $t \cdot \Delta$ and $(t+1) \cdot \Delta$ for a given time granularity Δ. However, the choice of an appropriate Δ is challenging, as too small values lead to trivial (almost empty) graphs G_t whereas too large values miss the dynamic nature of the data. In addition, studying such sequences of graphs is a challenge in itself and there is no consensus on an appropriate method for doing so. This approach has several other weaknesses, including the fact that appropriate Δ may vary over time or depend on the considered subset of nodes, the fact that the temporal relations within a given time window is lost, etc. Several works make interesting proposals for solving these issues [20,2,8], but current state-of-the-art remains far from satisfactory.

We propose here another approach, which consists in capturing the both temporal and structural nature of software execution traces by link streams directly. We do not transform them into graphs and then study the dynamics of obtained graphs; instead, we define properties directly over link streams and use these properties to describe our data in a way similar to what we presented in Section 4 for (static) graphs. For instance, as illustrated in Figure 5, in a link stream density should capture both temporal and structural features: while a (sub-)graph is dense if most possible links do exist, a (sub-)link stream is dense if most possible links exist *most of the time*. In other words, in a (sub-)graph, the density is the probability that two randomly chosen nodes are linked together. In a link stream, the density is the probability that two randomly chosen nodes are linked together at a randomly chosen time. We proposed a notion capturing precisely this intuition in [17].

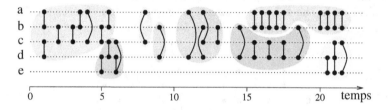

Fig. 6. Communities in a link stream: each shaded sub-stream is both temporally and structurally dense, and poorly connected to the rest of the stream. Such communities may represent discussions in a mailing-list, information spreading in a social network, or functions in a program execution trace.

Going further, just like communities in complex networks are dense sub-graphs poorly connected to the rest of the network, and just like communities in dynamic graphs are groups of nodes that remain strongly connected over time, one may define communities in link streams as group of links both temporally and structurally densely connected, and poorly connected to the rest of the stream. An illustration is given in Figure 6. In the context of a software trace, such communities may represent modules, concurrent threads, or parallel applications for instance. Interestingly, this notion of communities is very different from the notion of communities in dynamic graphs discussed above, although link streams are commonly studied as dynamic graphs. This shows that our direct link stream approach provides a new and complementary perspective on these objects.

7   Conclusion

This introductory paper presented an overview of (possible) relations between the recent field of network science and the empirical study of large software. It discussed in particular dynamical aspects, which are poorly captured by current approaches although they are crucial. We proposed a new approach, based on the direct study of link streams, as a promising direction for taking such dynamics into account. However, it must be clear that most perspectives remain open regarding the study of software as networks. Network science itself is an emerging field, and studying link streams is a recently proposed approach which is only at its very beginning.

References

1. Alawneh, L., Hamou-Lhadj, A.: Identifying computational phases from inter-process communication traces of hpc applications. In: Beyer, D., van Deursen, A., Godfrey, M.W. (eds.) ICPC, pp. 133–142 (2012)
2. Alvarez-Hamelin, J.I., Fleury, E., Vespignani, A., Ziviani, A.: Complex dynamic networks: Tools and methods. Computer Networks 56(3), 967–969 (2012)
3. Bhattacharya, P., Iliofotou, M., Neamtiu, I., Faloutsos, M.: Graph-based analysis and prediction for software evolution. In: Glinz, M., Murphy, G.C., Pezzè, M. (eds.) ICSE, pp. 419–429. IEEE (2012)
4. Cai, K.-Y., Yin, B.-B.: Software execution processes as an evolving complex network. Inf. Sci. 179(12), 1903–1928 (2009)
5. Caudwell, A.H.: Gource: visualizing software version control history. In: Cook, W.R., Clarke, S., Rinard, M.C. (eds.) SPLASH/OOPSLA Companion, pp. 73–74. ACM (2010)
6. Fortunato, S.: Community detection in graphs. CoRR, abs/0906.0612 (2009)
7. Guo, F., Wang, Y., Zhao, L., Zhang, M.: Introduction to the applications of complex networks in software engineering. In: ICEE, pp. 4162–4165. IEEE (2010)
8. Holme, P., Saramäki, J.: Temporal networks. CoRR, abs/1108.1780 (2011)
9. Latapy, M.: Main-memory triangle computations for very large (sparse (power-law)) graphs. Theor. Comput. Sci. 407(1-3), 458–473 (2008)
10. Li, B., Pan, W., Lu, J.: Multi-granularity dynamic analysis of complex software networks. In: ISCAS, pp. 2119–2124. IEEE (2011)
11. Li, D., Han, Y., Hu, J.: Complex network thinking in software engineering. In: CSSE (1), pp. 264–268. IEEE Computer Society (2008)
12. Li, H., Huang, B., Lu, J.: Dynamical evolution analysis of the object-oriented software systems. In: IEEE Congress on Evolutionary Computation, pp. 3030–3035. IEEE (2008)
13. Liu, J., Lu, J., He, K., Li, B., Tse, C.K.: Characterizing the structural quality of general complex software networks. I. J. Bifurcation and Chaos 18(2), 605–613 (2008)
14. Pan, W., Li, B., Ma, Y., Liu, J., Qin, Y.: Class structure refactoring of object-oriented softwares using community detection in dependency networks. Frontiers of Computer Science in China 3(3), 396–404 (2009)
15. Pan, W., Li, B., Ma, Y., Qin, Y., Zhou, X.-Y.: Measuring structural quality of object-oriented softwares via bug propagation analysis on weighted software networks. J. Comput. Sci. Technol. 25(6), 1202–1213 (2010)
16. Subelj, L., Bajec, M.: Software systems through complex networks science: review, analysis and applications. In: Software Mining, pp. 9–16. ACM (2012)
17. Viard, J., Latapy, M.: Identifying roles in an ip network with temporal and structural density. In: INFOCOM Workshops (2014)
18. Šubelj, L., Bajec, M.: Software systems through complex networks science: Review, analysis and applications. In: Proceedings of the First International Workshop on Software Mining, SoftwareMining 2012, pp. 9–16. ACM, New York (2012)

19. Wang, H., He, K., Li, B., Lü, J.: On some recent advances in complex software networks: Modeling, analysis, evolution and applications. I. J. Bifurcation and Chaos 22(2) (2012)
20. Wehmuth, K., Ziviani, A., Fleury, E.: A unifying model for representing time-varying graphs. CoRR, abs/1402.3488 (2014)
21. Wen, L., Kirk, D., Geoff Dromey, R.: Software systems as complex networks. In: Zhang, D., Wang, Y., Kinsner, W. (eds.) IEEE ICCI, pp. 106–115. IEEE (2007)
22. Zanetti, M.S., Scholtes, I., Tessone, C.J., Schweitzer, F.: Categorizing bugs with social networks: a case study on four open source software communities. In: Notkin, D., Cheng, B.H.C., Pohl, K. (eds.) ICSE, pp. 1032–1041. IEEE / ACM (2013)
23. Zanetti, M.S., Schweitzer, F.: A network perspective on software modularity. In: Mühl, G., Richling, J., Herkersdorf, A. (eds.) ARCS Workshops. LNI, vol. 200, pp. 175–186. GI (2012)
24. Zhang, X., Zhao, G., Lv, T., Yin, Y., Zhang, B.: Analysis on key nodes behavior for complex software network. In: Liu, B., Ma, M., Chang, J. (eds.) ICICA 2012. LNCS, vol. 7473, pp. 59–66. Springer, Heidelberg (2012)
25. Zhao, C., Ates, K., Kong, J., Zhang, K.: Discovering program's behavioral patterns by inferring graph-grammars from execution traces. In: ICTAI (2), pp. 395–402. IEEE Computer Society (2008)
26. Zhao, C., Kong, J., Zhang, K.: Program behavior discovery and verification: A graph grammar approach. IEEE Trans. Software Eng. 36(3), 431–448 (2010)

Soundness of Timed-Arc Workflow Nets

José Antonio Mateo[1,2], Jiří Srba[1], and Mathias Grund Sørensen[1]

[1] Department of Computer Science, Aalborg University,
Selma Lagerlöfs Vej 300, 9220 Aalborg East, Denmark
[2] Department of Computer Science, University of Castilla-La Mancha,
Campus Universitario s/n, Albacete, Spain

Abstract. Analysis of workflow processes with quantitative aspects like timing is of interest in numerous time-critical applications. We suggest a workflow model based on timed-arc Petri nets and study the foundational problems of soundness and strong (time-bounded) soundness. We explore the decidability of these problems and show, among others, that soundness is decidable for monotonic workflow nets while reachability is undecidable. For general timed-arc workflow nets soundness and strong soundness become undecidable, though we can design efficient verification algorithms for the subclass of bounded nets. Finally, we demonstrate the usability of our theory on the case studies of a Brake System Control Unit used in aircraft certification, the MPEG2 encoding algorithm, and a blood transfusion workflow. The implementation of the algorithms is freely available as a part of the model checker TAPAAL.

1 Introduction

Workflow nets [16,17] were introduced by Wil van der Aalst as a formalism for modelling, analysis and verification of business workflow processes. The formalism is based on Petri nets abstracting away most of the data while focusing on the possible flow in the system. Its intended use is in finding design errors like the presence of deadlocks, livelocks and other anomalies in workflow processes. Such correctness criteria can be described via the notion of *soundness* (see [18]) that requires the option to complete the workflow, guarantees proper termination and optionally also the absence of redundant tasks.

After the seminal work on workflow nets, researchers have invested much effort in defining new soundness criteria and/or improving the expressive power of the original model by adding new features and studying the related decidability and complexity questions (it is not in the scope of this paper to list all these works but we refer to [18] for a recent overview). In the present paper we consider a quantitative extension of workflow nets with timing features, allowing us to argue, among others, about the execution intervals of tasks, deadlines and urgent behaviour of workflow processes. Our workflow model is based on timed-arc Petri nets [3,9] where tokens carry timing information and arcs are labelled with time intervals restricting the available ages of tokens used for transition firing. Let us first informally introduce the model on our running example.

G. Ciardo and E. Kindler (Eds.): PETRI NETS 2014, LNCS 8489, pp. 51–70, 2014.

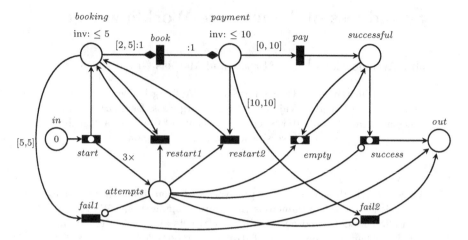

Fig. 1. Booking-payment workflow with timing constraints

The timed-arc workflow net in Figure 1 describes a simple booking-payment workflow where a web-service provides a booking form followed by online payment. Normal flow of the net executes the transition *start* followed by the transitions *book* and *pay*. The whole booking-payment procedure cannot last for more than 10 minutes and the booking phase takes at least 2 minutes and must be finished within the first 5 minutes. The process can fail at any moment and the service allows for three additional attempts before it will terminate with failure. The workflow net consists of six places drawn as circles and nine transitions drawn as rectangles. Places can contain timed tokens, like the one of age 0 in the place *in* (input place of the workflow). The tokens present in the net form a marking. Places and transitions are connected by arcs such that arcs from places to transitions contain time intervals restricting the possible ages of tokens that can be consumed by transition firing. For simplicity we do not draw time intervals of the form $[0, \infty]$ as they do not restrict the ages of tokens in any way.

In the initial marking of the net, the transition *start* is enabled as it has a token in its input place. The transition is urgent (marked with a filled circle), so no time delay is possible once it gets enabled. After the *start* transition is fired, a new token of age 0 arrives to the place *booking* (initiating the booking phase) and three new tokens of age 0 arrive to the place *attempts* (in order to count the number of attempts we have before the service fails). The transition *fail1* is not enabled as the place *attempts*, connected to *fail1* via the so-called inhibitor arc, contains tokens, inhibiting *fail1* from firing. The transition *book* is not enabled either as the token's age in the place *booking* does not belong to the interval [2, 5]. However, after waiting for example 3 minutes, *book* can fire. This consumes the token of age 3 from *booking* and transports it to the place *payment*, preserving its age. This is signalled by the use of transport arcs that contain the diamond-shaped tips with index :1 (denoting how these arcs are paired).

At any moment, the booking-payment part of the workflow can be restarted by firing the transitions *restart1* or *restart2*. This will bring the token back to the place *booking*, reset its age to 0, and consume one attempt from the place *attempts*. Once no more attempts are available and the age of the token in the place *booking* or *payment* reaches 5 resp. 10, we can fire the transition *fail1* resp. *fail2* and terminate the workflow by placing a token into the output place *out*. Note that the places *booking* and *payment* contain age invariants ≤ 5 resp. ≤ 10, meaning that the ages of tokens in these places should be at most 5 resp. 10. Hence if the service did not succeed within the given time bound, the workflow will necessarily fail. Finally, if the payment transition was executed within 10 minutes from the service initialization, the transition *empty* can now repeatedly remove any remaining tokens from the place *attempts* and the transition *success* terminates the whole workflow. As both the transitions *empty* and *success* are urgent, no further time delay is allowed in this termination phase.

We are concerned with the study of soundness and strong soundness, intuitively meaning that from any marking reachable from the initial one, it is always possible to reach a marking (in case of strong soundness additionally within a fixed amount of time), having just one token in the place *out*. Moreover, once a token appears in the place *out*, it is mandatory that the rest of the workflow net does not contain any remaining tokens. One can verify (either manually or using our tool mentioned later) that the workflow net of our running example is both sound and strongly sound.

Our contribution. We define a workflow theory based on timed-arc Petri nets, extend the notion of soundness from [16] to deal with timing features and introduce a new notion of strong soundness that guarantees time-bounded workflow termination. We study the decidability/undecidability of soundness and strong soundness and conclude that even though they are in general undecidable, we can still design efficient verification algorithms for two important subclasses: monotonic workflow nets (not using any inhibitor arcs, age invariants and urgent transitions) and for the subclass of bounded nets. This contrasts to the fact that for example the reachability question for monotonic workflow nets is already undecidable [19]. Moreover, our algorithms allow us to compute the minimum and maximum execution times of the workflow. The theory of timed-arc workflow nets is developed for discrete-time semantics. As remarked in Section 6, dealing with continuous-time semantics will require different techniques to argue about soundness of workflow nets. Last but not least, we implemented the algorithms given in this paper within the open-source tool TAPAAL [5] and successfully demonstrate on a number of case studies the applicability of the theory in real-world scenarios.

Related work. Soundness for different extensions of Petri nets with e.g. inhibitor arcs, reset arcs and other features have been studied before, leading often to undecidability results (for a detailed overview see [18]). We shall now focus mainly on time extensions of Petri net workflow models. Ling and Schmidt [10] defined timed workflow nets in terms of Time Elementary Nets (TENs). These nets are

1-bounded by definition and a net is sound iff it is live and the initial marking is a home marking in a net that connects the output place of the workflow with the input one. Du and Jiang [7] suggested Logical Time Workflow Nets (LTWN) and their compositional semantics. Here liveness together with boundedness is a necessary and sufficient condition for soundness. Moreover, the soundness of a well-structured LTWN can be verified in polynomial time. Tiplea et al. [13] introduced a variant of timed workflow nets in terms of timed Petri nets and showed the decidability of soundness for the bounded subclass. In subsequent work [14,15] they studied the decidability of soundness under different firing strategies. The papers listed above rely on the model of time Petri nets where timing information is associated to transitions and not to tokens like in our case. The two models are significantly different, in particular the number of timing parameters for time Petri nets is fixed, contrary to the dynamic creation of tokens with their private clocks in timed-arc Petri nets. We also see several modelling advantages of having ages associated to tokens as we can for example track the duration of sequentially composed tasks (via transport arcs) as demonstrated in our running example. We are not aware of other works developing a workflow theory and the corresponding notions of soundness based on timed-arc Petri nets. Finally, we implement the soundness checks within a user-friendly tool that permits easy GUI-based debugging of issues in workflows—something that is not that common for other workflow analysis tools (see [8] for more discussion).

2   Extended Timed-Arc Petri Nets

We shall start with the definition of extended timed-arc Petri nets in the discrete time setting and later on we recall some basic facts about the extrapolation technique applicable on this class of nets.

Let $\mathbb{N}_0 = \mathbb{N} \cup \{0\}$ and $\mathbb{N}_0^\infty = \mathbb{N}_0 \cup \{\infty\}$. A *discrete timed transition system* (DTTS) is a triple $(S, Act, \rightarrow)$ where S is the set of states, Act is the set of actions and $\rightarrow \subseteq S \times (Act \cup \mathbb{N}_0) \times S$ is the transition relation written as $s \xrightarrow{a} s'$ whenever $(s, a, s') \in \rightarrow$. If $a \in Act$ then we call it a *switch transition*, if $a \in \mathbb{N}_0$ we call it a *delay transition*. We also define the set of *well-formed time intervals* as $\mathcal{I} \stackrel{\text{def}}{=} \{[a, b] \mid a \in \mathbb{N}_0, b \in \mathbb{N}_0^\infty, a \leq b\}$ and its subset $\mathcal{I}^{\text{inv}} \stackrel{\text{def}}{=} \{[0, b] \mid b \in \mathbb{N}_0^\infty\}$ used in age invariants.

Definition 1 (Extended timed-Arc Petri Net). *An* extended timed-arc Petri net *(ETAPN) is a 9-tuple* $N = (P, T, T_{urg}, IA, OA, g, w, Type, I)$ *where*

- P *is a finite set of* places,
- T *is a finite set of* transitions *such that* $P \cap T = \emptyset$,
- $T_{urg} \subseteq T$ *is the set of* urgent transitions,
- $IA \subseteq P \times T$ *is a finite set of* input arcs,
- $OA \subseteq T \times P$ *is a finite set of* output arcs,
- $g : IA \rightarrow \mathcal{I}$ *is a time constraint function* assigning *guards to input arcs,*
- $w : IA \cup OA \rightarrow \mathbb{N}$ *is a function assigning* weights *to input and output arcs,*

- *Type* : $IA \cup OA \to$ **Types** *is a* type function *assigning a type to all arcs where* **Types** $= \{Normal, Inhib\} \cup \{Transport_j \mid j \in \mathbb{N}\}$ *such that*
  - *if* $Type(a) = Inhib$ *then* $a \in IA$ *and* $g(a) = [0, \infty]$,
  - *if* $(p, t) \in IA$ *and* $t \in T_{urg}$ *then* $g((p, t)) = [0, \infty]$,
  - *if* $Type((p, t)) = Transport_j$ *for some* $(p, t) \in IA$ *then there is exactly one* $(t, p') \in OA$ *such that* $Type((t, p')) = Transport_j$,
  - *if* $Type((t, p')) = Transport_j$ *for some* $(t, p') \in OA$ *then there is exactly one* $(p, t) \in IA$ *such that* $Type((p, t)) = Transport_j$,
  - *if* $Type((p, t)) = Transport_j = Type((t, p'))$ *then* $w((p, t)) = w((t, p'))$,
- $I : P \to \mathcal{I}^{inv}$ *is a function assigning* age invariants *to places.*

Remark 1. Note that for transport arcs we assume that they come in pairs (for each type $Transport_j$) and that their weights match. Also for inhibitor arcs and for input arcs to urgent transitions, we require that the guards are $[0, \infty]$. This restriction is important for some of the results presented in this paper and it also guarantees that we can use DBM-based algorithms in the tool TAPAAL [5].

The ETAPN model is not monotonic, meaning that adding more tokens to markings can disable time delays or transition firing. Therefore we define a subclass of ETAPN where the monotonicity breaking features are not allowed. In the literature such nets are often considered as the standard timed-arc Petri net model [3,9] but we add the prefix monotonic for clarity reasons.

Definition 2 (Monotonic timed-arc Petri net). *A* monotonic timed-arc Petri net *(MTAPN) is an extended timed arc Petri net with no urgent transitions* $(T_{urg} = \emptyset)$, *no age invariants* $(I(p) = [0, \infty]$ *for all* $p \in P)$ *and no inhibitor arcs* $(Type(a) \neq Inhib$ *for all* $a \in IA)$.

Before we give the formal semantics of the model, let us fix some notation. Let $N = (P, T, T_{urg}, IA, OA, g, w, Type, I)$ be an ETAPN. We denote by $^\bullet x \stackrel{\text{def}}{=} \{y \in P \cup T \mid (y, x) \in (IA \cup OA), \ Type((y, x)) \neq Inhib\}$ the preset of a transition or a place x. Similarly, the postset $x^\bullet$ is defined as $x^\bullet \stackrel{\text{def}}{=} \{y \in P \cup T \mid (x, y) \in (IA \cup OA)\}$. Let $\mathcal{B}(\mathbb{N}_0)$ be the set of all finite multisets over $\mathbb{N}_0$. A *marking* M on N is a function $M : P \longrightarrow \mathcal{B}(\mathbb{N}_0)$ where for every place $p \in P$ and every token $x \in M(p)$ we have $x \in I(p)$, in other words all tokens have to satisfy the age invariants. The set of all markings in a net N is denoted by $\mathcal{M}(N)$.

We write (p, x) to denote a token at a place p with the age $x \in \mathbb{N}_0$. Then $M = \{(p_1, x_1), (p_2, x_2), \ldots, (p_n, x_n)\}$ is a multiset representing a marking M with n tokens of ages x_i in places p_i. We define the size of a marking as $|M| = \sum_{p \in P} |M(p)|$ where $|M(p)|$ is the number of tokens located in the place p.

Definition 3 (Enabledness). *Let* $N = (P, T, T_{urg}, IA, OA, g, w, Type, I)$ *be an ETAPN. We say that a transition* $t \in T$ *is* enabled *in a marking* M *by the multisets of tokens* $In = \{(p, x_p^1), (p, x_p^2), \ldots, (p, x_p^{w((p,t))}) \mid p \in {}^\bullet t\} \subseteq M$ *and* $Out = \{(p', x_{p'}^1), (p', x_{p'}^2), \ldots, (p', x_{p'}^{w((t,p'))}) \mid p' \in t^\bullet\}$ *if*

– *for all input arcs except the inhibitor arcs, the tokens from In satisfy the age guards of the arcs, i.e.*

$$\forall (p,t) \in IA.\,Type((p,t)) \neq Inhib \Rightarrow x_p^i \in g((p,t)) \text{ for } 1 \leq i \leq w((p,t))$$

– *for any inhibitor arc pointing from a place p to the transition t, the number of tokens in p is smaller than the weight of the arc, i.e.*

$$\forall (p,t) \in IA.\,Type((p,t)) = Inhib \Rightarrow |M(p)| < w((p,t))$$

– *for all input arcs and output arcs which constitute a transport arc, the age of the input token must be equal to the age of the output token and satisfy the invariant of the output place, i.e.*

$$\forall (p,t) \in IA.\forall (t,p') \in OA.\,Type((p,t)) = Type((t,p')) = Transport_j$$
$$\Rightarrow \left(x_p^i = x_{p'}^i \wedge x_{p'}^i \in I(p') \right) \text{ for } 1 \leq i \leq w((p,t))$$

– *for all normal output arcs, the age of the output token is 0, i.e.*

$$\forall (t,p') \in OA.\,Type((t,p')) = Normal \Rightarrow x_{p'}^i = 0 \text{ for } 1 \leq i \leq w((p,t)).$$

A given ETAPN N defines a DTTS $T(N) \stackrel{\text{def}}{=} (\mathcal{M}(N), T, \rightarrow)$ where states are the markings and the transitions are as follows.

– If $t \in T$ is enabled in a marking M by the multisets of tokens In and Out then t can *fire* and produce the marking $M' = (M \smallsetminus In) \uplus Out$ where $\uplus$ is the multiset sum operator and $\smallsetminus$ is the multiset difference operator; we write $M \stackrel{t}{\rightarrow} M'$ for this switch transition.
– A time *delay* $d \in \mathbb{N}_0$ is allowed in M if
  • $(x + d) \in I(p)$ for all $p \in P$ and all $x \in M(p)$, and
  • if $M \stackrel{t}{\rightarrow} M'$ for some $t \in T_{urg}$ then $d = 0$.
  By delaying d time units in M we reach the marking M' defined as $M'(p) = \{x + d \mid x \in M(p)\}$ for all $p \in P$; we write $M \stackrel{d}{\rightarrow} M'$ for this delay transition.

Let $\rightarrow \stackrel{\text{def}}{=} \bigcup_{t \in T} \stackrel{t}{\rightarrow} \cup \bigcup_{d \in \mathbb{N}_0} \stackrel{d}{\rightarrow}$. The set of all markings reachable from a given marking M is denoted by $[M\rangle \stackrel{\text{def}}{=} \{M' \mid M \rightarrow^* M'\}$. By $M \stackrel{d,t}{\rightarrow} M'$ we denote that there is a marking M'' such that $M \stackrel{d}{\rightarrow} M'' \stackrel{t}{\rightarrow} M'$.

A marking M is a *deadlock* if there is no $d \in \mathbb{N}_0$, no $t \in T$ and no marking M' such that $M \stackrel{d,t}{\rightarrow} M'$. A marking M is *divergent* if for every $d \in \mathbb{N}_0$ we have $M \stackrel{d}{\rightarrow} M'$ for some M'.

In general, ETAPNs are infinite in two dimensions. The number of tokens in reachable markings can be unbounded and even for bounded nets the ages of tokens can be arbitrarily large. We shall now recall a few results that allow us to make finite abstractions for bounded ETAPNs, i.e. for nets where the maximum number of tokens in any reachable marking is bounded by a constant.

Let $N = (P, T, T_{urg}, IA, OA, g, w, Type, I)$ be a given ETAPN. In [1] the authors provide an algorithm for computing a function $C_{max} : P \rightarrow (\mathbb{N}_0 \cup \{-1\})$ returning for each place $p \in P$ the maximum constant associated to this place, meaning that the ages of tokens in place p that are strictly greater than $C_{max}(p)$ are irrelevant. In particular, places where $C_{max}(p) = -1$ are the so-called *untimed* places where the age of tokens is not relevant at all, implying that all the intervals on their outgoing arcs are $[0, \infty]$.

Let M be a marking of N. We split it into two markings $M_>$ and $M_\leq$ where $M_>(p) = \{x \in M(p) \mid x > C_{max}(p)\}$ and $M_\leq(p) = \{x \in M(p) \mid x \leq C_{max}(p)\}$ for all places $p \in P$. Clearly, $M = M_> \uplus M_\leq$.

We say that two markings M and M' in the net N are equivalent, written $M \equiv M'$, if $M_\leq = M'_\leq$ and for all $p \in P$ we have $|M_>(p)| = |M'_>(p)|$. In other words M and M' agree on the tokens with ages below the maximum constants and have the same number of tokens above the maximum constant.

The relation $\equiv$ is an equivalence relation and it is also a timed bisimulation where delays and transition firings on one side can be matched by exactly the same delays and transition firings on the other side and vice versa.

Theorem 1 ([1]). *The relation $\equiv$ is a timed bisimulation.*

We can now define canonical representatives for each equivalence class of $\equiv$.

Definition 4 (Cut). *Let M be a marking. We define its canonical marking $cut(M)$ by $cut(M)(p) = M_\leq(p) \uplus \underbrace{\{ C_{max}(p) + 1, \ldots, C_{max}(p) + 1 \}}_{|M_>(p)| \; times}.$*

Lemma 1 ([1]). *Let M, M_1 and M_2 be markings. Then (i) $M \equiv cut(M)$, and (ii) $M_1 \equiv M_2$ if and only if $cut(M_1) = cut(M_2)$.*

Let M and M' be two markings. We say that M' *covers* M, denoted by $M \sqsubseteq M'$, if $M(p) \subseteq M'(p)$ for all $p \in P$. We write $M \sqsubseteq_{cut} M'$ if $cut(M) \sqsubseteq cut(M')$.

For monotonic timed-arc Petri nets we can now show that adding more tokens to the net does not restrict its possible behaviour.

Lemma 2. *Let N be an MTAPN and $M, M' \in \mathcal{M}(N)$ be two of its markings such that $M \sqsubseteq_{cut} M'$. If $M \xrightarrow{d} M_1$ (resp. $M \xrightarrow{t} M_1$) then $M' \xrightarrow{d} M'_1$ (resp. $M' \xrightarrow{t} M'_1$) such that $M_1 \sqsubseteq_{cut} M'_1$ and $|M'| - |M| = |M'_1| - |M_1|$.*

Proof. Let $M \xrightarrow{d} M_1$, resp. $M \xrightarrow{t} M_1$. As $M \equiv cut(M)$ by Lemma 1(i), we can by Theorem 1 conclude that also $cut(M) \xrightarrow{d} M_2$, resp. $cut(M) \xrightarrow{t} M_2$, such that $M_1 \equiv M_2$. Recall that $cut(M) \sqsubseteq cut(M')$ by the assumption of the lemma.

- Time delay case ($cut(M) \xrightarrow{d} M_2$). As the net does not contain any nontrivial age invariants and there are no urgent transitions, we know that also $cut(M') \xrightarrow{d} M_3$ such that $M_2 \sqsubseteq M_3$ as time delay preserves the $\sqsubseteq$-relation.
- Transition firing case ($cut(M) \xrightarrow{t} M_2$). As the net does not have any inhibitor arcs, we can see that also $cut(M') \xrightarrow{t} M_3$ by consuming exactly the same tokens in $cut(M')$ as we did in $cut(M)$. Clearly, $M_2 \sqsubseteq M_3$.

Because $cut(M') \equiv M'$ due to Lemma 1(i), we know by Theorem 1 that $M' \xrightarrow{d}$ M_1', resp. $M' \xrightarrow{t} M_1'$, such that $M_3 \equiv M_1'$. Hence $M_1 \equiv M_2 \sqsubseteq M_3 \equiv M_1'$. By Lemma 1(ii) we get $cut(M_1) = cut(M_2)$ and $cut(M_3) = cut(M_1')$. Observe now a simple fact that $M_2 \sqsubseteq M_3$ implies that $cut(M_2) \sqsubseteq cut(M_3)$. This all together implies that $cut(M_1) = cut(M_2) \sqsubseteq cut(M_3) = cut(M_1')$ which is another way of saying that $M_1 \sqsubseteq_{cut} M_1'$ as required by the lemma. As time delays do not change the number of tokens in M and M' and transition firing adds or removes an equal number of tokens from both M and M', we can also conclude that $|M'| - |M| = |M_1'| - |M_1|$.   □

3   Timed-Arc Workflow Nets

We shall now formally define timed-arc workflow nets, introduce the soundness notion for this class of nets and answer the questions about the decidability of soundness.

Timed-arc workflow nets are defined similarly as untimed workflow nets [16]. Every workflow net has a unique input place and a unique output place. After initializing such a net by placing a token into the input place, it should be guaranteed that any possible workflow execution can be always extended such that the workflow terminates with just one token in the output place (also known as the soundness property).

Definition 5 (Extended timed-arc workflow net). *An ETAPN* $N = (P, T, T_{urg}, IA, OA, g, w, Type, I)$ *is called an* Extended Timed-Arc WorkFlow Net *(ETAWFN) if*

- *there exists a unique place* $in \in P$ *such that* $^{\bullet}in = \emptyset$ *and* $in^{\bullet} \neq \emptyset$,
- *there exists a unique place* $out \in P$ *such that* $out^{\bullet} = \emptyset$ *and* $^{\bullet}out \neq \emptyset$,
- *for all* $p \in P \setminus \{in, out\}$ *we have* $^{\bullet}p \neq \emptyset$ *and* $p^{\bullet} \neq \emptyset$, *and*
- *for all* $t \in T$ *we have* $^{\bullet}t \neq \emptyset$.

Remark 2. Notice that the conditions $^{\bullet}in = \emptyset$ and $^{\bullet}out \neq \emptyset$ necessarily imply that $in \neq out$. Moreover, we allow the postset of a transition to be empty $(t^{\bullet} = \emptyset)$. This is just a technical detail and an equivalent workflow net where all transitions satisfy $t^{\bullet} \neq \emptyset$ can be constructed by introducing a new place p_{new} so that any outgoing transition from the start place in puts a token into p_{new} and every incoming transition to the final place out consumes the token from p_{new}. Now for any transition t with $t^{\bullet} = \emptyset$ we add the pair of arcs (p_{new}, t) and (t, p_{new}) without influencing the behaviour of the net.

Decidability of soundness crucially depends on the modelling features allowed in the net. Hence we define a subclass of so-called monotonic workflow nets.

Definition 6 (Monotonic timed-arc workflow net). *A monotonic timed-arc workflow net (MTAWFN) is an ETAWFN with no urgent transitions, no age invariants and no inhibitor arcs.*

The marking $M_{in} = \{(in, 0)\}$ of a timed-arc workflow net is called *initial*. A marking M is *final* if $|M(out)| = 1$ and for all $p \in P \setminus \{out\}$ we have $|M(p)| = 0$, i.e. it contains just one token in the place *out*. There may be several final markings with different ages of the token in the place *out*.

We now provide the formal definition of soundness that formulates the standard requirement on proper termination of workflow nets [17,18].

Definition 7 (Soundness of timed-arc workflow nets). *An (extended or monotonic) timed-arc workflow net* $N = (P, T, T_{urg}, IA, OA, g, w, Type, I)$ *is sound if for any marking* $M \in [M_{in}\rangle$ *reachable from the initial marking* M_{in}:

a) *there exists some final marking* M_{out} *such that* $M_{out} \in [M\rangle$, *and*
b) *if* $|M(out)| \geq 1$ *then* M *is a final marking.*

A workflow is sound if once it is initiated by placing a token of age 0 in the place *in*, it has always the possibility to terminate by moving a token to the place *out* (option to complete) and moreover it is guaranteed that the rest of the workflow net is free of any remaining tokens as soon as the place *out* is marked (proper completion). We now define a subclass of bounded workflow nets.

Definition 8 (Boundedness). *A timed-arc workflow net* N *is* k-bounded *for some* $k \in \mathbb{N}_0$ *if any marking* M *reachable from the initial marking* M_{in} *satisfies* $|M| \leq k$. *A net is* bounded *if it is* k-bounded *for some* k.

A classical result states that any untimed sound net is bounded [16]. This is not in general the case for extended timed-arc workflow nets as demonstrated in Figure 2. Nevertheless, we recover the boundedness result for the subclass of monotonic timed-arc workflow nets.

Theorem 2. *Let* N *an MTAWFN. If* N *is sound then* N *is bounded.*

Proof. By contradiction assume that N is a sound and unbounded MTAWFN. Let M_{in} be the initial workflow marking. Now we can argue that there must exist two reachable markings $M, M' \in [M_{in}\rangle$ such that

i) $M \sqsubseteq_{cut} M'$, and
ii) $|M| < |M'|$.

This follows from the fact that $M \sqsubseteq_{cut} M'$ iff $cut(M) \sqsubseteq cut(M')$ and from Definition 4 where the cut function is given such that each token is placed into one of the finitely many places, say p, and its age is bounded by $C_{max}(p) + 1$. Thanks to Dickson's Lemma [6], saying that every set of n-tuples of natural numbers has only finitely many minimal elements, we are guaranteed that conditions i) and ii) are satisfied for some reachable markings M and M'.

Since N is a sound workflow net, we now use condition a) of Definition 7, implying that from M we reach some final marking M_{out}. Assume that this is achieved w.l.o.g. by the following sequence of transitions:

$$M \xrightarrow{d_1} M_1 \xrightarrow{t_1} M_2 \xrightarrow{d_2} M_3 \xrightarrow{t_2} M_4 \dots \xrightarrow{t_n} M_{out} .$$

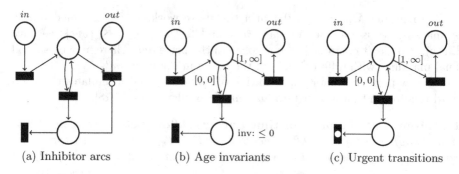

(a) Inhibitor arcs   (b) Age invariants   (c) Urgent transitions

Fig. 2. Sound and unbounded extended timed-arc workflow nets

We know that $M \sqsubseteq_{cut} M'$ and hence by repeatedly applying Lemma 2 also

$$M' \xrightarrow{d_1} M'_1 \xrightarrow{t_1} M'_2 \xrightarrow{d_2} M'_3 \xrightarrow{t_2} M'_4 \dots \xrightarrow{t_n} M'_{out}$$

such that at the end $M_{out} \sqsubseteq_{cut} M'_{out}$. The facts that $M_{out} \sqsubseteq_{cut} M'_{out}$ and M_{out} is a final marking imply that $|M'_{out}(out)| \geq 1$. By a repeated application of Lemma 2 we also get $|M'| - |M| = |M'_{out}| - |M_{out}|$. By condition ii) of this lemma we know that $|M| < |M'|$, this implies that also $|M_{out}| < |M'_{out}|$. However, now the place out in M'_{out} is marked and there is at least one more token somewhere else in the marking M'_{out}. This contradicts condition b) of Definition 7.   □

Next we show that soundness for extended timed-arc workflow nets is unde-cidable. The result has been known for the extension with inhibitor arcs [18], we prove it (by reduction from two counter Minsky machines) also for urgent transitions and age invariants.

Theorem 3. *Soundness is undecidable for extended timed-arc workflow nets. This is the case also for MTAWFNs that contain additionally only inhibitor arcs, age invariants or urgent transitions but not necessarily all of them together.*

We now prove decidability of soundness for workflow nets without any in-hibitor arcs, age invariants and urgency. This contrasts to undecidability of reachability for this subclass [19]. Algorithm 1 shows how to efficiently check soundness on this subclass and on the subclass of bounded nets. The algorithm first performs a standard forward search on the cut-extrapolated marking graph by using the sets *Waiting* and *Reached* for storing the discovered resp. already explored cut markings, while at the same time computing the shortest path from the initial marking to the reachable cut-markings in the net. The algorithm will terminate at line 7 if the k bound for a non-monotonic input net N is exceeded or at line 18 if we find a marking covering another already discovered marking in case the input net N is monotonic (note that monotonicity is a simple syntactic property of the net). In case a marking with a token in the output place is dis-covered, we report a problem if the marking is not a final marking; otherwise we

---

Algorithm 1: Soundness checking for timed-arc workflow nets

Input	: An MTAWFN or an ETAWFN with a positive integer bound k $N = (P, T, T_{urg}, IA, OA, g, w, Type, I)$ where $in, out \in P$.
Output	: "Not k-bounded" if the workflow net is not monotonic and not k-bounded; "true" together with the minimum execution time if N is sound; "false" if N is not sound.

```
 1  begin
 2  │  A marking M has an (initially empty) set of its parents M.parents and a
    │  minimum execution time M.min (initially ∞); M_in := {(in, 0)};
 3  │  Waiting := {M_in}; M_in.min = 0; Reached := Waiting; Final := ∅;
 4  │  while Waiting ≠ ∅ do
 5  │  │  Remove some marking M from Waiting with the smallest M.min;
 6  │  │  foreach M' s.t. M →¹ M' or M →ᵗ M' for some t ∈ T do
 7  │  │  │  if N is not monotonic and |M'| > k then return "Not k-bounded";
 8  │  │  │  M'_c := cut(M'); M'_c.parents := M'_c.parents ∪ {M};
 9  │  │  │  if M →¹ M' then M'_c.min := MIN(M'_c.min, M.min + 1);
10  │  │  │  else M'_c.min = MIN(M'_c.min, M.min);
11  │  │  │  if |M'_c(out)| ≥ 1 then
12  │  │  │  │  if M'_c is a final marking then Final := Final ∪ {M'_c};
13  │  │  │  │  else return false;
14  │  │  │  else
15  │  │  │  │  if M'_c ∉ Reached then
16  │  │  │  │  │  if M'_c is a deadlock then return false;
17  │  │  │  │  │  if N is monotonic and ∃M'' ∈ Reached. M'' ⊑_cut M'_c then
18  │  │  │  │  │  │  return false;
19  │  │  │  │  │  Reached := Reached ∪ {M'_c}; Waiting := Waiting ∪ {M'_c};
20  │  Waiting := Final;
21  │  while Waiting ≠ ∅ do
22  │  │  Remove some marking M from Waiting;
23  │  │  Waiting := Waiting ∪ (M.parents ∩ Reached);
24  │  │  Reached := Reached \ M.parents;
25  │  if Reached = ∅ then
26  │  │  time := ∞; foreach M ∈ Final do time = MIN(time, M.min);
27  │  │  return true and time;
28  │  else
29  │  │  return false;
```

---

store the final marking into the set *Final* (line 12). In case a deadlock non-final marking is discovered, we immediately return false at line 16.

If the first phase of the algorithm successfully terminates, we initiate in the second while-loop a backward search from the set *Final*, checking that all reachable states have a path leading to some final marking. If this is the case, we return at line 27 that the net is sound together with its minimum execution time.

Formally, the correctness of the algorithm is introduced by the following series of lemmas. The next loop invariants can be proved in a straightforward manner.

Lemma 3 (Loop Invariants). *The while-loop in lines 4-19 of Algorithm 1 satisfies the following loop-invariants:*

a) *Waiting $\subseteq$ Reached,*

b) *for any marking $M_c' \in$ Reached $\cup$ Final, there exists a computation of the net $M_{in} \rightarrow^* M'$ such that $M_c' = cut(M')$ and the accumulated delay on the computation $M_{in} \rightarrow^* M'$ is equal to $M_c'.min$, and*

c) *for any marking $M_c' \in$ Reached $\cup$ Final and any $M \in M_c'.parents$ there is a transition $M \rightarrow M'$ such that $M_c' = cut(M')$.*

Lemma 4 (End of Phase One). *After the first while loop (lines 4-19) of Algorithm 1 is finished, we have at line 20 that Reached $\cup$ Final $= \{cut(M') \mid M_{in} \rightarrow^* M'\}$. Moreover, if $M_{in} \rightarrow^* M'$ then the accumulated delay of this computation is greater or equal to $cut(M').min$ and there is at least one such computation ending in M' where the accumulated delay is equal to $cut(M').min$.*

Proof. Let us first argue for the fact $Reached \cup Final = \{cut(M') \mid M_{in} \rightarrow^* M'\}$. The inclusion "$\subseteq$" follows directly from claim b) of Lemma 3. The inclusion "$\supseteq$" follows from the fact that we search all possible successors of M_{in}; we do not provide further arguments as this is a standard graph searching algorithm. The optimality of the computation of the minimum delay is guaranteed because we explore the graph from the nodes with the smallest *min* value (line 5) and this is (up to the cut-equivalence) essentially the Dijkstra's algorithm for shortest path in a graph. □

Lemma 5 (Not k-bounded). *Let N be an MTAWFN or ETAWFN and $k > 0$. If Algorithm 1 returns "Not k-bounded" then N is not k-bounded.*

Proof. The algorithm returns "Not k-bounded" only at line 7, provided that the net is not monotonic and there is a marking M' reachable in one step from $M \in$ *Waiting* such that $|M'| > k$. By claim b) of Lemma 3, we know that there is a computation from M_{in} to M_1 such that $M = cut(M_1)$ and we also know that $M \rightarrow M'$ (line 6). By Lemma 1 and Theorem 1 also $M_1 \rightarrow M_2$ such that $M' = cut(M_2)$ and this means that M_2 is reachable from M_{in} and at the same time $|M_2| > k$ as cut preservers the number of tokens in a marking. Hence if the algorithm returns "Not k-bounded" then the net is not k-bounded. □

Lemma 6 (Return value false). *Let N be an MTAWFN or ETAWFN and $k > 0$. If Algorithm 1 returns false then N is not sound.*

Proof. By a simple analysis of the four places where the algorithm returns false (lines 13, 16, 18 and 29). □

Lemma 7 (Return value true). *Let N be an MTAWFN or ETAWFN and $k > 0$. If Algorithm 1 returns true then N is sound.*

Proof. Assume that the algorithm returned true at line 27 and we shall argue that N satisfies conditions a) and b) of Definition 7. Condition b) is straightforward as by Lemma 4 we know that Reached $\cup$ Final is the set of cut-markings of all the reachable markings of N and if some of them marks the place *out* then this must be a final marking, otherwise the algorithm would return false at line 13. For condition a) we realise that the set *Final* contains all final markings reachable from M_{in} and in the second-phase of the algorithm we run a backward search and remove from the reachable state-space all markings that have a computation leading to one of the final markings. We return true only if *Reached* is empty, meaning that all reachable markings have a computation to some final marking. This corresponds to condition a).   □

Lemma 8 (Termination). *Algorithm 1 terminates on any legal input.*

Proof. For non-monotonic nets there are only finitely many canonical markings with at most k tokens to be explored. For monotonic nets, similar arguments like in the proof of Theorem 2 imply that there cannot be infinitely many markings that are incomparable w.r.t. $\sqsubseteq_{cut}$.   □

We can so conclude with the main result claiming decidability of soundness for workflow nets that are either bounded or monotonic.

Theorem 4. *Soundness is decidable for monotonic timed-arc workflow nets and for bounded extended timed-arc workflow nets.*

Given a sound ETAWFN $N = (P, T, T_{urg}, IA, OA, g, w, Type, I)$, we can reason about its execution times (the accumulated time that is used to move a token from the place *in* into the place *out*). Let M_{in} be the initial marking of N and $\mathcal{F}(N)$ be the set of all final markings of N. Let $\mathcal{T}(N)$ be the set of all execution times by which we can get from the initial marking to some final marking. Formally,

$$\mathcal{T}(N) \stackrel{\text{def}}{=} \{\sum_{i=0}^{n-1} d_i \mid M_{in} = M_0 \stackrel{d_0,t_0}{\to} M_1 \stackrel{d_1,t_1}{\to} M_2 \stackrel{d_2,t_2}{\to} \cdots \stackrel{d_{n-1},t_{n-1}}{\to} M_n \in \mathcal{F}(N)\} \ .$$

The set $\mathcal{T}(N)$ is nonempty for any sound net N and the *minimum execution time* of N, defined by $\min \mathcal{T}(N)$, is computable by Algorithm 1 (correctness follows from Lemma 4).

Theorem 5. *Let N be a sound MTAWFN or a sound and bounded ETAWFN. The minimum execution time of N is computable.*

Notice that the set $\mathcal{T}(N)$ can be infinite for general timed-arc workflow nets, meaning that the *maximum execution time* of N, given by $\max \mathcal{T}(N)$, is not always well defined. This issue is discussed in the next section.

4 Strong Soundness

Soundness ensures the possibility of correct termination in a workflow net, however, it does not give any guarantee on a timely termination of the workflow.

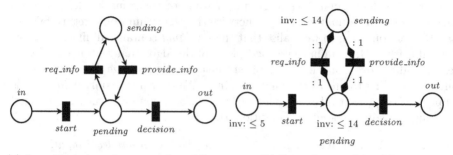

(a) Sound but strongly unsound workflow   (b) Strongly sound workflow

Fig. 3. Fragment of customer complaint workflow ($[0, \infty]$ guards are omitted)

The notion of strong soundness introduced in this section will provide us with such guarantees.

In untimed workflows, infinite behaviour can be used to model for instance repeated queries for further information until a decision can be taken. In a time setting, we usually have a deadline such that if the information is not acquired within the deadline, alternative behaviour in the net is executed (compensation). Consider the workflow nets presented in Figure 3. They represent a simple customer-complaint workflow where, before a decision is made, the customer can be repeatedly requested to provide additional information. The net in Figure 3a is sound but there is no time guarantee by when the decision is reached. On the other hand, the net in Figure 3b introduces additional timing, requiring that the process starts within 5 days and the request/provide loop takes no more than 14 days, after which a decision is made. The use of transport arcs enables us to measure the accumulated time since the place *pending* was entered the first time. It is clear that the workflow only permits behaviours up to 19 days in total. In fact, the net enables infinite executions never reaching any final marking, however, this only happens within a bounded time interval (producing a so-called *zeno run*) and we postulate that such a scenario is unrealistic in a real-world workflow execution. After disregarding the zeno runs, we are guaranteed that the workflow finishes within 19 days and we can call it *strongly sound*.

A formal definition of strong soundness follows. Recall that a marking is divergent if it allows for arbitrarily long delays.

Definition 9 (Strong soundness of TAWFN). *An (extended or monotonic) timed-arc workflow net N is strongly sound if*

a) *N is sound,*
b) *every divergent marking reachable in N is a final marking, and*
c) *there is no infinite computation starting from the initial marking*
$$\{(in, 0)\} = M_0 \overset{d_0, t_0}{\rightsquigarrow} M_1 \overset{d_1, t_1}{\rightsquigarrow} M_2 \overset{d_2, t_2}{\rightsquigarrow} \cdots \text{ where } \sum_{i \in \mathbb{N}_0} d_i = \infty.$$

As expected, strong soundness for general (unbounded) extended workflow nets is undecidable.

Theorem 6. *Strong soundness of ETAWFN is undecidable.*

The next lemma shows that strong soundness of bounded nets corresponds to the property that any execution of the workflow net is time bounded.

Lemma 9. *A sound and bounded ETAWFN is strongly sound if and only if the set of its execution times $\mathcal{T}(N)$ is finite.*

Proof. "$\Leftarrow$": By contradiction we assume that $\mathcal{T}(N)$ is finite while N is not strongly sound. This means that either (i) there is a reachable divergent marking of N that is not a final marking or (ii) the net contains an infinite time-divergent computation. In case (i) we can reach the divergent marking and perform an arbitrarily long delay after which (thanks to soundness of N) we can still reach some final marking. Hence $\mathcal{T}(N)$ is clearly infinite, contradicting our assumption. In case (ii) we can again follow the infinite execution for a sufficiently long time so that an arbitrary accumulated delay is achieved and again (thanks to soundness of N) we can reach some final marking, implying that $\mathcal{T}(N)$ is again infinite, contradicting our assumption.

"$\Rightarrow$": Let N be a strongly sound workflow net. From condition b) of Definition 9 we know that any reachable non-final marking in N cannot diverge. Moreover, there is a global bound B such that any reachable marking can delay at most B time units but not more. This is due to the fact that non-divergent behaviour is guaranteed either by age invariants (that have a fixed upper-bound limiting the maximum delay) or by urgent transitions with input arcs having $[0, \infty]$ guards only (prohibiting time delay as soon as a marking enables some urgent transition). Also, it is impossible to have a reachable marking with no tokens as the net cannot be sound in this case (Definition 5 requires that every transition has at least one input place).

Let S denote the number of reachable cut-markings in the net N. Hence any execution from the initial marking to some final one has either length of no more than S, meaning that its accumulated time duration is at most $S \cdot B$, or it contains the same cut marking twice, forming a loop on the execution. We know that there must be only zero delays on any such a loop as otherwise we would be able to repeat the cycle infinitely often, breaking condition c) of Definition 9 (of course, this loop is only on the cut markings but due to Theorem 1 it can be found also in the real execution of the net with exactly the same delays). This implies that the loop can be omitted while preserving the accumulated execution time of the path. So we are guaranteed that the set $\mathcal{T}(N)$ is bounded by $S \cdot B$ and hence it is finite. $\qquad\square$

Lemma 9 implies that for any bounded and strongly sound net N, the maximum execution time is well defined. Notice that for monotonic nets (even extended with inhibitor arcs), the answer to the strong soundness is always negative as all reachable markings are divergent.

We shall so focus on bounded ETAWFN where strong soundness is decidable and the maximum execution time computable, relying on Lemma 9. We prove this by reducing strong soundness of a given bounded ETAWFN N into a reachability problem on a bounded ETAPN $N(c)$, where c is a nonnegative integer;

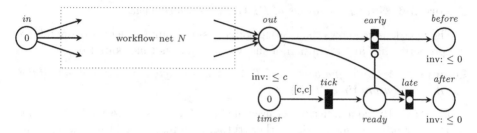

Fig. 4. Transformation of an ETAWFN N into an ETAPN $N(c)$

the translation is given in Figure 4. The token from the place *timer* has to move to the place *ready* exactly at the time c from the start of the workflow. If the workflow can finish (by marking the place *out*) after at least c time units passed, then we can fire the transition *late* and mark the place *after*. If a token is moved to *out* earlier, then the urgent transition *early* will have to fire immediately.

Lemma 10. *Let N be a sound ETAWFN. Let $M_{after} = \{(after, 0)\}$ be a marking in $N(c)$ with one token in the place after. If $c \in \mathcal{T}(N)$ then $N(c)$ can reach the marking M_{after}. If $N(c)$ can reach the marking M_{after} then $c' \in \mathcal{T}(N)$ for some $c' \geq c$.*

Proof. If $c \in \mathcal{T}(N)$ then we perform the execution lasting exactly c time units in the net N and at the moment c we fire the transition *tick*, enabling the transition *late* and marking the place *after*. If on the other hand the place *after* can be marked then necessarily the token in the place *out* arrived at time c' such that $c' \geq c$, otherwise the urgent transition *early* had to be fired instead.   □

Let $N = (P, T, T_{urg}, IA, OA, g, w, Type, I)$ be a given bounded ETAWFN. We can run Algorithm 1 to check for soundness of N. If it is not sound then N cannot be strongly sound either. Otherwise, let S be the number of non-final cut markings reachable in N (corresponding to the maximum cardinality of the set *Reached* in Algorithm 1). Let $B = \max\{b \mid p \in P,\ I(p) = [0, b],\ b \neq \infty\}$ be the maximum integer number used in any of the age invariants in N.

Lemma 11. *A sound and bounded ETAWFN N is strongly sound if and only if $N(S \cdot B + 1)$ cannot reach the marking $\{(after, 0)\}$.*

Proof. If the net N is strongly sound then there is no reachable divergent marking with the possible exception of final markings. Hence any reachable marking either contains some enabled urgent transition (and so no delay is possible) or the divergent behaviour is avoided by some age invariant, giving us the guarantee that no reachable marking can delay more than B units of time. As there are S reachable non-final cut markings, we know that any execution of N using more than $S \cdot B$ units of time must contain a loop with a non-zero time delay somewhere on the loop. Hence if $N(S \cdot B + 1)$ can mark the place *after*, then either there is a reachable divergent marking (and the net is not strongly sound) or there exists an execution with a non-zero delay loop and by repeating the loop infinitely often, we get an execution breaking the condition c) of Definition 9 and the net is not strongly sound either.

On the other hand, if the place *after* is not reachable in $N(S \cdot B + 1)$ then it is surely not reachable also for any other $c \geq S \cdot B + 1$, meaning that the set $\mathcal{T}(N)$ is finite by Lemma 10. Now Lemma 9 and the fact that N is sound implies that N is strongly sound. □

Theorem 7. *Strong soundness of bounded extended timed-arc workflow nets is decidable and the maximum execution time is computable.*

Proof. Let N be a given bounded ETAWFN. We first run Algorithm 1 to check for soundness of N. If it is not sound, we terminate and announce that N is not strongly sound. Otherwise, we check whether $N(S \cdot B + 1)$ can reach a marking containing just one token in the place *after* (this check is decidable for bounded ETAPN [1]). If this is the case, we return that N is not strongly sound due to Lemma 11. Otherwise the net is sound and we return the maximum accumulated delay in any marking discovered during the check as the maximum execution time (correctness follows from Lemma 10, soundness of N and the fact that once a token appears in the place *out* in $N(S \cdot B + 1)$, no further delay is possible). □

5   Implementation and Experiments

We demonstrate the usability of our framework on three case studies. The studied workflows were modelled and verified with the help of a publicly available, open-source tool TAPAAL [5], where the algorithms presented in this paper are efficiently implemented in C++. The tool provides a convenient GUI support and one of the main advantages of our tool is the visualization of traces disproving soundness (see [8] for more discussion on this topic).

In the Brake System Control Unit (BSCU) case study, a part of a Wheel Braking System (WBS) used for the certification of civil aircrafts in the SAE standard ARP4761 [12], we discovered in less than 1 second that the workflow is not sound due to unexpected deadlocks. The authors of [12] were able to detect these problems asking a reachability query, however, the error traces contradicting soundness were constructed manually. Our implementation allows a fully automatic detection and visualization of such situations. The workflow model contains 45 places, 33 transitions and 55 arcs.

In the second case study describing the workflow of MPEG2 encoding algorithm run on a multicore processor (Petri net model was taken from [11]), we verified in about 10 seconds both soundness and strong soundness, and computed the minimum and maximum encoding time for the IBBP frame sequence. The workflow model contains 44 places, 34 transitions and 82 arcs.

In the third case study, we checked the soundness of a larger blood transfusion workflow [4], the benchmarking case study of the little-JIL language. The Petri net model was suggested in [2] but we discovered several issues with improper workflow termination that were fixed and then both soundness and strong

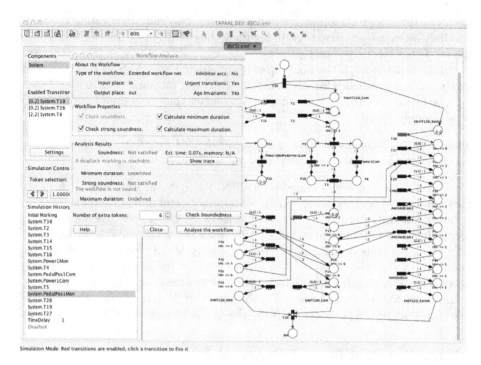

Fig. 5. TAPAAL screenshot of the workflow analysis tool

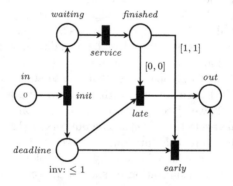

Fig. 6. A net sound in the discrete semantics but unsound in the continuous one

soundness was confirmed in about 1 second, including the information about the minimum and maximum execution times. The workflow model contains 115 places, 94 transitions and 198 arcs.

TAPAAL models of all case studies can be obtained from www.tapaal.net and Figure 5 shows a screenshot of the GUI in the trace debugging mode for workflow analysis of the brake system control unit mentioned above.

6   Conclusion

We presented a framework for modelling of timed workflow processes via timed-arc workflow nets and studied the classical problem of soundness and its extension to time-bounded (strong) soundness. We provided a comprehensive analysis of decidability/undecidability of soundness and strong soundness on different subclasses of timed-arc workflow nets. We also suggested efficient algorithms for computing minimum and maximum execution times of a given workflow and implemented all algorithms within the tool TAPAAL [5]. As a result we have a complete theory for checking soundness on timed workflow nets and contrary to many other papers studying different variants of workflow processes, we took a step further by providing efficient implementation of the algorithms, including a platform independent GUI support for modular design of timed workflow nets and visual error trace debugging. The tool is open-source and freely available at www.tapaal.net. The practical usability of the approach was documented on three industry-inspired case studies, demonstrating a promising potential for verification of larger timed workflows.

In our study we focused on the discrete semantics of workflow nets that is often sufficient and allows for modelling of workflows where events can happen in discrete steps. In case of continuous time semantics (delays are from the domain of nonnegative real numbers) the situation is, perhaps surprisingly, different. Consider the workflow net in Figure 6 (as before we do not draw the $[0, \infty]$ intervals). The workflow is clearly sound w.r.t. the discrete semantics as the age of the token in the place *finished* can be either 1 or 0, depending on whether the service was executed early or late, and then either the transition *early* or *late* is enabled and allows us to always reach a final marking. However, in the continuous semantics we can execute the sequence "*init*, delay 0.5, *service*, delay 0.5", bringing us into a deadlock situation. Hence the decidability of soundness in the continuous semantics cannot be derived from the results achieved in this paper. We nevertheless conjecture that soundness is decidable also in this case and the details are left for future work.

References

1. Andersen, M., Gatten Larsen, H., Srba, J., Grund Sørensen, M., Haahr Taankvist, J.: Verification of liveness properties on closed timed-arc Petri nets. In: Kučera, A., Henzinger, T.A., Nešetřil, J., Vojnar, T., Antoš, D. (eds.) MEMICS 2012. LNCS, vol. 7721, pp. 69–81. Springer, Heidelberg (2013)
2. Bertolini, C., Liu, Z., Srba, J.: Verification of timed healthcare workflows using component timed-arc Petri nets. In: Weber, J., Perseil, I. (eds.) FHIES 2012. LNCS, vol. 7789, pp. 19–36. Springer, Heidelberg (2013)
3. Bolognesi, T., Lucidi, F., Trigila, S.: From timed Petri nets to timed LOTOS. In: PSTV 1990, pp. 1–14. North-Holland, Amsterdam (1990)
4. Christov, S.C., Avrunin, G.S., Clarke, A.L., Osterweil, L.J., Henneman, E.A.: A benchmark for evaluating software engineering techniques for improving medical processes. In: SEHC 2010, pp. 50–56. ACM (2010)

5. David, A., Jacobsen, L., Jacobsen, M., Jørgensen, K.Y., Møller, M.H., Srba, J.: TAPAAL 2.0: Integrated development environment for timed-arc Petri nets. In: Flanagan, C., König, B. (eds.) TACAS 2012. LNCS, vol. 7214, pp. 492–497. Springer, Heidelberg (2012)
6. Dickson, L.E.: Finiteness of the odd perfect and primitive abundant numbers with distinct factors. American Journal of Mathematics 35, 413–422 (1913)
7. Du, Y., Jiang, C.: Towards a workflow model of real-time cooperative systems. In: Dong, J.S., Woodcock, J. (eds.) ICFEM 2003. LNCS, vol. 2885, pp. 452–470. Springer, Heidelberg (2003)
8. Flender, C., Freytag, T.: Visualizing the soundness of workflow nets. In: AWPN 2006, Department Informatics, University of Hamburg, vol. 267 (2006)
9. Hanisch, H.M.: Analysis of place/transition nets with timed-arcs and its application to batch process control. In: Ajmone Marsan, M. (ed.) ICATPN 1993. LNCS, vol. 691, pp. 282–299. Springer, Heidelberg (1993)
10. Ling, S., Schmidt, H.: Time Petri nets for workflow modelling and analysis. In: SMC 2000, vol. 4, pp. 3039–3044. IEEE (2000)
11. Pelayo, F.L., Cuartero, F., Valero, V., Macia, H., Pelayo, M.L.: Applying timed-arc Petri nets to improve the performance of the MPEG-2 encoding algorithm. In: MMM 2004, pp. 49–56. IEEE (2004)
12. Sieverding, S., Ellen, C., Battram, P.: Sequence diagram test case specification and virtual integration analysis using timed-arc Petri nets. In: FESCA 2013. EPTCS, vol. 108, pp. 17–31 (2013)
13. Tiplea, F.L., Macovei, G.: Timed workflow nets. In: SYNASC 2005, pp. 361–366. IEEE Computer Society (2005)
14. Tiplea, F.L., Macovei, G.: E-timed workflow nets. In: SYNASC 2006, pp. 423–429. IEEE Computer Society (2006)
15. Tiplea, F.L., Macovei, G.: Soundness for s- and a-timed workflow nets is undecidable. IEEE Trans. on Systems, Man, and Cybernetics 39(4), 924–932 (2009)
16. van der Aalst, W.M.P.: Verification of workflow nets. In: Azéma, P., Balbo, G. (eds.) ICATPN 1997. LNCS, vol. 1248, pp. 407–426. Springer, Heidelberg (1997)
17. van der Aalst, W.M.P.: The application of Petri nets to workflow management. Journal of Circuits, Systems, and Computers 8(1), 21–66 (1998)
18. van der Aalst, W.M.P., van Hee, K., ter Hofstede, A.H.M., Sidorova, N., Verbeek, H.M.W., Voorhoeve, M., Wynn, M.T.: Soundness of workflow nets: classification, decidability, and analysis. Formal Aspects of Comp. 23(3), 333–363 (2011)
19. Valero, V., Cuartero, F., de Frutos-Escrig, D.: On non-decidability of reachability for timed-arc Petri nets. In: PNPM 1999, pp. 188–196. IEEE (1999)

Process Model Discovery: A Method Based on Transition System Decomposition*

Anna A. Kalenkova[1], Irina A. Lomazova[1], and Wil M.P. van der Aalst[1,2]

[1] National Research University Higher School of Economics (HSE),
Moscow, 101000, Russia
{akalenkova,ilomazova}@hse.ru
[2] Eindhoven University of Technology,
P.O. Box 513, NL-5600 MB, Eindhoven, The Netherlands
w.m.p.v.d.aalst@tue.nl

Abstract. Process mining aims to discover and analyze processes by extracting information from event logs. Process mining discovery algorithms deal with large data sets to learn automatically process models. As more event data become available there is the desire to learn larger and more complex process models. To tackle problems related to the readability of the resulting model and to ensure tractability, various decomposition methods have been proposed. This paper presents a novel decomposition approach for discovering more readable models from event logs on the basis of a priori knowledge about the event log structure: regular and special cases of the process execution are treated separately. The transition system, corresponding to a given event log, is decomposed into a regular part and a specific part. Then one of the known discovery algorithms is applied to both parts, and finally these models are combined into a single process model. It is proven, that the structural and behavioral properties of submodels are inherited by the unified process model. The proposed discovery algorithm is illustrated using a running example.

1 Introduction

Process mining techniques can be used, amongst others, to discover process models (e.g., in the form of Petri nets) from event logs. Many discovery methods were suggested in order to obtain process models reflecting a behavior presented in event logs. Discovered process models may vary considerably depending on a chosen discovery method. For an overview of process discovery approaches and techniques see [15].

The main challenge of process discovery is to construct an adequate formal model reflecting behavior presented in an event log in a best possible way. Quality criteria for process models discovered from event logs are described in [2]. The first criterion is *(replay) fitness*: a process model should allow for behavior recorded in an event log. The next one is *precision*: a discovered process model

---

* This work is supported by the Basic Research Program of the National Research University Higher School of Economics.

G. Ciardo and E. Kindler (Eds.): PETRI NETS 2014, LNCS 8489, pp. 71–90, 2014.
© Springer International Publishing Switzerland 2014

should not allow for behavior which differs markedly from an event log records (no underfitting). The *generalization* criterion states that a discovered model should be general enough (no overfitting). And the last but not least quality criterion is *simplicity*: a discovered model should not be too complicate and confusing.

In this paper we focus on simplicity, fitness and precision. The goal of our work is to present a decomposition method for obtaining clearer and simpler models, trying to preserve their fitness and precision. The decomposition method proposed in this paper aim to exploit *modularity* in processes to obtain more readable process models. For other quality metrics for evaluation of simplicity see [22].

Most of process mining algorithms for discovering a model from an event log first build a (labeled) transition system from an event log, and then use different techniques to construct a model from this transition system. We also follow this approach. Methods for building transition systems based on event logs were proposed in [6] and are out of the scope of this paper. In this paper we assume that there is a transition system, already constructed from some event log, and concentrate on discovering a process model from a given transition system. Moreover, we assume that a transition system is decomposed into a regular and specific parts on base of some a priori knowledge about a modeled system. For each of the parts we apply existing process discovery algorithms to obtain corresponding (sub)process models. Then these models are combined into a single process model.

For discovering subprocess models we suggest to use state-based region algorithms and algorithms based on regions of languages. The state-based region approach was initially proposed by A. Ehrenfeucht and G. Rozenberg [16]. Later this approach was generalized by J. Cortadella et al. [12, 13]. An alternative generalization was proposed by J. Carmona et al. [11]. The application of state-based region algorithms to process mining was studied in [6, 9, 21]. Algorithms based on regions of languages were presented in [7, 14, 18] and then applied to process mining [8, 24]. State-based region algorithms and algorithms based on regions of languages map discovered regions into places of a target Petri net. The advantage of these algorithms is that they guarantee "perfect" fitness, i.e. every trace in a log (a transition system) can be reproduced in a model. However, a large degree of concurrency in a system and incompleteness of an event log (or corresponding transition system) may lead to a blowup of the diagram comparable to the the state explosion problem.

The paper is organized as follows. In Section 2 a motivating example is presented. Section 3 introduces basic definitions and notions, including traces, Petri nets and transition systems. In Section 4 we propose a decomposition algorithm for constructing a process model. In Section 5 we formally prove that the structural and behavioral properties of subprocess models constructed from the decomposed transition system are inherited by the unified process model. Section 6 presents related work. Section 7 concludes the paper.

2   Motivating Example

In this section we will consider booking a flight process. The log reflecting a history of process execution is presented in Fig. 1. The transition system constructed from this log is depicted in Fig. 2.

$L = \{\langle start\_booking, book\_flight, get\_insurance, send\_email, choose\_payment\_type,$
$\quad pay\_by\_card, complite\_booking\rangle,$
$\quad \langle start\_booking, get\_insurance, book\_flight, send\_email, choose\_payment\_type,$
$\quad pay\_by\_card, complite\_booking\rangle,$
$\quad \langle start\_booking, get\_insurance, book\_flight, send\_email, choose\_payment\_type,$
$\quad pay\_by\_web\_money, complite\_booking\rangle,$
$\quad \langle start\_booking, book\_flight, get\_insurance, send\_email, choose\_payment\_type,$
$\quad pay\_by\_web\_money, complite\_booking\rangle,$
$\quad \langle start\_booking, book\_flight, cancel, send\_email\rangle,$
$\quad \langle start\_booking, book\_flight, get\_insurance, send\_email, choose\_payment\_type,$
$\quad \langle cancel, send\_email\rangle\}.$

Fig. 1. An event log for a booking process

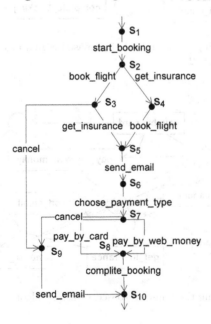

Fig. 2. A transition system for a booking process constructed from the event log depicted in Fig. 1

At the beginning of a booking process a customer needs to book a flight and to get an insurance, these actions are performed in parallel.

Then an email is sent to confirm the booking. After that the customer chooses a payment method, pays and the booking process successfully completes. If the booking was cancelled, an email is sent to notify the cancellation. These cancellations may occur during an execution of booking procedures as well as after the booking was accepted.

Let us consider the models produced by the standard state-based region algorithm[1] (Fig. 3) and the language-based synthesis algorithm[2] (Fig. 4) from original transition system and corresponding event log respectively.

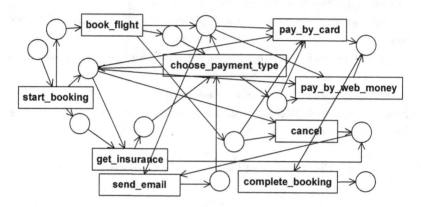

Fig. 3. The result of applying the standard state-based region algorithm to the transition system depicted in Fig. 2

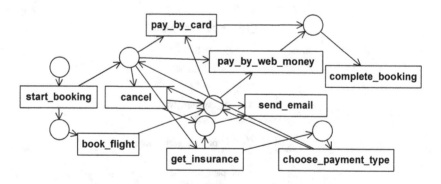

Fig. 4. The result of applying the language-based synthesis algorithm to the event log depicted in Fig. 1

---

[1] The *State-based regions Miner* plug-in is available in Prom framework [23]. This plug-in implements the standard state-based region algorithm presented in [12, 13].

[2] The *ILP Miner* [24] plug-in is implemented in Prom framework [23]. We choose such parameters that there are no tokens left after a case completion, and initial places don't have incoming arcs.

Figures 3 and 4 illustrate that region-based techniques may result in models that are more complicated than the corresponding transition system.

In this paper we present a method for discovering better structured and more readable process models by detecting a regular behavior in a given transition system. We split a transition system in two parts: one of them represents a regular behavior, and the other describes handling special cases (exceptions, cancellations, etc.)

3   Preliminaries: Petri Nets and Transition Systems

Let S be a finite set. A *multiset* m over a set S is a mapping $m : S \to Nat$, where Nat is the set of natural numbers (including zero), i.e. a multiset may contain several copies of the same element.

For two multisets m, m' we write $m \subseteq m'$ iff $\forall s \in S : m(s) \leq m'(s)$ (the inclusion relation). The sum of two multisets m and m' is defined as usual: $\forall s \in S : (m + m')(s) = m(s) + m'(s)$, the difference is a partial function: $\forall s \in S$ such that $m(s) \geq m(s') : (m - m')(s) = m(s) - m'(s)$. By $\mathcal{M}(S)$ we denote the set of all finite multisets over S.

Let S and E be two disjoint non-empty sets of *states* and *events*, and $B \subseteq S \times E \times S$ be a *transition relation*. A *transition system* is a tuple $TS = (S, E, B, s_{in}, S_{fin})$, where $s_{in} \in S$ is an initial state and $S_{fin} \subseteq S$ — a set of final states. Elements of B are called *transitions*. We write $s \xrightarrow{e} s'$, when $(s, e, s') \in B$.

A state s is *reachable* from a state s' iff there is a possibly empty sequence of transitions leading from s to s' (denoted by $s \xrightarrow{*} s'$).

A transition system must satisfy the following basic axioms:

1. every state is reachable from the initial state: $\forall s \in S : s_{in} \xrightarrow{*} s$;
2. for every state there is a final state, which is reachable from it: $\forall s \in S \, \exists s_{fin} \in S_{fin} : s \xrightarrow{*} s_{fin}$;

Let E be a set of events. A *trace* σ (over E) is a sequence of events, i.e., $\sigma \in E^*$. An *event log* L is a multiset of traces, i.e., $L \in \mathcal{M}(E^*)$.

A trace $\sigma = \langle e_1, \ldots, e_n \rangle$ is called *feasible* in a transition system TS iff $\exists s_1, \ldots, s_{n-1}, s_n \in S : s_{in} \xrightarrow{e_1} s_1 \xrightarrow{e_2} \ldots s_{n-1} \xrightarrow{e_n} s_n$, and $s_n \in S_{fin}$, i.e. a *feasible* trace leads from the initial state to some final state. A *language accepted by* TS is defined as the set of all traces feasible in TS, and is denoted by $L(TS)$.

We say that a transition system TS and an event log L are *matched* iff each trace from L is a feasible trace in TS, and inversely each feasible trace in TS belongs to L.

Let P and T be two finite disjoint sets of *places* and *transitions*, and $F \subseteq (P \times T) \cup (T \times P)$ — a flow relation. Let also E be a finite set of events, and $\lambda : T \to E$ be a labeling function. Then $N = (P, T, F, \lambda)$ is a *(labeled) Petri net*.

A *marking* in a Petri net is a multiset over the set of places. A marked Petri net (N, m_0) is a Petri net together with its *initial marking*.

Pictorially, places are represented by circles, transitions by boxes, and the flow relation F by directed arcs. Places may carry tokens represented by filled circles. A current marking m is designated by putting $m(p)$ tokens into each place $p \in P$.

For a transition $t \in T$ an arc (x, t) is called an *input arc*, and an arc (t, x) — an *output arc*; the *preset* ${}^\bullet t$ and the *postset* $t^\bullet$ are defined as the multisets over P such that ${}^\bullet t(p) = 1$, if $(p, t) \in F$, otherwise ${}^\bullet t(p) = 0$, and $t^\bullet(p) = 1$ if $(t, p) \in F$, otherwise $t^\bullet(p) = 0$. Note that we will also consider presets and postsets as sets of places. A transition $t \in T$ is *enabled* in a marking m iff ${}^\bullet t \subseteq m$. An enabled transition t may *fire* yielding a new marking $m' =_{\text{def}} m - {}^\bullet t + t^\bullet$ (denoted $m \xrightarrow{t} m'$, $m \xrightarrow{\lambda(t)} m'$, or just $m \to m'$).

We say that m' is *reachable* from m iff there is a (possibly empty) sequence of firings $m = m_1 \to \cdots \to m_n = m'$.

$\mathcal{R}(N, m)$ denotes the set of all markings reachable in N from the marking m.

A marked Petri net (N, m_0), $N = (P, T, F, \lambda)$ is called *safe* iff $\forall p \in P \; \forall m \in \mathcal{R}(N, m_0)\colon m(p) \leq 1$, i.e. at most one token can appear in a place.

A *reachability graph* for a marked Petri net (N, m_0) labeled with events from E is a transition system $TS = (S, E, B, s_{in}, S_{fin})$, with the set of states $S = \mathcal{R}(N, m_0)$, the event set E, and transition relation B defined by $(m, e, m') \in B$ iff $m \xrightarrow{t} m'$, where $e = \lambda(t)$. The initial state in TS is the initial marking m_0. If some reachable markings in (N, m_0) are distinguished as final markings, they are defined as final elements in TS. Note that TS may also contain other final states, to satisfy the axiom that for every state in TS there is a final state, which is reachable from it.

Workflow nets (WF-nets) [1] is a special subclass of Petri nets designed for modeling workflow processes. A workflow net has one initial and one final place, and every place or transition in it is on a directed path from the initial to the final place.

A (labeled) Petri net N is called a (labeled) *workflow net (WF-net)* iff

1. There is one source place $i \in P$ and one sink place $f \in P$ s. t. i has no input arcs and f has no output arcs.
2. Every node from $P \cup T$ is on a path from i to f.
3. The initial marking in N contains the only token in its source place.

We denote by $[i]$ the initial marking in a WF-net N. Similarly, we use $[f]$ to denote the final marking in a WF-net N, defined as a marking containing the only token in the sink place f.

A WF-net N with an initial marking $[i]$ and a final marking $[f]$ is *sound* iff

1. For every state m reachable in N, there exists a firing sequence leading from m to the final state $[f]$. Formally, $\forall m\colon [([i] \xrightarrow{*} m)$ implies $(m \xrightarrow{*} [f])]$;
2. The state $[f]$ is the only state reachable from $[i]$ in N with at least one token in place f. Formally, $\forall m\colon [([i] \xrightarrow{*} m) \wedge ([f] \subseteq m)$ implies $(m = [f])]$;
3. There are no dead transitions in N. Formally, $\forall t \in T \; \exists m, m'\colon (i \xrightarrow{*} m \xrightarrow{\lambda(t)} m')$.

4 Method for Constructing Structured and Readable Process Models

As shown by the example in the Section 2 straightforward application of the synthesis algorithms may give rather confounded process models. Prior knowledge of a modular process structure can be used to identify subprocesses and clarify the target process model. Our goal is to construct readable process models which will reflect modular structures of processes.

4.1 Decomposition of a Transition System

Assume that we can identify a regular and a special process behavior within the original transition system.

Let us consider a transition system $TS = (S, E, B, s_{in}, S_{fin})$ and divide the set of states into two non-overlapping subsets which correspond to a regular and a special behavior: $S = S_{reg} \cup S_{spec}$, $S_{reg} \cap S_{spec} = \emptyset$ (Fig. 5). Let B_{reg} denote a

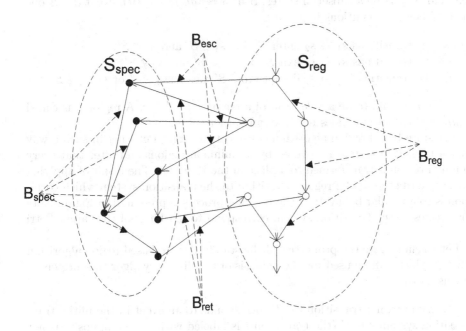

Fig. 5. Decomposition of a transition system

set of regular process transitions, B_{spec} denote a set of special transitions, B_{esc} and B_{ret} stand for transitions, which indicate escaping from the regular process flow and returning to the regular process flow respectively. Let E_{reg} and E_{spec} denote the set of events corresponding to B_{reg} and B_{spec} respectively. Note that E_{reg} and E_{spec} are not necessarily disjoint sets, i.e. the same label can appear in different parts of the transition system.

Formally, set of states S can be partitioned over S_{reg} and S_{spec} and then the tuple $TS_{dec} = (TS, S_{reg}, S_{spec})$ is called a *decomposed transition system* if the following additional conditions hold: $s_{in} \in S_{reg}$ and $S_{fin} \subseteq S_{reg}$.

The construction of such a transition system from an event log can be performed in two steps. Firstly, a transition system is constructed for the traces corresponding to a regular process behavior. Secondly, an additional behavior is added to the transition system, and new states are marked as special.

4.2   Region-Based Algorithms

An algorithm for synthesis of a marked Petri net from a decomposed transition system will be build on well-known region based algorithms. Therefore, we will give an overview of these algorithms and outline their properties, which will be used in the further analysis of the presented algorithm.

State-based region algorithm First, we briefly describe the standard state-based region algorithm [12,13]. Let $TS = (S, E, T, s_{in}, S_{fin})$ be a transition system and $S' \subseteq S$ be a subset of states. S' is a *region* iff for each event $e \in E$ one of the following conditions hods:

- all the transitions $s_1 \xrightarrow{e} s_2$ enter S', i.e. $s_1 \notin S'$ and $s_2 \in S'$,
- all the transitions $s_1 \xrightarrow{e} s_2$ exit S', i.e. $s_1 \in S'$ and $s_2 \notin S'$,
- all the transitions $s_1 \xrightarrow{e} s_2$ do not cross S', i.e. $s_1, s_2 \in S'$ or $s_1, s_2 \notin S'$.

A region r' is said to be a *subregion* of a region r iff $r' \subseteq r$. A region r is called a *minimal region* iff it does not have any other subregions.

The state-based region algorithm constructs a target Petri net in such a way that a transition system is covered by its minimal regions and after that every minimal region is transformed to a place in the Petri net. The result of applying the standard state-based region algorithm to the transition system which corresponds to a regular behavior of the booking process is presented in Fig. 6. Note that states in the transition system correspond to markings of the target Petri net.

Let us enumerate the properties of the standard state-based region algorithm [12,13], which will be used for the analysis of the discovery algorithm presented in this paper:

1. Every Petri net transition $t \in T$ corresponds to an event in the initial transition system $e \in E$ (the transition t is labeled with e), the opposite is not true (events of the initial transition system might be split).

2. There is a bisimulation between a transition system and a reachability graph of the target Petri net, this implies that every state in TS corresponds to a Petri net marking.

3. The target Petri net is safe, i.e. no more than one token can appear in a place.

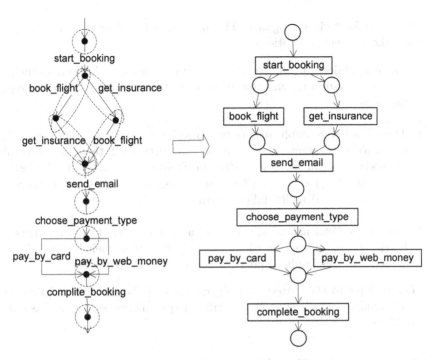

Fig. 6. Applying the state-based region algorithm to the transition system which corresponds to a regular behavior of the booking process

An algorithm based on regions of languages The aim of the different algorithms based on regions of languages [8,24] is to construct a Petri net, which is able to reproduce a given language (herein we will consider a language accepted by an initial transition system), reducing undesirable behavior by adding places. Addition of such places will not allow for construction of a Petri net, e.g. the flower-model (Fig. 7), which generates all the words in a given alphabet. A

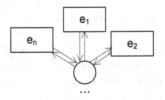

Fig. 7. A flower model

(language-based) region is defined as a $(2\,|T|+1)$-tuple of $\{0,1\}$, representing an initial marking and a number of tokens each transition consumes and produces in a place. Like in the previous approach each region corresponds to a place in a Petri net. Regions are defined as solutions of the linear inequation system, constructed for a given language. The algorithms based on regions of languages satisfy the following conditions:

1. There is a bijection between Petri net transitions T and events in the initial transition system E, such that every transition is labeled with a corresponding event.

2. There is a homomorphism ω from a transition system TS to the reachability graph RG of a target Petri net N, i.e. for every $s \in S$ there is a corresponding node - $\omega(s)$ in RG (every state in TS has a corresponding N marking), such that $\omega(s_{in}) = m_0$ and for every transition $(s_1 \xrightarrow{e} s_2) \in B$ there is an arc $(\omega(s_1), \omega(s_2))$ in RG labeled with e.

3. The target Petri net is safe. We will add constraints to obtain elementary Petri nets, in which transitions can only fire when their output places are empty [24], this implies that we will get a safe Petri net.

Let us refer to the state-based algorithms and the algorithms based on regions languages, which meet the specified requirements, simply as *basic region algorithms*.

4.3   Constructing Transition Systems

In this subsection we give a method for constructing two separate transition systems from a given decomposed transition system. Before applying *basic region algorithms* to parts of a decomposed transition system we have to be sure that these parts are transition systems as well, otherwise they should be repaired.

Let $TS_{dec} = ((S, E, B, s_{in}, S_{fin}), S_{reg}, S_{spec})$ be a decomposed transition system. As we can see from the example (Fig. 5) the subgraph formed by vertices from S_{reg} and transitions from B_{reg} may not define a transition system, since it contains states which are not on the path from the initial state to some final state, and should be repaired. A set of novel events E' and a set of transitions B' labeled with this events should be added to retrieve missing connections between S_{reg} states (see Fig. 8). For every pair of nodes from S_{reg} having a path between them with a starting transition from B_{esc}, a destination transition from B_{ret}, and containing exactly one transition from B_{esc}, such that there is no path between these nodes within the graph (S_{reg}, B_{reg}), a novel event $e' \in E'$ and a novel transition $b' \in B'$ labeled with this event should be added. One can note that after this transformation every state is on the path from s_{in} to $s_{fin} \in S_{fin}$, and we get a transition system $TS_{reg} = (S_{reg}, E_{reg} \cup E', B_{reg} \cup B', s_{in}, S_{fin})$.

The subgraph formed by vertices from S_{spec} and transitions from B_{spec} should be also repaired to form a transition system. As in the previous case each pair of states connected only through external nodes should be connected directly via transitions labeled with novel events (see Fig. 8). Note that a path through the external nodes should not contain transitions added to repair the transition system constructed for a normal flow. Let B'' denote the set of novel transitions,

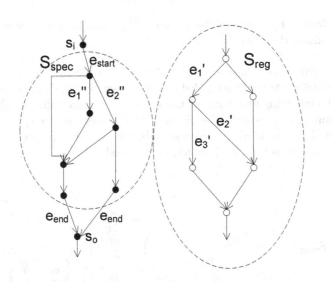

Fig. 8. Constructing transition systems, which correspond to subprocesses

E'' denote the set of corresponding events. In contrast to the transition system TS_{reg} constructed for the normal process flow in the previous step an initial state s_i and a final state (state without outgoing transitions) s_o should be added. All states having incoming transitions from B_{esc}, should be connected with s_i by incoming transitions labeled with a special event e_{start}. Let us denote the set of these transitions by B_{start}. Similarly, all states having outgoing transitions from B_{ret} should be connected with s_o by outgoing transitions labeled with the event e_{end}. The set of such transitions will be denoted by B_{end}. After these transformations every state lies on a path from s_{in} to $s_{fin} \in S_{fin}$, and, hence, we obtain a transition system $TS_{spec} = (S_{spec} \cup \{s_i, s_o\}, E_{spec} \cup E'' \cup \{e_{start}, e_{end}\}, B_{spec} \cup B'' \cup B_{start} \cup B_{end}, s_i, \{s_o\})$.

4.4 Discovery Algorithm

This algorithm uses some *basic region algorithm* **A**.

Algorithm [Discovery algorithm]. *(Constructing a marked Petri net for a decomposed TS).*
Input: A decomposed transition system $TS_{dec} = ((S, E, B, s_{in}, S_{fin}), S_{reg}, S_{spec})$.

Step 1: Construct two transition systems: $TS_{reg} = (S_{reg}, E_{reg} \cup E', B_{reg} \cup B', s_{in}, S_{fin})$ and $TS_{spec} = (S_{spec} \cup \{s_i\} \cup \{s_o\}, E_{spec} \cup E'' \cup \{e_{start}, e_{end}\}, B_{spec} \cup B'' \cup B_{start} \cup B_{end}, s_i, \{s_o\})$ form the decomposed transition system TS_{dec}.

Step 2: Apply algorithm **A** to retrieve a regular (N_{reg}) and a special (N_{spec}) process flow from TS_{reg} and TS_{spec} respectively.

Step 3: Restore the connections between N_{reg} and N_{spec} to create a so-called a unified Petri net N:

  – For every transition $(s \overset{e_{esc}}{\to} s') \in B_{esc}, s \in S_{reg}, s' \in S_{spec}$ add a novel Petri net transition labeled with e_{esc} (see Fig. 9). Connect this transition by incoming arcs with all the places $p \in P$, such that $m(p) > 0$, and by outgoing arcs with the places $p' \in P'$, such that $m'(p') > 0$, where m and m' are markings corresponding to s and s' respectively. Similarly, transitions from B_{ret} should be restored.

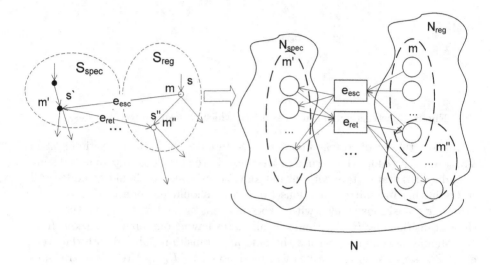

Fig. 9. A unified Petri net

  – Delete the following nodes along with their incident arcs from the result Petri net: transitions with labels from E' and E'', all the transitions labeled with e_{start} along with the places from their presets (if these places don't have other output arcs), and all the transitions labeled with e_{end} along with the places from their postsets (if these places don't have output arcs).

  – Initial marking for the result Petri net N is defined as an initial marking of N_{reg}, label function of the result N is defined on the basis of N_{reg} and N_{spec} label functions.

Output: Marked Petri net N.

Note that after partitioning of the initial transition system into two transitions systems (Step 1), each of the parts can be in turn divided into subsystems. After decomposition a discovery algorithm is applied to each part (Step 2) and required connections are restored within the entire model (Step 3).

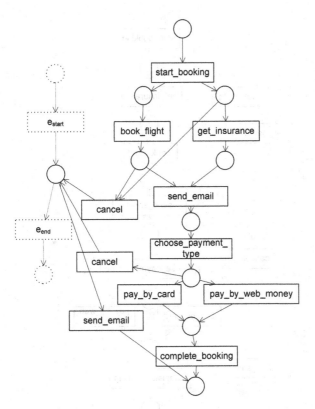

Fig. 10. The result of applying the discovery algorithm to the original transition system

Let us consider the initial transition system presented in Fig. 2. Suppose that we will divide the set of states in the following manner: $S = S_{reg} \cup S_{spec}, S_{reg} = \{s_1, s_2, s_3, s_4, s_5, s_6, s_7, s_8, s_{10}\}$, $S_{spec} = \{s_9\}$. A Petri net which is constructed for this decomposed transitions system according to the discovery algorithm is presented in Fig. 10. The subprocesses structures can be easily retrieved from this model. Note, that dashed nodes and arcs denote those parts which were deleted during an execution of the discovery algorithm.

Now assume that, we decided to divide the set of states as follows: $S = S_{reg} \cup S_{spec}, S_{reg} = \{s_1, s_2, s_4, s_5, s_6, s_7, s_8, s_{10}\}$, $S_{spec} = \{s_3, s_9\}$. The result of applying the discovery algorithm to the decomposed transition system is presented in Fig. 11. This example shows that the result depends on choosing a partition of the set of states. Expert knowledge can help to find an appropriate partition. For example, names of events, which correspond to an irregular behavior, can be helpful for that.

Note, that the models, presented in Fig. 10 and Fig. 11, can be constructed by both: the state-based region algorithm and the algorithm based on regions of languages, which meet the requirements, listed in Subsection 5.2, with the only difference, that the algorithm based on regions of languages doesn't produce final place.

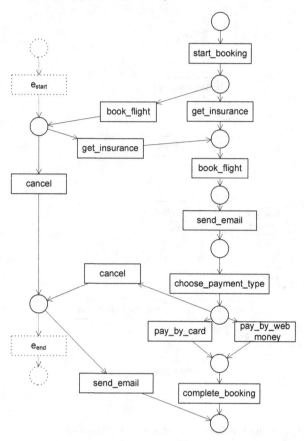

Fig. 11. The result of applying the discovery algorithm to the original transition system with different states partition

5   Structural and Behavioral Properties Preserved by Decomposed Discovery

In this section we will formally prove that the structural and behavioral properties of subprocess models constructed from a decomposed transition system are inherited by the unified process model. As was mentioned earlier the discovery algorithm use some *basic region algorithm*. A *basic region algorithm* is a state-based region algorithm, which guarantees the bisimilarity relation between an initial transition system and a reachability graph of the target Petri net, or an algorithm based on regions of languages, for which there is a homomorphism from a transition system to a reachability graph of the target Petri net. Bisimularity relation defined by the state-based region algorithm specifies exactly one state in a reachability graph for each state in a transition system, in such a case bisimularity implies homomorphism. So, our decomposition approach can use any of *basic region algorithms*, provided this algorithm outputs a safe Perti net, and there is a homomorphism from an initial transition system to the reachability graph of the target Petri net.

5.1   Structural Properties

First, we will show that the Discovery algorithm preserve connectivity properties of subprocess models, i.e. nodes connected within the subprocess model, obtained on the Step 2 of the Discovery algorithm, will be connected within the unified model.

Lemma 1 (Connectivity properties). *If there is a directed path between a pair of nodes (i.e., places or transitions) within subprocess model N_{reg} (N_{spec}) and these nodes were not deleted during the construction of the unified Petri net model $N = (P, T, F, \lambda)$, then there is a directed path between them within N.*

Proof. Let $TS_{dec} = (TS, S_{reg}, S_{spec})$ be a decomposed transition system. Let us consider two arbitrary nodes $u, v \in P' \cup T'$ within $N_{reg} = (P', T', F', \lambda_{reg})$. By construction there is a path between them before the deletion of unnecessary nodes. Let us prove that u, v will be connected after the deletion as well. Consider transition $t \in T'$ labeled with e', which should be deleted along with all incident arcs (see Fig. 12).

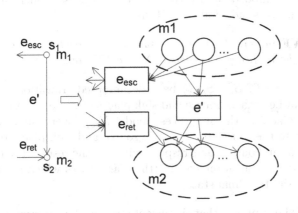

Fig. 12. Transition that should be deleted

Let us prove that the nodes from $^\bullet t$ and $t^\bullet$ are still connected with each other. If so, connection between arbitrary nodes u and v will be preserved. Consider transition $(s_1 \xrightarrow{e'} s_2), s_1, s_2 \in S_{reg}$, which was added to the transition system constructed for S_{reg} (see Fig. 12). Let $B_{spec}, B_{esc},$ and B_{ret} be transitions of the decomposed transition system, connecting nodes as it shown in Fig. 5. There is an alternative path within the transition system between s_1 and s_2 which contains transitions from B_{esc}, B_{spec} and B_{ret}. Since there is a homomorphism from the transition system to the reachability graph of the target Petri net, there is a path through N_{spec} nodes between Petri net transitions: $t_{esc} \in T$ and $t_{ret} \in T$ labeled with e_{esc} and e_{ret} respectively (inner transitions of this path are represented only by N_{spec} transitions), which corresponds to a firing sequence within N_{spec}, since N_{spec} contains no tokens before t_{esc} fires. Let us consider Petri net markings: m_1 and m_2 which correspond to s_1 and s_2 respectively. Since there is an arc corresponding to $(s_1 \xrightarrow{e'} s_2)$ within the reachability graph of N_{reg}, the following conditions hold: $\bullet t \subseteq m_1$ and $t^\bullet \subseteq m_2$. This implies that every place from $\bullet t$ connected with t_{esc}, and t_{ret} is connected with any place from $t^\bullet$, if so places from $\bullet t$ are still connected with places from $t^\bullet$ through Petri net transitions t_{esc}, and t_{ret}. Similarly, it may be proven that the deletion of unnecessary nodes within N_{spec} will not lead to a violation of nodes connectivity.   □

The standard state-based region algorithm could be extended to produce WF-nets by adding artificial initial and final states, connected by transitions with unique labels with the original initial and final states respectively. This follows from the definition of a region. In [24] the extensions for algorithms based on regions of languages were presented: the first extension produces models with places that contain no tokens after a case completion, the second extension doesn't allow for places to have initial markings, unless they have no incoming arcs. It is easier to transform a Petri net, which satisfies these conditions, to a WF-net. Thus, it is important to verify that if subprocess models are WF-nets then the unified process model also a WF-net.

Theorem 1 (WF-nets). *Assume that subprocess models N_{reg} and N_{spec} are WF-nets. Then the unified process model N is a WF-net.*

Proof. Let $TS_{dec} = (TS, S_{reg}, S_{spec})$ be a decomposed transition system. The proof follows from Lemma 1. Source and sink places of N are determined as the source and sink places of the subprocess model N_{reg}. Every node within N_{reg} is on the path from the source to sink. The source and sink places of N_{spec} are connected by input and output arcs respectively with the rest part of the system, otherwise TS is not a transition system (there are states which are not on the path from the initial to a final state).   □

For now, it has been proven that significant structural properties are inherited by the discovered unified process model.

5.2   Behavioral Properties

In this subsection we show that that unified process model also preserves some behavioral properties.

First we show that if a *basic region algorithm* constructs sound WF-nets, then the composite model will also be a sound WF-net. A reasonable decomposition of a transition system may help to construct a hierarchy of sound process models.

Theorem 2 (Sound WF-nets). *Let subprocess models N_{reg} and N_{spec} be sound WF-nets, then the unified process model N is also a sound WF-net.*

Proof. Using Theorem 1 we can show that N is a workflow net. By construction every state is reachable from the initial state and the final state is reachable from any state. No dead transitions are added by construction. □

The standard state-based region algorithm [12,13] guarantees that there is a bisimilarity relation between the initial transition system and the reachability graph of the target Petri net. This property is inherited by a regular transition system under the assumption that a *basic region algorithm* will not produce reachability graphs with markings which dominate one another ($m \subseteq m'$). Generally speaking, state-based region algorithms can produce Petri nets with reachability graphs, containing states with markings which dominate one another. In that case splitting of labels can be applied to separate the states from the same region.

Theorem 3 (Bisimulation). *If there are bisimilarity relations between transition systems, which correspond to subprocess models, and reachability graphs RG_{reg}, RG_{spec} of these subprocess models, then there is a bisimilarity relation between a decomposed transition system and the reachability graph of the unified process model N.*

Proof. Since reachability graphs RG_{reg} and RG_{spec} don't have common states and transitions, a reachability graph of the unified process model N will be built as a union of RG_{reg} and RG_{spec} with subsequent deletion of unnecessary transitions and addition of novel connecting transitions, corresponding to the transitions B_{reg} and B_{spec} of the decomposed transition system. Note that no extra transitions will be added, since we assume that there are no markings that dominate one another. This will guarantee bisimilarity. □

In contrast to the state-based region algorithm which guarantees fitness and precision, the algorithm based on regions of languages guarantees only fitness, i.e. every trace can be reproduced in a process model. Let us prove that the property of language inclusion is also preserved.

Theorem 4 (Language inclusion). *Let $TS_{dec} = (TS, S_{reg}, S_{spec})$ be a decomposed transition system. Assume that N_{reg} and N_{spec} are subprocess models constructed from transition systems TS_{reg} and TS_{spec} with corresponding reachability graphs RG_{reg} and RG_{spec}. Let Petri net N be the unified process model with a reachability graph RG. If $L(TS_{reg}) \subseteq L(RG_{reg})$ and $L(TS_{spec}) \subseteq L(RG_{spec})$, then $L(TS) \subseteq L(RG)$.*

Proof. Let us consider two transition systems: TS_{reg} and TS_{spec}. For each transition system there is a homomorphism to the corresponding reachability graph (see Fig. 8): $w_{reg} \colon TS_{reg} \to RG_{reg}$, $w_{spec} \colon TS_{spec} \to RG_{spec}$. Since RG_{reg} and RG_{spec} don't have common states and transitions, by construction of the unified process model N its reachability graph RG will be built as a union of RG_{reg} and

RG_{spec} reachability graphs with subsequent deletion of unnecessary transitions and addition of novel transitions, which corresponds to transitions connecting states from S_{reg} with states from S_{spec}. Note that we may get extra transitions connecting states, which dominate the states that should be connected. By construction there is a homomorphism from TS to RG, which implies language inclusion.   □

These theoretical observations are of great importance for application of region-based synthesis since state-based region algorithms can be decomposed and still produce Petri nets with reachability graphs bisimilar to original transition systems, language-based algorithms can be decomposed and still guarantee language inclusion.

6   Related Work

In this section we will give an overview of the process discovery techniques based on decomposition. An approach for partitioning activities over a collection of passages in accordance with so-called predefined causal structure was introduced in [3]. Using this approach discovery can be done per passage. A generic approach based on horizontal projections of an event log was proposed in [4], this approach can be combined with different process discovery algorithms and might be considered as a generalization of passages technique.

More related are approaches based on the decomposition analysis of an entire transition system [10,17,20]. In [20] an effective method for a union of transition systems which correspond to different log traces was presented. The main difference of [20] from the approach presented in this paper is that the aim of [20] was to distribute the computations, and subsystems were not considered as subprocesses. The idea proposed in [10] is to generate a set of state machines (Petri nets with transitions having at most one incoming and at most one outgoing arc) whose parallel composition can reproduce any trace from an event log. In contrast to the approach presented in this paper, the decomposition of a transition system was based only on its structural properties, additional information about an event log was not considered. An approach for the discovery of cancellation regions based on the analysis of a topological structure of an initial transition system was proposed in [17]. This approach uses state-based region algorithm to discover regular and exceptional behavior. Improvement of the algorithm proposed in this paper based on the addition of reset arcs in order to reduce the number of connections between subsystems might be considered as a generalization of [17].

In this paper we focus on producing readable process models and not on the decomposition of a transition system in order to distribute the computations, but the approach can be used for the decomposition of computations as well.

7   Conclusion

This paper presents a novel decomposition approach for discovering more readable process models from event logs. Using existing techniques we first produce a transition system. This transition system is decomposed into a regular and a special part on the basis of a priori knowledge about an event log. Then one of the region based discovery algorithms [8,12,13,24] is applied to each part of the transition system and after that the discovered subprocess models are combined into a unified model. It is proven that structural and behavioral properties of subprocess models are inherited by the unified process model.

The results presented in this paper can be used as a starting point for more advanced methods of discovering better structured and more readable process models from transition systems. The quality of the model obtained within the decomposition approach depends significantly on the choice of states partitioning in a given transition systems. Our future work aims at implementing the presented discovery algorithm and continue the research with real-life event logs. Also we plan applying the decomposition approach to discover and build process models in high-level process languages such as BPMN [19] or YAWL [5].

References

1. van der Aalst, W.M.P.: The application of Petri nets to workflow management. Journal of Circuits, Systems, and Computers 8(1), 21–66 (1998)
2. van der Aalst, W.M.P.: Process Mining - Discovery, Conformance and Enhancement of Business Processes. Springer (2011)
3. van der Aalst, W.M.P.: Decomposing Process Mining Problems Using Passages. In: Haddad, S., Pomello, L. (eds.) PETRI NETS 2012. LNCS, vol. 7347, pp. 72–91. Springer, Heidelberg (2012)
4. van der Aalst, W.M.P.: Decomposing Petri Nets for Process Mining: A Generic Approach. Distributed and Parallel Databases 31(4), 471–507 (2013)
5. van der Aalst, W.M.P., Aldred, L., Dumas, M., ter Hofstede, A.H.M.: Design and Implementation of the YAWL System. QUT Technical report, FIT-TR-2003-07, Queensland University of Technology, Brisbane (2003)
6. van der Aalst, W.M.P., Rubin, V., Verbeek, H.M.W., van Dongen, B.F., Kindler, E., Günther, C.W.: Process Mining: A Two-Step Approach to Balance Between Underfitting and Overfitting. Software and Systems Modeling 9(1), 87–111 (2010)
7. Badouel, E., Bernardinello, L., Darondeau, P.: Polynomial Algorithms for the Synthesis of Bounded Nets. In: Mosses, P.D., Nielsen, M., Schwartzbach, M.I. (eds.) TAPSOFT 1995. LNCS, vol. 915, pp. 364–378. Springer, Heidelberg (1995)
8. Bergenthum, R., Desel, J., Lorenz, R., Mauser, S.: Process Mining Based on Regions of Languages. In: Alonso, G., Dadam, P., Rosemann, M. (eds.) BPM 2007. LNCS, vol. 4714, pp. 375–383. Springer, Heidelberg (2007)
9. Carmona, J.A., Cortadella, J., Kishinevsky, M.: A Region-Based Algorithm for Discovering Petri Nets from Event Logs. In: Dumas, M., Reichert, M., Shan, M.-C. (eds.) BPM 2008. LNCS, vol. 5240, pp. 358–373. Springer, Heidelberg (2008)
10. Carmona, J., Cortadella, J., Kishinevsky, M.: Divide-and-Conquer Strategies for Process Mining. In: Dayal, U., Eder, J., Koehler, J., Reijers, H.A. (eds.) BPM 2009. LNCS, vol. 5701, pp. 327–343. Springer, Heidelberg (2009)
11. Carmona, J., Cortadella, J., Kishinevsky, M.: New Region-Based Algorithms for Deriving Bounded Petri Nets. IEEE Transactions on Computers 59(3), 371–384 (2010)

12. Cortadella, J., Kishinevsky, M., Lavagno, L., Yakovlev, A.: Synthesizing Petri Nets from State-Based Models. In: Proceedings of the 1995 IEEE/ACM International Conference on Computer-Aided Design (ICCAD 1995), pp. 164–171 (1995)
13. Cortadella, J., Kishinevsky, M., Lavagno, L., Yakovlev, A.: Deriving Petri nets for finite transition systems. IEEE Trans. Computers 47(8), 859–882 (1998)
14. Darondeau, P.: Deriving Unbounded Petri Nets from Formal Languages. In: Sangiorgi, D., de Simone, R. (eds.) CONCUR 1998. LNCS, vol. 1466, pp. 533–548. Springer, Heidelberg (1998)
15. van Dongen, B.F., Alves de Medeiros, A.K., Wen, L.: Process Mining: Overview and Outlook of Petri Net Discovery Algorithms. In: Jensen, K., van der Aalst, W.M.P. (eds.) Transactions on Petri Nets and Other Models of Concurrency II. LNCS, vol. 5460, pp. 225–242. Springer, Heidelberg (2009)
16. Ehrenfeucht, A., Rozenberg, G.: Partial (Set) 2-Structures - Part 1 and Part 2. Acta Informatica 27(4), 315–368 (1989)
17. Kalenkova, A.A., Lomazova, I.A.: Discovery of cancellation regions within process mining techniques. In: CS&P. CEUR Workshop Proceedings, vol. 1032, pp. 232–244. CEUR-WS.org (2013)
18. Lorenz, R., Juhás, G.: How to Synthesize Nets from Languages: A Survey. In: Proceedings of the Wintersimulation Conference (WSC 2007), pp. 637–647. IEEE Computer Society (2007)
19. OMG. Business Process Model and Notation (BPMN). Object Management Group, formal/2011-01-03 (2011)
20. Solé, M., Carmona, J.: Incremental process mining. In: ACSD/Petri Nets Workshops. CEUR Workshop Proceedings, vol. 827, pp. 175–190. CEUR-WS.org (2010)
21. Solé, M., Carmona, J.: Process Mining from a Basis of State Regions. In: Lilius, J., Penczek, W. (eds.) PETRI NETS 2010. LNCS, vol. 6128, pp. 226–245. Springer, Heidelberg (2010)
22. Vanderfeesten, I., Cardoso, J., Mendling, J., Reijers, H.A., van der Aalst, W.M.P.: Quality Metrics for Business Process Models. In: BPM and Workflow Handbook 2007, pp. 179–190. Future Strategies Inc., Lighthouse Point (2007)
23. Verbeek, H.M.W., Buijs, J.C.A.M., van Dongen, B.F., van der Aalst, W.M.P.: ProM 6: The Process Mining Toolkit. In: Proc. of BPM Demonstration Track 2010. CEUR Workshop Proceedings, vol. 615, pp. 34–39 (2010)
24. van der Werf, J.M.E.M., van Dongen, B.F., Hurkens, C.A.J., Serebrenik, A.: Process discovery using integer linear programming. Fundamenta Informaticae 94(3), 387–412 (2009)

Discovering Block-Structured
Process Models from Incomplete Event Logs

Sander J.J. Leemans, Dirk Fahland, and Wil M.P. van der Aalst

Eindhoven University of Technology, The Netherlands
{s.j.j.leemans,d.fahland,w.m.p.v.d.aalst}@tue.nl

Abstract One of the main challenges in process mining is to discover a process model describing observed behaviour in the best possible manner. Since event logs only contain example behaviour and one cannot assume to have seen all possible process executions, process discovery techniques need to be able to handle incompleteness. In this paper, we study the effects of such incomplete logs on process discovery. We analyse the impact of incompleteness of logs on behavioural relations, which are abstractions often used by process discovery techniques. We introduce probabilistic behavioural relations that are less sensitive to incompleteness, and exploit these relations to provide a more robust process discovery algorithm. We prove this algorithm to be able to rediscover a model of the original system. Furthermore, we show in experiments that our approach even rediscovers models from incomplete event logs that are much smaller than required by other process discovery algorithms.

Keywords: process discovery, block-structured process models, rediscoverability, process trees.

1 Introduction

Organisations nowadays collect and store considerable amounts of event data. For instance, workflow management systems log audit trails, and enterprise resource planning systems store transaction logs. From these event logs, process mining aims to extract information, such as business process models, social networks, bottlenecks and compliance with regulations [1]. In this paper we focus on the most challenging problem: discovering a process model from example traces. Learning a process model (e.g., a Petri net) from example traces in an event log, called *process discovery*, is one of the first and most challenging steps of process mining.

Two problems of logs are particularly challenging for process discovery algorithms. First, the log may contain *infrequent behaviour*, which forces algorithms to either exclude this behaviour or return complicated, unreadable models describing all behaviour [18]. Second, the log might contain insufficient information to discover a process model that represents the system well: the log might be *incomplete*. Incompleteness forces algorithms to either exclude the missing behaviour, thereby reducing the as yet unseen behaviour the model can produce, or include the missing, unknown, behaviour, thereby risk guessing wrong. In this paper, we focus on handling incomplete logs.

G. Ciardo and E. Kindler (Eds.): PETRI NETS 2014, LNCS 8489, pp. 91–110, 2014.

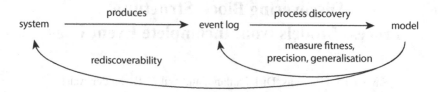

Fig. 1. Traditional model quality assessment (fitness, precision, generalisation) and rediscoverability

A notion closely related to incompleteness is rediscoverability. If a process discovery technique has *rediscoverability*, it is able to discover models that have the same language as the real-life process by which a log was produced [3,5,17]. Figure 1 shows the context of process discovery, rediscoverability, and how discovered models can be evaluated. Traditionally, models are evaluated with respect to the event log: *fitness* measures what part of the event log is described by the model, *precision* is high when the model does not allow too much behaviour that was not in the event log, and *generalisation* is high when the model allows more behaviour than just the behaviour in the event log. Although fitness, precision, and generalisation are intuitively clear, different formal definitions are possible [13,24,25]. Measuring the quality of a discovered model with respect to its event log might be useful, but whether the best model for the event log is the best model for the system is not captured by these measures. Therefore, to compare process discovery techniques it is useful to study rediscoverability, as that gives theoretical bounds to when a model is language-equivalent to its real-life system.

Rediscoverability is usually proven using assumptions about both log and model [3,5,17]. A model must be from a certain class, and a log must contain sufficient information. The notion what information is sufficient, *completeness*, depends on the discovery algorithm. Generally, the strongest completeness notion is *language-completeness*, i.e., each trace through the process must be present in the log. The weakest completeness notion is that each process step must occur at least once in the log: *activity-completeness* [17].

Typically, rediscoverability can only be guaranteed if the log is complete. In this paper, we investigate the problem of *rediscovering* process models from event logs, in particular from *incomplete* event logs.

Another desirable property of process discovery algorithms is that they return simple and sound models. A *simple* model needs few constructs to express its behaviour, and a *sound* model is a model free of deadlocks and other anomalies. While an unsound model might be useful, it is, for instance, not well suited for compliance evaluation and bottleneck analysis [18]. Therefore, in this paper we will focus on *process trees*: abstract hierarchical block-structured Petri nets that are guaranteed to be sound.

The Inductive Miner (IM) [17] is an example of an algorithm that discovers process trees and for which rediscoverability has been proven. IM applies a divide-and-conquer approach: it partitions the activities, selects the most important process construct, splits the log and recurses until a base case is encountered.

In this paper, we adapt IM to handle incomplete logs: we keep the divide-and-conquer approach, but replace the activity partition step by an optimisation problem. We introduce relations between activities, estimate probabilities of these relations and search for a partition of activities that is optimal with respect to these probabilities. Rediscoverability is proven assuming log completeness and a sufficiently large log; we give a lower bound for sufficiency.

In the remainder of this paper, we first explore related work. In Section 3, we introduce logs, Petri nets, process trees and completeness notions. We study effects of incompleteness on behavioural relations in Section 4 and describe behavioural probabilisations. Section 5 describes the algorithm, Section 6 proves rediscoverability for sufficiently large logs, and illustrates how incompleteness is handled by the new approach, compared with other approaches. Section 7 concludes the paper.

2 Related Work

Petri net synthesis aims to build an equivalent Petri net from a transition system or a language. Region theory, that characterises places in a Petri net, was introduced in [15], and several synthesis methods were proposed, for instance in [11,21,6,12].

Process discovery differs from Petri net synthesis in the assumption regarding completeness. Synthesis assumes that the complete language of the system is described in some form. For process discovery we cannot assume the log to be language-complete, as typically only a fraction of the possible behaviour can be observed in the event log, making language-completeness often impossible or infeasible. For example, the language of a model with a loop in it contains infinitely many traces, and the language of a model describing the parallel execution of 10 activities contains at least $10! = 3628800$ different traces [1]. In contrast, a typical log only contains a fraction of that.

Many process discovery techniques have been proposed. For instance, after a transition system has been constructed from the log, state-based region miner techniques construct a Petri net by folding regions of states into places [4,30]. Typically, state-based region techniques provide rediscoverability guarantees [10], but have problems dealing with incompleteness (concurrency is only discovered if sufficient/all interleavings are present).

Process trees, or block structures in general, have been used in process discovery, both inside the scope of Petri nets [8,2,22], as outside [26,27] the scope of Petri nets. They provide a natural, structured, well-defined way of describing processes that are often easily translatable to Petri nets. The process tree formalisms used in [8,17,18] guarantee soundness as well. Process tree discovery techniques have also been proposed before. For instance, the approach used by [28] constructs a process tree from a log by enumerating all traces, after which the process tree is simplified. The Evolutionary Tree Miner (ETM) [8] uses a genetic approach to discover a process tree, i.e., a random population is mutated until a certain stop criterion is met, but as it is steered by log-based metrics, fitness, precision, generalisation and simplicity, and by its random nature, it is unable to guarantee rediscoverability. A natural strategy when using block structures is to apply a divide-and-conquer strategy, which has been applied to process discovery in for instance [9,38,17,18].

In distinguishing languages of classes of Petri nets, behavioural relations have proved their worth [31], and they have been used to refine or coarsen models, i.e., making them more or less abstract [29,16], to compare process models [32], and to perform process discovery. For instance, the behavioural relation used in the α algorithm [3], its derivatives [35,36], and in [17,18], the directly-follows relation, holds for two activities if one activity can consecutively follow the other activity. A notion close to the directly-follows relation is the eventually-follows relation, which holds if one activity can eventually be followed by another. This eventually-follows relation has been used in the context of process discovery [28,31,18].

To the best of our knowledge, the influence of incompleteness has not been systematically studied either on behavioural relations or process discovery.

3   Traces, Event Logs, Petri Nets and Completeness

Traces, Event Logs. A *trace* is a sequence of activities: $\langle a, a, b \rangle$ denotes a trace in which first a occurred, then a again and finally b. Traces can be concatenated: $\langle a, b \rangle \cdot \langle c \rangle = \langle a, b, c \rangle$. An *event log* is a multiset of traces. For instance, $[\langle a, a, b \rangle^3, \langle b, b \rangle^2]$ denotes an event log in which the trace $\langle a, a, b \rangle$ happened 3 times and $\langle b, b \rangle$ happened 2 times. The function set transforms a multiset into a set: $set(L) = \{t | t \in L\}$; the function Σ gives the alphabet of the log, i.e., the activities used in it.

Petri Nets, Workflow Nets and Block-Structured Workflow Nets. A *Petri net* is a bipartite directed graph of interconnected *places* and *transitions*, in which *tokens* on places model the system state and transitions model process step execution. We use the standard semantics of Petri nets, see [23].

A *workflow net* is a Petri net having a single input and a single output place, modelling the initial and final states of the system. Moreover, each element is on a path from input to output [3]. A consecutive sequence of process executions that brings the system from the initial state into the final state, corresponds to a *trace*. The set of traces that can be produced by a model M, the *language* of M, is denoted by $\mathcal{L}(M)$.

A *block-structured workflow net* is a hierarchical workflow net: it can be divided recursively into workflow nets. An example is shown in Figure 2.

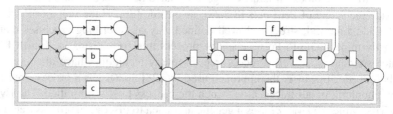

Fig. 2. A block-structured workflow net M_E; filled regions denote the block-structure; process tree $\rightarrow (\times (\wedge (a, b), c), \times (\circlearrowleft (\rightarrow (d, e), f), g))$ corresponds to this net

Process Trees. A *process tree* is an abstract hierarchical representation of a block-structured workflow net. The leaves of the tree are *activities*, representing transitions. The nodes of the tree, *operators*, describe how their children are combined. This paper uses four operators: $\times$, $\rightarrow$, $\wedge$ and $\circlearrowleft$. The $\times$ operator describes the exclusive choice between its children, $\rightarrow$ the sequential composition and $\wedge$ the parallel composition. The first child of a $\circlearrowleft$ tree is the loop *body*, the non-first children are *redo* parts. For instance, $\circlearrowleft(a, b)$ is the composition of a trace of the body a, then zero-or-more times a trace from a redo part b and a body a again: $a(ba)^*$.

Each process tree is easily translatable to a sound workflow net. For example, Figure 2 shows the block-structured workflow net corresponding to the process tree $M_E = \rightarrow(\times(\wedge(a, b), c), \times(\circlearrowleft(\rightarrow(d, e), f), g))$.

To define the semantics of process trees, we assume a finite set of activities Σ to be given. The language of an activity is the execution of that activity (a process step). The language of the *silent activity* τ contains only the empty trace: executing τ adds nothing to the log. The language of an operator is a combination of the languages of its children.

In the following definition, we use the standard language notations $|, \cdot$ and $*$ [20]. To characterise $\wedge$, we use the shuffle product $S_1 \sqcup \ldots S_n$, which takes sets of traces from $S_1 \ldots S_n$ and interleaves their traces $t_1 \in S_1, \ldots, t_n \in S_n$ while maintaining the partial order within each t_i [7]. For instance,

$$\{\langle a, b\rangle\} \sqcup \{\langle c, d\rangle\} = \{\langle a, b, c, d\rangle, \langle a, c, b, d\rangle, \langle a, c, d, b\rangle,$$
$$\langle c, d, a, b\rangle, \langle c, a, d, b\rangle, \langle c, a, b, d\rangle\}$$

Using this notation, we define the semantics of process trees:

$$\mathcal{L}(\tau) = \{\langle\rangle\}$$
$$\mathcal{L}(a) = \{\langle a\rangle\} \text{ for } a \in \Sigma$$
$$\mathcal{L}(\times(M_1, \ldots, M_n)) = \mathcal{L}(M_1)|\mathcal{L}(M_2)\ldots\mathcal{L}(M_n)$$
$$\mathcal{L}(\rightarrow(M_1, \ldots, M_n)) = \mathcal{L}(M_1) \cdot \mathcal{L}(M_2) \cdots \mathcal{L}(M_n)$$
$$\mathcal{L}(\wedge(M_1, \ldots, M_n)) = \mathcal{L}(M_1) \sqcup \mathcal{L}(M_2) \ldots \mathcal{L}(M_n)$$
$$\mathcal{L}(\circlearrowleft(M_1, \ldots, M_n)) = \mathcal{L}(M_1)(\mathcal{L}(\times(M_2, \ldots, M_n))\mathcal{L}(M_1))^*$$

As an example, the language of M_E is $(ab|ba|c)(de(fde)^*|g)$. The function Σ gives the alphabet of a process tree: $\Sigma(M_E) = \{a, b, c, d, e, f, g\}$. We use $\bigoplus$ to denote the set of operators, and often $\oplus$ to denote a process tree operator: $\oplus \in \bigoplus$, $\bigoplus = \{\times, \rightarrow, \wedge, \circlearrowleft\}$. Obviously, the order of children for $\times$ and $\wedge$ and the order of non-first children of $\circlearrowleft$ is arbitrary.

Directly-Follows Relation, Transitive Closure and Graphs. The *directly-follows relation* $\mapsto$ has been proposed in [3] as an abstraction of the behaviour described by a model or a log. From a model M, take two activities a and b. If b can follow a directly in M, $\langle\ldots, a, b, \ldots\rangle \in \mathcal{L}(M)$, then $a \mapsto_M b$. For a log L, $\mapsto_L$ is defined similarly. For logs, $\mapsto$ is monotonic: for a pair of activities, $\mapsto$ cannot cease to hold by adding more traces to the log.

A $\mapsto$-*path* is a sequence $a_1 \ldots a_k$ of activities such that $k \geqslant 2$ and $\forall_{1 \leqslant i < k} a_i \mapsto a_{i+1}$. The transitive closure of $\mapsto$ is denoted by $\mapsto^+$: for activities a and b, the relation $a \mapsto^+ b$ holds if there exists a $\mapsto$-path from a to b. [1] For a model M (resp. a log L), $Start(M)$

---

[1] We did not choose the eventually-follows/weak-order relation [18,31], as its completeness does not survive log splitting; Lemma 11 does not hold for it.

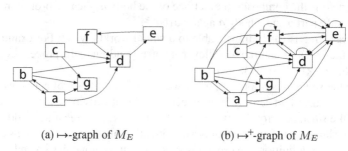

(a) ↦-graph of M_E (b) ↦⁺-graph of M_E

Fig. 3. Graphs of M_E showing its directly-follows relation ↦ and its transitive closure ↦⁺

(resp. $Start(L)$) denotes the start activities, found at the beginning of a trace, and $End(M)$ (resp. $End(L)$) the end activities, that can conclude a trace.

Figure 3a shows the directly-follows relation of M_E in graph notation: a directly-follows graph. In this graph, an edge is drawn between a pair of activities (x, y) if $x \mapsto y$. Similarly, Figure 3b shows the graph of ↦⁺ for M_E.

Completeness. Using these relations, we introduce two completeness notions, between a model M and a log L:

- L is *activity complete* to M ($L \diamond_\Sigma M$), if each activity of M is present in L at least once: $\Sigma(M) \subseteq \Sigma(L)$.
- L is *directly-follows complete* to M ($L \diamond_\mapsto M$), if L is activity-complete to M, its directly-follows relation is complete, and both start and end activities are complete: $L \diamond_\Sigma M$, $\mapsto_M \subseteq \mapsto_L$, $Start(M) \subseteq Start(L)$ and $End(M) \subseteq End(L)$.

Partitions and Cuts. A *partition* is a distribution of an activity set Σ into disjoint non-empty subsets $\Sigma_1 \ldots \Sigma_n$, with $n > 1$. A pair of activities (a, b) is *partitioned* by a partition $\Sigma_1, \ldots, \Sigma_n$ if a and b are not both in the same Σ_i. A *cut* is a partition combined with a process tree operator. If a pair of activities is partitioned by the partition in a cut, the pair *crosses* the cut. For example, $(\rightarrow, \{a\}, \{b, c, d, e, f\})$ is a cut, activity pair (a, b) crosses it and activity pair (b, d) does not.

Obviously, any process tree can be rewritten to a language-equivalent binary process tree. Therefore, without loss of generality, in this paper we consider only binary partitions and cuts.

4   Behavioural Relations

In many Petri net discovery algorithms, such as [3,17,18,35,36], a two-stage approach is used: first, an abstraction of the log is derived, and second, from this abstraction a model is generated. The directly-follows relation ↦ is often used as a behavioural relation. In this section, we first describe the influence of incompleteness on behavioural relations. To this end, we classify pairs of activities inspired by the process tree operators, by using the ↦ relation, after which we show the effect incompleteness has on this classification. Second, we introduce a probabilistic version of the classification that helps discovery techniques deal with incompleteness.

Figure 4 identifies nine cases for $\mapsto$ and $\mapsto^+$ between two given activities a and b, and organises these cases in a lattice. The structure of the lattice follows from $\mapsto$ and $\mapsto^+$: an edge in the lattice corresponds to an extension of the $\mapsto$-relation with one pair of activities.

The lattice yields five relations between activities: the commutative $\times$, $\wedge$ and $\circlearrowleft_i$, and the non-commutative $\rightarrow$ and $\circlearrowleft_s$. For instance, if $b \mapsto a$ and $a \not\mapsto^+ b$, then $\rightarrow(a, b)$, and if $a \mapsto^+ b$, $b \mapsto^+ a$, $a \not\mapsto b$ and $b \not\mapsto a$, then $\circlearrowleft_i(a, b)$. Informally, $\times(a, b)$ denotes that a and b are in an exclusive choice relation, $\rightarrow(a, b)$ denotes that a and b are in a sequence relation, and $\wedge(a, b)$ denotes that a and b are in a parallel relation. These are similar to the α-relations $\#_W$, $\rightarrow_W$ and $\|_W$ [3], but act globally instead of locally.

Both $\circlearrowleft_i(a, b)$ (*loop indirect*) and $\circlearrowleft_s(a, b)$ (*loop single*) denote that a and b are in a loop relation. If we combined them into a single relation, this single relation would not give sufficient information to partition the activities. Using the two relations $\circlearrowleft_s$ and $\circlearrowleft_i$ as given by the lattice does, as will be proven in Section 6.

We consider the commutative cases, for instance $\wedge(a, b)$ and $\wedge(b, a)$, to be equivalent.

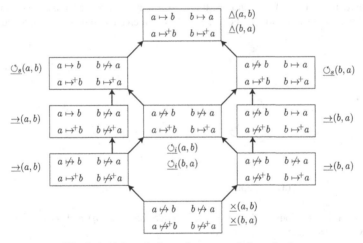

Fig. 4. Activity relations; the arrows define a lattice

Consider again Petri net M_E shown in Figure 2. Figure 5 shows the activity relations of M_E as graphs. Consider the log $L_E = [\langle c, d, e, f, d, e, f, d, e \rangle, \langle b, a, d, e \rangle, \langle a, b, d, e, f, d, e \rangle, \langle c, g \rangle]$, which we produced using M_E, but L_E is not directly-follows complete to M_E, as $a \mapsto g$, $b \mapsto g$, $a \mapsto^+ g$ and $b \mapsto^+ g$ hold in M_E but not in L_E. Therefore, $\times(a, g)$ and $\times(b, g)$ hold in L_E; Figure 6 shows how $\times$ and $\rightarrow$ change. For L_E, a process discovery algorithm will regard a and b to be exclusive to g, while M_E puts them in sequence, and thus be unable to rediscover M_E. The problem illustrated with these activity relations is inherent to any process discovery algorithm using behavioural relations; any technique that just uses behavioural relations is likely unable to rediscover a model if the behavioural relations of the log are not complete.

In the following, we explore ways to use information from incomplete logs that could help to rediscover the original model. Therefore, in the remainder of this paper we assume that the log only contains behaviour from its system, i.e., no noise is present. First,

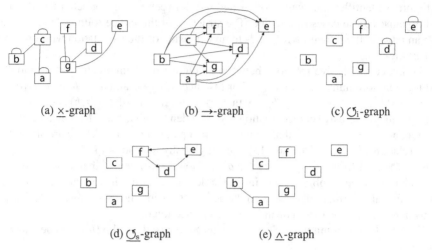

Fig. 5. Activity relations of M_E as graphs. In the $\rightarrow$-graph a directed edge is drawn from a to b if $\rightarrow(a, b)$ holds, and similar for $\circlearrowright_s$. For $\times$, $\wedge$ and $\circlearrowright_i$, which are commutative, undirected edges are drawn.

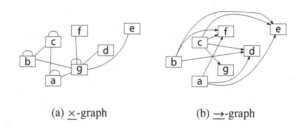

Fig. 6. Two activity relations of L_E as graphs. Notice that $\rightarrow(a, g)$ and $\rightarrow(b, g)$ do not hold anymore, while $\times(a, g)$ and $\times(b, g)$ now do.

some information in the log may allow us to conclude that a particular relation between two activities cannot hold. For instance, if the log contains a trace $\langle b, a \rangle$, then $\rightarrow(a, b)$ cannot hold. These violations follow from Figure 4: if the log contains information that a relation $\oplus$ holds, then any weaker relation, i.e., not reachable from $\oplus$, cannot hold; one can only move up in the lattice.

Second, the idea is, instead of using a binary choice, to rather use an estimated probability that a relation holds, an idea also used in for instance the Heuristics miner [33,34]. For each of the activity relations $\oplus$, we introduce a probabilistic version $p_\oplus$: for activities a and b, $p_\oplus(a, b)$ denotes an artificially estimated probability that (a, b) are in a $\oplus$-related. Using the probabilistic versions makes it easier for techniques to handle incompleteness: in our example, instead of a binary choice whether $\rightarrow(a, g)$ and $\rightarrow(b, g)$ hold or not, we can compare the probabilities $p_\rightarrow$ and $p_\times$ to make a choice.

Our choice for these $p_\oplus$ is shown in Table 1. Let M be a model and L a log of M. Then, using Figure 4, we distinguish three cases and choose $p_\oplus(a, b)$ as follows:

- if $\underline{\oplus}(a,b)$ holds in L, it makes sense to choose $p_\oplus(a,b)$ as the highest of all relations for the pair (a,b). The more frequent activities a and b occur in L, the more confident we are that $\underline{\oplus}(a,b)$ holds for M, and not some stronger relation. We choose $p_\oplus(a,b)$ as follows: let $z(a,b) = \frac{|a|+|b|}{2}$ denote the average number of occurrences of a and b, then we define $p_\oplus(a,b) = 1 - \frac{1}{z(a,b)+1}$, yielding a number between $\frac{1}{2}$ and 1.
- if some relation $\underline{\otimes}(a,b)$, holds in L from which $\underline{\oplus}(a,b)$ is unreachable, then L contains a violation to $p_\oplus(a,b)$, as we assumed L to be noise-free and the behavioural relations cannot cease to hold by adding observations. Therefore, we choose $p_\oplus(a,b)$ low: 0.
- if some relation $\underline{\otimes}'(a,b)$ holds in L from which $\underline{\oplus}(a,b)$ can be reached, i.e., $p_\oplus(a,b)$ could hold by adding more traces to L, we choose to divide the remaining $\frac{1}{z(a,b)+1}$ evenly over all remaining entries, such that the probabilities for each pair (a,b) sum up to 1.

For example, in case of L_E, we get $p_\times(a,g) = 0.6$ and $p_\to(a,g) = 0.07$.

Table 1. Our proposal for probabilistic activity relations for activities a and b, with $z(a,b) = (|a| + |b|)/2$. Negations of relations are omitted from the first column.

	$p_\times(a,b)$	$p_\to(a,b)$	$p_\to(b,a)$	$p_{\circlearrowleft_i}(a,b)$	$p_{\circlearrowleft_s}(a,b)$	$p_{\circlearrowleft_s}(b,a)$	$p_\wedge(a,b)$
(nothing)	$1-\frac{1}{z+1}$	$\frac{1}{6}\cdot\frac{1}{z+1}$	$\frac{1}{6}\cdot\frac{1}{z+1}$	$\frac{1}{6}\cdot\frac{1}{z+1}$	$\frac{1}{6}\cdot\frac{1}{z+1}$	$\frac{1}{6}\cdot\frac{1}{z+1}$	$\frac{1}{6}\cdot\frac{1}{z+1}$
$a\mapsto^+ b$	0	$1-\frac{1}{z+1}$	0	$\frac{1}{4}\cdot\frac{1}{z+1}$	$\frac{1}{4}\cdot\frac{1}{z+1}$	$\frac{1}{4}\cdot\frac{1}{z+1}$	$\frac{1}{4}\cdot\frac{1}{z+1}$
$b\mapsto^+ a$	0	0	$1-\frac{1}{z+1}$	$\frac{1}{4}\cdot\frac{1}{z+1}$	$\frac{1}{4}\cdot\frac{1}{z+1}$	$\frac{1}{4}\cdot\frac{1}{z+1}$	$\frac{1}{4}\cdot\frac{1}{z+1}$
$a\mapsto^+ b \wedge b\mapsto^+ a$	0	0	0	$1-\frac{1}{z+1}$	$\frac{1}{3}\cdot\frac{1}{z+1}$	$\frac{1}{3}\cdot\frac{1}{z+1}$	$\frac{1}{3}\cdot\frac{1}{z+1}$
$a\mapsto b$	0	$1-\frac{1}{z+1}$	0	0	$\frac{1}{2}\cdot\frac{1}{z+1}$	0	$\frac{1}{2}\cdot\frac{1}{z+1}$
$a\mapsto b \wedge b\mapsto^+ a$	0	0	0	0	$1-\frac{1}{z+1}$	0	$\frac{1}{z+1}$
$b\mapsto a$	0	0	$1-\frac{1}{z+1}$	0	0	$\frac{1}{2}\cdot\frac{1}{z+1}$	$\frac{1}{2}\cdot\frac{1}{z+1}$
$b\mapsto a \wedge a\mapsto^+ b$	0	0	0	0	0	$1-\frac{1}{z+1}$	$\frac{1}{z+1}$
$a\mapsto b \wedge b\mapsto a$	0	0	0	0	0	0	1

In the next section, we demonstrate how to use any system of probabilistic relations in a concrete algorithm; one could define Table 1 differently, as long as for each pair of activities (a,b) and each relation $\oplus$, a probability $p_\oplus(a,b)$ is available. In Section 6, we will show that our choices for $p_\oplus$ lead to a correct algorithm. We expect that the proofs given in Section 6 easily extend to other choices, but the precise class of acceptable $p_\oplus$ needs further research.

5 Algorithm

In this section, we demonstrate how the probabilistic activity relations defined in Section 4 can be used to discover process trees.

We use a divide-and-conquer approach and adapt ideas from IM [17] to introduce a new disovery algorithm that we call Inductive Miner - incompleteness (IMin). IMin consists of three steps that are applied recursively: first, the $\mapsto$-graph of the log and its transitive closure $\mapsto^+$ are computed. Second, a cut is chosen such that the relations between pairs crossing the cut have the highest probability according to Table 1. The operator of the chosen cut is recorded. Third, using the cut, the log is split into a sublog for each part and on each sublog, IMin recurses. The recursion ends when a base case, a log containing just a single activity, is encountered. The hierarchy of recorded operators is a process tree.

We first describe how to accumulate the probabilities of Table 1 to assess the probability of a cut. Second, we give the algorithm, an example and a description of our implementation.

5.1 Accumulated Estimated Probabilities for Cuts

Given activity relation probabilities, such as the ones defined in Table 1, we compute an accumulated probability for a cut. Informally, for $\oplus \in \{\times, \rightarrow, \wedge\}$, the accumulated probability $p_\oplus$ is the average $p_\oplus$ over all partitioned pairs of activities.

Definition 1 (accumulated probability for $\times$, $\rightarrow$ and $\wedge$). *Let $c = (\oplus, \Sigma_1, \Sigma_2)$ be a cut, with $\oplus \in \{\times, \rightarrow, \wedge\}$. Then $p_\oplus(\Sigma_1, \Sigma_2)$ denotes the accumulated probability of c:*

$$p_\oplus(\Sigma_1, \Sigma_2) = \frac{\sum_{a \in \Sigma_1, b \in \Sigma_2} p_\oplus(a, b)}{|\Sigma_1| \cdot |\Sigma_2|}$$

Note that a $\rightarrow$, $\times$, or $\wedge$ cut requires all pairs of activities to be in the same relation sufficiently often. For a loop cut, this is not sufficient, as all crossing pairs of activities in a loop are in a loop relation ($\underline{\circlearrowright_s} \cup \underline{\circlearrowright_i}$). This loop relation suffices to describe the probability whether all activities are indeed in a loop, but on its own cannot distinguish the body of a loop from its redo parts. For this, we have to explicitly pick the start and end activities of the redo parts, such that a *redo start activity* follows a *body end activity*, and a redo end activity is followed by a body start activity. This direct succession in a loop is expressed in $\underline{\circlearrowright_s}$. Hence, we obtain the following probability that $c = (\circlearrowright, \Sigma_1, \Sigma_2)$ is a loop cut for the chosen redo start activities S_2 and loop redo end activities E_2; the start and end activities of the body are the start and end activities of the log. In the next section, we show how S_2 and E_2 could be chosen.

Definition 2 (accumulated probability for $\circlearrowright$). *Let $c = (\circlearrowright, \Sigma_1, \Sigma_2)$ be a cut, L be a log, and S_2, E_2 be sets of activities. We aggregate over three parts: start of a redo part, end of a redo part and everything else:*

$$redo_{start} = \sum_{(a,b) \in End(L) \times S_2} p_{\underline{\circlearrowright_s}}(a, b)$$

$$redo_{end} = \sum_{(a,b) \in E_2 \times Start(L)} p_{\underline{\circlearrowright_s}}(a, b)$$

$$indirect = \sum_{\substack{a \in \Sigma_1, b \in \Sigma_2 \\ (a,b) \notin (End(L) \times S_2) \cup (E_2 \times Start(L))}} p_{\underline{\circlearrowright_i}}(a, b)$$

Then, $p_\circlearrowright(\Sigma_1, \Sigma_2, S_2, E_2)$ denotes the accumulated probability of c:

$$p_\circlearrowright(\Sigma_1, \Sigma_2, S_2, E_2) = \frac{redo_{start} + redo_{end} + indirect}{|\Sigma_1| \cdot |\Sigma_2|}$$

In this definition, $redo_{start}$ and $redo_{end}$ capture the strength of S_2 and E_2 really being the start and end of the redo parts; *indirect* captures the strength that all other pairs of activities that cross Σ_1, Σ_2 are in a loop relation.

For readability reasons, in the following, we will omit the parameters S_2 and E_2.

5.2 The Algorithm: Inductive Miner - Incompleteness (IMin)

Next, we introduce a process discovery algorithm that uses the accumulated estimations of definitions 1 and 2 in a divide-and-conquer approach.

For this, we introduce a parameter that influences a threshold of acceptable incompleteness. By default, a cut with highest $p_\oplus$ is to be selected at all times. However, a low $p_\oplus$ might indicate that the behaviour in the log cannot be described well by a block-structured Petri net. Therefore, a parameter h is included: if there is no cut with $p_\oplus \geqslant h$, a flower model $\circlearrowleft(\tau, a_1, \ldots, a_m)$ with $\{a_1, \ldots, a_m\} = \Sigma(L)$, allowing for any trace over $\Sigma(L)$ [17], is returned.

> **function** IMIN(L)
>   **if** $L = [\langle a \rangle^x]$ with $a \in \Sigma$ and $x \geqslant 1$ **then**
>   **return** a
>   **end if**
> $(\oplus, \Sigma_1, \Sigma_2) \leftarrow$ cut of $\Sigma(L)$ with highest $p_\oplus(\Sigma_1, \Sigma_2)$; $\oplus \in \bigoplus$
>   **if** $p_\oplus(\Sigma_1, \Sigma_2) \geqslant h$ **then**
> $L_1, L_2 \leftarrow$ SPLIT$(L, (\oplus, \Sigma_1, \Sigma_2))$
>   **return** $\oplus(\text{IMin}(L_1), \text{IMin}(L_2))$
>   **else**
>   **return** $\circlearrowleft(\tau, a_1, \ldots, a_m)$ where $\{a_1, \ldots, a_m\} = \Sigma(L)$
>   **end if**
> **end function**

IMin contains two non-trivial operations: selecting a cut with highest $p_\oplus$ and the SPLIT function. To select a cut with highest $p_\oplus$, and in case of $\circlearrowleft$ to choose S_2 and E_2, our implementation uses an SMT-solver. For more details of the translation to SMT, please refer to [19].

The function SPLIT splits a log L into sublogs L_1 and L_2, according to a given cut $c = (\oplus, \Sigma_1, \Sigma_2)$, by projecting the traces of L on Σ_1 and Σ_2. For example, SPLIT applied to a sequence cut $(\rightarrow, \{a\}, \{b\})$ and a trace $\langle a, a, b, b \rangle$ yields $\langle a, a \rangle$ and $\langle b, b \rangle$. In addition, for $\circlearrowleft$, traces are split on the points where the trace 'leaves' Σ_1 and 'enters' Σ_2. For example: SPLIT$([\langle a, b, a, a, b, a \rangle], (\circlearrowleft, \{a\}, \{b\}))$ yields $[\langle a \rangle^2, \langle a, a \rangle]$ and $[\langle b \rangle^2]$. For a more detailed formal description, please refer to [17].

IMin has been implemented as part of the Inductive Miner plug-in of the ProM framework [14], available at http://www.promtools.org.

Example 3. As an example, consider again the log $L_E = [\langle c, d, e, f, d, e, f, d, e \rangle$, $\langle b, a, d, e \rangle, \langle a, b, d, e, f, d, e \rangle, \langle c, g \rangle]$. If IMin is applied to L_E with $h = 0$, the first most likely cut is $(\rightarrow, \{a, b, c\}, \{d, e, f, g\})$, with a $p_\rightarrow$ of about 0.64. The choice for $\rightarrow$ is recorded, and L_E is split into $[\langle c \rangle^2, \langle b, a \rangle, \langle a, b \rangle]$ and $[\langle d, e, f, d, e, f, d, e \rangle, \langle d, e \rangle$, $\langle d, e, f, d, e \rangle, \langle g \rangle]$. Then, IMin recurses on both these sublogs. Figure 7 shows the recursive steps that are taken by IMin. The final result is $\rightarrow(\times(\wedge(a, b), c),$ $\times(\circlearrowleft(\rightarrow(d, e), f), g))$, which is equal to M_E.

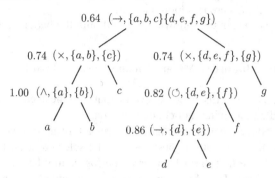

Fig. 7. Running example: IMin(L_E). As a first step, the cut with highest $p_\oplus$ is $(\rightarrow, \{a, b, c\}, \{d, e, f, g\})$, with $p_\oplus = 0.64$. Then, IMin recurses as shown.

6 Rediscoverability

In this section, we report on the rediscoverability of IMin. We first describe a class of process trees, for which we then prove that IMin has rediscoverability, given a directly-follows complete log in which each activity occurs sufficiently often. After that, we report on experiments showing that IMin manages to rediscover these process trees, even from smaller logs than those needed by other discovery algorithms.

6.1 Class of Rediscoverable Process Trees; Normal Form

The class of process trees C_R for which we will prove rediscoverability is as follows:

Definition 4 (Class C_R). *Let M be a process tree. Then M belongs to C_R if for each (sub)tree M' at any position in M, it holds that*
- *The subtree is not a silent activity: $M' \neq \tau$*
- *If $M' = \oplus(M'_1 \ldots M'_n)$, with $\oplus \in \bigoplus$, then no activity appears more than once: $\forall_{1 \leqslant i < j \leqslant n} \Sigma(M'_i) \cap \Sigma(M'_j) = \varnothing$*
- *If $M' = \circlearrowleft(M'_1 \ldots M'_n)$, then M'_1 is required to have disjoint start and end activities: $Start(M'_1) \cap End(M'_1) = \varnothing$*

In order to prove language-rediscoverability, we use a language-unique normal form. Each process tree can be converted into this normal form using the following language-preserving reduction rules. If no rule can be applied to a tree, the tree is in language-unique normal form [17].

Note that the order of children of $\times$ and $\wedge$, and redo children of $\circlearrowleft$, is arbitrary.

Definition 5 (Normal Form). *Let M be a process tree. Then applying the following reduction rules exhaustively on subtrees of M yields a language-unique normal form, in which $\oplus$ denotes a process tree operator:*

$$\oplus(M') \to M'$$
$$\times(\cdots_1, \times(\cdots_2), \cdots_3) \to \times(\cdots_1, \cdots_2, \cdots_3)$$
$$\to(\cdots_1, \to(\cdots_2), \cdots_3) \to \to(\cdots_1, \cdots_2, \cdots_3)$$
$$\wedge(\cdots_1, \wedge(\cdots_2), \cdots_3) \to \wedge(\cdots_1, \cdots_2, \cdots_3)$$
$$\circlearrowright(\circlearrowright(M', \cdots_1), \cdots_2) \to \circlearrowright(M', \cdots_1, \cdots_2)$$
$$\circlearrowright(M', \cdots_1, \times(\cdots_2), \cdots_3) \to \circlearrowright(M', \cdots_1, \cdots_2, \cdots_3)$$

Using this normal form, IMin can discover the language of any tree by searching for only binary cuts. For example, if $M = \to(M_1, M_2, M_3)$, it is perfectly fine to discover either $\to(M_1, \to(M_2, M_3))$ or $\to(\to(M_1, M_2), M_3)$.

We say that a cut c *conforms* to a model M in normal form if selecting c does not disable discovery of a tree equivalent to M:

Definition 6. *Let* $c = (\oplus, \Sigma_1, \Sigma_2)$ *be a cut and let* $M = \oplus(M_1 \ldots M_n)$ *be a model in normal form. Then* c conforms *to* M *if no* $\Sigma(M_i)$ *is partitioned:* $\forall_i \exists_j \Sigma(M_i) \subseteq \Sigma_j$. *Moreover, for non-commutative operators, order must be maintained.*

6.2 Formal Rediscoverability

The main theorem states that any model from class C_R can be rediscovered from a directly-follows complete log whose activities occur at least a certain number of times. Let $least(L)$ denote the number of times the least occurring activity occurs in a log L.

Theorem 7. *Assume a model* M *that is of class* C_R. *Then there exists a* $k \in \mathbb{N}$ *such that for all logs* L *with* $set(L) \subseteq \mathcal{L}(M)$, $L \diamond_{\mapsto} M$ *and* $least(L) \geqslant k$, *it holds that* $\mathcal{L}(IMin(L)) = \mathcal{L}(M)$.

We prove the theorem as follows: we first show that IMin selects the correct root operator (Lemma 9), then that IMin selects a partition corresponding to M (Lemma 10), and finally that log splitting yields correct directly-follows complete sublogs (Lemma 11), on which IMin recurses.

In these lemmas, we will use a very general property of partitions: any two partitions share at least one pair of activities that crosses both partitions.

Lemma 8. *Take two binary partitions* Σ_1, Σ_2 *and* Σ'_1, Σ'_2, *both of the same* Σ. *Then there is a pair of activities that is partitioned by both partitions.*

Proof. Towards contradiction, assume there is no pair that is partitioned by both Σ_1, Σ_2 and Σ'_1, Σ'_2. Take $a_1, a'_1 \in \Sigma_1$, $a_2 \in \Sigma_2$. Pairs (a_1, a_2) and (a'_1, a_2) are partitioned by Σ_1, Σ_2, so by assumption they are not partitioned by Σ'_1, Σ'_2. Thus, there is an $1 \leqslant i \leqslant 2$ such that $a_1, a'_1, a_2 \in \Sigma'_i$. As we posed no restrictions on a_1 and a'_1, for some $1 \leqslant i \leqslant 2$, $\Sigma_1 \subseteq \Sigma'_i$. By similar reasoning, $\Sigma_2 \subseteq \Sigma'_i$, so $\Sigma_1 \cup \Sigma_2 \subseteq \Sigma'_i$. Therefore, $\Sigma'_i = \Sigma$ and hence Σ'_1, Σ'_2 is not a partition. $\qquad \square$

In the following lemma, we prove that for each log for which $least$ is sufficiently large, IMin selects the correct root operator.

Lemma 9. *Assume a reduced model $M = \oplus(M_1, \ldots, M_n)$. Then there exists a $k \in \mathbb{N}$ such that for all logs L with $set(L) \subseteq \mathcal{L}(M)$, $L \diamond_{\hookrightarrow} M$ and $least(L) \geq k$, it holds that $IMin(L)$ selects $\oplus$.*

Proof. IMin selects binary cuts, while M can have an arbitrary number of children. Without loss of generality, assume that $c = (\oplus, \Sigma_1, \Sigma_2)$ is a binary cut conforming to M. Let $c' = (\otimes, \Sigma_1', \Sigma_2')$ be an arbitrary cut of M, with $\otimes \neq \oplus$. We need to prove that $p_\oplus(\Sigma_1, \Sigma_2) > p_\otimes(\Sigma_1', \Sigma_2')$, which we do by computing a lower bound for $p_\oplus(\Sigma_1, \Sigma_2)$ and an upper bound for $p_\otimes(\Sigma_1', \Sigma_2')$ and then comparing these two bounds. Apply case distinction on whether $\oplus = \circlearrowleft$:

– Case $\oplus \neq \circlearrowleft$. We start with the lower bound for $p_\oplus(\Sigma_1, \Sigma_2)$. By Definition 1,

$$p_\oplus(\Sigma_1, \Sigma_2) = \frac{\sum_{a \in \Sigma_1, b \in \Sigma_2} p_\oplus(a, b)}{|\Sigma_1| \cdot |\Sigma_2|}$$

By semantics of process trees, Figure 4, $set(L) \subseteq \mathcal{L}(M)$ and $L \diamond_{\hookrightarrow} M$, for each activity pair (a, b) that crosses c, $\oplus(a, b)$ holds. For each such pair, we chose $p_\oplus(a, b) \geq 1 - \frac{1}{z(a,b)+1}$ (note that this would be an equality, save for $p_\wedge(a, b)$, which is 1). Thus,

$$p_\oplus(\Sigma_1, \Sigma_2) \geq \frac{\sum_{a \in \Sigma_1, b \in \Sigma_2} 1 - \frac{1}{z(a,b)+1}}{|\Sigma_1| \cdot |\Sigma_2|}$$

For all a and b, $z(a, b) = \frac{|a|+|b|}{2} \geq \min(|a|, |b|) \geq least(L)$. Thus,

$$p_\oplus(\Sigma_1, \Sigma_2) \geq 1 - \frac{1}{least(L) + 1} \tag{1}$$

Next, we prove an upper bound for $p_\otimes(\Sigma_1', \Sigma_2')$. By Definition 1,

$$\frac{\sum_{a \in \Sigma_1', b \in \Sigma_2'} p_\otimes(a, b)}{|\Sigma_1'| \cdot |\Sigma_2'|} = p_\otimes(\Sigma_1', \Sigma_2')$$

Let (u, v) be a pair partitioned by both Σ_1, Σ_2 and Σ_1', Σ_2'. By Lemma 8, such a pair exists. For all other $(a, b) \neq (u, v)$, it holds that $p_\otimes(a, b) \leq 1$ (abusing notation a bit by combining $\circlearrowleft_i$ and $\circlearrowleft_s$), and there are $|\Sigma_1| \cdot |\Sigma_2| - 1$ of those pairs.

$$\frac{(|\Sigma_1'| \cdot |\Sigma_2'| - 1) \cdot 1 + 1 \cdot p_\otimes(u, v)}{|\Sigma_1'| \cdot |\Sigma_2'|} \geq p_\otimes(\Sigma_1', \Sigma_2')$$

As (u, v) crosses c, $\oplus(u, v)$ holds. Then by inspection of Table 1, $p_\otimes(u, v) \leq \frac{1}{z(u,v)+1}$. Define y to be $|\Sigma_1'| \cdot |\Sigma_2'|$.

$$\frac{(y - 1) + \frac{1}{z(u,v)+1}}{y} \geq p_\otimes(\Sigma_1', \Sigma_2')$$

From $z(a, b) = \frac{|a|+|b|}{2} \geq 1$ follows that $\frac{1}{z(u,v)+1} \leq \frac{1}{2}$. Thus,

$$\frac{(y - 1) + \frac{1}{2}}{y} \geq p_\otimes(\Sigma_1', \Sigma_2') \tag{2}$$

Using the two bounds (1) and (2), we need to prove that

$$1 - \frac{1}{least(L) + 1} > \frac{(y - 1) + \frac{1}{2}}{y} \tag{3}$$

Note that y is at most $\lfloor \Sigma(M)/2 \rfloor \cdot \lceil \Sigma(M)/2 \rceil$, which allows us to choose k such that $k > 2y - 1$. By initial assumption $least(L) \geqslant k$, and therefore (3) holds. Hence, $p_\oplus(\Sigma_1, \Sigma_2) > p_\otimes(\Sigma_1', \Sigma_2')$.

- Case $\oplus = \circlearrowleft$. Using reasoning similar to the $\oplus \neq \circlearrowleft$ case, we derive (1). We directly reuse (2) to arrive at (3) and conclude that $p_\oplus(\Sigma_1, \Sigma_2) > p_\otimes(\Sigma_1', \Sigma_2')$.

Thus, $p_\oplus(\Sigma_1, \Sigma_2) > p_\otimes(\Sigma_1', \Sigma_2')$ holds for all $\oplus$. As IMin selects the cut with highest $p_\oplus$, IMin selects $\oplus$. □

Next, we prove that for a log L, if $least(L)$ is sufficiently large, then IMin will select a partition conforming to M.

Lemma 10. *Assume a model $M = \oplus(M_1, \ldots, M_n)$ in normal form. Let $c = (\oplus, \Sigma_1, \Sigma_2)$ be a cut conforming to M, and let $c' = (\oplus, \Sigma_1', \Sigma_2')$ be a cut not conforming to M. Then there exists a $k \in \mathbb{N}$ such that for all logs L with $set(L) \subseteq \mathcal{L}(M)$, $L \diamond_\mapsto M$ and $least(L) \geqslant k$, holds that $p_\oplus(\Sigma_1, \Sigma_2) > p_\oplus(\Sigma_1', \Sigma_2')$.*

The proof strategy for this lemma is similar to the proof of Lemma 9: we prove that at least one "misclassified" activity pair (u, v) contributes to the average $p_\oplus(\Sigma_1', \Sigma_2')$. Please refer to [19] for a detailed proof.

As a last lemma, we show that log splitting produces correct and directly-follows complete sublogs.

Lemma 11. *Assume a model M in normal form and a log L such that $set(L) \subseteq \mathcal{L}(M)$ and $L \diamond_\mapsto M$. Let $c = (\oplus, \Sigma_1, \Sigma_2)$ be a cut corresponding to M, and let L_1, L_2 be the result of SPLIT(L, c). Then, there exist process trees M_1 and M_2, such that $\Sigma_1 = \Sigma(M_1), \Sigma_2 = \Sigma(M_2)$, the normal form of $\oplus(M_1, M_2)$ is M, $set(L_1) \subseteq \mathcal{L}(M_1)$, $L_1 \diamond_\mapsto M_1, set(L_2) \subseteq \mathcal{L}(M_2)$ and $L_2 \diamond_\mapsto M_2$.*

For this lemma, we use that M can be converted into a binary tree by using the reduction rules of Definition 5 reversed. As c conforms to M, it is possible to convert M to $\oplus(M_1, M_2)$ such that $\Sigma_1 = \Sigma(M_1)$ and $\Sigma_2 = \Sigma(M_2)$. The strategy for the remaining part of the proof is to show for each operator that SPLIT returns sublogs L_1 and L_2 that are valid for M_1 and M_2 ($\forall i : set(L_i) \subseteq \mathcal{L}(M_i)$). We then prove that L_1 and L_2 are directly-follows complete to M_1 and M_2 ($\forall i : L_i \diamond_\mapsto M_i$). Please refer to [19] for details.

Using these lemmas, we can prove rediscoverability for sufficiently large logs.

Proof (of Theorem 7). We prove the theorem by induction on model sizes, being $|\Sigma(M)|$.

- Base case: $M = a$. As $set(L) \subseteq \mathcal{L}(M)$, $L = [\langle a \rangle^x]$ for some $x \geqslant 1$. By code inspection, $\mathcal{L}(\text{IMin}(L)) = \mathcal{L}(M)$.

- Induction step: assume that the theorem holds for all models smaller than M. By Lemma 9 and 10, IMin selects a cut $c = (\oplus, \Sigma_1, \Sigma_2)$ conforming to M. Next SPLIT(L, c) returns an L_1 and L_2. By Lemma 11, there exists process trees M_1, M_2 such that $\mathcal{L}(\oplus(M_1, M_2)) = \mathcal{L}(M)$. By Lemma 11, $set(L_1) \subseteq \mathcal{L}(M_1)$, $L_1 \diamond_\mapsto M_1$, set(L_2) $\subseteq$ $\mathcal{L}(M_2)$ and $L_2 \diamond_\mapsto M_2$. As of the induction hypothesis and the fact that L_1 and L_2 are sufficiently large by construction, $\mathcal{L}(\oplus(\text{IMin}(L_1), \text{IMin}(L_2)))$ = $\mathcal{L}(\oplus(M_1, M_2))$ = $\mathcal{L}(M)$. Because $\text{IMin}(L)$ = $\oplus(\text{IMin}(L_1), \text{IMin}(L_2))$, there exists a $k \in \mathbb{N}$ such that if $least(L) \geqslant k$, then $\mathcal{L}(\text{IMin}(L))$ = $\mathcal{L}(M)$. $\qquad\square$

In the proofs of Lemmas 9 and 10, we chose $k > 2 \cdot \lfloor \Sigma(M)/2 \rfloor \cdot \lceil \Sigma(M)/2 \rceil - 1$. This gives an upper bound for the minimum $least(L)$ required, and a characterisation of sufficiency:

Corollary 12. *A bound for k and $least(L)$ as used in Theorem 7 is determined by the size of the alphabet: $least(L) \geqslant k \geqslant 2 \cdot \lfloor |\Sigma(M)|/2 \rfloor \cdot \lceil |\Sigma(M)|/2 \rceil$.*

Last, the unsolved question remaining is whether directly-follows completeness of a log implies that the log is sufficiently large, and that a generalised version of Theorem 7 holds:

Conjecture 13. *Assume a model M and a log L such that set(L) $\subseteq$ $\mathcal{L}(M)$ and $L \diamond_\mapsto M$. Then $\mathcal{L}(IMin(L))$ = $\mathcal{L}(M)$.*

The experimental results reported in the remainder of this paper support this conjecture.

6.3 Experimental Result

In this section, we show that IMin can rediscover models from small logs. In addition, we investigate how various process discovery algorithms, including IMin, handle incompleteness.

Experiment. In the experiment, we aim to answer three questions: 1) Can IMin rediscover the language of models? 2) How does IMin handle incomplete logs? 3) How do other algorithms handle incomplete logs?

To answer questions 1 and 2, we investigated how large the log of a given model M has to be to rediscover the language of M, by generating logs of various sizes and trying to rediscover M from these logs. For question 3, we investigated how large logs need to be for other algorithms, such that adding more traces to the log would not change the result of the algorithm.

Setup. For answering questions 1 and 2, we generated 25 random process trees with 15 activities from class C_R. For each tree M, 20 random, sufficiently large, directly-follows complete logs were generated. For each log L, we verified that $\mathcal{L}(M)$ was rediscovered from it: $\mathcal{L}(\text{IMin}(L))$ = $\mathcal{L}(M)$. Then we performed a binary search on L to find the smallest sublog of L from which, in normal form, M was rediscovered. These sublogs were obtained by removing traces from L, and on each smallest sublog found, we measured the number of traces and completeness of $\mapsto$.

To answer question 3, comparing IMin to other algorithms, we used a similar procedure: for each discovery algorithm D, we used the same randomly generated process trees to find, for each tree, the smallest logs L_D such that adding more traces to L_D would always return a model $D' = D(L_D)$ (up to isomorphism). We call the model

$D(L_D)$ for such a smallest log L_D a *top model* M_T. For this experiment, we considered the following discovery algorithms: Inductive Miner (IM) [17], Integer Linear Programming miner (ILP) [37], α-algorithm (α) [3], Region miner (RM) [30,4] and flower model, all plug-ins of the ProM framework [14]. The flower model was included as a baseline, as it will reach its top model if $L \diamond_\Sigma M$: it only depends on the presence of activities in the log. All miners were applied using their default settings, and for IMin h was set to 0. For both procedures, we experimentally observed that event logs with 16000 traces were directly-follows complete and sufficiently large to rediscover the original model (in case of IMin) or to find the top model (for other algorithms).

Results. Table 2 shows the results. For example, IM on average required 97% of the $\mapsto$-pairs of the model to be present in the log to discover its top model M_T. For some models, the ILP implementation we used did not return an answer. Averages are given without these models and are marked with a preceding *.

Table 2. Results of the experiments. Column 2: for how many models M was its language rediscovered in M_T, averaged over logs. Column 3: average number of traces in the smallest sublogs. Column 4: average ratio of $\mapsto$-pairs present in smallest sublogs compared to the models M.

miner	$\mathcal{L}(M) = \mathcal{L}(M_T)$	number of traces	$\mapsto$-completeness
α	0%	133.132	1.000
ILP	12%	*258.529	*0.980
RM	4%	132.896	1.000
IM	100%	85.256	0.971
IMin	100%	32.568	0.875
Flower	0%	11.620	0.641

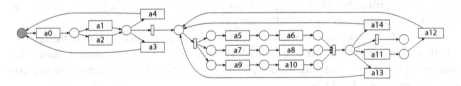

Fig. 8. Petri net representation of M_F: $\rightarrow(\circlearrowleft(\rightarrow(a_0, \times(a_1, a_2)),$ $a_3, a_4), \circlearrowleft(\wedge(\rightarrow(a_5, a_6), \rightarrow(a_7, a_8), \rightarrow(a_9, a_{10})), \rightarrow(a_{11}, a_{12}), a_{13}, a_{14})$

One of the randomly generated models is shown in Figure 8. To illustrate handling of incompleteness, we used this model to find the smallest sublog for which IMin rediscovered M_F, and applied other discovery algorithms to that sublog. The results are shown in Figure 9.

Discussion. Answering question 1, whether IMin can rediscover the language of models, for all models and logs, IMin discovered the original model or a language-equivalent one, and even did not require the log to be directly-follows complete, which supports Conjecture 13. IMin required on average 87.5% of the $\mapsto$-relation pairs to be present

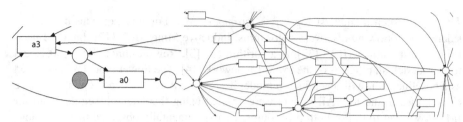

(a) Excerpt of α; a_0 cannot fire; (b) Excerpt of RM; labels have been removed; lots of
unsound.   places necessary to represent parallelism.

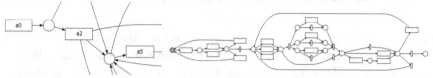

(c) Excerpt of ILP; a_0 can fire at any (d) IM; labels have been removed; misses the central
time.   parallelism.

Fig. 9. Models resulting from discovery of a smallest sublog of IMin

in the log to discover its top model. This suggests that IMin is able to handle directly-
follows incomplete logs, answering question 2.

The flower model provides a baseline: it discovers a model based on the activities
that are present in a log; no process discovery technique can be expected to reach its
top model without all activities being present in the log. For all models, IMin required
fewer or equally many traces than any other discovery algorithm, except for the flower
model, to reach its top model.

Remarkably, also IM did not require the $\mapsto$ relation to be complete at all times. A
possible explanation is that log splitting might help at times. For instance, $\wedge(a, b, c)$
could be rediscovered as $\wedge(a, \wedge(b, c))$. If a log lacks $\mapsto(b, c)$, it could be introduced
during log splitting: by splitting $\langle b, a, c \rangle$ with $\{a\}$ and $\{b, c\}$ yields the trace $\langle b, c \rangle$ for
which $b \mapsto c$ holds, enabling the rediscovery of $\wedge(b, c)$.

Figure 9 illustrates how other discovery algorithms handle models within the representational bias of IM and IMin, for which IMin rediscovers its language. It would be
interesting to see how these algorithms perform on process trees not derived from class
C_R, and on general Petri nets.

7   Conclusion

In this paper, we studied the effects of incompleteness on process discovery. We analysed the impact of incompleteness of logs on behavioural relations. We introduced
probabilistic behavioural relations to make them more stable when dealing with incompleteness, and defined an algorithm based on these probabilistic relations. This algorithm was proven to be able to rediscover the language of models, given sufficiently
large directly-follows complete logs. Moreover, in experiments it was shown to be able
to rediscover the language of models, even when given small incomplete logs, and to
need less information in the log to converge than other process discovery algorithms.

An open question remaining is whether rediscoverability holds for IMin (Conjecture 13). Other points of future research could be what characterises acceptable choices of probabilistic activity relations (Table 1), (that could even be able to handle noise), and, if directly-follows completeness is an upper bound for rediscoverability, and if activity-completeness is a lower bound for it, whether these bounds are tight. The experiments we conducted suggest that there is a tighter upper bound than directly-follows completeness.

References

1. van der Aalst, W.: Process Mining: Discovery, Conformance and Enhancement of Business Processes. Springer (2011)
2. van der Aalst, W., Buijs, J., van Dongen, B.: Towards improving the representational bias of process mining. In: Aberer, K., Damiani, E., Dillon, T. (eds.) SIMPDA 2011. LNBIP, vol. 116, pp. 39–54. Springer, Heidelberg (2012)
3. van der Aalst, W., Weijters, A., Maruster, L.: Workflow mining: Discovering process models from event logs. IEEE Trans. Knowl. Data Eng. 16(9), 1128–1142 (2004)
4. Badouel, E., Darondeau, P.: Theory of Regions. In: Reisig, W., Rozenberg, G. (eds.) APN 1998. LNCS, vol. 1491, pp. 529–586. Springer, Heidelberg (1998)
5. Badouel, E.: On the α-reconstructibility of workflow nets. In: Haddad, S., Pomello, L. (eds.) PETRI NETS 2012. LNCS, vol. 7347, pp. 128–147. Springer, Heidelberg (2012)
6. Bergenthum, R., Desel, J., Mauser, S., Lorenz, R.: Synthesis of Petri nets from term based representations of infinite partial languages. Fundam. Inform. 95(1), 187–217 (2009)
7. Bloom, S.L., Ésik, Z.: Free shuffle algebras in language varieties. Theor. Comput. Sci. 163(1&2), 55–98 (1996)
8. Buijs, J., van Dongen, B., van der Aalst, W.: A genetic algorithm for discovering process trees. In: IEEE Congress on Evolutionary Computation, pp. 1–8. IEEE (2012)
9. Carmona, J.: Projection approaches to process mining using region-based techniques. Data Mining and Knowledge Discovery 24(1), 218–246 (2012)
10. Cortadella, J., Kishinevsky, M., Lavagno, L., Yakovlev, A.: Deriving Petri nets for finite transition systems. IEEE Trans. Computers 47(8), 859–882 (1998)
11. Darondeau, P.: Region based synthesis of P/T-nets and its potential applications. In: Nielsen, M., Simpson, D. (eds.) ICATPN 2000. LNCS, vol. 1825, pp. 16–23. Springer, Heidelberg (2000)
12. Darondeau, P.: Unbounded Petri net synthesis. In: Desel, J., Reisig, W., Rozenberg, G. (eds.) Lectures on Concurrency and Petri Nets. LNCS, vol. 3098, pp. 413–438. Springer, Heidelberg (2004)
13. De Weerdt, J., De Backer, M., Vanthienen, J., Baesens, B.: A multi-dimensional quality assessment of state-of-the-art process discovery algorithms using real-life event logs. Information Systems 37, 654–676 (2012)
14. van Dongen, B.F., de Medeiros, A.K.A., Verbeek, H.M.W., Weijters, A.J.M.M.T., van der Aalst, W.M.P.: The proM framework: A new era in process mining tool support. In: Ciardo, G., Darondeau, P. (eds.) ICATPN 2005. LNCS, vol. 3536, pp. 444–454. Springer, Heidelberg (2005)
15. Ehrenfeucht, A., Rozenberg, G.: Partial (set) 2-structures. Acta Informatica 27(4), 343–368 (1990)
16. Günther, C.W., van der Aalst, W.M.P.: Fuzzy mining – adaptive process simplification based on multi-perspective metrics. In: Alonso, G., Dadam, P., Rosemann, M. (eds.) BPM 2007. LNCS, vol. 4714, pp. 328–343. Springer, Heidelberg (2007)
17. Leemans, S.J.J., Fahland, D., van der Aalst, W.M.P.: Discovering block-structured process models from event logs - A constructive approach. In: Colom, J.-M., Desel, J. (eds.) PETRI NETS 2013. LNCS, vol. 7927, pp. 311–329. Springer, Heidelberg (2013)

18. Leemans, S., Fahland, D., van der Aalst, W.: Discovering block-structured process models from event logs containing infrequent behaviour. In: Business Process Management Workshops. Springer (2013)
19. Leemans, S., Fahland, D., van der Aalst, W.: Discovering block-structured process models from incomplete event logs. Tech. Rep. BPM-14-05, Eindhoven University of Technology (March 2014)
20. Linz, P.: An introduction to formal languages and automata. Jones & Bartlett Learning (2011)
21. Lorenz, R., Mauser, S., Juhás, G.: How to synthesize nets from languages: a survey. In: Winter Simulation Conference, WSC, pp. 637–647 (2007)
22. Polyvyanyy, A., Vanhatalo, J., Völzer, H.: Simplified computation and generalization of the refined process structure tree. In: Bravetti, M. (ed.) WS-FM 2010. LNCS, vol. 6551, pp. 25–41. Springer, Heidelberg (2011)
23. Reisig, W., Schnupp, P., Muchnick, S.: Primer in Petri Net Design. Springer (1992)
24. Rozinat, A., de Medeiros, A.K.A., Günther, C.W., Weijters, A.J.M.M., van der Aalst, W.M.P.: The need for a process mining evaluation framework in research and practice. In: ter Hofstede, A.H.M., Benatallah, B., Paik, H.-Y. (eds.) BPM 2007 Workshops. LNCS, vol. 4928, pp. 84–89. Springer, Heidelberg (2008)
25. Rozinat, A., Veloso, M., van der Aalst, W.: Evaluating the quality of discovered process models. In: 2nd Int. Workshop on the Induction of Process Models, pp. 45–52 (2008)
26. Schimm, G.: Generic linear business process modeling. In: Mayr, H.C., Liddle, S.W., Thalheim, B. (eds.) ER Workshops 2000. LNCS, vol. 1921, pp. 31–39. Springer, Heidelberg (2000)
27. Schimm, G.: Process miner - A tool for mining process schemes from event-based data. In: Flesca, S., Greco, S., Leone, N., Ianni, G. (eds.) JELIA 2002. LNCS (LNAI), vol. 2424, pp. 525–528. Springer, Heidelberg (2002)
28. Schimm, G.: Mining most specific workflow models from event-based data. In: van der Aalst, W.M.P., ter Hofstede, A.H.M., Weske, M. (eds.) BPM 2003. LNCS, vol. 2678, pp. 25–40. Springer, Heidelberg (2003)
29. Smirnov, S., Weidlich, M., Mendling, J.: Business process model abstraction based on synthesis from well-structured behavioral profiles. Int. J. Cooperative Inf. Syst. 21(1), 55–83 (2012)
30. Solé, M., Carmona, J.: Process mining from a basis of state regions. In: Lilius, J., Penczek, W. (eds.) PETRI NETS 2010. LNCS, vol. 6128, pp. 226–245. Springer, Heidelberg (2010)
31. Weidlich, M., van der Werf, J.M.: On profiles and footprints – relational semantics for petri nets. In: Haddad, S., Pomello, L. (eds.) PETRI NETS 2012. LNCS, vol. 7347, pp. 148–167. Springer, Heidelberg (2012)
32. Weidlich, M., Polyvyanyy, A., Mendling, J., Weske, M.: Causal behavioural profiles - efficient computation, applications, and evaluation. Fundam. Inform. 113(3-4), 399–435 (2011)
33. Weijters, A., van der Aalst, W., de Medeiros, A.: Process mining with the heuristics miner-algorithm. BETA Working Paper series 166, Eindhoven University of Technology (2006)
34. Weijters, A., Ribeiro, J.: Flexible Heuristics Miner. In: CIDM, pp. 310–317. IEEE (2011)
35. Wen, L., van der Aalst, W., Wang, J., Sun, J.: Mining process models with non-free-choice constructs. Data Mining and Knowledge Discovery 15(2), 145–180 (2007)
36. Wen, L., Wang, J., Sun, J.: Mining invisible tasks from event logs. In: Dong, G., Lin, X., Wang, W., Yang, Y., Yu, J.X. (eds.) APWeb/WAIM 2007. LNCS, vol. 4505, pp. 358–365. Springer, Heidelberg (2007)
37. van der Werf, J., van Dongen, B., Hurkens, C., Serebrenik, A.: Process discovery using integer linear programming. Fundam. Inform. 94(3-4), 387–412 (2009)
38. Yzquierdo-Herrera, R., Silverio-Castro, R., Lazo-Cortés, M.: Sub-process discovery: Opportunities for process diagnostics. In: Poels, G. (ed.) CONFENIS 2012. LNBIP, vol. 139, pp. 48–57. Springer, Heidelberg (2013)

Synthesis of Persistent Systems

Eike Best[1,*] and Raymond Devillers[2]

[1] Department of Computing Science,
Carl von Ossietzky Universität Oldenburg, Germany
eike.best@informatik.uni-oldenburg.de
[2] Département d'Informatique, Université Libre de Bruxelles, Belgium
rdevil@ulb.ac.be

Abstract. This paper presents efficient, specialised synthesis and reengineering algorithms for the case that a transition system is finite, persistent and reversible. It also shows by means of a complex example that structural properties of the synthesised Petri nets may not necessarily be entailed.

Keywords: Cyclic Behaviour, Persistency, Labelled Transition Systems, Parikh Vectors, Petri Nets, Region Theory, System Synthesis, Reengineering.

1 Introduction

In the realm of (asynchronous) hardware, persistency [14] is a significant, desirable property, as it is related to the absence of hazards [12,18,19], as well as to arbiter-free synchronisation [13]. Persistency means that an enabled transition can never become disabled through occurrences of other transitions.

In this paper, we focus our attention on a class of persistent labelled transition systems (lts) generated by Petri nets. A relatively weak structural restriction for a Petri net to have a persistent reachability graph is that its places have at most one outgoing transition. Such Petri nets will be called ON in this paper, for "(place-)output-nonbranching".

We investigate conditions under which, conversely, a given persistent lts is isomorphic to the reachability graph of an unknown ON Petri net. Moreover, we define an algorithm that creates such a net in case it is theoretically possible. Eventually, such an algorithm could be useful in the automatic generation of asynchronous hardware from persistent specifications.

These results can be seen as a variant of the Petri net synthesis problem addressed by region theory [1,3]. Since one of the conditions we use is that the given lts is already generated by some Petri net, our results can also be seen as a variant of the reengineering problem, asking whether a given Petri net can be transformed – under invariance of its reachability graph – into an ON Petri net.

The paper is structured as follows. Labelled transition systems, Petri nets, and regions are briefly introduced in section 2. Section 3 delineates the class of

---

* The first author gratefully acknowledges the support of Université d'Évry-Val-d'Essonne and Université Paris-Est Créteil-Val-de-Marne.

G. Ciardo and E. Kindler (Eds.): PETRI NETS 2014, LNCS 8489, pp. 111–129, 2014.
© Springer International Publishing Switzerland 2014

lts we shall study and lists several auxiliary results about this class. Sections 4 and 5 contain the main results: a dedicated test which allows to check the ON implementability of a persistent lts specification; an efficient algorithm producing a generating ON Petri net if one exists; and examples demonstrating the necessity and (non-)sufficiency of various conditions. Section 6 concludes.

2   Labelled Transition Systems, Petri Nets, and Regions

Definition 1. LTS, REACHABILITY, PARIKH VECTORS, CYCLES, EQUIVALENCES

An lts (labelled transition system with initial state) is a tuple $(S, \rightarrow, T, s_0)$, where S is a set of *states*; T is a set of *labels* with $S \cap T = \emptyset$; $\rightarrow \subseteq (S \times T \times S)$ is the *transition relation*; and $s_0 \in S$ is an *initial state*. A label t is *enabled* in a state s, denoted by $s[t\rangle$, if there is some state s' such that $(s, t, s') \in \rightarrow$. We also use the notation $s[t\rangle s'$, meaning that s' is *reachable* from s through the execution of t, instead of $(s, t, s') \in \rightarrow$. We denote by $s^\bullet = \{t \in T \mid s[t\rangle\}$ the set of labels enabled at s, and by $^\bullet s = \{t \in T \mid s'[t\rangle s \text{ for some } s' \in S\}$ the set of labels leading to s. The definitions of enabledness and of the reachability relation are extended to label sequences (or directed paths) $\sigma \in T^*$:

$s[\varepsilon\rangle$ and $s[\varepsilon\rangle s$ are always true;

$s[\sigma t\rangle$ $(s[\sigma t\rangle s')$ iff there is some s'' with $s[\sigma\rangle s''$ and $s''[t\rangle$ $(s''[t\rangle s'$, respectively). A state s' is reachable from state s if there exists a label sequence σ such that $s[\sigma\rangle s'$. By $[s\rangle$, we denote the set of states reachable from s. For a finite sequence $\sigma \in T^*$ of labels, the *Parikh vector* $\Psi(\sigma)$ is a T-vector (i.e., a vector of natural numbers with index set T), where $\Psi(\sigma)(t)$ denotes the number of occurrences of t in σ. $s[\sigma\rangle s'$ is called a *cycle* (at state s) if $s = s'$. The cycle is *nontrivial* if $\sigma \neq \varepsilon$. A nontrivial cycle $s[\sigma\rangle s$ around a reachable state $s \in [s_0\rangle$ is called *small* if there is no nontrivial cycle $s'[\sigma'\rangle s'$ with $s' \in [s_0\rangle$ and $\Psi(\sigma') \lneqq \Psi(\sigma)$.

Two lts $(S_1, \rightarrow_1, T, s_{01})$ and $(S_2, \rightarrow_2, T, s_{02})$ over the same set of labels will be called *language-equivalent* if their initially enabled sequences coincide, i.e., if $\forall \sigma \in T^*: s_{01}[\sigma\rangle \iff s_{02}[\sigma\rangle$, and *isomorphic* if there is a bijection $\zeta: S_1 \rightarrow S_2$ with $\zeta(s_{01}) = s_{02}$ and $(s, t, s') \in \rightarrow_1 \iff (\zeta(s), t, \zeta(s')) \in \rightarrow_2$, for all $s, s' \in S_1$.

□ 1

Definition 2. BASIC PROPERTIES OF LTS

A labelled transition system $(S, \rightarrow, T, s_0)$ is called *finite* if S and T (hence also $\rightarrow$) are finite sets; *deterministic* if for any reachable state s and label a, $s[a\rangle s'$ and $s[a\rangle s''$ imply $s' = s''$; *totally reachable* if $S = [s_0\rangle$ and $\forall t \in T \exists s \in [s_0\rangle: s[t\rangle$; *reversible* if $\forall s \in [s_0\rangle: s_0 \in [s\rangle$; *persistent* if for all reachable states s and labels t, u, if $s[t\rangle$ and $s[u\rangle$ with $t \neq u$, then there is some state $r \in S$ such that both $s[tu\rangle r$ and $s[ut\rangle r$.

□ 2

Definition 3. PETRI NETS, MARKINGS, REACHABILITY GRAPHS

A (finite, initially marked, place-transition, arc-weigthed) Petri net is a tuple (P, T, F, M_0) such that P is a finite set of *places*, T is a finite set of *transitions*, with $P \cap T = \emptyset$, F is a *flow* function $F: ((P \times T) \cup (T \times P)) \rightarrow \mathbb{N}$, M_0 is the *initial marking*, where a *marking* is a mapping $M: P \to \mathbb{N}$, indicating the number of *tokens* in each place. A transition $t \in T$ is *enabled by* a marking M, denoted by $M[t\rangle$, if for all places $p \in P$, $M(p) \geq F(p,t)$. If t is enabled at M, then t can *occur* (or *fire*) in M, leading to the marking M' defined by $M'(p) = M(p) - F(p,t) + F(t,p)$ (notation: $M[t\rangle M'$, and $[M_0\rangle$ again denotes the set of reachable markings). The *reachability graph of N*, with initial marking M_0, is the labelled transition system with the set of vertices $[M_0\rangle$ and set of arcs $\{(M,t,M') \mid M,M' \in [M_0\rangle \wedge M[t\rangle M'\}$. If an lts TS is isomorphic to the reachability graph of a Petri net N, then we will say that N *solves TS*.   □ 3

Definition 4. BASIC PROPERTIES OF PETRI NETS
    For a place p of a Petri net $N = (P,T,F,M_0)$, let ${}^\bullet p = \{t \in T \mid F(t,p) > 0\}$ its pre-places, and $p^\bullet = \{t \in T \mid F(p,t) > 0\}$ its post-places. N is called *connected* if it is weakly connected as a graph; *plain* if $cod(F) \subseteq \{0,1\}$; *pure* or *side-condition free* if $p^\bullet \cap {}^\bullet p = \emptyset$ for all places $p \in P$; ON if $|p^\bullet| \leq 1$ for all places $p \in P$; a *marked graph* if it is plain and $|p^\bullet| \leq 1$ and $|{}^\bullet p| \leq 1$ for all places $p \in P$.
    N is called *weakly live* if $\forall t \in T \exists M \in [M_0\rangle : M[t\rangle$ (i.e., there are no unfireable transitions); *k-bounded*, for some $k \in \mathbb{N}$, if $\forall M \in [M_0\rangle \forall p \in P : M(p) \leq k$ (i.e., the number of tokens on any place never exceeds k); *bounded* if it is k-bounded for some k; *persistent* (*reversible*) if so is its reachability graph.   □ 4

The class of ON nets has also been called CF (for *Choice-Free* nets) in [16], but to avoid an easy confusion with free-choice nets [10] or conflict-free nets [14], we shall here stick to the above terminology.
    In the remainder of this paper, attention will be restricted to bounded and weakly live Petri nets. It is easy to see that the reachability graphs of such nets are finite (by boundedness), deterministic (coming from a Petri net), and totally reachable (by weak liveness).
    The synthesis problem consists of finding a Petri net solving a given lts in the sense of Definition 3. In order to study conditions for such solutions to exist, regions have been introduced as follows.

Definition 5. REGIONS OF LTS
    Let $TS = (S, \to, T, s_0)$ be an lts. A triple

$$\rho = (\mathbb{R}, \mathbb{B}, \mathbb{F}) \in (S \to \mathbb{N}, T \to \mathbb{N}, T \to \mathbb{N})$$

is a *region* of TS if, for all $s[t\rangle s'$ with $s \in [s_0\rangle$, $\mathbb{R}(s) \geq \mathbb{B}(t)$ and $\mathbb{R}(s') = \mathbb{R}(s) - \mathbb{B}(t) + \mathbb{F}(t)$.   □ 5

A region mimics, at the level of an lts, the properties of a Petri net place p. More precisely, $\mathbb{R}(s)$ mimics the marking of p in state s, $\mathbb{B}(t)$ the weight of the arc from p to t, and $\mathbb{F}(t)$ weight of the arc from t to p ($\mathbb{B}$ stands for "backward", $\mathbb{F}$ for "forward", as seen from transitions). For instance, suppose that TS is the reachability graph of a Petri net $N = (P,T,F,M_0)$, and let $p \in P$. For any $M \in [M_0\rangle$, define $\mathbb{R}_p(M) = M(p)$, and for any $t \in T$, define $\mathbb{B}_p(t) = F(p,t)$ and

$\mathbb{F}_p(t) = F(t, p)$. Then $(\mathbb{R}_p, \mathbb{B}_p, \mathbb{F}_p)$ is a region of TS. The region properties in Definition 5 correspond to the notions of enabling and firing in Definition 3.

An lts $TS = (S, \rightarrow, T, s_0)$ satisfies SSP (state separation property) iff

$$\forall s, s' \in [s_0\rangle:\; s \neq s' \;\Rightarrow\; \exists\, \text{region } \rho = (\mathbb{R}, \mathbb{B}, \mathbb{F}) \text{ with } \mathbb{R}(s) \neq \mathbb{R}(s')$$

meaning that it is possible to distinguish the various states in terms of markings. TS satisfies ESSP (event/state separation property) iff

$$\forall s \in [s_0\rangle\, \forall t \in T:\; (\neg s[t\rangle) \;\Rightarrow\; \exists\, \text{region } \rho = (\mathbb{R}, \mathbb{B}, \mathbb{F}) \text{ with } \mathbb{R}(s) < \mathbb{B}(t)$$

meaning that it is possible to exclude forbidden transitions through a marking.

Theorem 1. BASIC REGION THEOREM FOR PLACE/TRANSITION NETS
   A (finite, deterministic, totally reachable) lts TS is isomorphic to the reachability graph of a (possibly non-plain, or non-pure) Petri net iff TS satisfies SSP and ESSP.   □ 1

   In the proof of this result (e.g. [1,3]), it turns out that ESSP without SSP allows to build a Petri net with the same language as the given lts, but not necessarily satisfying the requested isomorphism.

3   Some Classes of Labelled Transition Systems

In section 3.1, the class of lts considered in this paper is motivated and introduced. In section 3.2, some basic properties of this class of lts are documented.

3.1   Persistency, Uniform Small Cycles, and the ON Property

Let $TS = (S, \rightarrow, T, s_0)$ be some lts. Let $\Upsilon: T \rightarrow \mathbb{N} \setminus \{0\}$ be a fixed vector with no zero entries. The principal properties we study are the following ones.

rg	TS is the reachability graph of some bounded Petri net.
r	TS is reversible.
p	TS is persistent.
PΥ	All small cycles of TS have Parikh vector Υ.

Special cases of **PΥ** are **P1** (Υ is the all-ones vector), **P2** (Υ is the all-twos vector), and so on. For instance, Figure 1 shows an lts satisfying all properties **rg** to **P1**. Two solutions of this lts are depicted: a plain non-ON one (in the middle of the figure), and a non-plain ON one (on the right-hand side). Figure 2 shows an lts satisfying **rg** to **P2**. This lts has a solution, as shown in the figure, but no ON solution, as will be proved later.

   The interest of property **PΥ** arises from results in [4]. These results show that if an lts satisfies **rg**, **r** and **p**, then it may essentially be expressed as a direct product of label-disjoint lts, each of which satisfies **PΥ**, for some vector Υ. It is

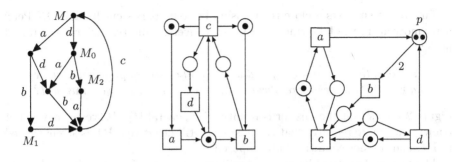

Fig. 1. An lts satisfying **rg**, **r**, **p**, and **P1**, with two different solutions

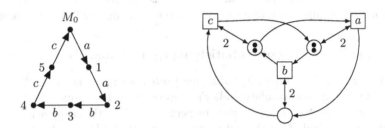

Fig. 2. An lts satisfying **rg**, **r**, **p**, and **P2**, but having no ON Petri net solution. A non-pure, non-plain, and non-ON solution is shown on the right-hand side.

also shown in the same paper that there is a small cycle around each state, and that the Parikh vector of each cycle is a linear combination of the Υ.

If some transition t is the only outgoing transition of a place p, then no other transition can reduce the number of tokens on p. Thus, ON Petri nets are a subclass of persistent Petri nets, and the results of [4] can be specialised as follows:

Theorem 2. PROPERTIES OF ON PETRI NETS
*The reachability graph TS of a connected, bounded, weakly live, reversible, ON Petri net N is finite and satisfies **rg**, **r**, **p**, and **PΥ**, for some Υ.*

Proof: All claims but **PΥ** are obvious.

If a place p is isolated (i.e., $p^{\bullet} = \emptyset = {}^{\bullet}p$), then since the net is connected, the transition set is empty, and **PΥ** is vacuously true.

If p is not isolated, it must have both input and output transitions, because the net is weakly live and reversible. Since the net is ON, p has a unique output transition; let it be t. From results in [4], t belongs to some small cycle; let T' be the unique set of labels occurring in this cycle. If p has an input transition t' not in T', p is not bounded, since there is a (small) cycle containing t' but not t; it is possible to reach it; and following indefinitely that cycle will indefinitely increase the marking of p. Hence, since the net is connected, $T' = T$, and **PΥ** is satisfied with Υ being the Parikh vector of any small cycle.   □ 2

This result suggests a close relationship between persistent lts and ON Petri nets, motivating the following (in a sense, converse) question which was raised in [5]:

*If an lts satisfies persistency and a set of other strong properties, viz. **rg** and **r** and **PΥ**, does there always exist an ON Petri net generating it?*

Figure 2 shows that the answer is negative for general **PΥ**. However, it was not known until more recently that the answer is still negative if **PΥ** is strengthened to **P1**, and further conditions are imposed.

The theory developed in section 4 will lead to an efficient algorithm allowing to synthesise (and reengineer, if possible) labelled transition systems satisfying **rg**, **r**, **p**, and **PΥ**, such as the one shown in Figure 1. The same theory also leads to a method for proving that examples such as the one shown in Figure 2, as well as a more complicated one we will exhibit later, do *not* have ON solutions.

3.2   Some Properties of lts Satisfying rg, r, p, and PΥ

Let $TS = (S, \to, T, s_0)$ be an lts satisfying properties **rg**, **r**, **p**, and **PΥ**.

First, we briefly recapitulate Keller's theorem [11]. For sequences $\sigma, \tau \in T^*$, $\tau \stackrel{\bullet}{-} \sigma$ denotes the *residue* of τ with respect to σ, i.e., the sequence left after cancelling successively in τ the leftmost occurrences of all symbols from σ, read from left to right. Formally and inductively: for $t \in T$, $\tau \stackrel{\bullet}{-} t = \tau$ if $\Psi(\tau)(t) = 0$; $\tau \stackrel{\bullet}{-} t = \tau_1 \tau_2$ if $\tau = \tau_1 t \tau_2$ and $\Psi(\tau_1)(t) = 0$; $\tau \stackrel{\bullet}{-} \varepsilon = \tau$; and $\tau \stackrel{\bullet}{-} (t\sigma) = (\tau \stackrel{\bullet}{-} t) \stackrel{\bullet}{-} \sigma$.

Theorem 3. KELLER'S THEOREM
If $s[\tau\rangle$ and $s[\sigma\rangle$ for some $s \in [s_0\rangle$, then $s[\tau(\sigma \stackrel{\bullet}{-} \tau)\rangle s'$ and $s[\sigma(\tau \stackrel{\bullet}{-} \sigma)\rangle s''$ as well as $\Psi(\tau(\sigma \stackrel{\bullet}{-} \tau)) = \Psi(\sigma(\tau \stackrel{\bullet}{-} \sigma))$ and $s' = s''$.   □ 3

Definition 6. SHORT PATHS, AND DISTANCES
Let r, s be two states of TS. A path $r[\tau\rangle s$ will be called *short* if $|\tau| \leq |\tau'|$ for every path $r[\tau'\rangle s$, where $|\tau|$ denotes the length of τ. We shall denote by $\Delta_{r,s}$ the Parikh vector of some short path from r to s, and call it the *distance* between r and s.   □ 6

According to Lemma 2 below, the definition of $\Delta_{r,s}$ does not depend on the choice of the short path from r to s. For a label t, the number $\Delta_{r,s}(t)$ thus simply indicates how often t occurs on *any* short path from r to s.

Lemma 1. CHARACTERISATION OF SHORT PATHS
Suppose that $s[\tau\rangle s'$. Then $s[\tau\rangle s'$ is short iff $\neg(\Upsilon \leq \Psi(\tau))$.

Proof: ($\Rightarrow$): By contraposition. Suppose that $s[\tau\rangle s'$ and that $\Upsilon \leq \Psi(\tau)$. By results in [4], there is some cycle $s[\kappa\rangle s$ with $\Psi(\kappa) = \Upsilon$. By Keller's theorem, $s[\tau\rangle s'[\kappa \stackrel{\bullet}{-} \tau\rangle s''$ and $s[\kappa\rangle s[\tau \stackrel{\bullet}{-} \kappa\rangle s''$. But $\Psi(\kappa) = \Upsilon \leq \Psi(\tau)$ implies $\kappa \stackrel{\bullet}{-} \tau = \varepsilon$. Therefore, $s' = s''$ and $s[\tau \stackrel{\bullet}{-} \kappa\rangle s'$. Since κ contains every transition at least once and $\Upsilon \leq \Psi(\tau)$, $|\tau \stackrel{\bullet}{-} \kappa| < |\tau|$. Hence $s[\tau\rangle s'$ is not short.

($\Leftarrow$): Suppose that $s[\tau\rangle s'$ and $\neg(\Upsilon \leq \Psi(\tau))$. Consider any other path $s[\tau'\rangle s'$; we show $|\tau| \leq |\tau'|$. By reversibility, there is some path ρ from s' to s. Both $s'[\rho\tau\rangle s'$ and $s'[\rho\tau'\rangle s'$ are cycles at s'. By results from [4], they can be permuted into sequences of small cycles. Therefore, $\Psi(\rho\tau) = \ell\cdot\Upsilon$ and $\Psi(\rho\tau') = \ell'\cdot\Upsilon$. If $\ell > \ell'$, then $\Psi(\tau) \geq \Psi(\tau)-\Psi(\tau') = \Psi(\rho\tau)-\Psi(\rho\tau') = (\ell-\ell')\cdot\Upsilon \geq \Upsilon$, contradicting $\neg(\Upsilon \leq \Psi(\tau))$. Hence $\ell \leq \ell'$ and $\Psi(\tau) \leq \Psi(\tau')$ and $|\tau| \leq |\tau'|$.   □ 1

Lemma 2. Uniqueness of short Parikh vectors
Suppose that $s[\tau\rangle s'$ and $s[\tau'\rangle s'$ are both short. Then $\Psi(\tau) = \Psi(\tau')$.

Proof: By Lemma 1($\Rightarrow$), both $\neg(\Upsilon \leq \Psi(\tau))$ and $\neg(\Upsilon \leq \Psi(\tau'))$. As in the proof of Lemma 1($\Leftarrow$), $\Psi(\tau) \leq \Psi(\tau')$ and $\Psi(\tau') \leq \Psi(\tau)$, hence $\Psi(\tau) = \Psi(\tau')$.   □ 2

Lemma 3. Characterisation of Parikh vectors of paths
Suppose that $s[\tau\rangle s'$. Then $\Psi(\tau) = \Psi(\tau') + m\cdot\Upsilon$, with some number $m \in \mathbb{N}$, where $s[\tau'\rangle s'$ is any short path from s to s'.

Proof: Assume that $s[\tau\rangle s'$. Let m be the maximal number in $\mathbb{N}$ such that $\Psi(m\cdot\Upsilon) \leq \Psi(\tau)$. Let $s[\kappa\rangle s$ be some cycle with $\Psi(\kappa) = \Upsilon$. Then also $s[\kappa^m\rangle s$, with $\Psi(\kappa^m) = m\cdot\Upsilon$. By Keller's theorem, $s[\kappa^m\rangle s[\tau'\rangle s'$, with $\tau' = \tau \stackrel{\bullet}{-} \kappa^m$. By the maximality of m, $s[\tau'\rangle s'$ is short, and by $\Psi(\kappa^m) \leq \Psi(\tau)$, $\Psi(\tau)$ can be written as $\Psi(\tau) = \Psi(\tau') + \Psi(\kappa^m)$. By Lemma 2, the choice of τ' is arbitrary.   □ 3

Lemma 4. Existence of short paths
Suppose that s, s' are states. There is a short path from s to s'.

Proof: By reversibility, $s[\tau\rangle s'$ for some τ. Just take the path $s[\tau'\rangle s'$ from the proof of Lemma 3.   □ 4

Lemma 5. A repeat lemma for plain nets
*Assume that the Petri net N generating TS by **rg** is plain, and that b does not occur in τ. If $s[\tau\tau'b\rangle$ and $\Psi(\tau) = \Psi(\tau')$, then also $s[\tau b\tau'\rangle$.*

Proof: Suppose $s[\tau\rangle s'[\tau'\rangle s''[b\rangle s'''$ and assume that b is not enabled in state s'. By plainness, this implies that in N, there is some pre-place p of b which has zero tokens in s'. The total effect of τ' on p is to create at least one token on p, because b is enabled at s''. But since $\Psi(\tau) = \Psi(\tau')$, the total effect of τ is the same as that of τ', which implies that at state s', place p has at least one token. Hence the assumption was wrong, and instead, b is enabled in s'. By persistency, since b does not occur in τ', also $s'[b\tau'\rangle$, and hence $s[\tau b\tau'\rangle$, as claimed.   □ 5

4   Solving an lts, Using rg, r, p, and PΥ

Throughout this section, we continue to assume that some given, finite lts $TS = (S, \rightarrow, T, s_0)$ satisfies all properties **rg**, **r**, **p**, and **PΥ**. Our aim will be to derive conditions under which an ON Petri net solution exists for TS. In section 4.1, we will identify important subsets of states. Using these sets, section 4.2

presents an algorithm which is able to produce an ON Petri net from TS, under certain conditions specifying exactly when this is possible. Section 4.3 contains the correctness proof of this algorithm. Finally, section 4.4 discusses how it may be checked that *no* ON Petri net can be constructed for TS.

The lts shown in Figures 1 and 2 will serve as motivating and as running examples. Note that both of them satisfy all required properties (one with **P1**, the other with **P2**), but for the first one, an ON solution exists while for the second one, *no* ON solution exists (although we still did not prove this). Henceforth, examples of the first type will be called *positive* while examples of the second kind will be called *negative*.

4.1   Sequentialising States

In Figure 1, state M does not enable b, but all of its successor states do, no matter whether they are reached by a or by d. We might say that state M *sequentialises* the set of labels $\{a, d\}$ with regard to b. The ON solution shown on the right-hand side of Figure 1 contains a place, called p, with ingoing transitions a, d (each with weight 1) and a single outgoing transition b (with weight 2). We might interpret this place as *realising* the sequentialisation of $\{a, d\}$ with regard to b.

The basic idea, to be developed in the following, is to generalise this observation: If all sequentialising states are enumerated and adequate corresponding places are introduced, does there result an ON net solving the original lts? In section 4.2, it will be shown that, upon closer inspection of this idea, the following definition plays a crucial role.

Definition 7. Unique input states and sequentialisation states
For any label $x \in T$, we shall denote by

$$
\begin{aligned}
NUI(x) &= \{s \in S \mid \neg s[x\rangle \wedge {}^\bullet s = \{x\}\} \\
Seq(x) &= \{s \in S \mid \neg s[x\rangle \wedge \forall t \in s^\bullet : s[tx\rangle\}
\end{aligned}
$$

the set of states with unique input x not enabling x, and the set of states from which x is sequentialised, respectively.   □ 7

Example: In Figure 1, $NUI(b) = \{M_1, M_2\}$ and $Seq(b) = \{M\}$.
In Figure 2, $NUI(a) = \{2\}$ and $Seq(a) = \{5\}$.   *End of example*

4.2   Checking ON-solvability

Assuming that $T = \{x, a_1, a_2, \ldots, a_m\}$ is the set of labels of TS, we now wish to determine under which conditions a pure place p with outgoing transition x and incoming transitions $a_1, a_2, \ldots, a_m$ can serve as a part of an ON Petri net solving TS. The general form of such a place is shown in Figure 3. For generality reasons, it is assumed that all transitions a_j but the outgoing one, x, are inputs of such a place, even if some of the weights k_j can possibly turn out to be zero.

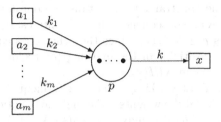

Fig. 3. A general pure ON place p

The parameters to be determined are the arc weights $k_1, k_2, \ldots, k_m, k$, all ≥ 0, and the initial marking $M_0(p)$ corresponding to the initial state s_0 of TS.

First, we may observe that we do not change the dynamics of the place if we multiply all the weights by some integer $n > 0$ and the initial marking by the same factor; we may even replace the initial marking by any value $n \cdot M_0(p) + \ell$ provided $0 \leq \ell < n$. Conversely, if all the weights have a common factor $n > 0$, the dynamics of the place is not modified if we divide the weights by n and replace the initial marking by $M_0(p) \div n$. Hence, we may always assume

$$\gcd\{k, k_1, k_2, \ldots, k_m\} = 1 \tag{1}$$

Next, since all cycles have a Parikh vector multiple of Υ, we must have

$$\sum_{1 \leq j \leq m} k_j \cdot \Upsilon(a_j) = k \cdot \Upsilon(x) \tag{2}$$

Example: The lts in Figure 1 satisfies **P1**. For place p, (2) becomes: sum of the weights of p's incoming arcs = weight of p's outgoing arc = 2. A similar equality is true for all other places in Figure 1.   *End of example*

Now, let us determine the constraints the initial marking of this place must satisfy. Since it is necessary that each path allowed by the lts is also allowed by the place, the initial marking must be large enough. By the shape of the place shown in Figure 3 and by the firing rule, the marking of place p at an arbitrary state r is $M_r(p) = M_0(p) + \sum_j k_j \cdot \Delta_{s_0,r}(a_j) - k \cdot \Delta_{s_0,r}(x)$. This sum must always be nonnegative, that is, we must have

$$\forall r \in S: \quad M_0(p) \geq k \cdot \Delta_{s_0,r}(x) - \sum_{1 \leq j \leq m} k_j \cdot \Delta_{s_0,r}(a_j) \tag{3}$$

In addition, since there is no side-condition around p, if these inequalities are satisfied for all states r, no path of the lts will be prevented by place p.

Another way to interpret the constraints (2) and (3) is to see that these are exactly the conditions to be satisfied such that the triple $(\mathbb{R}, \mathbb{B}, \mathbb{F})$ where $\mathbb{R}(r) = M_0(p) + \sum_j k_j \cdot \Delta_{s_0,r}(a_j) - k \cdot \Delta_{s_0,r}(x)$, $\mathbb{B}(x) = k$ (0 otherwise), and $\mathbb{F}(a_j) = k_j$ (for $j = 1, ..., m$; 0 otherwise) is a region in the sense of Definition 5.

The constraints (3) yield $|S|$ inequalities, but they are not all useful. If $r[x\rangle r'$, the constraint for r' entails the one for r since $M_{r'}(p) = M_r(p) - k < M_r(p)$.

Similarly, if $r[a_j\rangle r'$, the constraint for r entails the one for r' since $M_{r'}(p) = M_r(p) + k_j \geq M_r(p)$. As a consequence, the only interesting states for inequalities (3) are the states $r \in NUI(x)$, since the other ones correspond to higher markings, so that the positivity of the marking (or region) is ensured for the latter if it is for the states in $NUI(x)$.

The values for the initial marking which satisfy inequalities (3) are upward closed, and for any choice of the weights satisfying the equations (2) and (1), it is always possible to choose $M_0(p) = \max_{r \in NUI(x)}(k \cdot \Delta_{s_0,r}(x) - \sum_j k_j \cdot \Delta_{s_0,r}(a_j))$. This is the least possible value for $M_0(p)$ and, in that case, for at least one of the states $r \in NUI(x)$, the marking $M_r(p)$ is 0 (otherwise a lower value for $M_0(p)$ could have been chosen).

Example: For the lts in Figure 1, $\max_{r \in \{M_1,M_2\}}(2 \cdot \Delta_{M_0,r}(b) - (\Delta_{M_0,r}(a) + \Delta_{M_0,r}(d))) = 2$, the number of tokens initially on place p.   *End of example*

Next, let s be any state of the lts which does not enable x. In a pure ON solution of TS, and corresponding to ESSP, there must be at least one place p_s of the kind shown in Figure 3 that forbids this transition. Hence we must have:

$$M_0(p_s) \ < \ k \cdot (\Delta_{s_0,s}(x) + 1) - \sum_{1 \leq j \leq m} k_j \cdot \Delta_{s_0,s}(a_i) \tag{4}$$

because otherwise, due to the "+1", the marking $M_s(p_s)$ does not prevent x from occurring at state s. Note that we do not forbid that $p_s = p_{s'}$, if both s and s' exclude an x-move and the same place works for both. It could even happen that a single place works for all the exclusions of x.

Again, some of those constraints (hence some places) entail other ones. For instance, if $s[a_j\rangle s'$, while $\neg s[x\rangle$ and $\neg s'[x\rangle$, the place $p_{s'}$ also does the job for s, since its marking at state s is not higher than at state s', so that $p_{s'}$ excludes x from s if it does so from s'. As a consequence, we only have to consider the inequalities (4) for states $s \in Seq(x)$. For this reason, in view of (4), only the sequentialisation states for x are interesting.

The constraints (3) and (4) both concern the initial marking, but it is possible to express them without it, since the system (3) yields the minimal initial marking. One has to find, for each transition x and each state $s \in Seq(x)$, arc weights such that

$$\forall r \in NUI(x): k \cdot \Delta_{s_0,r}(x) - \sum_j k_j \cdot \Delta_{s_0,r}(a_j) < k \cdot (\Delta_{s_0,s}(x) + 1) - \sum_j k_j \cdot \Delta_{s_0,s}(a_j)$$

or equivalently

$$\forall r \in NUI(x): \ 0 \ < \ k \cdot (\Delta_{r,s}(x) + 1) - \sum_j k_j \cdot \Delta_{r,s}(a_j) \tag{5}$$

since, using Lemma 3, $\Delta_{r,s} = \Delta_{s_0,s} - \Delta_{s_0,r} + m \cdot \Upsilon$ for some integer m, and the coefficients satisfy equation (2). With the aid of equation (2), we may even eliminate k from these inequalities. As a result, for each state $s \in Seq(x)$ we obtain the system of inequations

$$\boxed{\forall r \in NUI(x): \ 0 \ < \ \sum_{1 \leq j \leq m} k_j \cdot (\Upsilon(a_j) \cdot (1 + \Delta_{r,s}(x)) - \Upsilon(x) \cdot \Delta_{r,s}(a_j))} \tag{6}$$

The reasoning above shows that, if the considered lts is solvable by a pure ON net, then for each label $x \in T$ and each state $s \in Seq(x)$ the system of inequations (6) is solvable in the $\mathbb{N}$ domain. A converse is also true. Assume that, for each label $x \in T$ and each state $s \in Seq(x)$, the system of inequations (6) is solvable. So, we get nonnegative integer values for all the weights k_j. It may still happen that they do not lead to an integer value for k satisfying equation (2). But since the inequations are homogeneous, any non-null set of integers proportional to a solution is also a solution (while there may be other, non-proportional, solutions as well). Hence it is always possible to choose a solution which may be extended with an integer k such that equation (2), as well as (1), is satisfied, and choose the initial marking $\max_{r \in NUI(x)} \{ \sum_{1 \le j \le m} k_j \cdot (\frac{\Upsilon(a_j)}{\Upsilon(x)} \cdot \Delta_{s_0,r}(x) - \Delta_{s_0,r}(a_j)) \}$.

Then, from (6) and (2), the constraints (3) and (4) are satisfied, and a pure ON place with integer weights on all of its adjacent arcs may be constructed.

First example: Consider label $x = b$ and state $s = M$ in the lts depicted in Figure 1. For states $r = M_1 \in NUI(b)$ and $r = M_2 \in NUI(b)$, inequations (6) respectively reduce to $0 < k_a$ and $0 < k_d$ after setting the Υ terms to 1 and evaluating the Δ terms on the lts. This system is simultaneously solvable by $k_a = 1$, $k_c = 0$ and $k_d = 1$, describing the interface at place p with regard to its incoming transitions. Using (2), the weight k of the arc from p to its outgoing transition b can then be set to $k = k_a + k_d = 2$. Observe that apart from the minimal solution given in this instance, there are plenty of other solutions arising, for instance, by uniform multiplication by a constant number. All of them serve the same purpose, and redundant ones can be omitted. *End of first example*

It can be verified that the system (6) of inequations can always be solved for this example, not just for $x = b$ and $s = M$. Moreover, the ON solution shown on the right-hand side of Figure 1 can be obtained by assembling places yielded by such solutions. In the next section, it will be shown that this is a general property of the construction defined in the present section.

Second example: Consider label $x = a$ and state $s = 5$ in the lts depicted in Figure 2. For the only state $r = 2 \in NUI(a)$, inequations (6) become $0 < k_b \cdot (-2)$, which is not solvable in the $\mathbb{N}$ domain. *End of second example*

This second example illustrates the opposite case. As we have just seen, there exists some label x and some state $s \in Seq(x)$ such that (6) is unsolvable. In the next section, it will be shown that this entails, in general, that no ON Petri net solving the given lts exists.

Note: The constructions also work in case $|T| = |\{x\}| = 1$ (then $Seq(x) = \emptyset$, and a single, isolated transition x is created) as well as in case $T = \emptyset$ (then an empty net with empty initial marking is created). *End of note*

Figure 4 summarises the resulting algorithm.

4.3 Correctness and Optimisations

In this section, the shorthand "(6) is solvable" means that for all pairs $x \in T$ and $s \in Seq(x)$, the system of inequations (6) is solvable in $\mathbb{N}$.

Theorem 4. LANGUAGE EQUIVALENCE

---

input an lts $TS = (S, \rightarrow, T, s_0)$ and a T-vector $\Upsilon \geq 1$ satisfying **rg, r, p, PΥ**;
initially T is the set of transitions, and $P := \emptyset$;
for every $x \in T$ and $s \in Seq(x)$ **do**
    construct the system (6) for x and s, as well as equations (1) and (2) for x;
    if $\neg \exists k_1, \ldots, k_m \in \mathbb{N}$ solving (6) **then**
        {**output** "TS not ON-solvable, due to x, s and system (6)"; **stop**};
    choose a set of integers $(k_1, \ldots, k_m, k)$ satisfying (6), (1) and (2);
    add to P a place as in Fig. 3, with weights $k_1, \ldots, k_m, k$ and initial marking
    $\max_{r \in NUI(x)}\{\sum_{1 \leq j \leq m} k_j \cdot (\frac{\Upsilon(a_j)}{\Upsilon(x)} \cdot \Delta_{s_0,r}(x) - \Delta_{s_0,r}(a_j))\}$
end for; **output** "The net with transitions T and places P ON-solves TS".

Fig. 4. An algorithm checking ON-solvability and constructing an adequate solution

A finite lts TS satisfying properties **rg, r, p** *and* **PΥ** *has the same language as some pure ON net if and only if* (6) *is solvable.*

Proof

($\Leftarrow$): Suppose that (6) can be solved. Then the construction exhibited in the previous section yields a pure ON Petri net N, whose set of places correspond to regions satisfying ESSP. As noted after Theorem 1, ESSP entails language-equivalence between TS and N.

($\Rightarrow$): Suppose that (6) cannot be solved, for some $x \in T$ and $s \in Seq(x)$. It was shown in the previous section that it is impossible to separate x at s by any pure ON place. Thus there is no pure ON net with the same language as TS (nor solving TS).   □ 4

It is possible to strengthen language-equivalence to isomorphism, as follows.

Theorem 5. REACHABILITY GRAPH ISOMORPHISM

A finite lts satisfying properties **rg, r, p** *and* **PΥ** *is isomorphic to the reachability graph of some pure ON net if and only if* (6) *is solvable.*

Proof: ($\Rightarrow$) follows from Theorem 4($\Rightarrow$).

($\Leftarrow$): Let N be a pure ON net as constructed by the algorithm in the previous section. From Theorem 4($\Leftarrow$), one only has to check also that no two states s_1 and s_2 of the lts correspond to the same marking of N. If it would be the case, since the lts is strongly connected, there would be a sequence σ of transitions leading from s_1 to s_2. Since both places correspond to the same marking of the net, the sequence σ should also be allowed iteratively from s_2, leading to states $s_3, s_4, \ldots$, and since the system is finite, at some point we will have $s_i = s_j$ with $i < j$. Hence, from s_i we have a cycle with Parikh vector $(j - i) \cdot \Psi(\sigma)$, and by **rg** (as successor markings depend only on Parikh vectors of paths), σ generates a cycle from s_1 and $s_2 = s_1$. Consequently, SSP holds and, by Theorem 1, the reachability graph of the constructed net is isomorphic to the lts we started from.   □ 5

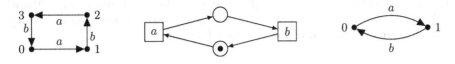

Fig. 5. An lts, the constructed Petri net, and its reachability graph

The significance of **rg** in part ($\Leftarrow$) of Theorem 5 is illustrated by the example shown in Figure 5. The lts on the left-hand side (which does not satisfy **rg**) leads to solvable systems (6). A corresponding net is shown in the middle of the figure, and its reachability graph on the right. In this case, the places of the constructed net yield regions of the given lts satisfying ESSP, but not SSP. The culprit is the fact that, in the lts we start from, $0[abab\rangle0$ form a cycle, with $\Psi(abab) = \Upsilon = (2, 2)$, but $0[ab\rangle2$ is not a cycle while $\Psi(ab) = (1, 1) = \Upsilon/2$.

Some remarks: The previous theorems hold even if "pure ON" is replaced by "ON" in their statements. That is, allowing side-conditions does not afford any true new degree of freedom.

If one is interested in synthesis problems, instead of reengineering ones, it is possible to weaken **rg**. For instance, it is possible to show that if **rg** is replaced by "the lts is finite, deterministic, and totally reachable" plus "$\gcd_{t\in T}\{\Upsilon(t)\} = 1$", Theorem 5 is still valid. Theorem 5 is also still valid if **rg** is replaced by "the lts is finite, deterministic, and totally reachable" plus a marginally stronger form of cycle-consistency [4]. One only has to make sure that the proof of 5($\Leftarrow$) goes through.

For these remarks, the details are described in [6].   *End of some remarks*

The aim of the algorithm exhibited in Figure 4 is correctness, not minimality. Various optimisations may be considered, such as:

- when a new place is constructed, for some $x \in T$ and $s \in Seq(x)$, it may happen that the arc weights around a place constructed for a previously considered $s' \in Seq(x)$ also satisfy the current system (6), as well as (1) and (2) since the latter have not changed; hence the new place the algorithm would construct is redundant and can be dropped;
- conversely, when a new place is constructed for some $x \in T$ and $s \in Seq(x)$, it may happen that its arcs weights also satisfy one or more systems (6) constructed for previous states $s' \in Seq(x)$, so that the places constructed from the latter are redundant and may be dropped;
- even if the algorithm does not produce redundant places, it can happen that a set of natural numbers $k_1, \ldots, k_m$ solves simultaneously many systems (6), for some x and many states s, leading to a place allowing to drop many redundant places; this kind of optimisation may be detected by searching for maximal subsets $S \subseteq Seq(x)$ such that the system $\cup_{s\in S}(6)_s$ is solvable, where $(6)_s$ denotes the system (6) constructed for x and s; then one only has to consider the subset $Seq(x) \setminus S$ for continuing the construction of places with output x;

- from the way we constructed a place from a solution of (6), or $\cup_{s\in S}(6)_s$, if $\Upsilon(x) > 1$, it may happen that a "better" place may be found when starting from a greater solution of the considered system.

4.4   Checking Non-ON-Solvability

Using the previous results, checking ON-solvability amounts to checking the *solvability* of the system of inequations (6) for all $x \in T$ and $s \in Seq(x)$, while checking non-ON-solvability amounts to checking the *unsolvability* of (6) for one such label x and state s. By means of linear-algebraic duality and by considering a dual system of inequalities, it is possible to exchange these two methods:

Theorem 6. ON INCOMPATIBILITY

A finite lts satisfying properties **rg, r, p** *and* **PΥ** *is not language-equivalent to the reachability graph of some (pure) ON Petri net if and only if, for some label* $x \in T$ *and sequentialising state* $s \in Seq(x)$, *the system of constraints in* y_r's

$$\forall j, 1 \leq j \leq m: \ 0 \geq \sum_{r\in NUI(x)} y_r \cdot (\Upsilon(a_j) \cdot (1 + \Delta_{r,s}(x)) - \Upsilon(x) \cdot \Delta_{r,s}(a_j)) \quad (7)$$

has a nonnull solution in $\mathbb{N}$.

Proof: This is an immediate consequence of Theorem 4 and the alternation result of Ville [17]. Among several similar results (e.g., Farkas's lemma), Ville's theorem has a convenient formulation to imply directly that the system of inequations (6) has a solution in $\mathbb{N}$ if and only if the system (7) has no other solution in $\mathbb{N}$ than $y_r = 0$ for each r.   □ 6

Specialising Theorem 6($\Leftarrow$) by considering solution vectors with only 0 and 1 for the unknowns, we obtain the following:

Corollary 1. BAD CONFIGURATIONS FOR ON NETS

If, for a finite lts TS *satisfying properties* **rg, r, p** *and* **PΥ**, *there exist a label* $x \in T$, *a state* $s \in Seq(x)$, *and a subset* $\emptyset \neq R \subseteq NUI(x)$ *such that*

$$\forall j, 1 \leq j \leq m: \ 0 \geq \sum_{r\in R}(\Upsilon(a_j) \cdot (1 + \Delta_{r,s}(x)) - \Upsilon(x) \cdot \Delta_{r,s}(a_j)) \quad (8)$$

then no ON net is language-equivalent (nor, a fortiori, reachability graph-isomorphic) to TS.   □ 1

Example: In Figure 2, there is a bad configuration corresponding to label $x = a$, state $s = 5$, and state set $R = \{2\}$.   *End of example*

Even though this corollary constitutes only a very special case, we mention it explicitly, because for all the examples we have considered up to now, checking (8) was sufficient to show non-ON-solvability, and we conjecture that this is a general property.

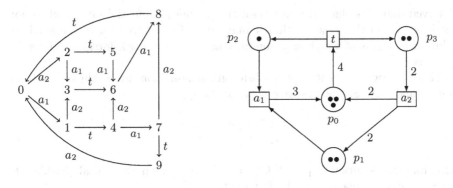

Fig. 6. An lts with unique Parikh cycle and a possible ON Petri net solution

5   Examples of the Constructions

We shall now illustrate the constructions (and optimisations) developed in section 4 on two rather more substantial examples.

5.1   A Worked, Positive Example

Let us consider the lts in Figure 6. It satisfies all the requested preconditions, with $\Upsilon = (a1 \mapsto 2, a2 \mapsto 1, t \mapsto 2)$. We get $NUI(a1) = \{1, 7\}$, $Seq(a1) = \{3, 8, 9\}$, $NUI(a2) = \{2\}$, $Seq(a2) = \{8\}$, $NUI(t) = \{4, 5, 9\}$ and $Seq(t) = \{0, 6\}$.

Let us first consider the sequentialisation of t at state 0 through $a1$ and $a2$, which should correspond to the place p_0 in the ON net on the right.
The system (6) has the form

$$0 < 2 \cdot k_{a1}$$
$$0 < 2 \cdot k_{a2}$$
$$0 < 2 \cdot k_{a1} - k_{a2}$$

the least solution is $k_{a1} = 1, k_{a2} = 1$, but this does not lead to an integer value for k_t; but multiplying it by 2 leads to a valid solution $k_{a1} = 2, k_{a2} = 2, k_t = 3$, with the initial marking 2.

For the sequentialisation of t at state 6 through a_1 we get the system:

$$0 < 2 \cdot k_{a1} - k_{a2}$$
$$0 < k_{a2}$$
$$0 < 2 \cdot k_{a1} - 2 \cdot k_{a2}$$

again, the least solution ($k_{a1} = 2, k_{a2} = 1$) is not adequate; twice it is adequate: $k_{a1} = 4, k_{a2} = 2, k_t = 5$, but there is a smaller one: $k_{a1} = 3, k_{a2} = 2, k_t = 4$, with the initial marking 3, corresponding to place p_0 in the Petri net. This shows that the least solution of the system (6) does not always lead to the smallest solution of (5) (but it leads nevertheless to an acceptable solution). Moreover, it may be observed that this place also works for the previous sequentialisation, while not the least one in this case, so that it may be useful not to stick to the smallest solution in terms of weights: a non-minimal one may work for many different systems.

There are two different sequentialisation configurations for a_1 through t: from state 3 and state 8. The first one leads to the system

$$0 < -k_{a2} + 2 \cdot k_t$$
$$0 < -2 \cdot k_{a2} + 2 \cdot k_t$$

with minimal solution $k_{a1} = 1, k_{a2} = 0, k_t = 1$, with the initial marking 1, corresponding to place p_2 in the Petri net.
The second one leads to a different system

$$0 < 2 \cdot k_t$$
$$0 < -k_{a2} + 2 \cdot k_t$$

but with the same minimal solution, and place.

However, there is another sequentialisation for a_1, from state 9 through a_2. Here the system to be solved is

$$0 < 2 \cdot k_{a2}$$
$$0 < k_{a2}$$

and the minimal solution is $k_{a1} = 1, k_{a2} = 2, k_t = 0$, with the initial marking 2, corresponding to place p_1 in the net.

Finally, the sequentialisation of a_2 from state 8 through t yields the (very simple) system

$$0 < k_t$$

with minimal solution $k_{a1} = 0, k_{a2} = 2, k_t = 1$, with the initial marking 2, corresponding to place p_3 in the net.

5.2   A Worked, Negative Example

In this section, the following assertion will be proved:

Proposition 1. A VERY REGULAR, PERSISTENT LTS WITHOUT ON SOLUTION
*There exists a finite lts, satisfying properties **r**, **p**, **P1**, and **rg** with a plain and pure solution, which cannot be solved by any ON Petri net.*

This proposition implies, amongst other things, that the class of persistent (plain, pure) Petri nets is "essentially larger" than the class of ON Petri nets, even if for the latter, arbitrary arc weights and side-conditions are allowed. Note that the latter class is, in turn, much larger than the class of marked graphs, as exemplified by Figure 1.

Proof: *By example.* The lts presented in Figure 7, where a triple (s, t, s') represents an arc $s[t\rangle s'$ and $s0$ is the initial state, has 10 labels, 89 states and 180 arcs. We have verified, with synet [8] and our own tools [9,15], that it satisfies **r**, **p**, **P1** and a strong form of **rg** since it is generated by a plain and pure net. However it has no ON solution. The culprit – by construction of the lts, and also found by [9] – is label $y1$ with sequentialising state $s6 \in Seq(y1)$ and states $NUI(y1) = \{s58, s83\}$. The system (6) yields the constraints

$$0 < -2 \cdot k_{b1} + k_{a2} - k_{b2} - k_{b3} \quad (\text{ from a short path } s58 \rightsquigarrow s6)$$
$$0 < -2 \cdot k_{a1} - k_{a2} + k_{b2} - k_{a3} \quad (\text{ from a short path } s83 \rightsquigarrow s6)$$

whose sum $0 < -2 \cdot k_{b1} - k_{b3} - 2 \cdot k_{a1} - k_{a3}$ has no solution in $\mathbb{N}$. In fact, this corresponds to a bad configuration in the sense of Corollary 1, with $x = y1$, $s = s6$, and $R = \{s58, s83\}$. □ 1

(s0,a1,s1) (s0,b1,s2) (s0,z,s3) (s1,b1,s25) (s1,z,s4) (s2,a1,s25) (s2,z,s5) (s3,a1,s4)
(s3,b1,s5) (s4,a2,s31) (s4,b1,s6) (s5,a1,s6) (s5,b2,s7) (s6,a2,s8) (s6,b2,s9) (s7,a1,s9)
(s7,y1,s26) (s8,b2,s10) (s8,y1,s11) (s9,a2,s10) (s9,y1,s87) (s10,y1,s12) (s11,b2,s12)
(s11,y2,s33) (s12,y2,s13) (s13,a3,s14) (s13,b3,s15) (s13,x,s16) (s14,b3,s17) (s14,x,s21)
(s15,a3,s17) (s15,x,s18) (s16,a3,s21) (s16,b3,s18) (s17,x,s0) (s18,a3,s0) (s18,b1,s19)
(s18,z,s20) (s19,a3,s2) (s19,z,s22) (s20,a3,s3) (s20,b1,s22) (s21,a1,s27) (s21,b3,s0)
(s21,z,s28) (s22,a3,s5) (s22,b2,s23) (s23,a3,s7) (s23,y1,s24) (s24,a3,s26) (s24,y2,s54)
(s25,z,s6) (s26,a1,s87) (s26,y2,s55) (s27,b3,s1) (s27,z,s29) (s28,a1,s29) (s28,b3,s3)
(s29,a2,s30) (s29,b3,s4) (s30,b3,s31) (s30,y1,s32) (s31,b1,s8) (s31,y1,s59) (s32,b3,s59)
(s32,y2,s44) (s33,a3,s34) (s33,b2,s13) (s33,x,s35) (s34,b2,s14) (s34,x,s36) (s35,a3,s36)
(s35,b2,s16) (s36,a1,s37) (s36,b2,s21) (s36,z,s38) (s37,b2,s27) (s37,z,s39) (s38,a1,s39)
(s38,b2,s28) (s39,a2,s40) (s39,b2,s29) (s40,b2,s30) (s40,y1,s41) (s41,b2,s32) (s41,y2,s42)
(s42,a3,s43) (s42,b2,s44) (s43,b2,s45) (s43,x,s49) (s44,a3,s45) (s44,b3,s46) (s45,b3,s47)
(s45,x,s48) (s46,a3,s47) (s46,b1,s33) (s46,x,s62) (s47,b1,s34) (s47,x,s50) (s48,b3,s50)
(s49,b2,s48) (s50,a1,s51) (s50,b1,s36) (s50,z,s52) (s51,b1,s37) (s51,z,s53) (s52,a1,s53)
(s52,b1,s38) (s53,a2,s57) (s53,b1,s39) (s54,a3,s55) (s54,b3,s56) (s55,a1,s78) (s55,b3,s63)
(s55,x,s79) (s56,a3,s63) (s56,x,s64) (s57,b1,s40) (s57,y1,s58) (s58,b1,s41) (s58,y2,s60)
(s59,b1,s11) (s59,y2,s46) (s60,a3,s61) (s60,b1,s42) (s61,b1,s43) (s61,x,s88) (s62,a3,s50)
(s62,b1,s35) (s63,a1,s65) (s63,x,s66) (s64,a3,s66) (s65,a2,s15) (s65,x,s67) (s66,a1,s67)
(s66,b1,s68) (s66,z,s69) (s67,a2,s18) (s67,b1,s70) (s67,z,s74) (s68,a1,s70) (s68,z,s71)
(s69,a1,s74) (s69,b1,s71) (s70,a2,s19) (s70,z,s72) (s71,a1,s72) (s71,b2,s82) (s72,a2,s22)
(s72,b2,s73) (s73,a2,s23) (s73,y1,s75) (s74,a2,s20) (s74,b1,s72) (s75,a2,s24) (s75,y2,s76)
(s76,a2,s54) (s76,b3,s77) (s77,a2,s56) (s77,x,s81) (s78,a2,s13) (s78,b3,s65) (s78,x,s80)
(s79,a1,s80) (s79,b3,s66) (s80,a2,s16) (s80,b3,s67) (s81,a2,s64) (s82,a1,s73) (s82,y1,s83)
(s83,a1,s75) (s83,y2,s84) (s84,a1,s76) (s84,b3,s85) (s85,a1,s77) (s85,x,s86) (s86,a1,s81)
(s87,a2,s12) (s87,y2,s78) (s88,b1,s49)

Fig. 7. An lts satisfying **rg** with a plain and pure net, **r**, **p**, and **P1**, without an ON solution

So far, we did not check whether the example shown in Figure 7 has a minimal number of states. Nevertheless, the following two arguments lead us to believe that the number of states cannot be reduced considerably.

- We found an example satisfying **rg**, **r**, **p**, **P1**, that has no plain or pure solution, cannot be reduced, and already has 23 states [6].

- This kind of counterexample is derived rather painstakingly from a skeleton, akin to a bad configuration, which ensures the unsolvability of (6) *in spite of* **rg**. Such a skeleton already has quite a few states, and Lemma 5 (in conjunction with persistency) adds more states to it. It is hard to see that considerably fewer states would suffice.

6   Concluding Remarks

In this paper, we have developed a synthesis / reengineering algorithm for lts satisfying several nice properties, which allows to create an ON Petri net whenever it is theoretically possible. Moreover, we have shown that the existence of structurally pleasant solutions cannot always be guaranteed. In parallel work [7], we were able to show, however, that the state spaces of live and bounded marked graphs (and their bounds) can actually be characterised by adding a single further property, namely **bp**, an analogue of persistency in backward direction.

Several questions remain open, and new ones have been detected.

Generalisations and extensions. Very simple examples show that persistency cannot be dropped (quite naturally not, since the ON property is intimately related to persistency). But what happens exactly if reversibility is weakened to liveness? What happens for unbounded nets? Can concurrency semantics, especially step semantics, play a useful role?

Restrictions. Can one find a weak (preferably, structural) property, to be imposed besides **rg**, **r**, **p**, and **PΥ** or **P1**, which is weak enough not to imply **bp**, but also strong enough to guarantee ON solvability? For example, it is not known whether Proposition 1 in section 5.2 remains true if the net which exists by **rg** is assumed, in addition, to be 1-bounded.

Simplifications. Can the crucial system of constraints, (6), be reduced further by considering only those $r \in NUI(x)$ from which x-free directed paths lead to s? Can the number of states be reduced in the example discussed in section 5.2?

Special cases. Can one find exact criteria for cyclic lts (generalising Figures 2 and 5), or for lts of other regular shapes?

Complexity analysis. As compared, for instance, with [2], our constructions are more efficient for two reasons. The first reason is that, as a synthesis method, the algorithm given in section 4.3 applies to a special case. This is reflected by the fact that we identify the two sets $NUI(x) \subseteq S$ and $Seq(x) \subseteq S$ which are normally much smaller than S, leading to much fewer linear-algebraic calculations needing to be done. However, it is still a matter of research to find out exactly how the sizes of these sets are related to each other in the average or worst cases. The second reason is that our algorithm comes with an in-built reengineering method, which is absent in the general synthesis algorithm. If one wanted to use the latter for reengineering in a brute-force way, one would have to cycle through all region bases in order to check whether there exists a "nice", desirable one. Such an additional loop implies a considerable additional layer of complexity to general synthesis. It is absent in our approach because it was specifically tailored to the desired "niceness" criterion, viz. ON solvability.

Acknowledgments. We are grateful to Philippe Darondeau and Hanna Klaudel for inspirations and discussions. The remarks of the anonymous reviewers allowed to improve the presentation of the paper.

References

1. Badouel, É., Bernardinello, L., Darondeau, P.: Petri Net Synthesis, 330 pages. Springer (in preparation, 2014)
2. Badouel, É., Bernardinello, L., Darondeau, P.: Polynomial Algorithms for the Synthesis of Bounded Nets. In: Mosses, P.D., Nielsen, M., Schwartzbach, M.I. (eds.) TAPSOFT 1995. LNCS, vol. 915, pp. 364–378. Springer, Heidelberg (1995)
3. Badouel, É.: Theory of Regions. In: Reisig, W., Rozenberg, G. (eds.) APN 1998. LNCS, vol. 1491, pp. 529–586. Springer, Heidelberg (1998)
4. Best, E., Darondeau, P.: A Decomposition Theorem for Finite Persistent Transition Systems. Acta Informatica 46, 237–254 (2009)
5. Best, E., Darondeau, P.: Petri Net Distributability. In: Clarke, E., Virbitskaite, I., Voronkov, A. (eds.) PSI 2011. LNCS, vol. 7162, pp. 1–18. Springer, Heidelberg (2012)
6. Best, E., Devillers, R.: Solving LTS with Parikh-unique Cycles. TR 2/14, Dep. Informatik, Carl von Ossietzky Universität Oldenburg, 80 pages (February 2014)
7. Best, E., Devillers, R.: Characterisation of the State Spaces of Live and Bounded Marked Graph Petri Nets. In: Dediu, A.-H., Martín-Vide, C., Sierra-Rodríguez, J.-L., Truthe, B. (eds.) LATA 2014. LNCS, vol. 8370, pp. 161–172. Springer, Heidelberg (2014)
8. Caillaud, B.: http://www.irisa.fr/s4/tools/synet/
9. Devillers, R.: plain.c, pure.c, frag.c: Specially tailored programs written in C++
10. Hack, M.: Analysis of production schemata by Petri nets, M.S. thesis, D.E.E. MIT. Cambridge Mass. Project MAC-TR 94 (1972)
11. Keller, R.M.: A Fundamental Theorem of Asynchronous Parallel Computation. In: Tse-Yun, F. (ed.) Parallel Processing. LNCS, vol. 24, pp. 102–112. Springer, Heidelberg (1975)
12. Kondratyev, A., Cortadella, J., Kishinevsky, M., Pastor, E., Roig, O., Yakovlev, A.: Checking Signal Transition Graph Implementability by Symbolic BDD Traversal. In: Proc. European Design and Test Conference, Paris, France, pp. 325–332 (1995)
13. Lamport, L.: Arbiter-Free Synchronization. Distributed Computing 16(2/3), 219–237 (2003)
14. Landweber, L.H., Robertson, E.L.: Properties of Conflict-Free and Persistent Petri Nets. J. ACM 25(3), 352–364 (1978)
15. Schlachter, U., et al.: https://github.com/renke/apt
16. Teruel, E., Colom, J.M., Silva, M.: Choice-Free Petri nets: a model for deterministic concurrent systems with bulk services and arrivals. IEEE Transactions on Systems, Man and Cybernetics, Part A, 73–83 (1997)
17. Ville, J.: Sur la théorie générale des jeux où intervient l'habileté des joueurs. In: Borel, E. (ed.) Traité du calcul des probabilités et de ses applications, vol. 4, pp. 105–113. Gauthiers-Villars (1938)
18. Yakovlev, A.: Designing control logic for counterflow pipeline processor using Petri nets. Formal Methods in Systems Design 12(1), 39–71 (1998)
19. Yakovlev, A.: Theory and practice of using models of concurrency in hardware design. DSc Thesis, University of Newcastle upon Tyne (August 2005)

Learning Transparent Data Automata*

Normann Decker[1], Peter Habermehl[2], Martin Leucker[1], and Daniel Thoma[1]

[1] ISP, University of Lübeck, Germany
{decker,leucker,thoma}@isp.uni-luebeck.de
[2] Univ Paris Diderot, Sorbonne Paris Cité, LIAFA, CNRS, France
peter.habermehl@liafa.univ-paris-diderot.fr

Abstract. This paper studies the problem of learning data automata (DA), a recently introduced model for defining languages of data words which are finite sequences of pairs of letters from a finite and, respectively, infinite alphabet. The model of DA is closely related to general Petri nets, for which no active learning algorithms have been introduced so far. This paper defines transparent data automata (tDA) as a strict subclass of deterministic DA. Yet, it is shown that every language accepted by DA can be obtained as the projection of the language of some tDA. The model of class memory automata (CMA) is known to be equally expressive as DA. However deterministic DA are shown to be strictly less expressive than deterministic CMA. For the latter, and hence for tDA, equivalence is shown to be decidable. On these grounds, in the spirit of Angluin's L* algorithm we develop an active learning algorithm for tDA. They are incomparable to register automata and variants, for which learning algorithms were given recently.

1 Introduction

Learning of formal languages is a fundamental problem in computer science. In the setting of active learning, where a *learner* can ask *membership queries* (i.e. is a given word in the language to be learned) and *equivalence queries* (i.e. is a learning hypothesis equivalent to the language to be learned) to an *oracle (teacher)*, it has been shown [1] that regular languages over a finite alphabet can be learned using the L* algorithm. However, in several application areas like program verification and database management it is important to be able to reason about data coming from an infinite domain. For that purpose *data words*, i.e. sequences of pairs (a, d) of letters a from a finite alphabet and data values d from an infinite alphabet, are used. The data values can contain for example process identifiers from an infinite domain allowing to model naturally parameterized systems with an unbounded number of components. For *data languages*, i.e. sets of data words, *data automata* have been introduced recently [2] as a computational model. A data automaton is a tuple $(\mathcal{A}, \mathcal{B})$ composed of a transducer $\mathcal{A}$, the *base automaton*, and a finite state automaton $\mathcal{B}$, the *class automaton*. A data word w is handled in two phases. First the transducer $\mathcal{A}$

---

* This work is partially supported by EGIDE/DAAD-Procope (LeMon).

G. Ciardo and E. Kindler (Eds.): PETRI NETS 2014, LNCS 8489, pp. 130–149, 2014.

reads w without data values and possibly modifies the individual (finite-domain) letters. This results in a data word w' where the data values have not changed. Then, the so called *class strings* of w' are individually checked by the class automaton $\mathcal{B}$. The class strings of a data word are the sub-strings of finite-domain letters carrying the same data value. Roughly, the base automaton enforces a *global property* whereas the class automaton enforces a *local property*. In [2] it is shown that emptiness of data automata and reachability in general Petri nets are polynomially equivalent.

An example of a data automaton, taken with minor changes from [3], is given in Figure 1. It will be used throughout this paper and corresponds to a system where a printer is shared by processes. Data values correspond here to process identifiers and each process can request (r), start (s) and terminate (t). The global property is that each started job must be terminated before the next one can be started and the local property is that each process can invoke one job ($\epsilon + rst$). An accepted data word is for example $\left(\begin{smallmatrix} rrstst \\ 121122 \end{smallmatrix}\right)$. Notice that the global property can be characterized by a transducer not modifying the letters but just copying them.

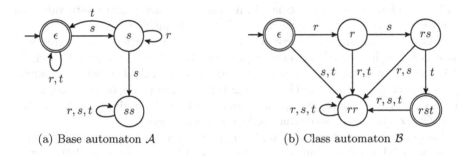

(a) Base automaton $\mathcal{A}$ (b) Class automaton $\mathcal{B}$

Fig. 1. Transparent data automaton $\mathcal{D} = (\mathcal{A}, \mathcal{B})$

The example illustrates two characteristics of many systems, namely the fact that (1) the local behaviour is not constrained by the global one. This means that a process can run on its own. Furthermore, (2) the global behaviour is just a filter, i.e. the transducer is not changing any letters.

Turning to the problem of learning of data automata which we tackle in this paper, we notice that learning the full class of data automata is difficult, as they are closely related to general unbounded Petri nets, a powerful model of computation. Furthermore in active learning it is desirable to have at least theoretically the possibility of answering equivalence queries. However, the equivalence problem for data automata is undecidable. Therefore, we have to look for a simpler but still expressive sub-class of data automata.

In this paper we introduce *transparent data automata* (tDA), which correspond to data automata with the conditions (1) and (2), i.e. $\mathcal{A}$ and $\mathcal{B}$ are finite state automata over the same input alphabet and $\mathcal{L}(\mathcal{B}) \subseteq \mathcal{L}(\mathcal{A})$. We show that tDA have a decidable equivalence problem in Section 2.

More precisely, we obtain decidability even for deterministic *class memory automata* (dCMA), a closely related automaton model for data words introduced in [3]. While general class memory automata (CMA) are expressively equivalent to DA, we show dCMA are strictly more expressive than deterministic DA that in turn are strictly more expressive than tDA. However, tDA are still quite powerful as we show that each DA can be encoded into a tDA that accepts the same language up to projection. This in turn induces the fact that a variant of the emptiness problem is still as hard as Petri net reachability. Furthermore, the class of complements of tDA exceeds the class of dCMA.

For tDA, we introduce several learning algorithms in Section 3. We first consider the case where the global behaviour $\mathcal{A}$ is known and the local behaviour $\mathcal{B}$ is to be learned. We handle that case by adapting Angluin's L^* algorithm. The case where $\mathcal{B}$ is known and $\mathcal{A}$ is to be learned is more difficult since membership queries cannot always be answered conclusively. We therefore adopt the approach of learning from inexperienced teachers [4,5] that may additionally answer membership queries with *don't know*. Finally, we combine the two algorithms in the case where neither $\mathcal{A}$ nor $\mathcal{B}$ are directly accessible.

Another well studied automaton model for data words are *register automata* (RA) [6]. They have a finite control and can additionally store data values in a finite set of registers. Transitions can depend on equality checks between the current data value and values from the registers. DA are strictly more expressive than RA which are strictly more expressive than their deterministic variant. RA and deterministic RA are both incomparable to tDA: The printer example (Figure 1) cannot be accepted by any register automaton and, on the other hand, dCMA are neither more nor equally expressive then deterministic RA [3]. This transfers to tDA as we show that dCMA subsume them.

There are a number of works on learning register automata and its variants [7–9] based all on extensions or adaptations of L*. For Workflow Petri Nets a learning algorithm has been given in [10]. However unlike our models these Petri Nets are bounded and for unbounded Petri Nets we are not aware of any active learning algorithm.

2   Transparent Data Automata

In this section we consider deterministic automata on data words. In particular, we introduce and study transparent data automata that we build on in the subsequent Section 3.

Data words and data languages. Let Σ be a finite alphabet and Δ an infinite set of *data values*. A *data word* is a finite sequence $w = w_1 w_n \in (\Sigma \times \Delta)^*$ of pairs $w_i = (a_i, d_i)$ of letters and data values. We call $\mathsf{str}(w) = a_1 a_n \in \Sigma^*$ the *string projection* of w. The *class string* of w for a data value $d \in \Delta$ is the maximal projected subsequence $w|_d := a_{i_1} a_{i_m} \in \Sigma^*$ of w with data value d, i.e., for all $1 \leq j \leq m$ we have $1 \leq i_j \leq n$, $d_{i_j} = d$, $i_j < i_{j+1}$ (for $j < m$) and for each $1 \leq k \leq n$ with $d_k = d$ there is some $i_j = k$.

We refer to the set of all (non-empty) class strings of w as $w\!\downarrow$. We use the data values $1, 2, 3$, as representatives for arbitrary data values. A data word where the sequence of data values is $d_1 d_n$ and with string projection u is written as $\left(\begin{smallmatrix} u \\ d_1 d_n \end{smallmatrix}\right)$. If all data values are 1 we may abbreviate that by $\left(\begin{smallmatrix} u \\ 1 \end{smallmatrix}\right)$.

For any automaton $\mathcal{A}$, $\mathcal{L}(\mathcal{A})$ denotes the set of all accepted (data) words but we may also write $w \in \mathcal{A}$ and $L \subseteq \mathcal{A}$ for $w \in \mathcal{L}(\mathcal{A})$ and $L \subseteq \mathcal{L}(\mathcal{A})$, respectively. We use $\overline{L}$ to denote the complement of a language L. A *(deterministic) letter-to-letter transducer* $\mathcal{T}$ is a (deterministic) finite state automaton over a finite input alphabet Σ that additionally outputs a letter from some finite output alphabet Γ for every letter it reads. For $u \in \Sigma^*$ we denote $\mathcal{T}(u)$ the set of possible outputs of $\mathcal{T}$ when reading u.

Data automata. A *data automaton* [2] (DA) is a tuple $\mathcal{D} = (\mathcal{A}, \mathcal{B})$. The *base automaton* $\mathcal{A}$ is a letter-to-letter transducer with input alphabet Σ and output alphabet Γ. The *class automaton* $\mathcal{B}$ is a finite state automaton with input alphabet Γ. A data word $w = \left(\begin{smallmatrix} u \\ d_1 d_n \end{smallmatrix}\right)$ is accepted by $\mathcal{D}$ if its string projection $u \in \mathcal{A}$ and there is an output $u' \in \mathcal{A}(u)$ of $\mathcal{A}$ s.t. every class string of $\left(\begin{smallmatrix} u' \\ d_1 d_n \end{smallmatrix}\right)$ is accepted by $\mathcal{B}$. We call a data automaton *deterministic* (dDA), if the base automaton $\mathcal{A}$ is deterministic.

Class Memory Automata. A *class memory automaton* [3] (CMA) over Σ is a tuple $\mathcal{C} = (Q, \Sigma, \delta, q_0, F_l, F_g)$ where Q is a finite set of states, $\delta : Q \times (Q \cup \{\bot\}) \times \Sigma \to 2^Q$ is the transition function, $q_0 \in Q$ is the initial state and $F_l \subseteq Q$ and $F_g \subseteq Q$ are the locally and globally accepting states, respectively. A configuration of $\mathcal{C}$ is a pair (q, f) where $q \in Q$ is a state and $f : D \to Q \times \{\bot\}$ is a *memory function* storing the state in which some data value has last been read. If d has not been read before $f(d) = \bot$. The initial configuration is (q_0, f_0) with $\forall_{x \in D} f_0(x) = \bot$. When reading a pair (a, d), the automaton can change from a configuration (q, f) to a configuration (q', f') if $q' \in \delta(q, f(d), a)$, $f'(d) = q'$ and $\forall_{x \in D \setminus \{d\}} f'(x) = f(x)$. A configuration (q, f) is accepting, if $q \in F_g$ and $\forall_{d \in D} f(d) \in (F_l \cup \{\bot\})$. For a configuration (q, f) we call q the global state and all states referred to by f the local states. $\mathcal{C}(w)$ denotes the set of configurations that $\mathcal{C}$ can reach reading a data word w and w is accepted by $\mathcal{C}$ if there is an accepting configuration in $\mathcal{C}(w)$. We call a CMA deterministic (dCMA) if $|\delta(q_g, q_l, a)| \leq 1$ for all $q_g \in Q$, $q_l \in Q \cup \{\bot\}$ and $a \in \Sigma$.

Expressiveness. As is shown in [3], DA and CMA are expressively equivalent. Also, the classes are effectively closed under intersection and union [2,3]. The emptiness problem for the automata models is shown to be equivalent to reachability in Petri nets and therefore decidable. However the classes are not closed under complementation. For the deterministic case, the classes are not equivalent anymore. Intuitively, DA can globally recognize data values only by means of non-deterministic guessing while CMA do not always rely on that as the present data value affects the transition function.

Lemma 1. $dDA \subsetneq dCMA$

Proof. The inclusion follows from the construction in [3] which translates DA into CMA and preserves determinism. The automaton classes are separated by the language $L \subseteq (\Sigma \times \Delta)^*$ containing the data words over $\Sigma = \{a\}$ with at least two different data values. L is accepted by the dCMA in Figure 2, whereas there is no dDA accepting L: As contradiction, assume some dDA $\mathcal{D} = (\mathcal{A}, \mathcal{B})$ accepts L and consider the words $w_1 = \binom{aa}{12}$, $w_2 = \binom{aaa}{112} \in L$. From w_1 we see that $\mathcal{A}$ accepts aa and from w_2 it follows that $\mathcal{B}$ accepts the corresponding projection $\mathcal{A}(aa)$. Then, however, $\mathcal{D}$ also accepts $\binom{aa}{11} \notin L$ as $\mathcal{A}$ is deterministic.   □

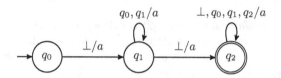

Fig. 2. A dCMA accepting data words with at least two data values. All states are accepting locally and q_2 is also accepting globally.

We now define transparent data automata. They form a sub-class of data automata that reflect the intuition that local behaviour is not constrained by the global one, i.e. any process can run on its own. Technically, we require, that the global language contains the local language as a subset. The condition will later in Section 3 allow us to use global observations for deducing information on the local automaton.

Definition 1 (Transparent Data Automaton). *A transparent data automaton (tDA) is a tuple $\mathcal{D} = (\mathcal{A}, \mathcal{B})$ where $\mathcal{A}$ and $\mathcal{B}$ are finite state automata over the same input alphabet Σ and $\mathcal{L}(\mathcal{B}) \subseteq \mathcal{L}(\mathcal{A})$.*

Note that, in fact, a tDA is a DA in the sense that the global automaton $\mathcal{A}$ can be interpreted as letter-to-letter transducer with $\Gamma = \Sigma$ that just outputs accepted input words unchanged.

2.1   Expressiveness of tDA

The transparency condition is a restriction designed to allow for active learning as will be discussed in Section 3. However, we remark in this section that tDA are nevertheless complex. But first, by extending Lemma 1, we obtain a strict hierarchy between tDA, dDA and dCMA.

Theorem 1. *tDA $\subsetneq$ dDA $\subsetneq$ dCMA*

Proof. Note that for every tDA there is an equivalent dDA as the base automaton is a finite automaton which can be determinized. To verify that tDA are strictly less expressive than dDA, consider the language of data words over $\Sigma = \{a\}$

where every second position carries a new data value. A dDA with internal alphabet $\Gamma = \{a, \hat{a}\}$ can accept that language by marking every other position using the base automaton whereas the class automaton checks that the first letter is marked. On the contrary the language is not accepted by any tDA since the base automaton is neither aware of the data values itself nor can it transmit any positioning information to the class automaton.   □

Checking tDA for emptiness boils down to checking the class automaton and is thus in NLogSpace. However, the slight modification of checking if there is an accepted word with at least two data values is still as hard as emptiness of DA. This follows from the possibility to encode any DA $\mathcal{D}$ into a tDA $\mathcal{D}'$ in such a way that $\mathcal{D}'$ accepts the same language as $\mathcal{D}$ up to some projection Π. We outline this connection more precisely in the following.

For the DA $\mathcal{D} = (\mathcal{A}, \mathcal{B})$, let Σ, Γ be the input and internal alphabet of the base automaton $\mathcal{A}$, respectively. $\mathcal{D}'$ employs an extended alphabet Σ' that is built from the product of Σ and Γ, an additional flag and a new symbol \$. Formally, we let $\Sigma' := (\Sigma \times \Gamma \times \{0,1\}) \cup \{\$\}$. Recall, that the input and internal alphabets are required to be equal for tDA.

The projection $\Pi : 2^{\Sigma' \times \Delta} \to 2^{\Sigma \times \Delta}$ basically removes all additional information stored in Σ'. For a data language $L \subseteq \Sigma' \times \Delta$ we let $\Pi(L) := \left\{ \binom{\pi(w)}{d_2 d_n} \mid \binom{\$\$w}{d_0 d_1 d_2 d_n} \in L \right\}$ where $\pi : \Sigma'^* \to \Sigma^*$ is the letter-wise projection to the first component, i.e. $\pi(a, g, x) = a$ for $(a, g, x) \in \Sigma'$ and $\pi(a_0 a_1 a_n) = \pi(a_0)\pi(a_1)\pi(a_n)$ for $a_i \in \Sigma'$.

Theorem 2. *For all DA $\mathcal{D}$ there exists (constructively) a tDA $\mathcal{D}'$ such that* $\mathcal{L}(\mathcal{D}) = \Pi(\mathcal{L}(\mathcal{D}'))$.

Proof. First we note that we can deafen the base automaton $\mathcal{A}$ by simply considering the output of $\mathcal{A}$ as additional input, i.e. we interpret $\mathcal{A}$ over the input alphabet $\Sigma \times \Gamma$. This yields a finite automaton $\hat{\mathcal{A}}$ over $\Sigma \times \Gamma$ accepting exactly the correct input/output combinations $(w, \mathcal{A}(w)) \in \Sigma \times \Gamma$ of $\mathcal{A}$. Now, we can define from the class automaton $\mathcal{B}$ a class automaton $\hat{\mathcal{B}}$ over the alphabet $\Sigma \times \Gamma$ which does the same on Γ as $\mathcal{B}$ while ignoring Σ. Then, $(\hat{\mathcal{A}}, \hat{\mathcal{B}})$ is a transparent data automaton in the sense of Definition 1.

From that we can construct $\mathcal{D}' = (\mathcal{A}', \mathcal{B}')$ as follows. Let $\$ \notin (\Sigma \times \Gamma)$ be a new symbol. For $\mathcal{A}'$ we take the deafened base automaton $\hat{\mathcal{A}}$ but extend the input alphabet by a new flag, 0 or 1, and the special symbol \$, i.e. $\Sigma' := (\Sigma \times \Gamma \times \{0,1\}) \cup \{\$\}$. $\mathcal{A}'$ checks that the input starts with \$\$ and then behaves as $\hat{\mathcal{A}}$ on the rest of the input ignoring the flag.

The class automaton $\mathcal{B}'$ behaves just like $\hat{\mathcal{B}}$ but checks that the first input symbol carries flag 1 and all following symbols carry flag 0. Additionally, it accepts a single \$ as input word.

In combination, this ensures that $\mathcal{D}'$ accepts only data words where exactly the first occurrence of every data value is marked by flag 1 (when considering the symbol \$ as carrying flag 1). If the original automaton $\mathcal{D}$ accepts some word w then the modified automaton $\mathcal{D}'$ accepts some word with at least two data values, namely $\left(\begin{smallmatrix}\$\$\\d_0d_1\end{smallmatrix}\right)w$ where the data values d_0, d_1 do not occur in w and the first occurrences of data values in w are marked by flag 1. On the other hand, if the modified automaton $\mathcal{D}'$ accepts some word w' then w' has the form $\left(\begin{smallmatrix}\$\$\\d_0d_1\end{smallmatrix}\right)\left(\begin{smallmatrix}w\\d_2d_n\end{smallmatrix}\right)$ and the original automaton $\mathcal{D}$ accepts $\left(\begin{smallmatrix}\pi(w)\\d_2d_n\end{smallmatrix}\right)$.

It remains to ensure the transparency condition $\mathcal{L}(\mathcal{B}') \subseteq \mathcal{L}(\mathcal{A}')$. This is done by letting the base automaton $\mathcal{A}'$ accept any word accepted by the new class automaton $\mathcal{B}'$. This potentially adds new data words to the represented language, however, they all do *not* start with $\$\$$. Thus these are excluded by the projection Π defined above. □

Despite Theorem 2 does not directly yield a hardness result, it provides evidence that the transparency restriction does not make the model trivial. The construction used in the proof yields a tDA that is only polynomial in the size of the DA. Using this technique we can proof the following corollary.

Corollary 1. *Given a tDA, deciding whether there is an accepted word containing at least two different data values is at least as hard as Petri net reachability.*

2.2   Complementation and Equivalence of tDA

As said earlier, DA and CMA are not closed under complementation. This is also the case for the deterministic versions. Moreover, even complements of the smallest class tDA may exceed the largest deterministic class dCMA.

Theorem 3. *dCMA do not capture the complements of tDA.*

Proof (Theorem 3). Let L be the language of data words over $\Sigma = \{a\}$ for which every class string is of even length. L is accepted by a tDA where the base automaton is universal and the class automaton just counts modulo two. For accepting the complement $\overline{L}$ of L, however, an automaton has to check for an input word, that there is a data value for which the class string is of odd length.

Assume there is a dCMA $\mathcal{C}$ that accepts $\overline{L}$. Since $\mathcal{C}$ has finitely many states, there are positions $m < n$ s.t. $\mathcal{C}$ is in the same state q after reading $u = \left(\begin{smallmatrix}aa\\1m\end{smallmatrix}\right)$ and after reading $uv = \left(\begin{smallmatrix}a\ a\\1mn\end{smallmatrix}\right)$. Because $u \in \overline{L}$, all local states as well as the global state in the configuration of $\mathcal{C}$ after reading u must be accepting. On the contrary, $uu \notin \overline{L}$ and so continuing by reading u again, $\mathcal{C}$ must change to some non-accepting state, either globally or locally. As the automaton is deterministic, appending u to uv must effect the same change as the data values in v are not present in u and the local states w.r.t. v do thus not influence the transitions taken by $\mathcal{C}$ when reading u. Therefore, after reading uvu, the configuration of $\mathcal{C}$ must contain some non-accepting local or global state which contradicts $uvu \in \overline{L}$. □

Even though neither the deterministic nor the non-deterministic class of data automata are closed under complementation, the complements of the deterministic classes can still be constructed in terms of CMA and thus allow for algorithmic analysis, in particular for emptiness checking.

Theorem 4. *For a deterministic CMA C we can construct a CMA accepting exactly the complement $\overline{\mathcal{L}(C)}$.*

Note that this result does not follow from [3]. There, a complementable variant called Presburger CMA is introduced and claimed to subsume dCMA but in fact it does not. Presburger CMA replace the acceptance condition of CMA by a *limited* Presburger formula, allowing essentially modulo constraints over the local states of a configuration. While this allows for complementation by complementing the Presburger formula, the original acceptance condition can no longer be encoded. Adding the original condition to Presburger CMA breaks closure under complementation.

Proof. Let $C = (Q, \Sigma, \delta, Q_0, F_\mathrm{l}, F_\mathrm{g})$ be a dCMA accepting the data language $L = \mathcal{L}(C)$. For the complement $\overline{L}$ of L, we observe that for some data word $w \in (\Sigma \times \Delta)^*$ and the configuration $C(w)$ of C after reading w we have $w \in \overline{L}$ iff (1) all local states in $C(w)$ are accepting and the global state is rejecting or (2) there is some local state in $C(w)$ that is rejecting.

Hence, we construct two CMA $\tilde{C}$ and $\hat{C}$ that accept all words obeying conditions (1) and (2), respectively. Then, the automaton $\overline{C} := \tilde{C} \cup \hat{C}$ accepts exactly $\overline{L}$ and is a CMA since this class is effectively closed under union.

To recognize data words satisfying the first condition, we simply complement the set of global accepting states: $\tilde{C} := (Q, \Sigma, \delta, q_0, F_\mathrm{l}, \overline{F}_\mathrm{g})$.

To recognize the second condition let $\hat{C} = (\hat{Q}, \Sigma, \hat{\delta}, \{(q_0, 0, 0)\}, \hat{F}_\mathrm{l}, \hat{F}_\mathrm{g})$ where the state space $\hat{Q} := Q \times B \times B$ is that of C enriched by two boolean flags from $B = \{0, 1\}$. The idea is that, whenever observing a new data value, the automaton guesses whether this is the data value for which the corresponding class causes the rejection in the original automaton C. The automaton then sets both flags to 1. The first flag is propagated globally, thereby keeping track of the fact that a data value has been guessed. The second flag is propagated locally, thereby marking the chosen data value. Except for the described guessing step and propagation of both flags, $\hat{C}$ just simulates C. The automaton accepts globally, once a data value has been chosen and thus the first flag is 1, i.e. for $\hat{F}_\mathrm{g} = Q \times \{1\} \times B$. The automaton accepts locally if the local state for the chosen data value would have been locally rejecting, i.e. if the second flag is 1 and the original state is in $\overline{F}_\mathrm{l}$. Formally, if $\hat{F}_\mathrm{l} = (Q \times B \times \{0\}) \cup (\overline{F}_\mathrm{l} \times B \times \{1\})$.

The transition function $\hat{\delta} : \hat{Q} \times (\hat{Q} \cup \{\bot\}) \times \Sigma \to 2^{\hat{Q}}$ is defined as follows. We use _ as placeholder for an arbitrary, irrelevant value.

$$\hat{\delta}((q, 0, \_), (q', \_, \_), a) := \{(\delta(q, q', a), 0, 0)\} \tag{1}$$

$$\hat{\delta}((q, 0, \_), \bot, a) := \{(\delta(q, \bot, a), 0, 0), (\delta(q, \bot, a), 1, 1)\} \tag{2}$$

$$\hat{\delta}((q, 1, \_), (q', \_, x), a) := \{(\delta(q, q', a), 1, x)\} \tag{3}$$

$$\hat{\delta}((q, 1, \_), \bot, a) := \{(\delta(q, \bot, a), 1, 0)\} \tag{4}$$

Equations 1 and 2 capture the case, that no data value has been guessed so far. In case of Equation 1 the present data value is not new. In case of Equation 2 the present data value is new. Thus, the automaton can progress just as for Equation 1 or choose to guess the present data value. Equations 3 and 4 capture that a data value has already been guessed. In case of Equation 3 the present data value is not new and the first flag in the global and the second flag in the local state have to be propagated. Thereby the information, that a value has been guessed is propagated globally, and the information, which value has been guessed is propagated locally. In case of Equation 4 the present data value is new and the first flag in the global state has to be propagated. As the value is new, it can not be the chosen value and thus the second flag is set to 0.   □

With the emptiness check for CMA, their closure under union and intersection [2,3] and the complement construction above, we can decide language inclusion and equivalence of dCMA and its subclasses.

Corollary 2. *Language inclusion and equivalence of dCMA, dDA and tDA is decidable.*

3   Learning Transparent Data Automata

In this section we develop learning algorithms for tDA. We first recall the classical active learning procedure, and a variation with inconclusive answers to membership queries along the lines of [5]. Based on these we show how the class automaton of some tDA can be learned assuming the base automaton is known. Then, we provide an algorithm for learning the base automaton assuming the class automaton is known. Finally, we combine the two developed approaches to obtain a learning procedure for a completely unknown tDA.

3.1   Learning of Finite Automata

The learning algorithm L*. Angluin's learning algorithm, called L* [1], is designed for learning a regular language, $L \subseteq \Sigma^*$, by constructing a minimal DFA $\mathcal{A}$ accepting precisely L. In this algorithm a *learner*, who initially knows nothing about L, is trying to learn L by asking an *oracle* (also called the *teacher*), that knows L, two kinds of queries: A *membership query* for a word $u \in \Sigma^*$ is the question whether u is in L. Given a DFA $\tilde{\mathcal{A}}$ as a *hypothesis*, an *equivalence query* is the question whether $\tilde{\mathcal{A}}$ is correct, i.e. $\mathcal{L}(\tilde{\mathcal{A}}) = L$. The oracle answers *yes* if $\tilde{\mathcal{A}}$ is correct, or else provides a *positive* or *negative counter-example* u from $L \setminus \mathcal{L}(\tilde{\mathcal{A}})$ or $\mathcal{L}(\tilde{\mathcal{A}}) \setminus L$, respectively.

The learner maintains a prefix-closed set $U \subseteq \Sigma^*$ of prefixes, which are candidates for identifying states, and a suffix-closed set $V \subseteq \Sigma^*$ of suffixes, which are used to distinguish such states. The sets U and V are extended when needed during the algorithm. The learner poses membership queries for all words in $(U \cup U\Sigma)V$, and organizes the results into a *table* $T : (U \cup U\Sigma) \times V \rightarrow \{\checkmark, \times\}$ where $(U \cup U\Sigma)$ are the row and V the column labels, respectively, and $\checkmark$ represents *accepted* and $\times$ *not accepted*. Where convenient, we write $T(u)$ for the complete row in T indexed by $u \in U \cup U\Sigma$.

When T is *closed*, i.e. for each $u \in U$, $a \in \Sigma$ there is a $u' \in U$ such that $T(ua) = T(u')$, and *consistent*, i.e. $T(u) = T(u')$ implies $T(ua) = T(u'a)$, the learner constructs a hypothesis $\tilde{\mathcal{A}} = (Q, q_0, \delta, F)$, where $Q = \{T(u) \mid u \in U\}$ is the set of distinct rows, q_0 is the row $T(\epsilon)$, δ is defined by $\delta(T(u), a) = T(ua)$, and $F = \{T(u) \mid u \in U, T(u)(\epsilon) = \checkmark\}$. The hypothesis is posed as an equivalence query to the oracle. If the answer is *yes*, the learning procedure is completed, otherwise the returned counter-example $c \in \Sigma^*$ is used to extend U by adding all prefixes of c to U, and subsequent membership queries are performed in order to make the new table closed and consistent producing a new hypothesis.

Concerning complexity, it can easily be seen that the number of membership queries can be bounded by $O(kn^2m)$, where n is the number of states of the automaton to learn, k is the size of the alphabet, and m is the length of the longest counter-example.

Learning from inexperienced teacher. In the setting of an *inexperienced teacher*, membership queries are no longer answered only by *yes* or *no*, but also by *don't know*, denoted ?. Angluin's algorithm can easily be adapted to work with an inexperienced teacher and we list the necessary changes [5]. The table can now also contain ?, i.e., $T : (U \cup U\Sigma) \times V \to \{\checkmark, \times, ?\}$. For $u, u' \in (U \cup U\Sigma)$, we say that rows $T(u)$ and $T(v)$ *look similar*, denoted by $T(u) \equiv T(u')$, iff, for all $v \in V$, $T(u)(v) \neq ?$ and $T(u')(v) \neq ?$ implies $T(u)(v) = T(u')(v)$. Otherwise, we say that $T(u)$ and $T(v)$ are *obviously different*. We call T *weakly closed* if for each $u \in U$, $a \in \Sigma$ there is a $u' \in U$ such that $T(ua) \equiv T(u')$, and *weakly consistent* if $T(u) \equiv T(u')$ implies $T(ua) \equiv T(u'a)$. Angluin's algorithm works as before, but using the weak notions of closed and consistent. While extracting a DFA from a weakly closed and weakly consistent table is no longer straightforward, it is possible using techniques developed by Biermann and Feldman [11] that infer an automaton from a sample set $S = (S^{\checkmark}, S^{\times})$ consisting of positive and negative examples $S^{\checkmark}$ and $S^{\times}$, respectively. As there is no longer a unique automaton for a weakly closed and weakly consistent table, the overall complexity of identifying a given automaton is no longer polynomial in the number of equivalence queries but may be exponential (see [5] for details).

3.2   Learning the Class Automaton

Let the base automaton $\mathcal{A}$ of some tDA $\mathcal{D} = (\mathcal{A}, \mathcal{B})$ over an alphabet Σ be known. For learning the class automaton $\mathcal{B}$ we can employ the classical L* algorithm as presented above. The algorithm, however, assumes direct access to an oracle for $\mathcal{B}$ that answers membership and equivalence queries. Given such an oracle for $\mathcal{D}$, we can answer queries for $\mathcal{B}$ using queries for $\mathcal{D}$ as follows.

Membership. To answer a membership query $u \overset{?}{\in} \mathcal{B}$ for $u \in \Sigma^*$, we can directly reuse the answer of the oracle for the query $\binom{u}{1} \overset{?}{\in} \mathcal{D}$. $\binom{u}{1} \in \mathcal{D}$ implies $u \in \mathcal{B}$ since u is a class string of $\binom{u}{1}$. Further, if $\binom{u}{1} \notin \mathcal{D}$ then $u \notin \mathcal{B}$ due to the transparency property $\mathcal{B} \subseteq \mathcal{A}$ meaning that $\mathcal{A}$ cannot reject u while $\mathcal{B}$ accepts it.

Algorithm 1. Learning the class automaton

1: **function** LEARNB(Automaton $\mathcal{A}$)
2:     **function** ISMEMBERB(Word u)
3:         **return** ISMEMBERD($\binom{u}{11}$)
4:     **function** ISEQUIVALENTB(Automaton $\tilde{\mathcal{B}}$)
5:         result := ISEQUIVALENTD($(\mathcal{A}, \tilde{\mathcal{B}})$)
6:         **if** ISPOSITIVECE(result) **then**
7:             **for all** c $\in$ CLASSSTRINGS(result) **do**
8:                 **if** $c \notin \tilde{\mathcal{B}}$ **then return** ASPOSITIVECE(c)
9:         **else if** ISNEGATIVECE(result) **then**
10:          **for all** c $\in$ CLASSSTRINGS(result) **do**
11:              **if** $\neg$ISMEMBERB(c) **then return** ASNEGATIVECE(c)
12:         **else return** true
13:     **return** ANGLUIN(ISMEMBERB, ISEQUIVALENTB)

Equivalence. To obtain the answer to an equivalence query $\tilde{\mathcal{B}} \stackrel{?}{\equiv} \mathcal{B}$ for some hypothesis $\tilde{\mathcal{B}}$ we can pose the query $(\mathcal{A}, \tilde{\mathcal{B}}) \stackrel{?}{\equiv} (\mathcal{A}, \mathcal{B})$ to the oracle for $\mathcal{D}$. A positive answer confirms that $\tilde{\mathcal{B}}$ is correct. A negative counter-example $c \in (\mathcal{A}, \tilde{\mathcal{B}})$ is accepted by the hypothesis but should be rejected. Thus, at least one of its class strings must be wrongly accepted by $\tilde{\mathcal{B}}$ since $\mathcal{A}$ is correct. To find it, we consider all class strings $u \in c\lfloor \cap \tilde{\mathcal{B}}$ accepted by the hypothesis and use membership queries $u \stackrel{?}{\in} \mathcal{B}$ for identifying one that must be rejected. This is returned as counter-example $\tilde{\mathcal{B}}$.

If $c \notin (\mathcal{A}, \tilde{\mathcal{B}})$ is a positive counter-example there must be some class string of c rejected by $\tilde{\mathcal{B}}$ whereas all should be accepted. Hence, we check all class strings $u \in c\lfloor$ for one being rejected by $\tilde{\mathcal{B}}$ to find the counter-example that is returned.

Algorithm 1 takes a base automaton as input and calls Angluin's L*, providing the functions for membership and equivalence queries. We assume the functions ISMEMBERD and ISEQUIVALENTD to be globally defined and represent the query to the oracle for $\mathcal{D}$. We suppose that ISEQUIVALENTD returns yes or either a positive or negative counter-example which can be checked by the functions ISPOSITIVECE and ISNEGATIVECE. The function CLASSSTRINGS takes a data word and returns all class strings of it.

Example. As an example, consider the transparent data automata $\mathcal{D} = (\mathcal{A}, \mathcal{B})$ for the printer example from Section 1 and assume $\mathcal{B}$ is unknown. L* first asks queries $\mathcal{B}$ for the empty word ϵ which is translated to the empty data word ϵ. Since $\mathcal{D}$ accepts, the answer is positive. For closing the table, we need to answer queries for all words in $\{\epsilon\} \cdot \Sigma$. Since $\binom{r}{1}, \binom{s}{1}, \binom{t}{1} \notin \mathcal{D}$ the answer is negative for all of them and we obtain a new state for which we choose e.g. r as representative. To close the table, L* asks for the words in $r \cdot \Sigma$ and we answer them by posing queries $\binom{rr}{1}, \binom{rs}{1}, \binom{rt}{1} \stackrel{?}{\in} \mathcal{D}$ to the oracle which are all negative. The resulting table consists of $U = \{\epsilon, r\}$ and $V = \{\epsilon\}$ with $T(\epsilon) = \checkmark$ and $T(r) = ✗$. It is closed and consistent and yields the hypothesis $\tilde{\mathcal{B}}_1$ shown in Figure 3a.

For the equivalence query, we ask $(\mathcal{A}, \tilde{\mathcal{B}}_1) \overset{?}{\equiv} \mathcal{D}$ and obtain a counter-example, say $c = \binom{rrstst}{122211} \in \mathcal{D}$. From the class strings $c\!\downarrow = \{rst\}$ we obtain rst as a positive counter-example as it is rejected by $\tilde{\mathcal{B}}_1$ and return that to the L^* instance. The prefixes rst, rs are added to U and the table is filled using queries for rst, rs as well as all words from $\{rst, rs\} \cdot \Sigma$. Apart from rst we answer all of them negatively using the oracle for $\mathcal{D}$ as before. We have now $T(rs) = T(r)$ but $T(rs \cdot t) \neq T(r \cdot t)$ and resolve this inconsistency by adding t to V and fill the table using membership queries. The table is now closed and consistent, the hypothesis $\tilde{\mathcal{B}}_2$ is shown in Figure 3b.

Asking $(\mathcal{A}, \tilde{\mathcal{B}}_2) \overset{?}{\equiv} \mathcal{D}$ we obtain, e. g., the positive counter-example $\binom{rrrsstt}{1211212} \in \mathcal{D}$. Membership queries for all class strings $\{rrst, rst\}$ yield that $rrst$ is not in $\mathcal{B}$ but in $\tilde{\mathcal{B}}_2$ and we can provide $rrst$ as negative counter-example for $\tilde{\mathcal{B}}_2$. Consequently, $rrst$ and its prefixes are added to U, the table is filled and we observe first the inconsistency $T(r) = T(rr)/T(r \cdot st) \neq T(rr \cdot st)$. After adding st to V and filling the table we handle the second inconsistency $T(\epsilon) = T(rst)/T(\epsilon \cdot rst) \neq T(rst \cdot rst)$ similarly adding rst to V. We finally have $U = \{\epsilon, r, rst, rs, rrst, rrs, rr\}$ and $V = \{\epsilon, t, st, rst\}$ leading to the correct hypothesis (Figure 1b). Note that rr, rrs and $rrst$ have equal rows in T and are thus represented by the same state. The final table is presented as Table 1.

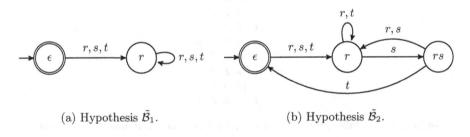

(a) Hypothesis $\tilde{\mathcal{B}}_1$.   (b) Hypothesis $\tilde{\mathcal{B}}_2$.

Fig. 3. Hypotheses while learning the class automaton $\mathcal{B}$ of the printer example

3.3   Learning the Base Automaton

In the previous section we assumed the base automaton $\mathcal{A}$ to be given and we now show how $\mathcal{A}$ can be learned when the class automaton $\mathcal{B}$ is known. The major difference is that we can not always answer membership queries for $\mathcal{A}$ conclusively. If some word is rejected due to the class automaton $\mathcal{B}$, the oracle for $\mathcal{D}$ will answer negatively but we do not gain any information on whether $\mathcal{A}$ also rejects. The approach (Algorithm 2) is therefore based on the learning procedure allowing for the additional answer *don't know* (**?**) [4,5].

Membership. To answer a membership query $u \overset{?}{\in} \mathcal{A}$ for a word $u \in \Sigma^*$ of length n, we consider the set $\mathsf{dw}(u)$ of all data words $\binom{u}{d_1 d_n}$ up to isomorphism on the data domain Δ. If there exists a data word $w \in \mathsf{dw}(u)$ where all class strings are accepted by $\mathcal{B}$, i.e. $w\!\downarrow \subseteq \mathcal{B}$, we can directly use the answer of the oracle for $\mathcal{D}$

		ε	t	st	rst
ε		✓	✗	✗	✓
r		✗	✗	✓	✗
rst		✓	✗	✗	✗
rs		✗	✓	✗	✗
rrst		✗	✗	✗	✗
rrs		✗	✗	✗	✗
rr		✗	✗	✗	✗
ε	r	✗	✗	✓	✗
	s	✗	✗	✗	✗
	t	✗	✗	✗	✗
r	r	✗	✗	✗	✗
	s	✗	✓	✗	✗
	t	✗	✗	✗	✗
rst	r	✗	✗	✗	✗
	s	✗	✗	✗	✗
	t	✗	✗	✗	✗
rs	r	✗	✗	✗	✗
	s	✗	✗	✗	✗
	t	✓	✗	✗	✗
rrst	r	✗	✗	✗	✗
	s	✗	✗	✗	✗
	t	✗	✗	✗	✗
rrs	r	✗	✗	✗	✗
	s	✗	✗	✗	✗
	t	✗	✗	✗	✗
rr	r	✗	✗	✗	✗
	s	✗	✗	✗	✗
	t	✗	✗	✗	✗

Table 1. The final table produced while learning the class automaton $\mathcal{B}$ of the printer example

to the query $w \stackrel{?}{\in} \mathcal{D}$ since acceptance of w, and therefore u, only depends on $\mathcal{A}$. If there is no such data word, we have to answer inconclusively (**?**).

Note that an inconclusive answer does not imply that the value is arbitrary. The answer of the base automaton does not matter *for acceptance* of a data word when the class automaton would always reject. However, choosing arbitrary answers, e.g., always no, can make the language that is factually learned non-regular. Hence, there would be no guarantee anymore that the learning procedure for the base automaton terminates as there might not exist an automaton with a finite state space.

Equivalence. To check a hypothesis $\tilde{\mathcal{A}}$ for equivalence we pose the query $(\tilde{\mathcal{A}}, \mathcal{B}) \stackrel{?}{\equiv} \mathcal{D}$ to the oracle. A positive answer confirms that $\tilde{\mathcal{A}}$ is correct. A positive or negative counter-example $w = \left(\begin{smallmatrix} u \\ d_1 d_n \end{smallmatrix}\right)$ directly yields the respective counter-example u for $\tilde{\mathcal{A}}$. If w is rejected by $(\tilde{\mathcal{A}}, \mathcal{B})$ but should be accepted, $\mathcal{B}$ has to accept all class strings and this is the case as $\mathcal{B}$ is correct. Thus $\tilde{\mathcal{A}}$ wrongly rejects u. Oth-

---

Algorithm 2. Learning the base automaton

1: **function** LEARNA(Automaton $\mathcal{B}$)
2:     **function** ISMEMBERA(Word u)
3:         **for all** $w \in \mathsf{dw}(u)$ **do**
4:             **if** $w\lfloor \subseteq \mathcal{B}$ **then return** ISMEMBERD(w)
5:         **return** ?
6:     **function** ISEQUIVALENTA(Automaton $\tilde{\mathcal{A}}$)
7:         result := ISEQUIVALENTD$((\tilde{\mathcal{A}}, \mathcal{B}))$
8:         **if** ISPOSITIVECE(result) **then**
9:             **return** ASPOSITIVECE(STRINGPROJECTION(result))
10:        **else if** ISNEGATIVECE(result) **then**
11:            **return** ASNEGATIVECE(STRINGPROJECTION(result))
12:        **else return** true
13:     **return** ANGLUININEXP(ISMEMBERA, ISEQUIVALENTA)

---

erwise, if w is accepted by the hypothesis but should be rejected, all class strings of w are accepted by $\mathcal{B}$. Hence, it must be $\mathcal{A}$ that causes the rejection of w by rejecting its string projection u. The function STRINGPROJECTION takes a data word and returns the string projection of it.

Note that we stop learning the base automaton as soon as the hypothesis $\tilde{\mathcal{A}}$ is equivalent to $\mathcal{A}$ in the context of $\mathcal{B}$. That is, $(\tilde{\mathcal{A}}, \mathcal{B})$ is a DA equivalent to $\mathcal{D}$ even though $\tilde{\mathcal{A}}$ and $\mathcal{A}$ are not necessarily language-equivalent.

L* with guided search. The setting of learning an automaton with potentially inconclusive membership queries does, in principle, work independently of the amount of conclusive answers. However, if many membership queries are answered inconclusively, i.e., the table is mostly filled by **?**, the algorithm essentially learns from counter-examples.

In our setting, we can improve the procedure using $\mathcal{B}$. L* explores the state space of the unknown automaton by following single edges: Inconsistencies in the table are generated by appending single letters to the access strings in U, i.e. asking additional membership queries for $U\Sigma$. A conclusive answer to these queries, however, is only possible if there is (by chance) an assignment of data values to the generated prefix s.t. all class strings are accepted by $\mathcal{B}$.

Hence it is reasonable to extend the prefixes $u \in U$ not only by the single letters from Σ but also by possibly longer suffixes that guarantee that there is indeed an assignment of data values s.t. all class strings are accepted by $\mathcal{B}$. For $u \in \Sigma^*$ we therefore let $\mathsf{ext}_{\mathcal{B}}(u)$ be the set of shortest suffixes $v \in \Sigma^*$ that can be appended to u s.t. there is a data word $\binom{uv}{d_1 d_n}$ that is not rejected locally, i.e. $\binom{uv}{d_1 d_n}\lfloor \subseteq \mathcal{B}$. By short we mean that the extensions of the single class strings are as short as possible to be accepted by $\mathcal{B}$. Formally, for $c \in \Sigma^*$, let $\mathsf{short}_{\mathcal{B}}(c) = \{v \in \Sigma^* \mid cv \in \mathcal{B}$ and $\forall_{v' \in \Sigma^*, |v'|<|v|} : cv' \notin \mathcal{B}\}$ be the shortest extensions of c accepted by $\mathcal{B}$ and $\bigsqcup_i L_i$ be the shuffle of (finitely many) languages $L_i \subseteq \Sigma^*$. Then $\mathsf{ext}_{\mathcal{B}}(u) := \bigcup_{w \in \mathsf{dw}(u)} \bigsqcup_{c \in w\lfloor} \mathsf{short}_{\mathcal{B}}(c)$ and additionally to filling the table for $U \cdot \Sigma$, as standard L* does, we also consider $U \cdot \mathsf{ext}_{\mathcal{B}}(u)$ for all $u \in U\Sigma$.

Example. We consider again the printer example (Section 1) and apply Algorithm 2 for learning the base automaton $\mathcal{A}$. The first query for the empty word ϵ gives a positive answer. The table is closed with $\{\epsilon\}\Sigma$. We must answer the respective queries with **?** since the only data words are $\binom{r}{1}, \binom{s}{1}, \binom{t}{1}$ for which the class strings are rejected by $\mathcal{B}$.

In the guided search step we do not find shortest extensions of s, t yielding definite results. For r we find st since $\binom{rst}{111} \lfloor = \{rst\} \subseteq \mathcal{B}$ which is added to V. For filling the table queries $st, sst, tst, rst \stackrel{?}{\in} \mathcal{A}$ have to be answered. We answer with **?** for st, sst, tst since no data values can be found to produce a query for $\mathcal{D}$ but posing $\binom{rst}{111} \stackrel{?}{\in} \mathcal{D}$ yields that $rst \in \mathcal{A}$.

The table is now weakly closed and weakly consistent giving $S_1 = (\{\epsilon, rst\}, \{\})$ as sample set and thereby the trivial hypothesis $\tilde{\mathcal{A}}_1$ accepting Σ^*. For the equivalence check, we pose $(\tilde{\mathcal{A}}_1, \mathcal{B}) \stackrel{?}{\equiv} \mathcal{D}$ to the oracle that returns a negative counter-example, e.g. $\binom{rrsstt}{111111} \notin \mathcal{D}$. Adding the counter-example to U and proceeding until the table is again weakly closed and weakly consistent yields Table 2 and the sample set $S_2 = (S_2^{\checkmark}, S_2^{\times})$ with

$$S_2^{\checkmark} = \{\epsilon, rst, rrstst, rrsrtstst, rrrststst\},$$
$$S_2^{\times} = \{rrsstt, rrssttrst, rrsstrtst, rrsstrstt, rrsrttst,$$
$$rrssrtstt, rrssrsttt, rrsrsttst, rrsrssttt, rrsrstst,$$
$$rrsrtsstt, rrrssttst, rrrstsstt, rrrsssttt\}.$$

The hypothesis $\tilde{\mathcal{A}}_2$ must now have at least three states and could thus already be correct.

3.4   Complete Learning of tDA

We have seen so far how both components, the base and the class automaton can be learned using the respective other. Now the approaches can be interleaved to obtain a complete learning procedure for transparent data automata as follows.

The two learning procedures for the base and the class automaton are started independently. Both processes synchronize only on equivalence queries. After providing a hypothesis, the process has to wait for the other process to come up with a hypothesis as well. These two form the query $(\tilde{\mathcal{A}}, \tilde{\mathcal{B}}) = \tilde{\mathcal{D}} \stackrel{?}{\equiv} \mathcal{D}$ which is posed to the oracle for $\mathcal{D}$. From a counter-example for $\tilde{\mathcal{D}}$ we can always generate a counter-example for at least one of the processes. This ensures that the hypothesis $\tilde{\mathcal{D}}$ improves in every step. If a counter-example is derived for only one of the processes, the respective other has to wait until a new hypothesis is provided.

Algorithm 3 presents the handling of membership and equivalence queries. The coordination is done by the function ANGLUINPARALLEL that takes the functions for handling both types of membership queries and the equivalence query for the complete hypothesis $\tilde{\mathcal{D}}$. For better readability, Algorithm 3 is simplified in the sense that it generates a counter-example for exactly one of the learning tasks, even though it may be possible to obtain one for each. Such parallelization and also the synchronization part that is omitted here can be implemented in a straight forward manner using, e.g., threads and message channels or an actor model.

Membership. Membership queries for the class automaton $\mathcal{B}$ can be handled as before since the base automaton $\mathcal{A}$ is not involved. For answering membership queries for $\mathcal{A}$ Algorithm 2 looked up a set of words in $\mathcal{B}$ which is now simulated using membership queries for $\mathcal{B}$ instead of a direct lookup.

Equivalence. The individual equivalence queries are handled together forming a hypothesis $\tilde{\mathcal{D}} = (\tilde{\mathcal{A}}, \tilde{\mathcal{B}})$ for $\mathcal{D}$. A positive answer confirms that the single hypotheses are correct. When the oracle provides a counter-example $w \in (\Sigma \times \Delta)^*$ we consider the following two cases.

If $w \in \tilde{\mathcal{D}}$ is a negative counter-example we check each class string $c \in w\!\downarrow$ of w that is rejected by the hypothesis $\tilde{\mathcal{B}}$ for membership in $\mathcal{B}$. That way we either find a counter-example for $\tilde{\mathcal{B}}$ and can proceed with learning $\mathcal{B}$ or $\tilde{\mathcal{B}}$ behaves correctly on w and its string projection $\mathsf{str}(w)$ must then be a counter-example for $\tilde{\mathcal{A}}$ that is used to continue learning $\mathcal{A}$.

A positive counter-example $w \notin \tilde{\mathcal{D}}$ is wrongly rejected by the hypothesis and we check if some class string $c \in w\!\downarrow$ of w is rejected by $\tilde{\mathcal{B}}$. If there is such c, it is supposed to be accepted and returned as counter-example for $\tilde{\mathcal{B}}$. Otherwise $\tilde{\mathcal{B}}$ correctly accepts all class strings of w and thus $\tilde{\mathcal{A}}$ must have wrongly rejected the string projection $\mathsf{str}(w)$ which we return as counter-example for $\tilde{\mathcal{A}}$. Note that with every equivalence query to the oracle we gain a counter-example for at least one of the sub-processes and as soon as one of the sub-processes learned the correct automaton, it does not change anymore until the other process finishes as well.

Example. We illustrate the complete learning procedure using again the printer example as above. The process for learning $\mathcal{B}$ is started and proceeds as described in Section 3.2 until the first hypothesis $\tilde{\mathcal{B}}_1$ is constructed. Next, the learning procedure for $\mathcal{A}$ starts as described in Section 3.3 except that for checking $r, s, t \in \mathcal{B}$, membership queries for $\mathcal{B}$ are used.

For the guided search, we use $\tilde{\mathcal{B}}_1$ to find suffixes for r, s, t. While knowing $\mathcal{B}$ led to the suffix st for r, we now obtain no suitable suffix at all as $\tilde{\mathcal{B}}_1$ does not accept any continuation. We still have $U = V = \{\epsilon\}$ and $T(u) = ?$ for all $u \in U\Sigma$. The sample sets are now $S_1 = (\{\epsilon\}, \emptyset)$ but that generates the same hypothesis $\tilde{\mathcal{A}}_1$ accepting Σ^*.

As $\tilde{\mathcal{B}}_1$ rejects any class string, the equivalence query $(\tilde{\mathcal{A}}_1, \tilde{\mathcal{B}}_1) \stackrel{?}{\equiv} \mathcal{D}$ returns a positive counter-example, e.g. $\binom{rst}{111} \in \mathcal{D}$. The string projection rst is a positive counter-example for $\tilde{\mathcal{B}}_1$ and the process proceeds as before finally coming up with hypothesis $\tilde{\mathcal{B}}_2$.

As rst is already accepted by $\tilde{\mathcal{A}}_1$, it is no counter-example for learning $\mathcal{A}$. The next equivalence query is $(\tilde{\mathcal{A}}_1, \tilde{\mathcal{B}}_2) \stackrel{?}{\equiv} \mathcal{D}$ yielding a negative counter-example, e.g. $\binom{rrsstt}{121212} \notin \mathcal{D}$. The only class string is rst which is accepted by $\mathcal{B}$ and so we do not obtain a counter-example for $\tilde{\mathcal{B}}_2$ but keep the hypothesis.

Table 2. The table produced while learning the base automaton $\mathcal{A}$ in the example presented in Section 3.3

Algorithm 3. Learning transparent data automata

1: **function** LEARNAB( )
2:     **function** ISMEMBERA(Word u)
3:         **for all** $w \in$ DATAWORDS(u) **do**
4:             **if** $\forall_{c \in w \downarrow}$: ISMEMBERB(c) **then return** ISMEMBERD(w)
5:         **return** ?
6:     **function** ISMEMBERB(Word u)
7:         **return** ISMEMBERD($\binom{u}{11}$)
8:     **function** ISEQUIVALENTAB(Automaton $\tilde{\mathcal{A}}$, Automaton $\tilde{\mathcal{B}}$)
9:         result := ISEQUIVALENTD($(\tilde{\mathcal{A}}, \tilde{\mathcal{B}})$)
10:         **if** ISPOSITIVECE(result) **then**
11:             **for all** $u \in$ result$\downarrow$ **do**
12:                 **if** $u \notin \tilde{\mathcal{B}}$ **then return** ASPOSITIVECEFORB(u)
13:             **return** ASPOSITIVECEFORA(STRINGPROJECTION(result))
14:         **else if** ISNEGATIVECE(result) **then**
15:             **for all** $u \in$ CLASSSTRINGS(result) **do**
16:                 **if** $\neg$ISMEMBERB(u) **then return** ASNEGATIVECEFORB(u)
17:             **return** ASNEGATIVECEFORA(STRINGPROJECTION(result))
18:         **else return** true
19:     **return** ANGLUINPARALLEL(ISMEMBERA, ISMEMBERB, ISEQUIVALENTAB)

For $\tilde{\mathcal{A}}$, $rrsstt \in \tilde{\mathcal{A}}_1$ must be a negative counter-example because $\tilde{\mathcal{B}}_2$ behaved correctly on all class strings. The process for learning $\mathcal{A}$ therefore adds $rrsstt$ and all prefixes to the table (U). In our case, the additional suffixes found by using $\tilde{\mathcal{B}}_2$ for the guided search are the same as we got using $\mathcal{B}$ in Section 3.3. The obtained table is thus also the same and we obtain a hypothesis with at least three states for which we assume to choose the correct one $\tilde{\mathcal{A}}_2 \equiv \mathcal{A}$

The following equivalence query $(\tilde{\mathcal{A}}_2, \tilde{\mathcal{B}}_2) \stackrel{?}{\equiv} \mathcal{D}$ yields a negative counter-example, e.g. $\binom{rrrstst}{1212211} \notin \mathcal{D}$. The class strings are $rrst$ and rst and querying them for membership in $\mathcal{B}$ yields $rrst \notin \mathcal{B}$ as negative counter-example for $\tilde{\mathcal{B}}_2$. As before, this leads to the correct hypothesis $\tilde{\mathcal{B}}_3 = \mathcal{B}$.

Theorem 5 (Termination). *The learning procedures (Algorithms 1, 2 and 3) terminate.*

The algorithms employ Angluin's learning algorithm L* which terminates for regular languages [1], also in the setting of possibly inconclusive answers by the oracle [5,11]. These results apply in our setting as the base and the class automata are finite automata and the algorithms simulate an oracle for the respective regular languages.

4 Conclusion

In this paper, we have presented an active learning algorithm for a subclass of deterministic data automata, which we called transparent data automata. To put this class into a general picture, we have shown that despite data automata being equally expressive to class memory automata, deterministic data automata are a strict subclass of deterministic class memory automata. For the latter, we have shown that their complement is within the class of (non-deterministic) data automata, which comes with a decidable emptiness problem. Thus, equivalence of deterministic class memory automata and thus transparent data automata is decidable, which guarantees that the oracle used within the active learning algorithm is in principle realizable. The transparency condition for data automata intuitively states that local behavior may not be restricted globally, following the idea that a single process should be able to operate especially when no further process is around.

Note that one could consider the case in which global behaviour is part of the local behaviour. Then, one would obtain a similar learning procedure without *don't knows* for the base automaton as for the local automaton in the transparent case. As we do not see any valuable practical setting in which this is satisfied, we do not list the results here.

References

1. Angluin, D.: Learning regular sets from queries and counterexamples. Inf. Comput. 75(2), 87–106 (1987)
2. Bojanczyk, M., David, C., Muscholl, A., Schwentick, T., Segoufin, L.: Two-variable logic on data words. ACM Trans. Comput. Log. 12(4), 27 (2011)
3. Björklund, H., Schwentick, T.: On notions of regularity for data languages. Theor. Comput. Sci. 411(4-5), 702–715 (2010)
4. Grinchtein, O., Leucker, M., Piterman, N.: Inferring network invariants automatically. In: Furbach, U., Shankar, N. (eds.) IJCAR 2006. LNCS (LNAI), vol. 4130, pp. 483–497. Springer, Heidelberg (2006)
5. Leucker, M., Neider, D.: Learning minimal deterministic automata from inexperienced teachers. In: Margaria, T., Steffen, B. (eds.) ISoLA 2012, Part I. LNCS, vol. 7609, pp. 524–538. Springer, Heidelberg (2012)
6. Kaminski, M., Francez, N.: Finite-memory automata. Theor. Comput. Sci. 134(2), 329–363 (1994)
7. Jonsson, B.: Learning of automata models extended with data. In: Bernardo, M., Issarny, V. (eds.) SFM 2011. LNCS, vol. 6659, pp. 327–349. Springer, Heidelberg (2011)
8. Howar, F., Steffen, B., Jonsson, B., Cassel, S.: Inferring canonical register automata. In: Kuncak, V., Rybalchenko, A. (eds.) VMCAI 2012. LNCS, vol. 7148, pp. 251–266. Springer, Heidelberg (2012)

9. Bollig, B., Habermehl, P., Leucker, M., Monmege, B.: A fresh approach to learning register automata. In: Béal, M.-P., Carton, O. (eds.) DLT 2013. LNCS, vol. 7907, pp. 118–130. Springer, Heidelberg (2013)
10. Esparza, J., Leucker, M., Schlund, M.: Learning workflow Petri nets. Fundam. Inform. 113(3-4), 205–228 (2011)
11. Biermann, A.W., Feldman, J.A.: On the synthesis of finite-state machines from samples of their behaviour. IEEE Transactions on Computers 21, 592–597 (1972)

A Programming Language for Spatial Distribution of Net Systems

Paweł Sobociński and Owen Stephens

ECS, University of Southampton, UK

Abstract. Petri nets famously expose concurrency directly in their statespace. Building on the work on the compositional algebra of nets with boundaries, we show how an algebraic decomposition allows one to expose both concurrency and spatial distribution in the statespace.

Concretely, we introduce a high-level domain specific language (DSL), PNBml, for the construction of nets in terms of their components. We use PNBml to express several well-known parametric examples.

Keywords: Modelling approaches, system design using nets, net-based semantical, logical and algebraic calculi.

Introduction

Composition of nets is of fundamental importance in constructing models of large systems [22]. A successful theory must combine simplicity, so as not to overburden users with unnecessary technicalities, with a rigorous formal semantics that can be harnessed for reasoning and automated verification, for example via model checking or theorem proving. The interplay between simplicity and rigorous, practical foundations allows the development of modelling languages, tools and techniques that support the user in model design and evaluation, the elimination of bugs, verification, refinement and finally code generation and deployment. The field of compositional concurrent/distributed system specification thus collects insights and techniques from the various communities: models of concurrency, process algebra and programming languages, amongst others.

While Petri nets [20] were introduced in part to study chemical and physical phenomena, their applications until recently have been chiefly in computing. Their popularity is now extending to other disciplines, both scientific and industrial, where distributed, concurrent systems abound [11,15,28]. Their vivid graphical formalism is intuitive, and clearly expresses the concurrency inherent in the systems they model. This information is moreover crucial in verification tasks: for instance, partial order reduction that can alleviate the state-explosion problem. The applicability of such methods relies on the fact that in nets, unlike in mere (interleaving) transition systems, *concurrency is explicit in their structure*: at any point in the computation, one can readily determine the enabled transitions that may be executed concurrently.

Process algebra [10,19] on the other hand, focusses on the study of syntax for component-wise composition of systems. The emphasis is usually on *compositionality*, whereby the behaviour of a composition system is defined exactly in

G. Ciardo and E. Kindler (Eds.): PETRI NETS 2014, LNCS 8489, pp. 150–169, 2014.

terms of its components' behaviour: there is no emergent behaviour when composing sub-systems, simplifying intuitive and formal reasoning. The practical focus is often on using behavioural pre-orders and equivalences to simplify global complexity. For the latter, the pre-orders and equivalences must be *congruences* with respect to the composition operation(s): one can switch two behaviourally equivalent components without affecting the behaviour of the system as a whole.

As opposed to process algebras, net models are often *monolithic*, with the entire system being modelled in one net. As opposed to Petri nets, the semantics of a process algebra specification is often given in terms of a transition system (TS), that "hides" the concurrency: a TS represents interleavings of concurrent events, thereby obscuring which events can occur concurrently.

In order to combine the advantages of both approaches, one needs to define composition operations on nets that:

- are as simple and intuitive for users as nets themselves,
- are supported by a suite of high-level specification languages and tools for modelling and verification,
- have a compositional formal semantics where typical behavioural pre-orders and equivalences are congruences, thus enabling the use techniques from process algebra,
- have an intuitive graphical presentation that qualitatively eases the task of modelling and quantitatively leads to efficient verification algorithms, for example through the use of partial order reduction.

There have been many proposals in the literature for net composition operators, some of which we discuss below. As observed by Reisig [22], many are quite technical and/or specific for a particular class of nets, making them inconvenient for use by practitioners. Some are equipped with a compositional semantics, yet no formalism has become standard nor widely used. The challenges of modelling large complex systems, given the increasing popularity of Petri nets in several fields, make the quest for a successful theory of net composition timely.

The algebra of Petri nets with boundaries [25,6,7] (PNB) gives a compositional algebra of Petri nets, allowing large nets to be constructed from smaller "components" in the style of process algebra. It features two associative but non-commutative composition operations, and it handles both 1-bounded elementary nets [25] as well as potentially infinite-state P/T nets [6]. The focus of research thus far has been on theory: for instance the algebra was shown to be compositional and lead to congruent behavioural pre-orders and equivalences. Moreover it was proved that all 1-bounded elementary nets can be composed from a small set of primitive PNBs (two nets that express a marked and unmarked place and eight primitive nets for "wiring" together transitions). In this paper, our aim is to demonstrate that PNBs are not merely a theoretical curiosity.

The "raw" algebra of PNBs is not convenient for describing real world systems directly. Syntactic repetition is unavoidable, and expressions soon grow to be unmanageably large; in a sense the algebra is too low-level, lacking abstraction techniques that give compact and expressive representations. In order to make progress in this direction, we use insights from the functional programming languages community: function abstraction, name binding, type-checking and iteration. The result is a Domain Specific Language, the *Petri Nets with Boundaries Meta Language* (PNBml), that is a central contribution of this paper. We show that programs written in PNBml allow us to construct PNB expressions, and thus nets in a compositional fashion. Programming language features such as type-checking can catch simple, yet important specification bugs.

The language is expressive enough to express all of the parametric examples we have come across in the literature. In order to support our claims, we include programs for a representative selection, including several of Corbett's [9]. These have proved to be popular as benchmark for model checkers and one immediate convenience is that our PNBml programs can generate arbitrary instances as input to a model checker. The type system and intuitive geometric nature of PNBs mean that using PNBml is more convenient and less likely to lead to specification errors than an ad-hoc solution for generating such nets.

Our chief claim is that PNBs retain the distinct benefits of process algebra and Petri nets - compositional reasoning and descriptive graphical representation, whilst allowing for interaction between (sub-)components of a larger net. In this paper, we take several steps to show that the algebra of PNB has what it takes to become a mainstream low-level foundation for the modular specification of complex concurrent and distributed systems. Concretely:

- we show that the algebra of PNBs can be used to write natural specification of realistic systems,
- we introduce of a high-level DSL called PNBml. Programs in PNBml evaluate to PNB expressions, yet PNBml provides a more expressive and convenient setting to specify realistic, parametric systems,
- we provide parametric PNBml programs that generate several well-known examples from the literature.

In our discussion above we have focussed on qualitative issues, and these indeed are an important consideration in this paper. The theoretically minded researcher or tool builder may ask what one gains by writing a PNB expression rather than a global net, apart from the convenience of a program that generates examples of arbitrary size. We believe that, just as one gains techniques such as partial order methods through the explicit treatment of concurrency in the statespace of nets, one can gain additional insight and techniques through expressing a system as an explicit network of synchronised Petri nets. As we show in our examples, the algebra allows the specification of systems constructed from spatially separated components, we have made initial investigations into how this information can be exploited by model checkers [27,26]: briefly, identifying identical components allows *memoisation* to be used when calculating and composing component reachability information. Further, component unreachability implies composite unreachability, allowing the reachability check to "fail fast".

Related work. While Petri nets are sometimes accused of being an inherently non-compositional theory, already Mazurkiewicz [17] defined a compositional algebra of nets, based on fusion of named transitions. While in PNBs it is also transitions that are fused, the composition operations are quite different in nature: for one, they are not commutative. Mazurkiewicz's composition is a commutative parallel composition in the spirit of CSP and CCS.

Similar operations were used for the development of the Petri Box calculus (PBC), a process algebra of labelled Petri nets [5]. The PBC features two kinds of composition: the first is a control-flow-style sequential composition that utilises certain places labelled as "entry" or "exit" places in order to enforce a computation order, the second a synchronising composition, introducing new transitions based on the global fusion of transitions with conjugate labels, whilst preserving the original transitions. The composition operations of PNBs, instead, are closely related to the geometry of nets, with no control-flow style composition and only local synchronisation through shared boundary ports.

Reisig's [22] simple composition of nets (SCN) is an elegantly simple way of composing nets and is conceptually quite close to our work. His nets, similarly to PNBs, have left and right interfaces that are made up of ports and ought not to be confused with notions of input and output, rather reflecting the structural geometry of nets. Differently, in SCN the interfaces typically expose places, whereas PNB interfaces expose only transitions. Another difference is that in PNB, composition $N_1 ; N_2$ is only defined when the right interface of N_1 is equal to the left interface of N_2. Nevertheless, Reisig's composition is intuitively quite similar to our composition operation ';'. While [22] demonstrates that the operation is very natural for composing real systems, the compositional semantic aspects of the theory have not, so far, been developed.

Component-wise construction of nets was emphasised by Kindler [14] who worked with a partial order semantics. The interfaces are a set of input and output places, that are connected with a transition when composed. The semantics was shown to be compositional with respect to this operation. Because the composition introduces additional transitions, it is not always clear how to divide a net into components with input and output places. This issue is also problematic in formalisms such as open Petri nets [4].

Structure of the paper. The remainder of this paper is organised as follows: in §1 we describe the component algebra of nets with boundaries, used to construct composite Petri nets. In §2 we motivate the use of a DSL for more convenient specification of net compositions, informally introducing our DSL, PNBml. In §3 we encode several of Corbett's parametric examples using our DSL. We formally introduce the syntax and semantics of PNBml in §4, and prove that type-correct expressions are guaranteed to correctly evaluate. Finally, we discuss future work and conclude in §5. We have tried to keep our presentation as intuitive and non-technical as possible, illustrating the theory with a large number of examples.

1 Nets with Boundaries

In this section we give an intuitive introduction to the algebra of Petri nets with boundaries [25,6,7] (PNB). The formal details can be found in [7]. There are two versions of the algebra, one for k-bounded elementary nets (in which the number of tokens at each place is restricted to a positive integer k, typically 1) and one for ordinary, potentially infinite-state P/T nets. While explanations and examples in this section can be understood in either version, the bounded version is typically used in applications, since it suffices to characterise the behaviour of safe nets, and its semantics is finite-state. The language of PNBs is inspired by the Span(Graph) algebra of transition systems [12] and the recent wave of formal graphical languages in various fields: for instance graphical languages for quantum information [2], boolean circuits [16], signal-flow graphs [23] etc.

We start by explaining the graphical notation used in this paper. The mathematical structure represented by a classical, unmarked Petri net is a *directed hypergraph*: a directed graph in which edges have arbitrarily many sources and targets. The usual graphical notation in net theory has a transition drawn as a rectangle with directed incoming and outgoing arrows, thus identifying the sources and targets. We use a different notation: instead of orienting transitions, each place is drawn as "directed," having an *in* and *out* port. Transitions are represented by undirected *links*—that is, sets of connected ports—that similarly identify the sources and targets. Indeed, the sources are those places to which it is connected via an out port, and the targets are those places to which it is connected via an in port. The out port of a place is represented by a small triangle pointing out of it, the in port by a triangle pointing out. This alternative notation is compact and particularly convenient when reasoning about transitions in composite PNBs. In order to distinguish individual links and increase legibility, transitions are drawn with a small perpendicular mark. For example, consider the graph with set of nodes $\{A, B, C, D\}$ and a single edge from $\{A, D\}$ to $\{B, C\}$. In the left part of Fig. 1 we illustrate the classical graphical notation of this structure, and the notation used in this paper is given on the right.

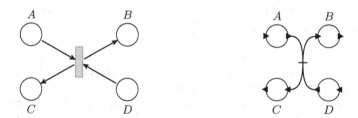

Fig. 1. Two ways of drawing hypergraphs

A PNB is a Petri net with extra structure: two finite ordinals of *boundary ports*, to which net transitions can connect. The two sets of ports are drawn, from top to bottom, on the left and right hand sides of an enclosing box. An example is given in Fig. 2: here the left set of boundary ports is empty and the right contains two ports. We use the notation $P : (0, 2)$ to mean that P is a PNB with left boundary of size 0 and right boundary of size 2. As in the classical graphical representation, the presence of a token at a place is represented by the small black disc. Now consider the two transitions of P, the first, t, which connects the first right boundary port with the out-port of place p, and the second, u, which connects the second right boundary port with the in-port of place q.

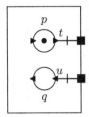

Fig. 2. An example PNB, $P : (0, 2)$

Intuitively, transitions t and u are not yet completely specified because they connect to a boundary port. Thus when composed into a larger net, t may result in several different transitions, all of which will include p in their pre-sets. There are two operations for composing PNBs: synchronisation along a common boundary and a non-commutative parallel composition.

The most interesting operation on PNBs is synchronisation along a common boundary; we illustrate this operation in Fig. 3. In each of the examples, the size of the right boundary of the first net agrees with the size of the left boundary of the second net—this is a general requirement for composition to be defined: nets that do not agree on the size of their common boundary cannot be synchronised. Given nets $X : (k, l)$ and $Y : (l, m)$, their composition is denoted $X ; Y : (k, m)$. In general, transitions of the composed net—called the *minimal synchronisations*—will be subsets of transitions of the individual component nets. We describe this operation informally with examples because the graphical presentation is quite intuitive.

Consider the top left quadrant of Fig. 3. The composed net $P ; Q$ has a transition $\{t, a\}$ that results from synchronising transitions t and a. The transition $\{t, a\}$ is now fully specified and will not be further altered because it is not connected to any boundary port in the composed net. The situation for transition $\{u, b\}$ is similar. In the top right quadrant, there are two separate transitions, c and d, that can synchronise with t. Both the choices are taken into account in the composed net and result in two different transitions $\{t, c\}$ and $\{t, d\}$, which intuitively mean that the transition t in the left net can synchronise in two different ways with transitions in the right net. The transition e does not connect to any places, only to the second boundary port. Thus the corresponding synchronised transition $\{u, e\}$ has precisely the same pre and post set as transition u. In the bottom left quadrant, the transitions t and u are fused into a single transition after composition. In the final example, u has no complementary transition to synchronise with and thus no composite transition results.

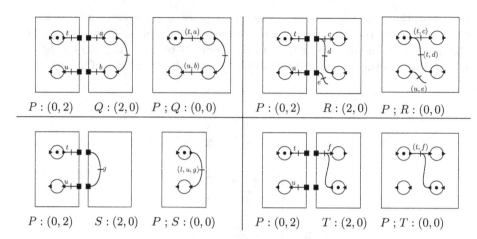

| $P : (0,2)$ | $Q : (2,0)$ | $P\,;Q : (0,0)$ | $P : (0,2)$ | $R : (2,0)$ | $P\,;R : (0,0)$ |

| $P : (0,2)$ | $S : (2,0)$ | $P\,;S : (0,0)$ | $P : (0,2)$ | $T : (2,0)$ | $P\,;T : (0,0)$ |

Fig. 3. Examples of compositions of PNBs

The second operation for composing PNBs is called tensor. Graphically, it can be described as "stacking" one net over the other, and intuitively, it acts as a non-communicating parallel composition. Differently from synchronisation along common boundary, any two nets can be tensored: given nets $X : (k, l)$ and $Y : (m, n)$, we have $X \otimes Y : (k + m, l + n)$. A simple example is given in Fig. 4. Both ';' and '$\otimes$' are associative, but neither is commutative.

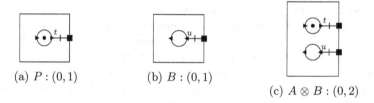

(a) $P : (0,1)$ (b) $B : (0,1)$ (c) $A \otimes B : (0,2)$

Fig. 4. Example of tensor

PNBs have a labelled transition semantics that is compositional in two ways. First, for any composable nets N and M, we have that $[\![N\,;M]\!] \cong [\![N]\!]\,;[\![M]\!]$. The relation $\cong$ is isomorphism of transition systems; on the left of the equation, ';' denotes composition of PNBs, illustrated in Fig. 3, while on the right, ';' denotes composition of their LTSs, see [7].

Similarly, we have that $[\![N \otimes M]\!] \cong [\![N]\!]\otimes[\![M]\!]$. This means that the *behaviour of a composed net depends only on the behaviours of its components*, an important principle in formal semantics of programming languages: there is no unexpected emergent behaviour in a composite net.

Secondly, the semantics is compositional w.r.t. several standard notions of behavioural equivalence $\sim$, (bisimilarity, weak bisimilarity, language equivalence, etc.): if $[\![N]\!] \sim [\![N']\!]$ then also $[\![N\,;M]\!] \sim [\![N'\,;M]\!]$, $[\![M\,;N]\!] \sim [\![M\,;N']\!]$, $[\![N \otimes M]\!] \sim [\![N' \otimes M]\!]$ and $[\![M \otimes N]\!] \sim [\![M \otimes N']\!]$, whenever the compositions are defined. In particular, this means that *behaviourally equivalent nets can be substituted for each other in any context*. This powerful principle of process algebra is useful when reasoning about the behaviour of complex systems.

1.1   Specifying Systems Algebraically

The examples we have considered thus far have not been of practical interest, having been chosen for their simplicity in order to illustrate the basic operations of PNBs. We now show how a more interesting system can be expressed with the algebra. We will consider other realistic examples in §3.

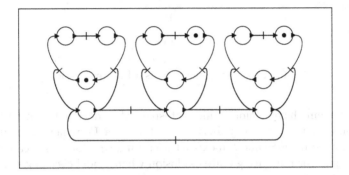

Fig. 5. Token ring network

Consider a model of simple token ring network, taken from [1], and illustrated in Fig. 5. Note that the (1-safe) net contains three identical components, which differ only in their "internal state" (the local marking). Initially, only the leftmost component can proceed: after it finishes its internal computation it relinquishes its token, meaning that the next component can proceed. The modular structure of the system is made explicit with the algebra of PNBs, illustrated in Fig. 6, where we show how the system can be expressed formally as a collection of component PNBs, wired together appropriately with simple connector PNBs. Indeed, when the expression (†) is evaluated by composing nets with boundaries, the resulting Petri net is isomorphic to the net in Fig. 5.

The example is an illustration of the fact that the operations for composing PNBs are closely linked to the underlying geometry of nets – the logical structure of the system is reflected in the structure of the algebraic expression.

1.2   Explicit Spatial Distribution

Using transition systems as a model of concurrency has a long history (see e.g. [3]). Indeed, the semantics of a Petri net is usually a transition system. Two reasons are often cited by researchers and practitioners in support of working with Petri nets, rather than, for example, products of automata. One is qualitative: the graphical syntax results in vivid, intuitive and informative models of real concurrent and distributed systems. A more empirical, quantitative reason is that

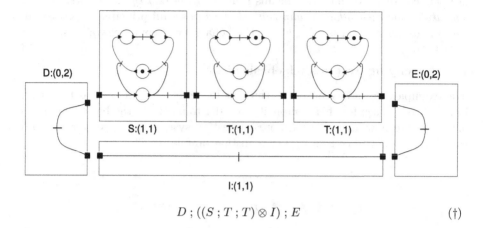

$$D \; ; \; ((S \; ; \; T \; ; \; T) \otimes I) \; ; \; E \tag{†}$$

Fig. 6. A token ring network as a PNB expression

transition systems have a monolithic statespace that does not contain inherent information about concurrency. Instead, a state of a Petri net, i.e. a marking, has structure from which one can extract useful information. This leads to practical techniques for mitigating state explosion when model checking, e.g. partial order reduction [18] and symmetry-reduction [24], that would not be possible if working with mere transitions systems.

$$\text{Transition system} \xleftarrow{\text{State graph}} \text{Petri net} \xleftarrow{\text{Composition}} \text{PNB expression} \tag{‡}$$

A PNB expression can be understood as representing a collection of Petri nets that synchronise with each other on shared transitions. Thus, while inheriting the explicit concurrency of Petri nets, PNB expressions add explicit spatial separation of state to individual component nets. Such a distribution can be obtained directly from the description of the problem and thus reflect the actual physical separation of a distributed system in terms of its components. Several of the examples in this paper (e.g. §3.3,§3.2 and §3.1) demonstrate this principle.

On the other hand, in general, a given Petri net can be described by several different PNB expressions, allowing a logical separation that may not necessarily reflect a physical separation (e.g. the n-bit counter example §3.4. One would usually not consider a counter to be distributed in this manner). Considering different *decompositions* [21] of a Petri net in this way, however, may be beneficial for algorithmic purposes, such as model checking.

Just as Petri nets can be evaluated into a transition system, forgetting the concurrency, a PNB expression can be composed into a Petri net, forgetting the spatial distribution. As we have shown, the close connection between the algebra and net geometry is a qualitative reason for working with PNB expressions. The information can also be exploited quantitatively [27,26] in order to improve the performance of model checking in suitable examples – the statespace of a PNB expression contains information both about concurrency (because the components are Petri nets) as well as spatial distribution.

2   A Language for Net Composition

In the previous section we demonstrated the algebraic description of Petri Net systems in terms of their component nets with boundaries. We now motivate using a Domain Specific Language (DSL), PNBml, that evaluates to the algebra of PNB, but adds expressive high-level functional programming language features.

Consider again the algebraic description of a token ring network, as illustrated in Fig. 6. An algebraic expression representing the network with 10 worker components can be written as follows:

$$D \; ; \; ((S \; ; \; T \; ; \; T \ldots ; \; T) \otimes id) \; ; \; E$$

where T appears precisely 10 times. However, this is clearly not scalable: for large numbers of components, or more complex components (that may themselves be formed of component compositions) it becomes inconvenient to construct such low-level expressions, and furthermore, ensure that they are correctly composed.

Indeed, consider the expression $t \; ; \; (t \otimes t)$ that we might (accidentally) write when composing task nets $t : (1,1)$. The result of evaluating this expression is undefined, since the two nets being sequentially composed have different size boundaries: it is easy to confirm that $t \otimes t : (2,2)$. Yet, for the sequential composition to be well-defined, we must have that $t \otimes t$ has boundaries $(1,i)$ for some i, a contradiction, indicating an invalid expression. To ensure we disallow such invalid expressions, we must use an appropriate notion of *type*, to ensure that incompatible nets are never composed during evaluation.

When describing complex components, we would like any repeated sub-components to be described only once, rather than each time they are used. For example, we might consider an extended token ring network model where each task, T, is comprised of two sub-components: T_1 and T_2. Using name binding, we might describe a sequence of such tasks by writing:

$$\textbf{bind } t = (t_1 \; ; \; t_2) \textbf{ in } t \; ; \; t \; ; \ldots ; \; t$$

Another improvement we can make is to abstract over procedures; in the previous example, we perform the procedure "sequentially compose with t" several times. Using a lambda notation common to functional programming languages, we might write this procedure as $\lambda x \, . \, x \; ; \; t$ that is, take a suitable net, represent it by the variable x and compose it with t. Using this abstraction, we can write:

$$\textbf{bind } t = (t_1 \; ; \; t_2) \textbf{ in}$$
$$\textbf{bind } addt = \lambda x \, . \, x \; ; \; t \textbf{ in}$$
$$addt \, (addt \, (\ldots (addt \, t)))$$

Finally, we introduce a way of compactly writing an expression to represent "apply a procedure n times to an initial argument", that is, allowing us to represent sequences of tasks as per Fig. 6, but with *parameterised* length.

The notion of repeating an same operation n times is described by "folding" over the number n and repeatedly performing the operation, until n becomes 0.

$$\textbf{bind } t = (t_1 \; ; \; t_2) \textbf{ in}$$
$$\textbf{bind } addt = \lambda x \; . \; x \; ; \; t \textbf{ in}$$
$$\textbf{fold } n \; addt \; t$$

where **fold** n f x is an expression that applies f to x, n times: $f(f(\dots(fx)))$. Other examples, such as all of those in §3, are naturally *parametric* and can thus be compactly represented for any particular parameter choice. As an example, we may represent the token ring network of Fig. 6, with the expression:

$$\textbf{bind } procs = \textbf{fold } 2 \; (\lambda x \; . \; x \; ; \; T) \; S \textbf{ in}$$
$$D \; ; \; (procs \otimes I) \; ; \; E$$

Since PNBml programs evaluate to PNB expressions, we can extend (‡):

$$\text{PNB expression} \xleftarrow{\text{Evaluation}} \text{PNBml program}$$

We defer formally introducing PNBml to §4. Instead, in the next section, we show how it is used to encode several well-known examples.

3 Examples

In the following examples we frequently use the "wiring" component nets of Fig. 7, which do not contain places, but are useful when connecting components.

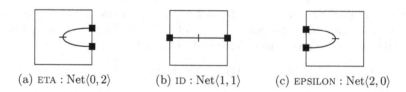

(a) ETA : $\text{Net}\langle 0, 2 \rangle$ (b) ID : $\text{Net}\langle 1, 1 \rangle$ (c) EPSILON : $\text{Net}\langle 2, 0 \rangle$

Fig. 7. Commonly-used wiring component nets

3.1 Hartstone

The Hartstone net models a program that starts i tasks in some order, lets them compute, before instructing them to stop them in the same order. In the original description of the problem, a central controller is directly connected to the i tasks. Using nets with boundaries, we can simplify this description: we construct i controllers, each responsible for a single task, with each controller passing signals to the next controller.

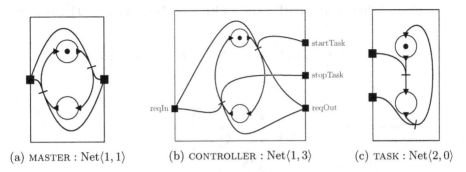

(a) MASTER : Net$\langle 1, 1 \rangle$ (b) CONTROLLER : Net$\langle 1, 3 \rangle$ (c) TASK : Net$\langle 2, 0 \rangle$

Fig. 8. Hartstone component nets

The PNBml expression to represent a Hartstone net, with i tasks is as follows:

$$HART(i) \stackrel{\text{def}}{=} \textbf{bind } contTask = \text{CONTROLLER} ; (\text{TASK} \otimes \text{ID}) \textbf{ in}$$
$$\textbf{bind } contTasks = \textbf{fold } i \ (\boldsymbol{\lambda} x : \text{Net}\langle 1, 1 \rangle . \ contTask ; x) \ \text{ID} \textbf{ in}$$
$$\text{ETA} ; (\text{MASTER} ; contTasks) \otimes \text{ID} ; \text{EPSILON}$$

This expression represents a sequence of controller/tasks, which are wired to a

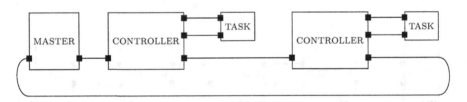

Fig. 9. Schematic of Hartstone(2)

master controller (that models the protocol of repeatedly starting all processes and then stopping them). Signals are looped back around (via ETA/EPSILON), such that MASTER receives the signal when all controllers have already received it. We show a schematic diagram of Hartstone for $i = 2$ in Fig. 9.

3.2   DAC: Divide and Conquer

The DAC nets [9] model the recursion in divide and conquer approaches to problem solving. The components of DAC are illustrated in Fig. 10. Each worker can chose to invoke a computation in a child process, or perform all computation itself. If a worker invokes a child process, it must then wait for it and all of its descendants to finish. Each layer in the recursion is modelled by the addition of a worker net. Varying the number of worker nets allows one to treat recursion up to any depth. The worker chain is terminated by a net without synchronising transitions, forcing the last worker to do any remaining work itself. The parametric PNBml expression for DAC with i workers (see Fig. 11), is given below:

$$DAC(i) \stackrel{\text{def}}{=} \text{CONT} ; \left(\textbf{fold } i \ (\lambda x : \text{Net}\langle 2,0\rangle . \text{WORKER} ; x) \ \text{TERM}\right)$$

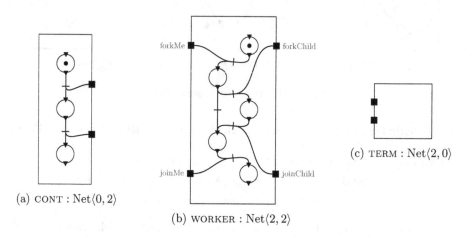

(a) CONT : Net$\langle 0,2\rangle$

(b) WORKER : Net$\langle 2,2\rangle$

(c) TERM : Net$\langle 2,0\rangle$

Fig. 10. DAC component nets

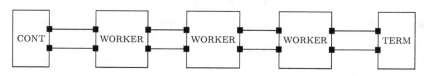

Fig. 11. Schematic of DAC(3)

3.3 Dining Philosophers

The dining philosophers is the classic example of a concurrent system modelled by Petri nets. The PNBml expression to represent a table of dining philosophers, with i philosophers and forks requires a simple $id2$ net, which is just $id \otimes id$:

$$
\begin{aligned}
DPH(i) \stackrel{\text{def}}{=} \ & \textbf{bind } phfk = \text{PH} ; \text{FK } \textbf{in} \\
& \textbf{bind } phfks = \textbf{fold } i \ (\lambda x : \text{Net}\langle 2,2\rangle . \ phfk ; x) \ id2 \ \textbf{in} \\
& \text{LEND} ; (id2 \otimes phfks) ; \text{REND}
\end{aligned}
$$

The expression represents the composition of a philosopher with a fork, before forming a sequence of i such compositions. Then, to form the "table", the last fork is wired together with the first philosopher, as illustrated in Fig. 13.

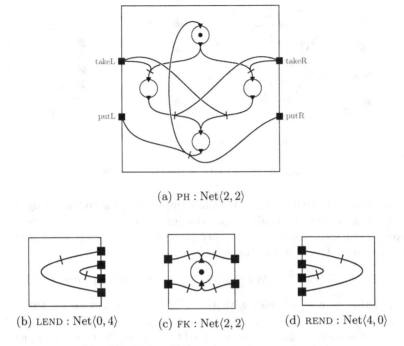

(a) PH : Net$\langle 2, 2 \rangle$

(b) LEND : Net$\langle 0, 4 \rangle$ (c) FK : Net$\langle 2, 2 \rangle$ (d) REND : Net$\langle 4, 0 \rangle$

Fig. 12. Dining Philosophers component nets

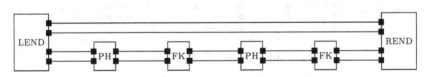

Fig. 13. Schematic of DPH(2)

3.4 n-bit Counter

An n-bit counter net models a "counter" from $0 - n$ that may be increment-ed/decremented. Counters make use of transitions connected to place "query" ports. Such transitions are represented graphically as an edge that connects to the side of a place — the semantics are that the corresponding transition can only fire if a token is present, and that no transitions connecting to the place's in/out ports are also being fired. Our query ports are equivalent to the read arcs [8] found in contextual nets.

An n-bit counter net is formed by sequentially composing n 1-bit counter nets, terminating with a net that always reports as being full, see Fig. 15. The intuitive description of a 1-bit component is that it is either "empty" or "full". A full component may be directly decremented, or may pass its token to the

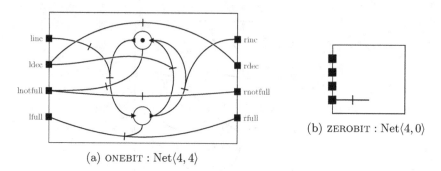

(a) ONEBIT : Net$\langle 4, 4 \rangle$

(b) ZEROBIT : Net$\langle 4, 0 \rangle$

Fig. 14. n-bit Counter component nets

next component, in either case it becomes empty. Passing tokens along a chain of components allows the chain to become full — a n-bit counter is not full if any component has a token in the empty place; it is full if all places have tokens in the full place. The PNBml expression is:

$$COUNT(i) \stackrel{\text{def}}{=} \textbf{fold } i \ (\boldsymbol{\lambda} x : \text{Net}\langle 4, 4 \rangle \ . \ \text{ONEBIT} \ ; \ x) \ \text{ZEROBIT}$$

Clients of the counter interact with the 4 boundary ports on its left boundary: they may increment, decrement and test for notfull/full (for example if the counter is at capacity, transitions connected to *lfull* may fire and otherwise not).

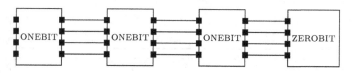

Fig. 15. Schematic of Counter(3)

4   PNBml: A DSL for Constructing Nets

In this section we give a formal description of the language PNBml for specifying net compositions. In particular, we show how PNBml expressions are evaluated to nets, and how the type system ensures that only valid expressions are processed.

PNBml is a monomorphic call-by-value functional language, following the tradition in classic functional programming languages such as ML of extending the syntax of the lambda calculus with convenient programming constructs. In particular, we add net literals and composition, syntax for variable binding and iterated function application.

The abstract syntax of PNBml is given in Fig. 16: x is drawn from a countable set of variables, n is a net literal (defined using a low-level syntax that we do not describe here) and $i \in \mathbb{N}$. Function application is indicated by simple juxtaposition: $(e_1 \, e_2)$. Following mathematical convention $;/\otimes$ associate to the left, and $\otimes$ binds tighter than $;$. We require type annotations on function abstractions to enable type checking, which is discussed in §4.2.

$$
\begin{aligned}
e = \; & x && \text{(variable)} \\
\mid \; & n && \text{(net literal)} \\
\mid \; & \mathbf{bind}\ x = e_1\ \mathbf{in}\ e_2 && \text{(variable binding)} \\
\mid \; & \lambda x : \tau\ .\ e && \text{(function abstraction)} \\
\mid \; & e_1\ e_2 && \text{(function application)} \\
\mid \; & e_1\ ;\ e_2 && \text{(sequential net composition)} \\
\mid \; & e_1 \otimes e_2 && \text{(tensor net composition)} \\
\mid \; & \mathbf{fold}\ i\ e_1\ e_2 && \text{(iterated function application)}
\end{aligned}
$$

Fig. 16. Syntax of PNBml

4.1 Operational Semantics

We define the big-step operational semantics of PNBml in Fig. 17, using an explicit variable binding environment E. The language is call-by-value, and the evaluation rules reduce PNBml expressions to values: either (composite) nets or function closures (an environment and lambda abstraction).

The evaluation rules are almost standard, with $E \vdash e \Downarrow v$ meaning that in environment E, expression e reduces to value v. Variables are simply looked up in the environment, nets evaluate to themselves and lambdas evaluate to a closure over the current environment. Bindings evaluate their body in an extended environment, similarly to applications. Sequential and tensor composition evaluate both expressions to nets, before applying the appropriate net operation. Finally, folds are implemented in terms of (iterated) function application until i reaches the base case, 0.

4.2 Static Type Checking

PNBml expressions are statically type-checked, allowing us to rule out errors before evaluation is performed. Such errors include treating a net as a function, sequentially composing incompatible nets, or trying to tensor two lambda abstractions. The (monomorphic) types assigned to PNBml expressions are shown in Fig. 18, with the corresponding typing rules in Fig. 19. As is standard for a monomorphic language, Γ is simply a sequence of bindings of variables to types, extended in the TBIND and TLAM rules.

As an example use of the typing rules, consider composing the three wiring nets illustrated in Fig. 7 to form a loop, with the expression:

$$\text{ETA} \; ; \; (\text{ID} \otimes \text{ID}) \; ; \; \text{EPSILON}$$

We can confirm that the expression is well-composed with the proof illustrated in Fig. 20 (using η, i, ϵ in place of ETA, ID, EPSILON).

$$(\text{EVAR}) \; \frac{}{E \vdash x \Downarrow E(x)} \qquad\qquad (\text{ELAM}) \; \frac{}{E \vdash \boldsymbol{\lambda} x : \tau \,.\, e \Downarrow \langle E, \boldsymbol{\lambda} x : \tau \,.\, e \rangle}$$

$$(\text{ENET}) \; \frac{}{E \vdash n \Downarrow n} \qquad\qquad (\text{EBIND}) \; \frac{E \vdash e_1 \Downarrow v_1 \qquad E, x \mapsto v_1 \vdash e_2 \Downarrow v_2}{E \vdash \mathbf{bind}\; x = e_1 \;\mathbf{in}\; e_2 \Downarrow v_2}$$

$$(\text{EAPP}) \; \frac{E \vdash e_1 \Downarrow \langle E', \boldsymbol{\lambda} x : \tau \,.\, e_3 \rangle \qquad E \vdash e_2 \Downarrow v_2 \qquad E', x \mapsto v_2 \vdash e_3 \Downarrow v_3}{E \vdash e_1 \, e_2 \Downarrow v_3}$$

$$(\text{ESEQ}) \; \frac{E \vdash e_1 \Downarrow n_1 \qquad E \vdash e_2 \Downarrow n_2 \qquad n_3 = n_1 \,;\, n_2}{E \vdash e_1 \,;\, e_2 \Downarrow n_3}$$

$$(\text{ETEN}) \; \frac{E \vdash e_1 \Downarrow n_1 \qquad E \vdash e_2 \Downarrow n_2 \qquad n_3 = n_1 \otimes n_2}{E \vdash e_1 \otimes e_2 \Downarrow n_3}$$

$$(\text{EFOLD0}) \; \frac{E \vdash e_2 \Downarrow v}{E \vdash \mathbf{fold}\; 0 \; e_1 \, e_2 \Downarrow v} \qquad\qquad (\text{EFOLDI}) \; \frac{E \vdash e_1 \,(\mathbf{fold}\;(i-1)\; e_1 \, e_2) \Downarrow v}{E \vdash \mathbf{fold}\; i \; e_1 \, e_2 \Downarrow v}$$

Fig. 17. Operational Semantics of PNBml

$$\tau = \text{Net}\langle i, j \rangle \;\; (i, j \in \mathbb{N}) \qquad\qquad\qquad (\text{Net Component})$$
$$\mid \tau_1 \to \tau_2 \qquad\qquad\qquad\qquad\qquad (\text{Function Type})$$

Fig. 18. Types of PNBml

Our type checker rules out *all* possible run-time failures for PNBml expressions. Indeed, the novel feature of our type system is the tracking of component boundary sizes, achieved by parametrising the Net base type: $\text{Net}\langle l, r \rangle$ by $l, r \in \mathbb{N}$, which describe the left and right boundary sizes respectively.

We say an expression e is *well-typed*, if there exists a type environment binding all free variables appearing in e, Γ, and a type, τ, such that $\Gamma \vdash e : \tau$. Furthermore, an operational environment (mapping lambda-bound-variables to values), E respects a type environment Γ iff the domains of Γ and E are equal and E point-wise respects Γ, as per Fig. 21.

Now we can state our formal notion of "well-typed expressions can always be evaluated to values":

Theorem 1 (Well-typed expressions are well-composed).
For a well-typed expression, $\Gamma \vdash e : \tau$, and operational environment E:

$$E : \Gamma \implies E \vdash e \Downarrow v \;\text{ with }\; \vdash v : \tau$$

Proof. Induction over the structure of the proof of $\Gamma \vdash e : \tau$.

$$(\text{TVar}) \;\frac{\Gamma(x) = \tau}{\Gamma \vdash x : \tau} \qquad (\text{TBind}) \;\frac{\Gamma \vdash e_1 : \tau_1 \qquad \Gamma, x \mapsto \tau_1 \vdash e_2 : \tau_2}{\Gamma \vdash \mathbf{bind}\ x = e_1\ \mathbf{in}\ e_2 : \tau_2}$$

$$(\text{TLam}) \;\frac{\Gamma, x \mapsto \tau_1 \vdash e : \tau_2}{\Gamma \vdash \boldsymbol{\lambda} x : \tau_1 \,.\, e : \tau_1 \to \tau_2} \qquad (\text{TApp}) \;\frac{\Gamma \vdash e_1 : \tau_1 \to \tau_2 \qquad \Gamma \vdash e_2 : \tau_1}{\Gamma \vdash e_1\, e_2 : \tau_2}$$

$$(\text{TTen}) \;\frac{\Gamma \vdash e_1 : \text{Net}\langle i, j \rangle \qquad \Gamma \vdash e_2 : \text{Net}\langle k, l \rangle}{\Gamma \vdash e_1 \otimes e_2 : \text{Net}\langle i + k, j + l \rangle}$$

$$(\text{TSeq}) \;\frac{\Gamma \vdash e_1 : \text{Net}\langle i, j \rangle \qquad \Gamma \vdash e_2 : \text{Net}\langle k, l \rangle \qquad j = k}{\Gamma \vdash e_1\, ;\, e_2 : \text{Net}\langle i, l \rangle}$$

$$(\text{TNet}) \;\frac{n : (i, j)}{\Gamma \vdash n : \text{Net}\langle i, j \rangle} \qquad (\text{TFold}) \;\frac{\Gamma \vdash e_1 : \tau \to \tau \qquad \Gamma \vdash e_2 : \tau}{\Gamma \vdash \mathbf{fold}\ i\ e_1\ e_2 : \tau}$$

Fig. 19. Typing of PNBml Expressions

$$\frac{\dfrac{\vdash i : \text{Net}\langle 1, 1 \rangle \qquad \vdash i : \text{Net}\langle 1, 1 \rangle}{\vdash i \otimes i : \text{Net}\langle 2, 2 \rangle} \qquad \vdash \epsilon : \text{Net}\langle 2, 0 \rangle}{\vdash \eta : \text{Net}\langle 0, 2 \rangle \qquad \dfrac{\vdash i \otimes i\, ;\, \epsilon : \text{Net}\langle 2, 0 \rangle}{\vdash \eta\, ;\, i \otimes i\, ;\, \epsilon : \text{Net}\langle 0, 0 \rangle}}$$

Fig. 20. Example typing proof

$$\frac{dom(E) = dom(\Gamma) \qquad \forall x \in dom(E) \vdash E(x) : \Gamma(x)}{\vdash E : \Gamma}$$

$$\frac{n : (i, j)}{\vdash n : \text{Net}\langle i, j \rangle} \qquad \frac{\vdash E : \Gamma \qquad \Gamma, x \mapsto \tau_1 \vdash e : \tau_2}{\vdash \langle E, \boldsymbol{\lambda} x : \tau_1 \,.\, e \rangle : \tau_1 \to \tau_2}$$

Fig. 21. Typing of values and operational environments

5 Conclusions and Future Work

We have shown that the algebra of Petri nets with boundaries can be used to write natural specification of realistic concurrent, distributed systems. We introduced a high-level DSL, PNBml, which provides an expressive and convenient setting to specify parametric systems, using several techniques: name binding, function abstraction, static types and iterated function application. Although

PNBml is a simple language, we have supported our claims of its applicability by providing succinct PNBml programs that generate arbitrary instances of well-known, parametric examples from the literature.

In future work we plan to investigate allowing *polymorphic* functions (w.r.t. parameter boundaries), allowing more expressions to be typed. With suitable *equational unification* and *type inference* type annotations could be omitted from lambda arguments. For example, the "design pattern" of closing a chain of nets using a loop (e.g. the Hartstone example, §3), could be typed:

$$\text{close} : \text{Net}\langle n+1, m+1 \rangle \to \text{Net}\langle n, m \rangle$$

that is, removing the last boundary on either side by connecting them to one another (here n and m are variables). Another example that could be typed with polymorphic boundaries (and a suitable algebra on boundary sizes) would be the n-way tensor:

$$\textbf{fold } n \ (\boldsymbol{\lambda} x : \text{Net}\langle i, j \rangle \ . \ x \otimes id) \ x$$

which, given an expression x, with type $\text{Net}\langle i, j \rangle$ would perform the n-way tensor of x with id giving type $\text{Net}\langle i+n, j+n \rangle$. A well-known example of a type system with similar features is Kennedy's dimension types [13].

References

1. Abdulla, P.A., Iyer, S.P., Nylén, A.: SAT-Solving the Coverability Problem for Petri Nets. Formal Methods in System Design 24(1), 25–43 (2004)
2. Abramsky, S., Coecke, B.: A categorical semantics of quantum protocols. In: LiCS 2004. IEEE Press (2004)
3. Arnold, A.: Nivat's processes and their synchronization. TCS 281(1-2), 31–26 (2002)
4. Baldan, P., Corradini, A., Ehrig, H., Heckel, R.: Compositional modelling of reactive systems using open nets. In: Larsen, K.G., Nielsen, M. (eds.) CONCUR 2001. LNCS, vol. 2154, pp. 502–518. Springer, Heidelberg (2001)
5. Best, E., Devillers, R., Koutny, M.: Petri Net Algebra. Springer (2001)
6. Bruni, R., Melgratti, H., Montanari, U.: A connector algebra for P/T nets interactions. In: Katoen, J.-P., König, B. (eds.) CONCUR 2011. LNCS, vol. 6901, pp. 312–326. Springer, Heidelberg (2011)
7. Bruni, R., Melgratti, H.C., Montanari, U., Sobociński, P.: Connector algebras for C/E and P/T nets' interactions. Log. Meth. Comput. Sci. 9(3:16), 1–65 (2013)
8. Christensen, S., Hansen, N.D.: Coloured Petri Nets Extended With Place Capacities, Test Arcs and Inhibitor Arcs. In: Ajmone Marsan, M. (ed.) ICATPN 1993. LNCS, vol. 691, pp. 186–205. Springer, Heidelberg (1993)
9. Corbett, J.C.: Evaluating Deadlock Detection Methods for Concurrent Software. IEEE Transactions on Software Engineering 22(3), 161–180 (1996)
10. Hoare, C.A.R.: Communicating Sequential Processes. Prentice Hall (1985)
11. Junker, B.H., Schreiber, F.: Analysis of Biological Networks. Wiley (2008)
12. Katis, P., Sabadini, N., Walters, R.F.C.: Span (Graph): A Categorical Algebra of Transition Systems. In: Johnson, M. (ed.) AMAST 1997. LNCS, vol. 1349, pp. 307–321. Springer, Heidelberg (1997)

13. Kennedy, A.: Relational Parametricity and Units of Measure. In: POPL 1997, pp. 442–455. ACM (1997)
14. Kindler, E.: A compositional partial order semantics for petri net components. In: Azéma, P., Balbo, G. (eds.) ICATPN 1997. LNCS, vol. 1248, pp. 235–252. Springer, Heidelberg (1997)
15. Koch, I.: Petri nets - a mathematical formalism to analyze chemical reaction networks. Molecular Informatics 29(12), 838–843 (2010)
16. Lafont, Y.: Towards an algebraic theory of boolean circuits. J. Pure. Appl. Alg. 184, 257–310 (2003)
17. Mazurkiewicz, A.: Compositional semantics of pure place/transition systems. In: Rozenberg, G. (ed.) APN 1988. LNCS, vol. 340, pp. 307–330. Springer, Heidelberg (1988)
18. McMillan, K.: A technique of a state space search based on unfolding. Form. Method Syst. Des. 6(1), 45–65 (1995)
19. Milner, R.: A Calculus of Communicating Systems. Prentice Hall (1989)
20. Petri, C.A.: Communication with automata. Technical report, Air Force Systems Command, Griffiss Air Force Base, New York (1966)
21. Rathke, J., Sobociński, P., Stephens, O.: Decomposing Petri nets. arXiv:1304.3121v1 (2013)
22. Reisig, W.: Simple composition of nets. In: Franceschinis, G., Wolf, K. (eds.) PETRI NETS 2009. LNCS, vol. 5606, pp. 23–42. Springer, Heidelberg (2009)
23. Rutten, J.: A tutorial on coinductive stream calculus and signal flow graphs. Theor. Comput. Sci. 343(3), 443–481 (2005)
24. Schmidt, K.: How to calculate symmetries of Petri nets. Acta. Inf. 36, 545–590 (2000)
25. Sobociński, P.: Representations of Petri net interactions. In: Gastin, P., Laroussinie, F. (eds.) CONCUR 2010. LNCS, vol. 6269, pp. 554–568. Springer, Heidelberg (2010)
26. Sobociński, P., Stephens, O.: Penrose: Putting Compositionality to Work for Petri Net Reachability. In: Heckel, R. (ed.) CALCO 2013. LNCS, vol. 8089, pp. 346–352. Springer, Heidelberg (2013)
27. Sobociński, P., Stephens, O.: Reachability via compositionality in Petri nets. arXiv:1303.1399v1 (2013)
28. van der Aalst, W.: Process Mining: Discovery, Conformance and Enhancement of Business Processes. Springer (2011)

Flow Unfolding of Multi-clock Nets*

Giovanni Casu and G. Michele Pinna

Dipartimento di Matematica e Informatica, Università di Cagliari, Cagliari, Italy
{giovanni.casu,gmpinna}@unica.it

Abstract. Unfoldings of nets are often related to event structures: each execution of a net can be viewed as a configuration in the associated event structure. This allows for a clear characterization of dependencies and the conflicts between occurrences of transitions in the net. This relation is somehow lost if more compact representations of the executions of nets are considered, *e.g.* in trellises or merged processes of multi-clock nets. In this paper we introduce an unfolding, called *flow unfolding*, that turns out to be related to flow event structures, hence dependencies and conflict are still represented. Furthermore, this unfolding gives also a more compact representation of the executions of a multi-clock net, similarly to what approaches like trellises or merged processes do.

1 Introduction

In recent years various new approaches have been proposed to unfold a Petri net. Unfoldings are meant to give a representation of the computations of a Petri net which can be used for several purposes, and among others we recall verification of properties [1], diagnosis of systems [2] and obviously modeling of systems computations [3]. The classical notion of unfolding as developed by Winskel in [3] and Engelfriet in [4] suffers of the state explosion problem, as each event in the unfolding has a unique history, thus possibly equivalent computations leading to the *same* state in the original net are kept distinct. To overcome this problem two main approaches have been pursued. One focuses in finding a *finite* representation of an unfolding, *e.g.* with the notion of prefix [5]. The other tries to identifies computations under suitable equivalences. To the latter approach *trellises* and *merged processes* can be ascribed. Indeed, with different motivations, both Fabre in [6] with his *trellises* and Khomenko, Kondratyev, Koutny, and Vogler in [7] with their *merged processes* have proposed two different ways to reduce dramatically the size of the unfolding of a safe net. In the first proposal a safe net is considered as the product of finite state automata (hence turned into a so called *multi-clock* net), and the unfolding of all the components are then glued together by merging conditions which have the same heights (the height of a condition being its history in the proper automata) and identifying

---

* Work partially supported by Aut. Region of Sardinia under grants LR 7/07 CRP-17285 (TRICS), PIA 2010 "Social Glue", by MIUR PRIN 2010-11 "Security Horizons"

G. Ciardo and E. Kindler (Eds.): PETRI NETS 2014, LNCS 8489, pp. 170–189, 2014.

transitions representing correct synchronizations among the various automata; whereas in the second proposal conditions representing the same occurrence of a token are identified and consequently transitions bearing the same label and having the same preset and postset are merged.

The classical notion of unfolding has a clear and useful connection with another central notion of concurrency theory, namely the one of *event structure* [3]. Indeed, to the classical unfolding of a safe net it is possible to associate a *prime event structure* and vice versa. Dependencies and conflicts among events are represented faithfully in prime event structure, but some prices have to be paid: possibly equivalent computations may be not *equate*, thus producing again the explosion of the states space.

To be able to relate unfoldings to event based models a minimal requirement should be verified: in the unfolding a transition can be executed only once in a run (see [8], where *configuration structures* are introduced). It is worth to stress that in some event based models dependencies and conflicts are not directly available, but have to be deduced (*e.g.* in [8] or [9]). We observe that there is no clear relation between trellises or merged processes and the more used notions of event structures (where dependencies and conflicts are represented). For merged process, even when restricted to multi-clock nets, there is no relation at all, as they do not fulfil the minimal requirement stated above, namely that each transition is executed only once in a run.

Boudol in [10] and with Castellani in [11] are among the first in proposing another notion of event structure, where an event may have several histories, namely *flow* event structures. Other variations of the basic concept of event structures have been proposed subsequently, with various purposes which we will not investigate here. We briefly recall among others: asymmetric event structure of Baldan, Corradini and Montanari [12], or inhibitor event structure of Baldan, Busi, Corradini and Pinna [13], bundle event structure of Langerak [14] or the one associated to the Muller's unfolding of Gunawardena [15]. The configurations of flow event structures and those of prime event structures ordered by inclusion form a prime algebraic domains. The notion of configuration in prime event structure is extremely natural, and modeling the causal relation as a partial order and stating the inheritance principle for the conflict relation (along the causal relation) have played a major rôle in the success of prime event structures, as they imply that each event has a unique history. In this respect flow event structures are less manageable. On the one hand the dependency relation and the conflict relation are required to be irreflexive the first one and symmetric the second one, but no clear interaction among them is foreseen. On the other hand the notion of configuration is much more complicated with respect to the one of prime event structure because it is on this level that a choice should be done among the various histories of an event: one which is compatible with the histories of the other events have to be selected. We observe that prime event structures can be seen as special cases of any other kind of event structures.

In this paper we propose a notion, flow unravel net, where a dependency relation and a conflict relation are easily defined, but many equivalent runs may be equated, similarly to merged processes or trellises. This is obtained by adding suitable *control* places. The notion of flow unravel net is a proper extension of that of causal net, as each causal net can be turned into a flow unravel net. Control places are used to define a relation of dependency among transitions of the net: a transition depends on another if in the preset of the transition there is a control place that is in the postset of the other. A conflict relation is instead defined stating an *immediate conflict* among two transitions that share an *internal* place *i.e.* a place which is not a control one, and that represents a shared resource, and this conflict is inherited along the dependency up to a certain point, which is identified as the point where two alternative histories determine the same future evolution.

Flow unravel nets are the basis to develop the notion of flow unfolding. We, similarly to what does Fabre in [6], unfold a multi-clock net, as the information provided by the various components of a multi-clock net eases the construction. The unfolding algorithm of Esparza, Römer and Vogler in [21], without cutoffs, can be easily adapted to our purposes, once it is understood when, in the construction, two elements are the same (both for places and transitions). In [16] some notions of equivalence among transitions based of the neighborhoods of transitions have been proposed. Here we adapt these equivalence to our purposes: two transitions are equivalent if they have compatible histories and have the same *future* evolution. The result of the unfolding algorithm of a multi-clock net N is a flow unravel net and a mapping that folds the flow unravel net onto N. It is worth to observe that each safe net can be turned into a multi-clock net having the same *behaviour*, *i.e.* the same firing sequences and with a (step) case graph isomorphic to the one of the original safe net.

The paper is organized as follows: in the next section we recall all the needed definitions concerning nets and we define what an unravel net and a flow unravel net are. In Section 3 we show how prime event structures and classical unfoldings are related as well as flow unravel nets and flow event structures. In Section 4 we present our unfolding algorithm and we show that indeed the algorithm gives a flow unravel net (hence a flow event structure can be associated to it). In Section 5 we compare our construction with trellises and merged process. Some conclusions are drawn in the final section.

2   Nets

Notations: With $\mathbb{N}$ we denote the set of natural numbers and with $\mathbb{N}^+$ the set of natural numbers without zero, i.e., $\mathbb{N} \setminus \{0\}$. Let X be a set, with $|X|$ we denote the cardinality of the set. Let A be a set, a *multiset* of A is a function $m : A \to \mathbb{N}$. The set of multisets of A is denoted by μA. The usual operations on multisets, like multiset union $+$ or multiset difference $-$, are used. We write $m \leq m'$ if $m(a) \leq m'(a)$ for all $a \in A$. If $m \in \mu A$, we denote by $\llbracket m \rrbracket$ the multiset defined as $\llbracket m \rrbracket(a) = 1$ if $m(a) > 0$ and $\llbracket m \rrbracket(a) = 0$ otherwise; sometimes we will use $\llbracket m \rrbracket$ as the denotation of the subset $\{a \in A \mid \llbracket m \rrbracket(a) = 1\}$ of A. Finally, when a multiset m of A is a set, *i.e.* $m = \llbracket m \rrbracket$, we write $a \in m$ to denote that $m(a) \neq 0$, namely that $a \in \llbracket m \rrbracket$, and often confuse the multi set m with the set $\{a \in A \mid m(a) \neq 0\}$.

Given an alphabet Σ, with Σ^* we denote as usual the set of words on Σ with ϵ as the empty word. The length of a word is defined as usual and, with abuse of notation, it is denoted with $|\cdot|$. Given a word w and a subset A of the alphabet, $proj(w, A)$ is the word obtained deleting all occurrences of symbols not belonging to A.

Given a partial order $(D, \sqsubseteq)$, with $\lfloor d \rfloor$ we denote the set $\{d' \in D \mid d' \sqsubseteq d\}$.

Nets: We first review the notions of Petri net and of the token game.

Definition 1. *A Petri net is a 4-tuple* $N = \langle S, T, F, m \rangle$*, where S is a set of places and T is a set of transitions (with $S \cap T = \emptyset$), $F: (S \times T) \cup (T \times S) \to \mathbb{N}$ is the* flow *mapping, and $m \in \mu S$ is called the* initial marking.

Subscripts or superscript on the net name carry over the names of the net components. Given an $x \in T$, with $^\bullet x$ we denote the multiset on S defined as $^\bullet x(s) = 1$ if $F(s, x)$ and 0 otherwise, and with $x^\bullet$ we denote the multiset on S defined as $x^\bullet(s) = 1$ if $F(x, s)$ and 0 otherwise. Similarly, given an $y \in S$, with $^\bullet y$ and $y^\bullet$ we denote the multisets on T defined respectively as $^\bullet y(t) = 1$ if $F(y, t)$ and 0 otherwise, and $x^\bullet(t) = 1$ if $F(t, y)$ and 0 otherwise. For $x \in S \cup T$, $^\bullet x$ and $x^\bullet$ are called the *preset* and *postset* respectively of x. Given a finite multiset of transitions $A \in \mu T$ we write $^\bullet A$ for $\sum_{t \in T} A(t) \cdot {}^\bullet t$ and $A^\bullet$ for $\sum_{t \in T} A(t) \cdot t^\bullet$.

A net $\langle S, T, F, m \rangle$ is as usual graphically represented as a bipartite directed graph where the nodes are the places and the transitions, and where an arc connects a place s to a transition t iff $F(s, t) > 0$ and an arc connects a transition t to a place s iff $F(t, s) > 0$. We assume that all nets we consider are such that $\forall t \in T$ $^\bullet t$ and $t^\bullet$ are not empty.

A finite multiset of transitions A is enabled at a marking m, if m contains the pre-set of A. Formally, a finite multiset $A \in \mu T$ is *enabled* at m if $^\bullet A \leq m$. In this case, to indicate that the execution of A in m produces the new marking $m' = m - {}^\bullet A + A^\bullet$ we write $m [A\rangle m'$. Steps and firing sequences, as well as reachable markings, are defined in the usual way. The set of reachable markings of a net N is denoted with $\mathcal{M}_N$. Each reachable marking can be obviously reached with a firing sequence where just a transition is executed at each step. Given a firing sequence $m [A_1\rangle m_1 \cdots m_{n-1} [A_n\rangle m_n$, we say that m_n it *reached* by $\sum_{i=1}^n A_i$.

A net is said *safe* whenever its places hold at most one token in all possible evolutions. Formally:

Definition 2. *A net* $N = \langle S, T, F, m \rangle$ *is said* safe *in the case that $F: (S \times T) \cup (T \times S) \to \{0, 1\}$ and each marking $m \in \mathcal{M}_N$ is such that $m = \llbracket m \rrbracket$.*

Subnet: A subnet of a net is a net obtained restricting places and transitions, and correspondingly also the multirelation F and the initial marking. We can restrict either the transitions or the places.

Definition 3. *Let* $N = \langle S, T, F, m \rangle$ *be a Petri net and let $T' \subseteq T$. Then the subnet generated by T' is the net* $N|_{T'} = \langle S', T', F', m' \rangle$*, where $S' = \{s \in$*

$S \mid F(t,s) > 0$ or $F(s,t) > 0$ for $t \in T'\} \cup \{s \in S \mid m(s) > 0\}$, F' is restriction of F to S' and T', and m' is the multiset on S' obtained by m restricting to places in S'.

Analogously we can restrict the net to a subset of places.

Definition 4. *Let* $N = \langle S, T, F, m \rangle$ *be a Petri net and let* $S' \subseteq S$. *Then the subnet generated by* S' *is the net* $N|_{S'} = \langle S', T', F', m' \rangle$, *where* $T' = \{t \in T \mid F(t,s) > 0$ *or* $F(s,t) > 0$ *for* $s \in S'\}$, F' *is restriction of* F *to* S' *and* T', *and* m' *is the multiset on* S' *obtained by* m *restricting to places in* S'.

Multi-clock nets: Safe nets can be seen as formed by various *sequential* components (automata) synchronizing on common transitions. This intuition is formalized in the notion of *multi-clock* nets, introduced by Fabre in [6].

Definition 5. *A* multi-clock *net* N *is the pair* $(\langle S, T, F, m \rangle, \nu)$ *where* $\langle S, T, F, m \rangle$ *is a safe net and* $\nu : S \to [\![m]\!]$ *is a mapping such that*

- *for all* $s, s' \in [\![m]\!]$, *it holds that* $s \neq s'$ *implies* $\nu^{-1}(s) \cap \nu^{-1}(s') = \emptyset$,
- $\bigcup_{s \in [\![m]\!]} \nu^{-1}(s) = S$,
- $\nu|_{[\![m]\!]}$ *is the identity, and*
- *for all* $t \in T$. ν *is injective on* $[\![{}^\bullet t]\!]$ *and on* $[\![t^\bullet]\!]$, *and* $\nu([\![{}^\bullet t]\!]) = \nu([\![t^\bullet]\!])$.

Given $s \in S$, with $\bar{s}$ we denote the subset of places defined by $\nu^{-1}(\nu(s))$. The consequences of the two requirements, namely (a) $\nu|_{[\![m]\!]}$ is the identity and (b) ν is injective on the preset (postset) of each transition and that $\nu([\![{}^\bullet t]\!]) = \nu([\![t^\bullet]\!])$, is that for each $s \in [\![m]\!]$, the net $\langle S, T, F, m \rangle|_{\bar{s}} = \langle \bar{s}, T_{\bar{s}}, F_{\bar{s}}, m_{\bar{s}} \rangle$ is a state-machine net, *i.e.* the preset and the postset of each transition has at most one element. State-machine nets can be considered as finite state automata, and the net $\langle S, T, F, m \rangle$ can be seen as the *union* of the various components. Sometimes multi-clock nets will be identified with the underlying safe net $N = \langle S, T, F, m \rangle$ and the partition

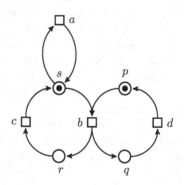

Fig. 1. A multi-clock net

mapping will be denoted with $\nu(N)$. It should be stressed that the partition is not unique. Consider the net in figure 1, the two partitions are identified by the following partition mapping $\nu(s) = s$, $\nu(r) = s$, $\nu(p) = p$ and $\nu(q) = p$.

Occurrence Nets: The notion of occurrence net we introduce here is the one called 1-occurrence net and proposed by van Glabbeek and Plotkin in [17]. First we need to introduce the notion of *state*.

Definition 6. *Let $N = \langle S, T, F, m \rangle$ be a Petri net, a* state *is any finite multiset X of transitions with the property that the function $m_X : S \to \mathbb{Z}$ given by $m_X(s) = m(s) + \sum_{t \in T} X(t) \cdot (t^\bullet(s) - {}^\bullet t(s))$, for all $s \in S$, is a reachable marking of the net which is reached by X. With $\mathcal{X}(N)$ we denote the states of the net N.*

A state contains (in no order) all the occurrences of the transitions that have been fired to reach a marking. Observe that a trace of a net is a suitable linearization of the elements of a state X. On the notion of state the notion of occurrence net is based:

Definition 7. *An* occurrence net *$O = \langle S, T, F, m \rangle$ is a Petri net where each state is a set, i.e. $\forall X \in \mathcal{X}(N)$ it holds that $X = [\![X]\!]$.*

The intuition behind this notion is the following: regardless how tokens are produced or consumed, an occurrence net *guarantees* that each transition can *occur* only once (hence the reason for calling them occurrence nets).

Causal Nets: The notion of causal net we use here is the classical one, though it is often called occurrence net. The different name is due to the other notion of occurrence net we use here. Given a net $N = \langle S, T, F, m \rangle$, we define $s <_N t$ iff $F(s, t)$ and $t <_N s$ iff $F(t, s)$, and $\leq_N$ is the transitive and reflexive closure of this relation. For denoting places and transitions we use B and E (see [18] and [3,19]) and call them conditions and events respectively. A causal net is essentially an acyclic net equipped with a conflict relation (which is deduced using the relation F, as causal nets are safe nets).

Definition 8. *A* causal net *$C = \langle B, E, F, m \rangle$ is a safe net satisfying the following restrictions:*

- *$\forall b \in m, \ {}^\bullet b = \emptyset$,*
- *$\forall b \in B. \ \exists b' \in m$ such that $b' \leq_C b$,*
- *$\forall b \in B. \ {}^\bullet b$ is either empty or a singleton,*
- *for all $e \in E$ the set $\{e' \in E \mid e' \leq_C e\}$ is finite, and*
- *$\#$ is an irreflexive and symmetric relation defined as follows:*
    - *$e \#_i e'$ iff $e, e' \in E$, $e \neq e'$ and ${}^\bullet e \cap {}^\bullet e' \neq \emptyset$,*
    - *$x \# x'$ iff $\exists y, y' \in E$ such that $y \#_i y'$ and $y \leq_C x$ and $y' \leq_C x'$.*

The intuition behind this notion is the following: each condition b represents the occurrence of a token, which is produced by the *unique* event in ${}^\bullet b$, unless b belongs to the initial marking, and it is used by only one transition (hence if $e, e' \in b^\bullet$, then $e \# e'$). On causal net it is natural to define a notion of *causality* among elements of the net: we say that x is *causally dependent* from y iff $y \leq_C x$. Given a causal net $C = \langle B, E, F, m \rangle$, if $\forall b \in B$ it holds that $b^\bullet$ is a singleton, we say that it is a *conflict-free* causal net. Observe that a conflict-free causal net may be considered as a net representing a non-interleaving execution of a system. The following observation essentially says that each transition (event) in a causal net is executed only once:

Proposition 1. *let C be a causal net, then C is also an occurrence net.*

Unravel Nets: Causal nets capture dependencies (and conflicts) whereas occurrence nets capture the unique occurrence property of each transition. We introduce now a notion of net which will turn to be, so to say, in between occurrence nets and causal nets. Like in the case of occurrence nets we want to assure that each transition happens just once, and similarly to causal nets we want still to be able to retrieve dependencies among the firings of transitions, though in a more *semantical* way, as we require that each state of the net (together with the adjacent arcs) induces a conflict-free causal net.

Definition 9. *An unravel net* $R = \langle S, T, F, m \rangle$ *is an occurrence net such that (a) R is safe, and (b) for each state $X \in \mathcal{X}(R)$ the net $R|_{[\![X]\!]}$ is a conflict-free causal net.*

This notion covers trivially the one of causal net.

Proposition 2. *Let C be a causal net. Then C is an unravel net.*

Flow Unravel Nets: Unravel nets are *locally* acyclic, *i.e.* for each execution of the net the causal dependencies are clear. We would like to have this information also *structurally* available. To this aim we introduce the notion of *flow unravel* nets.

Definition 10. *An unravel net* $R = \langle S, T, F, m \rangle$ *is a* flow unravel net *iff the set of places S can be divided into two subsets S_i and S_c (internal and control places respectively) such that*

1. $S_i \cup S_c = S$ and $S_i \cap S_c = [\![m]\!]$,
2. $\forall t \in T.$ $^\bullet t \cap S_x \neq \emptyset$ and $t^\bullet \cap S_x \neq \emptyset$, for $x \in \{i, c\}$,
3. $\forall t, t' \in T.$ $t^\bullet \cap {}^\bullet t' \cap S_c \neq \emptyset$ implies that $t^\bullet \cap {}^\bullet t' \cap S_i \neq \emptyset$,
4. $\forall t \in T. \forall s \in {}^\bullet t$ either $\exists t' \in T.$ $t'^\bullet \cap {}^\bullet t \cap S_c \neq \emptyset$ or $s \in [\![m]\!]$,
5. $\forall t, t' \in T.$ $t^\bullet \cap {}^\bullet t' \cap S_c \neq \emptyset$ implies that $|t^\bullet \cap {}^\bullet t' \cap S_c| = 1$, and
6. (S_c, T, F_c, m_c) is a connected and acyclic net, where F_c and m_c are the restriction of F and m to S_c respectively.

The idea behind flow unravel nets is to be able to keep track of dependencies among transitions, and this is achieved using the places in S_c. We require that each transition is connected both to internal places (which represent the used or produced resources) and control places (which are used to describe the dependencies). Requirement (5) is a kind of *economicity* criterion: among two transitions there may be at most one control place. Furthermore condition (4) guarantees that it a transition t consumes a resource (internal place) then there should be a transition t' connected to t (t depends on t') or the resource is the initial one. Observe that $\mathcal{X}(R) \subseteq \mathcal{X}(R|_{S_i})$ as each transition is connected to internal places. We stress that requiring that among two transitions there may be at most one control place does not imply that the control place must have just one outgoing arc.

Flow unravel nets are conservative extensions of causal net. $C = \langle B, E, F, m \rangle$ is turned into a flow unravel net as follows: for each pair of events e, e' such that

$e^\bullet \cap {}^\bullet e' \neq \emptyset$ add a place (e, e'), for each event e such that $\forall e' \in E$ ${}^\bullet e' \cap e^\bullet = \emptyset$ add a place $(e, -)$. These added places are the places in $S_c \setminus m$. The flow relation F' is obtained as expected: $F'(e, (e, e')) = 1 = F'((e, e'), e')$ for all $(e, e') \in S_c$ and $F(e, (e, -)) = 1$ for all $(e, -) \in S_c$.

We end this section introducing some auxiliary notions. Assume that there exists a set of labels $\mathcal{A}$ and a labelling function $l : S_i \to \mathcal{A}$. Then, for each state of a flow unravel net we can define a mapping that associates to each *internal* place the number of equally labeled internal places preceding it with respect to that state (and this is finite as a state of an unravel net gives a conflict-free causal net).

Definition 11. *Let $R = \langle S, T, F, m \rangle$ be a flow unravel net, and $l : S_i \to \mathcal{A}$ be a labelling function. For each $X \in \mathcal{X}(R)$ call $C_X = (R|_{S_i})|_X$ and S_i^X are the places of this causal net. Then for each $X \in \mathcal{X}(R)$ define $tok_X^l : S_i \to \mathbb{N}$ as follows:*
$$tok_X^l(s) = |\{s' \in S_i^X \mid s' \leq_C s \ \wedge \ l(s) = l(s')\}|.$$

Given a flow unravel net $R = \langle S, T, F, m \rangle$, $s \in S_i$ and $X \in \mathcal{X}(R)$, we say that s is *used* in X iff there exists $t \in X$ with $s \in t^\bullet$. A flow unravel net is *uniformly labelled* with respect to a given labelling function iff to each internal place a unique number can be associated, for every state. Formally:

Definition 12. *Let $R = \langle S, T, F, m \rangle$ be a flow unravel net, and $l : S_i \to \mathcal{A}$ be a labelling function. We say that R is* uniformly labelled *with respect to l iff for all $s \in S_i$ and for all $X, X' \in \mathcal{X}(R)$ such that s is used in X and X', then $tok_X^l(s) = tok_{X'}^l(s)$.*

The purpose of the labelling function is to identify token occurrences in the notion of flow unfolding as it will be clear later.

3   Event Structures and Nets

We recall now some basic notions on *event structures* and their relations with nets.

Prime event structures: Prime event structures (PES) [20,3] are a simple event-based model of concurrent computations in which events are considered as atomic and instantaneous steps, which can appear only once in a computation. The relationships between events are expressed by two binary relations: *causality* and *conflict*. The relevance of the notion of prime event structure is rooted in the well known relation with another central notion for modeling computations, namely the one of *domain*.

Definition 13. *A* prime event structure (PES) *is a tuple $P = (E, \leq, \#)$, where E is a set of events and $\leq$, $\#$ are binary relations on E called* causality relation *and* conflict relation *respectively, such that:*

1. *the relation $\leq$ is a partial order and $\lfloor e \rfloor$ is finite for all $e \in E$, and*
2. *the relation $\#$ is irreflexive, symmetric and hereditary with respect to $\leq$, i.e., $e\#e'$ and $e' \leq e''$ imply $e\#e''$ for all $e, e', e'' \in E$.*

An event can occur only after some other events (its causes) have taken place, and the execution of an event can prevent the execution of other events. This is formalized via the notion of *configuration* of a PES $P = \langle E, \leq, \# \rangle$, which is a subset of events $C \subseteq E$ such that for all $e, e' \in C \ \neg(e \# e')$ (*conflict-freeness*) and $\lfloor e \rfloor \subseteq C$ (*left-closedness*).

Causal nets and PES are closely related: let $C = \langle B, E, F, m \rangle$ be a causal net. Then $(E, \leq, \#)$ is a PES, where $\leq$ and $\#$ are the causality and conflict relations obtained by the causal net (see [3]). To a configuration of the associated PES it is possible to associate a marking in the causal net.

Proposition 3. *Let $C = \langle B, E, F, m \rangle$ be a causal net, and let $X \subseteq E$ be a configuration of $(E, \leq, \#)$. Then X is a state of C and $\mathbf{mark}(X) = m_X$ is the marking reached executing the events in X.*

We observe that, given a configuration X of the PES associated to a causal net C, the subnet $C|_X$ is a causal conflict-free net.

Flow event structures: Flow event structures (FES) are another event-based model for concurrent computations [10]. Like prime event structures also flow event structures have a clear relation with prime algebraic domains [11], but in a FES an event may have several histories, whereas in a PES $(E, \leq, \#)$ the history of the event e is simply $\lfloor e \rfloor$, which is a configuration.

Definition 14. *A flow event structure (FES) is a tuple $F = (E, \prec, \#)$, where E is a set of events and $\prec, \#$ are binary relations on E called precedence relation and conflict relation respectively such that $\prec$ is irreflexive and $\#$ is symmetric.*

With respect to PES, the causality is substituted with a precedence relation and it is stipulated that it is irreflexive, whereas for the conflict relation the inheritance principle is abandoned. Consider a FES $F = (E, \prec, \#)$. With $e \mathbin{\natural} e'$ we denote the reflexive closure of $\#$ and, given $X \subseteq E$, with $\leq_X$ the relation $(\prec \cap (X \times X))^*$. A configuration of flow event structure is a subset of events which is conflict-free and where each event e is *justified*: if an event preceding it is not in the configuration there must be another one preceding e. The precedence relation hence cover not only the immediate causality but also the various possible alternatives. Formally we have that X is a configuration iff $(X, \leq_X)$ is a partial order such that $\forall e \in X. \{e' \in X \mid e' \leq_X e\}$ is finite, and given any $e \in X$, if $e' \prec e$ and $e' \notin X$ then there exists $e'' \in X$ and $e' \mathbin{\natural} e'' \prec e$. In fact obviously $\prec$ is irreflexive and $\#$ is symmetric. Flow unravel nets are good candidates to be related to flow event structures. On a flow unravel net net $R = \langle S, T, F, m \rangle$ we can define the following relations, which can be considered as *dependency* and *conflict* relations:

- $t \prec t'$ iff $t^\bullet \cap {}^\bullet t' \cap S_c \neq \emptyset$,
- $t \# t'$ iff $\forall X \in \mathcal{X}(R) \ \{t, t'\} \not\subseteq [X]$.

Hence, a flow unravel net net has ingredients similar to the ones that a causal net has, namely a causality relation and a conflict relation, the main difference is that the conflict relation in a flow unravel net is obtained semantically. We can prove the following propositions:

Proposition 4. *Let $R = \langle S, T, F, m \rangle$ be a flow unravel net, then $(T, \prec, \#)$ is a flow event structure.*

Proposition 5. *Let $R = \langle S, T, F, m \rangle$ be a flow unravel net, and let X be a state of R. Then X is a configuration of $(T, \prec, \#)$.*

Proof. It is enough to show that, given any $t \in X$, if $t' \prec t$ and $t' \notin X$ then there is a $t'' \in X$ such that $t'' \prec t$ and $t' \# t''$, as the other requirements are met trivially by the definition of state and of unravel net. Assume that there is $t' \prec t$, $t' \notin X$ and there is no $t'' \in X$ which is $t'' \prec t$ and such that $t' \# t''$. But this would violate that $R|_{\llbracket X \rrbracket}$ is a causal net.

Proposition 6. *Let $R = \langle S, T, F, m \rangle$ be a flow unravel net, and let $X \subseteq T$ be a configuration of $(T, \prec, \#)$. Then X is a state of R and $\mathbf{mark}(X) = m_X$ is the marking reached executing the events in T.*

Proof. By induction on the size of X (the elements of X). If X is the empty set then $\mathbf{mark}(X) = m = m_X$. Assume it holds for X of size n and let us prove for $X \cup \{t\}$, with $t \notin X$. As $X \cup \{t\}$ is a configuration t is a maximum with respect to $\leq_X$ as otherwise X would not be a configuration, hence it remains to prove that $m_X[t\rangle$. Assume it is not, then there must be a place in ${}^\bullet t$ which is not marked in m_X. But this can happen only if there is a transition t' in X which have used the token in this place, which means that $t \# t'$ contradicting that $X \cup \{t\}$ is a configuration.

4   Flow Unfolding of a Multi-clock Net

In this section we construct a flow unravel net which turns out to be an unfolding of a multi clock net.

The unfolding of a net N is usually defined as a pair: a net with certain properties and a mapping that associate this net to N in such a way that to each state of N a state of the unfolding of N correspond and vice versa. We recall the notion of morphism between safe nets [3].

Definition 15. *Let $N = \langle S, T, F, m \rangle$ and $N' = \langle S', T', F', m' \rangle$ be nets. A morphism $h : N \to N'$ is a pair $\langle h_T, h_S \rangle$, where $h_T : T \to T'$ is a partial function and $h_S \subseteq S \times S'$ is a relation such that*

- *for each $s' \in m'$ there exists a unique $s \in S$ and $s \, h_S \, s'$,*
- *if $s \, h_S \, s'$ then the restriction $h_T : {}^\bullet s \to {}^\bullet s'$ and $h_T : s^\bullet \to s'^\bullet$ are total functions, and*
- *if $t' = h_T(t)$ then $h_S^{op} : {}^\bullet t' \to {}^\bullet t$ and $h_S^{op} : t'^\bullet \to t^\bullet$ are total functions, where h_S^{op} is the opposite relation to h_S.*

Morphisms among safe nets preserve the reachable markings: let $h: N \to N'$ be a net morphism. For each $m, m' \in \mathcal{M}_N$ and $A \in \mu T$, if $m\,[A\rangle\,m'$ then $h_S(m)\,[\mu h_T(A)\rangle\,h_S(m')$ where $h_S(m) = \{s' \in S' \mid \exists s \in m \text{ and } s\ h_S\ s'\}$.

The mapping which is the second component of the unfolding is a suitable morphism which is called folding:

Definition 16. *Let $N = \langle S, T, F, m \rangle$ and $N' = \langle S', T', F', m' \rangle$ be two nets and $h: N \to N'$ a net morphism. h is a folding iff h_T is total, h_S is a total function and for all $t \in T$, there are bijections between $^\bullet t$ and $^\bullet h_T(t)$, $t^\bullet$ and $h_T(t)^\bullet$ and between m and m'.*

Given a safe net $N = \langle S, T, F, m \rangle$, an unfolding is a pair (C, p) where $C = \langle B, E, F', m' \rangle$ is a causal net and p is a folding (see [3,4]). Observe that if N is a multi-clock net (the partition mapping being $\nu(N)$), also C is a multi-clock net, the $\nu(C)$ being defined as follows: for $b \in B$. $\nu(C)(b) = \nu(N)(h_s(b))$.

The notion of folding we have defined above has to be specialised when flow unravel nets are considered. Control places are used to enforce dependencies among transitions, but they do not represent *resources*.

Definition 17. *Let $R = \langle S_i^R \cup S_c^R, T^R, F^R, m^R \rangle$ be a flow unravel net and $N = \langle S, T, F, m \rangle$ be multi clock net. Then $p: R \to N$ is a flow-folding morphism iff $p': R|_{S_i^R} \to N$ is a folding morphism, where $p_T = p_T'$ and p_S' is the restriction of p_S to places in S_i^R, and for all $s_c \in S_c$ and for all $s \in S$. $\neg(s_c\ h_s\ s)$.*

A consequence of this definition is that in a flow-folding morphism control places are not associated to any place in the net onto which a flow unravel net is folded.

We are now ready to define a *flow* unfolding.

Definition 18. *Let $N = (\langle S, T, F, m \rangle, \nu)$ be a multi-clock net. Then a flow unfolding is the pair $(R = \langle S^r, T^r, F^r, m^r \rangle, p)$ where*

1. *$p: \langle S^r, T^r, F^r, m^r \rangle \to \langle S, T, F, m \rangle$ is a flow folding morphism,*
2. *$R = \langle S^r, T^r, F^r, m^r \rangle$ is a uniformly labelled flow unravel net with respect to $p_S|_{S_i^R}$,*
3. *$\forall\, t, t' \in T^R$. $^\bullet t = {^\bullet t'}$ and $p_T(t) = p_T(t') \Rightarrow t = t'$,*
4. *$\forall\, t, t' \in T^R$. $^\bullet t \cap S_i = {^\bullet t'} \cap S_i$ and $t^\bullet \cap S_i = t'^\bullet \cap S_i \Rightarrow t = t'$, and*
5. *$\forall\, t \in T^R$. $|^\bullet t \cap S_c| \le |^\bullet t \cap S_i|$.*

Condition (3) is the usual on unfoldings: two transitions that have the same preset and are mapped onto the same transition of the original net are the same. Internal places are meant to represent the $i - th$ occurrence of a token in a given place of the unfolded net. In this view Condition (2) states that each internal place bears the *same* occurrence of tokens. Condition (4) enforces two transitions consuming and producing the same tokens to be the same transition and the last condition puts a bound on the number of control places. This condition will be more clear when we will effectively construct the unfolding of a multi-clock net.

The algorithm to construct this unfolding is similar to the one devised in the construction of a branching process [4]. However, in order to adapt it to our purposes, we have to characterize the ingredients, namely the names of places (either control or internal ones), transitions, what a *co-set* of the net is and finally what the *possible extensions* are.

We start introducing the *neighborhood* of a transition.

Definition 19. *Let* $N = \langle S, T, F, m \rangle$ *be a net, and let* $t \in T$, *with* $\circlearrowright(t) = \{t' \mid t' \in {}^\bullet s \text{ or } t' \in s'^\bullet \text{ with } s \in {}^\bullet t \text{ and } s' \in t^\bullet\} \cup \{t\}$ *we denote the* neighborhood *of* t, *namely the transitions following and preceding* t, *including* t.

The transitions in the neighborhood of t are used to find the *local name* of the occurrence of the transition in the unfolding, and the name is used to characterize also internal and control places. To this aim, we introduce an equivalence on words (on alphabets containing the names of transitions in the net we have to unfold). Let $N = (\langle S, T, F, m \rangle, \nu)$ be a multi-clock net, and let $T' \subseteq T$ be a subset of transitions, and let w, w' two words on $(T')^+$, the for all $t \in T'$, we say that $w \sim_t w'$ iff for all $s \in [\![\,{}^\bullet t\,]\!]$, $|proj(w, {}^\bullet s)| = |proj(w', {}^\bullet s)|$ and for all $s \in [\![\,t^\bullet\,]\!]$, $|proj(w, {}^\bullet s)| = |proj(w', {}^\bullet s)|$, and with $(\!(w)\!)_{\sim_t}$ we denote the equivalence class of the word w. Control places and transitions are pairs where the first component is an equivalence class of words on an alphabet of transitions (restricted to the transitions of an automata forming the multi-clock net) and the second component is a transition. The first component of a control place, the equivalance class, encodes all the equivalent (local) histories leading to the same future, represented by the name of the transition in the second component.

The internal places of this unfolding are easy to identify: consider a multi-clock net $N = (\langle S, T, F, m \rangle, \nu)$, then these places are of the following form: $\{(s, i) \mid s \in S \text{ and } i \in \mathbb{N}^+\}$, meaning that the place s got its i-th token.

We characterise now the possible extensions of a flow unravel net. Let $R = \langle S, T, F, m \rangle$ be a flow unravel net and let $X \in \mathcal{X}(R)$, then $[\![m_X]\!]$ is a *cut* of R. With respect to causal nets, where a cut is a maximal subset of pairwise concurrent places (conditions), here we have to consider the reached marking of the execution of the elements of a state (a configuration in the corresponding FES). A *co-set* A is a subset of a cut of R such that there exists a transition $t \in T$ such that $[\![\,{}^\bullet t\,]\!] = A$.

Definition 20. *Let* (R, p) *be a flow unfolding, with* $R = \langle S_i \cup S_c, T, F, m \rangle$. *The* possible extensions *of* (R, p) *are the transitions* $((\!(w)\!)_{\sim_t}, t)$, $w \in \circlearrowright(t)^*$, *such that for all* $s \in [\![\,{}^\bullet t\,]\!]$

- *there exists* $((\!(\alpha_s)\!)_{\sim_t}, t) \in S_c$ *where* $\alpha_s = proj(w, \circlearrowright(t) \cap T_{\nu^{-1}(\nu(s))})$
- $A = \{((\!(\alpha_s)\!)_{\sim_t}, t) \mid s \in {}^\bullet t\} \cup \{(s, |proj(w, {}^\bullet s)| + m(s)) \mid s \in {}^\bullet t\}$ *is a co-set of* R *such that* ${}^\bullet t = p_S(A)$, *and*
- $((\!(w)\!)_{\sim_t}, t)$ *does not already belong to* (R, p).

Let us focus on the set of places $A = \{((\!(\alpha_s)\!)_{\sim_t}, t)\} \cup \{(s, |proj(w, {}^\bullet s)| + m(s))\}$, where clearly $\{((\!(\alpha_s)\!)_{\sim_t}, t)\} \subseteq S_c$ and $\{(s, |proj(w, {}^\bullet s)| + m(s))\} \subseteq S_i$. The internal places (those of the form (s, i)) are the instances of tokens consumed by the transition $((\!(w)\!)_{\sim_t}, t)$, whereas the $\{((\!(\alpha_s)\!)_{\sim_t}, t)\}$ are the control places used by this transition.

The algorithm to construct the flow unfolding is the one described in Table 1. In this algorithm, $NextPe(R,p)$ is used to find all the possible extensions according to Def. 20.

Table 1. The algorithm for constructing a flow unfolding

Input: A multi-clock net $N = (S, T, F, m)$
Output: The flow unfolding $\mathcal{FU} = (R, p), R = \langle S_i \cup S_c, T', F', m \rangle$
  begin:
  $\mathcal{FU} \leftarrow (\langle \{(s,1) \mid m(s) = 1\}, \emptyset, \emptyset, \{(s,1) \mid m(s) = 1\} \rangle, p)$ where $p_S((s,1)) = s$
  $pe \leftarrow NextPe(R,p)$
  while $pe \neq \emptyset$ **do**
    Add to $\mathcal{FU}$ a transition $((\langle w \rangle_{\sim_t}, t) \in pe$
    and compute the places:
    $S_i^{(\langle w \rangle_{\sim_t}, t)} = \{(s,k) \mid k = |proj(w, {}^\bullet s)| + 1 + m(s)\}, \quad \forall s \in \llbracket t^\bullet \rrbracket$
    $S_c^{(\langle w \rangle_{\sim_t}, t)} = \{((\langle \alpha_s \rangle_{\sim_{t'}}, t') \mid \alpha_s \sim_{t'} proj(wt, \circlearrowright(t) \cap T_{\overline{s}}), \forall s \in \llbracket t^\bullet \rrbracket$ and $\forall t' \in \llbracket s^\bullet \rrbracket$
    and extend F' with:
    $F'(x, (\langle w \rangle_{\sim_t}, t)) = 1, \forall x \in A$ (see Def. 20) and 0 otherwise
    $F'((\langle w \rangle_{\sim_t}, t), s) = 1, \forall s \in (S_c^{(\langle w \rangle_{\sim_t}, t)} \cup S_i^{(\langle w \rangle_{\sim_t}, t)})$ and 0 otherwise
    then update data structures
    $pe \leftarrow (pe \setminus (\langle w \rangle_{\sim_t}, t)) \cup NextPe(R,p)$
    $S_i \leftarrow S_i \cup S_i^{(\langle w \rangle_{\sim_t}, t)}$
    $S_c \leftarrow S_c \cup S_c^{(\langle w \rangle_{\sim_t}, t)}$
    $T' \leftarrow T' \cup \{(\langle w \rangle_{\sim_t}, t)\}$
    and extend p_T with $p_T((\langle w \rangle_{\sim_t}, t)) = t$ and p_S with $p_S((s,k)) = s$ with
    $(s,k) \in S_i^{(\langle w \rangle_{\sim_t}, t)}$ and undefined for the places in $S_c^{(\langle w \rangle_{\sim_t}, t)}$
  end while

The following proposition states that at each iteration the algorithm produces a flow unravel net, that means that no circularity is introduced among control places.

Proposition 7. *Let (R,p) be the result of the algorithm in Table 1. Then R is a flow unravel net.*

Proof. Algorithm initialization creates the net $R^0 = \langle S^0 = S_i^0 \cup S_c^0 = \{(s,1) \mid m(s) = 1\}, \emptyset, \emptyset, m = \{(s,1) \mid m(s) = 1\} \rangle$ and a set of possible extensions $pe = \{((\langle \epsilon \rangle_{\sim_t}, t)\}$, for all t enabled by the initial marking of N. R^0 is a trivial flow unravel net and equipped with p is a flow unfolding.

Assume that up to the n-th possible extension added we have a flow unravel net $R^n = \langle S_i^n \cup S_c^n, T^n, F^n, m = \{(s,1) \mid m(s) = 1\} \rangle$ and be $((\langle w \rangle_{\sim_t}, t)$ the $(n+1)$-th. We will show that adding $((\langle w \rangle_{\sim_t}, t)$ the properties of Def. 10 are fulfilled.

(1) and (2) follow from the definition of possible extensions, in particular, (2) holds because we always put a transition iff there is a co-set that can fire it and at least one internal place is created in the process of adding a transition. Conditions

(3) and (4) are proven similarly, hence we argue only for (3). In order to prove
(3) we must ensure that if $((\![\bar{w}]\!)_{\sim_{t'}}, t') \in T^m, m \le n$ and $s_c \in ((\![\bar{w}]\!)_{\sim_{t'}}, t')^\bullet \cap$
$^\bullet((\![w]\!)_{\sim_t}, t) \cap S_c$ then there exists $s_i \in ((\![\bar{w}, t']\!)_{\sim_{t'}})^\bullet \cap {}^\bullet((\![w]\!)_{\sim_t}, t) \cap S_i$. The possible
extension $((\![\bar{w}]\!)_{\sim_{t'}}, t')$ added a place (s, k') with $s \in t'^\bullet$, $k' = |proj(\bar{w}, {}^\bullet s)| + 1$,
and the equivalences $\bar{w}t' \sim_t s_c \sim_t w$ exhibit the existence of $(s, k) \in A$ co-set
of R^n, such that $s \in {}^\bullet t$ with $k = |proj(w, {}^\bullet s)|$. We show that $k = k'$ and thus
Condition 3 of Def. 10 holds. As $t' \in {}^\bullet s$, by using the definition of equivalence
on places, we obtain:

$$\bar{w}t' \sim_t s_c \sim_t w \Leftrightarrow |proj(\bar{w}t', {}^\bullet s)| = |proj(w, {}^\bullet s)|$$
$$\Leftrightarrow |proj(\bar{w}, {}^\bullet s)| + 1 = |proj(w, {}^\bullet s)|$$
$$\Leftrightarrow k' = k$$

To prove Condition (6) of Def. 10 consider the following net fragment:

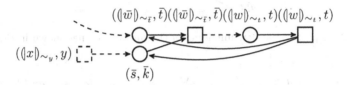

$$((\![\bar{w}]\!)_{\sim_{\bar{t}}}, \bar{t})((\![\bar{w}]\!)_{\sim_{\bar{t}}}, \bar{t})((\![w]\!)_{\sim_t}, t)((\![w]\!)_{\sim_t}, t)$$

$$((\![x]\!)_{\sim_y}, y)$$

$$(\bar{s}, \bar{k})$$

A cycle means that $\bar{w} \sim_{t'} wt$, where $((\![wt]\!)_{\sim_{t'}}, t')$ is one of the control places
created by adding the transition $((\![w]\!)_{\sim_t}, t)$. Before adding the possible extension
$((\![w]\!)_{\sim_t}, t)$ we can identify class representative of $u \sim_{\bar{t}}$ such that $|u|_t = n$ is the
maximum number of t and $u \sim_{\bar{t}} \bar{w}$. The number of t is bounded because we
assume that at least till $((\![w]\!)_{\sim_t}, t)$ the net restricted to control places has no
cycles. A state of $R^{n+1}|_{S_c^{n+1}}$ containing both $((\![\bar{w}]\!)_{\sim_{\bar{t}}, t})$ and $((\![w]\!)_{\sim_t}, t)$ would
have the internal place $(\bar{s}, \bar{k})$ marked twice since its token is put by $((\![x]\!)_{\sim_y, y})$
first, and then by $((\![w]\!)_{\sim_t}, t)$. As for $((\![\bar{w}]\!)_{\sim_{\bar{t}, \bar{t}}})$ we can find a class representative
of $v \sim_{\bar{t}}$ such that $|v|_t$ is maximum and $v \sim_{\bar{t}} w$. Since the word v takes into
account all the occurrences of t that u has, plus at least one, it is obvious that
$\bar{k} = |proj(v, \{t, \dots\})| \neq |proj(u, \{t, \dots\})|$ and this leads to a contradiction.
Hence a cycle cannot exist.

The algorithm does what it is expected: it gives a flow unfolding (it is routine
to check the various conditions of Def. 18).

Theorem 1. *Let $N = (\langle S, T, F, m \rangle, \nu)$ be a multi-clock net. The algorithm in
Table 1 constructs a flow unfolding for N.*

In Fig. 2 the result of few iterations of the algorithm applied to the multi-clock
net in Fig. 1 is shown. Control places are depicted with a gray background. The
transition $((\![a]\!)_{\sim_b}, b)$ depends on the transition $((\![\epsilon]\!)_{\sim_a}, a)$ as in the preset of the
former there is the control place $((\![a]\!)_{\sim_b}, b)$ that is in the postset of the latter.
The transitions $((\![a]\!)_{\sim_b}, b)$ and $((\![\epsilon]\!)_{\sim_b}, b)$ are in conflict as they share, in their
presets, the internal place $(p, 1)$, which is also a control place.

If we consider only internal places of a flow unfolding of a multi-clock net, we
have again a multi-clock net.

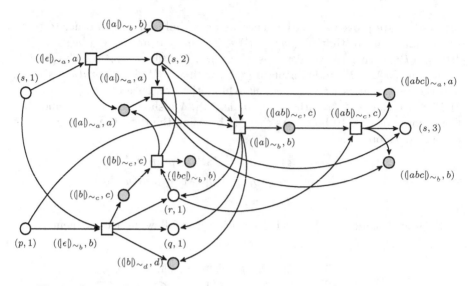

Fig. 2. A part of the flow unfolding of the multi-clock net shown in Fig. 1

Proposition 8. *Let $N = (\langle S, T, F, m\rangle, \nu)$ be a multi-clock net and let (R, p) be the flow unfolding of N, where $R = \langle S_i^R \cup S_c^R, T^R, F^R, m^R\rangle$. Then $R|_{S_i^R}$ is a multi-clock net.*

Proof. The internal places of R are mapped onto the places of a multi-clock net. By definition of flow folding morphism it is clear that also $R|_{S_i^R}$ is a multi-clock net, defining $\nu(R|_{S_i^R})((s, k)) = p_S^{-1}(\nu(s))$.

Our construction has the same property of other notions of unfoldings: it is the most general one, in the sense that any other *candidate* to be an unfolding is uniquely mapped onto our flow unfolding.

To prove this we first have to define the *depth* of a flow unravel net $R = \langle S_i \cup S_c, T, F, m\rangle$. As the net when restricted to control places is acyclic it is straightforward to define the depth as follows:

Definition 21. *Let $R = \langle S_i \cup S_c, T, F, m\rangle$ be a flow unravel net. We define the depth of control places and transitions as follows:*

- *$depth(s) = 0$ if $s \in m$,*
- *$depth(t) = max\{depth(s) \mid s \in {}^\bullet t \cap S_c\} + 1$ and for all $s \in S_c$, and*
- *$depth(s) = min\{depth(t) \mid s \in t^\bullet\}$.*

There are two relevant differences with respect to the classical notion of depth: it is calculated on control places and not on internal places (because of cycle it may arise when considering internal places) and it is taken as the minimum among those available. Control places may have several incoming arcs modeling the various alternatives but locally equivalent past histories of a transition. It is then enough to consider the *shortest*.

Theorem 2. *Let N be a multi-clock net and (R, p) its flow unfolding. Let R' be a flow unravel net, $g : R' \to N$ be a morphism and let R' be uniformly labelled flow unravel net with respect to g_S. Then there exists a unique morphism from R' to R.*

Proof. We sketch the proof. The proof is done by constructing a chain of morphisms from suitable subnets of R' to R. Subnets are defined accordingly to the notion of prefix, which is in this case calculated as follows. Consider the control places at depth less or equal to n, and call them S'_n. Take $T'_n = {}^\bullet S'_n = \bigcup_{s \in S'_n} {}^\bullet s$, then the subnet of depth n of R' is $R'|_{T'_n}$.

Let us construct the morphisms as follows: $h^0 \colon R'|_{T'_0} \to R$ is defined as $h^0_T = \emptyset$ and the relation on places is $s\ h^0_S\ (g_S(s), 1)$, as T'_0 is empty (as g_S is a bijection on the initial marking $g_S(s)$ is well defined).

The morphism $h^{n+1} \colon R'|_{T'_{n+1}} \to R$ is obtained from h^n. Take any $t_1 \in T'_{n+1} \setminus T'_n$. We have two possibilities: either $g_T(t_1)$ is undefined or $g_T(t_1) = t$. In the first case $h^{n+1}_T(t_1)$ is undefined and the the places in $t_1{}^\bullet$ are unrelated to any place in R. In the second case, consider ${}^\bullet t_1$, and the places in $s' \in S^R_i \cup S^R_c$ such that $s\ h^n_S\ s'$, for $s \in {}^\bullet t_1$. By construction of the flow unfolding, these places are a co-set of R, and then there is a $t' \in T^R$ such that ${}^\bullet t'$ is this co-set and $p_T(t') = t = g_T(t_1)$. It is then easy to stipulate $h^{n+1}_T(t_1) = t$ and for all $s \in t_1{}^\bullet \cap S^R_i$ put $s h^{n+1}_T(g_S(s), k)$, where k is number associated to s in R' (as R' is uniformly labelled with respect to g_S). It remains to define the relation h^{n+1} on control places. Consider then any $t'_1 \in T'$ for which h^n_T is defined and such that $h^n_T(t'_1){}^\bullet \cap {}^\bullet t' \cap S^R_c \neq \emptyset$. As N is multi-clock net $h^n_T(t'_1){}^\bullet \cap {}^\bullet t' \cap S^R_c$ is a singleton, say $\{s_{h^n_T(t'_1), t'}\}$. Relate then the place in $t'_1{}^\bullet \cap {}^\bullet t_1 \cap S'_c$ with $s_{h^n_T(t'_1), t'}$. It is routine then to check that this is a well defined morphism.

Uniqueness can be proved along the same line.

5   Relating Flow Unfoldings to Other Unfoldings

In this section we relate our construction with two other notions of unfolding presented in literature, namely the one of *merged process* [7] and *trellises* [6]. Clearly a classical unfolding can be *folded* onto a flow unfolding by transforming the causal net into a flow unravel net and using Th. 2.

Let $N = \langle S, T, F, m \rangle$ be a safe net, (C, p) be an unfolding of N where $C = \langle B, E, F', m' \rangle$ is a causal net and $p \colon C \to N$ is a folding morphism (*i.e.* $\forall\ e, e' \in E$. (${}^\bullet e = {}^\bullet e'$ and $p_T(e) = p_T(e')$) $\Rightarrow e = e'$), then (C, p) is called a *branching process* of N [4]. As p_S is a total function from B to S, it can be seen as a labelling function, hence we can associate to each place a number that it is called the *occurrence-depth* and that is defined as follows: the occurrence-depth of a condition $b \in B$ is the highest number of equally labelled conditions that are on a path from an initial condition to b. We recall the definition of merged process for safe nets:

Definition 22. *Let N be a safe net and (C, p) be branching process. The merged process of (C, p) is the net $\mathfrak{Merge}(C, p)$ defined by the following steps:*

1. *all the conditions bearing the same label and having the same* occurrence-depth *are* fused *together, and these conditions, called* mp-*conditions, inherits the same incoming and outgoing arcs of the conditions that are fused, finally an* mp-*condition inherit the same label of the fused conditions,*

2. *after performing the previous step, all the transitions with the same label, the same preset and the same postset are* fused *together, giving an* mp-*event, and they inherit the label from the fused as well as the incoming and outgoing arcs, and*

3. *the initial marking is given by the* mp-*conditions which are originated by conditions that were minimal in the causal net C.*

Interestingly enough, our construction is strongly related to this one:

Theorem 3. *Let N be a multi-clock net, (R, p) its flow unfolding, (C, f) be its branching process and $\mathfrak{Merge}(C, f)$ the associated merged process. Then $R|_{S_i}$ and $\mathfrak{Merge}(C, f)$ are the same net up to renaming of places and transitions.*

Proof. We give the proof idea. Clearly internal places of R are the same of $\mathfrak{Merge}(C, f)$, being N a multi-clock net (hence a place belongs to a unique automaton, as automata synchronize on common transitions). We have to show that the transitions are the same as well. Assume they are not, then R has at least two transitions t, t' which are identified in $\mathfrak{Merge}(C, f)$ but are not in R. As they are identified in $\mathfrak{Merge}(C, f)$ they the same *internal* preset and postset. But this is impossible. Assume now that there are two transitions t, t' in $\mathfrak{Merge}(C, f)$ which are identified in R. Then they have the same internal preset and postset hence they have to be identified also in $\mathfrak{Merge}(C, f)$. Hence the thesis.

A merged process of a multi-clock net can be transformed into a flow unfolding as well, but control places have to be added with a different criteria with respect to the one devised for causal net (*i.e.* by looking directly if two transitions have a place in common). The idea is that there is a control place among two transitions if they share a place and they belong to the same configuration. Consider the merged process in Fig. 3(d). The multiset of transition X defined as $X(a_1) = 1$, $X(c_1) = 2$ and $X(b_2) = 2$ is a state of the net depicted in Fig. 3(d), but it is not a configuration of the causal net in Fig. 3(c). In [7] a way to check if an *run* of the net is a configuration is provided without resorting to the branching process, that can be used to add the control places.

A different consideration have to be done for trellises. Trellises are defined for multi-clock nets, and they unfold properly the time but do not expand conflicts. In a trellis each execution corresponds to the synchronization of trajectories in each component, synchronization performed on appropriate equally labelled transitions. Now conditions in a trellis are fused only if they bear the same label (are occurrence of the same place) and have the same *time* and this time is calculated counting the conditions belonging to the same automata in the past. Thus they are not easily comparable with flow unfoldings, where time does not count.

In Fig. 3 we draw (parts) of the unfolding/branching process (c), merged process (d), trellis (e) and flow unfolding (b) of the net (a). Internal places and

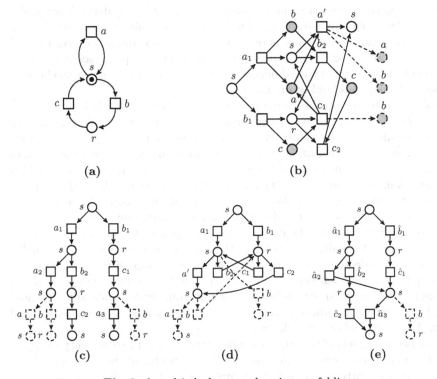

Fig. 3. A multi-clock net and various unfoldings

transitions of (b) give the net drawn in (d). In these unfoldings there is no concurrency, only conflicts and causal dependencies may be deduced. On the trellis the dependencies are deduced by going from the initial condition along a path, similarly to the flow unfolding, and conflicts arise from the use of a common resource (hence in the trellis (e) the events $\hat{a}_1$ and $\hat{b}_1$ are in conflict). In the merged process executable cycles are possible: b_2 can be executed twice (one after a_1 and the second after c_1), whereas this is impossible in the flow unravel net. The event a' is obtained fusing a_2 and a_3 in the branching process. In the flow unfolding b_2 can be executed only once, and again, like in trellises, conflicts arise by using the same resource: b_2 is in conflict with a' (which is again the result of fusing a_2 and a_3) but now b_2 cannot be executed twice, as it uses the token that the transition a_1 puts in the control place b. Dependencies are captured along the control places that in this figure are labelled with the name of the transitions they enable.

6   Conclusions

In this paper we have proposed a notion of unfolding of multi-clock nets that can be easily related to the class of flow event structures. This unfolding is proved to be the more general one among those for which a dependency and a conflict relation can be defined (see Th. 2), and this result gives, in our opinion, evidence that the construction is reasonable and useful. Indeed our result gives further substance from a theoretical viewpoint to merged processes (see Th. 3). Moreover the relation of causal dependency may be relevant for model checking performed using this kind of unfolding.

Still our construction has some weakeness. It relies on multi-clock nets, and though any safe net can be turned into a multi-clock net, as already noticed in the introduction, the construction as it is now cannot be applied to unsafe nets in general. The reason is that control places are used to equate histories leading to the same future, and these histories are easily identified just looking at transitions in a component. This information turn out to be rather crucial. The generalization we devise should consider an adequate equivalence to equate *local* histories. In this line, the decomposition approach proposed in [23] has to be pursued. Furthermore, the number of control places depends on the number of components of a multi-clock net, and the construction that associates a multi-clock net to a safe one creates a *component* for each place in the original net.

We have certainly left out the investigation on how to find *cut-off* events to obtain a *finite* and *complete* prefix of a flow unfolding, which is already presented in [22] for the merged processes. The clear dependency relation we propose could fit in the theoretical framework devised in [24].

Another advantage of having a dependency relation is the possibility of applying the approach pursued in [25] and [26]. We are confident that reveal relations can be defined starting from a flow unravel nets, and this will be the subject of future works.

Acknowledgement. We would like to thank Eric Fabre and Victor Khomenko for many useful discussions on the topic of this paper, and to the reviewers as well for the useful criticisms that have helped us in improving the paper.

References

1. Khomenko, V.: Model Checking based on Prefixes of Petri Net Unfoldings. PhD thesis, School of Computing Science, University of Newcastle upon Tyne (2003)
2. Fabre, E., Benveniste, A., Haar, S., Jard, C.: Distributed Monitoring of Concurrent and Asynchronous Systems. Discrete Event Dynamic Systems 15, 33–84 (2005)
3. Winskel, G.: Event Structures. In: Brauer, W., Reisig, W., Rozenberg, G. (eds.) APN 1986. LNCS, vol. 255, pp. 325–392. Springer, Heidelberg (1987)
4. Engelfriet, J.: Branching processes of Petri nets. Acta Informatica 28, 575–591 (1991)
5. McMillan, K.: A Technique of State Space Search Based on Unfolding. Formal Methods in System Design 6, 45–65 (1995)
6. Fabre, E.: Trellis processes: A compact representation for runs of concurrent systems. Discrete Event Dynamic Systems 17, 267–306 (2007)
7. Khomenko, V., Kondratyev, A., Koutny, M., Vogler, W.: Merged Processes: a new condensed representation of Petri net behaviour. Acta Informatica 43, 307–330 (2006)

8. van Glabbeek, R.J., Plotkin, G.D.: Configuration structures, event structures and Petri nets. Theoretical Computer Science 410, 4111–4159 (2009)
9. Pinna, G.M., Poigné, A.: On the nature of events: another perspective in concurrency. Theoretical Computer Science 138, 425–454 (1995)
10. Boudol, G.: Flow Event Structures and Flow Nets. In: Guessarian, I. (ed.) LITP 1990. LNCS, vol. 469, pp. 62–95. Springer, Heidelberg (1990)
11. Boudol, G., Castellani, I.: Flow models of distributed computations: Three equivalent semantics for CCS. Information and Computation 114, 247–314 (1994)
12. Baldan, P., Corradini, A., Montanari, U.: Contextual Petri nets, asymmetric event structures and processes. Information and Computation 171, 1–49 (2001)
13. Baldan, P., Busi, N., Corradini, A., Pinna, G.M.: Domain and event structure semantics for Petri nets with read and inhibitor arcs. Theoretical Computer Science 323, 129–189 (2004)
14. Langerak, R.: Bundle Event Structures: A Non-Interleaving Semantics for Lotos. In: Diaz, M., Groz, R. (eds.) Fifth International Conference on Formal Description Techniques for Distributed Systems and Communication Protocols, FORTE 1992, IFIP Transactions C-10, pp. 331–346. North-Holland (1992)
15. Gunawardena, J.: A generalized event structure for the Muller unfolding of a safe net. In: Best, E. (ed.) CONCUR 1993. LNCS, vol. 715, pp. 278–292. Springer, Heidelberg (1993)
16. Pinna, G.M.: How much is worth to remember? A taxonomy based on Petri Nets Unfoldings. In: Kristensen, L.M., Petrucci, L. (eds.) PETRI NETS 2011. LNCS, vol. 6709, pp. 109–128. Springer, Heidelberg (2011)
17. van Glabbeek, R.J., Plotkin, G.D.: Configuration structures. In: Kozen, D. (ed.) Proceedings of 10th Annual IEEE Symposium on Logic in Computer Science, pp. 199–209. IEEE Computer Society Press (1995)
18. Reisig, W.: Petri Nets: An Introduction. EACTS Monographs on Theoretical Computer Science. Springer (1985)
19. Hayman, J., Winskel, G.: The unfolding of general Petri nets. In: Hariharan, R., Mukund, M., Vinay, V. (eds.) IARCS Annual Conference on Foundations of Software Technology and Theoretical Computer Science (FSTTCS 2008), Dagstuhl, Germany, Schloss Dagstuhl - Leibniz-Zentrum fuer Informatik, Germany (2008)
20. Nielsen, M., Plotkin, G., Winskel, G.: Petri Nets, Event Structures and Domains, Part 1. Theoretical Computer Science 13, 85–108 (1981)
21. Esparza, J., Römer, S., Vogler, W.: An Improvement of McMillan's Unfolding Algorithm. Formal Methods in System Design 20, 285–310 (2002)
22. Khomenko, V., Mokhov, A.: Direct construction of Complete Merged Processes. The Computer Journal (2013) (to appear)
23. Rathke, J., Sobocinski, P., Stephens, O.: Decomposing Petri nets. CoRR abs/1304.3121 (2013)
24. Khomenko, V., Koutny, M., Vogler, W.: Canonical prefixes of Petri net unfoldings. Acta Informatica 40, 95–118 (2003)
25. Balaguer, S., Chatain, T., Haar, S.: Building occurrence nets from reveals relations. Fundamamenta Informaticae 123, 245–272 (2013)
26. Haar, S., Kern, C., Schwoon, S.: Computing the reveals relation in occurrence nets. Theoretical Computer Science 493, 66–79 (2013)

Non-interference by Unfolding[*]

Paolo Baldan[1] and Alberto Carraro[2]

[1] Università di Padova, Dipartimento di Matematica, Italy
baldan@math.unipd.it
[2] Università Ca' Foscari di Venezia, DAIS, Italy
and ANR Projet Récré, France
acarraro@pps.univ-paris-diderot.fr

Abstract. The concept of non-interference has been introduced to characterise the absence of undesired information flows in a computing system. Although it is often explained referring to an informal notion of causality - the activity involving the part of the system with higher level of confidentiality should not cause any observable effect at lower levels - it is almost invariably formalised in terms of interleaving semantics. Here we focus on Petri nets and on the BNDC property (Bisimilarity-based Non-Deducibility on Composition), a formalisation of non-interference widely studied in the literature. We show that BNDC admits natural characterisations based on the unfolding semantics - a classical true concurrent semantics for Petri nets - in terms of causalities and conflicts between high and low level activities. This leads to an algorithm for checking BNDC for safe Petri nets which relies on the construction of suitable complete prefixes of the unfolding. A prototype tool provides very promising results.

1 Introduction

The concept of non-interference has been introduced to characterise the absence of undesired information flows in a computing system. The underlying idea is simple: a system is viewed as consisting of components at different levels of confidentiality, in the simplest case a high part H, which intuitively should be secret, and a low part L, which is public. The absence of a flow of information from H to L is captured by asking that the activity of H does not determine visible effects, according to some selected observational semantics, at low level L. Originally the notion of non-interference [1] has been defined for deterministic programs, using a trace semantics. Since then, several variants have been studied, dealing with non-deterministic systems and finer observations, notably bisimilarity. In the setting of process calculi, a popular formulation is the so-called NDC (Non-Deducibility on Composition), which states that a process S is free of interferences whenever S running in isolation, seen from the low level, is behaviourally equivalent to S interacting with any parallel high level process. A

---

[*] Work supported by the project Récré (ANR) and the MIUR PRIN project CINA.

G. Ciardo and E. Kindler (Eds.): PETRI NETS 2014, LNCS 8489, pp. 190–209, 2014.

systematic presentation of non-interference notions for concurrent systems can be found, e.g., in [2,3,4].

Although the definition of non-interference often informally refers to some notion of causality – the activity at high level should not cause visible effects on the behaviour at low level – it has been almost invariably formalised in terms of interleaving semantics.

The value of a characterisation of non-interference in terms of a true concurrent semantics can be twofold. At a conceptual level, it can unveil the relation between causality and interferences. On the pragmatic side, the use of a true concurrent semantics, which represents concurrency of computational steps explicitly, rather than by their possible interleavings, can be helpful for facing the state explosion problem which affects the verification of concurrent systems.

A first step towards a causal characterisation of non-interference can be found in [5], where several notions of non-interference, in particular BNDC (Bisimilarity-based NDC), are formulated over Petri nets. More specifically, the authors consider contact-free elementary nets (or equivalently, safe P/T nets without self-loops), and they prove that a net satisfies the BNDC property when it does not include neither causal nor conflict places, i.e., places satisfying semi-structural conditions intended to identify undesired interactions between high and low transitions on those places. The result is also generalised to trace nets which extend elementary nets with arcs for testing the presence/absence of tokens in a place, and arcs for filling/emptying a place regardless of its previous content. The notions of causal and conflict place, however, are formulated by requiring the presence of suitable reachable markings and firing sequences, i.e., referring to an interleaving semantics rather than to a causal, true concurrent semantics. In [6] the authors face the question of decidability of BNDC over general P/T nets, providing a positive answer, but leaving aside the problem of providing a causal characterisation.

In this paper we study the notion of non-interference for Petri nets, formalised in terms of BNDC, aiming at a characterisation in terms of a causal semantics.

We first provide a characterisation of BNDC for P/T nets based on notions of causal and conflict places. Our definition slightly simplifies that given in [5] for elementary and safe nets, in a way that is later useful for the development of BNDC checking algorithms.

Focusing on safe nets, the above results are then exploited for obtaining a causal characterisation of BNDC in terms of a classical true concurrent semantics of Petri nets, the unfolding semantics [7]. More precisely, we prove that a safe net is BNDC if and only if its unfolding does not reveal a direct causality from a high level to a low level transition or a direct conflict between a high and a low level transitions. This enables the checking of the BNDC property on a suitably defined complete prefix of the unfolding of a safe net. In fact, we prove that it is possible to build a finite prefix of the unfolding which includes an interference witness if and only if the original net is not BNDC. As mentioned above, checking the property on an unfolding prefix rather than on the reachability graph can improve greatly the efficiency of the check for concurrent systems, since unfolding-based partial order verification techniques have been proven effective in facing the state explosion problem (see, e.g., [8], and references therein).

We developed a prototype tool UBIC (Unfolding-Based Interference Checker) for checking BNDC on safe nets which implements the algorithm proposed in the paper. The prototype is based on CUNF [9], a toolset for carrying out unfolding-based verification on Petri nets. Some preliminary experimental results are extremely promising in comparison to those provided by existing tools for checking BNDC based on interleaving semantics, like ANICA [10].

The rest of the paper is organised as follows. In §2 we define Petri nets and BNDC, the non-interference notion we will work with. In §3 we give a characterisation of BNDC based on causal and conflict places. After recalling in §4 the basics of the unfolding semantics, in §5 we provide an unfolding-based characterisation of BNDC on safe nets which is exploited for devising a corresponding algorithm for checking BNDC. In §6 we report some experimental results obtained with the tool UBIC, implementing the proposed algorithm. Finally, in §7 we draw some conclusions.

2   Preliminaries

A *(Petri) net* is a tuple $N = (P, T, F)$ where P, T are two disjoint sets of *places* and *transitions*, respectively, and $F : (P \times T) \cup (T \times P) \to \mathbb{N}$ is the *flow function*, representing a set of directed edges with non-negative integer weights, such that for every $t \in T$ there exists $p \in P$ such that $F(p, t) > 0$.

A *marking* of N is a function $m : P \to \mathbb{N}$. A transition $t \in T$ is *enabled* at a marking m, denoted $m[t\rangle$, if $m(p) \geq F(p, t)$ for all $p \in P$. If $m[t\rangle$ then t can be *fired* leading to a new marking m', written $m[t\rangle m'$, defined by $m'(p) = m(p) + F(t, p) - F(p, t)$ for all places $p \in P$. The enabling and firing relations are extended to $\sigma \in T^*$ (set of all finite sequences of elements of T) by defining $m[\varepsilon\rangle m$ (where ε is the empty sequence) and $m[\sigma t\rangle m''$ when $m[\sigma\rangle m'$ and $m'[t\rangle m''$. For a marking m, we denote $m^\circ = \{t \in T : m[t\rangle\}$.

A *marked net* is a pair $\mathbf{N} = (N, m_0)$ where N is a net and m_0 is a marking of N. A marking m' is *reachable* if there exists $\sigma \in T^*$ such that $m_0[\sigma\rangle m'$. The set of reachable markings of $\mathbf{N}$ is denoted by $[m_0\rangle$. When $m[t\rangle m'$, the marking m', uniquely determined by m and t, is denoted by $\langle m[t\rangle$. Analogously, for $\sigma \in T^*$, if $m[\sigma\rangle$ we can define the marking $\langle m[\sigma\rangle$.

A *net system* is a net N where T is partitioned into two disjoint sets H and L. We sometimes write $N = (P, H, L, F)$ making the two sets of transitions explicit. The idea is to model a system with two distinguished classes of "users": high level users and low level users. Transitions in H, called *high transitions*, are thought of as visible only to the high level users, while the *low transitions* in L are globally visible. A net system N is called *high* when $L = \emptyset$.

The *low view* (see [5, Definition 3.1]) of a sequence $\sigma \in T^*$ represents the view of a low level user on the run σ w.r.t. the system N. It is defined inductively by $\nu_N(\varepsilon) = \varepsilon$ and $\nu_N(t\sigma) = t\nu_N(\sigma)$ if $t \in L$ and $\nu_N(t\sigma) = \nu_N(\sigma)$ if $t \in H$.

An example of a net system, used also in [11], can be found in Fig. 1(a). It intuitively consists of a high and a low level subsystem, accessing in mutual

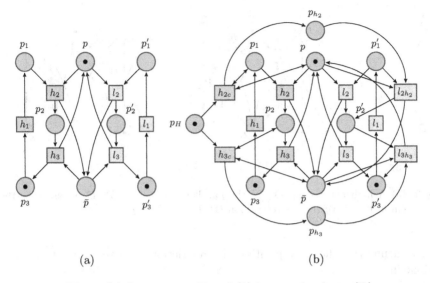

(a)   (b)

Fig. 1. (a) A net system $\mathbf{R}$ and (b) its causal reduct $\gamma(\mathbf{R})$

exclusion a common resource, represented by places p and $\bar{p}$. When place p is marked, the resource is free, when place $\bar{p}$ is marked, the resource is taken. Transitions h_1, l_1 represent the non-critical sections of the subsystems: they do not need the resource and they can run in parallel. Transitions h_2 and l_2 enter the critical section, hence they compete for the token in p. The resource is released and the critical section left by firing h_3, resp. l_3.

Following [5,6] we focus on a notion of non-interference known as BNDC (Bisimilarity-based NDC). The discriminating power of a low level user is formalised by means of a bisimulation equivalence based on the low views.

Definition 1 (low view bisimulation). *Let* $\mathbf{N}$ *and* $\mathbf{N}'$ *be two marked net systems. A* view simulation *of* $\mathbf{N}$ *by* $\mathbf{N}'$ *is a relation* $R \subseteq [m_0\rangle \times [m_0'\rangle$ *such that:*

- *$(m_0, m_0') \in R$;*
- *if $(m, m') \in R$ and $m[\sigma\rangle$ then there exists σ' such that $m'[\sigma'\rangle$, $(\langle m[\sigma\rangle, \langle m'[\sigma'\rangle) \in R$ and $\nu_N(\sigma) = \nu_{N'}(\sigma')$.*

A low view bisimulation *between* $\mathbf{N}$ *and* $\mathbf{N}'$ *is a relation* $R \subseteq [m_0\rangle \times [m_0'\rangle$ *such that both R and R^{-1} are view simulations. If there exists a low view bisimulation between* $\mathbf{N}$ *and* $\mathbf{N}'$, *we say that they are* low view bisimilar *and we write* $\mathbf{N} \approx \mathbf{N}'$.

We remark that Definition 1 above is an instance of [6, Definition 2.5], which introduces a notion of weak bisimilarity for general partially observed labelled transition systems.

A net system $\mathbf{N}$ is deemed free of interferences when the behaviour of $\mathbf{N}$ interacting with any parallel high system is low view bisimilar to the behaviour of $\mathbf{N}$, restricted to the low transitions. In order to formalise this intuition we

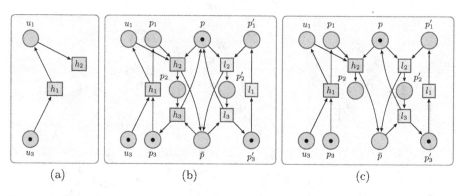

Fig. 2. (a) A high net system **D**; (b) the parallel composition **R | D**, where **R** is the net system in Fig. 1(a); (c) the restriction $(\mathbf{R} | \mathbf{D}) \setminus (H - H_D)$

need to define (parallel) composition and restriction operators on net systems, as done in [6].

Definition 2 (composition). *Let N and N' be two net systems such that $P \cap P' = \emptyset$, $(H' \cap L) \cup (H \cap L') = \emptyset$, and $(P \cap T') \cup (P' \cap T) = \emptyset$. The composition of N and N' is the net system $N | N' = (P \cup P', H \cup H', L \cup L', F | F')$ where $F | F'$ is the least (w.r.t. inclusion) flow function on $P \cup P'$ and $T \cup T'$ that extends both F and F'. The composition of two marked net systems $\mathbf{N} = (N, m_0)$ and $\mathbf{N}' = (N', m_0')$ is the marked net system $\mathbf{N} | \mathbf{N}' = (N | N', m_0 | m_0')$ where $m_0 | m_0'$ is the marking on $N | N'$ that extends both m_0 and m_0'.*

Intuitively, $N | N'$ is the parallel composition of N and N', synchronised on the common transitions. Whenever we consider two net systems N and N' we shall implicitly assume that the disjointness requirements are satisfied so that $N | N'$ is always defined. Note that this may require some "renaming".

Definition 3 (restriction). *Given a net system N and a subset $T_1 \subseteq T$, the restriction of N by T_1 is the net system $N \setminus T_1 = (P, H - T_1, L - T_1, F \setminus T_1)$ where $F \setminus T_1$ is the restriction of F to $(P \times (T - T_1)) \cup ((T - T_1) \times P)$. For a marked net system $\mathbf{N}$, the restriction $\mathbf{N} \setminus T_1$ is $(N \setminus T_1, m_0)$.*

The restricted net system is thus obtained by simply removing the restricted transitions. For instance, the net system $\mathbf{R} | \mathbf{D}$ - where $\mathbf{R}$ is the net in Fig. 1(a) and $\mathbf{D}$ is the high net system in Fig. 2(a) - is depicted in Fig. 2(b). The restriction of $\mathbf{R} | \mathbf{D}$ with respect to $\{h_3\}$, namely $(\mathbf{R} | \mathbf{D}) \setminus \{h_3\}$ is depicted in Fig. 2(c).

We can now recall the definition of the BNDC property on net systems.

Definition 4 (BNDC [6]). *A marked net system $\mathbf{N}$ is BNDC if for every high marked net system $\mathbf{N}'$ we have that $\mathbf{N} \setminus H \approx (\mathbf{N} | \mathbf{N}') \setminus (H - H')$.*

Intuitively, a net system $\mathbf{N}$ is BNDC when no behavioural difference can be detected by a low level observer between $\mathbf{N} \setminus H$ (i.e. $\mathbf{N}$ running in isolation and without firing high level transitions) and $(\mathbf{N} | \mathbf{N}') \setminus (H - H')$ (i.e., $\mathbf{N}$ running in parallel with an arbitrary high net $\mathbf{N}'$, thus possibly synchronising on high level transitions).

For instance, the net system $\mathbf{R}$ in Fig. 1(a) is not BNDC. In fact, $\mathbf{R} \setminus H$ is clearly not bisimilar to $(\mathbf{R} \,|\, \mathbf{D}) \setminus (H - H_D)$, since the latter has a deadlock (reached, e.g., by firing $h_1 h_2$). The intuition is that if the high level component deadlocks in the critical zone (after firing h_2) then this is detectable by the low level component because it will no longer be able to enter the critical section and access the resource.

3   BNDC through Causal and Conflict Places

In this section we start describing the contributions of this paper, showing how the BNDC property can be characterised in terms of the absence of suitably defined causal and conflict places. Roughly speaking, a net system is BNDC when there is no causal flow between high and low transitions, and high and low transitions are never in conflict, competing for a token. An analogous characterisation for elementary Petri nets without self-loops has been originally provided in [5]. Our characterisation works for P/T nets, possibly with self-loops, and it is based on a simpler notion of causal and conflict place.

For $x \in P \cup T$ we define $^\bullet x = \{y \in P \cup T : F(y, x) > 0\}$ (the *pre-set* of x) and $x^\bullet = \{y \in P \cup T : F(x, y) > 0\}$ (the *post-set* of x).

Definition 5 (causal place). *A place p of a net system $\mathbf{N}$ is* causal *if there exist transitions $l \in L$, $h \in H$ and a sequence $\tau \in L^*$ such that (1) $p \in {}^\bullet l \cap h^\bullet$; (2) there is $m \in [m_0\rangle$ satisfying $m[h\tau l\rangle$, $m[\tau\rangle$ and $\langle m[\tau\rangle(p) < F(p, l)$.*

Intuitively, in Definition 5, the fact that $p \in {}^\bullet l \cap h^\bullet$ means that in the place p a token can be potentially produced by a high transition and consumed by a low one, thus determining a flow of information from high to low level. Condition (2) ensures that this indeed happens in some computation starting from a reachable marking. In fact, transition l is enabled by $m[h\tau\rangle$ but not by $m[\tau\rangle$, since $\langle m[\tau\rangle(p) < F(p, l)$. This means that h puts at least one token in p which can be later used by the firing of l. In the spirit of [5] a place satisfying the conditions of Definition 5 should be called *active causal* but we preferred a more concise terminology.

Similarly, a *conflict place* is defined as a place where a low and a high transitions compete for a token in some computation.

Definition 6 (conflict place). *A place p of a net system $\mathbf{N}$ is* conflict *if there exist transitions $l \in L$, $h \in H$ and a sequence $\tau \in L^*$ such that (1) $p \in {}^\bullet l \cap {}^\bullet h$; (2) there is $m \in [m_0\rangle$ satisfying $m[h\tau\rangle$, $m[\tau l\rangle$ and $\langle m[h\tau\rangle(p) < F(p, l)$.*

We can now prove that for a net system the absence of causal or conflict places is a necessary and sufficient condition for being BNDC.

Theorem 1 (BNDC by causal/conflict places). *A marked net system $\mathbf{N}$ is not BNDC iff $\mathbf{N}$ has either a causal place or a conflict place.*

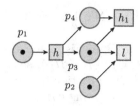

Fig. 3. Weak causal places are not always causal places

3.1   Safe Nets

Recall that a net $\mathbf{N}$ is *safe* if for every $p \in P$ and $m \in [m_0\rangle$ we have $m(p) \leq 1$. In a safe net, any marking m can be seen a subset of places and we write $p \in m$ instead of $m(p) = 1$. For safe net systems we can characterise BNDC in terms of a weaker notion of conflict and causal place (Definitions 7 and 8); these notions are novel and are motivated by the fact that images of these places are easily recognisable in the *unfolding* of the net (see §4), which is the main object of study in this paper.

Notation. Given a net system $\mathbf{N}$, a place $p \in P$ and a transition $t \in T$, we set $\delta_t(p) = F(t, p) - F(p, t)$, $t^- = \{p \in P : \delta_t(p) < 0\}$ and $t^+ = \{p \in P : \delta_t(p) > 0\}$.

Definition 7 (weak causal place). *A place p of a net system $\mathbf{N}$ is* weak causal *if there exist transitions $l \in L$, $h \in H$ and a sequence $\tau \in (L \cup H)^*$ such that (1) $p \in {}^\bullet l \cap h^+$; (2) there is $m \in [m_0\rangle$ such that $m[h\tau\rangle$.*

In words, we require the existence of a computation in which h precedes l, and of a place $p \in {}^\bullet l \cap h^+$, namely in the pre-set of l and where h contributes positively. Intuitively, in this way the firing of l could depend on the firing of h. A notion of weak conflict place can be defined along the same lines.

Definition 8 (weak conflict place). *A place p of a net system $\mathbf{N}$ is* weak conflict *if there exist transitions $l \in L$, $h \in H$ and a sequence $\tau \in (L \cup H)^*$ such that (1) $p \in {}^\bullet l \cap h^-$; (2) there is $m \in [m_0\rangle$ satisfying $m[h\rangle$ and $m[\tau l\rangle$.*

Every causal/conflict place is also a weak causal/conflict place. The converse implication does not hold in general, i.e., the presence of a weak causal/conflict place does not imply the existence of a causal/conflict place. For instance, consider the net system in Fig. 3: p_3 is a weak causal place, as witnessed by the firing sequence $h\,h_1\,l$, but p_3 is not a causal place and, actually, the net is BNDC.

Remarkably, in safe net systems, the existence of a weak causal (resp. conflict) place, implies the existence of a causal (resp. conflict) place. This fact is at the basis of the following theorem.

Theorem 2 (BNDC in safe nets). *Let $\mathbf{N}$ be a safe marked net system. The following statements are equivalent :*

(i) $\mathbf{N}$ contains either a causal place or a conflict place

(ii) **N** *contains either a weak causal place or a weak conflict place*
(iii) **N** *is not BNDC*

Moreover for every safe net **N** all interferences can be reduced to causal ones in the following sense. We can build a safe net $\gamma(\mathbf{N})$ such that **N** contains a weak causal or conflict place iff $\gamma(\mathbf{N})$ contains a weak causal place.

Definition 9 (causal reduct). *Given a net system* **N**, *we define its* causal reduct $\gamma(\mathbf{N})$ *as the net system* $(\gamma(N), \gamma(m_0))$ *obtained from* **N** *as follows. Let* $H_\# = \{h \in H : \ ^\bullet l \cap h^- \neq \emptyset \text{ for some } l \in L\}$. *Then:*

- *add a new place* p_H;
- *add a new place* p_h *for each transition* $h \in H_\#$;
- *for each transition* $h \in H_\#$, *add a new high transition* h_c, *setting* $F(p, h_c) = F(h_c, p) = F(p, h)$ *for every* $p \in P$; *moreover set* $F(p_H, h_c) = 1$ *and* $F(h_c, p_h) = 1$;
- *for each pair of transitions* $h \in H$, $l \in L$ *such that* $^\bullet l \cap h^- \neq \emptyset$, *insert a new low transition* l_h *setting* $F(p, l_h) = F(p, l)$ *and* $F(l_h, p) = F(l, p)$ *for every* $p \in P$; *moreover set* $F(p_h, l_h) = 1$;
- *finally* $\gamma(m_0)$ *is the unique extension of* m_0 *that assigns* 1 *to* p_H *and* 0 *to all other new places.*

In words, each h_c is a copy of the corresponding high transition h. It is enabled when h is enabled but its firing does not change the marking (it puts all consumed tokens back), apart from generating a token in the new place p_h which can later be used by a new transition l_h. Transition l_h is in turn a copy of l whose pre-set is extended with the addition of place p_h. The fact that each h_c inputs a token from p_H implies than every firing sequence will include at most one newly added high transition and at most one newly added low transition.

As an example, the causal reduct $\gamma(\mathbf{R})$ of the net **R** can be found in Fig. 1(b). E.g., the fact that $p \in h_2^- \cap \ ^\bullet l_2 \neq \emptyset$ in **R** leads to the creation of a copy h_{2c} of h_2, place p_{h_2} and a copy l_{2h_2} of transition l_2.

Proposition 1 (BNDC via the causal reduct). *Let* **N** *be a safe net system. Then* **N** *is not BNDC iff* $\gamma(\mathbf{N})$ *contains a weak causal place.*

Roughly, the core of the proof relies on the fact that every firing sequence $m_1[\tau\rangle m_2$ in **N** is also a firing sequence in $\gamma(\mathbf{N})$. A weak causal place in **N** is also a weak causal place in $\gamma(\mathbf{N})$. Given a weak conflict place p in **N**, with $p \in \ ^\bullet l \cap h^-$, and $m[h\rangle$, $m[\tau l\rangle$ for some reachable marking $m \in [m_0\rangle$, we can construct in the net $\gamma(\mathbf{N})$ the firing sequence $m'[h_c \tau l_h\rangle$ with $p \in \ ^\bullet l_h \cap h_c^+$, witnessing that p_h is a weak causal place in $\gamma(\mathbf{N})$. For an example of this phenomenon see Fig. 4(b), where the weak causal place p_{h_2} witnesses the presence of a weak conflict place p. Vice versa the presence of a weak causal place p in $\gamma(\mathbf{N})$ implies that either p itself is a weak causal place in **N** or that there is some weak conflict place in **N** (none of the newly added places can be a weak conflict place).

4   Unfolding Semantics and Related Notions

We recall the definition of the unfolding semantics for safe P/T nets, which is used to develop the results of the next section §5. The expert reader can quickly browse the current section for notation and jump to the next one.

The dynamics of a net system **N** can be represented by its *marking graph*, a directed graph whose nodes are the reachable markings of **N**. When **N** is safe, its marking graph is finite but its size can still be exponential in the size of **N**. An implicit representation of the marking graph is given by the *unfolding* of **N**, a possibly infinite net which, when **N** is safe, admits a finite fragment containing a representation of all the reachable markings. Moreover the size of such a fragment is, in presence of many concurrent transitions, considerably smaller than the marking graph [12,13,8].

The following relations can be defined on arbitrary nets, but they assume particular significance on net unfoldings.

Definition 10 (causality/conflict/concurrency). *Let N be a net. The causality relation $<$ is the least transitive binary relation on $P \cup T$ such that $x < y$ if $x \in {}^\bullet y$ (or, equivalently, if $y \in x^\bullet$). By $\leq$ we denote the reflexive closure of $<$. The conflict relation $\sharp$ is the least symmetric binary relation on $P \cup T$ such that:*
(1) if $t, t' \in T$, $t \neq t'$ and ${}^\bullet t \cap {}^\bullet t' \neq \emptyset$ then $t \sharp t'$;
(2) if $x < x'$ and $x \sharp y$ then $x' \sharp y$.
Finally the concurrency relation $\parallel$ is the complement of $(\sharp \cup \leq \cup >)$.

The relation $\parallel$ is symmetric and irreflexive. Given a subset $X \subseteq P \cup T$, we write $\mathsf{co}(X)$ when X is pairwise concurrent, i.e., $x \parallel y$ for all $x, y \in X$, $x \neq y$.

Net unfoldings fall into the class of *occurrence nets* [7]: their main properties are that causality is acyclic and well-founded, conflict is irreflexive and the arcs of the flow relation have weight at most 1 (i.e. F is a relation). Moreover their initial marking is often left implicit as it is identified as the set of minimal places.

Given a net **N**, an unfolding construction produces a net $\mathcal{U}(\mathbf{N})$ whose places are a reification of the tokens that circulate in **N** and whose transitions are copies of the transitions of **N**, representing their possible firings. The unfolding is constructed inductively starting from the initial marking of **N** and then adding, at each step, an occurrence of each transition of **N** which is enabled by (the image of) a concurrent subset of the places already generated.

For the sake of the presentation, hereafter we restrict to safe net systems **N**, where all reachable markings are (equivalent to) subsets of P and $F(x, y) \leq 1$ for $x, y \in P \cup T$, so that the flow function F is completely determined by the pre- and post-sets of transitions. In what follows we indicate by π_1 and π_2, respectively, the standard projection functions over the first and second component of pairs.

Definition 11 (unfolding). *Let $\mathbf{N} = ((P, T, F), m_0)$ be a safe marked net and let $\perp$ be an element not in P, T, F. Define the net $U^{(0)} = (T^{(0)}, P^{(0)}, F^{(0)})$ as:*

$$T^{(0)} = \emptyset ; \qquad P^{(0)} = \{(p, \perp) : p \in m_0\} ; \qquad F^{(0)} = \emptyset .$$

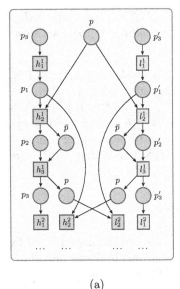
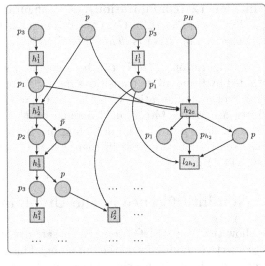

(a)   (b)

Fig. 4. (a) A fragment of the unfolding $\mathcal{U}(R)$ of the net system in Fig. 1(a); (b) a fragment of the unfolding $\mathcal{U}(\gamma(R))$ of its causal reduct $\gamma(R)$ in Fig. 1(b)

Then the unfolding is the least net $\mathcal{U}(\mathbf{N}) = (P^{(\omega)}, T^{(\omega)}, F^{(\omega)})$ containing $U^{(0)}$ and such that

- if $t \in T$ and $X \subseteq P^{(\omega)}$ is such that $\mathsf{co}(X)$ and $\pi_1(X) = {}^\bullet t$ then $(t, X) \in T^{(\omega)}$;
- if $e \in T^{(\omega)}$, $p \in \pi_1(e)^\bullet$ then $(p, e) \in P^{(\omega)}$;
- $F^{(\omega)}(x, y) = \begin{cases} 1 & \text{if } x \in T^{(\omega)}, \ y \in P^{(\omega)} \text{ and } x = \pi_2(y) \\ 1 & \text{if } x \in P^{(\omega)}, \ y \in T^{(\omega)} \text{ and } x = \pi_2(y) \\ 0 & \text{otherwise} \end{cases}$

The unfolding of a marked net system is an occurrence net system. We set $H^{(\omega)} = \{e \in T^{(\omega)} : \pi_1(e) \in H\}$ and $L^{(\omega)} = \{e \in T^{(\omega)} : \pi_1(e) \in L\}$. Places and transitions in the unfolding represent tokens and firing of transitions, respectively, of the original net. Each place in the unfolding is a tuple recording the place in the original net and the "history" of the token. By historical reasons the transitions in the unfolding are also called *events*. The projection π_1 over the first component maps places and transitions of the unfolding to the corresponding items of the original net $\mathbf{N}$.

For instance, a fragment of the unfolding of the net system in Fig. 1(a) can be found in Fig. 4(a). Different occurrences of a transition are distinguished using a superscript. E.g., h_2^1 and h_2^2 are two different occurrences of transition h_2.

For a transition $e \in T^{(\omega)}$ we define its *causal closure* $[e] = \{e' \in T^{(\omega)} : e' \le e\}$. We write $[e)$ for the set of strict causes, i.e., $[e) = [e] - \{e\}$. The runs of $\mathbf{N}$ are represented by the configurations of $\mathcal{U}(\mathbf{N})$, i.e., subsets of $T^{(\omega)}$ that are causally closed and conflict-free.

Definition 12 (configuration). *A configuration of $\mathcal{U}(\mathbf{N})$ is a finite subset $C \subseteq T^{(\omega)}$ such that $(C \times C) \cap \sharp = \emptyset$ and $[e] \subseteq C$ for all $e \in C$. The set of all configurations of $\mathcal{U}(\mathbf{N})$ is denoted by $\mathcal{C}(\mathcal{U}(\mathbf{N}))$.*

A configuration of $\mathcal{U}(\mathbf{N})$ can be associated with a reachable marking of $\mathbf{N}$, obtained by firing all its transitions in any order compatible with causality. The *frontier* of a configuration C is the set $C^{\circ} = (P^{(0)} \cup \bigcup_{e \in C} e^{\bullet}) - (\bigcup_{e \in C} {}^{\bullet}e)$; it induces a marking $\mathsf{M}(C)$ on $\mathbf{N}$ defined by $\mathsf{M}(C)(p) = |\{b \in C^{\circ} : \pi_1(b) = p\}|$, for every place p in $\mathbf{N}$. The unfolding has been shown to be marking complete in the sense that $m \in [m_0\rangle$ iff there exists $C \in \mathcal{C}(\mathcal{U}(\mathbf{N}))$ such that $\mathsf{M}(C) = m$ (see [7,14,12]).

5   Non-interference in the Unfolding

We show that the BNDC property for safe net systems can be characterised by quite effective conditions on the unfolding. This is later used to devise unfolding-based algorithms for checking BNDC on this class of net systems.

5.1   Images of Weak Causal and Weak Conflict Places in the Unfolding

Notation. For a place b and a transition e in $\mathcal{U}(\mathbf{N})$ we set $e^{+} = \{b \in P^{(\omega)} : \pi_1(b) \in \pi_1(e)^{+}\}$ and $e^{-} = \{b \in P^{(\omega)} : \pi_1(b) \in \pi_1(e)^{-}\}$. Moreover transitions denoted by h and l, possibly with subscripts, will be implicitly assumed to be high and low, respectively.

Theorem 3. *Let $\mathbf{N}$ be a net system.*

(i) *If p is a weak causal place in $\mathbf{N}$, then there are transitions h', l' and a place b in $\mathcal{U}(\mathbf{N})$ such that $b \in {}^{\bullet}l' \cap h'^{+}$ and $\pi_1(b) = p$;*

(ii) *if p is a weak conflict place in $\mathbf{N}$, then there are transitions h', l' and a place b in $\mathcal{U}(\mathbf{N})$ such that $b \in {}^{\bullet}l' \cap h'^{-}$, $[h'] \cup [l'] \in \mathcal{C}(\mathcal{U}(\mathbf{N}))$ and $\pi_1(b) = p$.*

Theorem 3 gives structural conditions that the unfolding $\mathcal{U}(\mathbf{N})$ necessarily satisfies if $\mathbf{N}$ contains either a weak causal or a weak conflict place. Conversely, the next theorem gives structural conditions on $\mathcal{U}(\mathbf{N})$ which are sufficient for $\mathbf{N}$ to contain either a weak causal or a weak conflict place.

Theorem 4. *Let $\mathbf{N}$ be a net system and let b a place in its unfolding $\mathcal{U}(\mathbf{N})$.*

(i) *If there are transitions h', l' in $\mathcal{U}(\mathbf{N})$ such that $b \in {}^{\bullet}l' \cap h'^{+}$, then $\pi_1(b)$ is a weak causal place in $\mathbf{N}$;*

(ii) *if there are transitions h', l' in $\mathcal{U}(\mathbf{N})$ such that $b \in {}^{\bullet}l' \cap h'^{-}$ and $[h'] \cup [l'] \in \mathcal{C}(\mathcal{U}(\mathbf{N}))$, then $\pi_1(b)$ is a weak conflict place in $\mathbf{N}$.*

Putting Theorem 3 and Theorem 4 together we get a characterisation of BNDC for safe nets in terms of the absence, in the unfolding, of places satisfying certain structural conditions.

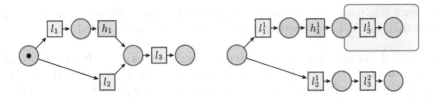

Fig. 5. A net system and a marking complete prefix not including an interference

Theorem 5 (BNDC in the unfolding of safe nets). *A safe net system* **N** *is not BNDC iff there are transitions* h', l' *and a place* b *in* $\mathcal{U}(\mathbf{N})$ *such that either (1)* $b \in {}^{\bullet}l' \cap h'^{+}$ *or (2)* $b \in {}^{\bullet}l' \cap h'^{-}$ *and* $[h'] \cup [l'] \in \mathcal{C}(\mathcal{U}(\mathbf{N}))$.

Remark 1. From the algorithmic point of view condition (1) above is very local and easy to check, while condition (2) involves the exploration of event histories. Notably, if we also assume that **N** does not contain self-loops on high transitions, it is no longer necessary to check that $[h'] \cup [l']$ is a conflict-free set so that condition (2) becomes local. Further insights will be given at the end of the section, but a thorough treatment of this case cannot be included here for space limitations and is deferred to an extended version of this paper.

5.2 Complete Prefixes for Interferences

A *prefix* of an occurrence net N is a causally closed subnet of N. In McMillan's seminal work [12] the focus is on reachability and a prefix U of the unfolding is deemed *complete* when any marking reachable in **N** is in the image of the marking produced by some configuration of U. This has been later extended to more general properties [13].

A prefix which is complete for reachability (and also for executability of transitions), could not include relevant information for interferences. Consider for instance the net in Fig. 5 (left) and its unfolding on the right. The unfolding prefix not including the boxed part is marking complete, but it excludes a direct causality between h_1^1 and l_3^1, which witnesses the presence of a weak causal place and thus the fact that the net system is not BNDC.

In order to capture all interferences, our idea is to build a prefix of the unfolding which contains a variety of configurations sufficient to witness all markings of the original net, taking into account also the confidentiality level of transitions producing the tokens. More precisely, we associate with each configuration C a so-called *extended marking*, $\mathsf{M}^{*}(C) = \langle \mathsf{M}(C), \mathsf{H}(C) \rangle$, where $\mathsf{H}(C) = \{\pi_1(b) \in P : \exists h' \in H^{(\omega)}. \ b \in \pi_1(h')^{+} \cap C^{\circ}\}$. In words $\mathsf{H}(C)$ is the set of places in the frontier of C that have been produced by some high transition that contributes positively. This extra information is needed to avoid the phenomenon illustrated in Fig. 5.

Definition 13 (e-complete prefix). *A prefix U of $\mathcal{U}(\mathbf{N})$ is complete for extended marking reachability, or simply e-complete, when for any configuration $C \in \mathcal{C}(\mathcal{U}(\mathbf{N}))$ there exists $C' \in \mathcal{C}(U)$ such that $\mathsf{M}^{*}(C) = \mathsf{M}^{*}(C')$.*

Given a safe net system **N**, an e-complete prefix U of $\mathcal{U}(\mathbf{N})$ contains sufficient information for deciding whether or not **N** contains a weak causal place.

Theorem 6 (completeness for weak causal places). *Let* **N** *be a safe net system and let* U *be an e-complete prefix of* $\mathcal{U}(\mathbf{N})$. *Then* p *is a weak causal place in* **N** *iff there exist high and low transitions* h', l' *and a place* b *in* U *such that* $b \in {}^{\bullet}l' \cap h'^{+}$ *and* $\pi_1(b) = p$.

As a consequence of Proposition 1 and of the above theorem the BNDC property for safe net systems can be checked on an e-complete prefix of the unfolding of the causal reduct.

Corollary 1 (BNDC on e-complete prefixes). *Let* **N** *be a safe net system and let* U *be an e-complete prefix of* $\mathcal{U}(\gamma(\mathbf{N}))$. *Then* **N** *is not BNDC iff there exist high and low transitions* h', l' *in* U *and a place* $b \in {}^{\bullet}l' \cap h'^{+}$.

5.3   Unfolding-based Algorithms

Corollary 1 naturally leads to an algorithm for checking the BNDC property for safe net systems: it consists in generating an e-complete prefix of the unfolding of the causal reduct while checking for the presence of a place produced by a high transition and consumed by a low one.

A key notion for constructing an e-complete prefix is that of cut-off, which is roughly a transition in the unfolding that produces an extended marking already produced by other transitions with smaller history. The idea of cut-off events goes back to [12]. The word "smaller" is formalised by fixing an order $\prec$ on configurations. For example we can take $C \prec C'$ is $|C| < |C'|$, as in [12], but finer adequate orders (see [13]) can be considered for reducing the size of complete prefixes and improving the efficiency.

Definition 14 (cut-off). *An event* e *of the prefix* U *is called a* cut-off *when there exists another event* e' *such that* $\mathsf{M}^*([e']) = \mathsf{M}^*([e])$ *and* $[e'] \prec [e]$.

A procedure that unfolds a net system by adding events with $\prec$-minimal history and stopping at cut-offs produces an e-complete prefix of the unfolding. This follows from the general theory in [13].

On these bases we developed the algorithm in Fig. 6. It first computes the causal reduct $\gamma(\mathbf{N})$ of **N**. Then it builds an e-complete prefix of the unfolding of $\gamma(\mathbf{N})$, looking, at each step, for the presence of direct causalities between high and low transitions satisfying the conditions in Theorem 6. The initial part of the unfolding is simply the initial marking of $\gamma(\mathbf{N})$. If U is an unfolding prefix, a *possible extension* of U is any transition $t' \in \gamma(T)^{(\omega)}$ such that ${}^{\bullet}t' \subseteq C^{\circ}$ for some configuration C of U. The set of possible extensions of U is denoted $PE(U)$.

Theorem 7 (correctness of the algorithm for safe nets). *Let* **N** *be a safe net system. Then the algorithm in Fig. 6 always terminates and provides the answer 'yes' iff* **N** *is BNDC.*

Data: A safe net system $\mathbf{N}$.
compute $\gamma(\mathbf{N})$
$U = \gamma(m_0)$
$pe = PE(U)$
while $pe \neq \emptyset$ **do**
    take $t \in pe$ such that $[t]$ is $\prec$-minimal;
    if $\pi_1(t) \in L$ **then**
        if $\exists h, b \in U.\ \pi_1(h) \in H.$
        $b \in {}^\bullet t \cap h^+$
        then
           | **return** '*no*'
        end
    end
    add t to U
    if t *is not a cut-off* **then**
      | add $t^\bullet$ to U
    end
    $pe = PE(U)$
end
return '*yes*';

Fig. 6. Algorithm to decide BNDC on safe net systems

For example, when applied to the safe net system $\mathbf{R}$ in Fig. 1(a), the algorithm first computes the causal reduct $\gamma(\mathbf{R})$ of Fig. 1(b). Then it starts generating the unfolding $\mathcal{U}(\gamma(\mathbf{R}))$ of Fig. 4(b) until the weak causal place p_{h_2} and the transitions l_{2h_2}, h_{2c} are discovered, corresponding to the fact that $p \in {}^\bullet l_2 \cap h_2{}^-$ is a (weak) conflict place. At this point, the algorithm returns the answer 'no'.

The size of the e-complete prefix of $\mathcal{U}(\gamma(\mathbf{N}))$ produced by the algorithm in Fig. 6 and thus the efficiency of the algorithm are highly influenced by the "level of concurrency" in $\mathbf{N}$. In absence of concurrency the size of the prefix can equate that of the marking graph, which is exponential in the number of places. It has been shown in [13] that, when dealing with standard marking completeness, the use of a total adequate order ensures that the prefix will be never larger than the marking graph. Here the situation is similar, but the reference marking graph is that of the causal reduct of $\gamma(\mathbf{N})$, whose size is at most $|H|$ times the size of the marking graph of $\mathbf{N}$.

Consider for example a generalisation of $\mathbf{R}$ with k low and high components competing for the resource: the marking graph would be of size exponential in k, thus impacting on the performance of algorithms based on the interleaving semantics, while the size of an e-complete prefix would be of the order of k^2. We will consider these kind of examples in § 6, where experiments corroborate our hypothesis about the efficiency of our approach.

We conclude this section with a further explanation of Remark 1. If $\mathbf{N}$ is safe and without self-loops on high transitions we can prove that a place b in $\mathcal{U}(\mathbf{N})$ is the image of a conflict place of $\mathbf{N}$ iff there are a high and a low transition h', l' such that $b \in {}^\bullet l' \cap h'^-$ and $\mathsf{co}({}^\bullet l' \cup {}^\bullet h')$. Moreover Theorem 6 can be extended saying that if such a place b occurs in $\mathcal{U}(\mathbf{N})$, then another place b', instance of the same conflict place, already occurs in an e-complete prefix U of $\mathcal{U}(\mathbf{N})$. For example, adding the check for conflict places, the modified algorithm would directly compute $\mathcal{U}(\mathbf{R})$ in Fig. 4(a) and then stop (returning the answer 'no') after generating transitions $h_1^1, l_1^1, h_2^1, l_2^1$ in the unfolding, since it identifies the place $p \in {}^\bullet l_2^1 \cap h_2^{1-}$, with the union of pre-sets ${}^\bullet l_2^1 \cup {}^\bullet h_2^1 = \{p_1, p, p_1'\}$ pairwise concurrent.

6   Experimental Results

We developed a prototype tool UBIC (Unfolding-Based Interference Checker) for checking the BNDC property for safe Petri nets according to the algorithm devised in this paper. The tool is based on CUNF [9], a toolset for unfolding and verifying low level nets with read arcs.

The tool UBIC takes as input a safe net $\mathbf{N}$, in the PEP ll_net format [15]. The confidentiality level of transitions is determined by the transition name: transitions whose name starts by "h" are of high level, and all the others are low level transitions. The tool constructs the causal reduct $\gamma(\mathbf{N})$ of the input net and then it starts the unfolding procedure. It can stop once the first weak causal place is found (if one is interested only in checking whether a net is or not BNDC) or it can produce a prefix of the unfolding of $\gamma(\mathbf{N})$ (when one is interested in complete information about the interferences in the net $\mathbf{N}$). A preliminary version of the tool UBIC is available at the page http://www.math.unipd.it/~baldan/UBIC.

Other algorithms have been proposed for checking BNDC on Petri nets and we are aware of two other tools that actually implement them. The tool Petri Net Security Checker (PNSC) [16] (written in Java), based on the work [5], basically generates the marking graph of the input net and then performs path searches in order to find interference situations.

In contrast, the tool ANICA [10] (Automated Non-Interference Check Assistant, written in C++) does not create the whole marking graph. Rather, it reduces each potential interfering place to a single reachability problem, which is then handled with the tool LOLA [17] (Low Level Petri Net Analyzer). According to the authors, this approach leads to a gain of efficiency with respect to PNSC, which allows ANICA to handle larger inputs. ANICA works on safe Petri nets.

Our tool UBIC (Unfolding-Based Interference Checker) provides very promising performances, especially in terms of speed. Here we illustrate some preliminary experimental results, in which we compare the performances of UBIC and ANICA on the same set of nets. All tests have been run on a laptop mounting an Intel®Core™i3 CPU (2.27GHz) and 3GB of RAM, in a Linux 13.10 environment. In each test we collect the execution time required by the two tools.

The tests have been conducted on three families of net systems:

(1) generalisations of the mutual exclusion net system $\mathbf{R}$ (see Fig. 1(a)), obtained by considering variants $\mathbf{R}(m, n)$, parametric with respect to the numbers m and n of high and low level components, respectively, competing for

Table 1. Experimental results on the parametric variants of the net system **R** in Fig. 1(a)

Input net	Places	Transitions	UBIC Time(sec)	ANICA Time(sec)
$\mathbf{R}(5,5)$	34	32	0.005	0.060
$\mathbf{R}(10,10)$	64	62	0.016	0.490
$\mathbf{R}(15,15)$	94	92	0.018	1.950
$\mathbf{R}(20,20)$	124	122	0.043	4.880
$\mathbf{R}(25,25)$	154	152	0.086	10.650
$\mathbf{R}(30,30)$	184	182	0.177	16.220
$\mathbf{R}(35,35)$	214	212	0.337	24.380
$\mathbf{R}(50,50)$	304	302	1.708	76.080
$\mathbf{R}(75,75)$	454	452	9.251	324.190
$\mathbf{R}(100,100)$	604	602	29.618	929.330

the resource. Net $\mathbf{R}(m,n)$ has $4+3(n+m)$ places and $2+3(n+m)$ transitions. Table 1 contains the results concerning these nets.

(2) "line-shaped" nets consisting of a sequence of low transitions ending with a high transition (see Fig. 7). The net $\mathbf{L}(n)$ contains $n-1$ low transitions and one high transition. Table 2 contains the results concerning these nets.

(3) nets $\mathbf{K}(m)$ implementing Dijkstra's mutual exclusion algorithm [18], parametric with respect to the number m of processes competing for the resource. Net $\mathbf{K}(m)$ has $12m$ places and $3m + 3m^2$ transitions. In each example we inserted exactly one high transition. This example is taken from the set of experiments provided with the toolset Cunf. In each net exactly one transition has been made high. Table 3 contains the results concerning these nets.

In all the examples we required the tools to stop as soon as the answer "yes BNDC" or "no BNDC" is found. These example nets are provided with the UBIC package. For example the net $\mathbf{R}(5,5)$ is encoded in file `netR5-5.ll_net` for UBIC and in file `netR5-5.ifn` for ANICA. The net $\mathbf{L}(5)$ is in file `netLine-5.ll_net` for UBIC, and in file `netLine-5.ifn` for ANICA. Similarly, net $\mathbf{K}(5)$ is in file `netDijkstra-5.ll_net` for UBIC and in file `netDijkstra-5.ifn` for ANICA.

Let us first focus on Table 1, which reports the experimental results for deciding BNDC on $\mathbf{R}(m,n)$, with UBIC and ANICA. All these nets are not BNDC. Note that UBIC is uniformly more efficient than ANICA and, although this is not reported, the difference becomes even more evident when full information about interferences (complete prefix for UBIC and all causal/conflict places for ANICA) are looked for.

The second class of examples, namely the nets $\mathbf{L}(n)$ are those for which the performances of the two tools differ the least, because there is no concurrency at all, so the unfolding of these nets is isomorphic to the marking graph. All these nets, but $\mathbf{L}(1)$, are not BNDC.

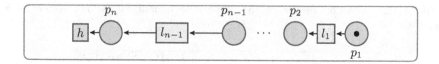

Fig. 7. Line-shaped net system $\mathbf{L}(n)$

Table 2. Experimental results on line-shaped net in Fig. 7 with variable size

Input net	Places	Transitions	UBIC Time(sec)	ANICA Time(sec)
L(50)	53	52	0.004	0.000
L(75)	78	77	0.004	0.010
L(100)	103	102	0.005	0.010
L(200)	203	202	0.009	0.030
L(300)	303	302	0.015	0.050
L(400)	403	402	0.016	0.080
L(1000)	1003	1002	0.104	0.430
L(2000)	2003	2002	0.424	2.340
L(3000)	3003	3002	1.057	5.390
L(4000)	4003	4002	2.224	10.020
L(5000)	5003	5002	4.261	15.660
L(10000)	10003	10002	31.642	78.410

Finally, the last set of tests on the nets $\mathbf{K}(m)$ (implementing Dijkstra's mutual exclusion algorithm with m processes) produced the results in Table 3. All these nets, but $\mathbf{K}(1)$, are not BNDC. These experiments confirm that the efficiency of unfolding-based algorithms tend to increase when the system is highly concurrent. In the case of the nets $\mathbf{K}(m)$ the performance gap is so large that, for $m \geq 8$, such nets could not be processed within one entire night by ANICA.

We also performed a preliminary comparison concerning memory usage for the tests described above. The comparison seems to reveal that on "small" input nets UBIC requires less memory than ANICA, but as the size of input nets grows, the increase of the memory required by ANICA is less than proportional. The memory required by UBIC instead is essentially proportional to the number of transitions. As a consequence for large inputs ANICA requires less memory than UBIC. A proper analysis of memory usage is not trivial and some further investigation is needed (e.g., ANICA throws subprocesses and we did not yet manage to analyse the use of memory of both tools in a uniform way). Indeed ANICA first isolates all potential interfering places and then for each one creates a reachability problem which is then passed over to LOLA. The memory used for processing a reachability problem can then be reused for the next one, until all potential interfering places have been analysed. In contrast, UBIC has a "global" approach: it checks all places while they are being added to the growing unfolding of the input net. Hence the memory is released only when the entire process stops.

Table 3. Experimental results on the net systems $\mathbf{K}(m)$

			UBIC	ANICA
Input net	Places	Transitions	Time(sec)	Time(sec)
$\mathbf{K}(1)$	12	6	0.000	0.000
$\mathbf{K}(2)$	24	18	0.000	0.004
$\mathbf{K}(3)$	36	36	0.003	0.016
$\mathbf{K}(4)$	48	60	0.003	0.028
$\mathbf{K}(5)$	60	90	0.006	2.608
$\mathbf{K}(6)$	72	126	0.010	42.136
$\mathbf{K}(7)$	84	168	0.019	608.856
$\mathbf{K}(8)$	96	216	0.020	$\perp$
$\mathbf{K}(9)$	108	270	0.025	$\perp$
$\mathbf{K}(10)$	120	330	0.040	$\perp$
$\mathbf{K}(20)$	240	1260	1.292	$\perp$
$\mathbf{K}(30)$	360	2790	16.257	$\perp$
$\mathbf{K}(40)$	480	4920	156.210	$\perp$
$\mathbf{K}(50)$	600	7650	728.522	$\perp$

7   Conclusions and Future Work

Non-interference is a strong property, and often proper weakenings of it are studied (e.g., based on declassification or downgrading). Still, it plays a basic role as a reference, conceptual notion.

We provided a "causal" characterisation of non-interference by focusing on Petri nets and on Bisimilarity-based Non-Deducibility on Composition (BNDC), a classical formalisation of non-interference. For the class of safe nets, we characterised BNDC on the unfolding, in terms of causalities and conflicts between high and low level activities. More general results, which apply also to non-safe nets, have not been included for space limitations and are deferred to an extended version of this paper.

Our work led to an algorithm for checking BNDC based on the generation of a suitable finite prefix of the unfolding. Other algorithms exist for checking BNDC on Petri nets and we are aware of two tools that actually implement them. The tool Petri Net Security Checker [16] (written in Java), based on the work [5], basically generates the marking graph of the input net and then performs path searches in order to find interference situations. In contrast, the tool ANICA [10] (Automated Non-Interference Check Assistant, written in C++) does not create the whole marking graph. Rather, it reduces each potential interfering place to a single reachability problem, which is then handled with the tool LOLA [17] (Low Level Petri Net Analyzer). According to the authors, their technique allows not only to handle larger inputs, but also to parallelize the checks. ANICA works on safe Petri nets.

We developed a prototype tool UBIC (Unfolding-Based Interference Checker) based on CUNF [9], that provides very promising results, in terms of time efficiency, when compared to ANICA. Some preliminary experiments reveal a gain which can reach orders of magnitude. This fact, in some cases, allows us to treat much larger examples, on which ANICA does not respond at all within hours. We believe that resorting to true concurrent semantics of Petri nets really helps in devising efficient algorithms, alleviating the state explosion problem.

The idea of using a true concurrent semantics to check the possibility of deducing the occurrence of non-observable transitions from the occurrence of observable ones has been proposed in [19], in the context of asynchronous diagnosis of discrete event event systems. The *diagnosability* properties studied in [19] - or better, their negations - are similar in spirit to noninterference properties. Although non-diagnosability and BNDC properties surely differ (e.g., the former are trace-based while the latter is bisimulation-based), the relation between diagnosability and noninterference properties deserves to be deepened.

As future lines of research, we intend to explore the possibility of providing causal characterisations of known notions of non-interference, e.g., including downgrading, possibly defined on other formalisms. E.g., for imperative languages, by considering Petri net encodings, where the control and data flow is suitably captured by causality. Or for process calculi, for which there are several Petri net encodings (see, e.g., [20,21,22]).

Another venue of research consists in considering formalisations of non-interference obtained from the classical ones, by replacing interleaving observational semantics with true-concurrent ones [23]. The higher distinguishing power of such semantics could allow to identify new forms of interference which cannot be captured in an interleaving setting.

Acknowledgements. We are grateful to César Rodríguez for developing the tool CUNF and for his suggestions on its use for producing UBIC. We also thank the anonymous reviewers who contributed to the improvement of this paper with their valuable suggestions.

References

1. Goguen, J.A., Meseguer, J.: Security policies and security models. In: Proceedings of the IEEE Symposium on Security and Privacy, pp. 11–20. IEEE Computer Society (1982)
2. Focardi, R., Gorrieri, R.: Classification of security properties (Part I: Information flow). In: Focardi, R., Gorrieri, R. (eds.) FOSAD 2000. LNCS, vol. 2171, pp. 331–396. Springer, Heidelberg (2001)
3. Ryan, P., Schneider, Y.: Process algebra and non-interference. Journal of Computer Security 9, 75–103 (2001)
4. Mantel, H.: Possibilistic definitions of security - an assembly kit. In: CSFW, pp. 185–199. IEEE Computer Society (2000)
5. Busi, N., Gorrieri, R.: Structural non-interference in elementary and trace nets. Mathematical Structures in Computer Science 19, 1065–1090 (2009)

6. Best, E., Darondeau, P., Gorrieri, R.: On the decidability of non interference over unbounded Petri nets. In: Proceedings of SecCo 2010. EPTCS, vol. 51, pp. 16–33 (2010)

7. Nielsen, M., Plotkin, G., Winskel, G.: Petri Nets, Event Structures and Domains, Part 1. TCS 13, 85–108 (1981)

8. Esparza, J., Heljanko, K.: Unfoldings - A Partial order Approach to Model Checking. EACTS Monographs in Theoretical Computer Science. Springer (2008)

9. Rodríguez, C., Schwoon, S.: Cunf: A tool for unfolding and verifying Petri nets with read arcs. In: Van Hung, D., Ogawa, M. (eds.) ATVA 2013. LNCS, vol. 8172, pp. 492–495. Springer, Heidelberg (2013)

10. Accorsi, R., Lehmann, A.: Automatic information flow analysis of business process models. In: Barros, A., Gal, A., Kindler, E. (eds.) BPM 2012. LNCS, vol. 7481, pp. 172–187. Springer, Heidelberg (2012)

11. Frau, S., Gorrieri, R., Ferigato, C.: Petri net security checker: Structural non-interference at work. In: Degano, P., Guttman, J., Martinelli, F. (eds.) FAST 2008. LNCS, vol. 5491, pp. 210–225. Springer, Heidelberg (2009)

12. McMillan, K.L.: A technique of state space search based on unfolding. Form. Methods Syst. Des. 6, 45–65 (1995)

13. Khomenko, V., Koutny, M., Vogler, W.: Canonical prefixes of Petri net unfoldings. Acta Informatica 40, 95–118 (2003)

14. Meseguer, J., Montanari, U., Sassone, V.: Representation theorems for petri nets. In: Freksa, C., Jantzen, M., Valk, R. (eds.) Foundations of Computer Science. LNCS, vol. 1337, pp. 239–249. Springer, Heidelberg (1997)

15. Best, E., Grahlmann, B.: PEP Documentation and User Guide 1.8 (1998)

16. Frau, S., Gorrieri, R., Ferigato, C.: Petri net security checker: Structural non-interference at work. In: Degano, P., Guttman, J., Martinelli, F. (eds.) FAST 2008. LNCS, vol. 5491, pp. 210–225. Springer, Heidelberg (2009)

17. Wolf, K.: Generating Petri net state spaces. In: Kleijn, J., Yakovlev, A. (eds.) ICATPN 2007. LNCS, vol. 4546, pp. 29–42. Springer, Heidelberg (2007)

18. Dijkstra, E.: Solution of a problem in concurrent programming control. Communication of the ACM 8, 569 (1965)

19. Haar, S.: Types of asynchronous diagnosability and the reveals-relation in occurrence nets. IEEE Transactions on Automatic Control 55, 2310–2320 (2010)

20. Gorrieri, R., Montanari, U.: SCONE: A simple calculus of nets. In: Baeten, J.C.M., Klop, J.W. (eds.) CONCUR 1990. LNCS, vol. 458, pp. 2–30. Springer, Heidelberg (1990)

21. Devillers, R., Klaudel, H., Koutny, M.: A compositional Petri net translation of general pi-calculus terms. Formal Asp. Comput. 20, 429–450 (2008)

22. Meyer, R., Khomenko, V., Hüchting, R.: A polynomial translation of π-calculus (FCP) to safe Petri nets. In: Koutny, M., Ulidowski, I. (eds.) CONCUR 2012. LNCS, vol. 7454, pp. 440–455. Springer, Heidelberg (2012)

23. van Glabbeek, R., Goltz, U.: Refinement of actions and equivalence notions for concurrent systems. Acta Informatica 37, 229–327 (2001)

The 4C Spectrum of Fundamental Behavioral Relations for Concurrent Systems

Artem Polyvyanyy[1], Matthias Weidlich[2], Raffaele Conforti[1],
Marcello La Rosa[1,3], and Arthur H.M. ter Hofstede[1,4]

[1] Queensland University of Technology, Brisbane, Australia
[2] Imperial College London, London, United Kingdom
[3] NICTA Queensland Lab, Brisbane, Australia
[4] Eindhoven University of Technology, Eindhoven, The Netherlands
{artem.polyvyanyy,raffaele.conforti,m.larosa,a.terhofstede}@qut.edu.au,
m.weidlich@imperial.ac.uk

Abstract. The design of concurrent software systems, in particular process-aware information systems, involves behavioral modeling at various stages. Recently, approaches to behavioral analysis of such systems have been based on declarative abstractions defined as sets of behavioral relations. However, these relations are typically defined in an ad-hoc manner. In this paper, we address the lack of a systematic exploration of the fundamental relations that can be used to capture the behavior of concurrent systems, i.e., co-occurrence, conflict, causality, and concurrency. Besides the definition of the spectrum of behavioral relations, which we refer to as the 4C spectrum, we also show that our relations give rise to implication lattices. We further provide operationalizations of the proposed relations, starting by proposing techniques for computing relations in unlabeled systems, which are then lifted to become applicable in the context of labeled systems, i.e., systems in which state transitions have semantic annotations. Finally, we report on experimental results on efficiency of the proposed computations.

1 Introduction

Process models play a key role in the development of concurrent software systems as they describe the functionality of a system by means of actions and their interdependencies for the coordination of action execution. On the one hand, such models are used to document system requirements, thereby guiding implementation efforts [1]. On the other hand, process-aware information systems rely on process models as implementation artifacts that are deployed in an execution environment, e.g., a workflow engine or a service orchestration framework [2,3].

Process models are *system models* according to the classification of models of concurrency presented by Sassone et al. [4], i.e., they feature an explicit representation of states and define how actions lead to state changes. This stands in contrast to *behavior models* that define occurrences of actions over time while abstracting from states. As such, the interpretation of a process model, e.g., a Labeled Transition System (LTS) [5], a Petri net [6], or a UML activity diagram [7], under a certain semantics defines a behavior model, e.g., a language over actions [8] or an event structure [9]. Semantics, in turn, are broadly classified in two dimensions [4]. First, a semantics is *concurrent* or *interleaving*, depending on whether the difference between concurrency and non-determinism is

G. Ciardo and E. Kindler (Eds.): PETRI NETS 2014, LNCS 8489, pp. 210–232, 2014.
© Springer International Publishing Switzerland 2014

considered to be important. Second, a semantics is *linear time* or *branching time*, which ignores or captures the moments of choice between the occurrences of different actions.

Given that process models are system models, analysis techniques are often grounded on actions (system model level) and not on action occurrences (behavior model level). However, recent work advocated to ground such analysis not directly in the procedural description that is inherent to every system model, but rather to rely on a declarative characterization of the behavior model that is induced by the process model under a certain semantics, cf. [10] for details. Then, different sets of behavioral relations are defined over pairs of actions (system model level), but capture *characteristics*, or *features* in data mining terminology [11], of the occurrences of these actions (behavior model level). Examples of these relations include different notions of exclusiveness, concurrency, successorship, co-occurrence, or precedence. A specific example would be a binary exclusiveness relation defined over actions represented by transition labels in an LTS that holds if the language of the LTS does not comprise a word that contains both labels. Such behavioral relations may be used to judge the consistency of process models, conduct similarity search and querying in a process model repository, or to realize change propagation between process models, cf. [12].

The benefit of relying on a declarative approach for the analysis of process models is clearly witnessed by existing work. However, there is a plethora of specific definitions of behavioral relations. Even for a single semantics and, thus, for a single behavior model that acts as the interpretation of the process model, we observe a lack of understanding of subtle differences in the definition of behavioral relations and their interplay. In this paper, therefore, we provide a rigorous analysis of the spectrum of possible behavioral relations. We base our analysis on two well-established formalisms for representing system models and behavior models, i.e., Petri nets [6] and their interpretation in terms of concurrent runs (or *processes* for short) [13]. We focus on four fundamental properties that are of particular relevance for behavioral analysis: co-occurrence, conflict, causality, and concurrency, jointly referred to in this paper as the 4C relations. For each of these relations, we define a spectrum of relations over actions (transitions of Petri net systems or transition labels) that are based on action occurrences (events of processes of Petri net systems). As such, our work provides the foundation for selecting specific behavioral relations for the analysis of a process model with a declarative characterization of the behavior model induced under a certain semantics.

More specifically, this paper makes the following contributions:

o It defines sets of co-occurrence, conflict, causality, and concurrency relations for Petri nets and shows that these relations give rise to implication lattices.

o It provides operationalizations of the proposed behavioral relations, i.e., it shows how these relations can be computed.

o It lifts the proposed behavioral relations, as well as the proposed computation techniques, to labeled systems.

o It presents an implementation and evaluation of the proposed computations.

The remainder of the paper is structured as follows. The next section illustrates the application of behavioral relations with an example. Section 3 presents preliminaries for our work. Section 4 defines a spectrum of fundamental behavioral relations. The computation of these relations is addressed in Section 5. Subsequently, we extend the

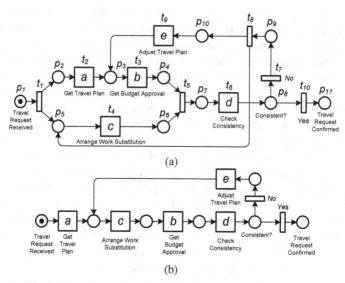

Fig. 1. Two behavioral specifications given as Petri net systems

class of considered models by lifting the relations, as well as their operationalizations, to labeled systems. We evaluate the proposed computation methods in Section 7. Finally, Section 8 reviews related work before Section 9 concludes the paper.

2 Motivating Example

We illustrate the application of fundamental behavioral relations for the analysis of process models with two use cases, process model search and querying. Fig. 1 shows two Petri net systems. Both models describe operations as they may be implemented in a process-aware information system to realize the handling of a travel request. While we define the formal semantics for Petri net systems later, here it suffices to see that both models describe similar behaviors. For instance, in both models, action a is executed at most once and always before action b, which may be repeated. However, the model in Fig. 1(a) defines that actions a and b may be executed concurrently to action c, whereas these actions are executed in a sequential order in Fig. 1(b).

Management of large process model collections requires effective search and querying techniques [12]. Since process models specify behaviors, search and querying should not be limited to the syntax of process models but should also consider semantics [14,15]. Behavioral relations have been used as the formal grounding for many search and querying techniques. For instance, behavioral similarity of two models can be defined as the Jaccard coefficient, i.e., the size of the intersection divided by the size of the union of exclusiveness, order, and interleaving relations, defined for trace semantics [16]. Then, the pair (b,c) would be in the intersection and union of order relations of both models in Fig. 1 and, thus, account for similar behavior. However, the relations defined in [16] do not distinguish concurrent and interleaved occurrences, so that the pair (b,c) would also be in the intersection of the relations representing interleaving. Similar approaches have been defined on other behavioral relations, cf. [17,18], raising the question of the underlying spectrum of relations for similarity assessment.

Turning to querying of process models, APQL [14] has been presented as a rich query language that supports 16 different forms of causal relations between actions, grounded in trace semantics. As an example, a relation may require that occurrences of b are succeeded by occurrences of c *immediately* in some occurrence sequence, which is the case in Fig. 1(a), but not in Fig. 1(b). Another relation captures that occurrences of b may be succeeded by occurrences of c *eventually*, which holds true in Figs. 1(a) and 1(b).

These examples illustrate that the benefit of using a declarative characterization of the behavior model induced by the process model under a certain semantics is clearly recognized. However, the choice of behavioral relations to use in a certain setting is taken in an ad-hoc manner. By precisely defining and exploring the spectrum of relations that may qualify as a formal grounding, our work, thus, lays the foundation for a rigorous application of behavioral relations in various use cases.

3   Preliminaries

This section introduces *Petri nets*, *net systems*, and *processes* of net systems.

3.1   Petri Nets and Net Systems

Petri nets are a well-established formalism for describing process models, i.e., system models [6]. They allow for the rigorous definition of semantics of systems and reuse of the well-developed mathematical theory for analysis of systems.

Definition 3.1 (Petri net)
A *Petri net*, or a *net*, is an ordered triple $N := (P,T,F)$, where P and T are finite disjoint sets of *places* and *transitions*, respectively, and $F \subseteq (P \times T) \cup (T \times P)$ is a *flow* relation. ⌐

An element $x \in P \cup T$ is a *node* of N. A *node* $x \in P \cup T$ is an *input* (an *output*) node of a node $y \in P \cup T$ iff $(x,y) \in F$ $((y,x) \in F)$. By $\bullet x$ $(x\bullet)$, $x \in P \cup T$, we denote the *preset* (the *postset*) of x, i.e., the set of all input (output) nodes of x. For a set of nodes $X \subseteq P \cup T$, $\bullet X := \bigcup_{x \in X} \bullet x$ and $X\bullet := \bigcup_{x \in X} x\bullet$. A node $x \in P \cup T$ is a *source* (a *sink*) node of N iff $\bullet x = \varnothing$ $(x\bullet = \varnothing)$. Given a net $N := (P,T,F)$, by $Min(N)$ we denote the set of all source nodes of N. For convenience considerations, we require all nets to be T-restricted. A net N is *T-restricted* iff the preset and postset of every transition is not empty, i.e., $\forall t \in T : \bullet t \neq \varnothing \neq t\bullet$.

The execution semantics of Petri nets is proposed in terms of states and state transitions and can be regarded as a 'token game'. A state of a net is captured by the concept of a *marking*, which specifies a distribution of *tokens* on the net's places.

Definition 3.2 (Marking of a net) A *marking*, or a *state*, of a net $N := (P,T,F)$ is a function $M : P \rightarrow \mathbb{N}_0$ that assigns to each place $p \in P$ a number $M(p)$ of *tokens* at p.[1] ⌐

---

[1] $\mathbb{N}_0$ denotes the set of all natural numbers including zero.

For M and M' being two markings of $N := (P,T,F)$, it holds that M is *covered* by M', denoted by $M \leq M'$, iff $M(p) \leq M'(p)$, for every $p \in P$. We shall often refer to a marking M as to the multiset of places that contains $M(p)$ copies of place p for every $p \in P$. Additionally, we shall use the symbol $\uplus$ to denote the union of multisets.

A *net system* is a Petri net at a certain state/marking.

Definition 3.3 (Net system) A *net system*, or a *system*, is an ordered pair $S := (N,M)$, where N is a net and M is a marking of N.

In the graphical notation, places are usually visualized as circles, transitions are drawn as rectangles, the flow relation is given as directed edges, and tokens are depicted as black dots inside assigned places; refer to Fig. 1(a) for a visualization of a net system with transitions $t_1 \ldots t_{10}$, places $p_1 \ldots p_{11}$, and a single token at place p_1.

A transition can be *enabled* at a given marking of a net. An enabled transition can *occur*. An occurrence of a transition leads to a new marking of the net.

Definition 3.4 (Semantics of a system) Let $S := (N,M)$, $N := (P,T,F)$, be a net system.
  ○ A transition $t \in T$ is *enabled* in S, denoted by $S[t\rangle$, iff every input place of t contains at least one token, i.e., $\forall p \in \bullet t : M(p) > 0$.
  ○ If a transition $t \in T$ is enabled in S, then t can *occur*, which leads to a *step* from S to $S' := (N,M')$ via t, where M' is a fresh marking such that $M'(p) := M(p) - \mathbf{1}_F((p,t)) + \mathbf{1}_F((t,p))$, for every $p \in P$, i.e., transition t 'consumes' one token from every input place of t and 'produces' one token for every output place of t.[2]

The fact that there exists a step from S to S' via a transition t is denoted by $S[t\rangle S'$. A marking M of a net N is a *terminal* marking iff there are no enabled transitions in (N,M). A net system induces a set of its *occurrence sequences/executions*.

Definition 3.5 (Occurrence sequence, Execution) Let $S_0 := (N,M_0)$ be a net system.
  ○ A sequence of transitions $\sigma := t_1 \ldots t_n$, $n \in \mathbb{N}_0$, of N is an *occurrence sequence* in S_0 iff there exists a sequence of net systems $S_0, S_1 \ldots S_n$, such that for every position i in σ, $1 \leq i \leq n$, it holds that $S_{i-1}[t_i\rangle S_i$; we say that σ *leads* from S_0 to S_n.
  ○ An occurrence sequence σ in S_0 is an *execution* iff σ leads from S_0 to (N,M), where M is a terminal marking in (N,M).

A marking M' is a *reachable* marking in a net system $S := (N,M)$, $N := (P,T,F)$, iff there exists an occurrence sequence σ in S that leads from S to (N,M'). By $[S\rangle$, we denote the set of all reachable markings in S. A marking M' is a *home* marking in S iff it is reachable from every reachable marking in S, i.e., $\forall M'' \in [S\rangle : M' \in [(N,M'')\rangle$. S is n-*bounded*, or *bounded*, iff there exists a number $n \in \mathbb{N}_0$ such that for every reachable marking M' in S and for every place $p \in P$ it holds that the number of tokens at p is at most n, i.e., $\forall M' \in [S\rangle \, \forall p \in P : M'(p) \leq n$. It is easy to see that the set of all reachable markings in a bounded net system is finite. Finally, a transition $t \in T$ is *dead* in S iff there does not exist a reachable marking in S that enables t.

3.2 Processes of Net Systems

Occurrence sequences and executions suit well when it comes to capturing *orderings* of transition occurrences. This section presents *processes* of net systems [19]. One can

---

[2] $\mathbf{1}_F$ denotes the characteristic function of F on the set $(P \times T) \cup (T \times P)$.

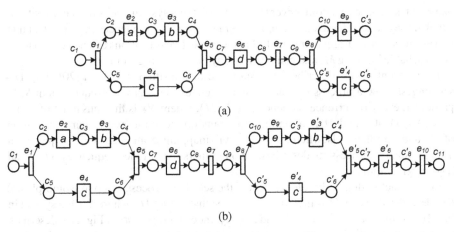

(a)

(b)

Fig. 2. Two processes of the net system in Fig. 1(a)

use processes to adequately represent *causality* and *concurrency* relations on transition occurrences. A process of a net system is a net of a particular kind, called a *causal net*, together with a mapping from nodes of the causal net to nodes of the net system.

Definition 3.6 (Causal net) A net $N := (B,E,G)$ is a *causal* net iff: (i) for every $b \in B$ it holds that $|{\bullet}b| \le 1$ and $|b{\bullet}| \le 1$, and (ii) N is acyclic, i.e., G^+ is irreflexive.[3]

Elements of B and E are called *conditions* and *events* of N, respectively. Two nodes x and y of a causal net $N := (B,E,G)$ are *causal*, or x is a *cause* for y, iff $(x,y) \in G^+$. They are *concurrent*, iff $x \ne y$, $(x,y) \notin G^+$, and $(y,x) \notin G^+$. A *cut* of a causal net is a maximal (with respect to set inclusion) set of its pairwise concurrent conditions.

Events of causal nets can be used to describe transition occurrences.

Definition 3.7 (Process, adapted from [19])
A *process* of a system $S := (N,M)$, $N := (P,T,F)$, is an ordered pair $\pi := (N_\pi, \rho)$, where $N_\pi := (B,E,G)$ is a causal net and $\rho : B \cup E \to P \cup T$ is such that:
- $\rho(B) \subseteq P$ and $\rho(E) \subseteq T$, i.e., ρ preserves the nature of nodes,
- $Min(N_\pi)$ is a cut and $\forall p \in P : M(p) = |\rho^{-1}(p) \cap Min(N_\pi)|$, i.e., π starts at M, and
- for every event $e \in E$ and for every place $p \in P$ it holds that
  $$\mathbf{1}_F((p,\rho(e))) = |\rho^{-1}(p) \cap {\bullet}e| \text{ and } \mathbf{1}_F((\rho(e),p)) = |\rho^{-1}(p) \cap e{\bullet}|,$$
  i.e., ρ respects the environment of transitions.[4]

Given a process π, we shall often write E_π and ρ_π to denote the set of events E and the mapping function ρ of π, respectively. We lift the aforementioned relations to processes by defining $\|_\pi$ and $\twoheadrightarrow_\pi$ as the concurrency relation and the causality relation on nodes of the causal net of π, respectively. We shall omit the subscripts where the context is clear.

Figs. 2(a) and 2(b) show processes π_1 and π_2 of the net system in Fig. 1(a), respectively. When visualizing processes, conditions $c_i, c_i' \dots$ refer to place p_i, i.e., $\rho(c_i) = \rho(c_i') = p_i$. Similarly, we assume events $e_j, e_j' \dots$ to refer to transition t_j, i.e., $\rho(e_j) = \rho(e_j') = t_j$. In Fig. 2(a), for example, it holds that $e_2 \| e_4$, $e_4 \twoheadrightarrow e_4'$, and $e_4' \| e_9$. Intuitively, the fact that

---

[3] R^+ denotes the transitive closure of binary relation R.

[4] $\rho(X) := \{\rho(x) \mid x \in X\}$ and $\rho^{-1}(z) := \{y \in Y \mid \rho(y) = z\}$, where X is a subset of ρ's domain Y.

one event is a cause for another event in a process π of a system S tells us that transitions which these events refer to can occur in order in occurrence sequences in S. The fact that two events are concurrent in π signals that the respective transitions can be both enabled at a reachable marking M, and can occur in any order starting from M.

Every event $e \in E_\pi$ describes an occurrence of transition $\rho_\pi(e)$. In [20], Jörg Desel suggests how a process of a net system S relates to occurrence sequences in S. In particular, every occurrence sequence in (N_π, M), where N_π is the causal net of a process (N_π, ρ) of S and M is a marking that puts one token at every source condition of N_π and no tokens elsewhere, *describes* via mapping ρ an occurrence sequence in S. For instance, process π_1 describes, among others, occurrence sequences $t_1 t_4 t_2$ and $t_1 t_2 t_3 t_4 t_5 t_6 t_7 t_8 t_9 t_4$.

Given a net system S, by Π_S we denote the set of all processes (up to isomorphism) that describe all executions in S. It is easy to see that the set Π_S, where S is the system in Fig. 1(a), is *infinite*, where $\pi_1 \notin \Pi_S$ and $\pi_2 \in \Pi_S$. Indeed, process π_2 in Fig. 2(b) describes, among nine executions, execution $t_1 t_2 t_3 t_4 t_5 t_6 t_7 t_8 t_9 t_3 t_4 t_5 t_6 t_{10}$ in the system in Fig. 1(a).

4   Definition of the 4C Spectrum

This section explores the definition of fundamental behavioral relations along two dimensions: occurrences of actions and their ordering. The first aspect is covered by different notions of conflict and co-occurrence relations (Section 4.1). Given two actions of a process model, these two relations relate to the presence or absence of joint occurrences of the two actions in the behavior model under a certain semantics. The second aspect is addressed by causality and concurrency relations (Section 4.2). Whenever there are joint occurrences of two actions, their ordering can be described by means of these relations.

4.1   Conflict and Co-occurrence

We start our study of behavioral relations on transitions of systems with a close look at the phenomena of conflict and co-occurrence. We noticed that every relation which characterizes how transition occurrences correlate across executions in systems can be captured in terms of two basic relations; one that checks if two transitions can both occur in some execution in the system, and the other that explores whether a transition can occur without some other transition.

Definition 4.1 (Basic conflict and co-occurrence)
Let $S := (N, M)$, $N := (P, T, F)$, be a system and let $x, y \in T$ be transitions of N.

   ○ x *can conflict with* y in S, denoted by $x \dashrightarrow_S y$, iff there exists an execution σ of S such that $x \in \sigma$ and $y \notin \sigma$.

   ○ x and y *can co-occur* in S, denoted by $x \leftrightsquigarrow_S y$, iff there exists an execution σ of S such that $x \in \sigma$ and $y \in \sigma$.[5]

---

[5] Given a sequence σ, $x \in \sigma$ denotes the fact that x is an element of σ.

We shall often omit subscripts where the context is clear (for all the subsequently proposed relations). For each transition x it holds that $\overline{x \dashrightarrow x}$. If a transition x is dead, then it holds that $\overline{x \rightsquigarrow x}$; otherwise $x \rightsquigarrow x$.

To give some examples we consider the net system in Fig. 3. Here, among other relations, it holds that $t_1 \dashrightarrow t_2$, $t_2 \dashrightarrow t_5$, $t_2 \dashrightarrow t_6$, $\overline{t_3 \dashrightarrow t_4}$, $\overline{t_1 \rightsquigarrow t_2}$, $t_2 \rightsquigarrow t_6$, and $t_3 \rightsquigarrow t_4$.

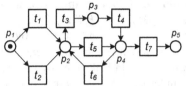

Fig. 3. A net system

Given a pair of transitions, one can use basic conflict and basic co-occurrence checks (refer to Definition 4.1) as atomic propositions, or *atoms*, in propositional logic formulas. These formulas can express 'rich' behavioral relations between pairs of transitions of a system. For instance, given two transitions x and y for which it holds that x can conflict with y, y can conflict with x, and x and y cannot co-occur, i.e., $x \dashrightarrow y \wedge y \dashrightarrow x \wedge \overline{x \rightsquigarrow y}$ evaluates to true, one can conclude that occurrences of x and y are *mutually exclusive*, or in *conflict*, in all executions in the system, e.g., transitions t_1 and t_2 are mutually exclusive in all executions in the system in Fig. 3.

Every well-formed propositional formula has an equivalent formula that is in disjunctive normal form (DNF), i.e., it is a disjunction of *conjunctive clauses*, where a conjunctive clause is a conjunction of one or more *literals*[6]. We are interested in *satisfiable* formulas that are not *tautologies*, as formulas that are either false or true in all interpretations are useless when it comes to characterizations of systems. A formula in DNF is satisfiable iff at least one of its conjunctive clauses is satisfiable.[7] Clearly, a conjunctive clause cannot be satisfied if it contains both the atoms a and $\bar{a}$. Thus, every satisfiable conjunctive clause that is composed of checks from Definition 4.1 (for a fixed pair of transitions) can never contain more than three literals.

A propositional formula is in *perfect* DNF if it is in DNF and each of its conjunctive clauses contains exactly one occurrence of each of the atoms. Every well-formed propositional formula has a *unique* equivalent formula that is in perfect DNF. Indeed, every elementary truth function over a set of atoms can be expressed as a formula in DNF where each conjunctive clause corresponds to one of the rows in the truth table for which the function is true. For each atom a that is made true in the row, the conjunctive clause should contain a and for atom a that is made false in that row, the conjunctive clause should contain $\bar{a}$. For example, formula $(x \dashrightarrow y \wedge y \dashrightarrow x \wedge \overline{x \rightsquigarrow y}) \vee (x \dashrightarrow y \wedge y \dashrightarrow x \wedge x \rightsquigarrow y)$ is an equivalent perfect DNF of formula $x \dashrightarrow y \wedge y \dashrightarrow x$.

Since every formula that exploits basic conflict and basic co-occurrence checks between a fixed pair of transitions operates with at most three literals, it has a unique equivalent formula in perfect 3DNF, i.e., a formula that is in DNF with each of its conjunctive clauses composed of exactly three different literals. These formulas in 3DNF can be seen as *canonical* forms of all propositional formulas over atoms induced by checks specified in Definition 4.1. Next, we take a closer look at all possible conjunctive clauses that can appear as parts of canonical formulas. These conjunctive clauses constitute fundamental

---

[6] A *literal* is an atomic proposition or its negation.

[7] A formula is *satisfiable* if it is possible to find an interpretation that makes the formula true.

conflict and co-occurrence checks between a fixed pair of transitions of a system, while disjunctions of these clauses allow one to obtain the 'relaxed' forms.

Definition 4.2 (Conflict and co-occurrence)

Let $S := (N,M)$, $N := (P,T,F)$, be a system and let $x, y \in T$ be transitions of N.

○ x and y *co-occur* in S, denoted by $x \leftrightarrow_S y$, iff $\overline{x \dashrightarrow_S y} \wedge \overline{y \dashrightarrow_S x} \wedge x \leftharpoonup_S y$.

○ x and y are in *conflict* in S, denoted by $x \,\#_S\, y$, iff $x \dashrightarrow_S y \wedge y \dashrightarrow_S x \wedge \overline{x \leftharpoonup_S y}$.

○ x *requires* y in S, denoted by $x \rightharpoonup_S y$, iff $\overline{x \dashrightarrow_S y} \wedge y \dashrightarrow_S x \wedge x \leftharpoonup_S y$.

○ x and y are *independent* in S, denoted by $x \rightleftharpoons_S y$, iff $x \dashrightarrow_S y \wedge y \dashrightarrow_S x \wedge x \leftharpoonup_S y$.

It is easy to check that transitions t_3 and t_4 co-occur in the system in Fig. 3, i.e., it holds that $t_3 \leftrightarrow t_4$, t_1 and t_2 are in conflict, i.e., $t_1 \,\#\, t_2$, t_5 requires t_7, i.e., $t_5 \rightharpoonup t_7$, and t_3 and t_5 are independent, i.e., $t_3 \rightleftharpoons t_5$. Note that $\rightharpoonup_S$ is asymmetric, whereas all other relations in Definition 4.2 are symmetric. In a system that is free from dead transitions every pair of transitions is in exactly one of the relations from Definition 4.2. Clearly, the relations in Definition 4.2 are disjoint. The fact that in the absence of dead transitions other conjunctive clauses (those not put into use in Definition 4.2) over the basic conflict and co-occurrence relations never evaluate to true is justified by the next proposition.

Proposition 4.3 (Basic conflict and co-occurrence) *If $S := (N,M)$, $N := (P,T,F)$, is a system without dead transitions, and $x, y \in T$ are transitions of N, then it holds that: (a) $\overline{x \dashrightarrow_S y}$ implies $x \leftharpoonup_S y$, and (b) $\overline{x \leftharpoonup_S y}$ implies $x \dashrightarrow_S y$ and $y \dashrightarrow_S x$.*

The proof of Proposition 4.3 is immediate. If x cannot conflict with y, i.e., $\overline{x \dashrightarrow_S y}$, then x and y can co-occur; otherwise x is a dead transition. Similarly, if x and y cannot co-occur, i.e., $\overline{x \leftharpoonup_S y}$, then there exist executions in S in which occurrences of x and y are mutually exclusive; otherwise either x, or y, or both x and y are dead transitions.

Next, we explore the remaining conjunctive clauses. These can relate dead transitions.

Definition 4.4 (Never (co-)occur)

Let $S := (N,M)$, $N := (P,T,F)$, be a system and let $x, y \in T$ be transitions of N.

○ x and y *never occur* in S, denoted by $x \mid_S y$, iff $\overline{x \dashrightarrow_S y} \wedge \overline{y \dashrightarrow_S x} \wedge \overline{x \leftharpoonup_S y}$.

○ x *but not* y *occurs* in S, denoted by $x \vdash_S y$, iff $x \dashrightarrow_S y \wedge \overline{y \dashrightarrow_S x} \wedge \overline{x \leftharpoonup_S y}$.

Indeed, in the general case, it is possible that either both transitions x and y are dead, in which case it holds that $x \mid y$, or one of the two transitions is dead, in which case it holds that $x \vdash y$ or $y \vdash x$. Definitions 4.2 and 4.4 propose 'strong' relations, i.e., every pair of transitions of a system is exactly in one of the proposed relations (they partition the Cartesian product of transitions). If one is interested in 'relaxed' forms of conflicts and co-occurrences, one can rely on the full spectrum of those, see the next definition.

Definition 4.5 (Spectrum of conflict and co-occurrence relations)

Let $S := (N,M)$, $N := (P,T,F)$, be a system, let $x, y \in T$ be transitions of N, and let Ω be a propositional formula on atomic propositions $x \dashrightarrow_S y$, $y \dashrightarrow_S x$, and $x \leftharpoonup_S y$.

○ Ω specifies a *conflict* relation between x and y iff each conjunctive clause of the perfect 3DNF of Ω contains either $x \dashrightarrow_S y$ or $y \dashrightarrow_S x$ among its literals.

○ Ω specifies a *co-occurrence* relation between x and y iff each conjunctive clause of the perfect 3DNF of Ω contains $x \leftharpoonup_S y$ as a literal.

Given a system S, by $\otimes_S$ and $\oplus_S$, we shall denote the sets of all, as per Definition 4.5, conflict and co-occurrence relations of S, respectively. For example, $x \leftrightarrow y \vee x \rightharpoonup y$ specifies a co-occurrence check between transitions x and y. Given two transitions x and y, there exist four conjunctive clauses (of the above discussed form) that contain literal $x \leftrightarrow y$; these are (i) $x \dashrightarrow y \wedge y \dashrightarrow x \wedge x \leftrightarrow y$, (ii) $\overline{x \dashrightarrow y} \wedge y \dashrightarrow x \wedge x \leftrightarrow y$, (iii) $x \dashrightarrow y \wedge \overline{y \dashrightarrow x} \wedge x \leftrightarrow y$, and (iv) $\overline{x \dashrightarrow y} \wedge \overline{y \dashrightarrow x} \wedge x \leftrightarrow y$. Thus, there are in total $2^4 - 1$, i.e., fifteen, distinct co-occurrence relations; each co-occurrence relation is either a single, or a disjunction of several, above proposed conjunctive clauses. By applying the same rationale, one can conclude that there are 63 distinct conflict relations.

4.2   Causality and Concurrency

This section looks into causality and concurrency phenomena. Similarly to the co-occurrence relations from Section 4.1, which report whether or not two actions can both occur in some execution in a system, causality and concurrency study situations when two actions occur in the same execution. However, causality and concurrency additionally enforce orderings on action occurrences.

Causality and concurrency are well-studied concepts in the context of behavior models [13,9,19]. These models focus on patterns of occurrences of actions, i.e., every occurrence of an action within a behavior model is supported with a dedicated modeling construct. Thus, there can exist several events in a process of a system which describe different occurrences of the same transition of the system, see the process in Fig. 2(b) and the corresponding net system in Fig. 1(a). This modeling approach has a simple characterization in terms of causality and concurrency relations on events, i.e., every two distinct events from a causal net that underpins the process are either causal or concurrent. Two concurrent events can be enabled at the same time, i.e., the corresponding actions can be executed simultaneously, while two causal events indicate the presence of an order, i.e., one action is a prerequisite of the other. In fact, both representations, i.e., (i) a process, and (ii) its causality and concurrency relations, are equivalent; given a causal net one can construct its causality and concurrency relations, and vice versa [9].

In what follows, we systematically discover causality and concurrency relations (of different 'strengths') by projecting the corresponding phenomena from action occurrences of behavior models into actions of system models, i.e., from events of processes into transitions of net systems. This way a comprehensive classification of causality and concurrency relations for system models is obtained. Given two transitions x and y of a system, the classification is founded on three 'dimensions'. Intuitively, these dimensions correspond to: (i) whether a relation holds in some or all processes of a net system, (ii) whether a relation holds for one or all occurrences of x, and (iii) whether a relation holds for one or all occurrences of y. Before proceeding, for convenience considerations, we define a filter that selects those processes that describe occurrences of x and y, i.e., $\Delta_S(x,y) := \{\pi \in \Pi_S \mid \exists e_1 \in E_\pi \, \exists e_2 \in E_\pi : e_1 \neq e_2 \wedge \rho_\pi(e_1) = x \wedge \rho_\pi(e_2) = y\}$. The constraint $e_1 \neq e_2$ is introduced to allow excluding those processes from $\Delta_S(x,x)$ that contain only one event that describes an occurrence of x. Thus, $\Delta_S(x,y)$ contains processes that are of interest when checking causality and concurrency. Note that the causality and concurrency relations on events of a causal net are irreflexive. Next, we propose concurrency checks between transitions x and y that imply checks in all processes that describe occurrences of x and y to obtain *total* relations.

Definition 4.6 (Total concurrency)

Let $S := (N,M)$, $N := (P,T,F)$, be a system and let $x,y \in T$ be transitions of N.

- x and y are *total (mutual) concurrent* in S, denoted by $x \parallel_S^{\forall\forall\forall} y$, iff:

    $\forall \pi \in \Delta_S(x,y) \ \forall e_1 \in E_\pi \ \forall e_2 \in E_\pi : (e_1 \neq e_2 \wedge \rho_\pi(e_1) = x \wedge \rho_\pi(e_2) = y) \Rightarrow e_1 \parallel_\pi e_2$.

- x is *total functional concurrent* for y in S, denoted by $x \parallel_S^{\forall\forall\exists} y$, iff:

    $\forall \pi \in \Delta_S(x,y) \ \forall e_1 \in E_\pi \ \exists e_2 \in E_\pi : \rho_\pi(e_1) = x \Rightarrow (\rho_\pi(e_2) = y \wedge e_1 \parallel_\pi e_2)$.

- x is *total dominant concurrent* for y in S, denoted by $x \parallel_S^{\forall\exists\forall} y$, iff:

    $\forall \pi \in \Delta_S(x,y) \ \exists e_1 \in E_\pi \ \forall e_2 \in E_\pi : \rho_\pi(e_1) = x \wedge ((\rho_\pi(e_2) = y \wedge e_1 \neq e_2) \Rightarrow e_1 \parallel_\pi e_2)$.

- x and y are *total existential concurrent* in S, denoted by $x \parallel_S^{\forall\exists\exists} y$, iff:

    $\forall \pi \in \Delta_S(x,y) \ \exists e_1 \in E_\pi \ \exists e_2 \in E_\pi : \rho_\pi(e_1) = x \wedge \rho_\pi(e_2) = y \wedge e_1 \parallel_\pi e_2$.

Instead of checking concurrency patterns in all processes where two transitions co-occur, one can ask if these patterns hold in at least one process. Such an intent results in the next definition of existential concurrent relations.

Definition 4.7 (Existential concurrency)

Let $S := (N,M)$, $N := (P,T,F)$, be a system and let $x,y \in T$ be transitions of N.

- x and y are *existential total concurrent* in S, denoted by $x \parallel_S^{\exists\forall\forall} y$, iff:

    $\exists \pi \in \Delta_S(x,y) \ \forall e_1 \in E_\pi \ \forall e_2 \in E_\pi : (e_1 \neq e_2 \wedge \rho_\pi(e_1) = x \wedge \rho_\pi(e_2) = y) \Rightarrow e_1 \parallel_\pi e_2$.

- x is *existential functional concurrent* for y in S, denoted by $x \parallel_S^{\exists\forall\exists} y$, iff:

    $\exists \pi \in \Delta_S(x,y) \ \forall e_1 \in E_\pi \ \exists e_2 \in E_\pi : \rho_\pi(e_1) = x \Rightarrow (\rho_\pi(e_2) = y \wedge e_1 \parallel_\pi e_2)$.

- x is *existential dominant concurrent* for y in S, denoted by $x \parallel_S^{\exists\exists\forall} y$, iff:

    $\exists \pi \in \Delta_S(x,y) \ \exists e_1 \in E_\pi \ \forall e_2 \in E_\pi : \rho_\pi(e_1) = x \wedge ((\rho_\pi(e_2) = y \wedge e_1 \neq e_2) \Rightarrow e_1 \parallel_\pi e_2)$.

- x and y are *existential (mutual) concurrent* in S, denoted by $x \parallel_S^{\exists\exists\exists} y$, iff:

    $\exists \pi \in \Delta_S(x,y) \ \exists e_1 \in E_\pi \ \exists e_2 \in E_\pi : \rho_\pi(e_1) = x \wedge \rho_\pi(e_2) = y \wedge e_1 \parallel_\pi e_2$.

Similarly, one can talk about causality relations of different strengths. These relations can be trivially obtained by replacing all the concurrent checks $e_1 \parallel_\pi e_2$ in Definitions 4.6 and 4.7 with the causal checks $e_1 \rightarrowtail_\pi e_2$.

For instance, the *total (mutual) causal* check between transitions x and y verifies if for every process π of the respective system and for every two distinct events e_1 and e_2 of π it holds that if e_1 describes an occurrence of x and e_2 describes an occurrence of y, then e_1 is a cause for e_2, i.e., it holds that $e_1 \rightarrowtail_\pi e_2$. The concurrency relations from Definitions 4.6 and 4.7 give rise to a lattice induced by logical implications; the same holds for the corresponding causality relations. It is easy to see that $x \parallel^{\forall\forall\forall} y$ implies $x \parallel^{\forall\forall\exists} y$. Clearly, if in every process that

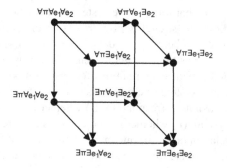

Fig. 4. The lattice of causality/concurrency

describes occurrences of x and y it holds that every occurrence of x is concurrent with some occurrence of y, and vice versa, then in each of these processes it also trivially holds that for every occurrence of x one can find a corresponding concurrent occurrence of y. Fig. 4 summarizes all the implications; transitive implications are not visualized. Here, every arrow specifies a logical implication between relations encoded in its endpoints, e.g., the implication from the above example is highlighted with a thicker arrow in the figure.

Finally, we define the spectrum of all causal and concurrent relations where each relation stems from a particular combination of co-occurrence and causal/concurrent patterns of action occurrences. Let $\Phi := \{\forall\forall\forall, \forall\forall\exists, \forall\exists\forall, \forall\exists\exists, \exists\forall\forall, \exists\forall\exists, \exists\exists\forall, \exists\exists\exists\}$.

Definition 4.8 (Spectrum of causality and concurrency relations)
Let $S := (N,M)$, $N := (P,T,F)$, be a system and let $x, y \in T$ be transitions of N.

○ x and y are *causal*, denoted by $x \rightsquigarrow^{\phi}_{S,\diamond} y$, iff it holds that

$(x \diamond_S y) \wedge (x \rightsquigarrow^{\phi}_S y)$, where $\diamond_S \in \oplus_S$ and $\phi \in \Phi$.

○ x and y are *concurrent*, denoted by $x \parallel^{\phi}_{S,\diamond} y$, iff it holds that

$(x \diamond_S y) \wedge (x \parallel^{\phi}_S y)$, where $\diamond_S \in \oplus_S$ and $\phi \in \Phi$.

It is easy to see that Definition 4.8 can be used to induce $15 \times 8 = 120$ distinct causal relations and the same number of concurrent relations on transitions of net systems. Definitions 4.5 and 4.8 jointly specify the 4C spectrum of behavioral relations.

Coming back to our motivating example in Section 2, one can clearly differentiate systems in Fig. 1 by using the above proposed behavioral relations on transitions. For instance, in Fig. 1(a), one can verify that the only transition with label b and the only transition with label c are existential causal, existential total concurrent, as well as total functional concurrent. In the system in Fig. 1(b), it also holds that the only transition with label b and the only transition with label c are existential causal. However, these transitions are not concurrent as per Definitions 4.6 and 4.7.

Table 1. Behavioral relations in Fig. 1(a)   **Table 2.** Beh. relations in Fig. 1(b)

Table 1. Behavioral relations in Fig. 1(a)

	a	b	c	d	e
a	↹	⤳^∀∀∀	⤳^∃∀∃ ∥^∃∀∀_∀∀∃	⤳^∀∀∀	⤳^∀∀∀
b	↹	↹	⤳^∀∃∃	⤳^∃∃∃ ∥^∃∀∀_∀∀∃	⤳^∃∀∀ ∀∀∃ ∀∃∀	⤳^∀∃∀
c	∥^∃∀∀_∀∃∀	⤳^∃∃∃ ∥^∃∀∀_∀∀∃	⤳^∀∃∃	⤳^∃∀∀ ∀∀∃ ∀∃∀	⤳^∀∃∀ ∥^∃∃∀_∀∃∃
d	↹	⤳^∃∃∃	⤳^∃∃∃	⤳^∀∃∃	⤳^∀∃∀
e	↹	⤳^∀∀∃	⤳^∃∃∃ ∥^∀∀∃	⤳^∀∀∃	⤳^∀∃∃

Table 2. Beh. relations in Fig. 1(b)

	a	b	c	d	e
a	↹	⤳^∀∀∀	⤳^∀∀∀	⤳^∀∀∀	⤳^∀∀∀
b	↹	⤳^∀∃∃	⤳^∃∃∃	⤳^∃∀∀ ∀∀∃ ∀∃∀	⤳^∀∃∀
c	↹	⤳^∃∀∀ ∀∀∃ ∀∃∀	⤳^∀∃∃	⤳^∃∀∀ ∀∀∃ ∀∃∀	⤳^∀∃∀
d	↹	⤳^∃∃∃	⤳^∃∃∃	⤳^∀∃∃	⤳^∀∃∀
e	↹	⤳^∀∀∃	⤳^∀∀∃	⤳^∀∀∃	⤳^∀∃∃

Tables 1 and 2 summarize all the fundamental relations for the systems in Fig. 1. Note that only *strong* relations are proposed, where a relation is classified as strong iff it is not implied by any other relation. Tables 1 and 2 do not suggest *can conflict* relations. For both systems in Fig. 1 it trivially holds that a, b, c, and d can conflict with e.

5 Computation of Behavioral Relations

This section addresses the problem of computing behavioral relations.

5.1   Conflict and Co-occurrence

Section 4.1 introduced a spectrum of conflict and co-occurrence relations. Despite the large number of relations that aim at recognizing small differences between patterns of action occurrences, all the relations are founded on two basic checks from Definition 4.1. In what follows, we show how one can reduce these basic checks to the *reachability problem* [8]. To this end, we rely on the next transformation of net systems.

Definition 5.1 (Transition guarding)
Let $S := (N,M)$, $N := (P,T,F)$, be a system and let $x \in T$ be one of its transitions. An *injection of a guard* for x in S results in a system $S' := (N',M')$, $N' := (P',T',F')$, where:
  ○ $P' := P \cup \{p,p'\}$, $T' := T \cup \{x'\}$, where p,p',x', are fresh nodes in N, $M' := M \uplus \{p\}$,
  ○ $F' := F \cup \{(y,x') \mid y \in \bullet x\} \cup \{(x',y) \mid y \in x\bullet\} \cup \{(p,x'),(x',p'),(p',x),(x,p')\}$.

We say that fresh transition x' is the *guard* for x, whereas fresh places p and p' are the *guard* and the *control* place for x, respectively. It is easy to see that different orderings of injections of guards for all transitions from some set of transitions lead to the same system. Finally, computations of conflicts and co-occurrences are due to the next result.

Proposition 5.2 (Basic conflict and co-occurrence check)
Let $S := (N,M)$, $N := (P,T,F)$, be a net system with a unique reachable terminal marking M_t. Let $x,y \in T$, $x \neq y$, be transitions of N. Let $S' := (N',M')$, $N' := (P',T',F')$, be a net system obtained via injections of guards for x and y, where $p' \in P'$ and $q' \in P'$ are the control places for x and y, respectively, and $q \in P'$ is the guard place for y.
  1. x can conflict with y in S, i.e., $x \to_S y$, iff $M_t \uplus \{p',q\}$ is a reachable marking in S'.
  2. x and y can co-occur in S, i.e., $x \to_S y$, iff $M_t \uplus \{p',q'\}$ is a reachable marking in S'.

Fig. 5(a) visualizes the construction of the proof of Proposition 5.2. In the figure, transitions x' and y' are the guards for transitions x and y, respectively, whereas p,q and p',q' are the corresponding guard and control places. The box with the dashed borderline demarcates boundaries of the original (not augmented) net system S. It holds that in every occurrence sequence in the augmented system S' transition x' can occur at most once (instead of the first occurrence of transition x in S). Indeed, the preset of x' consists of the preset of x and one additional place p, which is marked in S'. An occurrence of x' implements the effect of the occurrence of x, i.e., the postset of x' contains that of x. Additionally, an occurrence of x' marks place p' that allows subsequent occurrences of x. The same principles apply to occurrences of transitions y and y' in S'. Thus, it appears that every execution σ in S can be trivially transformed into an execution σ' in S' by replacing the first occurrences of x and y with those of x' and y', respectively. Moreover, the presence and absence of transitions x and y in σ is clearly witnessed by the presence and absence of tokens at places p' and q', respectively, in a marking that is reachable via σ' in S'. The above proposed rationale justifies both statements in Proposition 5.2.

Note that the *reachability problem*, which given a net system S and a marking M consists of deciding if M is a reachable marking in S, is decidable [21,22].

5.2   Causality and Concurrency

This section proposes computations of causality and concurrency relations. To demonstrate feasibility, this section addresses the computation of two extreme cases (as per Section 4). We start by showing how to compute existential concurrency.

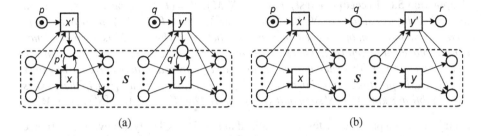

Fig. 5. Visualizations of: (a) the proof of Proposition 5.2, and (b) the proof of Proposition 5.6

Proposition 5.3 (Existential concurrency check)
Let $S := (N,M), N := (P,T,F)$, be a net system with a unique reachable terminal marking M_t, such that M_t is a home marking in S. Let $x,y \in T$ be transitions of N. Transitions x and y are existential concurrent in S, i.e., $x \parallel_S^{\exists\exists\exists} y$, iff there exists a reachable marking M' in S such that $\bullet x \uplus \bullet y$ is covered by M', i.e., $\exists M' \in [S\rangle : \bullet x \uplus \bullet y \leq M'$.

The statement in Proposition 5.3 follows immediately from the process construction principles described in [19,20]; refer to the proof of Theorem 3.6 in [19]. Note that the fact that M_t is a home marking ensures that every process of S that contains two concurrent events that refer to transitions x and y can indeed be extended to a process that describes an execution in S. Next, we propose a solution for checking total causality.

Proposition 5.4 (Total causality check) *Let $S := (N,M), N := (P,T,F)$, be a net system with a unique reachable terminal marking M_t, such that M_t is a home marking in S. Let $x,y \in T$ be transitions of N. Transitions x and y are total causal in S, i.e., $x \rightarrowtail_S^{\forall\forall\forall} y$, iff for every occurrence sequence $\sigma := t_1 \ldots t_n, n \in \mathbb{N}_0$, in S and for every two positions i and j in σ, $1 \leq i,j \leq n, i \neq j$, such that $t_i = x$ and $t_j = y$ it holds that $i < j$.*

Again, the existence of a reachable terminal marking M_t, which is a home marking, ensures that every occurrence sequence of interest can be extended to an execution. It is immediate that if x and y are total causal then in every occurrence sequence y can never be observed before x. As for the converse statement, assume that there exists an occurrence sequence σ in which y precedes x and it holds that $x \rightarrowtail_S^{\forall\forall\forall} y$. Then, it also holds that $x \parallel_\pi y$ or $y \rightarrowtail_\pi x$, where π is a process induced by σ, refer to [20] for details, which leads to a contradiction. Thus, one can verify total causality between x and y by testing for the absence of an occurrence sequence in which y precedes x. To this end, we suggest to rely on the next transformation of net systems.

Definition 5.5 (Precedence test) Let $S := (N,M)$, $N := (P,T,F)$, be a system and let $x,y \in T$, be its transitions. *An injection of a precedence test for x before y in S results in a system $S' := (N',M'), N' := (P',T',F')$, where:*

- $P' := P \cup \{p,q,r\}, T' := T \cup \{x',y'\}$, *where p,q,r and x',y' are fresh nodes in N,*
- $F' := F \cup \{(z,x') \mid z \in \bullet x\} \cup \{(x',z) \mid z \in x\bullet\} \cup \{(z,y') \mid z \in \bullet y\} \cup \{(y',z) \mid z \in y\bullet\} \cup \{(p,x'),(x',q),(q,y'),(y',r)\}$, *and $M' := M \uplus \{p\}$.*

We say that the fresh place r is the *precedence control* place for x before y. Given transitions x and y of a net system, the injection of a precedence test for x before y can be used to check if x can precede y in some occurrence sequence in the net system.

Proposition 5.6 (Precedence test) *Let* $S := (N,M)$, $N := (P,T,F)$, *be a net system and let* $x,y \in T$ *be transitions of* N. *Let* $S' := (N',M')$, $N' := (P',T',F')$, *be a net system obtained via injection of a precedence test for* x *before* y, *where* $r \in P'$ *is the precedence control place for* x *before* y. *There exists an occurrence sequence* $\sigma := t_1 \ldots t_n$, $n > 1$, *where* $t_i \in T$, $i \in 1..n$, *in* S *such that an occurrence of* x *precedes an occurrence of* y *in* σ, *i.e., there exist positions* i *and* j *in* σ, $1 \leq i < j \leq n$, *such that* $t_i = x$ *and* $t_j = y$, *iff there exists a reachable marking* M' *in* S' *such that* $\{r\}$ *is covered by* M', *i.e.*, $\exists M' \in [S'\rangle : \{r\} \leq M'$. ⌋

An injection of a precedence test is visualized in Fig. 5(b). Clearly, for every occurrence sequence in the augmented net system which leads to a marking that covers the precedence control place r it holds that transition x' precedes transition y'. As transition x and y can always occur instead of x' and y', both in the original and in the augmented net system, it holds that there exists an occurrence sequence in the original net system in which x precedes y, refer to the discussion in Section 5.1 for the intuition.

Note that the *covering problem*, which given a net system S and a marking M consists of deciding if there exists a reachable marking M' in S such that $M \leq M'$, i.e., M is covered by M', is decidable [23]. Moreover, the *home state problem*, which given a net system S and a reachable marking M in S consists of deciding if M is a home marking in S, is decidable [24]. Finally, one can often ensure the existence of a unique reachable terminal marking in a given net system, e.g., if the system is bounded.

6   The 4C Spectrum for Labeled Net Systems

So far we discussed behavioral relations for systems in which actions are represented by transitions. We now turn to labeled systems that represent actions by (transition) labels, for which we first recall basic notions. We then lift the relations of the 4C spectrum to labels and show how their operationalizations are traced back to the unlabeled case.

6.1   Labeled Net Systems

In the context of process models, the motivation for labeled net systems is twofold. First, it is often convenient to distinguish between *observable* and *silent* transitions, separating actions that carry semantics in the application domain from those that have no domain interpretation. Second, one may wish to assign a certain semantics in the application domain to different transitions. Note that the models in Fig. 1 are, in fact, labeled systems, although so far the labels have not been considered in our investigations. Fig. 6 depicts another labeled system, in which two transitions are assigned the same label.

We briefly recall notions and notations for labeled net systems as follows.

Definition 6.1 (Labeled net) A *labeled net* is an ordered tuple $N := (P,T,F,\mathcal{T},\lambda)$, where (P,T,F) is a net, $\mathcal{T}$ is a set of labels, where $\tau \in \mathcal{T}$ is a special label, and $\lambda : T \to \mathcal{T}$ is a function that assigns to each transition in T a *label* in $\mathcal{T}$.   ⌋

If $\lambda(t) \neq \tau$, $t \in T$, then t is *observable*; otherwise, t is *silent*. Labeling directly extends to systems, i.e., a *labeled net system*, or a *labeled system*, is an ordered pair $S := (N,M)$, where N is a labeled net and M is a marking of N.

In the graphical notation, a label of a transition is shown next to the transition rectangle with its short form shown inside of the rectangle, whereas silent transitions are

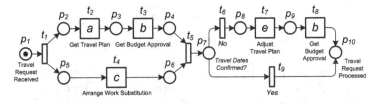

Fig. 6. A behavioral specification given as a labeled Petri net system

visualized as empty rectangles. For instance, two transitions in the system in Fig. 6 'wear' label *"Get Budget Approval"*, which we also refer to via its short form b. Note that Fig. 3 visualizes a regular, i.e., unlabeled, net system.

For a labeled system $S := (N, M)$, $N := (P, T, F, \mathcal{T}, \lambda)$, any occurrence sequence $\sigma := t_1 \ldots t_n$, $n \in \mathbb{N}_0$, of N can be interpreted as a sequence of observable labels. Let $\Theta(\sigma, k) := |\{t_i \in \sigma \mid i \leq k \wedge \lambda(t_i) = \tau\}|$ be the number of silent transitions of σ up to and including position k. Then, the *observable sequence* induced by σ, denoted by $\lambda(\sigma) := \lambda_1 \ldots \lambda_m$, $m \leq n$, is such that $\lambda_i := \lambda(t_j)$, $j = i + \Theta(\sigma, j)$, for $0 \leq i \leq m$, and $n = m + \Theta(\sigma, n)$.

In the same vein, processes of a labeled system can be interpreted in terms of transition labels. That is, given a process $\pi := (N_\pi, \rho)$, $N_\pi := (B, E, G)$, of a labeled net system $S := (N, M)$, $N := (P, T, F, \mathcal{T}, \lambda)$, each event $e \in E$ is not only related to a transition $\rho(e) \in T$, but also to a label $(\lambda \circ \rho)(e) \in \mathcal{T}$.

6.2 Relations over Transition Labels

Conflict & Co-occurrence. All the proposed conflict and co-occurrence relations from Section 4.1 are based on the binary *can conflict* and *can co-occur* relations that are defined over transitions, see Definition 4.1. Once any occurrence sequence and, thus, any execution in a labeled system $S := (N, M)$, $N := (P, T, F, \mathcal{T}, \lambda)$, is interpreted as a sequence of observable labels, both relations can be naturally lifted to labels. Label λ_x *can conflict with* label λ_y in S, $\lambda_x, \lambda_y \in \mathcal{T} \setminus \{\tau\}$, denoted by $\lambda_x \dashrightarrow_{\lambda,S} \lambda_y$, iff there exists an execution σ of S such that $\lambda_x \in \lambda(\sigma)$ and $\lambda_y \notin \lambda(\sigma)$. Labels λ_x and λ_y *can co-occur* in S, denoted by $\lambda_x \leftrightsquigarrow_{\lambda,S} \lambda_y$, iff there exists an execution σ in S such that $\lambda_x \in \lambda(\sigma)$ and $\lambda_y \in \lambda(\sigma)$. E.g., for the net system in Fig. 6 it holds that $c \dashrightarrow_\lambda e$, $\overline{e \dashrightarrow_\lambda c}$, and $c \leftrightsquigarrow_\lambda e$.

Causality & Concurrency. The causality and concurrency relations from Section 4.2 test for processes that contain events related to certain transitions. For the case of labeled systems, these tests can refer to events that relate to certain observable labels. We exemplify how the relations are lifted with the total (mutual) concurrency relation. For a labeled system $S := (N, M)$, $N := (P, T, F, \mathcal{T}, \lambda)$ and two labels $\lambda_x, \lambda_y \in \mathcal{T} \setminus \{\tau\}$, let $\Delta_{\lambda,S}(\lambda_x, \lambda_y) := \{\pi \in \Pi_S \mid \exists e_1 \in E_\pi \exists e_2 \in E_\pi : e_1 \neq e_2 \wedge (\lambda \circ \rho_\pi)(e_1) = \lambda_x \wedge (\lambda \circ \rho_\pi)(e_2) = \lambda_y\}$ be the set of processes containing events of interest. Then, two labels λ_x and λ_y are total (mutual) concurrent in S, denoted by $\lambda_x \parallel_{\lambda,S}^{\forall\forall\exists} \lambda_y$, iff $\forall \pi \in \Delta_{\lambda,S}(\lambda_x, \lambda_y) \, \forall e_1 \in E_\pi \forall e_2 \in E_\pi :$ $(e_1 \neq e_2 \wedge (\lambda \circ \rho_\pi)(e_1) = \lambda_x \wedge (\lambda \circ \rho_\pi)(e_2) = \lambda_y) \Rightarrow e_1 \parallel_\pi e_2$. For example, for the net system in Fig. 6 it holds that $c \parallel_\lambda^{\forall\forall\exists} b$ and $c \not\parallel_\lambda^{\exists\forall\exists} b$.

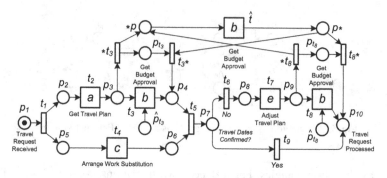

Fig. 7. The system of Fig. 6 after applying unification of label b

6.3 Computation

Computation of the relations defined over labels can be traced back to the computation of the relations defined over transitions, as introduced in Section 5. The idea behind our approach is to implement *label unification*, such that every occurrence of the same label is manifested in the occurrence of a specific (possibly newly introduced) transition. To this end, we perform structural transformations of labeled net systems.

Definition 6.2 (Label unification) Let $S := (N, M)$, $N := (P, T, F, \mathcal{T}, \lambda)$, be a labeled net system and let $\lambda_x \in \mathcal{T}$ be a label. Let $T_{\lambda_x} := \{t \in T \mid \lambda(t) = \lambda_x\}$ be the set of all transitions of N labeled with λ_x. A *label unification* of λ_x in S results in a labeled net system S', such that: (i) if $\lambda_x = \tau$ or $|T_{\lambda_x}| \leq 1$ then $S' := S$, i.e., the net system is not changed, and (ii) if $\lambda_x \neq \tau$ and $|T_{\lambda_x}| > 1$ then $S' := (N', M')$, $N' := (P', T', F', \mathcal{T}, \lambda')$, where:

- $P' := P \cup \{*p, p*\} \cup \bigcup_{t \in T_{\lambda_x}} \{p_t, \hat{p}_t\}$, $T' := T \cup \{\hat{t}\} \cup \bigcup_{t \in T_{\lambda_x}} \{*t, t*\}$, such that
  $(\{*p, p*, \hat{t}\} \cup \bigcup_{t \in T_{\lambda_x}} \{p_t, \hat{p}_t, *t, t*\}) \cap (P \cup T) = \varnothing$,
- $F' := F \cup \{(*p, \hat{t}), (\hat{t}, p*)\} \cup \bigcup_{t \in T_{\lambda_x}} \{(p, *t) \mid p \in \bullet t\} \cup \bigcup_{t \in T_{\lambda_x}} \{(t*, p) \mid p \in t \bullet\} \cup$
  $\bigcup_{t \in T_{\lambda_x}} \{(\hat{p}_t, t), (*t, p_t), (p_t, t*), (*t, *p), (p*, t*)\}$,
- $\lambda'(t) := \lambda(t)$, for every $t \in T$, $\lambda'(\hat{t}) := \lambda_x$, $\lambda'(*t) := \lambda'(t*) := \tau$, for every $t \in T_{\lambda_x}$, and
- $M'(p) := M(p)$, for every $p \in P$, $M'(*p) := M'(p*) := 0$, $M'(p_t) := M'(\hat{p}_t) := 0$, for every $t \in T_{\lambda_x}$.

If $\lambda_x \neq \tau$ and $|T_{\lambda_x}| > 1$, we say that transition $\hat{t}$ is the *solitary* transition for label λ_x in S'. Additionally, we say that transition t is the *solitary* transition for label λ_x in S' if $\lambda_x \neq \tau$ and $T_{\lambda_x} = \{t\}$. If $\lambda_x \neq \tau$ and $|T_{\lambda_x}| > 1$, all transitions in T_{λ_x} are dead in S'; since places $\hat{p}_{t_1}$ to $\hat{p}_{t_n}$ have empty presets and are not marked in M'. Thus, given a label λ_x, the solitary transition for λ_x (if such a transition exists) is the only transition with label λ_x that may appear in an occurrence sequence in S'. If $\lambda_x \neq \tau$, $|T_{\lambda_x}| > 1$, and $t \in T$ is such that $\lambda(t) = \lambda_x$, we say that $*t$ and $t*$ are the *presolitary* and the *postsolitary* transition of t for λ_x, respectively. For the example net system shown in Fig. 6, the result of applying unification of label b is illustrated in Fig. 7. It is easy to see that all applications of the same set of unification operations (in different orders) result in the same system.

In what follows, we argue that an original net system and its augmented version that is obtained via unification of every label in a given set of labels induce – from the point of view of an external observer – equivalent behaviors. In order to facilitate subsequent discussions, we rely on the next auxiliary definition.

Definition 6.3 (Labeled elementary event structure)
A *labeled elementary event structure* is an ordered tuple $\mathcal{E} := (E, <, \mathcal{T}, \lambda)$, where E is a set of *events*, $<$ is a partial order over E, called the *causality relation*, $\mathcal{T}$ is a set of labels, and $\lambda : E \rightarrow \mathcal{T}$ is a function that assigns to each event in E a *label* in $\mathcal{T}$.

The ordered pair $(E, <)$ is a partially ordered set of events, also known as an *elementary event structure*. In [9], the authors show that elementary event structures are alternative representations of causal nets and, thus, of processes of net systems [19]. Consequently, every labeled elementary event structure is a partially ordered set of labeled events that can be used to encode essential information about observable transition occurrences.

Let $\pi := (N_\pi, \rho)$, $N_\pi := (B, E, G)$, be a process of a labeled system $S := (N, M)$, $N := (P, T, F, \mathcal{T}, \lambda)$, and let $E' := \{e \in E \mid (\lambda \circ \rho)(e) \neq \tau\}$ be the set of events of N_π that correspond to observable transitions of N. Then, $\mathcal{E}[\pi] := (E, \rightarrowtail_\pi |_E, \mathcal{T}, \lambda \circ (\rho|_E))$ is the labeled elementary event structure induced by π, and $\mathcal{O}[\mathcal{E}[\pi]] := (E', \rightarrowtail_\pi |_{E'}, \mathcal{T} \setminus \{\tau\}, \lambda \circ (\rho|_{E'}))$ is the *observable* elementary event structure induced by $\mathcal{E}[\pi]$. Note that similar transformations are proposed in [9,25]; for instance, in [25], the authors propose the λ-*abstraction* of π. Given a process π, the observable elementary event structure $\mathcal{O}[\mathcal{E}[\pi]]$ describes all occurrences of observable transitions that are also captured in π, as well as the causality and the concurrency relations on the corresponding events.

Intuitively, two event structures describe the same observable behavior if they are *order-isomorphic*, refer to [25] for details.

Definition 6.4 (Order-isomorphism) Let $\mathcal{O}_1 := (E_1, <_1, \mathcal{T}, \lambda_1)$ and $\mathcal{O}_2 := (E_2, <_2, \mathcal{T}, \lambda_2)$ be two observable elementary event structures (both with labels in $\mathcal{T}$). Then, $\mathcal{O}_1$ and $\mathcal{O}_2$ are *order-isomorphic*, denoted by $\mathcal{O}_1 \cong \mathcal{O}_2$, iff there exists a bijection $\beta : E_1 \rightarrow E_2$, such that : (i) $\forall e \in E_1 : \lambda_1(e) = (\lambda_2 \circ \beta)(e)$ and (ii) $\forall e, e' \in E_1 : e <_1 e' \Leftrightarrow \beta(e) <_2 \beta(e')$.

Using the notion of observable elementary event structures, we show that, indeed, label unification does not change the behavior of a net system.

Lemma 6.5 (Equivalence of observable behaviors)
Let $S := (N, M)$, $N := (P, T, F, \mathcal{T}, \lambda)$, and S' be labeled net systems, where S' is obtained from S via label unification of every label in $\mathcal{T}' \subseteq \mathcal{T}$. For every process π of S there exists a process π' of S', such that $\mathcal{O}[\mathcal{E}[\pi]] \cong \mathcal{O}[\mathcal{E}[\pi']]$, and vice versa.

Proof. (Sketch) Let $S' := (N', M')$, $N' := (P', T', F', \mathcal{T}, \lambda')$. Let $\pi := (N_\pi, \rho)$, $N_\pi := (B, E, G)$, be a process of S, and let $\mathcal{E}[\pi] := (E, <, \mathcal{T}, \eta)$ be the labeled elementary event structure induced by π. We prove the statement by induction on the structure of $\mathcal{E}[\pi]$. It is easy to see that the empty processes of S and S', i.e., processes without a single event, induce order-isomorphic observable elementary event structures. By the induction hypothesis, there exists a process π' of S' such that $\mathcal{O}[\mathcal{E}[\pi']]$ is order-isomorphic with $\mathcal{O}[(E', < |_{E'}, \mathcal{T}, \eta|_{E'})]$, where E' is a *left-closed* subset of E, i.e., $e \in E'$ and $e' < e$, $e' \in E$, implies $e' \in E'$. Let $d \in E$ be an event such that $d \notin E'$ and $E'' := E' \cup \{d\}$ is a left-closed subset of E. Next, we construct a process π^* from π' by appending to π' a fresh event, refer to [19] for details. When appending a fresh event that refers to transition t, we also append conditions that map to places in the postset of t. Additionally, the flow relation of the causal net of the process under construction is completed to respect the environment of t. We distinguish the following two cases:

(i) $(\lambda \circ \rho)(d) = \tau$ or $|\{t \in T \mid \lambda(t) = (\lambda \circ \rho)(d)\}| = 1$ or $(\lambda \circ \rho)(d) \notin T'$.

We construct π^* by appending a fresh event f to π' that maps to transition $\rho(d)$.

(ii) Otherwise, we construct π^* by appending three fresh events f, f', and f'' to π' such that f maps to the solitary transition for label $(\lambda \circ \rho)(d)$, whereas f' and f'' map to the presolitary and the postsolitary transition of $\rho(d)$ for $(\lambda \circ \rho)(d)$, respectively. Event f' must be appended first. Then, f can be appended before appending f''.

It is easy to see that, because of Definition 6.2, both proposed constructions can be implemented and in both cases it holds that $\mathcal{O}[\mathcal{E}[\pi^*]] \cong \mathcal{O}[(E'', <|_{E''}, \mathcal{T}, \eta|_{E''})]$.

The proof of the converse statement proceeds similarly to the one proposed above.   ∎

Given a label λ_x, $\lambda_x \neq \tau$, and a labeled system S, unification of λ_x in S results in a system with at most one transition that carries label λ_x and is not dead. Thus, it is enforced that all occurrences of λ_x result from occurrences of a single transition. This allows to trace back the relations of the 4C spectrum over labels to those over transitions. To this end, it suffices to consider basic conflict, basic co-occurrence, and the eight instantiations ($\Phi := \{\forall\forall\forall, \forall\forall\exists, \forall\exists\forall, \forall\exists\exists, \exists\forall\forall, \exists\forall\exists, \exists\exists\forall, \exists\exists\exists\}$) of causality and concurrency.

Proposition 6.6 (Relations on labels) *Let* $S := (N, M)$, $N := (P, T, F, \mathcal{T}, \lambda)$, *and* $S' := (N', M')$, $N' := (P', T', F', \mathcal{T}, \lambda')$, *be labeled systems, where* S' *is obtained from* S *via label unification of every label in* $\mathcal{T} \subseteq range(\lambda')$.[8] *Let* $\lambda_x, \lambda_y \in \mathcal{T} \setminus \{\tau\}$ *be two labels. Let* $t_x \in T'$ *and* $t_y \in T'$ *be the solitary transitions for* λ_x *and* λ_y, *respectively.*

o *t_x can conflict with t_y in S', i.e., $t_x \rightarrow_{S'} t_y$, iff λ_x can conflict with λ_y in S, $\lambda_x \rightarrow_{\lambda,S} \lambda_y$.*

o *t_x and t_y can co-occur in S', i.e., $t_x \leftrightsquigarrow_{S'} t_y$, iff λ_x and λ_y can co-occur in S, $\lambda_x \leftrightsquigarrow_{\lambda,S} \lambda_y$.*

o *t_x and t_y are in the causality relation $\rightsquigarrow^{\phi}_{S'}$ in S' iff λ_x and λ_y are in the causal relation $\rightsquigarrow^{\phi}_{\lambda,S}$ in S, where $\phi \in \Phi$.*

o *t_x and t_y are in the concurrency relation $\|^{\phi}_{S'}$ in S' iff λ_x and λ_y are in the concurrency relation $\|^{\phi}_{\lambda,S}$ in S, where $\phi \in \Phi$.*   ⌟

Proposition 6.6 is a consequence of Lemma 6.5. Recalling our earlier examples in Figs. 6 and 7, for instance, we observe that $c \|^{\forall\forall\exists}_{\lambda} b$ and $c \rightsquigarrow^{\exists\forall\exists}_{\lambda} b$ in the system in Fig. 6 since it holds that $t_4 \|^{\forall\forall\exists}_{\lambda} \hat{t}$ and $t_4 \rightsquigarrow^{\exists\forall\exists}_{\lambda} \hat{t}$ in the system in Fig. 7, respectively.

Finally, note that the transformation presented in this section has value beyond the operationalization of behavioral relations on labels. Since each label occurrence in the resulting system relates to the occurrence of a unique transition while preserving the observable behaviors of the original system (Lemma 6.5), this result allows for the grounding of any computation over processes of labeled systems in the unlabeled case.

7 Evaluation

The approach for computing behavioral relations from Section 5 has been implemented and is publicly available as part of the jBPT initiative [26].[9] Using this implementation, we conducted an experiment to assess the performance of the technique. The experiment was carried out on a laptop with a dual core Intel CPU with 2.26 GHz, 4GB of memory, running Windows 7 and SUN JVM 1.7 (with standard allocation of memory).

---

[8] $range(f)$ denotes the range of function f, i.e., the image of f's domain under f.

[9] http://code.google.com/p/jbpt/

To eliminate load time, each check of a behavioral relation between a pair of transitions was executed six times, and we recorded average times of the second to sixth execution.

The study was conducted on a set of 367 systems that model financial services and processes from the telecommunication domain. The systems were selected from a collection of 735 models [27]. To ensure that each system has a unique terminal marking, unsound systems [28] were filtered out. In the experiment, the reachability and the covering problem (for bounded systems) were tackled using the LoLA tool ver. 1.14.[10]

Table 3 reports average times (in milliseconds) for checking behavioral relations. The first two columns report on the characteristics of the collection by providing information on the number 'n' of systems within a given 'Size' range (measured as the number of nodes). In order to obtain average values, checks of behavioral relations between random pairs of different transitions were performed. Each value was measured as the average time of checking 1000 random transition pairs and is recorded in the last four columns. The last row in the table shows average computation times over all systems in the collection. Note that the significant increase in computation times for $x \parallel^{\exists\exists\exists} y$ (1 626 ms) and $x \rightsquigarrow^{\forall\forall\forall} y$ (1 544 ms) in the fourth row of the table is due to a single system for which checks of each behavioral relation took approximately seven seconds.

Table 3. Average computation times (in ms)

Size	n	$x \rightarrow y$	$x \rightsquigarrow y$	$x \parallel^{\exists\exists\exists} y$	$x \rightsquigarrow^{\forall\forall\forall} y$
1–50	211	45	45	44	44
51–100	106	50	49	50	50
101–150	39	95	97	351	492
151–200	5	182	187	1 626	1 544
201–250	3	66	70	90	82
251–548	3	65	128	145	132
1–548	367	54	55	101	115

8 Related Work

We already discussed how our work is embedded in existing classifications of models of concurrency, i.e., fundamental behavioral relations provide a declarative characterization of the behavior model induced by a process model under a certain semantics, cf. [4]. Below, we focus on other declarative behavioral formalisms and their applications.

For interleaving semantics, declarative characterizations of behavior models can be formalized using temporal logic, most prominently Linear Temporal Logic (LTL) for linear time semantics and Computational Tree Logic (CTL) for branching time, see [5] for an overview. Then, behavioral relations are directly grounded in logic formulas over actions as realized, for instance, in the DecSerFlow language for process modeling [29]. For concurrent semantics, in turn, rewrite logics have been used as a formal grounding [30]. While all these approaches provide the basis for declarative characterizations of behavior models, they do not specify which characteristics shall be captured, which is the question addressed in this work. Also, only very few works target completeness of such declarative characterizations under a certain semantics. For process models given

---

[10] http://service-technology.org/lola/

as net systems of a particular class (free-choice, live, and bounded), completeness of a certain declarative characterization of interleaving, linear time semantics was demonstrated in [10]. However, we lack more general results for larger classes of process models under concurrent or branching time semantics.

Applications of basic behavioral relations for process model search and querying have been discussed in Section 2 already. Many more applications have been explored in the literature. Basic behavioral relations are at the core of many techniques in process mining, which connects process models with events that represent action occurrences [31]. These techniques include discovery algorithms, such as the α-algorithm [32], as well as methods for checking conformance between models and events [33]. Also, basic behavioral relations are the foundation for techniques for model synchronization [34]. Here, a change that is located using behavioral relations in one model helps to locate a region for applying the change in another model.

9   Conclusion

In this paper, we addressed the lack of a systematic exploration of fundamental behavioral relations for the analysis of concurrent systems. To this end, we defined a set of relations that capture co-occurrence, conflict, causality, and concurrency, proved that the proposed relations give rise to implication lattices of relations, and suggested operationalizations of these relations. Further, we lifted the relations as well as the operationalizations to labeled net systems. The computation of behavioral relations was evaluated with real-world process models. As such, our work builds a rigorous formal foundation for analysis techniques that are based on behavioral relations.

Some immediate directions for future work include: (i) development of techniques for computing the remaining causality and concurrency relations of the 4C spectrum (beyond the proposed extreme cases), (ii) generalization, and subsequent operationalization, of the proposed behavioral relations, e.g., one may be willing to generalize results to weighted nets, as well as to lift the proposed behavioral relations from executions to fair runs [35], and (iii) application of the relations as behavioral abstractions for modeling of, reasoning over, and analysis of systems.

Acknowledgments. This work is partly funded by the ARC Linkage Project LP110100252. NICTA is funded by the Australian Government (Department of Broadband, Communications and the Digital Economy) and the Australian Research Council through the ICT Centre of Excellence program.

References

1. Winkler, S.: Information flow between requirement artifacts. Results of an empirical study. In: Sawyer, P., Heymans, P. (eds.) REFSQ 2007. LNCS, vol. 4542, pp. 232–246. Springer, Heidelberg (2007)
2. Dumas, M., van der Aalst, W.M.P., ter Hofstede, A.H.M.: Process-Aware Information Systems: Bridging People and Software Through Process Technology. Wiley (2005)
3. ter Hofstede, A.H.M., van der Aalst, W.M.P., Adams, M., Russell, N. (eds.): Modern Business Process Automation — YAWL and its Support Environment. Springer (2010)

4. Sassone, V., Nielsen, M., Winskel, G.: Models for concurrency: Towards a classification. TCS 170(1-2), 297–348 (1996)
5. Baier, C., Katoen, J.P.: Principles of Model Checking. MIT Press (2008)
6. Reisig, W.: Elements of Distributed Algorithms: Modeling and Analysis with Petri Nets. Springer (1998)
7. Object Management Group (OMG): Unified Modeling Language: Superstructure. Version 2.1.2. Technical report (November 2007)
8. Hack, M.: Decidability Questions for Petri Nets. Outstanding Dissertations in the Computer Sciences. Garland Publishing, New York (1975)
9. Nielsen, M., Plotkin, G.D., Winskel, G.: Petri nets, event structures and domains, Part I. TCS 13, 85–108 (1981)
10. Weidlich, M., van der Werf, J.M.: On profiles and footprints – relational semantics for Petri nets. In: Haddad, S., Pomello, L. (eds.) PETRI NETS 2012. LNCS, vol. 7347, pp. 148–167. Springer, Heidelberg (2012)
11. Dunham, M.H.: Data Mining: Introductory and Advanced Topics. Prentice-Hall (2002)
12. Dijkman, R.M., La Rosa, M., Reijers, H.A.: Managing large collections of business process models — current techniques and challenges. Computers in Industry 63(2), 91–97 (2012)
13. Petri, C.A.: Non-Sequential Processes. ISF, GMD (1977)
14. ter Hofstede, A.H.M., Ouyang, C., La Rosa, M., Song, L., Wang, J., Polyvyanyy, A.: APQL: A process-model query language. In: Song, M., Wynn, M.T., Liu, J. (eds.) AP-BPM 2013. LNBIP, vol. 159, pp. 23–38. Springer, Heidelberg (2013)
15. Polyvyanyy, A., La Rosa, M., ter Hofstede, A.H.M.: Indexing and efficient instance-based retrieval of process models using untanglings. In: Jarke, M., Mylopoulos, J., Quix, C., Rolland, C., Manolopoulos, Y., Mouratidis, H., Horkoff, J. (eds.) CAiSE 2014. LNCS, vol. 8484, pp. 439–456. Springer, Heidelberg (2014)
16. Kunze, M., Weidlich, M., Weske, M.: Behavioral similarity – A proper metric. In: Rinderle-Ma, S., Toumani, F., Wolf, K. (eds.) BPM 2011. LNCS, vol. 6896, pp. 166–181. Springer, Heidelberg (2011)
17. van Dongen, B.F., Dijkman, R., Mendling, J.: Measuring similarity between business process models. In: Bellahsène, Z., Léonard, M. (eds.) CAiSE 2008. LNCS, vol. 5074, pp. 450–464. Springer, Heidelberg (2008)
18. Zha, H., Wang, J., Wen, L., Wang, C., Sun, J.: A workflow net similarity measure based on transition adjacency relations. Computers in Industry 61(5), 463–471 (2010)
19. Goltz, U., Reisig, W.: The non-sequential behavior of Petri nets. IANDC 57(2/3) (1983)
20. Desel, J.: Validation of process models by construction of process nets. In: van der Aalst, W.M.P., Desel, J., Oberweis, A. (eds.) Business Process Management. LNCS, vol. 1806, pp. 110–128. Springer, Heidelberg (2000)
21. Mayr, E.W.: Persistence of vector replacement systems is decidable. Acta Inf. 15, 309–318 (1981)
22. Kosaraju, S.R.: Decidability of reachability in vector addition systems (preliminary version). In: STOC, pp. 267–281. ACM (1982)
23. Rackoff, C.: The covering and boundedness problems for vector addition systems. TCS 6, 223–231 (1978)
24. Escrig, D.F.: Decidability of home states in place transition systems, Internal Report. Dpto. Informatica y Automatica. Univ. Complutense de Madrid (1986)
25. Best, E., Devillers, R.R., Kiehn, A., Pomello, L.: Concurrent bisimulations in Petri nets. Acta Inf. 28(3), 231–264 (1991)
26. Polyvyanyy, A., Weidlich, M.: Towards a compendium of process technologies: The jBPT library for process model analysis. In: CAiSE Forum. CEUR, vol. 998 (2013)
27. Fahland, D., Favre, C., Koehler, J., Lohmann, N., Völzer, H., Wolf, K.: Analysis on demand: Instantaneous soundness checking of industrial business process models. DKE (5), 448–466 (2011)

28. van der Aalst, W.M.P.: Verification of workflow nets. In: Azéma, P., Balbo, G. (eds.) ICATPN 1997. LNCS, vol. 1248, pp. 407–426. Springer, Heidelberg (1997)
29. van der Aalst, W.M.P., Pesic, M.: DecSerFlow: Towards a truly declarative service flow language. In: Bravetti, M., Núñez, M., Zavattaro, G. (eds.) WS-FM 2006. LNCS, vol. 4184, pp. 1–23. Springer, Heidelberg (2006)
30. Meseguer, J., Talcott, C.: A partial order event model for concurrent objects. In: Baeten, J.C.M., Mauw, S. (eds.) CONCUR 1999. LNCS, vol. 1664, pp. 415–430. Springer, Heidelberg (1999)
31. van der Aalst, W.M.P.: Process Mining — Discovery, Conformance and Enhancement of Business Processes. Springer (2011)
32. van der Aalst, W.M.P., Weijters, T., Maruster, L.: Workflow mining: Discovering process models from event logs. TKDE 16(9), 1128–1142 (2004)
33. Weidlich, M., Polyvyanyy, A., Desai, N., Mendling, J., Weske, M.: Process compliance analysis based on behavioural profiles. IS 36(7), 1009–1025 (2011)
34. Weidlich, M., Mendling, J., Weske, M.: Propagating changes between aligned process models. JSS 85(8), 1885–1898 (2012)
35. Kindler, E., van der Aalst, W.M.P.: Liveness, fairness, and recurrence in Petri nets. IPL 70(6), 269–274 (1999)

On Weighted Petri Net Transducers

Robert Lorenz[1], Markus Huber[1], and Günther Wirsching[2]

[1] Department of Computer Science
University of Augsburg, Germany
firstname.lastname@informatik.uni-augsburg.de
[2] Mathematisch-Geographische Fakultät
Catholic University of Eichstätt, Germany
guenther.wirsching@ku.de

Abstract In this paper we present a basic framework for weighted Petri net transducers (PNTs) for the translation of partial languages (consisting of partial words) as a natural generalisation of finite state transducers (FSTs).

Concerning weights, we use the algebraic structure of continuous concurrent semirings which is based on bisemirings and induces a natural order on its elements. Using the operations of this algebra, it is possible to define the weight of sequential parallel partial words in a standard way. We define the weight of a general partial word as the supremum of the weights of all of its sequential parallel extensions. As a fundamental result we show that concurrent semirings are the least restrictive idempotent bisemiring structure such that partial words with fewer dependencies have bigger weights. Moreover, the weight definition turns out to be compositional, i.e. the weight of (sequential or parallel) composed partial words equals the corresponding bisemiring composition of the weights of its components.

To be able to create complex PNTs through composition of simple PNTs, we introduce clean PNTs and the composition operations union, product, closure, parallel product and language composition on clean PNTs, lifting standard composition operations on FSTs. Composed PNTs yield a compositional computation of weights, where in the case of language composition such a compositional computation is possible only in restricted cases. Moreover, we give definitions for equivalent PNTs and show that all composition operations preserve equivalence. We also show that under certain conditions concerning the algebraic weight structure an FST can be represented by an equivalent PNT.

Keywords: Petri Net, Petri Net Transducer, Weighted Transducer, Labelled Partial Order, Weighted Labelled Partial Order, Partial Language, Semiring, Bisemiring, Concurrent Semiring, Cleanness.

1 Introduction

Weighted finite automata are classical non-deterministic finite automata in which transitions carry weights [6]. These weights may represent cost, time consumption or probability of a transition execution. The behaviour of such automata is defined by a function associating with each word the weight of its execution. For a uniform definition of the behaviour, the set of weights is equipped with the underlying algebraic structure of a

G. Ciardo and E. Kindler (Eds.): PETRI NETS 2014, LNCS 8489, pp. 233–252, 2014.

semiring. A semiring provides two operations of binary addition and multiplication of weights. The multiplication is used for determining the weight of a path, and the weight of a word is obtained by the sum of the weights of its underlying paths. If each transition additionally is equipped with an output symbol, the resulting automaton is called a transducer. Transducers are used for the translation between languages over different alphabets for example in natural language processing. For weighted finite automata and transducers (also called finite state transducers or FSTs) there are efficient implementations of composition and optimisation operations in standard libraries [17,27].

There are generalisations to weighted automata over discrete structures other than finite words, some of them introducing concurrency into the model through considering labelled partial orders (LPOs) (also called *partial words* [11] or *pomsets* [18]), not consisting of a total order on their symbols but of a partial order. In [9] an overview is given on weighted finite automata (and transducers) processing tree structures. They are used to recognise weighted context-free languages with weights coming from semirings and do not consider concurrency. In [8] weighted asynchronous cellular automata accepting weighted traces, a special restricted kind of LPOs, are described. Here also only semirings are used to describe weights, i.e. no difference is made between the combination of weights of transitions occurring in sequential order and occurring in parallel. In [14] weighted branching automata accepting weighted sequential parallel LPOs (sp-LPOs), which can be constructed from singletons using operations of sequential and parallel composition, are introduced. Weights now come from bisemirings where the algebraic structure of semirings is extended by a third operation of parallel multiplication (which in this case needs no unit) used for the combination of weights of concurrent transition occurrences. For all these automata models there are widely developed theories concerning equivalent representations as rational expressions or logic formulae, useful composition operations and closure properties [6]. Another extended automata model are Q-Automata [4] whose computations are step sequences. Q-Automata are coined for application in quality management with weights modelling costs and coming from a bisemiring, whose parallel multiplication may not be commutative.

The aim of this paper is the generalisation of automata based weighted transducers through weighted Petri net transducers (PNTs). A PNT is essentially a *place/transition net (PT-net)* having transitions equipped with input symbols, output symbols and weights. An LPO over the set of input symbols is translated into an LPO over the set of output symbols via weighted LPO-runs of the net, where weights are coming from an algebraic bisemiring structure. Thus, PNTs define (in a natural way) the translation between partial languages, consisting of general LPOs instead of words, over different alphabets. In this sense PNTs are a natural generalisation of automata based transducers working on finite words, traces or sp-LPOs. There are already several publications introducing PNTs and applying them in different application areas [24,23,21], however these are mainly case studies. Up to now there is no common basic formal definition and no theoretical development. Moreover, all existing definitions only make use of sequential semantics of PNTs and do not consider weights. In [15,16] we introduced first rather informal definitions of syntax and semantics of PNTs and of composition operations applied to small case studies in the area of semantic dialogue modelling. Another Petri net model with transitions having assigned weights are stochastic Petri nets (SPNs). SPNs introduce a temporal specification of probabilistic nature and are applied to the performance analysis of timed systems. The weights have no underlying algebraic structure and are used to compute firing probabilities of untimed transitions.

We use a special bisemiring structure called *concurrent semirings* [13][1] to represent weights. Concurrent semirings are a bisemiring structure with some additional laws interrelating its operations. They where already used by Gischer [10], who showed that the set of all extension closed sets of LPOs can be equipped with algebraic operations yielding a concurrent semiring. In particular, concurrent semirings have an idempotent addition inducing a natural order on the set of weights. This feature allows to define the weight of a general LPO in a natural way as the supremum of all weights of its sequential parallel extensions w.r.t. this order. As a fundamental result we show that concurrent semirings are the least restrictive idempotent bisemiring structure such that LPOs with fewer dependencies have bigger weights. Moreover, this weight definition turns out to be compositional, i.e. the weight of (sequential or parallel) composed LPOs equals the corresponding bisemiring composition of the weights of its components.

In practical applications, it is important to be able to create complex transducers through composition of simple ones. To this end we introduce *cleanness* of PNTs and composition operations of union, product, closure, parallel product and language composition on clean PNTs, lifting standard composition operations on FSTs. Cleanness ensures that runs always terminate properly and is shown to be preserved by the above operations. Concerning language composition, we consider different possible adaptions of the FST case and show that concrete constructions yield a compositional computation of weights only in restricted cases.

Since transitions also may have empty input and/or empty output, there are always (infinitely) many PNTs having the same input output behaviour. Such PNTs are equivalent (adapting the notion of equivalent FSTs). We show that the mentioned composition operations preserve equivalence of PNTs. Under certain conditions concerning the algebraic weight structure an FST can be represented by an equivalent PNT.

The presented framework mainly aims at an application in the field of semantic dialogue modelling as described in [26]. In [15,16] we propose the translation between utterances and meanings using PNTs. Since meanings are represented by arbitrary LPOs which need not be sequential parallel, it is not possible to use one of the mentioned weighted automata models. Additionally, PNTs also may be used to model quantitative aspects of computation by adding bisemiring costs to process calculi represented by arbitrary LPOs, generalising the models from [8,14,4].

The paper is organised as follows: In section 2 we recall basic definitions, including LPOs, Petri nets and weighted FSTs. In section 3 we introduce concurrent semirings and weighted LPOs, and examine fundamental relationships between the weight of LPOs and the algebraic weight structure of concurrent semirings. Then we give syntax and semantics of PNTs, define cleanness of PNTs and equivalences on PNTs and examine the representation of FSTs by equivalent PNTs. In section 4 we consider several composition operations of clean PNTs and the preservation of cleanness and equivalence

---

[1] In [13] concurrent semirings are applied in a trace model of programme semantics. Another axiomatic approach to partial order semantics using algebraic structures extending semirings by an additional operation of concurrent composition is [3] using the notion of trioids.

under these operations. Finally, we give a brief conclusion and outlook on future work in section 5.

All figures in this paper showing PNTs were generated with $PNT_\varepsilon^{\text{OOL}}$. $PNT_\varepsilon^{\text{OOL}}$ is a python library for the modular construction of PNTs through composition operations. Constructed PNTs can be exported in all standard picture formats and in an XML-format based on the standard PNML format. $PNT_\varepsilon^{\text{OOL}}$ will serve as a basis for the implementation and evaluation of algorithms for analysis, simulation and optimisation of PNTs. Its basic functionalities were developed in the bachelor thesis [20].

2   Basic Definitions and Notations

In this section we recall basic definitions and mathematical notations.

2.1   Mathematical Preliminaries

By $\mathbb{N}_0$ we denote the set of *non-negative integers*, by $\mathbb{N}$ the set of *positive integers*. Given a finite set X, the symbol $|X|$ denotes the *cardinality* of X.

The set of all *multisets* over a set X is the set $\mathbb{N}_0^X$ of all functions $f : X \to \mathbb{N}_0$. Addition $+$ on multisets is defined by $(m + m')(x) = m(x) + m'(x)$. The relation $\leq$ between multisets is defined through $m \leq m' \iff \exists m''(m + m'' = m')$. We write $x \in m$ if $m(x) > 0$. A set $A \subseteq X$ is identified with the multiset m satisfying $m(x) = 1 \iff x \in A \wedge m(x) = 0 \iff x \notin A$. A multiset m satisfying $m(a) > 0$ for exactly one element a we call *singleton multiset* and denote it by $m(a)a$.

Given a binary relation $R \subseteq X \times Y$ and a binary relation $S \subseteq Y \times Z$ for sets X, Y, Z, their composition is defined by $R \circ S = \{(x, z) \mid \exists y \in Y ((x, y) \in R \wedge (y, z) \in S)\} \subseteq X \times Z$. For $X' \subseteq X$ and $Y' \subseteq Y$ the restriction of R onto $X' \times Y'$ is denoted by $R|_{X' \times Y'}$. For a binary relation $R \subseteq X \times X$ over a set X, we denote $R^1 = R$ and $R^n = R \circ R^{n-1}$ for $n \geq 2$. The symbol R^+ denotes the *transitive closure* $\bigcup_{n \in \mathbb{N}} R^n$ of R.

Let A be a finite set of symbols. A *(linear) word* over A is a finite sequence of symbols from A. For a word w its length $|w|$ is defined as the number of its symbols. The symbol ε denotes the *empty word* satisfying $|\varepsilon| = 0$. The empty word is the neutral w.r.t. concatenation of words: $w\varepsilon = \varepsilon w = w$. By A^* we denote the set of all words over A, including the empty word. A *language over A* is a (possibly infinite) subset of A^*. A *step over A* is a multiset over A. A *step sequence* or *step-wise linear word* over A is an element of $(\mathbb{N}_0^A)^*$ and a *step language over A* is a (possibly infinite) subset of $(\mathbb{N}_0^A)^*$.

A *directed graph* is a pair $G = (V, \to)$, where V is a finite *set of nodes* and $\to \subseteq V \times V$ is a binary relation over V, called the *set of edges*. The *preset* of a node $v \in V$ is the set $^\bullet v = \{u \mid u \to v\}$. The *postset* of a node $v \in V$ is the set $v^\bullet = \{u \mid v \to u\}$. A *path* is a sequence of (not necessarily distinct) nodes $v_1 \ldots v_n$ $(n > 1)$ such that $v_i \to v_{i+1}$ for $i = 1, \ldots, n-1$. A path $v_1 \ldots v_n$ is a *cycle* if $v_1 = v_n$. A directed graph is called *acyclic* if it has no cycles. An acyclic directed graph $(V, \to')$ is an *extension* of an acyclic directed graph $(V, \to)$ if $\to \subseteq \to'$. An acyclic directed graph $(V', \to)$ is a *prefix* of an acyclic directed graph $(V, \to)$ if $V' \subseteq V$ and $(v' \in V') \wedge (v \to v') \Rightarrow (v \in V')$.

An *irreflexive partial order* over a set V is a binary relation $< \subseteq V \times V$ which is irreflexive $(\forall v \in V : v \not< v)$ and transitive $(< = <^+)$. We identify a finite irreflexive partial order $<$ over V with the directed graph $(V,<)$. Two nodes $v,v' \in V$ of a irreflexive partial order $po = (V,<)$ are called *independent* if $v \not< v'$ and $v' \not< v$. By $co_< \subseteq V \times V$ we denote the set of all pairs of independent nodes of V. A *reflexive partial order* over V is a binary relation $\leq \subseteq V \times V$ which is reflexive ($\forall v \in V : v \leq v$), transitive and antisymmetric ($\forall v \in V : v \leq w \wedge w \leq v \implies v = w$).

2.2   Labelled Partial Orders

We use irreflexive partial orders labelled by action names to represent single non-sequential runs of concurrent systems. The nodes of such a labelled partial order represent events and its arrows an 'earlier than'-relation between them in the sense that one event can be observed earlier than another event. If there are no arrows between two events, then these events are independent and are called *concurrent*. Concurrent events can be observed in arbitrary sequential order and simultaneously.

Formally, a *labelled partial order (LPO) over a set* X is a 3-tuple $(V,<,l)$, where $(V,<)$ is a irreflexive partial order and $l : V \to X$ is a labelling function on V. LPOs over X are also called *partial words over* X. In most cases, we only consider LPOs up to isomorphism, i.e. only the labelling of events is of interest, but not the event names. Formally, two LPOs $(V,<,l)$ and $(V',<',l')$ are *isomorphic* if there is a bijective renaming function $I : V \to V'$ satisfying $l(v) = l'(I(v))$ and $v < w \Leftrightarrow I(v) <' I(w)$. If an LPO lpo is of the form $(\{v\}, \emptyset, l)$, then it is called a *singleton LPO* and denoted by $lpo = l(v)$. We call a set of pairwise non-isomorphic LPOs a *partial language*. If L is a partial language, then an LPO $lpo \in L$ is called *minimal (in L)* if there is no extension of lpo in L. In figures, in general we do not show the names of the nodes of an LPO, but only their labels and we often omit transitive arrows of LPOs for a clearer presentation.

A *step-wise linear LPO* is an LPO $(V,<,l)$ where the relation $co_<$ is transitive. The maximal sets of independent events are called *steps*. The steps of a step-wise linear LPOs are linearly ordered. Thus, step-wise linear LPOs can be identified with step sequences. A *step-linearisation* of an LPO lpo is a step-wise linear LPO which is an extension of lpo. The set of *sequential parallel* LPOs (sp-LPOs) is the smallest set of LPOs containing all singleton LPOs (over a set X) and being closed under the sequential and parallel product of LPOs. The *sequential product* of two LPOs $lpo_1 = (V_1,<_1,l_1)$ and $lpo_2 = (V_2,<_2,l_2)$ is defined by $lpo_1 ; lpo_2 = (V_1 \cup V_2, <_1 \cup <_2 \cup V_1 \times V_2, l_1 \cup l_2)$, where V_1 and V_2 are assumed to be disjoint. Their *parallel product* is defined by $lpo_1 \parallel lpo_2 = (V_1 \cup V_2, <_1 \cup <_2, l_1 \cup l_2)$, where again V_1 and V_2 are assumed to be disjoint. For an LPO lpo we denote by $SP(lpo)$ the set of all sequential parallel extensions of lpo and by $SP_{min}(lpo)$ the set of all minimal sequential parallel extensions of lpo in $SP(lpo)$. If lpo is an extension of lpo', we write $lpo \leq lpo'$.

The sequential and parallel product of LPOs is extended to sets of LPOs A,B in the obvious way: $A \parallel B = \{a \parallel b \mid a \in A, b \in B\}$ and $A;B = \{a;b \mid a \in A, b \in B\}$. Moreover, we define the closure of a set of LPOs A by $A^* = \{a_1 ; \ldots ; a_n \mid n \in \mathbb{N}, a_i \in A\} \cup \{\varepsilon\}$, where ε denotes the empty LPO.

2.3 Petri Nets

A *net* is a 3-tuple $N = (P,T,F)$, where P is a finite set of *places*, T is a finite set of *transitions* disjoint from P and $F \subseteq (P \times T) \cup (T \times P)$ is the *flow relation*. A *marking* of a net assigns to each place $p \in P$ a number $m(p) \in \mathbb{N}_0$, i.e. a marking is a multiset over P. A *marked net* is a net $N = (P,T,F)$ together with an *initial marking* m_0.

A *place/transition Petri net (PT-net)* is a 4-tuple $N = (P,T,F,W)$, where (P,T,F) is a net and $W : (P \times T) \cup (T \times P) \to \mathbb{N}_0$ is a *flow weight function* satisfying $W(x,y) > 0 \Leftrightarrow (x,y) \in F$. For (transition) steps τ over T we introduce the two multisets of places ${}^\bullet\tau(p) = \sum_{t \in T} \tau(t)W(p,t)$ and $\tau^\bullet(p) = \sum_{t \in T} \tau(t)W(t,p)$. A transition step τ *can occur* in m if $m \geq {}^\bullet\tau$. If a transition step τ occurs in m, then the resulting marking m' is defined by $m' = m - {}^\bullet\tau + \tau^\bullet$. We write $m \xrightarrow{\tau} m'$ to denote that τ can occur in m and that its occurrence leads to m'. A *step execution in m* of a PT-net is a finite sequence of multisets of transitions $\sigma = \tau_1 \ldots \tau_n$ such that there are markings $m_1, \ldots, m_n$ satisfying $m \xrightarrow{\tau_1} m_1 \xrightarrow{\tau_2} \ldots \xrightarrow{\tau_n} m_n$. The markings which can be reached from the initial marking m_0 via step executions are called *reachable*.

We use LPOs over T to represent single non-sequential runs of PT-nets, i.e. the events of an LPO represent transition occurrences. An LPO $lpo = (V,<,l)$ over T is an *LPO-run* of a marked PT-net $N = (P,T,F,W,m_0)$ if each step-linearisation of lpo is a step execution of N in m_0. If an LPO-run $lpo = (V,<,l)$ occurs in a marking m, the resulting marking m' is defined by $m' = m - \sum_{v \in V} {}^\bullet l(v) + \sum_{v \in V} l(v)^\bullet$. We write $m \xrightarrow{lpo} m'$ to denote the occurrence of an LPO-run lpo.

2.4 Weighted Finite State Transducers

Finite-state transducers (FSTs) are finite automata in which each transition is augmented with an output label in addition to the familiar input label. Output labels are concatenated along a path to form an output sequence. Weighted transducers are finite-state transducers in which each transition additionally carries some weight. The weights are elements of an algebraic structure called semiring.

A *semiring* is a quintuple $\mathscr{S} = (S, \oplus, \otimes, \bar{0}, \bar{1})$, where $(S, \oplus, \bar{0})$ is a commutative monoid, $(S, \otimes, \bar{1})$ is a monoid, $\otimes$ (the *S-multiplication*) distributes over $\oplus$ (the *S-addition*) from both sides of $\otimes$ and the zero $\bar{0}$ is absorbing w.r.t. $\otimes$ ($\bar{0} \otimes x = x \otimes \bar{0} = \bar{0}$). If $\otimes$ is commutative, then the semiring is called *commutative*.

The $\otimes$-operation is used to compute the weight of a path of an FST by multiplying the weights of the transitions along that path. The $\oplus$-operation is used to compute the weight of a pair of input and output sequences (u,v) by summing up the weights of all paths labelled with (u,v). A *weighted finite state transducer (FST)* over a semiring $\mathscr{S}$ is an 8-tuple $T = (\Sigma, \Delta, Q, I, F, E, \lambda, \rho)$, where Σ is a finite alphabet of input symbols, Δ is a finite alphabet of output symbols, Q is a finite set of states, $I \subseteq Q$ is the set of initial states, $F \subseteq Q$ is the set of final states, $E \subseteq Q \times (\Sigma \cup \{\varepsilon\}) \times (\Delta \cup \{\varepsilon\}) \times S \times Q$ is the finite set of transitions, $\lambda : I \to S$ is the initial weight function and $\rho : F \to S$ is the final weight function. For a transition $e = (q_1, x, y, s, q_2)$, we denote $p(e) = q_1$ to be its *start state*, $n(e) = q_2$ its *next state*, $\omega(e) = s$ its *weight*, $\sigma(e) = x$ its *input label* and $\delta(e) = y$ its *output label*. Two transitions e_1 and e_2 are *consecutive* if $n(e_1) = p(e_2)$. A sequence $\pi = e_1 \ldots e_k \in E^*$ of consecutive transitions is called a *path* with start state $p(\pi) = p(e_1)$ and next state $n(\pi) = n(e_k)$. The input label of a path $e_1 \ldots e_k$ is the word $\sigma(e_1) \ldots \sigma(e_k)$. The output label of a path $e_1 \ldots e_k$ is the word $\delta(e_1) \ldots \delta(e_k)$. For subsets $Q_1, Q_2 \subseteq Q$, $u \in \Sigma^*$ and $v \in \Delta^*$, we denote by $P(Q_1, Q_2)$ the set of all paths from states in Q_1 to states in Q_2, $P(Q_1, u, Q_2)$ the subset of all paths from $P(Q_1, Q_2)$ with input label u, $P(Q_1, u, v, Q_2)$ the subset of all paths from $P(Q_1, u, Q_2)$ with output label v. The weight of a path is defined by $\omega(e_1 \ldots e_k) = \omega(e_1) \otimes \ldots \otimes \omega(e_k)$. The *output weight* of a pair of words $(u, v) \in \Sigma^* \times \Delta^*$ is defined by

$$T(u, v) = \bigoplus_{\pi \in P(I, u, v, F)} \lambda(p(\pi)) \otimes \omega(\pi) \otimes \rho(n(\pi)),$$

when the sum is well-defined in S. This is the case, for example, if the considered semiring is *complete* (see subsection 3.1). If $P(I, u, v, F) = \emptyset$, we set $T(u, v) = \overline{0}$. For a detailed overview on weighted FSTs see for example [17].

3 Definition of Weighted Petri Net Transducers

In this section we introduce weighted Petri net transducers (PNTs) for the translation between partial languages. For taking weights into account, we consider weighted LPOs (WLPOs) which are LPOs with additional node weights. Then the total weight of a WLPO is computed from the node weights using binary operations on the set of weights. We shall infer from a result of Gischer [10] that the algebraic structure of the set of possible weights is not arbitrary: If we postulate that the binary operations on the weights reflect sequential and parallel product of LPOs, then the set of possible weights must admit the algebraic structure *concurrent semiring* [13]. For the translation of input words into output words we equip transitions with input symbols, output symbols and weights and consider weighted LPO-runs. Based on this idea, we define syntax and semantics of PNTs. Then, we define equivalence of PNTs and examine the connection between PNTs and FSTs.

3.1 Continuous Concurrent Semirings

A binary operation $\oplus$ on a set S defines a binary relation on S via $a \leq_\oplus b :\Leftrightarrow a \oplus b = b$. If $\oplus$ is idempotent, associative, and commutative, then this relation is reflexive, transitive, and antisymmetric, hence a reflexive partial order. Moreover, if S is equipped with the partial order $\leq_\oplus$, then $\forall a, b \in S : a \oplus b = \sup\{a, b\}$, where the supremum is taken w.r.t. $\leq_\oplus$. If $(S, \oplus, \overline{0})$ is a monoid, and if $T \subseteq S$ is an arbitrary subset, then $\bigoplus T := \bigoplus_{t \in T} t :=$ $\sup(T)$, where the supremum of the empty set is understood to be the neutral element of the monoid. A semiring $(S, \oplus, \otimes, \overline{0}, \overline{1})$ is called *idempotent* if $\oplus$ is idempotent. An idempotent semiring is called *continuous* [5] if, for any subset $T \subseteq S$, the supremum is well-defined in S (that means the semiring is *complete*), and $\otimes$ distributes over the supremum from both sides: $\forall s \in S : s \otimes \bigoplus T = \bigoplus_{t \in T} s \otimes t$ and $(\bigoplus T) \otimes s = \bigoplus_{t \in T} t \otimes s$.

A *bisemiring* is a six-tuple $\mathscr{S} = (S, \oplus, \otimes, \boxtimes, \overline{0}, \overline{1})$, where $(S, \oplus, \otimes, \overline{0}, \overline{1})$ is a semiring and $(S, \oplus, \boxtimes, \overline{0}, \overline{1})$ is a commutative semiring.[2] The binary operation $\boxtimes$ on the set S is called *S-parallel multiplication*. If $\otimes$ distributes over $\boxtimes$ from both sides, the bisemiring is called *distributive*, if $\oplus$ is idempotent, the bisemiring is called *idempotent*, and if both semirings $(S, \oplus, \otimes, \overline{0}, \overline{1})$ and $(S, \oplus, \boxtimes, \overline{0}, \overline{1})$ are continuous, the bisemiring is called *continuous*. According to [13], a *concurrent semiring* is an idempotent bisemiring $(S, \oplus, \otimes, \boxtimes, \overline{0}, \overline{1})$ satisfying

$$\forall a, b, c, d \in S: \quad (a \boxtimes b) \otimes (c \boxtimes d) \leq_\oplus (a \otimes c) \boxtimes (b \otimes d). \tag{CS}$$

Concurrent semirings will be used to define the weight of a run of a Petri net transducer. $\otimes$ will be used to model the composition of weights of a sequence of runs (as in the case of FSTs) and $\boxtimes$ models the composition of weights of concurrent runs. Therefore, $\boxtimes$ is required to be commutative. The unit $\overline{1}$ can be thought of as the weight of the empty run (the analogue of the empty word). It is shared by $\otimes$ and $\boxtimes$, since the sequential or concurrent execution of a run r and the empty run does not change r. Using $\otimes$ and $\boxtimes$, the weight of a sequential parallel run can be defined in the standard way.

Idempotence of $\oplus$ induces a natural order on the set of weights. We will define the weight of a general run in a natural way as the supremum of all weights of its sequential parallel extensions w.r.t. this order. Condition (CS) will ensure that runs with fewer dependencies have bigger weights.

Example 1. If $\mathscr{S} = (S, \oplus, \otimes, \overline{0}, \overline{1})$ is an idempotent semiring such that $\leq_\oplus$ is a total order and $\overline{1}$ is maximal w.r.t. to that order, then we have $\mathscr{S} = (S, \max, \otimes, \overline{0}, \overline{1})$, and $(S, \max, \otimes, \min, \overline{0}, \overline{1})$ is a concurrent semiring extending $\mathscr{S}$.

If $\mathscr{S} = (S, \oplus, \otimes, \overline{0}, \overline{1})$ is an idempotent and commutative semiring, then the *doubled semiring* $(S, \oplus, \otimes, \otimes, \overline{0}, \overline{1})$ is a concurrent semiring extending $\mathscr{S}$.

Example 2. Based on the well-known *Viterbi semiring* $([0,1], \max, \cdot, 0, 1)$ representing probabilities of actions, the structure $\mathscr{V} := ([0,1], \max, \cdot, \min, 0, 1)$ yields a continuous concurrent semiring.

The structure $\mathscr{T} := ([0, \infty], \min, +, \max, \infty, 0)$ is a continuous concurrent semiring. It is based on the well-known *tropical semiring* $([0, \infty], \min, +, \infty, 0)$ representing execution times of actions.

Note that $\mathscr{V}$ and $\mathscr{T}$ are isomorphic, e.g. an isomorphism is given by $t = -\log(v)$. Both concurrent semirings extend a semiring as in the first construction of example 1.

An example of a concurrent semiring, which is not of the above kind, is $\mathscr{A} := (\{-\infty\} \cup [0, \infty[, \max, +, \boxtimes, -\infty, 0)$, where $a \boxtimes b := a + b + \min(a, b)$. It is based on the *arctic semiring*.

3.2 Weighted LPOs

We use LPOs extended by weights from a bisemiring to model runs of PNTs. By definition, a *weighted LPO* (WLPO) over a alphabet $\mathscr{A}$ and a bisemiring $\mathscr{S} = (S, \oplus, \otimes, \boxtimes,$

---

[2] In particular, both multiplications share the same unit. A similar algebraic structure without requiring commutativity of the second semiring is defined in [4], where it is called *Q-Algebra* and coined for application in quality management. In [14] a slightly different notion of bisemirings is used where parallel multiplication may miss a unit.

$\overline{0}, \overline{1})$ is a quadruple $(V, <, l, v)$ such that $(V, <, l)$ is an LPO over $\mathscr{A}$ and $v : V \to S$ is an additional *weight function*. We use all notions introduced for LPOs also for WLPOs.

The weight of sp-WLPOs can be defined similar as in [14] for runs of so called weighted branching automata. The total weight of an sp-WLPO is computed from the weights of their nodes through applying $\otimes$ to the sequential product and $\boxtimes$ to the parallel product of sub-WLPOs.

Definition 1 (Weight of sp-WLPOs). *The weight* $\omega(wlpo)$ *of an sp-WLPO* $wlpo = (V, <, l, v)$ *over a bisemiring is defined inductively as follows:*

- *If* $V = \{v\}$, *then* $\omega(wlpo) = v(v)$.
- *If* $wlpo = wlpo_1 ; wlpo_2$, *then* $\omega(wlpo) = \omega(wlpo_1) \otimes \omega(wlpo_2)$.
- *If* $wlpo = wlpo_1 \parallel wlpo_2$, *then* $\omega(wlpo) = \omega(wlpo_1) \boxtimes \omega(wlpo_2)$.

This is the standard technique to define weights of sequential parallel LPOs [14] with weights coming from a bisemiring. In particular, the given weight of sp-WLPOs is well-defined, since the set of sp-WLPOs as well as the sub-structure $(S, \otimes, \boxtimes)$ of a bisemiring $(S, \oplus, \otimes, \boxtimes, \overline{0}, \overline{1})$ form an sp-algebra admitting an sp-algebra homomorphism from the set of sp-WLPOs into the bisemiring. Note that for WLPOs $wlpo = (V, <, l, v)$ with underlying total order $V = \{v_1 < \cdots < v_n\}$ the weights computes $\omega(wlpo) = \bigotimes_{i=1}^n v(v_i)$, i.e. the above definition is compatible with the weight definition of paths of an FST. We now propose a weight definition for general WLPOs.

Definition 2 (Sequential-Parallel Weight of WLPOs). *Let* $wlpo = (V, <, l, \omega)$ *be a WLPO. Then its* sp-weight *is defined by* $\omega_{sp}(wlpo) = \bigoplus_{wlpo' \in SP(wlpo)} \omega(wlpo')$.

If the bisemiring of weights is idempotent, then the sp-weight of a WLPO-run equals the maximal weight of its sequential parallel extensions. As a fundamental result we will show that condition **(CS)** of concurrent semirings are the minimal requirement on idempotent bisemirings such that less restrictive weighted LPOs yield bigger weights. Moreover, the use of concurrent semirings ensures that the sp-weight of WLPOs can be computed in a modular way using bisemiring-operations.

Theorem 1. *Let* $\mathscr{A}$ *be an alphabet and* $\mathscr{S} = (S, \oplus, \otimes, \boxtimes, \overline{0}, \overline{1})$ *an idempotent bisemiring. Then the following assertions are equivalent:*

(A) *If* u_1, u_2 *are sp-WLPOs over* $\mathscr{A}$ *and* $\mathscr{S}$ *and if* u_1 *is an extension of* u_2, *then* $\omega(u_1) \leq_\oplus \omega(u_2)$.
(B) $\mathscr{S}$ *is a concurrent semiring.*

Proof. (A) $\Rightarrow$ (B): Let $\mathscr{I}$ be the set of sets of sp-LPOs over $\mathscr{A}$ which are *ideals* as introduced by Gischer [10] as extension-closed sets of sp-LPOs. As proved by Gischer, $(\mathscr{I}, \cup, ;, \parallel_I, \emptyset, \{\varepsilon\})$ is a concurrent semiring, where $A \parallel_I B$ is defined as the least ideal containing $A \parallel B$ and ε is the empty LPO. We show that the mapping $\omega : \mathscr{I} \to S$ defined by $\omega(A) = \bigoplus_{a \in A} \omega(a)$ is a bisemiring-homomorphism. Let $A, B \in \mathscr{I}$, then

- $\omega(A \cup B) = \omega(A) \oplus \omega(B)$, since $\oplus$ is assumed to be idempotent, commutative and associative.

- $\omega(A;B) = \omega(A) \otimes \omega(B)$ follows from $\omega(a;b) = \omega(a) \otimes \omega(b)$ for $a \in A, b \in B$ and because $\otimes$ distributes over $\oplus$.
- We claim that $\omega(A \parallel_I B) = \bigoplus_{a \in A, b \in B} \omega(a \parallel b) = \omega(A) \boxtimes \omega(B)$. The second equation follows from $\omega(a \parallel b) = \omega(a) \boxtimes \omega(b)$ for $a \in A, b \in B$ and because $\boxtimes$ distributes over $\oplus$. The first equation follows from (A), since each LPO in $A \parallel_I B$ is an extension of an LPO of the form $a \parallel b$ with $a \in A, b \in B$.

This proves that $\mathscr{S}$ also is a concurrent semiring.

(B) $\Rightarrow$ (A): Let u_1 be a proper extension of u_2 such that u_1, u_2 are non-isomorphic. Gischer shows in [10] in the Interpolation Lemma that the least ideal containing u_1 can be transformed in finitely many steps into the least ideal containing u_2 using one of the concurrent semiring equations w.r.t. the operations of $(\mathscr{I}, \cup, ;, \parallel_I, \emptyset, \{\varepsilon\})$ in each step, where at least once the equation $(a \parallel_I b);(c \parallel_I d) <_\cup (a;c) \parallel_I (b;d)$ (which corresponds to condition (CS) of concurrent semirings) is applied. Denote $u_i = (V_i, <_i, l_i)$ and equip the nodes of each u_i with the weight function ω yielding WLPOs. Then both $u'_i = (V_i, <_i, \omega)$ are sp-LPOs over S. Since $\mathscr{S}$ is a concurrent semiring, it is now possible to transform u'_1 into u'_2 using the same sequence of concurrent semiring equations as for the transformation of u_1 into u_2, but now w.r.t. the concurrent semiring operations of $\mathscr{S}$. We deduce $\omega(u_1) = u'_1 \leq_\oplus u'_2 = \omega(u_2)$. $\qquad\square$

We deduce that the sp-weight can be computed in a modular way.

Lemma 1. *The following holds for LPOs lpo_1 and lpo_2:*

(i) $SP(lpo_1; lpo_2) = \{lpo'_1; lpo'_2 \mid lpo'_1 \in SP(lpo_1), lpo'_2 \in SP(lpo_2)\}$,
(ii) $SP_{min}(lpo_1 \parallel lpo_2) = \{lpo'_1 \parallel lpo'_2 \mid lpo'_1 \in SP_{min}(lpo_1), lpo'_2 \in SP_{min}(lpo_2)\}$.

Proof. Straightforward observation. $\qquad\square$

Theorem 2. *Let $\mathscr{A}$ be an alphabet and $\mathscr{S} = (S, \oplus, \otimes, \boxtimes, \bar{0}, \bar{1})$ a concurrent semiring. Then the following assertions hold for weighted LPOs $wlpo_1, wlpo_2$ over $\mathscr{A}$ and $\mathscr{S}$:*

(C) $\omega_{sp}(wlpo_1; wlpo_2) = \omega_{sp}(wlpo_1) \otimes \omega_{sp}(wlpo_2)$.
(D) $\omega_{sp}(wlpo_1 \parallel wlpo_2) = \omega_{sp}(wlpo_1) \boxtimes \omega_{sp}(wlpo_2)$.

Proof. ad (C): We apply distributivity of $\otimes$ over $\oplus$ in the formula given in definition 2, and use the set equation (i) of the previous lemma.

ad (D): We claim $\omega_{sp}(wlpo_1 \parallel wlpo_2) = \bigoplus_{wlpo'_i \in SP_{min}(wlpo_i)} \omega(wlpo'_1) \boxtimes \omega(wlpo'_2)$. This equation follows from (A) in the previous theorem using the set equation (ii) of the previous lemma in the formula given in definition 2. The statement follows now from distributivity of $\boxtimes$ over $\oplus$. $\qquad\square$

Example 3. Consider the concurrent semiring $\mathscr{V}$ defined in subsection 3.1. The decision for min as parallel multiplication can be interpreted as follows: If $wlpo = wlpo_1 \parallel wlpo_2$, then $wlpo_1$ and $wlpo_2$ are both necessary but independent parts of the run $wlpo$ of a concurrent system and the probability of $wlpo$ cannot be better than the probability of one of its parts. In [25] we give a justification for that choice of min in the context of semantic dialogue modelling.

Consider the concurrent semiring $\mathscr{T}$ defined in subsection 3.1. It can be used to compute the minimal execution time of a run given by an arbitrary WLPO $wlpo$ of a concurrent system.

3.3   Syntax of Petri Net Transducers

A PNT is a Petri net which, for every transition occurrence, may read a symbol x from an input alphabet Σ and may print a symbol y from an output alphabet Δ. Additionally, a weight s from a bisemiring is assigned to each transition. If no input symbol should be read or no output symbol should be printed, we use the empty word symbol ε as annotation. We use the basic Petri net class of PT-nets to define PNTs.

Definition 3 (Petri Net Transducer). *A Petri net transducer (PNT)* over a bisemiring $\mathscr{S} = (S, \oplus, \otimes, \boxtimes, \overline{0}, \overline{1})$ *is a tuple* $N = (P, T, F, W, p_I, p_F, \Sigma, \sigma, \Delta, \delta, \omega)$, *where*

- *(P, T, F, W) is a marked PT-net (called the* underlying *PT-net), $p_I \in P$ is the* source place *satisfying* $^\bullet p_I = \emptyset$ *and $p_F \in P$ is the* sink place *satisfying* $p_F^\bullet = \emptyset$,
- *Σ is a set of* input symbols *and $\sigma : T \to \Sigma \cup \{\varepsilon\}$ is the* input mapping,
- *Δ is a set of* output symbols *and $\delta : T \to \Delta \cup \{\varepsilon\}$ is the* output mapping.
- *$\omega : T \to S$ is the* weight function.

We call the marking $m_0 = p_I$ the initial marking *and $m_F = p_F$ the* final marking. *A PNT is called* clean *if the final marking is the only reachable marking m with $m(p_F) > 0$.*

A WLPO $wlpo = (V, <, l, v)$ over T is a weighted LPO-run *of N if the underlying LPO $lpo = (V, <, l)$ is an LPO-run of N with $m_0 \xrightarrow{lpo} m_F$ and if $v(v) = \omega(l(v)))$. We denote by $WLPO(N)$ the set of all weighted LPO-runs of N.*

The cleanness property is similar to cleanness of Boxes [2] or soundness of workflow nets [22] and ensures that PNT semantics are closed under (sequential) product and closure. The final marking can be reached only from a finite set of reachable markings [12]. There are some obvious differences to the syntax of FSTs. There is only one initial state instead of multiple initial states, one final state instead of multiple final states and there are no initial and final weight functions. It is obvious that these restrictions are no real limitation. Figure 1 shows examples of PNTs, where an input symbol x, output symbol y and weight s are annotated to a transition in the form $x{:}y/s$, and annotations of the form $\varepsilon{:}\varepsilon/1$ are not shown.

3.4   Semantics of Petri Net Transducers

Considering non-sequential semantics of Petri nets, a PNT can be used to translate a partial language into another partial language, where so called input words are related to so called output words. Input and output words are defined as LPOs $(V, <, l)$ with a labelling function $l : V \to \mathscr{A} \cup \{\varepsilon\}$ for some input or output alphabet $\mathscr{A}$. Such LPOs we call ε-*LPOs*. For each ε-LPO $(V, <, l)$ we construct the *corresponding ε-free LPO* $(W, < |_{W \times W}, l|_W), W = V \setminus l^{-1}(\varepsilon)$ by deleting ε-labelled nodes together with their adjacent edges. Since partial orders are transitive, this does not change the order between the remaining nodes.

Definition 4 (Input and Output Labels of Runs). *Let $N = (P, T, F, W, p_I, p_F, \Sigma, \sigma, \Delta, \delta, \omega)$ be a PNT and let $wlpo = (V, <, l, v) \in WLPO(N)$. The* input label *of wlpo is the LPO $\sigma(wlpo)$ corresponding to the ε-LPO $(V, <, \sigma \circ l)$. The* output label *of wlpo is the LPO $\delta(wlpo)$ corresponding to the ε-LPO $(V, <, \delta \circ l)$.*

For LPOs u over Σ and v over Δ, we denote by WLPO(N,u) the subset of all WLPOs wlpo from WLPO(N) with input label $\sigma(wlpo) = u$, and by WLPO(N,u,v) the subset of all WLPOs from WLPO(N,u) with output label $\delta(wlpo) = v$.

The input language $L_I(N)$ *of N is the set of all input labels of weighted LPO-runs. Its elements are called* input words. *The* output language $L_O(N)$ *of N is the set of all output labels of weighted LPO-runs. Its elements are called* output words.

The language $L(N)$ *of N is the set of all pairs of LPOs (u,v) over $\Sigma \times \Delta$ with* WLPO$(N,u,v) \neq \emptyset$.

Note that the input and output language of a PNT N are extension closed, since WLPO(N) is extension closed. The *output weight* of a PNT assigned to all pairs of LPOs u over Σ and v over Δ is based on weights of its WLPO-runs.

Definition 5 (Output Weight of PNTs). *Let $N = (P,T,F,W,p_I,p_F,\Sigma,\sigma,\Delta,\delta,\omega)$ be a PNT over a concurrent semiring $\mathscr{S} = (S,\oplus,\otimes,\boxtimes,\overline{0},\overline{1})$, u be an LPO over Σ and v be an LPO over Δ. The output weight $N(u,v)$ is defined by*

$$N(u,v) = \bigoplus_{wlpo \in WLPO(N,u,v)} \omega_{sp}(wlpo),$$

when this sum is well-defined in S (note that the sum may be infinite). We set $N(u,v) = \overline{0}$ if WLPO$(N,u,v) = \emptyset$.

Note that the output weight equals the supremum of all weights of corresponding runs, since $\oplus$ is idempotent. If the concurrent semiring is continuous, the supremum always exists in S [5]. From the considerations in subsection 3.2 we immediately deduce that it is enough to consider minimal weighted sp-runs in the defining sum of the output weight using condition **(CS)** of concurrent semirings.

Corollary 1. *Let $N = (P,T,F,W,p_I,p_F,\Sigma,\sigma,\Delta,\delta,\omega)$ be a PNT over a concurrent semiring $\mathscr{S} = (S,\oplus,\otimes,\boxtimes,\overline{0},\overline{1})$, u be an LPO over Σ and v be an LPO over Δ. Then $N(u,v) = \bigoplus_{wlpo \in WLPO_{min}(N,u,v),wlpo' \in SP_{min}(wlpo)} \omega(wlpo')$, when this sum is well-defined in S, where WLPO$_{min}(\cdot)$ is the subset of all minimal WLPOs in WLPO$(\cdot)$.*

3.5 Equivalent PNTs

Concerning PNT semantics, only the input output behaviour is relevant. Since transitions also may have empty input and/or empty output, there are always (infinitely) many PNTs having the same semantics. For practical application, such PNTs are equivalent. We introduce equivalent PNTs lifting the corresponding notion for FSTs.

Definition 6 (Equivalent PNTs). *Let N_1,N_2 be two PNTs.*

(a) N_1 and N_2 are called structure equivalent *if $L(N_1) = L(N_2)$.*

(b) If N_1 and N_2 are structure equivalent, then they are called output equivalent *if $N_1(u,v) = N_2(u,v)$ for all $(u,v) \in L(N_1) = L(N_2)$.*

Two structure equivalent PNTs perform the same translation between input and output words, but the weights of these translations may be different. Two output equivalent PNTs perform the same weighted translation between input and output words, but the distribution of weights within WLPO-runs may be different. Output equivalence is usually used in the context of FSTs in order to push weights along paths [17]. Weight pushing leads to output equivalent FSTs which allow for more efficient FST-algorithms.

Example 4. In the following, consider a fixed concurrent semiring serving as the set of weights. We denote by $N(a,b,w)$ the clean PNT consisting of no other places than the source and sink place and exactly one transition with input symbol a, output symbol b and weight w connecting the source with the sink place. Then the following PNTs are structure equivalent: $N_1 = N(a,b,w)$, $N_2 = N(a,\varepsilon,u) \otimes N(\varepsilon,b,v)$ and $N_3 = N(a,\varepsilon,x) \boxtimes N(\varepsilon,b,y)$. They are output equivalent if $w = u \otimes v = x \boxtimes y$. The following PNTs in general also are output equivalent: $N_2 = N(a,\varepsilon,u) \otimes N(\varepsilon,b,v)$, $N_5 = N(a,\varepsilon,v) \otimes N(\varepsilon,b,u)$ and $N_6 = N(a,\varepsilon,u \otimes v) \otimes N(\varepsilon,b,\overline{1})$.

Since not each semiring can be extended to a concurrent semiring, not each FST can be represented by an equivalent PNT. On the other side, each finite automaton can be represented by a special PT-net, a so called *state machine*, having the same set of runs. This means, if a semiring can be extended to a concurrent semiring, then an FST over this semiring is output equivalent to a PNT. Given an FST over a semiring satisfying the preconditions in one of the cases considered in example 1, the constructions given in the example may be used to define an equivalent PNT:

Proposition 1. *Let FST $T = (\Sigma,\Delta,Q,I,F,E,\lambda,\rho)$ be a weighted FST over a semiring $\mathscr{S} = (S,\oplus,\otimes,\overline{0},\overline{1})$ satisfying one of the following conditions: (1) $\mathscr{S}$ is idempotent and commutative, (2) $\mathscr{S}$ is idempotent such that $\leq_\oplus$ is a total order and $\overline{1}$ is maximal w.r.t. to that order. Then there is a PNT $N = (P,T,F,W,p_I,p_F,\Sigma,\sigma,\Delta,\delta,\omega)$ satisfying $T(I,u,v,F) = N(u,v)$ for each pair of words $(u,v) \in \Sigma^* \times \Delta^*$.*

4   Composition of Petri Net Transducers

In practical applications, it is important to be able to create complex transducers through composition of simple ones. To this end we lift the FST standard composition operations of union, product, closure and parallel product to clean PNTs (the parallel product is a new operation which cannot be applied to FSTs but is natural in case of PNTs). Cleanness ensures that runs always terminate properly and is shown to be preserved by the above operations. Moreover, we show that these composition operations preserve equivalence of PNTs.

Finally, we consider the central transducer composition operation of language composition. While the adaption of the previously mentioned composition operations for PNTs is more or less straightforward, there are several different possible adaptions of FST language composition.

In the following we consider a fixed concurrent semiring $\mathscr{S} = (S,\oplus,\otimes,\boxtimes,\overline{0},\overline{1})$.

4.1   Union, Sequential Product, Closure, Parallel Product

In this subsection we briefly lift the standard FST composition operations of union, (sequential) product and closure to clean PNTs and additionally define the parallel product of clean PNTs. All definitions and constructions are in the spirit of the FST case and rather straightforward. For each operation, first a functional definition is given defining the output weight of the composed PNT based on the output weights of the original PNTs and bisemiring-operations and generalising the corresponding FST definitions. Then an effective construction is given, showing that there is a composed PNT having the intended output weight. The constructions are illustrated in Figure 1, where for a compact presentation input symbols, output symbols and weights of transitions are omitted if possible. For the correspondence of the functional definitions and the constructions essentially theorem 2 can be used.

The *sum (or union)* $N_1 \oplus N_2$ of two PNTs N_1 and N_2 over $\mathscr{S}$ with the same input alphabet Σ and output alphabet Δ is defined as a PNT over $\mathscr{S}$ in such a way that for each pair of LPOs u over Σ and v over Δ:

$$(N_1 \oplus N_2)(u,v) = N_1(u,v) \oplus N_2(u,v).$$

The sum $N = N_1 \oplus N_2$ can be constructed in a straightforward way as the union of N_1 and N_2 together with additional new source and sink places and connecting transitions having empty input symbol, empty output symbol and weight $\bar{1}$. The construction yields that $WLPO(N_1 \oplus N_2)$ equals $WLPO(N_1) \cup WLPO(N_2)$ if events labelled by additional transitions are omitted.

The *product (concatenation)* $N_1 \otimes N_2$ of two PNTs N_1 and N_2 over $\mathscr{S}$ with the same input alphabet Σ and output alphabet Δ is defined as a PNT over $\mathscr{S}$ in such a way that for each pair of LPOs u over Σ and v over Δ:

$$(N_1 \otimes N_2)(u,v) = \bigoplus_{u=u_1;u_2,\, v=v_1;v_2} N_1(u_1,v_1) \otimes N_2(u_2,v_2).$$

The product of $n > 0$ instances of a PNT N we denote by N^n. By convention $N^0 = \mathscr{I}$, where $\mathscr{I}$ is the PNT satisfying $\mathscr{I}(u,v) = \bar{1}$ if u and v are both the empty LPO $(\emptyset, \emptyset, \emptyset)$ and $\mathscr{I}(u,v) = \bar{0}$ otherwise.

If N_1 is clean, the product $N = N_1 \otimes N_2$ can be constructed as the union of N_1 and N_2 together with a new transition having empty input symbol, empty output symbol and weight $\bar{1}$ and connecting the sink place of N_1 with the source place of N_2. The construction yields that $WLPO(N_1 \otimes N_2)$ equals $WLPO(N_1); WLPO(N_2)$ if events labelled by additional transitions are omitted.

The *closure* N^* of a PNT N over $\mathscr{S}$ with input alphabet Σ and output alphabet Δ is defined as PNT over $\mathscr{S}$ in such a way that for each pair of LPOs u over Σ and v over Δ:

$$N^*(u,v) = \bigoplus_{n=0}^{\infty} N^n(u,v).$$

If N is clean, $\bigoplus_{n=1}^{\infty} N^n(u,v)$ can be constructed by adding a transition with empty input label, empty output label and weight $\bar{1}$, which connects the sink place of N with the source place of N and by adding additional new source and sink places and connecting transitions. Then N is the union of the resulting PNT and N^0. The construction yields that $WLPO(N^*)$ equals $WLPO(N)^*$ if events labelled by additional transitions are omitted.

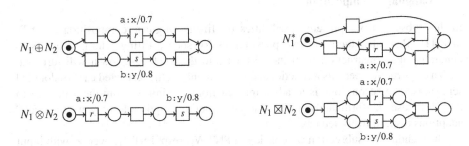

Fig. 1. Illustration of the union, (sequential) product, closure and parallel product of PNTs $N_1 = N(a,x,.7)$ and $N_2 = N(b,y,.8)$ over $\mathcal{V}$

The *parallel product* $N_1 \boxtimes N_2$ of two PNTs N_1 and N_2 over $\mathcal{S}$ with the same input alphabet Σ and output alphabet Δ is defined as a PNT over $\mathcal{S}$ in such a way that for each pair of LPOs u over Σ and v over Δ:

$$(N_1 \boxtimes N_2)(u,v) = \bigoplus_{u=u_1\|u_2,\,v=v_1\|v_2} N_1(u_1,v_1) \boxtimes N_2(u_2,v_2).$$

The parallel product $N = N_1 \boxtimes N_2$ can be constructed as the union of N_1 and N_2 together with additional new source and sink places and appropriate connecting transitions having empty input symbol, empty output symbol and weight $\overline{1}$. The construction yields that $WLPO(N_1 \boxtimes N_2)$ equals $WLPO(N_1) \parallel WLPO(N_2)$ if events labelled by additional transitions are omitted.

Theorem 3 (Composition Operations Preserve Cleanness). *Let N_1 and N_2 be clean PNTs. Then the PNTs $N_1 \oplus N_2$, $N_1 \otimes N_2$, N_1^* and $N_1 \boxtimes N_2$ are also clean.*

Proof. Clear by construction. □

An important application of equivalence in practise is the transformation of a PNT into an equivalent and simpler PNT. A central technique to do this is to replace parts of a complex composed PNT by equivalent parts. This technique requires that equivalence is consistent with composition operations.

Theorem 4 (Composition Operations Preserve Equivalence). *If N_1, N_1' and N_2, N_2' are (structure, output) equivalent, then also $N = N_1 \,\text{op}\, N_2$ and $N' = N_1' \,\text{op}\, N_2'$ with $\text{op} \in \{\oplus, \otimes, \boxtimes\}$, as well as $N = N_1^*$ and $N' = (N_1')^*$ are (structure, output) equivalent.*

Proof. (sketch) As previously argued, in each case the set $WLPO(N,u,v)$ can be constructed from the sets $WLPO(N_1,u,v)$ and $WLPO(N_2,u,v)$ using some additional transitions which do not influence input label, output label and weight. Moreover, $N(u,v)$ can be computed from $N_1(u,v)$ and $N_2(u,v)$ through bisemiring operations.

We deduce that $WLPO(N,u,v) \neq \emptyset \Leftrightarrow WLPO(N',u,v) \neq \emptyset$, if $WLPO(N_i,u,v) \neq \emptyset \Leftrightarrow WLPO(N_i',u,v) \neq \emptyset$ for $i = 1,2$. If additionally $N_i(u,v) = N_i'(u,v)$ for $i = 1,2$, then also $N(u,v) = N'(u,v)$.   □

4.2 Language Composition

In this subsection we present possibilities for lifting language composition of FSTs to PNTs. Basically, there are two possibilities for such a lifting. The first one is to generalise the construction from the FST case to the PNT case. As it will turn out, such a construction permits a functional definition only in the restricted case of doubled semirings. The second one is to adapt the functional definition from the FST case to the PNT case. Unfortunately, a concrete construction is possible only w.r.t. "weak" adaptions resp. in restricted cases.

Throughout this subsection we consider a PNT N_1, resp. FST T_1, over $\mathscr{S}$ with input alphabet Σ_1 and output alphabet Δ_1 and a PNT N_2, resp. FST T_2, over $\mathscr{S}$ with input alphabet $\Sigma_2 = \Delta_1$ and output alphabet Δ_2. In the FST case, the language composition $T_1 \circ T_2$ of T_1 and T_2 is essentially constructed from the Cartesian product of the two sets of states, the transitions of T_1 without output, the transitions of T_2 without input and transitions which are merged from a transition t_1 of T_1 and a transition t_2 of T_2 such that the output of t_1 equals the input of t_2, where the weights of t_1 and t_2 are multiplied. Finally, transitions which are not merged are put into an arbitrary but fixed sequence, i.e. weights are sequentially multiplied. This way, if $\otimes$ is commutative, $T_1 \circ T_2$ yields the functional equation

$$(T_1 \circ T_2)(u,w) = \bigoplus_v T_1(u,v) \otimes T_2(v,w),$$

where the sum runs over all words v over $\Sigma_2 = \Delta_1$ representing both output labels of paths of T_1 and input labels of paths of T_2.

We start with a generalisation of the FST construction to PNTs. The FST construction corresponds to the parallel product of N_1 and N_2 and merging each transition t_1 from N_1 with each transition t_2 from N_2 satisfying $\delta(t_1) = \sigma(t_2)$ to a transition t with input symbol $\sigma(t) = \sigma(t_1)$ and output symbol $\delta(t) = \delta(t_2)$, weight $\omega(t) = \omega(t_1) \otimes \omega(t_2)$ and connections $^\bullet t = {}^\bullet t_1 + {}^\bullet t_2$ and $t^\bullet = t_1^\bullet + t_2^\bullet$. Moreover, we keep all transitions of N_1 having empty output symbol, as well as all transitions of N_2 having empty input symbol (with unchanged input symbols, output symbols, weights and connections). All other transitions of N_1 or N_2 are omitted. We denote the constructed PNT by $N_1[\otimes]N_2$. If $\boxtimes$ is used to define the weight of merged transitions, we denote the resulting PNT by $N_1[\boxtimes]N_2$. Figure 2 illustrates the construction.

Theorem 5. *The PNT $N_1[\cdot]N_2$ satisfies the following properties:*

(i) *If N_1 and N_2 are clean, then also $N_1[\cdot]N_2$ is clean.*

(ii) *If $\mathscr{S}$ is the doubled semiring, then $(N_1[\otimes]N_2)(u,w) = \bigoplus_v N_1(u,v) \otimes N_2(v,w)$, where the sum runs over all LPOs v over $\Sigma_2 = \Delta_1$ representing output labels of weighted LPO-runs of N_1 and input labels of weighted LPO-runs of N_2. In particular $N_1[\otimes]N_2$ generalises FST language composition.*

(iii) If $(N_1[\otimes]N_2)(u,w) = \bigoplus_v N_1(u,v) \text{ op } N_2(v,w)$, *where the sum runs over all LPOs* v *over* $\Sigma_2 = \Delta_1$ *representing output labels of weighted LPO-runs of* N_1 *and input labels of weighted LPO-runs of* N_2 *and op is a semiring operation, then* op $= \otimes$ *and* $\mathscr{S}$ *is the doubled semiring.*

(iv) If N_1, N_1' *and* N_2, N_2' *are structure equivalent, then also* $N = N_1[\cdot]N_2$ *and* $N' = N_1'[\cdot]N_2'$ *are structure equivalent.*

(v) If N_1, N_1' *and* N_2, N_2' *are output equivalent, then* $N = N_1[\cdot]N_2$ *and* $N' = N_1'[\cdot]N_2'$ *need not be output equivalent.*

Proof. (sketch)

ad (i): By construction, every reachable marking m of $N_1[\cdot]N_2$ – except for the initial and final marking – is of the form $m = m_1 + m_2$ for some reachable marking m_1 of N_1 and some reachable marking m_2 of N_2. Since both N_1 and N_2 are clean the only reachable marking which marks the sink places $p_{1,F}$ and $p_{2,F}$ of N_1 and N_2 is $p_{1,F} + p_{2,F}$. The only transition step which can occur in this marking leads to the new sink place of $N_1[\cdot]N_2$. It follows that $N_1[\cdot]N_2$ is clean.

ad (ii): Follows from $\omega_{sp}(wlpo) = \bigotimes_{x \in V} v(x)$ for WLPOs $wlpo = (V, <, l, v)$.

ad (iii): Consider $N_1 = N(x, y, a) \boxtimes N(u, v, b)$ and $N_2 = N(y, z, c) \boxtimes N(v, w, d)$. Then $(a \otimes c) \boxtimes (b \otimes d) = (N_1[\otimes]N_2)(x \parallel u, z \parallel w) = N_1(x \parallel u, y \parallel v) \text{ op } N_2(y \parallel v, z \parallel w) = (a \boxtimes b) \text{ op } (c \boxtimes d)$. Putting $b = d = \bar{1}$ yields $a \text{ op } c = a \otimes c$. Putting $a = d = \bar{1}$ yields $b \otimes c = b \boxtimes c$.

ad (iv): Follows from $L(N_1[\cdot]N_2) = \{(u,w) \mid \exists v : (u,v) \in L(N_1), (v,w) \in L(N_2)\}$. This can be seen as follows: If $wlpo \in L(N_1[\cdot]N_2, u, w)$, then the restriction to nodes which are labelled by transitions from N_i and by merged transitions and the relabelling of merged transition labels by corresponding transition labels from N_i yields WLPO-runs $wlpo_1 \in L(N_1, u, v_1)$ and $wlpo_2 \in L(N_2, v_2, w)$ with $v_1 = v_2$. If on the other side $wlpo_1 \in L(N_1, u, v)$ and $wlpo_2 \in L(N_2, v, w)$, then $wlpo \in L(N_1[\cdot]N_2, u, w)$ can be constructed from the union of $wlpo_1$ and $wlpo_2$ through merging events corresponding to merged transitions of $N_1[\cdot]N_2$.

ad (v): Consider the PNTs $N_1 = N(a, x, .4) \boxtimes N(b, y, .8)$, $N_1' = N(a, x, .8) \boxtimes N(b, y, .4)$ and $N_2 = N(x, r, .5) \boxtimes N(y, s, 1)$ over the concurrent semiring $\mathscr{V}$. Then N_1 and N_1' are output equivalent, but $N_1[\otimes]N_2$ and $N_1'[\otimes]N_2$ are not. In a similar way, using sequential composition of PNTs, a counterexample for $N_1[\boxtimes]N_2$ can be found. $\qquad\square$

Remark 1. In case of part (ii) of the previous theorem the construction for the language composition of two PNTs is different and much simpler than the construction in the case of FSTs. In particular, if N_1 and N_2 are PNTs representing FSTs T_1 and T_2, then $N_1[\otimes]N_2$ does not represent an FST, since it is no state machine. Namely, transitions of N_1 with empty output and transitions of N_2 with empty input may be concurrent. Nevertheless $N_1[\otimes]N_2$ is output equivalent to the PNT representing $T_1 \circ T_2$ on pairs of sequences (u, v).

We now consider possible adaptions of the functional definition of FST language composition. A direct adaption yields

$$(N_1 \circ N_2)(u, w) = \bigoplus_{v \in L_O(N_1) \cap L_I(N_2)} N_1(u, v) \otimes N_2(v, w). \tag{1}$$

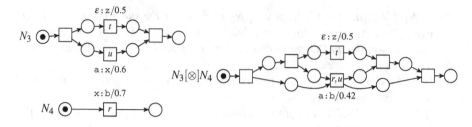

Fig. 2. Language composition for $N_3 = N(x,b,.6) \boxtimes N(\varepsilon,z,.5)$ and $N_4 = N(a,x,.7)$ over $\mathscr{V}$

Our belief is, that there is no construction satisfying this functional equation within the considered framework of PT-net based PNTs over general concurrent semirings. A proof of such a result is topic of further research, but there are constructions for some relaxations of equation 1.

Theorem 6. *It holds:*

(i) *There is a PNT N with $N(u,w) = \bigoplus_{v,v' \in L_O(N_1) \cap L_I(N_2): l(v)=l(v')} N_1(u,v) \otimes N_2(v',w)$, where $l(v)$ is the multiset of transition labels of an LPO v. The construction of N preserves structure and output equivalence, but not cleanness.*

(ii) *If the state graph of $N_1[\cdot]N_2$ is acyclic, then there is a PNT N satisfying $N(u,w) = \bigoplus_{v,v' \in L_O(N_1) \cap L_I(N_2): v \leq v' \vee v' \leq v} N_1(u,v) \otimes N_2(v',w)$, where $v \leq v'$ means that v is an extension of v'. The construction of N preserves structure and output equivalence and cleanness. In particular N generalises FST language composition.*

Proof. (sketch)

The basic idea for the constructions is to consider the sequential product of two PNTs N_1' and N_2', such that $L_O(N_1') = L_O(N_1) \cap L_I(N_2)$ and N_1' behaves like N_1 on its output words, and N_2' has similar properties. The sequential product of N_1' and N_2' satisfies

$$(N_1' \otimes N_2')(u,w) = \bigoplus_{v,v' \in L_O(N_1) \cap L_I(N_2)} N_1(u,v) \otimes N_2(v',w).$$

It is easy to observe that such N_1' and N_2' both can be constructed from $N_1[\cdot]N_2$, such that N_1' and N_2' have isomorphic underlying PT-nets, but different input and output symbols and weights, such that N_1' reads u but writes nothing and N_2' reads nothing but writes w w.r.t. the same LPO-run. Since $\bar{1}$ is the unit of both multiplications, this can be done for N_1' (and similar for N_2') as follows:

- Each transition gets ε as output symbol.
- Each transition t merged from t_1 of N_1 and t_2 of N_2 gets the weight of t_1.
- All transitions coming from N_2 get weight $\bar{1}$.

ad (i): Through adding additional places connecting transitions of N_1' with their isomorphic images in N_2' it is possible to restrict the behaviour in such a way that after executing an LPO-run of N_1' only LPO-runs of N_2' having the same set of transition occurrences can be executed. If the state graph of $N_1[\cdot]N_2$ contains cycles, the construction does not preserve cleanness, since additional places may be unbounded. The preservation of equivalences follows since $L(N)$ can be constructed from $L(N_1)$ and $L(N_2)$ and $N(u, w)$ is computed from $N_1(u, v)$ and $N_2(v', w)$ through bisemiring operations.

ad (ii): In the special case of an acyclic state graph, it is possible to add transition copies and places ensuring that transitions, which are in structural conflict in N_1' and which are executed in a specific order within an LPO-run of N_1', are executed in the same order afterwards in N_2'. Moreover, cleanness is preserved. The preservation of equivalences follows similar to (i).

$\square$

Remark 2. Note that $l(v) = l(v')$ but $v \neq v'$ is possible. For example, the PNT $(N(a, b, \omega) \oplus N(c, d, v))^*$ allows the outputs bd and db. This means, there are different LPO-runs of a PNT with equal sets of transition occurrences if there are transitions which are in structural conflict, but occur together within an LPO-run due to cycles in the PNT. The equation mentioned in property (i) of theorem 6 is not a generalisation of the FST case.

5   Conclusion and Outlook

In this paper we introduced weighted Petri net transducers for the translation of partial languages. As a central result we have shown that the used weight structure of concurrent semirings is the least restrictive idempotent bisemiring structure such that partial words with fewer dependencies have bigger weights. Moreover, we defined composition operations of union, product, closure, parallel product and language composition on PNTs which preserve equivalence of PNTs. The output weights of a composed PNT can be computed from the output weights of its components using bisemiring operations, where in the case of language composition such a compositional computation is possible only in restricted cases.

There are important further steps in several directions. Due to lack of space we only mention here that there are still several central aspects of the framework of FSTs which need to be examined also w.r.t. PNTs, for example additional composition operations (inversion, reversal), optimisation algorithms (ε-elimination, weight-pushing) and on-the-fly simulation algorithms.

References

1. Azéma, P., Balbo, G. (eds.): ICATPN 1997. LNCS, vol. 1248. Springer, Heidelberg (1997)
2. Best, E., Devillers, R.R., Hall, J.G.: The box calculus: a new causal algebra with multi-label communication. In: Rozenberg [19], pp. 21–69
3. Boudol, G., Castellani, I.: On the semantics of concurrency: Partial orders and transition systems. In: Ehrig, H., Levi, G., Montanari, U. (eds.) CAAP 1987 and TAPSOFT 1987. LNCS, vol. 249, pp. 123–137. Springer, Heidelberg (1987)
4. Chothia, T., Klejin, J.: Q-automata: Modelling the resource usage of concurrent components. Electronic Notes in Theoretical Computer Science 175(175), 153–167 (2007)
5. Droste, M., Kuich, W.: Semirings and Formal Power Series. In: Droste, et al. (eds.) [6], ch.1, pp. 3–28 (2009)

6. Droste, M., Kuich, W., Vogler, H. (eds.): Handbook of Weighted Automata. Monographs in Theoretical Computer Science. Springer (2009)
7. Esposito, A., Esposito, A.M., Vinciarelli, A., Hoffmann, R., Müller, V.C. (eds.): COST 2102. LNCS, vol. 7403. Springer, Heidelberg (2012)
8. Fichtner, I., Kuske, D., Meinecke, I.: Traces, Series-Parallel Posets, and Pictures: A Weighted Study. In: Droste, et al. (eds.) [6], ch. 10, pp. 405–452 (2009)
9. Füllöp, Z., Vogler, H.: Weighted Tree Automata and Tree Transducers. In: Droste, et al. (eds.) [6], ch. 9, pp. 313–404 (2009)
10. Gischer, J.L.: The equational theory of pomsets. Theoretical Computer Science 61, 199–224 (1988)
11. Grabowski, J.: On Partial Languages. Fundamenta Informaticae 4(2), 428–498 (1981)
12. Hack, M.: Petri net languages. Technical Report Memo 124, computation structures group, massachusetts institute of technology (1975)
13. Hoare, T., Möller, B., Struth, G., Wehrman, I.: Concurrent Kleene algebra and its foundations. The Journal of Logic and Algebraic Programming 80, 266–296 (2011)
14. Kuske, D., Meinecke, I.: Branching automata with costs - a way of reflecting parallelism in costs. Theoretical Computer Science 328, 53–75 (2004)
15. Lorenz, R., Huber, M.: Petri net transducers in semantic dialogue modelling. In: Proceedings of "Elektronische Sprachsignalverarbeitung (ESSV)". Studientexte zur Sprachkommunikation, vol. 64, pp. 286–297 (2012)
16. Lorenz, R., Huber, M.: Realizing the Translation of Utterances into Meanings by Petri Net Transducers. In: Proceedings of "Elektronische Sprachsignalverarbeitung (ESSV)". Studientexte zur Sprachkommunikation, vol. 65 (2013)
17. Mohri, M.: Weighted Automata Algorithms. In: Droste, et al. (eds.) [6], ch. 6, pp. 213–254 (2009)
18. Pratt, V.: Modelling Concurrency with Partial Orders. Int. Journal of Parallel Programming 15, 33–71 (1986)
19. Rozenberg, G. (ed.): Advances in Petri Nets 1992, The DEMON Project. Springer (1992)
20. Straßner, D.: Prototypische Implementierung von Petrinetz-Transduktoren mit SNAKES. Bachelor thesis, Augsburg University (2013)
21. van Biljon, W.R.: Extending Petri nets for specifying man-machine dialogues. Int. J. Man-Mach. Stud. 28(4), 437–455 (1988)
22. van der Aalst, W.M.P.: Verification of workflow nets. In: Azéa, Balbo (eds.) [1], pp. 407–426
23. Wang, F.-Y., Mittmann, M., Saridis, G.N.: Coordination specification for CIRSSE robotic platform system using Petri net transducers. Journal of Intelligent and Robotic Systems 9, 209–233 (1994)
24. Wang, F.-Y., Saridis, G.N.: A model for coordination of intelligent machines using Petri nets. In: Proceedings of the IEEE International Symposium on Intelligent Control, pp. 28–33. IEEE Comput. Soc. Press (1989)
25. Wirsching, G., Huber, M., Kölbl, C.: Zur Logik von Bestenlisten in der Dialogmodellierung. In: Proceedings of "Elektronische Sprachsignalverarbeitung (ESSV)". Studientexte zur Sprachkommunikation, vol. 61, pp. 309–316 (2011)
26. Wirsching, G., Huber, M., Kölbl, C., Lorenz, R., Römer, R.: Semantic dialogue modeling. In: Esposito, et al. (eds.) [7], pp. 104–113
27. Wolff, M.: Akustische Mustererkennung. Habilitation (2009)

Exhibition of a Structural Bug with Wings

Florent Avellaneda and Rémi Morin

Aix Marseille Université, CNRS, LIF UMR 7279, 13288, Marseille, France

Abstract. Checking the structural boundedness and the structural termination of vector addition systems with states boils down to detecting pathological cycles. As opposed to their non-structural variants which require exponential space, these properties need polynomial time only. The algorithm searches for a counter-example in the form of a multiset of arcs computed by means of linear programming. Yet the minimal length of a pathological cycle can be exponential in the size of the system which makes it difficult to visualize and to analyze the detected bug in details. Further minimizing the length or the number of distinct arcs in pathological paths is NP-hard.

In this paper we propose to represent pathological cycles in the form of a multiset of particular cycles called wings. We present an algorithm that builds in polynomial time a multiset of wings with a common starting point from the multiset of arcs that represents a pathological cycle. Interestingly the number of distinct wings we need is at most equal to the dimension of vectors which helps to describe in a concise way the underlying bug and to analyse it.

Next we tackle the problem of computing a pathological multiset built over wings with a bounded length. We show how to solve this problem in polynomial time by a reduction to a linear program using a separation algorithm.

1 Introduction

Consider a set of reactions that takes place among a collection of particles such that each reaction consumes a multiset of available particles and produces a linear combination of other particle types. This kind of framework can be formalized by a vector addition system [10] or, equivalently, a (pure) Petri net. In this case, particles are called *tokens* and particle types are called *places*. Consider in addition a control state that determines which reactions can occur, and such that the occurrence of a reaction leads to a possibly distinct control state. Then the model becomes formally a vector addition system with states (a VASS), a notion introduced in [8]. Checking reachability properties of these systems is equivalent to checking a Petri net using a well-known and simple simulation technique. In this paper we are interested in two *structural properties* for VASS, that is, properties that do not depend on a particular initial distribution of particles among places. In this way, we consider the initial marking as a parameter of the system. Interestingly, we give an example that shows that the usual simulation of a VASS by a Petri net does not preserve these properties in general. As a consequence, the analysis of structural properties of Petri nets by a reduction to linear programming [14,16,17] does not apply to the framework of VASS.

The first problem we consider asks whether the number of particles in the system remains bounded for each initial configuration. In other words only finitely many distinct configurations can be reached. Since particles often represent the consumption of

G. Ciardo and E. Kindler (Eds.): PETRI NETS 2014, LNCS 8489, pp. 253–272, 2014.

resources, such as messages in channels, this first problem asks whether there exists some amount of resources sufficient to cope with all configurations reachable from any fixed *finite* set of potential initial configurations. A second basic issue is to check that a given system terminates, i.e. whether there is no infinite execution, for each initial configuration. Thus we aim at checking that a system eventually deadlocks. Although one usually tries to avoid deadlocks in concurrent systems, termination remains in some cases a basic problem in formal verification: In particular non-termination can result from livelocks in concurrent programs when components fail to achieve their tasks.

Verifying the structural boundedness or the structural termination of a given VASS boils down to checking the costs of cycles within the system viewed as a weighted directed graph: A cycle is pathological for structural boundedness (resp. structural termination) if its arc weights sum to a positive (resp. non-negative) vector. Consequently these two problems are very close to the detection of a zero-cycle in dynamic graphs [9], which asks if there exists a cycle with a zero cost. In [11] Kosaraju and Sullivan showed how to decide the existence of such a cycle in polynomial time. Besides this problem was proved later to be equivalent to the general linear programming problem [4]. The idea is twofold. First cycles are identified with particular multisets of arcs. Second multisets of arcs with zero cost appear as solutions to some linear program. This technique adapts easily to the detection of pathological cycles for structural boundedness or structural termination. The resulting algorithm returns in polynomial time a multiset of arcs that represents a pathological cycle if such a cycle exists.

Structural properties consider systems with an arbitrary initial configuration. However, they can be checked for systems provided with an initial configuration, because a structurally bounded (resp. structurally terminating) system is bounded (resp. terminating) for any initial configuration. This abstraction approach can prove to be useful because the non-structural variants require both exponential space [2,13]. In this direction, we give in Section 2.3 an example that shows that it can be appropriate in some cases to split the set of places into two parts: The places that are known to be bounded for the given initial marking and those that are considered to have no specific initial content. One can then unfold the system into a new system in which the former places are encoded within control states and the remaining places are checked for structural properties. When the property is not satisfied, the analysis of a computed pathological cycle is necessary to detect a false counter-example, that is to say, to verify the validity of the abstraction.

When the model of a system does not satisfy a given property, formal verification tools usually provide users with a counter-example execution in the form of a sequence of atomic steps that describes an unexpected behaviour. In this paper, we tackle the problem of providing a useful description of a pathological cycle for a structural property. The point is that the number of times an arc occurs in a pathological cycle can be exponential in the size of the given VASS, even though the time needed to compute the corresponding multiset of arcs is only polynomial. Consequently listing the sequence of arcs occurring along such a cycle is prohibitive in general. A first approach consists in providing a partial description of the detected pathological cycle as the set of all arcs occurring in this cycle —or simply the set of places interacting in the reactions performed by these arcs. However, this information may not be sufficient to understand fully the detected bug.

In the particular case of a VASS with a single state —that is to say: a pure Petri net— a multiset of arcs can be regarded as a multiset of cycles with a common starting state. Moreover, due to Carathéodory's theorem [15, Cor. 7.7i], we need at most p distinct arcs to describe a structural bug if the given VASS has p places. Then each pathological cycle is decomposed into p elementary cycles of length 1 and with a common starting state. In this work, we want to extend this property to any VASS: *We aim at decomposing a given pathological cycle in the form of a multiset of particular cycles starting from a common fixed state. Moreover each component cycle should be easy to depict and the number of distinct cycles in this multiset should be at most equal to the number of places in the given VASS.*

We introduce in Section 3 a class of particular cycles, called *wings*, that are used as component cycles for the decomposition of a pathological cycle. Roughly speaking, a wing consists of a cycle provided with two paths back and forth from a fixed starting state to some particular state within the cycle. We require that the length of the three component paths of a wing is at most equal to the number of states in the given VASS. Actually we will often consider *simple wings*, that is, wings whose component paths are simple paths. Additionally, the *valuation* of a wing determines the number of iterations of its cyclic component. Indeed we can describe a wing to the user of a verification tool by listing the sequence of arcs of its three component paths and giving its valuation.

Our first main result is established in Section 4. We show how to compute in polynomial time a multiset of simple wings with a common starting state that corresponds to a given multiset of arcs that represents a pathological cycle. Moreover the number of distinct simple wings we need is at most equal to the number of places. Thus we propose to describe a structural bug to the user in the form of a small number of wings together with the number of times each wing occurs. Note that this information allows us to compute the minimal configuration required to execute the pathological cycle resulting of the iteration of each wing in some arbitrary order. This information is useful to the user when structural properties are checked instead of their non-structural variants, if the abstraction process yields a false counter-example. Then the analysis of the detected pathological cycle can lead to a refined model with a reduced set of non-initialized places.

Finding shortest counter-examples is often desirable in automated verification, because they are easier to analyse, see e.g. [3,12]. Unfortunately, searching for a pathological cycle built over a minimal number of arcs, or a minimal number of interacting places, is NP-hard (Prop. 18 and 19). Yet we show in Section 5 that we can minimize in polynomial time the length of the component paths in wings used to describe a pathological path. To do so, we fix a starting state q and a natural number ℓ and we focus on wings starting from q whose component paths have a length at most ℓ. By means of an encoding in linear programming and a separation algorithm, we show how to decide whether there exists a pathological multiset of such wings, and if so, to compute one (Theorem 23). In the rest of this paper, we focus on structural termination for simplicity's sake. However, all results adapt easily to structural boundedness.

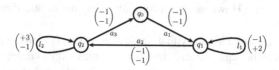

Fig. 1. A vector addition system with states

2 Background

Let p be a fixed non-zero natural number. A vector addition system with states is simply a directed graph whose arcs are labeled by vectors from $\mathbb{Z}^p$.

Definition 1. *[8] A* vector addition system with states *(for short, a VASS) is a pair* $\mathcal{S} = (Q, A)$ *where Q is a finite set of states, and $A \subseteq Q \times \mathbb{Z}^p \times Q$ is a finite set of arcs labeled by vectors from $\mathbb{Z}^p$.*

Throughout the paper we let $\mathcal{S} = (Q, A)$ be a VASS. We let $|Q|$ and $|A|$ denote the cardinalities of Q and A respectively. The source and the target of a labeled arc $a \in A$ are denoted by $\mathrm{dom}(a)$ and $\mathrm{cod}(a)$ respectively. We let $\mathrm{cost}(a) \in \mathbb{Z}^p$ denote the column vector labeling each arc $a \in A$. The size of a VASS $\mathcal{S} = (Q, A)$ is $\mathrm{size}(\mathcal{S}) = |A| \times (2 \times \lceil \log_2(|Q| + 1) \rceil + p \times (1 + \lceil \log_2(1 + v_{\max}) \rceil))$ where $v_{\max}$ is the maximal absolute value of coefficients of vectors labeling arcs in $\mathcal{S}$.

2.1 Basics and Notations

Let $\mathcal{S} = (Q, A)$ be a VASS. A path is a sequence of arcs $\gamma = a_1...a_n \in A^\star$ such that we have $\mathrm{dom}(a_{i+1}) = \mathrm{cod}(a_i)$ for each $i \in [1..n-1]$. A path $\gamma = a_1...a_n \in A^\star$ is closed if $n \geqslant 1$ and $\mathrm{dom}(a_1) = \mathrm{cod}(a_n)$. A closed path is called a *cycle*. A path $\gamma = a_1...a_n \in A^\star$ is *simple* if $\mathrm{dom}(a_i) \neq \mathrm{dom}(a_j)$ for all distinct i, j. A *circuit* is a simple and closed path. The cost of a path $\gamma = a_1...a_n$ is the vector $\mathrm{cost}(\gamma) = \sum_{i=1}^{i=n} \mathrm{cost}(a_i)$. Further the cost of a multiset of arcs $x \in \mathbb{N}^A$ is $\mathrm{cost}(x) = \sum_{a \in A} x[a] \cdot \mathrm{cost}(a)$ and the cost of a finite multiset of paths $\mathcal{F}$ is $\mathrm{cost}(\mathcal{F}) = \sum_{\gamma \in A^\star} \mathcal{F}[\gamma] \cdot \mathrm{cost}(\gamma)$. Let v and v' be two integral vectors with n coordinates: $v = (v[1], ..., v[n])$ and $v' = (v'[1], ..., v'[n])$. We put as usual $v \geqslant v'$ if $v[i] \geqslant v'[i]$ for each i; $v > v'$ if $v[i] > v'[i]$ for each i; and $v \gneqq v'$ if $v \geqslant v'$ and $v \neq v'$.

A configuration is a pair $(q, r) \in Q \times \mathbb{N}^p$ consisting of a control state q and a multiset of available particles r. A labeled arc $a \in A$ is enabled at the configuration (q, r) and leads to the configuration (q', r') if $\mathrm{dom}(a) = q$, $\mathrm{cod}(a) = q'$, and $r + \mathrm{cost}(a) = r'$. An execution of $\mathcal{S}$ from an initial configuration $(q_{\mathrm{in}}, r_{\mathrm{in}})$ is a sequence of labeled arcs $a_1...a_n \in A^\star$ such that there are configurations $(q_0, r_0), ..., (q_n, r_n)$ for which $(q_0, r_0) = (q_{\mathrm{in}}, r_{\mathrm{in}})$ and for each $i \in [1..n]$, the labeled arc a_i is enabled at (q_{i-1}, r_{i-1}) and leads to (q_i, r_i). Then the configuration (q_n, r_n) is reachable from $(q_{\mathrm{in}}, r_{\mathrm{in}})$.

In this paper we are mainly interested in checking the structural termination of a given VASS: We want to verify that for each initial configuration $(q_{\mathrm{in}}, r_{\mathrm{in}})$ the length of executions from $(q_{\mathrm{in}}, r_{\mathrm{in}})$ is bounded. It is easy to observe with the help of Dickson's lemma [10, Lemma 4.1] that this property is equivalent to the condition that there exists no cycle γ with $\mathrm{cost}(\gamma) \geqslant 0$. Thus we aim at detecting pathological cycles in $\mathcal{S}$.

Definition 2. *A cycle γ in a VASS $\mathcal{S}$ is pathological if $cost(\gamma) \geqslant 0$.*

Example 3. Along this paper, we shall use as a running example the 2-dimensional VASS depicted in Figure 1 with three states q_0, q_1, and q_2 and five weighted arcs a_1, a_2, a_3, l_1, and l_2. The cost of the cycle $\gamma = a_1.l_1^5.a_2.l_2^3.a_3$ is $\text{cost}(\gamma) = (1, 4)^\top$. So this cycle is pathological.

2.2 Multisets of Arcs vs. Cycles

We shall represent cycles of a VASS $\mathcal{S}$ as particular multisets of arcs. Let $x \in \mathbb{N}^A$ be a multiset of arcs. We denote by $\|x\| = |\{a \in A \mid x[a] \geqslant 1\}|$ the number of distinct arcs in x and by A_x the *support of x*, that is to say the set of arcs $a \in A$ such that $x[a] \geqslant 1$. Thus $\|x\| = |A_x|$. The *underlying graph G_x* of x is the (undirected) graph $G_x = (Q_x, E_x)$ where the set of vertices $Q_x = \{\text{dom}(a) \mid a \in A_x\} \cup \{\text{cod}(a) \mid a \in A_x\}$ collects the source and the target of all arcs in x and the set of edges $E_x = \{\{\text{dom}(a), \text{cod}(a)\} \mid a \in A_x \text{ and } \text{dom}(a) \neq \text{cod}(a)\}$ keeps track of all connections induced by arcs in x.

A multiset of arcs $x \in \mathbb{N}^A$ is called *connected* if G_x is a connected graph. Let $x \in \mathbb{N}^A$ and $C_1, ..., C_n \subseteq Q_x$ be the connected components of G_x. For each $1 \leqslant i \leqslant n$ and each $a \in A$, we put $x_i[a] = x[a]$ if $\text{dom}(a) \in C_i$ and $x_i[a] = 0$ otherwise. Then $x = x_1 + ... + x_n$ and the multisets $x_i \in \mathbb{N}^A$ are called the *connected components of x*. A multiset of arcs x is called *Eulerian* if for each state $q \in Q$ the number of arcs incident from q equals the number of arcs incident to q, i.e. $\sum_{\text{dom}(a)=q} x[a] = \sum_{\text{cod}(a)=q} x[a]$. A connected and Eulerian multiset of arcs is called a *circulation*. Note that if x and y are Eulerian, then $x + y$ is Eulerian. If moreover $x \leqslant y$ then $y - x$ is Eulerian, too. The *multiplicity* of a non-zero multiset $x \in \mathbb{N}^A \setminus \{0\}$ within a multiset $y \in \mathbb{N}^A$ is the greatest natural number k such that $k \cdot x \leqslant y$.

Each cycle $\gamma = a_1...a_n$ of $\mathcal{S}$ is represented by the multiset of arcs $x_\gamma = \sum_{i=1}^{i=n} a_i$, i.e. $x_\gamma[a]$ is the number of occurrences of a in γ. Since γ is a cycle, the multiset of arcs x_γ is non-empty, Eulerian and connected. For instance, continuing Example 3, the multiset of arcs $a_1 + a_2 + a_3 + 5 \cdot l_1 + 3 \cdot l_2$ is the circulation corresponding to the cycle $\gamma = a_1.l_1^5.a_2.l_2^3.a_3$. Conversely, each non-empty circulation corresponds to a cycle of $\mathcal{S}$: This is an immediate variant of Euler's theorem [5, Th. 1.8.1].

Proposition 4. *Let $x \in \mathbb{N}^A$ be a non-empty circulation. Then there exists a cycle γ such that $x_\gamma = x$.*

In [11], Kosaraju and Sullivan showed how to detect a cycle with a zero cost in polynomial time. Basically their algorithm searches for a non-empty circulation with a zero cost recursively by alternatively solving homogeneous linear programs and computing strongly connected components. It is straightforward to adapt this technique to the detection of pathological cycles. In fact it is sufficient to replace a vector equality $x = 0$ by $x \geqslant 0$ in part of the linear programs considered. Moreover we can require that the resulting algorithm returns a circulation that represents a pathological cycle if such a cycle exists. Note here that this algorithm remains polynomial although it does not boil down to solving a linear program as in the particular case of a Petri net [17].

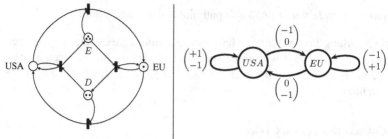

Fig. 2. A terminating Petri net   **Fig. 3.** A structurally terminating VASS

2.3   Semi-structural Properties of Petri Nets

When modeling a message-passing system as a Petri net, one often distinguishes two types of places:

- *control places* whose bounded marking describes the current global state;
- *container places* whose tokens represent pending messages.

It may be then interesting to check termination for a fixed initial marking of control places but an arbitrary initial marking of container places. In this way, semi-structural termination generalises both termination and structural termination by specifying a subset of places with an arbitrary initial marking.

A simple approach allows us to check semi-structural termination. First we erase the container places and check that the resulting Petri net is bounded. Next we build the corresponding finite marking graph viewed as a VASS and re-incorporate the constraints of container places. If the resulting VASS is structurally terminating, then the original Petri net is semi-structurally terminating, i.e. it terminates for any initial marking of its container places. Recall that checking termination of a Petri net requires exponential space [17] whereas we can check structural termination of a VASS in polynomial time. Thus, considering semi-structural termination of a Petri net and hence structural termination of a VASS can turn out to be efficient to check that a Petri net terminates.

Example 5. Consider the currency change Petri net depicted in Fig. 2. The container places E and D collect euros and dollars respectively. An additional token walks around between the two control places EU and USA. When the control token is in EU then euros can be changed into dollars, and conversely if the control token is in USA then dollars can be changed into euros. Moving from EU to USA (resp. from USA to EU) requires to pay a tax in dollars (resp. in euros). This Petri net is not structurally terminating because currency can circulate between euros and dollars provided that there is a token in both control places EU and USA. However, the resulting unfolded VASS, depicted in Fig. 3, consists of two states and is obviously structurally terminating. Thus the currency change Petri net from Fig. 2 terminates for any initial amount. Note that the usual Petri net associated with the VASS from Fig. 3 is precisely the Petri net from Fig. 2. Therefore the classical simulation of a VASS by a Petri net does not preserve structural termination.

3   Representation of a Circulation by a Multiset of Cycles

3.1   Exponential Length of Minimal Pathological Cycles

The algorithm to detect pathological paths can provide us with a circulation that corresponds to a pathological cycle. Moreover the *size* of the natural coefficients of such a circulation is polynomial. In order to help the understanding of a structural bug detected in the form of a circulation, it is useful to represent this counter-example as a pathological cycle. Then the length of this pathological cycle equals the sum of the circulation coefficients. Consequently the minimal length of the resulting cycle can be exponential in the size of the VASS as illustrated by the next example.

Example 6. Consider the VASS with a single state and six arcs labeled by the six following 6-dimensional vectors:

$$
t_1 = \begin{pmatrix} 2 \\ 0 \\ 0 \\ 0 \\ 0 \\ -1 \end{pmatrix} ; t_2 = \begin{pmatrix} -1 \\ 2 \\ 0 \\ 0 \\ 0 \\ 0 \end{pmatrix} ; t_3 = \begin{pmatrix} 0 \\ -1 \\ 2 \\ 0 \\ 0 \\ 0 \end{pmatrix} ; t_4 = \begin{pmatrix} 0 \\ 0 \\ -2 \\ 1 \\ 0 \\ 0 \end{pmatrix} ; t_5 = \begin{pmatrix} 0 \\ 0 \\ 0 \\ -2 \\ 1 \\ 0 \end{pmatrix} ; t_6 = \begin{pmatrix} 0 \\ 0 \\ 0 \\ 0 \\ -2 \\ 1 \end{pmatrix}
$$

It is easy to see that each pathological cycle needs all arcs because of their pairwise dependencies. Moreover a pathological cycle that contains one occurrence of t_6 needs 2 occurrences of t_5, 4 occurrences of t_4 and hence 4 occurrences of t_3, 2 occurrences of t_2 and one occurrence of t_1. Therefore the pathological cycle $\gamma = t_1 + 2 \cdot t_2 + 4 \cdot t_3 + 4 \cdot t_4 + 2 \cdot t_5 + t_6$ has a minimal length. We can easily generalize this example to a VASS made of $2 \times m$ arcs whose pathological cycles have a length greater than $2 \times (2^m - 1)$.

Thus listing the sequence of arcs occurring along a pathological cycle is prohibitive. For that reason we need to design a *compact representation* of pathological cycles.

3.2   Looking for a Format

It is clear that a pathological cycle γ (or a circulation) can be decomposed into a multiset $\mathcal{F}$ of circuits with $\text{cost}(\mathcal{F}) = \text{cost}(\gamma)$. Then Caratheodory's theorem [15, Cor. 7.7i] allows us to compute a multiset $\mathcal{F}'$ over at most p circuits (where p stands for the dimension of vectors) such that $\text{cost}(\mathcal{F}') = m \cdot \text{cost}(\gamma)$ for some $m \in \mathbb{N} \setminus \{0\}$. However, the connectedness of the underlying set of arcs may be lost at this point, that is, $\mathcal{F}'$ does not represent a pathological cycle any longer.

A natural idea is to use an additional connecting cycle on which the component circuits would hang. In other words it would be nice to find

- a sequence of circuits $\sigma_0, \ldots, \sigma_{k-1}$, with $k \leqslant p$,
- a sequence of fixed connection states $q_0, \ldots, q_{k-1}$ with $q_i \in Q_{\sigma_i}$
- a connecting cycle $w_0 \ldots w_{k-1}$, where w_i is a simple path from q_i to $q_{i+1 \pmod{k}}$,
- and a sequence $n_0, \ldots, n_{k-1}$ of natural numbers

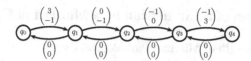

Fig. 4. Counter-example

such that the cycle $\gamma' = \sigma_0^{n_0} w_0 \sigma_1^{n_1} \ldots \sigma_{k-1}^{n_{k-1}} w_{k-1}$ satisfies $\mathrm{cost}(\gamma') = m \cdot \mathrm{cost}(\gamma)$ for some $m \in \mathbb{N} \setminus \{0\}$. Example 3 shows that in some cases pathological circulations can effectively be decomposed in this way. However, till now, it remains open whether it exists such a pathological cycle for every non structurally terminating VASS. For that reason, we consider in the sequel of this paper another kind of representation for pathological circulations. Before that, we would like to stress that we cannot require additionally that the connecting cycle $w_0.w_1 \ldots w_k$ is simple, as the next example shows.

Example 7. Consider the 2-dimensional VASS with 5 states from Fig. 4. Each pathological cycle in this VASS makes use of each arc. Such cycles cannot be decomposed in the above considered form with a *simple* connecting cycle.

3.3   From Multisets of Arcs to Multisets of Wings

At present we propose to describe pathological cycles of a VASS in the form of a multiset of particular cycles called wings. Roughly speaking, a wing with valuation k is a cycle which consists of k iterations of a circuit plus a path back and forth from one state of the circuit to some fixed starting state. This shared starting state will ensure that a multiset of wings remains connected.

Definition 8. *Let $q, q' \in Q$ be two states of $\mathcal{S}$. Let γ_0 be a cycle of $\mathcal{S}$ starting from q'. Let γ_1 be a path from q to q' and γ_2 be a path from q' to q. Let $k \in \mathbb{N}$. We assume that the length of each path γ_0, γ_1 and γ_2 is at most equal to the number of states $|Q|$. Let $W = \gamma_1.\gamma_0^k.\gamma_2$ be the cycle which starts from q and which consists of γ_1, followed by k iterations of the cycle γ_0, followed by γ_2. Then W is called a* wing *of $\mathcal{S}$ with valuation k. A wing is said to be* simple *if its three component paths γ_0, γ_1, and γ_2 are simple.*

A simple wing is often represented by a multiset of arcs $W = D + k \cdot C$ where C is the set of arcs occurring in the cycle γ_0 while D is the multiset of arcs occurring in γ_1 and γ_2. Then the multiset W is connected and Eulerian. Note that the path $\gamma_1.\gamma_2$ from q to q in a simple wing need not be simple (nor non-empty). However, each arc occurs *at most twice* in $\gamma_1.\gamma_2$.

Example 9. We continue Example 3 with $p = 2$. We have observed that the cost of the cycle γ is $\mathrm{cost}(\gamma) = (1,4)^\top$. Consider the two simple wings $W_1 = a_1.l_1^{10}.a_2.a_3$ with valuation 10 and $W_2 = a_1.a_2.l_2^6.a_3$ with valuation 6. Noteworthy $2 \cdot \mathrm{cost}(\gamma) = \mathrm{cost}(W_1) + \mathrm{cost}(W_2)$. This equality illustrates precisely how simple wings can represent a cycle up to a scalar multiplication factor of its cost.

Our first result asserts that there exists such a representation by wings with a shared starting state for any pathological circulation.

Theorem 10. *Let $\hat{H}$ be a non-empty circulation and $\hat{q} \in Q_{\hat{H}}$. There exists a non-empty multiset $\mathcal{F}$ of simple wings starting from $\hat{q}$ such that $\mathrm{cost}(\mathcal{F}) = m \cdot \mathrm{cost}(\hat{H})$ for some $m \in \mathbb{N} \setminus \{0\}$; moreover $\mathcal{F}$ is built over at most p distinct wings.*

The next section is devoted to the proof of Theorem 10. The factor m is necessary to make sure that the simple wings obtained share the common starting state $\hat{q}$ and hence to get an obvious cycle made of this multiset of wings. This factor m is not a drawback of this approach because we search for pathological cycles and moreover the actual length of the resulting pathological cycle is not relevant. It allows us also to ensure additionally that $\mathcal{F}$ is built over of at most p distinct wings.

4 Construction of Representative Wings from a Circulation

In this section we fix a non-empty circulation $\hat{H} \in \mathbb{N}^A$ and a state $\hat{q} \in Q_{\hat{H}}$. We show how to compute in polynomial time a non-empty multiset $\mathcal{F}$ of simple wings starting from $\hat{q}$ such that $\mathrm{cost}(\mathcal{F}) = m \cdot \mathrm{cost}(\hat{H})$ for some $m \in \mathbb{N} \setminus \{0\}$.

The construction of $\mathcal{F}$ proceeds inductively over the size of $A_{\hat{H}}$. At each step, a wing $W = D + k \cdot C \leqslant \hat{H}$ with valuation k is added to $\mathcal{F}$ and removed from $\hat{H}$ until $\hat{H}$ is empty. This wing should satisfy the three following properties:

1. Some arc in the cyclic component C has multiplicity k within $\hat{H}$; in this way, at least one arc is removed from the support of $\hat{H}$ at each step: $\|\hat{H} - W\| < \|\hat{H}\|$.
2. The Eulerian multiset of remaining arcs $\hat{H} - W$ is connected; this ensures that we can proceed recursively.
3. The fixed state $\hat{q}$ belongs to the new circulation $\hat{H} - W$, so that all wings share this common starting state —except of course if $\hat{H} - W$ is already empty.

The first idea for the search of such a wing W within $\hat{H}$ is that it is sufficient to find a circuit C satisfying these conditions. This leads us to the following central notion of an *adequate* circuit.

Definition 11. *Let $H \in \mathbb{N}^A$ be a non-empty circulation and $q_0 \in Q_H$. A circuit C with multiplicity $k \geqslant 1$ in H is* adequate *for H and q_0 if it satisfies the two next conditions:*

- *the multiset of arcs $H - k \cdot C$ is connected;*
- *if $H - k \cdot C$ is not empty then $Q_{H-k\cdot C}$ contains q_0.*

Example 12. Continuing Example 3, we consider the circulation $H = a_1 + a_2 + a_3 + 5 \cdot l_1 + 3 \cdot l_2$ for the VASS depicted in Figure 1. Then the two circuits l_1 and l_2 are adequate for H and q_0 whereas the circuit $a_1.a_2.a_3$ is not.

Note that $\|H - k \cdot C\| < \|H\|$ for any circuit C with multiplicity k in H. The construction of $\mathcal{F}$ relies on two independent algorithms presented in the two next subsections. The first algorithm shows how to find an adequate circuit for any non-empty circulation $H \in \mathbb{N}^A$ and any state $\hat{q} \in Q_H$. The second one is much easier. It explains how to build the expected multiset $\mathcal{F}$ of wings with the help of adequate circuits as inputs.

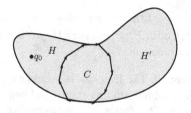

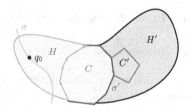

Fig. 5. Searching for an adequate circuit | **Fig. 6.** Induction step

4.1 Finding an Adequate Circuit in a Circulation for a Fixed State

The search for a circuit C adequate for H and q_0 proceeds non-deterministically and inductively over the number of arcs in A_H. Each step distinguishes two main cases. The simpler case assumes that all circuits within H contain q_0. Then each circuit is adequate for H and q_0. The reason is that any connected component of the Eulerian multiset $H - k \cdot C$ contains a circuit, and hence contains q_0.

The more interesting case considers that there exists a circuit $C \leqslant H$ that does not contain q_0. Let k be the multiplicity of C within H. Then $q_0 \in Q_{H-k\cdot C}$ because q_0 does not occur in C. Hence $H - k \cdot C$ is not empty. Then the circuit C is adequate if $H - k \cdot C$ is connected. In this case, the search is terminated. Otherwise we consider a connected component H' of $H - k \cdot C$ that does not contain q_0, as illustrated in Fig. 5. We will show how to find in H' a circuit C', with multiplicity k' in H', such that

1. at least one arc $a \in A_{C'} \setminus A_C$ satisfies $H'[a] = k'$. Then $H'[a] = H[a]$ and k' is also the multiplicity of a in H; hence $\|H - k' \cdot C'\| < \|H\|$.
2. each connected component of $H' - k' \cdot C'$ contains a state from C. Then $H - k' \cdot C'$ is connected; moreover $q_0 \in Q_{H-k'\cdot C'}$ because q_0 does not occur in H'.

It follows that C' is adequate for H and q_0.

The search for an appropriate circuit C' within H' is regarded as a generalisation of the search for an adequate circuit C within H where the connectivity of $H - k \cdot C$ is replaced by the connectivity of $H' - k' \cdot C'$ if one incorporates the circuit C. Actually, for simplicity's sake, we will consider at this point a simple path σ made of all but one arcs from C. Intuitively, σ will play the role of C. However we shall also consider a special case where σ is the empty path to deal with adequate circuits.

Definition 13. *Let $H \in \mathbb{N}^A$ be a non-empty circulation, $q_0 \in Q_H$, and $\sigma \in A^*$ be a simple path. A circuit C with multiplicity $k \geqslant 1$ in H is appropriate for H and (q_0, σ) if it satisfies the two next conditions:*

1. there exists an arc $a \in A_C \setminus A_\sigma$ such that $H[a] = k$;
2. each connected component of $H - k \cdot C$ contains a state from $Q_\sigma \cup \{q_0\}$.

Observe that a circuit C is appropriate for H and (q_0, ϵ) where ϵ denotes the empty path (Def. 13) if, and only if, it is adequate for H and q_0 (Def. 11). For that reason, the search for an adequate circuit will simply ask for an appropriate circuit w.r.t. the empty path ϵ in Algorithm 2 below.

We present now in Algorithm 1 a way to compute circuits appropriate for H and (q_0, σ), provided that σ is not a circuit and $q_0 \in Q_\sigma$ if σ is not empty.

Algorithm 1. AppropriateCircuit(H, q_0, σ)

Require: $H \in \mathbb{N}^A$ is a non-empty circulation.
Require: σ is a simple path consisting of arcs from A and such that σ is not a circuit.
Require: $q_0 \in Q_H$ and $q_0 \in Q_\sigma$ if the path σ is non-empty.
  if all circuits $C \leqslant H$ satisfy $Q_C \cap (Q_\sigma \cup \{q_0\}) \neq \emptyset$ **then**
    Let $b \in A_H \setminus A_\sigma$
    $\beta \leftarrow b$ # Initially β is a path of length 1
    while β contains no circuit **do**
      if there exists some arc $b' \in A_H \setminus A_\sigma$ with $\text{dom}(b') = \text{cod}(b)$ **then**
        Choose some $b' \in A_H \setminus A_\sigma$ with $\text{dom}(b') = \text{cod}(b)$
      else
        Choose some $b' \in A_H \cap A_\sigma$ such that $\text{dom}(b') = \text{cod}(b)$
      end if
      $b \leftarrow b'$
      Add the arc b to the end of the path β
    end while
    return a circuit C within β
  else
    Let $C \leqslant H$ be such a circuit such that $Q_C \cap (Q_\sigma \cup \{q_0\}) = \emptyset$
    Let k be the multiplicity of C in H
    if each connected component of $H - k \cdot C$ contains a state from $Q_\sigma \cup \{q_0\}$ **then**
      return C # In particular if $H = k \cdot C$.
    else
      Let H' be a connected component of $H - k \cdot C$ with $Q_{H'} \cap (Q_\sigma \cup \{q_0\}) = \emptyset$.
      Let q_0' be a state from $Q_{H'} \cap Q_C$ and a be an arc from A_C with $H[a] = k$.
      Let σ' be the path made of all arcs from $A_C \setminus \{a\}$
      return AppropriateCircuit(H', q_0', σ') # Then $\|H'\| < \|H\|$
    end if
  end if

Proposition 14. *Let $H \in \mathbb{N}^A$ be a circulation. Let $q_0 \in Q_H$ and $\sigma \in A^\star$ be a simple path such that $q_0 \in Q_\sigma$ if σ is not empty. Provided that σ is not a circuit, Algorithm 1 returns a circuit that is appropriate for H and (q_0, σ).*

Assume that $H \in \mathbb{N}^A$ is a non-empty circulation and $\sigma = a_1...a_n$ is a simple path consisting of arcs from A such that σ is not a circuit. Let $q_0 \in Q_H$ be a state of H such that $q_0 \in Q_\sigma$ if σ is non-empty. Searching for an appropriate circuit C for H and (q_0, σ) is slightly more involved than searching for an adequate one. However, Algorithm 1 proceeds similarly to the above discussion and distinguishes two main cases.

We need first to determine whether all circuits in H contain a state from $Q_\sigma \cup \{q_0\}$. To do so, one considers the subset $A' \subseteq A$ consisting of all arcs from A_H whose source and target do not belong to $Q_\sigma \cup \{q_0\}$. Let $A_1',..., A_n'$ be the strongly connected components of A'. Then there exists a circuit C in H with $Q_C \cap (Q_\sigma \cup \{q_0\}) = \emptyset$ if, and only if, A' contains a self-loop arc or one of the strongly connected components A_i' has two states. Depending on whether this condition is satisfied, we investigate one of the following two cases:

1. We assume first that all circuits in H contain a state from $Q_\sigma \cup \{q_0\}$. Algorithm 1 builds a circuit $C = a_0 a_1 ... a_{n-1}$ in H using preferably arcs that do not appear in σ. Since σ is not a circuit and H is a non-empty circulation, we can choose an arbitrary arc $b \in A_H \setminus A_\sigma$ and consider first the path $\beta = b$. This path is extended iteratively by adding arcs from A_H to the end of β until β contains a circuit C. At each iteration, there are potential candidates to complete β because H is Eulerian. However, we require that arcs from $A_H \setminus A_\sigma$ are preferred to the others in this extension process. Clearly this loop terminates after at most $|Q_H|$ iterations. At this point, we claim that C is appropriate for H and (q_0, σ).

   Proof. Let $k \geqslant 1$ be the multiplicity of C in H. Since H is Eulerian, $H - k \cdot C$ is Eulerian. Let H' be a connected component of $H - k \cdot C$. Since $H - k \cdot C$ is Eulerian, H' is Eulerian. Therefore there is some circuit in H' and hence H' contains a state from $Q_\sigma \cup \{q_0\}$. Thus, all connected components of $H - k \cdot C$ contain a state from $Q_\sigma \cup \{q_0\}$.

   Since the simple path σ is not closed, the circuit C within β cannot be made of arcs from σ only. In other words, C contains at least one arc that does not belong to A_σ. Assume that there is an arc $a_i \in A_\sigma \cap A_C$. Due to the priority of arcs adopted, the arc a_i is the single arc with $\mathrm{dom}(a_i) = \mathrm{cod}(a_{i-1 \ (\mathrm{mod}\ n)})$. Since H is Eulerian, we have $H[a_{i-1 \ (\mathrm{mod}\ n)}] \leqslant H[a_i]$. Since C contains at least one arc that does not belong to A_σ, there exists an arc $a \in A_C \setminus A_\sigma$ such that $H[a] \leqslant H[a_i]$. It follows that there exists $a \in A_C \setminus A_\sigma$ such that $H[a]$ is equal to the multiplicity C in H. ∎

2. We assume now that there exists some circuit C in H with $Q_C \cap (Q_\sigma \cup \{q_0\}) = \emptyset$. Let $k \geqslant 1$ be the multiplicity of C in H. If each connected component of $H - k \cdot C$ contains at least one state from $Q_\sigma \cup \{q_0\}$ then C is appropriate for H and (q_0, σ). Therefore we assume now that $H - k \cdot C$ is non-empty and admits some connected component H' of $H - k \cdot C$ that contains no state from $Q_\sigma \cup \{q_0\}$. Let $a \in A_C$ be such that $H[a] = k$. Then $H'[a] = 0$ and hence $\|H'\| < \|H\|$. Moreover $Q_{H'} \cap Q_C \neq \emptyset$, otherwise there would be no path from $Q_{H'}$ to Q_C in the circulation H. We fix some state $q_0' \in Q_{H'} \cap Q_C$. We let also σ' denote the simple path made of all arcs from $A_C \setminus \{a\}$. Then σ' contains all arcs from $A_C \cap A_{H'}$. Moreover σ' is not a circuit and $q_0' \in Q_{\sigma'}$ as soon as σ' is not empty. At this point we claim that any circuit C' appropriate for H' and (q_0', σ') is also appropriate for H and (q_0, σ).

   Proof. The situation is illustrated in Fig. 6. Let $k' \geqslant 1$ be the multiplicity of C' in H'. Then,
   - Each connected component of $H' - k' \cdot C'$ contains a state from $Q_{\sigma'} \cup \{q_0'\}$.
   - There exists an arc $a' \in A_{C'} \setminus A_{\sigma'}$ such that $H'[a'] = k'$.

   Since σ' contains all arcs from C that occur in H', we have $a' \notin A_C$. Therefore $H[a'] = (H - k \cdot C)[a'] = H'[a'] = k'$. It follows that k' is also the multiplicity of C' in H. Since H' contains no state from $Q_\sigma \cup \{q_0\}$, C' contains no state from $Q_\sigma \cup \{q_0\}$ either. Further, we have $a' \in A_{C'} \setminus A_\sigma$. Since $q_0 \in H$ and $q_0 \notin H'$, q_0 appears in $H - k' \cdot C'$. To conclude the proof, we show simply that $H - k' \cdot C'$ is connected.

   Since $H - k \cdot C \geqslant k' \cdot C'$, we have $H - k' \cdot C' \geqslant k \cdot C \geqslant C$. Thus all states of Q_C are strongly connected to each other in $H - k' \cdot C'$. Let $q'' \in Q_{H - k' \cdot C'}$. It remains to show that there exists a path from q'' to a state from C made of arcs from $H - k' \cdot C'$. The claim is trivial if $q'' \in Q_C$. If $q'' \notin Q_C$ then q'' belongs to one of the connected components of $H - k \cdot C$. We distinguish two cases:

- $q'' \in Q_{H'}$. Since $q'' \in Q_{H-k' \cdot C'}$, there exists some arc $a'' \in H - k' \cdot C'$ such that $q'' = \text{dom}(a'')$ or $q'' = \text{cod}(a'')$. Since $q'' \notin Q_C$, we have $a'' \notin C$ and hence $H[a''] = H'[a'']$. Then $H'[a''] - k' \cdot C'[a''] = H[a''] - k' \cdot C'[a''] \geqslant 1$. It follows that $q'' \in Q_{H'-k' \cdot C'}$. Since each connected component of $Q_{H'-k' \cdot C'}$ contains a state from $Q_{\sigma'} \cup \{q'_0\}$ and $Q_{\sigma'} \cup \{q'_0\} \subseteq Q_C$, there exists a path from q'' to C in $H' - k' \cdot C'$ and hence in $H - k' \cdot C'$.
- $q'' \in Q_{H''}$ where H'' is a connected component of $H - k \cdot C$ different from H'. Then $Q_{H''} \cap Q_C \neq \emptyset$ otherwise there would be no path from the set of states $Q_{H''}$ to the set of states Q_C in H. Therefore there exists a path from q'' to C in H'' and hence in $H - k' \cdot C'$.

Thus $H - k' \cdot C'$ is connected and the circuit C' is appropriate for H and (q_0, σ). ∎

4.2 Building a Multiset of Simple Wings from a Pathological Circulation

The construction of a representative multiset $\mathcal{F}$ of simple wings from the multiset $\hat{H}$ of arcs is described in Algorithm 2. Initially $\mathcal{F}$ is empty and we put $H = \hat{H}$. Hence $\text{cost}(\mathcal{F}) + \text{cost}(H) = m \cdot \text{cost}(\hat{H})$ with $m = 1$. This equality will act as a loop invariant of the main iterating process. First, a circuit C adequate for $\hat{H}$ and $\hat{q}$ is found with the help of Algorithm 1. Recall here that a circuit C is appropriate for H and $(\hat{q}, \epsilon)$ (where ϵ denotes the empty path) if, and only if, it is adequate for H and $\hat{q}$. Let k be the multiplicity of C in H. Then the Eulerian multiset $H - k \cdot C$ is connected and $\hat{q} \in Q_{H-k \cdot C}$ provided that $H - k \cdot C$ is not empty. Moreover $\|H - k \cdot C\| < \|H\|$.

We build from C a wing W starting from $\hat{q}$ with C as its cyclic component. If $\hat{q}$ appears in C then $W = k \cdot C$ is a simple wing starting from $\hat{q}$. Assume that $\hat{q} \notin Q_C$. Then $\hat{q} \in Q_{H-k \cdot C}$. Since H is connected, there is a state $q \in Q_C \cap Q_{H-k \cdot C}$. Since $H - k \cdot C$ is connected, there are a simple path γ_1 from $\hat{q}$ to q and a simple path γ_2 from q to $\hat{q}$ made of arcs from $A_{H-k \cdot C}$. We let D denote the multiset of arcs that corresponds to the cycle $\gamma_1.\gamma_2$. Then the multiset $W = D + k \cdot C$ represents a simple wing which starts from $\hat{q}$. Moreover $D[a] \leqslant 2$ for each $a \in A$ because γ_1 and γ_2 are simple paths, hence $W \leqslant 3 \cdot H$, because $k \cdot C \leqslant H$. Furthermore, each arc $a \in A_C$ with multiplicity k in H does not occur in $\gamma_1.\gamma_2$, since it does not occur in $H - k \cdot C$. We distinguish then three cases:

1. If $W = H$ then the simple wing W is added to $\mathcal{F}$ and removed from H leading to the empty multiset $H' = 0$.
2. If $W \leqslant H$, $H - W$ is connected and $\hat{q} \in Q_{H-W}$ then the simple wing W is added to $\mathcal{F}$ and removed from H leading to the new circulation $H' = H - W$ such that $\hat{q} \in Q_{H'}$. Since k is the multiplicity of C in H, we get $\|H'\| < \|H\|$.
3. Otherwise the multiset of wings $\mathcal{F}$ is multiplied by 3. Then we have $\text{cost}(\mathcal{F}) + \text{cost}(3 \cdot H) = m \cdot \text{cost}(\hat{H})$ for some $m \in \mathbb{N} \setminus \{0\}$. Let a be an arc from C such that $H[a] = k$. Then $3 \cdot H[a] - D[a] = 3k$ because a does not occur in $\gamma_1.\gamma_2$. On the other hand, for each arc a' from C with $H[a'] \geqslant k+1$, we have $3 \cdot H[a'] - D[a'] \geqslant 3k + 1$ because $D[a'] \leqslant 2$. It follows that $3k$ is the multiplicity of C in $3 \cdot H - D$. We consider the new wing $W' = D + 3k \cdot C$. The wing W' is added to $\mathcal{F}$ and

---

Algorithm 2. Computing a multiset of simple wings

Require: A non-empty circulation $\hat{H}$ and a state $\hat{q} \in Q_{\hat{H}}$

$\quad \mathcal{F} \leftarrow \mathbf{0}$ # Initially $\mathcal{F}$ is the empty multiset of simple wings

$\quad H \leftarrow \hat{H}$ # Initially $\mathrm{cost}(\mathcal{F}) + \mathrm{cost}(H) = m \cdot \mathrm{cost}(\hat{H})$ with $m = 1$

$\quad$ **while** $H \neq \mathbf{0}$ **do**

$\quad\quad C \leftarrow$ AppropriateCircuit$(H, \hat{q}, \epsilon)$ # C is adequate for H and $\hat{q}$.

$\quad\quad$ Let k be the multiplicity of C in H # $k \cdot C \leqslant H$ and $H - k \cdot C$ is connected

$\quad\quad$ **if** $\hat{q} \in Q_C$ **then**

$\quad\quad\quad D \leftarrow \mathbf{0}$ # $D \in \mathbb{N}^A$ is the empty multiset of arcs

$\quad\quad\quad W \leftarrow k \cdot C$ # The multiset W represents a simple wing such that $W \leqslant H$

$\quad\quad$ **else**

$\quad\quad\quad$ Let q be some state in $Q_C \cap Q_{H-k \cdot C}$.

$\quad\quad\quad$ Let γ_1 be a simple path from $\hat{q}$ to q made of arcs from $A_{H-k \cdot C}$.

$\quad\quad\quad$ Let γ_2 be a simple path from q to $\hat{q}$ made of arcs from $A_{H-k \cdot C}$.

$\quad\quad\quad$ Let D be the multiset of arcs that corresponds to the cycle $\gamma_1.\gamma_2$.   # Then $D \leqslant 2 \cdot H$

$\quad\quad\quad W \leftarrow D + k \cdot C$ # The multiset W represents a simple wing such that $W \leqslant 3 \cdot H$

$\quad\quad$ **end if**

$\quad\quad$ **if** $(H = W)$ or $(W \leqslant H$ and $H - W$ is connected and $\hat{q} \in Q_{H-W})$ **then**

$\quad\quad\quad$ Add the simple wing W to $\mathcal{F}$.

$\quad\quad\quad H \leftarrow H - W$ # $\mathrm{cost}(\mathcal{F}) + \mathrm{cost}(H) = m \cdot \mathrm{cost}(\hat{H})$ for some $m \geqslant 1$

$\quad\quad$ **else**

$\quad\quad\quad W' \leftarrow D + 3k \cdot C$ # We have $A_{H-k \cdot C} = A_{3 \cdot H - W'}$

$\quad\quad\quad \mathcal{F} \leftarrow 3 \cdot \mathcal{F}$ # $\mathrm{cost}(\mathcal{F}) + \mathrm{cost}(3 \cdot H) = m \cdot \mathrm{cost}(\hat{H})$ for some $m \geqslant 1$

$\quad\quad\quad$ Add the simple wing W' to $\mathcal{F}$.

$\quad\quad\quad H \leftarrow 3 \cdot H - W'$ # $\mathrm{cost}(\mathcal{F}) + \mathrm{cost}(H) = m \cdot \mathrm{cost}(\hat{H})$ for some $m \geqslant 1$

$\quad\quad$ **end if**

$\quad$ **end while**

$\quad$ **return** $\mathcal{F}$

---

removed from $3 \cdot H$ leading to the new Eulerian multiset of arcs $H' = 3 \cdot H - W'$. For each $a \in A$, we have $3(H - k \cdot C)[a] \geqslant H'[a] \geqslant 3(H - k \cdot C)[a] - 2$, because $D[a] \leqslant 2$. Hence $A_{H'} = A_{H-k \cdot C}$. Consequently, H' is connected, $\|H'\| < \|H\|$, and $\hat{q} \in Q_{H'}$ if $H' \neq \mathbf{0}$.

Thus, in all cases we get that H' is Eulerian and connected. Moreover $\hat{q} \in Q_{H'}$ provided that H' is not empty and hence the next iteration of the algorithm can proceed analogously. Furthermore we have $\|H'\| < \|H\|$ henceforth Alg. 2 terminates after at most $|A|$ iterations.

Example 15. We continue Examples 3 and 12 to illustrate an execution of Alg. 2 with the VASS depicted in Figure 1, the circulation $\hat{H} = a_1 + a_2 + a_3 + 5 \cdot l_1 + 3 \cdot l_2$, and the base state $\hat{q} = q_0$. First, the adequate circuit l_1 with multiplicity 5 can be chosen which leads to the wing $W_1 = a_1 + a_2 + a_3 + 5 \cdot l_1$. Since $\hat{H} - W_1$ does not contain $\hat{q}$, we put $W_1' = a_1 + a_2 + a_3 + 15 \cdot l_1$ and get $\mathcal{F} = \{W_1'\}$ and $H = 3 \cdot \hat{H} - W_1' = 2 \cdot a_1 + 2 \cdot a_2 + 2 \cdot a_3 + 9 \cdot l_2$ at the end of the first iteration.

In the second iteration, l_2 is the unique adequate circuit for H and $\hat{q}$. Therefore we put $W_2 = a_1 + a_2 + a_3 + 9 \cdot l_2$ and get $\mathcal{F} = \{W_1', W_2\}$ and $H' = H - W_2 = a_1 + a_2 + a_3$

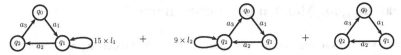

Fig. 7. Multiset of wings computed in Example 15

because this Eulerian multiset of arcs is connected and contains $\hat{q}$. The third and last iteration selects the adequate circuit $W_3 = a_1 + a_2 + a_3$ which yields the multiset of wings $\mathcal{F} = \{W_1', W_2, W_3\}$ depicted in Fig. 7. Observe here that $\mathrm{cost}(\mathcal{F}) = (3, 12)^\top = 3 \cdot \mathrm{cost}(\hat{H})$.

It is clear that the property that $\mathrm{cost}(\mathcal{F}) + \mathrm{cost}(H) = m \cdot \mathrm{cost}(\hat{H})$ for some $m \in \mathbb{N} \setminus \{0\}$ is a loop invariant of Algorithm 2. Consequently,

Theorem 16. *Let $\hat{H}$ be a non-empty circulation and $\hat{q} \in Q_{\hat{H}}$. Algorithm 2 returns a non-empty multiset $\mathcal{F}$ of simple wings starting from $\hat{q}$ such that $\mathrm{cost}(\mathcal{F}) = m \cdot \mathrm{cost}(\hat{H})$ for some $m \in \mathbb{N} \setminus \{0\}$.*

Clearly $\mathcal{F}$ is made of at most $|A|$ wings. Moreover the valuation of each wing in $\mathcal{F}$ is at most $3^{|A|} \times \max_{a \in A} \hat{H}[a]$. Since $\hat{H}$ is obtained from our variant of Kosaraju and Sullivan's algorithm, the size of $\hat{H}$ is polynomial in the size of $\mathcal{S}$. Thus, the size of the valuation of each wing in $\mathcal{F}$ is also polynomial in the size of $\mathcal{S}$.

4.3 An Upper Bound for the Number of Distinct Simple Wings

Since Algorithm 2 terminates in less than $|A|$ iterations, it provides us with a multiset $\mathcal{F}$ of simple wings starting from the arbitrarily fixed state $\hat{q}$ with at most $|A|$ distinct wings. We can make sure that the representative multiset $\mathcal{F}$ contains at most p distinct wings.

This results essentially from Carathéodory's theorem [15, Cor. 7.7i] which states that for each set $X \subseteq \mathbb{Q}^p$ of p-dimensional rational vectors, any rational vector $v \in \mathbb{Q}^p$ that lies in $\mathrm{Cone}(X) = \{\lambda_1 \cdot x_1 + \ldots + \lambda_n \cdot x_n \mid n \geqslant 1; x_1, \ldots, x_n \in X; \lambda_1, \ldots, \lambda_n \in \mathbb{Q}^+\}$ lies in $\mathrm{Cone}(X')$ for some $X' \subseteq X$ with $|X'| \leqslant p$, i.e. $v = \lambda_1 \cdot x_1 + \ldots + \lambda_n \cdot x_n$ with $p \geqslant n \geqslant 1$, $x_1, \ldots, x_n \in X$ and $\lambda_1, \ldots, \lambda_n \in \mathbb{Q}^+$.

Consider a multiset of wings $\mathcal{F} = k_1 \cdot W_1 + \ldots + k_n \cdot W_n$ with $\mathrm{cost}(\mathcal{F}) \geqslant 0$. Carathéodory's theorem ensures that there are rational numbers $\lambda_1, \ldots, \lambda_n \in \mathbb{Q}^+$ such that $\mathrm{cost}(\mathcal{F}) = \lambda_1 \cdot \mathrm{cost}(W_1) + \ldots + \lambda_n \cdot \mathrm{cost}(W_n)$ and $\lambda_i \neq 0$ for at most p values of i. Actually these rational numbers λ_i can be found using linear programming. Further Euclid's algorithm enables us to compute the least common multiple m of the denominators of all λ_i. Then we get $m \cdot \mathrm{cost}(\mathcal{F}) = k_1' \cdot \mathrm{cost}(W_1) + \ldots + k_n' \cdot \mathrm{cost}(W_n) \geqslant 0$ with $k_i' \in \mathbb{N}$ and $k_i' \neq 0$ for at most p values of i. Hence,

Corollary 17. *Let $\hat{H}$ be a non-empty circulation and $\hat{q} \in Q_{\hat{H}}$. We can compute in polynomial time a multiset $\mathcal{F}$ built over at most p distinct simple wings starting from $\hat{q}$ such that $\mathrm{cost}(\mathcal{F}) = m \cdot \mathrm{cost}(\hat{H})$ for some $m \in \mathbb{N} \setminus \{0\}$.*

Since our algorithm is polynomial, the size of the valuation of these wings and the size of the number of occurrences of these wings are polynomial in the size of $\mathcal{S}$.

5   Searching for Minimal Counter-Examples

Shortest counter-examples are usually more valuable in the debugging phase, because they focus on the actual causes of the bug and hence they are easier to understand [3,12]. That is why many verification tools offer to search for an erroneous path with a minimal length, see e.g. with Spin [7]. Several directions can be followed to describe a structural bug of a VASS in a minimal way. Pathological cycles with a minimal length are not that interesting in general because their length can be exponential in the size of the system (Example 6). The first natural approach we consider consists in searching for pathological cycles with a minimal number of distinct arcs. However, with no surprise,

Proposition 18. *Computing a pathological cycle of a VASS with a minimal number of distinct arcs is NP-hard.*

Since multisets of wings with a common starting state are a particular case of cycles and each pathological cycle can be represented by a pathological multiset of wings over the same set of arcs, Prop. 18 applies to the particular case of multisets of wings with a common starting state.

A coordinate $i \in [1..p]$ is said to be *involved* in an arc a if $\mathrm{cost}(a)[i] \neq 0$. The set of interacting coordinates in a cycle collects all coordinates involved in its arcs. A second natural approach aims at minimizing the number of interacting coordinates in a pathological cycle. Again, with no surprise,

Proposition 19. *Computing a pathological cycle of a VASS with a minimal number of interacting coordinates is NP-hard.*

Similarly to Prop. 18, this result applies to pathological multisets of wings with a common starting state. Thus searching for minimal multisets of wings appears to be hard in general.

In this section, we consider the problem of finding a pathological multiset of wings whose component paths have a minimal length. We show how to solve this problem in polynomial time using a separation algorithm. To do so, we fix a starting state $\hat{q}$ and a natural number ℓ and we focus on wings starting from $\hat{q}$ whose component paths have length at most ℓ. We show how to decide whether there exists a pathological multiset made of these wings, and if so, to compute one in polynomial time. In this way, we can minimize the length of the component paths used in a pathological multiset of wings.

5.1   An Upper Bound for the Valuations of Wings

Let $\mathcal{S} = (Q, A)$ be a VASS, $\hat{q} \in Q$ be a fixed state of $\mathcal{S}$ and $\ell \in \mathbb{N}$. For simplicity's sake, *we call length of a wing the maximal length of its component paths*. However, the results presented here can be adapted to the case where the length of a wing is the sum of the lengths of its component paths. We want to determine whether there exists a multiset $\mathcal{F}$ made of wings starting from $\hat{q}$ with length at most ℓ such that $\mathrm{cost}(\mathcal{F}) \geqslant \mathbf{0}$. We observe first that we can restrict the search to wings with a valuation at most equal to 2^{Φ} where Φ is polynomial in the size of $\mathcal{S}$.

Lemma 20. *Let $\mathcal{F}$ be a non-empty multiset of wings starting from $\hat{q}$ with length at most ℓ such that $cost(\mathcal{F}) \geqslant 0$. Let $\Phi = 96 \times p^4 \times size(\mathcal{S})$. Then there exists a non-empty finite multiset $\mathcal{F}'$ of wings starting from $\hat{q}$ with length at most ℓ and valuation at most 2^{Φ} such that $cost(\mathcal{F}') \geqslant 0$.*

Proof. By Cor. 17, there are a positive natural number $n \leqslant p$ and n wings $W_1, ..., W_n$ such that the system (Sys1) of $p + n$ inequalities

$$\sum_{i=1}^{n} k_i \cdot cost(W_i) \geqslant 0$$
$$k_i > 0 \text{ for each } i \in [1..n]$$

has an integral solution. We put $W_i = D_{2i} + k'_i \cdot C_{2i+1}$ where k'_i is the valuation of the wing W_i. We consider now the new system (Sys2) of $p + 2n$ inequalities

$$\sum_{i=1}^{n} k_{2i} \cdot cost(D_{2i}) + k_{2i+1} \cdot cost(C_{2i+1}) \geqslant 0$$
$$k_{2i} > 0 \text{ for each } i \in [1..n]$$
$$k_{2i+1} \geqslant 0 \text{ for each } i \in [1..n]$$

Since (Sys1) has an integral solution, (Sys2) has an integral solution. Any integral solution to (Sys2) corresponds to some multiset $\mathcal{F}$ of wings starting from $\hat{q}$ such that $cost(\mathcal{F}) \geqslant 0$ and for each i, the wing $D_{2i} + k_{2i+1} \cdot C_{2i+1}$ appears once and the wing D_{2i} with valuation 0 appears $k_{2i+1} - 1$ times if $k_{2i+1} \geqslant 1$.

Recall that solving a system of linear Diophantine inequalities is NP-complete. Moreover some integral solution of such a system use polynomial space, only. The matrix from (Sys2) has $p + 2 \times n$ rows and $2 \times n$ columns. The absolute value of each component of this matrix is at most $2 \times |Q| \times v_{\max}$ where $v_{\max}$ is the maximal absolute value of components in vectors carried by arcs in $\mathcal{S}$. We can assume of course that $|A| \geqslant 1$, $|Q| \geqslant 1$ and $p \geqslant 1$. Then $size(\mathcal{S}) \geqslant \lceil \log_2(2 \times |Q| \times v_{\max} + 1) \rceil$. The size of each row is $2 \times n \times \lceil \log_2(2 \times |Q| \times v_{\max} + 1) \rceil \leqslant 2 \times p \times size(\mathcal{S})$. By [15, Cor.17.1b], there exists some integral solution to (Sys2) whose size is at most $6 \times (2 \times p)^3 \times \varphi$, where the facet complexity φ is smaller than $2 \times p \times size(\mathcal{S})$. Thus there is a solution to (Sys2) whose size is at most $96 \times p^4 \times size(\mathcal{S}) = \Phi$. Consequently there exists some integral solution of (Sys2) where each variable k_i satisfies $k_i \leqslant 2^{\Phi}$.   ∎

Note here that the number N of wings starting from $\hat{q}$ with length at most ℓ and valuation at most 2^{Φ} is exponential in the size of $\mathcal{S}$. Let $W_1, ..., W_N$ be an enumeration of these wings. Then the linear program $\sum_{i=1}^{i=N} x[i] \cdot cost(W_i) \geqslant 0$ with $x \in \mathbb{Q}^N$ and $x \geqslant 0$ has a solution if and only if there exists a non-empty multiset $\mathcal{F}$ of wings starting from $\hat{q}$ with length at most ℓ (and valuation at most 2^{Φ}) such that $cost(\mathcal{F}) \geqslant 0$.

We consider actually a kind of dual problem. We define the linear program $LP_{\mathcal{S},\hat{q},\ell}$ for a vector $w \in \mathbb{Q}^p$ of p unknown which consists of the following two sets of constraints:

- $w[i] > 0$, for each $i \in [1..p]$;
- $-cost(W)^{\top} w > 0$, for each wing W starting from $\hat{q}$ with length at most ℓ and valuation at most 2^{Φ}.

By Gordan Theorem [15, p. 95], the linear program $LP_{\mathcal{S},\hat{q},\ell}$ has no solution if and only if there exists some non-negative non-zero linear combination of its row vectors that

---

Algorithm 3. (Separation algorithm)

Require: $\mathcal{S} = (Q, A)$ is a VASS, $w \in \mathbb{Q}^p$, $\hat{q} \in Q$.
Ensure: returns `true` if w is a solution to $LP_{\mathcal{S}, \hat{q}, \ell}$ and some violated inequality otherwise
  if $w \not> \mathbf{0}$ **then**
    return some $i \in [1..p]$ such that $w[i] \leqslant 0$.
  end if
  for $q, q' \in Q$ **do**
    Compute $\mathrm{blmw}_{q,q'}(w) \in \mathbb{Q}$ and a path $\gamma_{q,q'} \in A^*$ in polynomial time
  end for
  for $q \in Q$ **do**
    if (*) $\mathrm{blmw}_{\hat{q},q}(w) + 2^\Phi \times \mathrm{blmw}_{q,q}(w) + \mathrm{blmw}_{q,\hat{q}}(w) \geqslant 0$ **then**
      return the row vector $\mathrm{cost}(\gamma_{\hat{q},q}) + 2^\Phi \cdot \mathrm{cost}(\gamma_{q,q}) + \mathrm{cost}(\gamma_{q,\hat{q}})$
    end if
  end for
  return `true`

---

sum to a non-negative vector, i.e. there exists a non-empty multiset $\mathcal{F}$ of these wings with $\mathrm{cost}(\mathcal{F}) \geqslant \mathbf{0}$.

Corollary 21. *The linear program $LP_{\mathcal{S}, \hat{q}, \ell}$ has no solution iff there exists a non-empty multiset $\mathcal{F}$ of wings starting from $\hat{q}$ with length at most ℓ such that $\mathrm{cost}(\mathcal{F}) \geqslant 0$.*

5.2 Separation of Solutions

The linear program $LP_{\mathcal{S}, \hat{q}, \ell}$ consists of exponentially many inequalities. So we shall not build the whole set of its inequalities. However, we show here how to decide in polynomial time whether a given vector $w \in \mathbb{Q}^p$ is a solution to $LP_{\mathcal{S}, \hat{q}, \ell}$ or not, and, in the latter case, to compute an inequality of $LP_{\mathcal{S}, \hat{q}, \ell}$ for which w fails.

If some component $w[i]$ of w is non-positive, then the constraint $w[i] > 0$ is not satisfied. Thus we may assume that $w > 0$. We denote by $\mathcal{S}/w = (Q, A/w)$ the directed graph obtained from the VASS $\mathcal{S}$ by replacing the label $\mathrm{cost}(a) \in \mathbb{Z}^p$ of each arc $a \in A$ by $\mathrm{cost}(a)^\top w$. For any two states $q, q' \in Q$, we compute the maximal weight $\mathrm{blmw}_{q,q'}(w) \in \mathbb{Q}$ of the paths from q to q' in $\mathcal{S}/w$ with length at most ℓ. We compute also a path $\gamma_{q,q'} \in A^*$ from q to q' with length at most ℓ and such that its weights sum to $\mathrm{blmw}_{q,q'}(w)$ if it is regarded as a path in $\mathcal{S}/w$, i.e. $\mathrm{cost}(\gamma_{q,q'})^\top w = \mathrm{blmw}_{q,q'}(w)$. Note that $\mathrm{blmw}_{q,q}(w) \geqslant 0$ for each $q \in Q$. Let $q \in Q$ be some state of $\mathcal{S}$. If $\mathrm{blmw}_{\hat{q},q}(w) + 2^\Phi \times \mathrm{blmw}_{q,q}(w) + \mathrm{blmw}_{q,\hat{q}}(w) \geqslant 0$ then the wing W built with the path $\gamma_{\hat{q},q}$, followed by 2^Φ iterations of the cycle $\gamma_{q,q}$ and the path $\gamma_{q,\hat{q}}$ satisfies $\mathrm{cost}(W)^\top w \geqslant 0$. Otherwise w is a solution to $LP_{\mathcal{S}, \hat{q}, \ell}$.

Proposition 22. *Let $w \in \mathbb{Q}^p$. We can decide in polynomial time whether w is a solution to $LP_{\mathcal{S}, \hat{q}, \ell}$ or not, and, in the latter case, return an inequality of $LP_{\mathcal{S}, \hat{q}, \ell}$ for which w fails.*

5.3 Computing a Pathological Multiset of Wings with Length at most ℓ

Although the linear program $LP_{\mathcal{S}, \hat{q}, \ell}$ consists of exponentially many inequalities, the fundamental result due to Grötschel, Lovász and Schrijver [15, Th. 14.1] asserts that it is sufficient to design a separation oracle in order to solve this linear program in polynomial time. Given a vector $w > 0$, the separation oracle must decide whether w is a solution to $\mathrm{LP}_{S,\hat{q},\ell}$ or not, and, in the latter case, compute an inequality of $\mathrm{LP}_{S,\hat{q},\ell}$ for which w fails; in other words the separation oracle must compute a wing W with length at most ℓ and valuation at most 2^Φ for which $\mathrm{cost}(W)^\top w \geqslant 0$ whenever w is not a solution to $\mathrm{LP}_{S,\hat{q},\ell}$. We have shown in Subsection 5.2 above how to design such an oracle. As a consequence, we get our second main result:

Theorem 23. *Let $S = (Q, A)$ be a VASS, $\hat{q} \in Q$ be a particular state and ℓ be a natural number. We can decide in polynomial time whether there exists a non-empty multiset $\mathcal{F}$ of wings starting from $\hat{q}$ with length at most ℓ such that $\mathrm{cost}(\mathcal{F}) \geqslant 0$.*

With no surprise, the algorithm designed by Grötschel, Lovász and Schrijver to prove [15, Th. 14.1] can provide us with a certificate that $\mathrm{LP}_{S,\hat{q},\ell}$ has no solution in the form of polynomially many constraints from $\mathrm{LP}_{S,\hat{q},\ell}$ that have no solution. By Gordan Theorem again, we can derive from this certificate a multiset $\mathcal{F}$ of wings with $\mathrm{cost}(\mathcal{F}) \geqslant 0$. Consequently we can find in polynomial time a multiset of wings with a minimal size that describes a pathological cycle for structural termination. Further, we can guarantee that this multiset consists of at most p distinct wings.

6   Conclusion and Future Work

In this paper we tackle the problem of illustrating a structural bug detected in the form of a pathological circulation in a concise way. We propose to represent pathological cycles for structural termination as a set of wings that share a common starting state. Our main result shows how to compute a pathological multiset of wings in polynomial time (Th. 16) from any pathological circulation. Further we need only p distinct wings in such a multiset due to Carathéodory's theorem.

In practice it is interesting to search for pathological cycles (or pathological multisets of wings) with a minimal number of arcs or a minimal number of interacting places. Yet, both problems are NP-hard. Our second result is more theoretical: We have applied the separation technique from [15, Th. 14.1] to prove that one can search for wings whose component paths have a minimal length in polynomial time, too. Interestingly all results presented in this paper apply —or can be easily adapted— to structural boundedness: A VASS is said to be structurally bounded if for each initial configuration the number of reachable configurations is finite. This property corresponds to the non-existence of cycles with a non-negative non-zero cost.

Message Sequence Graphs (MSGs) are a popular formalism to describe communication protocols by means of partial orders of events called Message Sequence Charts [6]. As discussed in [1], MSGs can be regarded as a special case of VASSs when the latter are provided with a partial-order semantics. In this way, new features can be stirred into message sequence graphs such as message loss, message duplication, dynamic process creation, bounded counters or timers, etc. For that reason we found it useful to develop a prototype that implements the model-checking and the reachability techniques from [1]. In the near future our verification tool will benefit from the description of structural bugs by wings presented in this paper.

Acknowledgements. We would like to thank the anonymous reviewer who detected a mistake in the previous version of this paper and whose observations helped us to improve Algorithm 2 and to simplify its proof.

References

1. Avellaneda, F., Morin, R.: Checking partial-order properties of vector addition systems with states. In: International Conference on Application of Concurrency to System Design, pp. 100–109 (2013)
2. Carstensen, H.: Decidability questions for fairness in Petri nets. In: Brandenburg, F.J., Wirsing, M., Vidal-Naquet, G. (eds.) STACS 1987. LNCS, vol. 247, pp. 396–407. Springer, Heidelberg (1987)
3. Clarke, E.M., Grumberg, O., McMillan, K.L., Zhao, X.: Efficient generation of counterexamples and witnesses in symbolic model checking. In: DAC, pp. 427–432 (1995)
4. Cohen, E., Megiddo, N.: Strongly polynomial-time and NC algorithms for detecting cycles in dynamic graphs (preliminary version). In: Johnson, D.S. (ed.) STOC, pp. 523–534. ACM (1989)
5. Diestel, R.: Graph Theory. Springer, Heidelberg (2010)
6. Henriksen, J.G., Mukund, M., Narayan Kumar, K., Sohoni, M.A., Thiagarajan, P.S.: A theory of regular MSC languages. Information and Computation 202(1), 1–38 (2005)
7. Holzmann, G.: The Spin model checker: primer and reference manual, 1st edn. Addison-Wesley Professional (2003)
8. Hopcroft, J.E., Pansiot, J.-J.: On the reachability problem for 5-dimensional vector addition systems. Theoretical Computer Science 8, 135–159 (1979)
9. Iwano, K., Steiglitz, K.: Testing for cycles in infinite graphs with periodic structure (extended abstract). In: Aho, A.V. (ed.) STOC, pp. 46–55. ACM (1987)
10. Karp, R.M., Miller, R.E.: Parallel program schemata. Journal of Computer and System Sciences 3(2), 147–195 (1969)
11. Kosaraju, S.R., Sullivan, G.F.: Detecting cycles in dynamic graphs in polynomial time (preliminary version). In: Simon, J. (ed.) STOC, pp. 398–406. ACM (1988)
12. Kupferman, O., Sheinvald-Faragy, S.: Finding shortest witnesses to the nonemptiness of automata on infinite words. In: Baier, C., Hermanns, H. (eds.) CONCUR 2006. LNCS, vol. 4137, pp. 492–508. Springer, Heidelberg (2006)
13. Lipton, R.J.: The reachability problem requires exponential space. Technical Report 63, Yale University (1976)
14. Memmi, G., Roucairol, G.: Linear algebra in net theory. In: Brauer, W. (ed.) Net Theory and Applications. LNCS, vol. 84, pp. 213–223. Springer, Heidelberg (1980)
15. Schrijver, A.: Theory of linear and integer programming. John Wiley & Sons, Inc., New York (1986)
16. Sifakis, J.: Structural properties of Petri nets. In: Winkowski, J. (ed.) MFCS 1978. LNCS, vol. 64, pp. 474–483. Springer, Heidelberg (1978)
17. Sleator, D.D.: Data structures and terminating Petri nets. In: Simon, I. (ed.) LATIN 1992. LNCS, vol. 583, pp. 488–497. Springer, Heidelberg (1992)

Analysis of Petri Net Models
through Stochastic Differential Equations

Marco Beccuti[1], Enrico Bibbona[2], Andras Horvath[1], Roberta Sirovich[2],
Alessio Angius[1], and Gianfranco Balbo[1]

[1] Università di Torino, Dipartimento di Informatica
{beccuti,angius,horvath,balbo}@di.unito.it
[2] Università di Torino, Dipartimento di Matematica
{roberta.sirovich,enrico.bibbona}@unito.it

Abstract. It is well known, mainly because of the work of Kurtz, that density dependent Markov chains can be approximated by sets of ordinary differential equations (ODEs) when their indexing parameter grows very large. This approximation cannot capture the stochastic nature of the process and, consequently, it can provide an erroneous view of the behavior of the Markov chain if the indexing parameter is not sufficiently high. Important phenomena that cannot be revealed include non-negligible variance and bi-modal population distributions. A less-known approximation proposed by Kurtz applies stochastic differential equations (SDEs) and provides information about the stochastic nature of the process.

In this paper we apply and extend this diffusion approximation to study stochastic Petri nets. We identify a class of nets whose underlying stochastic process is a density dependent Markov chain whose indexing parameter is a multiplicative constant which identifies the population level expressed by the initial marking and we provide means to automatically construct the associated set of SDEs. Since the diffusion approximation of Kurtz considers the process only up to the time when it first exits an open interval, we extend the approximation by a machinery that mimics the behavior of the Markov chain at the boundary and allows thus to apply the approach to a wider set of problems. The resulting process is of the jump-diffusion type. We illustrate by examples that the jump-diffusion approximation which extends to bounded domains can be much more informative than that based on ODEs as it can provide accurate quantity distributions even when they are multi-modal and even for relatively small population levels. Moreover, we show that the method is faster than simulating the original Markov chain.

1 Introduction

Stochastic Petri Nets (SPNs) are a well-known formalism widely used for the performance analysis of complex Discrete Event Dynamic Systems [1,3]. The advantages of modeling with SPNs include their well defined time semantics which often allows the direct definition of the Continuous Time Markov Chain (CTMC) that represents the SPN's underlying stochastic process whose state space is isomorphic to the reachability set of the net. The analysis of real systems often requires the construction of SPN models with huge state spaces that may hamper the practical relevance of the formalism

G. Ciardo and E. Kindler (Eds.): PETRI NETS 2014, LNCS 8489, pp. 273–293, 2014.
© Springer International Publishing Switzerland 2014

and have motivated the development of many techniques capable of reducing the impact of this problem. However, when the model includes large groups of elements (e.g., Internet users, human populations, molecule quantities) most of these techniques may turn out to be insufficient, so that expected values and probability distributions must be estimated with Discrete Event Simulation [7,8]. An alternative to simulation is the approximation of the stochastic model with a deterministic one in which its time evolution is represented with a set of Ordinary Differential Equations (ODEs) whose solution is interpreted as the approximate expected value of the quantities of interest.

The convergence of the solution of the system of ODEs to the expected values of their corresponding quantities, when the sizes of the involved populations grow very large has been the subject of many papers. Most of these are based on the work of Kurtz [13] and have shown that the accuracy of its approximation is acceptable when the model represents a system of large interacting population quantities [18,19]. Unfortunately, there are many cases in which the deterministic approximation is not satisfactory because the obtained approximate expected values give little or even erroneous information about the actual population levels. This happens either when the population sizes are not large enough to rule out the variability of the process and the obtained expected values are not reliable, or when the population distributions are multi-modal, a case in which the mean does not provides much information [17].

In this paper we extend a stochastic approximation of the CTMC that has been introduced in [14] by Kurtz. There, the fluidisation is augmented by a suitable noise term which accounts for the stochasticity of the original system yielding a system of Stochastic Differential Equations (SDEs). Unfortunately the proposed diffusion approximation is only valid up to the first time the system exits a suitable open domain. In real systems however the boundaries of the state space are repeatedly visited (the buffer of a queue may get full, all resources of a system may be in use) and the system can stay there for a finite time and come back to the interior again and again. In these cases, the diffusion approximation proposed in [14] gives a totally incomplete description. We propose an improved approximation which results in a jump diffusion process that visits the boundaries and with jumps that push back the process to the interior of its state space.

The paper is organized as follows. In Section 2, in order to provide the theoretical background of our exposition, we review some of Kurtz's results regarding deterministic and diffusion approximations. In Section 3 we apply these results to SPNs and extend Kurtz's results to treat the barriers of the state space. Numerical experiments are provided in Section 4 and conclusions are drawn in Section 5.

2 Two Fluid Approximations for Density Dependent CTMCs

In this section we give a brief overview of two possible approximations of density dependent CTMCs. Both of these are "fluid" in the sense that the state space of the approximating process is continuous. The first one is the well-known deterministic fluid limit introduced in [13] which employs a set of ordinary differential equations. The second one is the so-called diffusion approximation introduced in [14] which uses SDEs. The decisive difference between the two approximations is that, at any time, the first one provides a single number per random variable of interest (e.g., number of customers in service, number of molecules in a cell), which is usually interpreted as the approximate expected value, while the second one leads to an approximate joint distribution of all the variables of interest.

2.1 Density Dependent CTMCs

In the following we will denote $\mathbb{R}$, $\mathbb{Z}$ and $\mathbb{N}$ the set of real, integer and natural numbers, respectively. Given a positive constant, r, we will denote by $\mathbb{R}^r$ the r–dimensional cartesian product of the space $\mathbb{R}$. The letter u will be dedicated to the time index ranging continuously between $[0,+\infty)$ or $[0,T]$ when specified. The discrete states of a continuous time Markov chain will be denoted as k or h and range in the state space that is included in $\mathbb{Z}^r$. We will always consider the abstract probability space to be given as $(\Omega, \mathscr{F}, \mathbb{P})$, where $\mathbb{P}$ is the probability measure. Furthermore, $\mathbb{E}$ will denote the expectation with respect to $\mathbb{P}$.

Definition 1. *A family of Markov chains $X^{[N]}(u)$ with indexing parameter N and with state space $S^{[N]} \subseteq \mathbb{Z}^r$, is called* density dependent *iff there exists a continuous non-zero function $f : \mathbb{R}^r \times \mathbb{Z}^r \to \mathbb{R}$ such that the instantaneous transition rate (intensity) from state k to state $k+l$ can be written as*

$$q^{[N]}_{k,k+l} = N f\left(\frac{k}{N}, l\right), \quad l \neq 0. \tag{1}$$

In the previous definition, the first argument of the function f can be seen as a normalized state (with respect to the indexing parameter N) of the CTMC and the second argument as a vector that describes the effect of a transition (change of state). Consequently, eq. (1) states that, given a vector l, the intensities depend on the normalized state, k/N, and are proportional to the indexing parameter N. In the following we denote the set of possible state changes by C, i.e., $C = \{l : l \in \mathbb{Z}^r, l \neq 0, q^{[N]}_{k,k+l} \neq 0\}$.

Some important models do not satisfy Definition 1 exactly but are still treatable in the same framework. For this reason we introduce the following more general definition.

Definition 2. *A family of Markov chains $X^{[N]}(u)$ with parameter N and with state space $S^{[N]} \subseteq \mathbb{Z}^r$, is called* nearly density dependent *iff there exists a continuous non-zero function $f : \mathbb{R}^r \times \mathbb{Z}^r \to \mathbb{R}$ such that the instantaneous transition rate (intensity) from state k to state $k+l$ can be written as:*

$$q^{[N]}_{k,k+l} = N\left[f\left(\frac{k}{N}, l\right) + O\left(\frac{1}{N}\right)\right], \quad l \neq 0. \tag{2}$$

Example 1. As an example consider a closed network of r infinite server queues with exponential service time distributions and with N jobs circulating in it. The state space is thus $S^{[N]} = \{k : k \in \mathbb{Z}^r, 0 \leq k_i \leq N, \Sigma_i k_i = N\}$. Let μ_i denote the service intensity of the ith queue, $r_{i,j}$ the routing probabilities with $r_{i,i} = 0$, and $l_{i,j}, i \neq j$, a vector with -1 in position i, $+1$ in position j and 0s elsewhere. Then the transition rates and the functions f are

$$q^{[N]}_{k,k+l} = \begin{cases} k_i \mu_i r_{i,j} & \text{if } l = l_{i,j} \\ 0 & \text{otherwise} \end{cases} \qquad f(y,l) = \begin{cases} y_i \mu_i r_{i,j} & \text{if } l = l_{i,j} \\ 0 & \text{otherwise} \end{cases} \tag{3}$$

and thus that the transition rates are in the form given in eq. (1), with $y = k/N$. For this simple example the transition rates depend only on one component of the state. This is not a necessary condition for a CTMC to be density dependent and in Section 4 we show examples for which this condition does not hold.

In order to gain a better understanding of the property of density dependence, let us introduce some general concepts from the theory of Markov chains. Among the many books devoted to this topic, we refer the reader to [6].

For a general Markov chain $M(u)$ with state space $S \subseteq \mathbb{Z}^r$ and instantaneous transition rates $q_{k,h}$, let us introduce the following key object

$$F_M(k) = \sum_{h \in S} (h - k) q_{k,h} \quad k \in S. \tag{4}$$

The function F_M will be referred to as the *generator* of the chain. Under suitable hypothesis the expectation of $M(u)$ solves the following *Dynkin equation* cf. [6, Chapter 9, Theorem 2.2]

$$\frac{d\mathbb{E}[M(u)]}{du} = \mathbb{E}[F_M(M(u))]. \tag{5}$$

Example 2. For the density dependent CTMC introduced in Example (1), the mth entry of the generator is

$$(F_{X^{[N]}}(k))_m = \sum_{i=1, i \neq m}^{r} k_i \mu_i r_{i,m} - k_m \mu_m$$

Define by $\pi_k(u)$ the transient probabilities and apply the Dynkin equation. We obtain

$$\frac{d(\mathbb{E}[M(u)])_m}{du} = \sum_{k \in E_N} \pi_k(u) \left(\sum_{i=1, i \neq m}^{r} k_i \mu_i r_{i,m} - k_m \mu_m \right)$$

$$= \sum_{i=1, i \neq m}^{r} (\mathbb{E}[M(u)])_i \mu_i r_{i,m} - (\mathbb{E}[M(u)])_m \mu_m$$

which provides a set of ODEs that can be used to calculate the mean queue length of each queue. Note that in general it is not the case that applying the Dynkin equation leads to such ODEs from which the mean quantities can be directly obtained.

In order to bring to the same scale the state spaces of all the CTMCs $X^{[N]}(u)$, it may be convenient to introduce the family of normalized CTMCs as $Z^{[N]}(u) = \frac{X^{[N]}(u)}{N}$, which is also referred to as the density process. Notice that the density process will have state space $\{\frac{k}{N}, k \in \mathbb{Z}^r\}$. Two invariance properties of density dependent CTMCs can then be stated using the normalized chains.

Property 1. If the set of possible state changes C does not depend on N, the density dependence property of the family $X^{[N]}(u)$ is equivalent to require that for the family of the normalized CTMCs, $Z^{[N]}(u)$, the generator does not depend on N. Indeed

$$F_{Z^{[N]}}\left(\frac{k}{N}\right) = \sum_{l \in C} \frac{l}{N} \cdot p_{\frac{k}{N}, \frac{k}{N} + \frac{l}{N}}^{[N]} = \sum_{l \in C} \frac{l}{N} \cdot q_{k,k+l}^{[N]} = \sum_{l \in C} l f\left(\frac{k}{N}, l\right) = F\left(\frac{k}{N}\right) \tag{6}$$

where $p^{[N]}_{\frac{k}{N},\frac{h}{N}}$ and $q^{[N]}_{k,h}$ are the instantaneous transition rates of the processes $Z^{[N]}$ and $X^{[N]}$, respectively. Hence, if the increments l are constant with N, i.e. the set C does not depend on N and comprises elements which are all independent of N, the generator is a function that depends on N only through the state $\frac{k}{N}$. Let us notice that if the family $X^{[N]}(u)$ is only nearly density dependent then $F_{Z^{[N]}}\left(\frac{k}{N}\right) = F\left(\frac{k}{N}\right) + O\left(\frac{1}{N}\right)$.

Property 2. Each element of the family $Z^{[N]}$ solves the same Dynkin equation

$$\frac{d\mathbb{E}[Z^{[N]}(u)]}{du} = \mathbb{E}[F(Z^{[N]}(u))]. \tag{7}$$

The results reported in the following two subsections was demonstrated by Kurtz exploiting the above properties.

2.2 From CTMCs to ODEs

In [13] Kurtz has shown that given a nearly density dependent family of CTMCs $X^{[N]}(u)$, if $\lim_{N\to\infty} Z^{[N]}(0) = z_0$, then, under relatively mild conditions on the generator F given in eq.(6), the density process $Z^{[N]}$ converges (in a sense to be precised) to a deterministic function z which solves the ODE [1]

$$dz(u) = F(z(u))du, \qquad z(0) = z_0. \tag{8}$$

In [13] the following convergence in probability is used: for every $\delta > 0$

$$\lim_{N\to\infty} \mathbb{P}\left\{ \sup_{u\leq T} \left| Z^{[N]}(u) - z(u) \right| > \delta \right\} = 0. \tag{9}$$

where T is the upper limit of the finite time horizon.

The function $z(u)$ is usually interpreted as the asymptotic mean of the process as it solves an equation which is analogous to eq. (7). The difference $Z^{[N]}(u) - z(u)$ can be interpreted as the "noisy" part of $Z^{[N]}(u)$. It was shown in [13] that for $N \to \infty$ the density process $Z^{[N]}(u)$ flattens at its mean value and that the magnitude of the noise is

$$Z^{[N]}(u) - z(u) = O\left(\frac{1}{\sqrt{N}}\right). \tag{10}$$

The result expressed by eq.(9) is often used to approximate the density dependent process $X^{[N]}(u) = N Z^{[N]}(u)$ with the deterministic function $x^{[N]}(u) = N z(u)$, in case of a finite N. In doing so, this approximation disregards the noise term which is now of order $\sqrt{N}$ that is small compared with the order of the mean (that is N), but not in absolute terms. Moreover, it ignores every details of the probability distribution of $X^{[N]}(u)$ except for the mean. It is easy to see that there are cases, e.g., multi-modal distributions, where the mean gives too little information about the location of the probability mass, cf [17].

Let us stress that the convergence holds only if $\lim_{N\to\infty} Z^{[N]}(0) = z_0$, meaning that the corresponding sequence of initial conditions $X^{[N]}(0)$ needs to grow linearly with N. In particular if $X^{[N]}(u)$ is multivariate, each component should grow with the same rate.

---

[1] Eq. (8) is equivalent to the form $\frac{dz(u)}{du} = F(z(u))$. We have chosen the "differential" form written in (8) to be consistent with the notation that will be introduced in Section 2.3 for the stochastic differential equations.

2.3   From CTMCs to SDEs

An approximation of a density dependent family $X^{[N]}$ which preserves its stochastic nature and has a better order of convergence was proposed in [14,15]. It has been shown in [14] that, given an open set $S \subset \mathbb{R}^r$, the density process $Z^{[N]}$ can be approximated by the diffusion process $Y^{[N]}$ with state space S and solution of the following SDE

$$dY^{[N]}(u) = F(Y^{[N]}(u))du + \sum_{l \in C} \frac{l}{\sqrt{N}} \sqrt{f(Y^{[N]}(u), l)} \, dW_l(u) \tag{11}$$

where W_l are independent standard one-dimensional Brownian motions and f is given in eq. (1). The approximation holds up to the first time $Y^{[N]}$ leaves S. A rigorous mathematical treatment of SDEs can be found in [11]. In the physical literature the notation $\frac{dW(u)}{du} = \xi(u)$ is often used even if Brownian motion is nowhere differentiable and $\xi(u)$ is called a *gaussian white noise*. This SDE approach that goes back to the already cited [14,15] has been applied in many contexts, e.g., it is used under the name of *Langevin equations* to model chemical reactions in [9].

The structure of eq. (11) is the following: the first term is the same that appears in eq. (8), while the second term represents the contribution of the noise and is responsible for the stochastic nature of the approximating process $Y^{[N]}$. A further relation between eq. (11) and eq. (8) can be obtained by considering that the stochastic part of the equation is proportional to $1/\sqrt{N}$, meaning that as $N \to \infty$ this term becomes negligible and $Y_\infty(u)$ solves the same ODE written in eq. (8). Let us remark that the construction of such noise is not based on an ad hoc assumption, but is derived from the structure of the generator of the original Markov chain.

As for the relation between the diffusion approximation and the original density process, in [14], it has been proven that, for any finite N, we have

$$Z^{[N]}(u) - Y^{[N]}(u) = O\left(\frac{\log N}{N}\right) \tag{12}$$

which, compared to eq. (10), is a better convergence rate. Thus, the processes $NY^{[N]}(u)$ approximates the density dependent CTMCs $X^{[N]}(u)$ with an error of order $\log N$, much better than the $\sqrt{N}$ of the deterministic fluid approximation.

Finally, let us stress that the approximation is valid only up to the first exit time from the open set S. For many applications the natural state space is bounded and closed and the process may reach the boundary of S in a finite time τ with non-negligible probability. In such cases, since the approximating process $Y^{[N]}(u)$ is no longer defined for any $u \geq \tau$, this approximation is not applicable. To overcome this limitation suitable boundary conditions must be set and this problem, that was considered neither in [14] nor in [15], will be tackled in Section 3.4, representing our main contribution.

3   From SPNs to Fluid Approximations

In this section we first introduce stochastic Petri nets and give a condition under which their underlying CTMC is density dependent. Then, we reinterpret the results discussed in Section 2.2 and 2.3 in terms of SPNs. Finally, we extend the diffusion approximation to bounded domains by adding jumps to the diffusion that mimics the behavior of the original CTMC at the barrier.

3.1 Density Dependent SPNs

Petri Nets (PNs) are bipartite directed graphs with two types of nodes: places and transitions. The places, graphically represented as circles, correspond to the state variables of the system (e.g., number of jobs in a queue), while the transitions, graphically represented as rectangles, correspond to the events (e.g., service of a client) that can induce state changes. The arcs connecting places to transitions (and vice versa) express the relations between states and event occurrences. Places can contain tokens (e.g., jobs) drawn as black dots within the places. The state of a PN, called marking, is defined by the number of tokens in each place. The evolution of the system is given by the occurrence of enabled transitions, where a transition is enabled iff each input place contains a number of tokens greater or equal than a given threshold defined by the multiplicity of the corresponding input arc. A transition occurrence, called firing, removes a fixed number of tokens from its input places and adds a fixed number of tokens to its output places (according to the multiplicity of its input/output arcs).

The set of all the markings that the net can reach, starting from the initial marking through transition firings, is called the Reachability Set (RS). Instead, the dynamic behavior of the net is described by means of the Reachability Graph (RG), an oriented graph whose nodes are the markings of the RS and whose arcs represent the transition firings that produce the corresponding marking changes.

Stochastic Petri Nets (SPNs) are PNs where the firing of each transition is assumed to occur after a delay (firing time) from the time it is enabled. In SPNs these delays are assumed to be random variables with negative exponential distributions [16]. Each transition of an SPN is thus associated with a rate that represents the parameter of its firing delay distribution. Firing rates may be marking dependent. When a marking is entered an exponentially distributed random delay is sampled for each enabled transition according to its intensity. The transition with the lowest delay fires and the system changes marking accordingly.

Here we recall the notation and the basic definitions used in the rest of the paper.

Definition 3. *A stochastic Petri net (SPN) system is a tuple* $\mathcal{N} = (P,T,I,O,\mathbf{m}_0,\lambda)$:

- $P = \{p_i\}_{1 \leq i \leq n_p}$ *is a finite and non empty set of* places.
- $T = \{t_i\}_{1 \leq i \leq n_t}$ *is a finite, non empty set of* transitions *with* $P \cap T = \emptyset$.
- $I,O : P \times T \to \mathbb{N}$ *are the* input, output *functions that define the arcs of the net and that specify their multiplicities.*
- $\mathbf{m}_0 : P \to \mathbb{N}$ *is a multiset on P representing the* initial marking,
- $\lambda : T \to \mathbb{R}$ *gives the* firing intensity *of the transitions.*

The overall effect of a transition is described by the function $L = O - I$. The values assumed by the function I,O and L can be collected in $n_p \times n_t$ matrices (which we still call I,O and L) whose entries are $I(p_i,t_j), O(p_i,t_j)$ and $L(p_i,t_j)$, respectively. By $I(t)$

we denote the column of I corresponding to transition t (the same holds for O and L). The matrix $L = O - I$ is called the *incidence matrix*.

A *marking* (or state) $\mathbf{m}$ is a function $\mathbf{m} : P \to \mathbb{N}$ identified with a multiset on P which can be seen also as a vector in $\mathbb{N}^{n_p}$. A transition t is *enabled* in marking $\mathbf{m}$ iff $\mathbf{m}(p) \geq I(p,t)$, $\forall p \in P$ where $\mathbf{m}(p)$ represents the number of tokens in place p in marking $\mathbf{m}$. Enabled transitions may *fire*, so that the firing of transition t in marking $\mathbf{m}$ yields a new marking $\mathbf{m}' = \mathbf{m} - I(t)^T + O(t)^T = \mathbf{m} + L(t)^T$. Marking $\mathbf{m}'$ is said to be reachable from $\mathbf{m}$ because of the firing of t and is denoted by $\mathbf{m}[t\rangle\mathbf{m}'$. The firing of a *sequence* σ of transitions enabled at $\mathbf{m}$ and yielding $\mathbf{m}'$ is denoted similarly: $\mathbf{m}[\sigma\rangle\mathbf{m}'$.

Let $E(\mathbf{m})$ be the set of transitions enabled in marking $\mathbf{m}$. The enabling degree of transition t in marking $\mathbf{m}$ is defined as

$$\forall t \in E(\mathbf{m}): \ e(t,\mathbf{m}) = \min_{j:I(p_j,t)\neq 0} \left\lfloor \frac{\mathbf{m}(p_j)}{I(p_j,t)} \right\rfloor. \tag{13}$$

which implies that a transition $t \in E(\mathbf{m})$ is enabled in marking $\mathbf{m} - (e(t,\mathbf{m}) - 1)I(t)^T$, but not in marking $\mathbf{m} - e(t,\mathbf{m})I(t)^T$. The notion of enabling degree is particularly useful when a transition intensity is proportional to the number of tokens in the input places of the transition, i.e., when the transition models the infinite server mechanism [1].

In the CTMC that underlies the behavior of an SPN, states are identified with markings and a change of marking of the SPN corresponds to a change of state of the CTMC. If we assume that all the transitions of the SPN use an infinite server policy, then the transition rate from state $\mathbf{m}$ to state $\mathbf{m}'$ in the CTMC can be written as

$$q_{\mathbf{m},\mathbf{m}'} = \sum_{t:L(t)=(\mathbf{m}'-\mathbf{m})} \lambda(t)e(t,\mathbf{m}) \tag{14}$$

where $\lambda(t)$ depends only on the transition and the marking dependence is determined by the enabling degree $e(t,\mathbf{m})$.

A vector $v \in \mathbb{N}^{n_p}$ is called a *P–semiflow* of the SPN if it satisfies $vL = 0$. All P–semiflows of an SPN can be obtained as linear combination of the P–semiflows that are elements of a minimal set. Given a marking $\mathbf{m}$, the quantities $\mathbf{m}v^T$ are invariant and hence equal to $\mathbf{m}_0 v^T$ where $\mathbf{m}_0$ is the initial marking.

Proposition 1. *Let $\mathcal{N} = (P,T,I,O,\mathbf{m}_0,\lambda)$ be an SPN model where all places are covered by P–semiflows and all transitions use an infinite server policy. Let us consider the family $\mathcal{N}^{[N]}$ of SPN models with indexing parameter N obtained from $\mathcal{N}$ by considering an increasing sequence of initial markings $\mathbf{m}_0^{[N]} = N\alpha$ for a given vector α. The corresponding family of CTMCs is nearly density dependent and the marking in each place has a bound which grows at most linearly with N. If the multiplicity of the input arcs are all unitary, the family is also density dependent.*

Proof. Let $\{v^{(\eta)}\}_{\eta=1}^{\kappa}$ denote a minimal set of P–semiflows for $\mathcal{N}$ and, consequently, for any $\mathcal{N}^{[N]}$ (P–semiflows are independent of the initial marking). For each place the marking is bounded by

$$\mathbf{m}(p_j) \leq \min_{\eta:v_j^{(\eta)}\neq 0} \left\{ \frac{\mathbf{m}_0^{[N]}v^{(\eta)T}}{v_j^{(\eta)}} \right\} = N \min_{\eta:v_j^{(\eta)}\neq 0} \left\{ \frac{\alpha v^{(\eta)T}}{v_j^{(\eta)}} \right\}, \tag{15}$$

where $v_j^{(\eta)}$ is the component of the P–semiflow vector $v^{(\eta)}$ that corresponds to the place p_j. By eq. (14) and (13)

$$q_{m,m+l} = \sum_{t:L(t)=l} \lambda(t) \min_{j:I(p_j,t)\neq 0} \left\lfloor \frac{m(p_j)}{I(p_j,t)} \right\rfloor.$$

For any j we have

$$\left\lfloor \frac{m(p_j)}{I(p_j,t)} \right\rfloor = \frac{m(p_j)}{I(p_j,t)} - \frac{R_j}{I(p_j,t)},$$

where $R_j < I(p_j,t)$ is the remainder of the division of $m(p_j)$ by $I(p_j,t)$. So

$$q_{m,m+l} = N \sum_{t:L(t)=l} \lambda(t) \min_{j:I(p_j,t)\neq 0} \left\{ \frac{m(p_j)}{NI(p_j,t)} - \frac{R_j}{N} \right\}$$

$$= N \left[\sum_{t:L(t)=l} \lambda(t) \min_{j:I(p_j,t)\neq 0} \left\{ \frac{m(p_j)}{NI(p_j,t)} \right\} + O\left(\frac{1}{N}\right) \right].$$

By Definition 2, the proposition follows. Notice that when the input arcs are all unitary the remainder is null, $R_j = 0$ for any j, and hence the term disappears and the chain is density dependent.

Let us notice that the hypothesis $m_0^{[N]} = N\alpha$ implies that the initial number of tokens in any place should grow with the same rate N. This means that a family of systems with finite resources cannot be modeled in this framework.

As shown in the proof of Proposition 1, for an SPN in which all places are covered by a P–semiflow, the number of tokens in a place is bounded. The minimal and maximal number of tokens in place p_i will be denoted by $\text{MIN}(p_i)$ and $\text{MAX}(p_i)$, respectively. If $S^{[N]}$ denotes the state space of the CTMC associated to the SPN $\mathcal{N}^{[N]}$, then

$$\text{MIN}(p_i) = \min_{x\in S^{[N]}} x_i, \quad \text{MAX}(p_i) = \max_{x\in S^{[N]}} x_i,$$

where x_i denotes the i–th component of the vector $x \in S^{[N]}$. The following set is a (possibly improper) superset of $S^{[N]}$

$$\hat{S}^{[N]} = \left\{ x \in \mathbb{Z}^{n_p} : \forall i, \text{MIN}(p_i) \leq x_i \leq \text{MAX}(p_i) \text{ and } \forall \eta, x v^{(\eta)T} = m_0 v^{(\eta)T} \right\}. \tag{16}$$

which will help us to define the state space of the approximate models.

3.2   From SPNs to ODEs

Having characterized, in Proposition 1, a family of SPNs whose underlying CTMC family is nearly density dependent, we can apply the results reported in Section 2.2 to construct an approximation by ODEs. In order to provide a direct relation between the SPN family and the ODE approximation, we construct the approximation not for the normalized process $Z^{[N]}$, as it was done by Kurtz, but for the unnormalized $X^{[N]}$.

The state of the system in the ODE approximation will be denoted by $x^{[N]}(u) \in \mathbb{R}^{n_p}$. A given infinite server transition t_i moves "fluid" tokens in state $x^{[N]}(u)$ with speed

$$\sigma(t_i, x^{[N]}(u)) = \lambda(t_i) \min_{j:I(p_j,t_i)\neq 0} \frac{x_j^{[N]}(u)}{I(p_j,t_i)} \qquad (17)$$

which depends on the rate of the transition, $\lambda(t_i)$, and on its *enabling degree*, calculated now at the "fluid" state. The number of tokens in the i-th place is then approximated by the following ODE system:

$$dx_i^{[N]}(u) = \sum_{j=1}^{n_t} \sigma(t_j, x^{[N]}(u)) L(p_i, t_j) du \qquad (18)$$

so that if place p_i is an input (output) place of transition t_j, then transition t_j is removing (adding) tokens from (to) place p_i according to the current speed of the transition and the multiplicity given by function I (O).

It is easy to see that the ODE approximation maintains the same invariance properties, expressed by the P–semiflows, that the original SPN enjoys. Therefore the ODE system is redundant and each P–semiflow in the minimal set can be used to derive one of its components from the others and hence the system can be reduced by as many equations as the number of P–semiflows in the minimal set.

The fluid state space $\hat{G}^{[N]} \in \mathbb{R}^{n_p}$ of the deterministic approximation $x^{[N]}$ is

$$\hat{G}^{[N]} = \left\{ x \in \mathbb{R}^{n_p} : \forall i, \text{MIN}(p_i) \leq x_i \leq \text{MAX}(p_i) \text{ and } \forall \eta, x v^{(\eta)^T} = m_0 v^{(\eta)^T} \right\} \quad (19)$$

that is the convex hull of the set $\hat{S}^{[N]}$ given in eq. (16). Theoretically, the fluid approximation may visit all the points between the boundaries that are compatible with the P–semiflows and the initial markings (gaps are filled). In practice, however, as the model follows a deterministic trajectory, only a n_p dimensional curve is covered. Moreover, if the initial marking belongs to the interior of $\hat{G}^{[N]}$, denoted by $\mathring{G}^{[N]}$, where all the components are strictly between the bounds, then the approximation cannot visit the boundary defined as

$$\overset{\star}{G}^{[N]} = \{ x \in \hat{G}^{[N]} : x_i = \text{MAX}(p_i) \text{ or } x_i = \text{MIN}(p_i), \text{for at least one } i. \} \qquad (20)$$

3.3   From SPNs to SDEs

Under the hypothesis of density dependence, the procedure illustrated in Section 2.3 can be applied in this case too, and the number of tokens in each place can be approximated by the diffusion process $\Upsilon^{[N]}(u) = NY^{[N]}(u)$, with components $\Upsilon_i^{[N]}$ given by the following system of SDEs:

$$d\Upsilon_i^{[N]}(u) = \sum_{j=1}^{n_t} \sigma(t_j, \Upsilon^{[N]}(u)) L(p_i, t_j) du + \sum_{j=1}^{n_t} \sqrt{\sigma(t_j, \Upsilon^{[N]}(u))} L(p_i, t_j) dW_j(u) \quad (21)$$

where each W_j is an independent one-dimensional Brownian motion.

Just like the ODE approximation, also the diffusion approximation enjoys the invariance properties present in the SPN. Thus the size of the system can be reduced by removing one equation for each minimal P–semiflow.

As already remarked, the diffusion approximation $Y^{[N]}$ introduced in Section 2.3 is defined only up to the first exit from an open set and the same holds for $\Upsilon^{[N]}$. The natural state space for the process $\Upsilon^{[N]}$ would be the closed set $\hat{G}^{[N]}$ as defined in eq. (19). However the diffusion approximation is only valid up to the first exit from $\mathring{G}^{[N]}$. If the underlying CTMC is only nearly density dependent a suitable extension of approximation (21) can still be applied.

3.4   From SPNs to SDEs in Bounded Domains

We have already stressed that for an SPN model satisfying the hypothesis of Proposition 1 the number of tokens in each place is bounded between a minimal and a maximal value. In many real examples the CTMC visits some of the states corresponding to a minimal/maximal marking quite often. From a modeling point of view this is not surprising: in Section 4 we revise the epidemiological Susceptible-Infectious-Recovered (SIR) model where it is natural (at least for some ranges of parameters) that the number of infected people is zero for a non-negligible time. We claim that for this kind of processes, both the fluid limit in eq. (18) and the diffusion process in eq. (21) fail to give satisfactory approximations of the original process $X^{[N]}(u)$ for finite N. Numerical evidence of this fact is given in Section 4, Table 2.

An explanation for such a failure is that, when the (possibly improper) state space $\hat{S}^{[N]}$ of the chain is embedded into the fluid state space $\hat{G}^{[N]}$, each state where the marking of a place is minimal or maximal is mapped to the boundary $\hat{G}^{[N]}$. While for finite N the original CTMC may visit the "boundary" often and eventually stay there for a long time, the deterministic fluid limit of Section 3.2 always remains in the interior. On the other hand the diffusion approximation of Section 3.3 is valid only up to the first time it leaves $\mathring{G}^{[N]}$ and hence cannot give a good approximation.

To overcome these difficulties, we abandon the ODE approach and propose here a new approximation that improves the SDE method by carefully introducing a suitable behavior at the boundaries with which we mimic the original chain. In the original CTMC, indeed, the system is described as a pure jump process with discrete events which perfectly takes into account the "boundaries". The SDE approximation of Section 3.3 is a less complex continuous model, but it does not deal with the behavior at the boundaries. The new approximation we propose aims at taking the best from both: time by time that part of the system which is not at the boundary is still fluidified with the SDE approach and the rest, which involves the boundaries, are kept discrete. In particular the resulting process is a jump–diffusion $\tilde{\Upsilon}^{[N]}(u)$ that we will describe in details.

If the process is initialized in $\mathring{G}^{[N]}$, the new approximating process $\tilde{\Upsilon}^{[N]}(u)$ evolves as the diffusion $\Upsilon^{[N]}(u)$ up to the first time it reaches $\overset{\star}{G}{}^{[N]}$. From now on, the set of places P is (dynamically, depending on the current value of $\tilde{\Upsilon}^{[N]}(u)$) split into those that are at the boundary

$$\overset{\star}{P} = \{p_i \in P : \tilde{\Upsilon}_i^{[N]}(u) = \text{MAX}(p_i) \text{ or } \tilde{\Upsilon}_i^{[N]}(u) = \text{MIN}(p_i)\}$$

and those that remain in the interior $\mathring{P} = P - \overset{*}{P}$. At the same time we (dynamically) split the set T of the transitions into those that might move one of the components currently at the boundary

$$\overset{*}{T} = \{t \in T : \exists p_i \in \overset{*}{P} \text{ such that } L(p_i, t) \neq 0\} \tag{22}$$

and those in $\mathring{T} = T - \overset{*}{T}$ that do not affect the places currently in $\overset{*}{P}$. As far as the transitions in $\overset{*}{T}$ do not fire, the subsystem made of the places in $\mathring{P}$ and the transitions in $\mathring{T}$ can still be approximated by a fluid SDE system (in the reduced state space that does not include the components in $\overset{*}{P}$) whose equations are analogous to eq. (21) except that the sums are restricted to the transitions in $\mathring{T}$. The transitions in $\overset{*}{T}$ cannot be fluidified since they include the dynamics of the components at the boundary. We keep them discrete and we encode them into a jump process which is responsible for all the events of the type "place p_i leaves the boundary". The amplitudes and the intensities of the jumps are formally taken from the original CTMC and depend on the complete state of the process. Finally, the approximating jump-diffusion $\tilde{Y}^{[N]}(u)$ which embodies both the fluid evolution and the discrete events solves the following system of SDEs

$$d\tilde{Y}^{[N]}(u) = \sum_{j: t_j \in \mathring{T}} L(t_j) \left(\sigma(t_j, \tilde{Y}^{[N]}(u)) du + \sqrt{\sigma(t_j, \tilde{Y}^{[N]}(u))} \, dW_j(u) \right) + \sum_{i: t_i \in \overset{*}{T}} L(t_i) dM_i^{[N]}(u)$$

$$\tag{23}$$

where $M_i^{[N]}(u)$ is the counting process that describes how many times transition t_i has fired in the time interval $(0, u]$ and whose intensity is given by

$$\mu_i(\tilde{Y}_j^{[N]}(u-)) = \lambda(t_i) \min_{j: I(p_j, t_i) \neq 0} \left\lfloor \frac{\tilde{Y}_j^{[N]}(u-)}{I(p_j, t_i)} \right\rfloor$$

which depends on the actual state of the process $\tilde{Y}^{[N]}$ right before the jump.

Equation (23) has a component for each place in the net. This might seem contradictory with the description we have given above according to which only the places in $\mathring{P}$ are fluidified. Let us however remark that the fluid increments in the first sum of equation (23) do not affect the component at the boundary since if $t_j \in \mathring{T}$ then $L(t_j, p_i) = 0$ for any p_i in $\overset{*}{P}$: their dynamics is solely affected by the jumps. On the other hand a component that is not at the boundary at a given time can reach it due to the continuous compounding of the fluid increments that sums up with the effect of the jumps.

Equation (23) is self-explanatory, but not rigorous since the splitting of T depends on the state and needs to be updated continuously with the evolution of the system. According to the definition (22), at any time u we can decide if a transition t belongs to $\overset{*}{T}$ by looking at the state $\tilde{Y}^{[N]}(u)$ of the system and calculating the following quantity

$$\theta\left(t, \tilde{Y}^{[N]}(u)\right) = \sum_{i=1}^{n_p} |L(p_i, t)| \cdot \mathbf{1}\left(\tilde{Y}_i^{[N]}(u) = \text{MAX}(p_i) \text{ or } \tilde{Y}_i^{[N]}(u) = \text{MIN}(p_i)\right)$$

where $\mathbf{1}(\cdot)$ is the indicator function of the event in parentheses.

Algorithm 1. Algorithm for solving SDE systems

```
 1: function SOLVESSDE(SSDE, step, MaxRuns, FinalTime)
    SSDE = SDE system.
    step = step used in the Euler-Maruyama solution.
    MaxRuns = maximum number of runs.
    FinalTime = maximum time for each run.
    Value= a matrix encoding for each run the SDE value at the current step.
 2:    run=1;
 3:    SSDE.Init(Value);
 4:    while (run ≤ MaxRuns) do
 5:       u = 0.0;
 6:       while (u ≤ FinalTime) do
 7:          Value[run].Copy(PrValue);
 8:          h = step;
 9:          P̊ = SSDE.splitP(Value);
10:          ⟨T̃,T̊⟩=P̊.SplitT();
11:          ⟨t,h⟩ = T̃.Jump(step);
12:          for (SDE ∈ SSDE) do
13:             SDE.computeJump(t,h,Value[run],PrValue);
14:             SDE.computeEuler-Maruyama(Value[run],PrValue,T̊,h);
15:          SSDE.Norm(Value);
16:          u += h;
17:       run++;
18:    return Value.distribution();
19: end function
```

If $\theta\left(u, \tilde{Y}^{[N]}(u)\right) = 0$ then $t \in \mathring{T}$. Accordingly, equation (23) can be recast into the following form

$$
d\tilde{Y}^{[N]}(u) = \sum_{j=1}^{n_t} \mathbf{1}\left\{\theta\left(t_j, \tilde{Y}^{[N]}(u)\right)=0\right\} L(t_j)\left(\sigma(t_j, \tilde{Y}^{[N]}(u))du + \sqrt{\sigma(t_j, \tilde{Y}^{[N]}(u))}\, dW_j(u)\right)
$$
$$
+ \sum_{j=1}^{n_t} \mathbf{1}\left\{\theta\left(t_j, \tilde{Y}^{[N]}(u)\right)\neq 0\right\} L(t_j)\, dM_j^{[N]}(u).
$$

Now we provide in Algorithm 1 a pseudo-code which describes the implementation of the solution of this approximating jump-diffusion, which extends the standard Euler-Maruyama method [12] in order to solve SDEs in which fluid evolution and discrete events coexist. We assume that the reader is familiar with the standard Euler-Maruyama method; for an its complete description the reader can refer to [12].

The algorithm takes in input the model definition represented by the system of SDEs (i.e., SSDE) corresponding to Eq. (23), the maximum Euler-Maruyama step (i.e., step), the maximum number of runs (i.e., MaxRuns), and a final time (i.e., FinalTime) for which the solution is computed; and it returns the distribution of the variables at Final-Time time. A floating point matrix (i.e. Value) of dimensions MaxRuns × |SSDE| is used to store for each run the current value of the variables. In line 3 the method init()

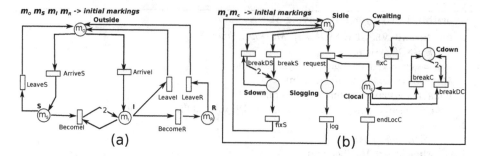

Fig. 1. (a) SPN net inspired by SIR model;   (b) SPN model inspired by PEPA client-server model

initializes the matrix *Value* according to the initial state, so that each run will start from the same initial values. Then for each run, the SDEs are recursively solved until the final solution time (i.e., *FinalTime*) is reached (from line 6 to 16). As previously described the SDEs solution at time u requires some steps: first the set of places is split in the two sub-sets $\overset{\circ}{P}$ and $\overset{*}{P}$ (i.e. line 9, method *SplitP()*), secondly the sets $\overset{*}{T}$ and $\overset{\circ}{T}$ are computed (i.e. line 10, method *SplitT()*). After that the method *Jump()* in line 11 is called to model the jump process which is responsible for all the events moving a place outside its boundaries. Its output is a tuple $\langle t, h \rangle$ which specifies which transition $t \in \overset{*}{T}$ will fire at time $u + h$ with $h \leq step$. Obviously in a time interval $(u, u + step)$ no discrete events could happen (even if $\overset{*}{T} \neq \emptyset$), in this case the method *Jump()* returns the tuple $\langle -1, step \rangle$. Then, for each equation in *SSDE* the method *computeJump()* updates the variables considering the discrete event modeled by t; while the method *computeEuler-Maruyama()* updates the variables considering the fluid evolution accounting only for the events in $\overset{\circ}{T}$. In the end of each step the method *Norm()* is called to normalize all the new computed variables taking into account the P-invariants. Finally the method *distribution()* generates from the final value of the variables the distribution of all the involved quantities.

4   Experimental Results

In this section we report the results obtained from the analysis of two SPN models, to show the quality and the robustness of the approximations obtained with our new approach. The first model depicted in Fig. 1(a) is inspired by the epidemiological Susceptible-Infectious-Recovered (SIR) mathematical representation of this problem originally introduced in [10] and discussed with respect to some of its variants in [4,5]. It describes the diffusion of an epidemic on a large population, and assumes that the population members are part of three sub-populations according to their health status: (a) *susceptible members* (represented in the model by tokens in place S) that are not ill, but that are susceptible to the disease; (b) *infected members* (i.e., tokens in place I) that are subject to the disease and can spread it among susceptible members; (c) *recovered members* (i.e., tokens in place R) that were previously ill and are now immune. Each member of the population typically progresses from susceptible to infectious (i.e., firing of transition *BecomeI*) depending on the number of infected members, and from

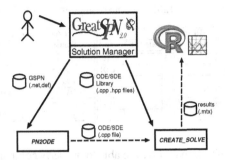

Fig. 2. Framework architecture

infectious to recovered (i.e., firing of transition *BecomeR*). Moreover, members of the population can leave the infected area (i.e., firing of transitions *LeaveS*, *LeaveI* and *LeaveR*) to reach the "outside world" (i.e., place *Outside*) and members of the outside world can enter into the infected area joining the sub-population of the susceptible (i.e., transition *ArriveS*) or infected members (i.e., transition *ArriveI*).

The second model represented in Fig. 1(b) is derived from the the PEPA representation of a Client-Server system studied in [17]. It describes an environment where servers, initially idle (tokens in place *Sidle*), are waiting for a client synchronization (represented by transition *request*). When the synchronization is completed, the client returns to its local computation (i.e., place *Clocal*) until the occurrence of the next synchronization (i.e., transition *endLocCl*), while the server executes an action log before becoming idle again (i.e., transition *log*). An idle server or a client in local computation may fail due to a virus infection (i.e., transitions *breakS* and *breakC*). Moreover an infected server or client can also infect other machines (i.e., transition *breakDS* and *breakDC*). Finally a server or a client recovers only when an anti-malware software discovers the virus (transitions *fixS* and *fixC*). All the experiments performed on these two models have been carried on with a prototype implementation integrated in Great-SPN framework [2], which allows the generation of the ODE/SDE system from an SPN model and then the computation of its solution. The architecture of this prototype is depicted in Fig. 2 where the framework components are presented by rectangles, the component invocations by solid arrows, and the models/data exchanges by dotted arrows. More specifically, GreatSPN is used to design the SPN model and to activate the solution process, which comprises the following two steps:

1. *PN2ODE* generates from an SPN model a C++ file implementing the corresponding ODE/SDE system;
2. *CREATE_SOLVE* compiles the previously generated C++ code with the library implementing the SDE/ODE solvers, and executes it.

Finally the computed results are processed through the R framework to derive statistical information and graphics. All the results have been obtained running these programs on a 2.13 GHz Intel I7 processor with 8GB of RAM.

In the first set of experiments performed on the model of Fig. 1(a), we consider a situation in which the effect of barriers does not influence the correctness/quality of the

Table 1. Transition rates

SIR model			Client Server model	
Transition	rate (1° exp.)	rate (2° 3° exp.)	Transition	rate
ArriveS	0.5	1.0	*log*	12
ArriveI	0.5	0.01	*request*	1
BecomeI	1.0	1.0	*endLocC*	0.2
BecomeR	0.5	0.5	*breakS, breakC*	0.0007 0.00002
LeaveS, LeaveR	0.02	0.02	*breakDS, breakDC*	0.8 1.4
LeaveI	0.1	0.1	*fixS, fixC*	0.001 0.001

solution computed by ODEs, so that we are able to properly compare the ODE approach with our new one. For this purpose, we assume that the initial marking of the model corresponds to a total of 200 people equally distributed over all the places of the model ($m_O = m_S = m_I = m_R = 50$)[2] and that the transition rates are chosen as reported in the second column of Table 1. Observe that we consider only 200 people since we want to compare the results obtained by the ODE and SDE approaches with those derived by solving the CTMC underlying the same SPN model[3], and because we want to stress the reliability of these methods even for cases of large, but not infinite, populations as it would instead be requested by Kurtz's theorem for ensuring the accuracy of the approximations. Fig. 3(a) shows the temporal behavior (i.e., between 0 to 10 time units) of the SIR members computed solving the ODE system. Similar figures obtained from the transient solution of the CTMC at different time points are not explicitly reported on these diagrams, but ensure the reliability of the method in this case. Figs. 3(b) and (c) show instead the temporal behavior of the Infected members as it is obtained by solving the SDE system with 1000 runs and Euler step equal to 0.001. In details, Fig. 3(b) plots the SDE traces (black lines) with respect to the ODE trace that is represented as the white line in the middle of the tick cloud of black lines; Fig. 3(c) reports the average SDE trace computed at specific points in time by considering the values obtained from the Euler simulations and augmented by confidence intervals that support the reliability of the method. The averages of the SDE results are represented in the diagram with the dashed black line. The results obtained with the ODEs are represented instead with a solid red line that lies next to the previous one and that is covered (in any case) by the confidence intervals obtained from the Euler Simulation. Figs. 3(b) and (c) show that the solution quality of both approaches are comparable, but it is important to highlight that the execution time for the two approaches are quite different. Indeed the solution for the ODE system requires $\sim$ 1sec., while that for the SDE model is six times slower ($\sim$ 6sec.). However, we can observe that this overhead in the SDE solution can be justified by the fact that the SDEs provide also the probability distribution of each sub-population at desired specific times. For instance, Fig.3(d) compares the probability distribution of Infected members at time 10 computed with GreatSPN solving the CTMC underlying the same SPN (grey dotted bars) with that computed by the SDEs (black lines) with 1000 runs. A good approximation is obtained with the SDE approach reducing the execution time by a factor of $\sim$ 30 with respect to that of the CTMC solution.

---

[2] This choice is done to avoid the initial barrier effect due to empty places.

[3] The generation of a CTMC from a SPN model and its solution are obtained using the GSPN solvers available in the GreatSPN suite.

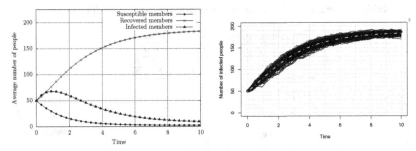

(a) Temporal behavior of the SIR members computed solving ODEs.

(b) Comparison between SDE traces (solid lines) and ODE one (dashed line)

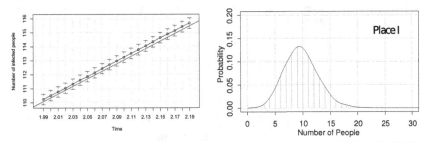

(c) Comparison between average SDE traces (black line) and ODE one (red line)

(d) Comparison between SDEs and CTMC for infected members.

Fig. 3. First SIR experiment

The second set of experiments addresses instead a case where the presence of barriers has a negative effect on the correctness/quality of the solution computed by ODEs, while it is handled correctly by our SDE solution algorithm which is still able to reproduce the expected of the model. To stress this result, we performed this new set of experiments using the same basic model discussed before, where we changed the transition rates as reported in the third column of Table 1 and we assumed that all the population members were originally concentrated in place *Outside* ($m_O = 200$ and $m_S = m_I = m_R = 0$). With this configuration of the model, we can observe that the temporal behavior of the SIR members derived by solving the ODE system disagree with those computed solving the CTMC (see Table 2 second and third columns). This does not contradict Kurzt's theorem since it cannot be directly applied due to the choice of these transition rate values which leads the number of Infected members to be equal to 0 (i.e., corresponding to the lower bound of this quantity) most of the time. Instead our approach based on SDE is still able to cope with this case providing a good approximation for the CTMC solution (i.e., Table 2 second and fourth columns).

In Fig.4 the probability distributions of SIR members at time 100 derived by the CTMC (grey dotted bars) are compared with those computed on the same model by SDE (black lines) with 5000 runs and step 0.01. From these graphs it is clear how our approach is still able to reproduce with a high precision these complex probability

Table 2. Average number of members in each sub-population at time 100

Sub-population	CTMC	ODE	SDE
S	62.636	4.367	61.906 +/-1.55
I	127.965	183.825	128.780 +/-1.48
R	4.280	4.454	4.268 +/-0.04

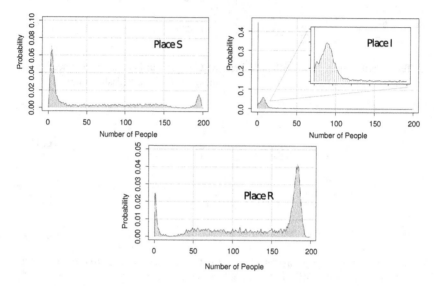

Fig. 4. Second SIR experiment: Comparison between SDEs and CTMC for SIR members

distributions reducing the memory demand (from $\sim$162MB to $\sim$1MB) and the execution time (from $\sim$600s. to $\sim$28s.).

Table 3. Comparing SDE approach with simulation varying the population size

Population	SDE		Simulation	
	Exec. Time	$E[I]_{T=100}$	Exec. Time	$E[I]_{T=100}$
200	128.78 +/-1.48	26s.	128.02+/-1.48	12s.
2,000	73.78 +/-0.19	26s.	73.51+/-0.19	155s.
20,000	735.31+/-0.62	27s.	735.03+/-0.61	20m.
200,000	7352.62+/-0.62	27s.	7352.32+/-0.62	5h.

Finally, to show how our approach scales when increasing the population, we report in Table 3. the results obtained with our method and those computed with (standard) Discrete Event Simulation. The first column of Table 3 reports the population size, the second and third show the average number of infected members at time 100 computed with the SDE approach and the execution time needed for its computation; similarly, the last two columns contain the same information referred to the Discrete Event Simulation. From these results it is clear how our approach is able to obtain a speed-up with respect to the Discrete Event Simulation requiring the same used memory. Obviously this speed-up depends on the characteristic of the model and increases/decreases proportionally to the time spent by the quantities of interest on their boundaries. Indeed, as

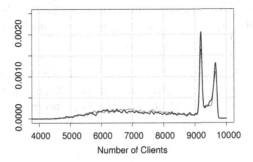

Fig. 5. First client server experiment: comparison between SDEs and Discrete Event Simulation for the distribution of tokens in place *Cwaiting* at time 18

explained in Sec.3, every time that a quantity of interest reaches one of its bounds, our approach uses a classical Discrete Event Simulation to derive its next evolution step.

The last set of experiments is related to the Client Server system and shows how the SDE approach deals with models exhibiting *multi-modal* behavior. Indeed, choosing the transition rates as reported in the last two columns of Table 1 and an initial marking with 120 idle servers and 10,000 clients in local computation, we can observe that the probability distribution of tokens in place *Cwaiting* at time 18, computed thought Discrete Event Simulation, has a multi-modal shape (see Fig.5 dashed light line). In particular, the first mode corresponds to the situation where most of the clients failed, the second one to the situation where only few servers are down and few clients are failed, and the last mode to the situation where most of the servers are down and only few clients are failed. Comparing this dashed line with the black solid line plotting the same measure computed by the SDE approach, we can observe that a good level of approximation is attained by such an approach reducing the computation time by a factor of ~ 13. Indeed, the two lines are often difficult to distinguish (thus showing the good level of agreement between the two methods) thus identifying the modes (picks) of the distributions in a satisfactory manner, even if the absolute values of the two lines are not perfectly matched in these cases.

5   Conclusion

In this paper we considered approximations of SPNs. We identified a class of SPNs for which the underlying stochastic process is a density dependent CTMC. Consequently, it is possible to apply to these SPNs both a deterministic approximation based on ODEs and a diffusion approximation based on SDEs, both being introduced by Kurtz. The diffusion approximation, as presented in its original form, is defined only up to the first exit from an open set. Since in many applications barriers are important, we extended the diffusion approximation by jumps that take into account the behavior of the process on the barriers. We showed by numerical examples that the resulting jump diffusion approximation provides precise information about the distribution of the involved quantities and outperforms the deterministic approach when the original process is with significant variability or it involves distributions whose mean value does not carry much information. Future work will investigate the numerical aspects of the prototype implementation used for the experiments and the possibility of applying these idea to the analysis of hybrid models.

Acknowledgments. We gratefully acknowledge the anonymous referees for their useful suggestions that helped improving the final version of the paper. This work has been supported in part by project "AMALFI " sponsored by Università di Torino and Compagnia di San Paolo.

References

1. Ajmone Marsan, M., Balbo, G., Conte, G., Donatelli, S., Franceschinis, G.: Modelling with Generalized Stochastic Petri Nets. J. Wiley, New York (1995)
2. Babar, J., Beccuti, M., Donatelli, S., Miner, A.S.: GreatSPN enhanced with decision diagram data structures. In: Proceedings of Applications and Theory of Petri Nets, 31st Int. Conference, Braga, Portugal, June 21-25, pp. 308–317. IEEE Computer Society (2010)
3. Balbo, G.: Introduction to Stochastic Petri Nets. In: Brinksma, E., Hermanns, H., Katoen, J.-P. (eds.) FMPA 2000. LNCS, vol. 2090, pp. 84–155. Springer, Heidelberg (2001)
4. Beccuti, M., Franceschinis, G.: Efficient simulation of stochastic well-formed nets through symmetry exploitation. In: Proceedings of the Winter Simulation Conference, WSC 2012, pp. 296:1–296:13. IEEE Computer Society (December 2012)
5. Beccuti, M., Fornari, C., Franceschinis, G., Halawani, S.M., Ba-Rukab, O., Ahmad, A.R., Balbo, G.: From symmetric nets to differential equations exploiting model symmetries. The Computer Journal (2013)
6. Brémaud, P.: Markov chains. Gibbs fields, Monte Carlo simulation, and queues. Texts in Applied Mathematics, vol. 31. Springer, New York (1999)
7. Fishman, G.S.: Principles of Discrete Event Simulation. John Wiley & Sons, Inc., New York (1978)
8. Gaeta, R.: Efficient Discrete-Event Simulation of Colored Petri Nets. IEEE Transactions on Software Engineering 22(9), 629–639 (1996)
9. Gillespie, D.T.: The chemical langevin equation. J. Chem. Phys. 113, 297 (2000)
10. Kermack, W., McKendrick, A.: A contribution to the mathematical theory of epidemics. Proceedings of the Royal Society of London. Series A 115(772), 700–721 (1927)
11. Klebaner, F.C.: Introduction to stochastic calculus with applications, 3rd edn. Imperial College Press, London (2012)
12. Kloeden, P.E., Platen, E.: Numerical solution of stochastic differential equations, vol. 23. Springer (1992)
13. Kurtz, T.G.: Solutions of ordinary differential equations as limits of pure jump Markov processes. Journal of Applied Probability 1(7), 49–58 (1970)
14. Kurtz, T.G.: Limit theorems and diffusion approximations for density dependent Markov chains. In: Stochastic Systems: Modeling, Identification and Optimization, I, pp. 67–78. Springer (1976)
15. Kurtz, T.G.: Strong approximation theorems for density dependent markov chains. Stochastic Processes and Their Applications 6(3), 223–240 (1978)

16. Molloy, M.K.: Performance analysis using stochastic Petri Nets. IEEE Transactions on Computers 31(9), 913–917 (1982)
17. Pourranjbar, A., Hillston, J., Bortolussi, L.: Don't just go with the flow: Cautionary tales of fluid flow approximation. In: Tribastone, M., Gilmore, S. (eds.) UKPEW 2012 and EPEW 2012. LNCS, vol. 7587, pp. 156–171. Springer, Heidelberg (2013)
18. Tribastone, M.: Scalable differential analysis of large process algebra models. In: 7th Int. Conference on the Quantitative Evaluation of Systems, p. 307. IEEE Computer Society, Williamsburg (2010)
19. Tribastone, M., Gilmore, S., Hillston, J.: Scalable differential analysis of process algebra models. IEEE Trans. Software Eng. 38(1), 205–219 (2012)

Dynamic Networks
of Timed Petri Nets

María Martos-Salgado and Fernando Rosa-Velardo*

Sistemas Informáticos y Computación, Universidad Complutense de Madrid
mrmartos@ucm.es, fernandorosa@sip.ucm.es

Abstract. We study dynamic networks of infinite-state timed processes, modelled as unbounded Petri nets. These processes can evolve autonomously, synchronize with each other (e.g., in order to gain access to some shared resources) and be created or become garbage dynamically. We introduce dense time in two different ways. First, we consider that each token in each process carries a real valued clock. We prove that this model can faithfully simulate Turing-complete formalisms and, in particular, safety properties are undecidable for them. Second, we consider locally-timed processes, where each process carries a single real valued clock. For them, we prove decidability of safety properties by a non-trivial instantiation of the framework of Well-Structured Transition Systems.

1   Introduction

Perhaps the most widely known model of real-time systems is that of Timed Automata [6]. Several tools like UPPAAL or KRONOS are available for them. Natural extensions of Timed Automata are Networks of Timed Automata (NTA) [6] or the Networks of Timed Processes in [3]. Both models consider parameterized systems of finite-state processes, each of which is endowed with a real clock.

Petri nets are one of the best known models for concurrent and distributed systems. They have been extended with discrete or continuous time in many works [20,18,21,19,9,5]. In some, transitions have a duration, while in others they fire atomically in some time interval. They also differ in whether time is considered relative to places, transitions or arcs. In [8] an exhaustive comparison of these models is done, and in particular it is proved that the class of Petri nets obtained by adding time constrains to the arcs is more expressive than the classes obtained from adding them to places or transitions. Among this class, in Timed-Arc Petri Nets (*TPN*) [5] each token is endowed with a real-valued clock. In particular, clocks can be dynamically created or destroyed.

Under the so called counting abstraction, one can think that each token in a place s of a Petri net represents a process in state s. Hence, Petri nets can be seen as networks (or products) of finite-state automata. With this intuition in mind, in *TPN* each (finite-state) process has a real-valued clock. Therefore,

---

* Authors supported by the Spanish projects STRONGSOFT TIN2012-39391-C04-04 and PROMETIDOS S2009/TIC-1465.

G. Ciardo and E. Kindler (Eds.): PETRI NETS 2014, LNCS 8489, pp. 294–313, 2014.

they encompass two infinite dimensions: infinitely-many (finite-state) processes and clocks over an infinite (uncountable) domain. In *TPN* arcs are labeled with intervals. Thus, when a token is taken from a place by a transition the value of the clock of the token must be in the interval labeling the corresponding arc, and when a token is put in a place, its clock is set to any real value in the corresponding interval. Moreover, it follows the so called weak semantics in timed systems, in which time delays may happen even when they disable transitions.

We extend the work in [5] by allowing each process to be infinite-state in turn. Hence, our model manages infinitely-many timed processes, each of which is infinite-state (a potentially unbounded Petri net). In this way we can for example easily model dynamic networks of processes accessing shared resources, that can be potentially unbounded.

Dynamic process creation is closely related to parametric verification, when the number of processes is a parameter of the system. Indeed, a standard approach for parametric verification is the addition of an "initialization phase" that spawns an unbounded number of processes (see e.g. [11] for a recent discussion). Hence, our results on verifying dynamic systems can also be seen as results on parametric verification of systems with a fixed number of processes.

As a starting point we consider an untimed model we have developed in previous work [22,23], called ν-*PN*. In ν-*PN* tokens are names, that can be created fresh and matched with other names. Therefore, there can be an unbounded number of different names, each of which can appear an unbounded number of times. Each name can be understood as a process identifier. Hence, ν-*PN* encompass infinitely-many (untimed) processes, each of which can be infinite-state.

We consider two ways in which to introduce time. In the first way we assign a clock to each token in each process. Then, each process is a *TPN*, that can be created fresh and can synchronize with others. We call this model *Timed ν-PN (ν-TPN)*. As in *TPN*, the clock value of each token consumed by a transition must belong to a given interval, as well as for the produced tokens. Moreover, as in ν-*PN*, names can be created and matched. We prove that this model can simulate Turing-complete formalisms and, in particular, even the control-state reachability problem (that of deciding if a given place can be marked) is undecidable.

In the second variant we consider that each process has a single real-valued clock. Since each process is a (concurrent) Petri net, we say these are locally-timed processes, and call them *locally-timed ν-PN (ν-lTPN)*. Hence, we still encompass infinitely-many processes, each of which is infinite-state and is endowed with a real-valued clock.

For ν-*lTPN* we successfully apply the theory of regions of [3]. More precisely, we prove that working with regions we can give ν-*lTPN* a well-structure, so that they belong to the class of Well-Structured Transition Systems [10,1], for which the coverability problem is decidable. This proves that control-state reachability (which can be reduced to coverability) is decidable for them. Moreover, safety properties can be reduced to control-state reachability by standard techniques.

Outline: Section 2 gives notations and results we use throughout the paper. Section 3 defines ν-*TPN* and proves undecidability of control-state reachability for them. In Section 4 we define ν-$lTPN$, and we prove decidability of control-state reachability for them. Finally, in Section 5 we present our conclusions.

2   Preliminaries

Let $\mathbb{N} = \{0, 1, 2, \ldots\}$ and for each $n \in \mathbb{N}$ let us denote $n^+ = \{1, \ldots, n\}$ and $n^* = \{0, \ldots, n\}$. We denote open, closed and mixed intervals of real numbers as (a, c), $[a, b]$ and $[a, c)$ or $(a, b]$, respectively, where $a, b \in \mathbb{N}$ and $c \in \mathbb{N} \cup \{\infty\}$. The set of intervals is denoted by $\mathcal{I}$. Let $\mathbb{R}_{\geq 0} = [0, \infty)$ and for each $x \in \mathbb{R}_{\geq 0}$ we denote by $\lfloor x \rfloor$ and $frct(x)$ the integer and the fractional part of x, respectively.

Well Orders: $(X, \leq)$ is a *partial order* (po)[1] if $\leq$ is a reflexive, transitive and antisymmetric binary relation on X. Let $A \subseteq X$. An element $x \in A$ is *minimal* in A if $x' \in A$ with $x' \leq x$ implies $x = x'$. We denote by $\min(A)$ the set of minimal elements in A. The *upward closure* of $A \subseteq X$ is defined as $\uparrow A = \{x \in X \mid \exists x' \in A,\ x' \leq x\}$. We say A is *upward closed* iff $\uparrow A = A$. A po $(X, \leq)$ is a *well partial order* (wpo) if for every infinite sequence $x_0, x_1, \ldots \in X$ there are i and j with $i < j$ such that $x_i \leq x_j$. Equivalently, a po is a wpo iff $\min(U)$ is finite for every upward closed set U. If X is finite, then $(X, =)$ is a wpo. If $(X, \leq_X)$ and $(Y, \leq_Y)$ are wpos, their product $X \times Y$ is well ordered by $(x, y) \leq (x', y')$ iff $x \leq_X x'$ and $y \leq_Y y'$.

Multisets: A (finite) *multiset* m over X is a mapping $m : X \to \mathbb{N}$ with finite support, that is, such that $supp(m) = \{x \in X \mid m(x) > 0\}$ is finite. We denote by $X^\oplus$ the set of finite multisets over X. For $m_1, m_2 \in X^\oplus$ we define $m_1 + m_2 \in X^\oplus$ by $(m_1 + m_2)(x) = m_1(x) + m_2(x)$ and $m_1 \subseteq m_2$ if $m_1(x) \leq m_2(x)$ for every $x \in X$. When $m_1 \subseteq m_2$ we can define $m_2 - m_1 \in X^\oplus$ by $(m_2 - m_1)(x) = m_2(x) - m_1(x)$. We denote by $\emptyset$ the empty multiset, that is, $\emptyset(x) = 0$ for every $x \in X$, and $|m| = \sum_{x \in supp(m)} m(x)$. We use set notation for multisets when convenient, with repetitions to account for multiplicities greater than one. Given a po $\leq$ over X, we define the po $\leq^\oplus$ over $X^\oplus$ as $\{x_1, \ldots, x_n\} \leq^\oplus \{y_1, \ldots, y_m\}$ if there is an injection $h : n^+ \to m^+$ such that $x_i \leq y_{h(i)}$ for each $i \in n^+$. If $(X, \leq)$ is a wpo then so is $(X^\oplus, \leq^\oplus)$ [13].

Words: Any $u = x_1 \cdots x_n$ with $n \geq 0$ and $x_i \in X$ for all $i \in n^+$ is a (finite) *word* over X. We denote by $X^\circledast$ the set of words over X. If $n = 0$ then u is the empty word, denoted by ϵ. If X is a wpo then so is $X^\circledast$ [13] ordered by $\leq^\circledast$, defined as $x_1 \ldots x_n \leq^\circledast y_1 \ldots y_m$ if there is a strictly increasing mapping $h : n^+ \to m^+$ such that $x_i \leq y_{h(i)}$ for each $i \in n^+$.

Transition Systems: A *transition system* is a tuple $\mathcal{S} = \langle X, \to, x_0 \rangle$ where X is the set of states, $x_0 \in X$ is the initial state and $\to \subseteq X \times X$ is the transition relation. We write $x \to x'$ instead of $(x, x') \in \to$ and we denote by $\to^*$ the reflexive and transitive closure of $\to$. We say $A \subseteq X$ is *reachable* if $x_0 \to^* x$ for some $x \in A$. For $x \in X$ we define $Pre(x) = \{x' \mid x' \to x\}$ and $Pre^*(x) = \{x' \mid x' \to^* x\}$, and extend them pointwise to sets of states. If X is

---

[1] We only work with po (and not quasi-orders).

a po, we can define the *coverability problem*, that of deciding, given U upward closed, whether U is reachable, or equivalently, whether $x_0 \in Pre^*(U)$. All the models in the paper induce transition systems in the obvious way if we provide them with an initial state.

Timed-Arc Petri Nets: A *Timed-Arc Petri Net (TPN)* is a tuple $N = \langle P, T, F, H \rangle$, where P and T are finite disjoint sets of places and transitions, respectively, and $F, H : P \times T \to \mathcal{I}^{\oplus}$. A marking of a *TPN* is a finite multiset M over $P \times \mathbb{R}_{\geq 0}$. Abusing notation, we define $M(p)$ as the multiset of clocks of tokens in place p at M. There are two types of transitions: timed transitions and discrete transitions. Given a marking $M = \{(p_1, d_1) \ldots (p_n, d_n)\}$ and $d \geq 0$, we write $M \xrightarrow{d} M'$ if $M' = \{(p_1, d_1 + d) \ldots, (p_n, d_n + d)\}$. Given $t \in T$ and a marking M we write $M \xrightarrow{t} M'$, if for each $p \in P$ with $F(p,t) = \{I_1, \ldots, I_n\}$ and $H(p,t) = \{J_1, \ldots, J_m\}$, there are $In = \{r_1, \ldots, r_n\}$ and $Out = \{r'_1, \ldots, r'_m\}$ such that $In \subseteq M(p)$, $r_i \in I_i$ for any $i \in n^+$, $r'_j \in J_j$ for any $j \in m^+$ and $M'(p) = (M(p) - Out) + In$. Finally, we write $M \to M'$ iff there is $d \geq 0$ with $M \xrightarrow{d} M'$ or $t \in T$ with $M \xrightarrow{t} M'$.

For an example see the nets in Fig. 1, in which F and H are represented by labelled arcs. Disregard the variables labelling the arcs and the different names in places, considering that all the names are plain tokens • instead. The superscripts of the tokens represent their clocks. In the first net, transition t cannot be fired, as the clocks of tokens do not fit in the intervals of the arcs. However, after an elapse of 1 unit of time, transition t can be fired from the marking represented in the second net, reaching the marking in the third one.

ν-**Petri Nets:** We fix infinite sets Id of names, Var of variables and a subset of special variables $\Upsilon \subset Var$ for fresh name creation. A *ν-Petri Net (ν-PN)* [23] is a tuple $N = \langle P, T, F, H \rangle$, where P and T are finite disjoint sets, and $F, H : T \to (P \times Var)^{\oplus}$ are the input and output functions, respectively. If $(p, x) \in F(t)$ $((p, x) \in H(t))$, we say that there is an arc from p to t (from t to p) labelled by x (among possibly other variables).[2] We call $Var(t) = \{x \in Var \mid \exists p \in P, (p, x) \in F(t) + H(t)\}$. A *marking* is a multiset over $P \times Id$. A *mode* is an injection $\sigma : Var(t) \to Id$. Modes are extended homomorphically to $(P \times Var(t))^{\oplus}$. A transition t is *enabled* with mode σ for a marking M if $\sigma(F(t)) \subseteq M$ and for every $\nu \in \Upsilon$, $(p, \sigma(\nu)) \notin M$ for any p. In that case we have $M \xrightarrow{t} M'$, where $M' = (M - \sigma(F(t)) + \sigma(H(t))$ and $M \to M'$ if $M \xrightarrow{t} M'$ for some $t \in T$. We interpret each name as (the identifier of) a process that can be created, synchronize with other processes or become garbage.

Again, for an example see the second and the third nets in Fig. 1. Tokens are represented as names in places. Disregard the intervals in the arcs and the superscripts of the tokens. Transition t can be fired from the marking represented in the second net, reaching the marking in the third one, with mode σ, with $\sigma(x) = a$, $\sigma(y) = b$ and $\sigma(\nu) = c$. In particular, note that the firing of t creates a new name c in place p_4. See [23,22] for more details.

---

[2] We use this notation following [15].

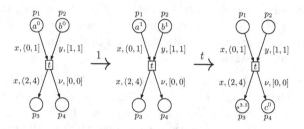

Fig. 1. Firing of transitions in a ν-*TPN*

3 Timed ν-Petri Nets

In this section we define the first extension of ν-*PN* with time, namely Timed ν-Petri nets (ν-*TPN* for short) and we prove the undecidability of control-state reachability for them.

Basically, a ν-*TPN* is a ν-*PN* in which each token has a clock, or equivalently, a *TPN* in which each token has a name. Arcs are labelled by intervals, meaning that the value of the clock of the tokens consumed and produced by the transition must be in these intervals. In Fig. 1 the nets depicted show the same ν-*TPN* with three different markings, in which tokens are depicted as names with its clock as superscript. In the first marking the transition t is not enabled, since the value of the clock of the only token in p_2 is not in $[1, 1]$. After a delay of one unit of time, t becomes enabled, and can be fired reaching, for example, the marking depicted in the right.

Let us define ν-*TPN* formally. Let *Var* be a set of variables with $\Upsilon \subset Var$.

Definition 1 (Timed ν-Petri Nets). *A Timed ν-Petri net (ν-*TPN*) is a tuple $N = \langle P, T, F, H \rangle$, where:*

- *P and T are finite disjoint sets,*
- *$F : T \to (P \times Var \times \mathcal{I})^{\oplus}$ is the input function,*
- *$H : T \to (P \times Var \times \mathcal{I})^{\oplus}$ is the output function.*

For a transition $t \in T$, we take $Var(t)$ as the set of variables adjacent to t, that is, $Var(t) = \{x \in Var \mid \exists p \in P, I \in \mathcal{I}, (p, x, I) \in F(t) + H(t)\}$. In figures, for each $(p, x, I) \in F(t)$ we draw an arc from p to t, labeled by x, I (and analogously for postconditions). For the next definition we consider a fixed infinite set Id of names.

Definition 2 (Markings). *A token of a ν-*TPN* is an element of $P \times Id \times \mathbb{R}_{\geq 0}$. A marking is a finite multiset of tokens.*

We write $p(a, r)$ instead of (p, a, r) to denote tokens. Intuitively, $p(a, r)$ is a token in p, carrying the name a, with clock value r. We use $M, M', M_1, \ldots$ to range over markings. We say M *marks* $p \in P$ if there are $a \in Id$ and $r \in \mathbb{R}_{\geq 0}$

such that $p(a,r) \in M$. We denote $Id(M) = \{a \mid \exists p, r, \ p(a,r) \in M\}$. We assume $\bullet \in Id$, so that black tokens can appear in markings as in ordinary Petri nets. If an arc is not labeled by any variable we assume that the token involved is $\bullet$. Moreover, in figures we do not write the interval $[0, \infty)$. Hence, ordinary notations in Petri nets can be used.

Now, let us define the semantics of ν-TPN. As expected, markings may evolve in two different ways: time elapsing and firing of transitions. Time elapsing is accomplished by simply adding the same amount of time to each token in the net. In order to fire a transition $t \in T$, we assign an identifier to each of the variables in $Var(t)$, and we need to ensure that for each $(p, x, I) \in F(t)$, there is a token $p(a, r)$ in the current marking such that $r \in I$.

Definition 3 (Semantics of ν-TPN). Time elapsing: *Given a marking* $M = \{p_1(a_1, r_1), \ldots, p_n(a_n, r_n)\}$ *and a delay* $d \in \mathbb{R}_{\geq 0}$, *we write* M^{+d} *to denote the marking* $\{p_1(a_1, r_1 + d), \ldots, p_n(a_n, r_n + d)\}$ *in which the value of the clocks of all tokens has increased by* d. *Then we write* $M \xrightarrow{d} M^{+d}$.

Firing of transitions: *Let* $t \in T$ *be a transition with* $F(t) = \{p_1(x_1, I_1), \ldots, p_n(x_n, I_n)\}$ *and* $H(t) = \{q_1(y_1, J_1), \ldots, q_m(y_m, J_m)\}$. *We say* t *is* enabled *or can be fired in marking* M, *evolving to* M', *and we denote it by* $M \xrightarrow{t} M'$, *if there is an injection* $\sigma : Var(t) \to Id$, $r_1, \ldots, r_n \in \mathbb{R}_{\geq 0}$ *and* $r'_1, \ldots, r'_m \in \mathbb{R}_{\geq 0}$ *such that:*

- $r_i \in I_i$ *for all* $i \in n^+$ *and* $r'_j \in J_j$ *for all* $j \in m^+$,
- $\sigma(\nu) \notin Id(M)$ *for all* $\nu \in \Upsilon$,
- $\{p_1(\sigma(x_1), r_1), \ldots, p_n(\sigma(x_n), r_n)\} \subseteq M$,
- $M' = (M - \{p_1(\sigma(x_1), r_1), \ldots, p_n(\sigma(x_n), r_n)\}) + \{q_1(\sigma(y_1), r'_1), \ldots, q_m(\sigma(y_m), r'_m)\}$.

We write $M \to M'$ *if* $M \xrightarrow{t} M'$ *for some* $t \in T$ *or* $M \xrightarrow{d} M'$ *for some* $d \in \mathbb{R}_{\geq 0}$.

As an example, let M_1, M_2 and M_3 be the markings represented in the first, second and third nets in Fig. 1, respectively. Note that $M_1 \xrightarrow{1} M_1^{+1} = M_2$ and $M_2 \xrightarrow{t} M_3$ with mode σ, where $\sigma(x) = a$, $\sigma(y) = b$ and $\sigma(\nu) = c$. We remark that we are defining a weak semantics, in which time elapsings can happen even if they disable transitions. For instance, from M_1 in Fig. 1 two units of time can elapse, which disables the firing of t forever.

The *control-state reachability* problem is that of deciding, given a place p, whether p is marked in some reachable marking (the same definition applies to the rest of the models in the paper).[3] Let us prove undecidability of control-state reachability for ν-TPN. Instead of giving a reduction from a well-known Turing-complete model (as Minsky or Turing machines), we first present a Turing complete model based on Petri nets with identifiers, called ν-RN systems in [22]. Then we reduce control-state reachability in ν-RN, which is undecidable, to our problem. Considering ν-RN considerably simplifies our reduction, since the

---

[3] We use this terminology, even if places are not necessarily control-states.

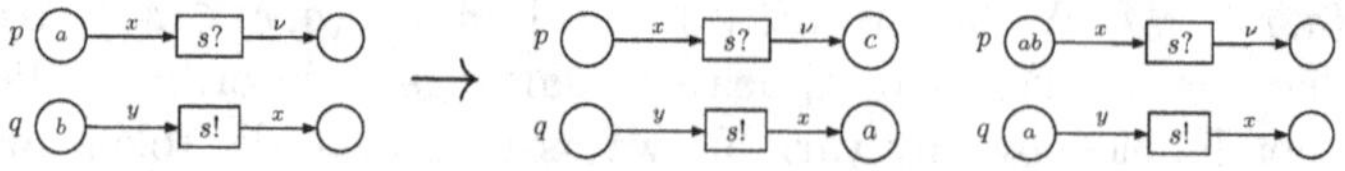

Fig. 2. A ν-RN system and the synchronous firing of the compatible transitions t_1 and t_2, assuming it creates M with $M(p) = \{a, b\}$ and $M(q) = \{a\}$

representation gap between both models is certainly smaller than that obtained if we considered a better known Turing-complete formalism.[4]

We briefly present ν-RN systems. For more details see [16,22]. Intuitively, a ν-RN system is just a collection of ν-PN that can synchronize with each other, and that can create replicas of themselves (hence the name, ν-Replicated Nets). For synchronization purposes, we consider a set $\mathcal{L}$ of transition labels.

A ν-RN *system* is a tuple $N = \langle P, T, F, H, \lambda \rangle$, where $\langle P, T, F, H \rangle$ is a ν-PN and $\lambda : T \to \mathcal{L}$ labels transitions for two different purposes. On the one hand, it specifies how a transition can be fired: whether it is an autonomous transition, that can be fired in isolation, or a synchronizing transition, that must be fired synchronously with another transition. On the other hand, it indicates which new instances (if any) are created by its firing. An *instance* of N is a multiset over $P \times Id$ (i.e., a marking of the underlying ν-PN). A *marking* of N is a multiset of instances of N. Therefore, in ν-RN each instance contains tokens, possibly with different names. A synchronous firing can happen whenever two compatible transitions (having labels $s?$ and $s!$) are enabled, according to the enabling condition of ν-PN. In that case they can both be fired simultaneously, following the ordinary token game of ν-PN. In particular, names can be moved along the nets, be communicated between instances and be created fresh. Moreover, firings may create new instances (see Fig. 2).

The control-state reachability problem for ν-RN is that of deciding whether some reachable marking marks a given place. The model of ν-RN is Turing-complete [22], and termination for Turing machines can be easily reduced to control-state reachability for ν-RN. Hence control-state reachability is undecidable for ν-RN.

Proposition 1. *Control-state reachability is undecidable for ν-TPN.*

Proof. We reduce control-state reachability for ν-RN systems to our problem. Given a ν-RN $N = \langle P, T, F, H, \lambda \rangle$, we build a ν-TPN $N' = \langle P', T', F', H' \rangle$ which simulates it. In particular, we build N' such that $P \subset P'$, and a place $p \in P$ can be marked in N iff it can be marked in N'. Without loss of generality, we suppose that the initial marking of every instance consists of a single (black) token in a place $p_0 \in P$. Moreover, we assume that only autonomous transitions may create new instances.

---

[4] Even a reduction from Petri nets with inhibitor arcs, which are also Turing-complete, needs to fill a much bigger representation gap. Informally, inhibitor nets are close to counter machines, while ν-RN systems and ν-TPN are somewhat close to Turing machines.

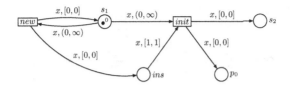

Fig. 3. Creation of instances

Intuitively, we represent each instance of N by a multiset of tokens with the same clock value in N'. The construction guarantees that all the transitions in N' use only tokens with clocks set to 1. Hence, tokens with clocks older than 1 are dead tokens, that cannot be used for the firing of transitions. In order to allow instances not to become dead, we will add transitions that reset tokens with clock 1 to 0. These transitions may not reset every token with clock 1, in which case some tokens are lost (after the elapsing of time). Therefore, in some simulations some tokens are lost, but there are also perfect simulations in which no tokens are lost. In this sense our simulation is lossy, though it preserves control-state reachability, since loosing tokens can only remove behavior (no spurious behavior is introduced). We also guarantee in our construction that we do not merge instances, that is, that no two tokens with different clock values may end up having the same value.

Executions in N' simulate executions of N in two steps: In the first step N' creates an unbounded number of tokens with different clock values, which represent all the instances that may take part in the simulation. The second step is the simulation itself. We consider in N' two places s_1 and s_2 (marked in mutual exclusion) to specify in which of the two steps the simulation currently is.

Step 1 (creation of instances): In the first step, depicted in Fig. 3, we repeatedly fire a transition new, which creates new tokens with clock 0 in place ins. The clock of each token in ins will represent a different instance of N, so that we need to ensure that they are all different. We do that by forcing some time elapsing between two consecutive firings of new, by demanding that the token in s_1 is strictly older than 0 when new is fired (and setting it back to 0). Initially, there is only one token in place s_1, with clock 0.

The firing of a transition $init$ concludes step 1, by moving the token in s_1 to s_2 when the token in s_1 has a non-null clock. It also sets the initial marking of N, by taking a token of clock vale 1 from ins and putting it in p_0, with clock 0. Notice that this guarantees that the clock value of the token in the initial instance is different from all the clock values of the tokens in ins.

Step 2 (simulation of transitions): As mentioned before, only tokens with clocks between 0 and 1 (both included) are valid tokens, that represent a token in some instance. Step 1 guarantees that at the beginning of step 2 there are no two tokens having clocks set to 0 and 1, respectively. Moreover, at any point in step 2, two tokens in P with clocks 0 and 1 belong to the same instance. Now we show how we reset the clock of tokens, and how we simulate the firing of autonomous transitions (possibly creating a fresh instance), and the synchronization of two compatible transitions.

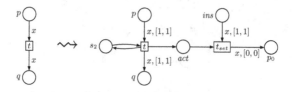

Fig. 4. Simulation of the firing of t, assuming t creates a fresh instance

Reseting Tokens: In order to be able to perform perfect (non-lossy) simulations, we need to be able to reset the clock of tokens with value 1. For that purpose, for each place $p \in P'$ we add a transition t_p which takes from p a token of clock 1 and puts it back with clock set to 0.[5] Formally, $F'(t_p) = \{(p, x, [1, 1])\}$ and $H'(t_p) = \{(p, x, [0, 0])\}$. Notice that this is correct because before reseting there are no tokens with clock set to 0.

Simulation of the Firing of a Transition: The simulation of the (autonomous) transition $t \in T$ is simply achieved by demanding that the clock of all tokens involved in the firing is set to 1. Thus, we consider $t \in T'$, and we attach the interval $[1, 1]$ to every arc adjacent to t. More precisely, if $(p, x) \in F(t)$ then $(p, x, [1, 1]) \in F'(t)$ (and analogously for postconditions). We also add s_2 as pre/postcondition of t. Moreover, if t creates a fresh instance, it puts a token in a new place act. Intuitively, we store in act a token for each instance that the simulation has created, but that has not been initialized yet. In order to initialize new instances, we add a new transition t_{set}, which takes a token from act and a token with clock value 1 from ins, and puts a token in p_0 with clock set to 0, analogously as $init$ (see Fig.4). Again, notice that when there is a token with clock value 1 in ins there is no token with clock 0 in the whole net, so that we are correctly creating the new instance.

Simulation of Synchronizing Transition: Let us see how we simulate the firing of $u = (t_1, t_2) \in T \times T$, where t_1 and t_2 are two compatible transitions according to λ.(see Fig. 5). We simulate u by means of the consecutive firing of transitions $start_u^1$, $start_u^2$, $\overline{u}$, end_u^1 and end_u^2 in T'. We guarantee (thanks to s_2 and new control places, not shown in Fig. 5) that these transitions can only be fired in the order shown, and that $start_u^1$ can only be fired when there is a token in s_2 (no simultaneous simulations of firings can take place).

Let us consider in P' new places, $role^1$ and $role^2$ (whose content can also be reseted, as explained above), and for each $p \in P$ let us consider $\overline{p} \in P'$. The firing of $start_u^1$ removes the tokens from the preconditions p of t_1 with clock value 1 and puts them in the corresponding $\overline{p}$ (with any value for the clock). More precisely, if $(p, x) \in F(t_1)$ then $(p, x, [1, 1]) \in F'(start_u^1)$ and $(\overline{p}, x, [0, \infty)) \in H'(start_u^1)$. Moreover, a token (with any name, e.g. a black token) is added to $role^1$ with clock value 1. The case of $start_u^2$ is analogous.

---

[5] It is enough to reset places in which the clock is meaningful, unlike e.g. s_2.

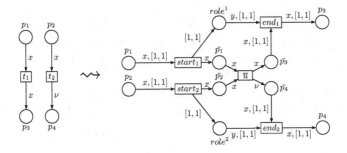

Fig. 5. Synchronizing transitions

The firing of $\overline{u}$ simulates the firing of u (that is, the simultaneous firing of t_1 and t_2) in the overlined places. More precisely, if $(p, x) \in F(t_i)$ for $i \in \{1, 2\}$ then $(\overline{p}, x, [0, \infty)) \in F'(\overline{u})$ (and analogously for postconditions). In particular, it checks that names in different places are matched according to the variables in the arcs, and new names are created if needed. Notice that if the names selected by $start_u^1$ and $start_u^2$ do not match then $\overline{u}$ is disabled. Hence, our simulation may introduce deadlocks, though it still preserves control-state reachability. Notice also that this firing can take place independently of the clocks of the tokens involved.

Finally, transitions end_u^1 and end_u^2 set the clocks of the tokens involved in the firing of u to their correct values. For that purpose, end_u^i takes the token from $role^i$ with clock value 1, and for every p postcondition of t_i it takes the token in $\overline{p}$ and puts it in p with clock value 1. More precisely, for $i = 1, 2$, $(role^i, y, [1, 1]) \in F'(t_i)$ (where y is a *fresh* variable), and if $(p, x) \in H(t_i)$ then $(\overline{p}, x, [0, \infty)) \in F'(end_u^i)$ and $(p, x, [1, 1]) \in H'(end_u^i)$.

The previous simulation preserves control-state reachability. Indeed, if p is marked by some execution of N, then that execution can be perfectly simulated, ending up in a marking that marks p. Conversely, if p is marked by some execution of N', by construction that execution corresponds to the simulation of some execution of N which also marks p (possibly with more tokens, if some were lost).

4   Locally-Timed ν-*PN*

In the previous section we have seen that even control-state reachability is undecidable for ν-*TPN*. Now we define the class of locally-timed ν-*PN* (ν-*lTPN*), for which each instance has a single clock. ν-*lTPN* can be obtained as a syntactic restriction of ν-*TPN*, ensuring that each instance uses only one clock. One way to do it is to consider a special place in which we store a token of each name in the net, whose clocks represents the age of the corresponding instance. However, in order to have simpler notations, we prefer to define ν-*lTPN* from scratch[6].

---

[6] Read-only constraints could also be considered within the same setting. However, for simplicity, we do not consider them in this paper.

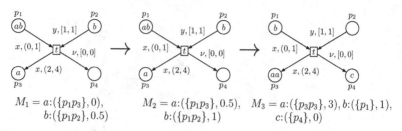

$$M_1 = a{:}(\{p_1p_3\},0),$$
$$b{:}(\{p_1p_2\},0.5)$$

$$M_2 = a{:}(\{p_1p_3\},0.5),$$
$$b{:}(\{p_1p_2\},1)$$

$$M_3 = a{:}(\{p_3p_3\},3), b{:}(\{p_1\},1),$$
$$c{:}(\{p_4\},0)$$

Fig. 6. Firing of a transition in a ν-$lTPN$

Definition 4 (Locally-timed ν-PN). *A* locally-timed ν-PN *(ν-lTPN) is a tuple $N = \langle P, T, F, H, \mathcal{G}\rangle$, where:*

- *P and T are finite disjoint sets,*
- *for $t \in T$, $F_t, H_t : Var \to P^\oplus$ are the input and output functions of t,*
- *for $t \in T$, $\mathcal{G}_t : Var \to \mathcal{I} \times \mathcal{I}$ is the time constraints function of t.*

For each $t \in T$ we define $Var(t) = \{x \in Var \mid F_t(x) + H_t(x) \neq \emptyset\}$, which is assumed to be finite, and we split it into $nfVar(t) = Var(t) \setminus \Upsilon$ and $fVar(t) = Var(t) \cap \Upsilon$. In fact, $\mathcal{G}_t$ only needs to be defined in $Var(t)$.

Definition 5 (Markings). *A marking M of a ν-lTPN is an expression of the form $a_1{:}(m_1, r_1), ..., a_n{:}(m_n, r_n)$, where $Id(M) = \{a_1, ..., a_n\} \subset Id$ are pairwise different names, and for each $i \in n^+$, $\emptyset \neq m_i \in P^\oplus$ and $r_i \in \mathbb{R}_{\geq 0}$.*

We treat markings of ν-lTPN as multisets over elements of the form $a{:}(m, r)$, which we call *instances*. Hence, $a : (m, r)$ is an instance with name a, tokens according to m, and clock with value r. We assume that each m_i in each instance is not empty. We use M, M',... to range over markings, and say a marking M *marks* $p \in P$ if there is $a{:}(m, r) \in M$ such that $p \in m$.

Definition 6 (Time delay). *Given $M = a_1{:}(m_1, r_1), ..., a_n{:}(m_n, r_n)$ and $d \in \mathbb{R}_{\geq 0}$, we write M^{+d} to denote the marking $a_1{:}(m_1, r_1 + d), ..., a_n{:}(m_n, r_n + d)$, in which the clock of every instance has increased by d. We write $M \xrightarrow{d} M^{+d}$.*

Again, we are defining a weak timed semantics. Now we define the firing of transitions, for which we need the following notations. We denote by $\mathcal{G}_t^1(x)$ and $\mathcal{G}_t^2(x)$ the first and second component of $\mathcal{G}_t(x)$, respectively. Intuitively, for a transition to fire the instance corresponding to x must have a clock value in $\mathcal{G}_t^1(x)$. This clock is set to any value in $\mathcal{G}_t^2(x)$. We say M' is an $\emptyset$-*expansion* of a marking M (or M is the $\emptyset$-*contraction* of M') if M is obtained by adding instances $a{:}(\emptyset, r)$ to M.

Definition 7 (Firing of transitions). *Let $t \in T$ with $nfVar(t) = \{x_1, ..., x_n\}$ and $fVar(t) = \{\nu_1, ..., \nu_k\}$. We say t is enabled at marking M if:*

- *$M = a_1 : (m_1, r_1), ..., a_n : (m_n, r_n) + \overline{M}$, for some $\overline{M}$,*
- *for each $i \in n^+$, $F_t(x_i) \subseteq m_i$ and $r_i \in \mathcal{G}_t^1(x_i)$.*

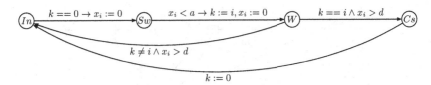

Fig. 7. Timed automaton modelling the i-th process of Fischer's mutual exclusion protocol

Then, t can be fired, *and taking*

- $\{b_1, ..., b_k\}$ *pairwise different names not in* $Id(M)$,
- $m_i' = (m_i - F_t(x_i)) + H_t(x_i)$ *for all* $i \in n^+$,
- $m_j'' = H_t(\nu_j)$ *for all* $j \in k^+$,
- r_i' *any value in* $\mathcal{G}_t^2(x_i)$, *for all* $i \in n^+$,
- r_j'' *any value in* $\mathcal{G}_t^2(\nu_j)$, *for all* $j \in k^+$,

we can reach M', *denoted by* $M \xrightarrow{t} M'$, *where* M' *is the* $\emptyset$-*contraction of*

$$a_1:(m_1', r_1'), ..., a_n:(m_n', r_n'), b_1:(m_1'', r_1''), ..., b_k:(m_k'', r_k'') + \overline{M}$$

Let us give two examples to illustrate the previous definitions.

Example 1. Fig. 6 depicts a ν-*lTPN* with three different markings. In the first marking the transition t is not fireable, because no instance with a clock value in $[1, 1]$ has a token in place p_2. However, after waiting 0.5 units of time, the marking M_2 is reached, and t becomes enabled. Then, we can fire t reaching, for example, the marking M_3 in the figure.

Example 2. Fischer's protocol: We model a parameterized version of Fischer's protocol for mutual exclusion, which considers n processes p_i (where n is a parameter), each of those endowed with a real clock x_i. Moreover, a shared integer variable $k \in \{1, ..., n\}$ is considered, in order to set the turn for entering the critical section. Each process p_i can be modelled by the timed automaton of Fig. 7, and behaves as follows:

```
1  repeat
2    non critical section          7    until k==i;
3    repeat                        8    critical section;
4      await k==0;                 9    k:=0;
5      k:=i;                       10   non critical section
6      delay(d);                   11 until false;
```

Process p_i repeatedly tries to enter the critical section (state In). For that purpose, it waits until $k = 0$, which means that no other process is in the critical section (state Sw). Then, it sets $k := i$, to ask for permission to enter (state W). After a delay of d units of time, if k is still i, the process enters the critical section (state Cs), setting $k = 0$ when it leaves. Otherwise, it repeats lines $4-6$. In order to make the algorithm satisfy the mutual exclusion property, it is important to fix a proper delay d, greater than the time a it takes each process to execute line 5. Then in Fig. 7 we take $a < d$.

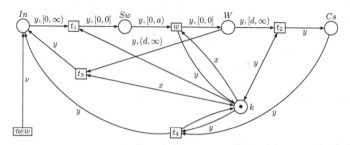

Fig. 8. Fischer's mutual exclusion protocol as a ν-$lTPN$

Let us define our model: We consider the net depicted in Fig 8. Intuitively, each token in places In, Sw, W and Cs represents a different instance. The variable k is represented by a place k that contains a black token if $k = 0$ or a token with the identifier that changed its value last. When a transition t is fired, if there are two different variables $x, y \in Var(t)$, then the names of the tokens associated to x and y in the firing are different (hence checking if $k == i$). Notice the transition new, that can create any number of processes in their initial state. To prove mutual exclusion, we have to prove that no marking with two tokens in place Cs can be reached, which can be easily reduced to control-state reachability.

You can note that the timed automaton in Fig. 7 modelling Fischer's protocol and our parametric model are very similar. In [2], the authors model Fischer's protocol using TPN. As they do not use colors, they need to use the counting abstraction (hence considering the state space of each process and the shared variable), and the obtained model is far more complicated than ours.

The state space of ν-$lTPN$ is infinite in various dimensions. It encompasses infinitely-many instances, each of which is potentially unbounded, and contains a clock over an uncountable domain. Moreover, as any marking has infinitely-many successors due to time delays, the transition system induced by a ν-$lTPN$ is not finitary. Next, we use the theory of regions to obtain a finitary transition system over a countable domain. Moreover, this transition system will be a Well-Structured Transition System [1,10], so that we can solve the control-state reachability problem by reducing it to a coverability problem. The proofs omitted from this section can be found in [16].

We fix a ν-$lTPN$ $N = \langle P, T, F, H, \mathcal{G} \rangle$ and simply denote by max the maximum integer bound appearing in the intervals of the net. Also, we write n_∞^* to denote $n^* \cup \{\infty\}$. Following [3,5], we represent markings of N using *regions*.

Definition 8 (Regions). *A region is an expression of the form $A_0 * A_1 * \ldots A_n * A_\infty$ with $n \geq 0$, where $A_i \in (P^\oplus \times I_i)^\oplus$ for every $i \in n_\infty^*$ and $I_0 = \max^*$, $I_i = (\max -1)^*$ for $i \in n^+$ and $I_\infty = \{\max +1\}$. We write $|R| = \sum_{i \in n_\infty^*} |A_i|$.*

We assume $A_i \neq \emptyset$ for any $i \in n^+$, and $m \neq \emptyset$ for all $(m, r) \in A_i$, for any $i \in n_\infty^*$. We use $R, R', \ldots$ to range over regions and $\mathcal{R}, \mathcal{R}', \ldots$ to range over sets of regions. Let us intuitively explain their meaning. Each marking M of a ν-$lTPN$ has a region R_M associated to it. To obtain it, we partition the instances in M into three multisets:

- The multiset M_1 of instances with an integer clock value of at most max,
- The multiset M_2 of instances younger than max, with a non-integer clock value,
- The multiset M_3 of instances older than max.

Then we put instances in M_1 in A_0, with the information about their clocks (though forgetting their names). Moreover, we keep in $A_1 \ldots A_n$ the instances in M_2, ordered according to the fractional part of their clocks, and storing only their integer part. Finally, we put instances in M_3 in A_∞, abstracting its clocks to max $+1$. Let us see it formally.

Definition 9 (Region of a marking). *Let M be a marking. We define the region $R_M = A_0 * A^{x_1} * \ldots * A^{x_n} * A_\infty$ where:*

- $|R_M| = |M|$, $x_1, \ldots, x_n \in (0,1)$ *and* $i < j$ *iff* $x_i < x_j$,
- $A_0 = \{(m,r) \mid a{:}(m,r) \in M, \ r \in \max^*\}$,
- $A^x = \{(m, \lfloor r \rfloor) \mid a{:}(m,r) \in M, r < \max, frct(r) = x\}$,
- $A_\infty = \{(m, \max +1) \mid a{:}(m,r) \in M, \ r > \max\}$.

Example 3. Let $M = a_1{:}(\{p\}, 1), a_2{:}(\{p\}, 1.1), a_3{:}(\{q\}, 2.1), a_4{:}(\{p,q\}, 1.2), a_5{:}$ $(\{pq\}, 3.1), a_6{:}(\{p,q\}, 3)$, and max $= 3$. Then, $R_M = A_0 * A_1 * A_2 * A_\infty$, with $A_0 = \{(\{p\}, 1), (\{p,q\}, 3)\}$ (which represents the two instances with integer clock value), $A_1 = \{(\{p\}, 1), (\{q\}, 2)\}$, $A_2 = \{(\{p,q\}, 1)\}$ (corresponding to the two different fractional parts, ordered) and $A_\infty = \{(\{pq\}, 4)\}$ (the only instance with clock value greater than max). Note that $x_1, \ldots, x_n$ above are not part of the definition of R_M.

Let us define the transition system over regions induced by N.

Time Elapsing: There are two ways in which time may elapse in regions. If $A_0 \neq \emptyset$, the region may evolve to $\emptyset * A_0^< * A_1 * \ldots * A_n * (A_\infty + A_0^=)$, where $A^< = \{(m,r) \in A \mid r < \max\}$ and $A^= = \{(m, \max +1) \mid (m, \max) \in A\}$, which corresponds to a small elapsing of time that makes all the instances in A_0 to have a non-integer clock value, and so that the instances in A_n do not reach an integer value. Notice that instances in A_0 with clock max are added to A_∞. Otherwise, when $A_0 = \emptyset$, the region may evolve to $A_n^{+1} * A_1 * \ldots * A_{n-1} * A_\infty$, where $A^{+1} = \{(m, r + 1) \mid (m, r) \in A\}$, which represents an elapsing of time that causes the instances in A_n (those with a higher fractional part) to reach the next integer part. Formally:

Definition 10 (Time elapsing for regions). *Let $R = A_0 * A_1 * \ldots * A_n * A_\infty$ be a region. We write $R \xrightarrow{\delta} R'$, where*

$$R' = \begin{cases} \emptyset * A_0^< * A_1 * \ldots * A_n * (A_\infty + A_0^=) & \text{if } A_0 \neq \emptyset \\ A_n^{+1} * A_1 * \ldots * A_{n-1} * A_\infty & \text{otherwise} \end{cases}$$

Example 4. Consider the region $R_M = A_0 * A_1 * A_2 * A_\infty$ of Ex.3. As $A_0 \neq \emptyset$ and $max = 3$, according to the first case of the previous definition, it holds that $R_M \xrightarrow{\delta} R'$, where $R' = \emptyset * A_0^< * A_1 * A_2 * (A_\infty + A_0^=)$, $A_0^< = \{(\{p\}, 1)\}$ and $A_0^= = \{(\{p, q\}, 4)\}$.

Firing of Transitions: In order to define the firing of transitions for regions we first need to define $\emptyset$-expansions/contractions for them.

Definition 11 ($\emptyset$-expansion/contraction). *We say R' is an $\emptyset$-expansion of a region $R = A_0 * A_1 * \ldots * A_n * A_\infty$ (or R is the $\emptyset$-contraction of R') if R' is of the form $A_0' * u_0 * A_1' * u_1 * \ldots * A_n' * u_n * A_\infty'$ and for each i:*

- *$A_i' = A_i + B_i$ with $m = \emptyset$ for all $(m, r) \in B_i$,*
- *$u_i = B_1^i * \ldots * B_{k_i}^i$ with $k_i \geq 0$ and $m = \emptyset$ for all $(m, r) \in B_j^i$.*

Example 5. Consider again the region R_M of Ex.3. $R_\emptyset = A_0 * A_1' * B * A_2 * A_\infty$, with $A_1' = \{(\{p\}, 1), (\{q\}, 2), (\emptyset, 1)\}$ and $B = \{(\emptyset, 1), (\emptyset, 2)\}$ is an $\emptyset$-expansion of R_M. Note that we have added to A_1 the pair $(\emptyset, 1)$, and a new multiset B, with only empty instances.

Now, we define the firing of transitions for regions. Intuitively, a transition t is enabled at a region if we can assign to each variable $x \in Var(t)$ with $x \notin \Upsilon$ a pair (m, r) in some multiset A_i of the region, in such a way that $F_t(x) \subseteq m$ and the clock that represents the pair is in $\mathcal{G}_t^1(x)$. Then, the transition can be fired, reaching a new region in which we update the markings of the pairs assigned to each variable according to F_t and H_t, and we update the clocks of the pair according to $\mathcal{G}_t^2$. Moreover, we possibly need to remove some of the pairs we have chosen from some A_i they are in, and put them in a different A_j, according to one of the possible clocks they may represent. Finally, for each $\nu \in \Upsilon$, we put a new pair $(H_t(\nu), r)$ in a proper (and maybe new) multiset of the region. In order to make the previous assignments, we define *modes* for regions. For any interval I, we call *left closure of I* the result of replacing the left delimiter of I by a closed one (for instance, the left closure of (a, b) is $[a, b)$).

Definition 12. *Given a transition $t \in T$ and an $\emptyset$-expansion $A_0 * A_1 * \ldots * A_n * A_\infty$ of a region R, let $l = |Var(t)|$. A mode for t and R is any tuple $\tau = (\tau_1, \tau_2, \tau_3)$ where $\tau_1 : Var(t) \to (n_\infty^* \times l^+)$ is an injection, and $\tau_2 : Var(t) \to (\max + 1)^*$ and $\tau_3 : Var(t) \to n_\infty^* \cup (n^* \times l^+)$ are mappings such that:*

- *For all $x \in Var(t)$, $\tau_2(x)$ is in the left closure of $\mathcal{G}_t^2(x)$,*
- *if $\tau_2(x) > \max$ then $\tau_3(x) = \infty$,*
- *if $\mathcal{G}_t^2(x) = (a, b]$ or $\mathcal{G}_t^2(x) = (a, b)$ and $\tau_2(x) = a$ then $\tau_3(x) \neq 0$.*

Intuitively, τ_1, τ_2 and τ_3 assign to each variable of t an instance of the region to perform the firing, the clock value to which we update this instance and the new position in the region that the instance takes, respectively. The first condition above ensures that the integers we choose to update the clocks of the instances are correct according to $\mathcal{G}_t^2(x)$. The second condition makes sure that instances older than max are stored in A_∞. The third condition ensures that the created instances with a clock value of integer part a, but not exactly a, are not stored in A_0. Let us now define the firing of transitions for regions.

Definition 13. *We say a transition t is enabled at a region R if there is an $\emptyset$-expansion $A_0 * A_1 * \ldots * A_n * A_\infty$ of R and a mode $\tau = (\tau_1, \tau_2, \tau_3)$ such that for each $i \in n_\infty^*$ there is $\bar{A}_i = \{(m_{ij}, r_{ij}) \mid \tau_1(x) = (i, j)\} \subseteq A_i$ and for each $x \in Var(t)$ with $\tau_1(x) = (i, j)$:*

- *If $x \in \Upsilon$, then $m_{ij} = \emptyset$,*
- *$F_t(x) \subseteq m_{ij}$,*
- *$r_{ij} \in \mathcal{G}_t^1(x)$ if $i \in \{0, \infty\}$, and $r_{ij} + 0.5 \in \mathcal{G}_t^1(x)$, otherwise.*

Then, we define $m'_{ij} = (m_{ij} - F_t(x)) + H_t(x)$ and take for all $k \in n^*$ and $b \in l^+$:

- *$B_k = A_k - \bar{A}_k$,*
- *$D_k = \{(m'_{ij}, r) \mid \exists x \in Var(t) \text{ with } \tau_1(x) = (i, j), \tau_2(x) = r, \tau_3(x) = k\}$,*
- *$C_k = B_k + D_k$ and*
- *$C_{kb} = \{(m'_{ij}, r) \mid \exists x \in Var(t) \text{ with } \tau_1(x) = (i, j), \tau_2(x) = r, \tau_3(x) = (k, b)\}$.*

Then, we write $R \xrightarrow{t} R'$, where R' is the $\emptyset$-contraction of $C_0 * C_{01} * \ldots * C_{0l} * C_1 * C_{11} * \ldots * C_{1l} * \ldots * C_n * C_{n1} * \ldots * C_{nl} * C_\infty$.

Intuitively, for each $i \in n_\infty^*$, $\bar{A}_i$ represents the multiset of instances selected by τ_1 from the multiset A_i which take part in the firing. Therefore, B_i is the multiset obtained after removing from A_i the instances corresponding to the preconditions. Finally, C_i represents B_i after adding the postconditions, and the C_{ij}s represent multisets of instances which we assign to clocks with fractional parts not appearing in R. Note that between two C_is we add l C_{ij}s. This is so to handle the case in which all the instances update their clocks to values with a fractional part between the ones represented by C_i and C_{i+1}.

Example 6. Let t be a transition with:

- $F_t(x) = \{p\}$,
- $H_t(x) = \{q\}$, $H_t(\nu) = \{pq\}$,
- $\mathcal{G}_t^1(x) = (0, 3]$, $\mathcal{G}_t^2(x) = (1, 2)$ and $\mathcal{G}_t^2(\nu) = (1, 3)$.

Then, we could consider the mode $\tau = (\tau_1, \tau_2, \tau_3)$ for t and the region R_M in Ex.3, where:

- $\tau_1(x) = (2, 1)$,
- $\tau_2(x) = 1$, $\tau_2(\nu) = 2$,
- $\tau_3(x) = (2, 1)$ and $\tau_3(\nu) = 1$.

According to the previous definition, we can fire t from R_M with mode τ, reaching a new marking $R' = A_0 * A'_1 * A_{21} * A_\infty$, where $A'_1 = \{(\{p\}, 1), (\{q\}, 2), (\{pq\}, 2)\}$ and $A_{21} = \{(\{q^2\}, 1)\}$. Note that A'_1 comes from adding $(\{pq\}, 2)$ to A_1, which represents that the new instance (associated to ν) is created with a clock with fractional part as the ones represented in A_1. Moreover, the multiset A_2 dissapears, as we have removed from it the only instance it contained. Finally, a new multiset A_{21} is created, with the instance associated to variable x.

Let $\overset{\Delta}{\twoheadrightarrow}$ be the reflexive and transitive closure of $\overset{\delta}{\twoheadrightarrow}$ and $\twoheadrightarrow = \overset{\Delta}{\twoheadrightarrow} \cup \bigcup_{t \in T} \overset{t}{\twoheadrightarrow}$.

Proposition 2. *The following relations between $\rightarrow$ and $\twoheadrightarrow$ hold:*

- *If $M \longrightarrow^* M'$ then $R_M \twoheadrightarrow^* R_{M'}$,*
- *If $R_M \twoheadrightarrow^* R'$ then there is M' with $R' = R_{M'}$ and $M \longrightarrow^* M'$.*

The proof of the previous proposition can be found in [16]. We omit it from this paper because it is rather technical. However, there is a point which would be interesting to focus in, which is how we manage the elapsings of time. In Def. 10 there are two ways time may elapse, depending on the region we consider. Both ways correspond to a small elapse, of less than a unit of time. However, we need to be able to represent longer elapsings. Prop. 2 can be proved because $\overset{\Delta}{\twoheadrightarrow}$ is defined as the reflexive and transitive closure of $\overset{\delta}{\twoheadrightarrow}$, and therefore, we can concatenate as many small elapsings as we need, in order to represent longer elapsings of time.

Let us next see that we can reduce the control-state reachability problem to a coverability problem in ν-$lTPN$ using regions. In the first place, we must define an order over regions, which induces the corresponding coverability problem.

Definition 14 (Order over regions). *We define $(m, r) \leq (m', r')$ iff $m \subseteq m'$ and $r = r'$. Then, we define $A_0 * A_1 * \ldots * A_n * A_\infty \sqsubseteq B_0 * B_1 * \ldots * B_m * B_\infty$ iff $A_0 \leq^\oplus B_0$, $A_\infty \leq^\oplus B_\infty$ and $A_1 \ldots A_n \leq^{\oplus \circledast} B_1 \ldots B_m$.*

Notice that we are using the word order induced by the multiset order, and therefore $\sqsubseteq$ is a decidable wpo. The order $\sqsubseteq$ induces a coverability problem in the transition system with regions as states, and we can reduce control-state reachability to it.

Proposition 3. *Given $p \in P$ we can compute a finite set of regions $\mathcal{R}_p$ such that p is marked by some reachable marking iff $\uparrow \mathcal{R}_p$ can be reached.*

A *Well Structured Transition System* (WSTS) is a tuple $\mathcal{S} = \langle X, \rightarrow, x_0 \leq \rangle$, where $\langle X, \rightarrow, x_0 \rangle$ is a transition system, and $\leq$ is a decidable wpo on X, such that (i) for all $x_1, x_2, x_1' \in X$ such that $x_1 \leq x_1'$ and $x_1 \rightarrow x_2$ there is $x_2' \in X$ such that $x_1' \rightarrow x_2'$ and $x_2 \leq x_2'$ (compatibility); (ii) $\min(\uparrow Pre(\uparrow x))$ is computable for every $x \in X$ (effective *Pre*-basis).[7] Coverability is decidable for WSTS [1,10].

Since $\sqsubseteq$ is a decidable wpo, in order to prove that the transition system over regions induced by a ν-$lTPNN$ is a WSTS, it only remains to prove that the transition relation is compatible with the order, and that the effective *Pre*-basis property holds. We prove both properties by first proving that they hold for $\overset{\Delta}{\twoheadrightarrow}$ and $\overset{t}{\twoheadrightarrow}$, and then considering the union of them. In particular, in order to prove the effective *Pre*-basis, we split *Pre* into $Pre_\Delta(R) = \{R' \mid R' \overset{\Delta}{\twoheadrightarrow} R\}$ and $Pre_t(R) = \{R' \mid R' \overset{t}{\twoheadrightarrow} R\}$, and we we define $\overline{Pre}_\Delta$ and $\overline{Pre}_t$ for each $t \in T$, so

---

[7] This class is actually referred to as effective WSTS with strong compatibility and effective *Pred*-basis in the literature.

that $Pre_\Delta(\uparrow R) = \uparrow\overline{Pre}_\Delta(R)$ and $Pre_t(\uparrow R) = \uparrow\overline{Pre}_t(R)$. These proofs are rather technical, and therefore, we prefer to omit them from this paper. From the fact that the transition system we have defined is a WSTS and Prop. 3 above, we obtain the following result:

Corollary 1. *Control-state reachability is decidable for ν-lTPN.*

5   Conclusions and Future Work

We have introduced real time in a model of dynamic networks of processes that encompasses two sources of infinity: processes can be infinite-state, and there can be infinitely-many such processes. Despite there are previous works in which real time is studied in such Turing-powerful concurrent systems, as in [7], up to our knowledge, this is the first work in which real time is considered for this kind of concurrent systems, in which safety properties are still decidable. In the first model considered, ν-TPN, each process is endowed with an arbitrary amount of real clocks, while in the second one, ν-lTPN, only one clock per process is allowed. While control-state reachability (whether a given place can be marked) is undecidable in the first model, we have shown that we can use the theory of regions to prove decidability of this property in the second. With regions as state space, we prove that ν-lTPN belong to the class of WSTS, for which coverability is decidable. In [17], we compare ν-lTPN with other classes of WSTS, proving that they are the most expressive of the studied classes. In particular, we prove that *TPN* are strictly less expressive than ν-lTPN, using coverability languages for their comparison.

As future work, we plan to study the expressive power of models in between ν-TPN and ν-lTPN, in which a fixed number (possibly greater than one) of clocks is allowed, and the relation of ν-lTPN to the existing works that model GALS (globally asynchronous locally synchronous) systems using Petri nets [14]. In a different line, we have assumed that processes (or their identifiers) are not ordered in any way. It would be interesting to see whether our work scales in the case of ordered processes, which amounts to extend Data Nets [15] with time.

Regarding complexity, since ν-lTPN are more expressive than Data Nets or *TPN* [17], we can already obtain a lower bound for coverability and termination at level $F_{\omega^{\omega^\omega}}$ [12] in the fast-growing hierarchy. It would be interesting to know if this lower bound is tight, though we may expect it is not, due to the higher order types of the state space in ν-lTPN.

Although we have not discussed properties other than control-state reachability, the properties of termination and boundedness are still decidable for ν-lTPN. Indeed, termination is decidable for WSTS under rather general hypothesis, as well as boundedness.[8] Other directions for further study include other properties, as the existence of Zeno behaviors [4] (actually, the first step in the proof of Prop. 1 exhibits such behavior), or liveness properties, although negative results in the untimed case are discouraging [23].

---

[8] For boundedness compatibility must be strict, as we claim is the case for ν-lTPN.

References

1. Abdulla, P.A., Cerans, K., Jonsson, B., Tsay, Y.-K.: Algorithmic analysis of programs with well quasi-ordered domains. Inf. Comput. 160(1-2), 109–127 (2000)
2. Abdulla, P.A., Deneux, J., Mahata, P., Nylén, A.: Forward reachability analysis of timed Petri nets. In: Lakhnech, Y., Yovine, S. (eds.) FORMATS/FTRTFT 2004. LNCS, vol. 3253, pp. 343–362. Springer, Heidelberg (2004)
3. Abdulla, P.A., Jonsson, B.: Verifying networks of timed processes (Extended abstract). In: Steffen, B. (ed.) TACAS 1998. LNCS, vol. 1384, pp. 298–312. Springer, Heidelberg (1998)
4. Abdulla, P.A., Mahata, P., Mayr, R.: Dense-timed Petri nets: Checking zenoness, token liveness and boundedness. Logical Methods in Computer Science 3(1) (2007)
5. Abdulla, P.A., Nylén, A.: Timed Petri Nets and BQOs. In: Colom, J.-M., Koutny, M. (eds.) ICATPN 2001. LNCS, vol. 2075, pp. 53–70. Springer, Heidelberg (2001)
6. Alur, R., Courcoubetis, C., Henzinger, T.A.: The observational power of clocks. In: Jonsson, B., Parrow, J. (eds.) CONCUR 1994. LNCS, vol. 836, pp. 162–177. Springer, Heidelberg (1994)
7. Bashkin, V.A., Lomazova, I.A., Novikova, Y.A.: Timed resource driven automata nets for distributed real-time systems modelling. In: Malyshkin, V. (ed.) PaCT 2013. LNCS, vol. 7979, pp. 13–25. Springer, Heidelberg (2013)
8. Boyer, M., Roux, O.H.: On the compared expressiveness of arc, place and transition time Petri nets. Fundam. Inform. 88(3), 225–249 (2008)
9. de Frutos Escrig, D., Ruiz, V.V., Marroquín Alonso, O.: Decidability of properties of timed-arc Petri nets. In: Nielsen, M., Simpson, D. (eds.) ICATPN 2000. LNCS, vol. 1825, pp. 187–206. Springer, Heidelberg (2000)
10. Finkel, A., Schnoebelen, P.: Well-structured transition systems everywhere! Theor. Comput. Sci. 256(1-2), 63–92 (2001)
11. Geeraerts, G., Heussner, A., Praveen, M., Raskin, J.-F.: ω-petri nets. In: Colom, J.-M., Desel, J. (eds.) PETRI NETS 2013. LNCS, vol. 7927, pp. 49–69. Springer, Heidelberg (2013)
12. Haddad, S., Schmitz, S., Schnoebelen, P.: The ordinal-recursive complexity of timed-arc Petri nets, data nets, and other enriched nets. In: LICS, pp. 355–364. IEEE (2012)
13. Higman, G.: Ordering by Divisibility in Abstract Algebras. Proc. London Math. Soc. s3-2(1), 326–336 (1952)
14. Kleijn, J., Koutny, M.: Localities in systems with a/sync communication. Theoretical Computer Science 429, 185 (2012)
15. Lazic, R., Newcomb, T., Ouaknine, J., Roscoe, A.W., Worrell, J.: Nets with tokens which carry data. Fundam. Inform. 88(3), 251–274 (2008)
16. Martos-Salgado, M., Rosa-Velardo, F.: Dynamic networks of timed Petri nets. Technical Report 9/13, DSIC Universidad Complutense de Madrid (2013), http://antares.sip.ucm.es/~frosa/
17. Martos-Salgado, M., Rosa-Velardo, F.: Expressiveness of dynamic networks of timed petri nets. In: Dediu, A.-H., Martín-Vide, C., Sierra-Rodríguez, J.-L., Truthe, B. (eds.) LATA 2014. LNCS, vol. 8370, pp. 516–527. Springer, Heidelberg (2014)
18. Merlin, P., Farber, D.: Recoverability of communication protocols–implications of a theoretical study. IEEE Transactions on Comm. 24(9), 1036–1043 (1976)

19. Pezzè, M.: Time Petri nets. In: Proceedings of the Multi-Workshop on Formal Methods in Performance Evaluation and Applications (1999)
20. Ramchandani, C.: Analysis of asynchronous concurrent systems by timed Petri nets. Technical report, Cambridge, MA, USA (1974)
21. Razouk, R.R., Phelps, C.V.: Performance analysis using timed Petri nets. In: Yemini, Y., Strom, R.E., Yemini, S. (eds.) PSTV, pp. 561–576. North-Holland (1984)
22. Rosa-Velardo, F., de Frutos-Escrig, D.: Name creation vs. replication in Petri net systems. Fundam. Inform. 88(3), 329–356 (2008)
23. Rosa-Velardo, F., de Frutos-Escrig, D.: Decidability and complexity of Petri nets with unordered data. Theor. Comput. Sci. 412(34), 4439–4451 (2011)

A Framework for Classical Petri Net Problems: Conservative Petri Nets as an Application

Ernst W. Mayr and Jeremias Weihmann

Technische Universität München, 85748 Garching, Germany
{mayr,weihmann}@informatik.tu-muenchen.de
http://www14.in.tum.de/personen/index.html.en

Abstract. We present a framework based on permutations of firing sequences and on canonical firing sequences to approach computational problems involving classes of Petri nets with arbitrary arc multiplicities. As an example of application, we use these techniques to obtain **PSPACE**-completeness for the reachability and the covering problems of conservative Petri nets, generalizing known results for ordinary 1-conservative Petri nets. We also prove **PSPACE**-completeness for the RecLFS and the liveness problems of conservative Petri nets, for which, in case of ordinary 1-conservative Petri nets, **PSPACE**-membership but no matching lower bound has been known. Last, we show **PSPACE**-completeness for the containment and equivalence problems of conservative Petri nets. **PSPACE**-hardness of the problems mentioned above still holds if they are restricted to ordinary 1-conservative Petri nets.

1 Introduction

In [14], Mayr presented a non-primitive recursive algorithm for the general Petri net reachability problem, thus proving its decidability. For many restricted Petri net classes, a better complexity of the reachability problem can be shown. However, the nets of most Petri net classes for which the complexity of the reachability problem could be refined are forward-ordinary, i. e., they are subject to the restriction that all arcs from places to transitions have multiplicity 1. Well-known examples for such classes with **NP**-complete reachability problems are communication-free Petri nets (cf-PNs, also known as BPP-PNs), [2, 19], conflict-free Petri nets [6], normal Petri nets, and sinkless Petri nets [7] (for the latter two, the promise problem variation of the reachability problem was considered). Notable examples for Petri net classes without restrictions on arc multiplicities, and with matching lower and upper bounds for the reachability problem are single-path Petri nets [5] (**PSPACE**-complete), reversible Petri nets [1, 15] (**EXPSPACE**-complete), and generalized communication-free Petri nets (gcf-PNs, **PSPACE**-complete) [16] (which are also known as join-free Petri nets [17], and are similar to forward-concurrent-free Petri nets [13]). For a more comprehensive overview we refer to [3].

It is well known that the reachability problem of Petri nets with arbitrary arc multiplicities can be reduced in polynomial time to the reachability problem of ordinary Petri nets. However, such reductions usually do not conserve

G. Ciardo and E. Kindler (Eds.): PETRI NETS 2014, LNCS 8489, pp. 314–333, 2014.

given (topological) restrictions. Hence, the existence of such reductions does not automatically imply that such a reduction can be performed for a class of general Petri nets that are, for instance, topologically restricted to the corresponding problem involving the corresponding class of ordinary Petri nets. Furthermore, it cannot be ruled out (in particular as long as common assumptions like $\mathbf{NP} \subsetneq \mathbf{PSPACE}$ are not proven to be false) that such a reduction conserving given restrictions is either impossible to begin with or needs superpolynomial time. An example for this observation is the case of cf-PNs and gcf-PNs. Another problem in context of Petri nets with arbitrary arc multiplicities is that nice characterizations of, for instance, reachable markings are hard to find. In some cases, even if such characterizations exist, they are algorithmically hard to check.

One reason is the relationship between places and transitions: In forward-ordinary Petri nets, the firing of a transitions puts enough tokens to each output place such that these places are not responsible for preventing any of their output transitions. This intrinsic property of forward-ordinary Petri nets, which is usually (implicitly) used for such characteriziations, is lost in case of Petri nets with arbitrary arc multiplicities. If a transition t of such a net puts tokens onto a place p, then the answer to the question whether p prevents some transition t' depends on many different aspects: the number of tokens p contained before t took place, the number of tokens t removed from p and put onto p, and the number of tokens t' needs from p in order to be enabled. These mutual dependencies often make it difficult or even impossible to characterize enabled firing sequences, enabled Parikh vectors, or reachable markings in terms of elegant and easily checkable structural and behavioral properties.

This paper aims to provide a mathematical framework to approach many of the classical problems for classes of Petri nets with arbitrary arc multiplicities, like reachability, boundedness, covering, liveness, equivalence, and containment.

In Section 3, we define the concept of simple structurally f-g-canonical classes of Petri nets, which is based on (canonical) firing sequences leading to reachable markings. We show that for classes that are simple structurally f-g-canonical, the problems named above are decidable within certain space bounds, depending on the concrete values for the functions f and g used to specify the class. Furthermore, we present a sufficient condition for a class to be f-f-canonical. This condition is based on the existence of certain permutations of firing sequences leading to the empty marking in the wipe-extensions of the nets of the class. We previously used similar ideas in a less general form in [16] for generalized communication-free Petri nets. Here, we extend the set of problems for which complexity results are provided, and focus on the essential properties that are sufficient for providing these results.

In Section 4, we use conservative Petri nets as an example of application of the framework presented in Section 3. Jones et al. [10] showed that the reachability, and the covering problems of ordinary 1-conservative Petri nets are **PSPACE**-complete, and that the liveness problem of this class is in **PSPACE**. Furthermore, Mayr and Weihmann [16] showed that the RecLFS problem of Petri nets in general is **PSPACE**-complete. We improve on these results in the following way: We show that the reachability, covering, liveness, equivalence, and containment problems of conservative Petri nets are **PSPACE**-complete in the strong sense, even if restricted to ordinary 1-conservative Petri nets. Furthermore, we show that the RecLFS problem is **PSPACE**-complete, even under the same restriction as before.

2   Preliminaries

Throughout this paper, we use the following notation to avoid confusion between elements of vectors or of sequences and indexed elements of a set. We use $v_{[i]}$ in the few occasions we need to refer to the i-th element of a vector or a sequence v. The notation v_i is reserved for indexed elements of a set (e. g., p_1, p_2, ...). $\mathbb{Z}$, $\mathbb{N}_0$, and $\mathbb{N}$ denote the set of all integers, all nonnegative integers, and all positive integers, respectively, and we define $[a, b] = \{a, a+1, \ldots, b\} \subsetneqq \mathbb{Z}$, and $[k] = [1, k] \subsetneqq \mathbb{N}$. When k is understood, $\boldsymbol{a}$ denotes, for a number $a \in \mathbb{R}$, the k-dimensional vector with $\boldsymbol{a}_{[i]} = a$ for all $i \in [k]$. For two vectors $u, v \in \mathbb{Z}^k$, we write $u \geq v$ if $u_{[i]} \geq v_{[i]}$ for all $i \in [k]$, and $u > v$ if $u \geq v$ and $u_{[i]} > v_{[i]}$ for some $i \in [k]$. We write $\max(u) := \max_{i \in [k]} u_{[i]}$ ($\min(u) := \min_{i \in [k]} u_{[i]}$, resp.) for the maximum component (minimum component, resp.) of u. For two functions $f, g : X \to \mathbb{R}$, we write $f(a) \overset{P}{\leq} g(a)$ if there is a polynomial p such that $f(x) \leq p(g(x))$ for all $x \in X$. Note that $\overset{P}{\leq}$ is transitive.

For $\zeta, \pi_1, \ldots, \pi_\ell \in \mathbb{N}_0^k$, the *linear set representation* (LSR) $\mathcal{L}(\zeta, \{\pi_1, \ldots, \pi_\ell\})$ is the encoding of the tuple $(\zeta, \pi_1, \ldots, \pi_\ell)$, and represents the set $\{\zeta + a_1\pi_1 + \ldots + a_\ell\pi_\ell \mid a_1, \ldots, a_\ell \in \mathbb{N}_0\}$. A set is *linear*, if it is represented by some LSR. The vector ζ is called the *constant vector* of the LSR, while the vectors π_i are its *periods*. $\boldsymbol{\mathcal{L}}(\zeta, \{\pi_1, \ldots, \pi_\ell\})$ ($\boldsymbol{\mathcal{L}}$, resp.) denotes the linear set represented by $\mathcal{L}(\zeta, \{\pi_1, \ldots, \pi_\ell\})$ ($\mathcal{L}$, resp.). A *semilinear set representation* (SLSR) $\mathcal{SL} = \bigodot_{i=1}^k \mathcal{L}(\zeta_i, \{\pi_{i,1}, \ldots, \pi_{i,\ell_i}\})$ is the concatenation of LSRs, and represents $\bigcup_{i \in [k]} \boldsymbol{\mathcal{L}}(\zeta_i, \{\pi_{i,1}, \ldots, \pi_{i,\ell_i}\})$. Here, $\odot$ is a concatenation operator used to concatenate two SLSRs. A set is *semilinear* if it is represented by some SLSR. $\boldsymbol{\mathcal{SL}}$ denotes the semilinear set represented by an SLSR $\mathcal{SL}$. We remark that each (infinite) semilinear set has an infinite number of representations.

Throughout this paper we use a succinct encoding scheme. Every number is encoded in binary representation. A vector of $\mathbb{N}_0^k$ is encoded as a k-tuple. If we regard a tuple as an input, then it is encoded as a tuple of the encodings of the particular components. Under this encoding scheme, size(x) denotes the encoding size of an object x.

We remark that the input size of a problem instance consists of the encodings of all entities that are declared as being "given" in the respective problem statement. A problem is **NP**-hard (**PSPACE**-hard) in the strong sense if the problem is still **NP**-hard (**PSPACE**-hard, resp.) under a unary encoding scheme for the numbers appearing in the inputs. Note that if, for each language $L \in \mathbf{NP}$ ($L \in \mathbf{PSPACE}$), there is a polynomial time reduction from L to A such that all numbers encoded in the instances of A produced by the reduction are polynomial in the size of the respective instance, then A is **NP**-hard (**PSPACE**-hard, resp.) in the strong sense.

2.1 Petri Nets

A *Petri net* N is a 3-tuple (P, T, F) where P is a finite set of n *places*, T is a finite set of m *transitions* with $P \cap T = \emptyset$, and $F : (P \times T) \cup (T \times P) \to \mathbb{N}_0$ is a *flow function*. Throughout this paper, n and m will always refer to the number of places resp. transitions of the Petri net under consideration, and $W = \max\{F(p, t),$ $F(t, p) \mid p \in P, t \in T\}$ to the largest value of its flow function. Usually, we assume an arbitrary but fixed order on P and T, respectively. With respect to this order on P, we can consider an n-dimensional vector v as a function of P, and, abusing the notation, write $v(p)$ for the entry of v corresponding to place p. Analogously, we write $v(t)$ in context of an m-dimensional vector v and a transition t.

A *marking* μ (of N) is a vector of $\mathbb{N}_0^n$. A pair (N, μ_0) such that μ_0 is a marking of N is called a *marked Petri net*, and μ_0 is called its *initial marking*. We will omit the term "marked" if the presence of a certain initial marking is clear from the context. N or (N, μ_0) is called *ordinary* if $F(p, t), F(t, p) \in \{0, 1\}$ for all $p \in P$ and $t \in T$.

A Petri net naturally corresponds to a directed bipartite graph with arcs from P to T and vice versa such that there is an arc from $p \in P$ to $t \in T$ (from t to p, resp.) labeled with w if $0 < F(p, t) = w$ (if $0 < F(t, p) = w$, resp.). The label of an arc is called its *multiplicity*. If a Petri net is visualized, places are usually drawn as circles and transitions as bars. If the Petri net is marked by μ, then, for each place p, the circle corresponding to p contains $\mu(p)$ so called *tokens*. For a transition $t \in T$, ${}^{\bullet}t$ is the *preset* of t and denotes the set of all places p such that $F(p, t) > 0$.

For a Petri net $N = (P, T, F)$ and a marking μ of N, a transition $t \in T$ can be *applied* at μ, producing a vector $\mu' \in \mathbb{Z}^n$ with $\mu'(p) = \mu(p) - F(p, t) + F(t, p)$ for all $p \in P$. The transition t is *enabled* at μ or in (N, μ) if $\mu(p) \geq F(p, t)$ for all $p \in P$. We say that t is *fired* at marking μ if t is enabled and applied at μ. If t is fired at μ, then the resulting vector μ' is a marking, and we write $\mu \xrightarrow{t} \mu'$. Intuitively, if a transition is fired, it first removes $F(p, t)$ tokens from p and then adds $F(t, p)$ tokens to p.

An element σ of T^* is called a *transition sequence*, and $|\sigma|$ denotes its length. We write $\sigma_{[i..j]}$ for the subsequence $\sigma_{[i]} \cdot \sigma_{[i+1]} \cdots \sigma_{[j]}$, and $\sigma_{[..i]}$ for the prefix of length i of σ, i.e., $\sigma_{[..i]} = \sigma_{[1..i]}$. A *Parikh vector* Φ, also known as *firing count vector*, is simply an element of $\mathbb{N}_0^m$. The *Parikh map* $\Psi : T^* \to \mathbb{N}_0^m$ maps each transition sequence σ to its *Parikh image* $\Psi(\sigma)$ where $\Psi(\sigma)(t) = k$ for a transition t if t appears exactly k times in σ. Note that each Parikh vector Φ is the Parikh image of some transition sequence. Moreover, we write, abusing notation, $t \in \Phi$ if $\Phi(t) > 0$, and $t \in \sigma$ if $t \in \Psi(\sigma)$.

The *displacement* $\Delta : \mathbb{N}_0^m \to \mathbb{Z}^n$ maps Parikh vectors $\Phi \in \mathbb{N}_0^m$ onto the change of tokens at the places $p_1, \ldots, p_n$ when applying transition sequences with Parikh image Φ. That is, we have $\Delta(\Phi)(p) = \sum_{t \in T} \Phi(t) \cdot (F(t,p) - F(p,t))$ for all places p. Accordingly, we define the displacement $\Delta(\sigma)$ of a transition sequence σ by $\Delta(\sigma) := \Delta(\Psi(\sigma))$. For a marking μ and a transition sequence σ, we define $\max(\mu, \sigma) := \max_{i \in [0, |\sigma|]} \max(\mu + \Delta(\sigma_{[..i]}))$. The system matrix D of a Petri net $\mathcal{P} = (P, T, F, \mu_0)$ has, for all $i \in [m]$, $\Delta(t_i)$ as its i-th column.

For the empty transition sequence ϵ, we define $\mu \xrightarrow{\epsilon} \mu$. For a transition t, we write $\mu \xrightarrow{t} \mu'$ if t is enabled at μ and $\mu + \Delta(t) = \mu'$. For a nonempty transition sequence σ, we write $\mu \xrightarrow{\sigma} \mu'$ if $\mu \xrightarrow{\sigma_{[..|\sigma|-1]}} \mu'' \xrightarrow{\sigma_{[|\sigma|]}} \mu'$ for some marking μ''. We also say that σ is enabled at μ and leads from μ to μ'.

For a marked Petri net (N, μ_0), we call a transition sequence that is enabled at μ_0 a *firing sequence*. A marking μ is called *reachable* if $\mu_0 \xrightarrow{\sigma} \mu$ for some σ. The *reachability set* $\mathcal{R}(N, \mu_0)$ of (N, μ_0) consists of all reachable markings. We say that a marking μ can be *covered* if there is a reachable marking $\mu' \geq \mu$. A Petri net $\mathcal{P}$ is called *bounded* if $\mathcal{R}(\mathcal{P})$ is finite. Analogously, $\mathcal{P}$ is bounded if there is a $k \in \mathbb{N}$ such that $\max(\mu) \leq k$ for each $\mu \in \mathcal{R}(\mathcal{P})$. A Petri net $\mathcal{P}$ is called *live* if, for each transition t of $\mathcal{P}$ and each marking $\mu \in \mathcal{R}(\mathcal{P})$, there is a transition sequence enabled at μ that contains t.

A Parikh vector or a transition sequence with nonnegative displacement at all places is called *loop* (also known as *self-covering sequence*). A loop with positive displacement at some place p is a *positive loop* (for p). A loop with displacement 0 at all places is a *zero-loop*.

The *wipe-extension* $\widehat{\mathcal{P}} = (P, \widehat{T}, \widehat{F}, \mu_0)$ of a Petri net $\mathcal{P} = (P, T, F, \mu_0)$ is obtained from $\mathcal{P}$ by adding, for each place $p \in P$, a transition $\widehat{t}_p$ with $\widehat{F}(p, \widehat{t}_p) = 1$. These new transitions can be used to remove tokens from the net.

A Petri net is encoded as an enumeration of places $p_1, \ldots, p_n$ and transitions $t_1, \ldots, t_m$ followed by an enumeration of the arcs with their respective arc multiplicity.

In this paper, we consider the following decision problems for classes $\mathcal{C}$ of Petri nets.

- RecLFS: Given a PN $\mathcal{P} \in \mathcal{C}$ and a Parikh vector Φ, is Φ enabled in $\mathcal{P}$?
- Reachability: Given a PN $\mathcal{P} \in \mathcal{C}$ and a marking μ, is μ reachable in $\mathcal{P}$?
- Covering: Given a PN $\mathcal{P} \in \mathcal{C}$ and a marking μ, is μ coverable in $\mathcal{P}$?
- Boundedness: Given a PN $\mathcal{P} \in \mathcal{C}$, is $\mathcal{P}$ bounded?
- Liveness: Given a PN $\mathcal{P} \in \mathcal{C}$, is $\mathcal{P}$ live?
- Containment: Given two PNs $\mathcal{P}, \mathcal{P}' \in \mathcal{C}$, is $\mathcal{R}(\mathcal{P}) \subseteq \mathcal{R}(\mathcal{P}')$?
- Equivalence: Given two PNs $\mathcal{P}, \mathcal{P}' \in \mathcal{C}$, is $\mathcal{R}(\mathcal{P}) = \mathcal{R}(\mathcal{P}')$?

We remark that the input size of a problem instance consists of the encodings of all entities that are declared as being "given" in the respective problem statement.

3   A Framework for Classes of General Petri Nets

In this section, we present a framework that can be used to obtain complexity results for a number of computational problems, in particular involving classes of Petri nets with arbitrary arc multiplicities.

Definition 1 (f-g-canonical class of Petri nets). *A class $\mathcal{C}$ of Petri nets is f-g-canonical for two monotonically increasing functions f, $g : \mathbb{N}_0^4 \to \mathbb{N}$ if, for each $\mathcal{P} = (P, T, F, \mu_0) \in \mathcal{C}$ and each marking μ reachable in $\mathcal{P}$, there are $k \in [0, n(\max(\mu) + uW)]$ and some transition sequences ξ, $\bar{\xi}$, $\alpha_1, \ldots, \alpha_{k+1}$, τ_1, $\ldots, \tau_k$ with the following properties, where $u = f(n, m, W, \max(\mu_0))$:*

(a) $\xi = \alpha_1 \cdot \tau_1 \cdot \alpha_2 \cdot \tau_2 \cdots \alpha_k \cdot \tau_k \cdot \alpha_{k+1}$ *is a firing sequence of length at most $(k+1)u$ leading from μ_0 to μ,*
(b) $\bar{\xi} = \alpha_1 \cdot \alpha_2 \cdots \alpha_{k+1}$ *is a firing sequence of length at most u,*
(c) *at most $g(n, m, W, \max(\mu_0))$ elements of $\{\alpha_1, \ldots, \alpha_{k+1}\}$ are nonempty sequences, and*
(d) *each τ_i, $i \in [k]$, is a positive loop of length at most u, enabled at some marking μ^* with $\max(\mu^*) \le u$ and $\mu^* \le \mu_0 + \Delta(\alpha_1 \cdot \alpha_2 \cdots \alpha_i)$.*

An f-g-canonical class is

- *structurally f-g-canonical if, for each $(N, \mu_0) \in \mathcal{C}$ and each marking μ of N, the Petri net (N, μ) is also in $\mathcal{C}$ (i.e., it does not depend on the initial marking whether a Petri net is part of $\mathcal{C}$), and*
- *simple if it can be determined in polynomial space if a given Petri net $\mathcal{P}$ belongs to $\mathcal{C}$, and if f and g are computable functions.*

We remark that each reachable marking μ could have many different firing sequences satisfying the properties of Definition 1, i.e., ξ is usually not unique. We still call ξ *the* canonical firing sequence of μ. The sequence $\bar{\xi}$ is called the *backbone* of ξ.

The following theorem provides a sufficient condition for a class to be f-f-canonical.

Theorem 1. *Let $\mathcal{C}$ be a class of Petri nets for which there is a monotonically increasing function $h : \mathbb{N}_0^4 \to \mathbb{N}_0$ such that, for each $\mathcal{P} \in \mathcal{C}$ with $n > 0$ and each firing sequence σ of $\mathcal{P}$'s wipe-extension $\widehat{\mathcal{P}}$ leading to the empty marking $\mathbf{0}$, there is a permutation φ of σ enabled in $\widehat{\mathcal{P}}$ with $\max(\mu_0, \varphi) \le h(n, m, W, \max(\mu_0))$, where m is the number of transitions of $\mathcal{P}$, and W is the largest arc multiplicity of $\mathcal{P}$. Then, $\mathcal{C}$ is f-f-canonical, where f is defined by $f(n, m, W, K) = (h(n, m, W, K) + 1)^{2n}$.*

Proof. Let $\mathcal{P} = (P, T, F, \mu_0) \in \mathcal{C}$. If one of the values n, m, W is 0, then μ_0 is the only reachable marking, which means that $\mathcal{P}$ can be added to any f-g-canonical class such that the resulting class is still f-g-canonical. Hence, we assume in the following that n, m, $W > 0$. Let $b := h(n, m, W, \max(\mu_0))$, and let μ be a reachable marking of $\mathcal{P}$. Then, there is a firing sequence σ leading to μ. Consider the wipe-extension $\widehat{\mathcal{P}} = (P, \widehat{T}, \widehat{F}, \mu_0)$ of $\mathcal{P}$ with n places, $m + n$ transitions, and largest arc multiplicity W. The sequence σ is also a firing sequence in $\widehat{\mathcal{P}}$, leading to μ, and can be extended by transitions of $\widehat{T} \setminus T$ to a firing sequence σ' leading to the empty marking $\mathbf{0}$. By the assumption of the theorem, there is a permutation φ of σ' enabled in $\widehat{\mathcal{P}}$ with $\max(\mu_0, \varphi) \le b$.

Let $M := \{\nu \mid \mu_0 \xrightarrow{\varphi_{[..i]}} \nu, i \in [0, |\varphi|]\}$ be the set of all markings obtained when firing φ. We partition φ into contiguous non-overlapping subsequences $\varphi_1, \ldots, \varphi_\ell$ with $\varphi = \varphi_1 \cdots \varphi_\ell$ such that the markings $\mu_i^* := \mu_0 + \Delta(\varphi_1 \cdots \varphi_i)$, $i \in [0, \ell]$, satisfy the following property: for each $\nu \in M$, there is exactly one $i \in [0, \ell]$ with $\mu_i^* = \nu$. In particular, this means $\mu_i^* \neq \mu_j^*$ for all distinct $i, j \in [0, \ell]$ and $M = \bigcup_{i \in [0, \ell]} \{\mu_i^*\}$. Note that $\ell \leq (b+1)^n$ since there are at most $(b+1)^n$ markings ν with $\max(\nu) \leq b$. In the following, we will iteratively cut out short zero-loops from these subsequences and collect them in a multiset L^*.

Consider the following condition: for all zero-loops $\tau^* \in L^*$, we have $|\tau^*| \leq (b+1)^n$, and there is a marking $\mu^* \in M$ such that τ^* is enabled at μ^* in $\widehat{\mathcal{P}}$. At the beginning, L^* is empty, implying that the above condition is satisfied. Now, assume that, for some sequence $\rho := \varphi_i$, $i \in [\ell]$, we observe $|\rho| \geq (b+1)^n$. Then, with the same argument as before, there are indices i_1, i_2 with $i_1 < i_2$ and $i_2 - i_1 \leq (b+1)^n$ such that both firing sequences $\varphi_1 \cdots \varphi_{i-1} \cdot \rho_{[..i_1]}$ and $\varphi_1 \cdots \varphi_{i-1} \cdot \rho_{[..i_2]}$ lead to the same marking $\mu^* \in M$. Let $\varphi_j' := \varphi_j$ for all $j \in [\ell] \setminus \{i\}$, and $\varphi_i' := \rho_{[..i_1]} \cdot \rho_{[i_2+1..]}$. If the zero-loop $\rho_{[i_1+1..i_2]}$ contains some transition of $\widehat{T} \setminus T$, then we add it to L^*, and discard it otherwise. Then, $\mu_0 \xrightarrow{\varphi_1' \cdots \varphi_i'} \mu_i^*$, $i \in [\ell]$, since we merely removed a zero-loop (which has no effect on the markings). In particular, the zero-loop $\rho_{[i_1+1..i_2]}$, which is enabled at $\mu^* \in M$, as well as all zero-loops which were contained in L^* before, (still) satisfy the condition given above.

Iterating this argument yields sequences $\varphi_1^*, \ldots, \varphi_\ell^*$ and multisets L_i^*, $i \in [0, \ell]$, consisting of zero-loops, where $L^* := \bigcup_{i=0}^{\ell} L_i^*$, such that

- $\mu_0 = \mu_0^* \xrightarrow{\varphi_1^*} \mu_1^* \xrightarrow{\varphi_2^*} \cdots \mu_{\ell-1}^* \xrightarrow{\varphi_\ell^*} \mu_\ell^* = \mathbf{0}$ in $\widehat{\mathcal{P}}$,
- $\tau^* \in L_i^*$ is enabled at μ_i^* in $\widehat{\mathcal{P}}$ and $\max(\mu_i^*) \leq b$ for all $i \in [0, \ell]$,
- $|\varphi_i^*| \leq (b+1)^n$ for all $i \in [\ell]$, and
- $|\tau^*| \leq (b+1)^n$ for all $\tau^* \in L^*$.

All these sequences potentially contain transitions of $\widehat{T} \setminus T$ since they are sequences of $\widehat{\mathcal{P}}$. Furthermore, each $\tau^* \in L^*$ certainly contains such transitions which implies $k := |L^*| \leq n \cdot \max(\mu)$. We obtain the sequences α_i^*, $i \in [\ell]$, from φ_i^*, and the multisets L_i, $i \in [0, \ell]$, from the sets L_i^* by removing all transitions $\widehat{T} \setminus T$ from the respective sequences. Let $L := \bigcup_{i=0}^{\ell} L_i$, and $\mu_i := \mu_0 + \Delta(\alpha_1^* \cdots \alpha_i^*)$, $i \in [\ell]$. We define the function $f : \mathbb{N}_0^4 \to \mathbb{N}$ by $f(n, m, W, K) := (h(n, m, W, K) + 1)^{2n}$. The following properties are satisfied:

- $\bar{\xi} := \alpha_1^* \cdots \alpha_\ell^*$ is a firing sequence of $\mathcal{P}$ with length $|\bar{\xi}| \leq (b+1)^{2n} = f(n, m, W, \max(\mu_0))$,
- $\tau \in L_i$, $i \in [0, \ell]$, is enabled in $\mathcal{P}$ at $\mu_i^* \leq \mu_i$, where $\max(\mu_i^*) \leq b \leq f(n, m, W, \max(\mu_0))$, and
- $|\tau| \leq (b+1)^n \leq f(n, m, W, \max(\mu_0))$ for all $\tau \in L$.

Now, we obtain $\tau_1, \ldots, \tau_k$ by numbering the sequences of L, where we number the sequences of L_i before the sequences of L_{i+1}. Furthermore, we obtain the sequences α_i, $i \in [k+1]$, by splitting $\bar{\xi}$ at appropriate positions (where at most $f(n, m, W, \max(\mu_0))$ of the sequences α_i are nonempty). Note that $\xi :=$ $\alpha_1 \cdot \tau_1 \cdot \alpha_2 \cdot \tau_2 \cdots \alpha_k \cdot \tau_k \cdot \alpha_{k+1}$ is indeed a firing sequence. In total, all properties of the theorem are satisfied.   □

The next theorem provides upper bounds for the reachability, covering, and boundedness problems in terms of f and g.

Theorem 2. *Let $\mathcal{C}$ be a simple f-g-canonical class of Petri nets. Then, the reachability, and the covering problems are decidable in space polynomial in*

$$\text{size}(\mathcal{P}) + \text{size}(\mu) + n \operatorname{ld} f(n, m, W, \max(\mu_0)) + r,$$

and the boundedness problem is decidable in space polynomial in

$$\text{size}(\mathcal{P}) + n \operatorname{ld} f(n, m, W, \max(\mu_0)) + r,$$

where r is the space needed to compute $f(n, m, W, \max(\mu_0))$.

Proof. Let $u := f(n, m, W, \max(\mu_0))$. In the following, we assume n, m, W, $u > 0$ since otherwise μ_0 is the only reachable marking and the problems of the theorem can trivially be decided in polynomial space.

Reachability Problem. Let μ be a reachable marking, and let ξ, $\bar{\xi}$, α_i, and τ_i be as in Definition 1. We observe that $\max(\mu_0 + \Delta(\alpha_1 \cdot \tau_1 \cdots \alpha_i)) \leq \max(\mu) + uW$ for each $i \in [k+1]$, as well as $\max(\mu_0 + \Delta(\alpha_1 \cdot \tau_1 \cdot \alpha_2 \cdots \tau_i)) \leq \max(\mu) + uW$ for each $i \in [k]$ since all τ_j are loops, and $\min(\Delta(\bar{\xi}_{[q..r]})) \geq -uW$ for all q, $r \in [|\bar{\xi}|]$. Together with $\max(\mathbf{0}, \tau_i) \leq uW$ for all $i \in [k]$, and $\max(\mathbf{0}, \alpha_i) \leq uW$ for all $i \in [k + 1]$, we find $\max(\mu_0, \xi) \leq \max(\mu) + 2uW$. Hence, we can decide the reachability problem (nondeterministically) in space polynomial in

$$\text{size}(\mathcal{P}) + n \operatorname{ld}(\max(\mu) + 2uW) + r \overset{P}{\leq} \text{size}(\mathcal{P}) + \text{size}(\mu) + n \operatorname{ld}(u) + r$$

by guessing the transitions of ξ one after another, while only storing the last marking.

Boundedness Problem. Let $\delta := \max(\mu_0) + uW + 1$. Assume that $\mathcal{P}$ is unbounded. Then, there is a reachable marking μ with $\max(\mu) \geq \delta$. Let ξ, $\bar{\xi}$, α_i, and τ_i be the sequences corresponding to μ as of Definition 1. Let p be a place with $\mu(p) = \max(\mu)$. Since $|\bar{\xi}| \leq u$ and $|\tau_i| \leq u$, $i \in [k]$, we can find coefficients $a_i \in \{0, 1\}$, $i \in [k]$, such that the reachable marking $\mu' := \mu_0 + \Delta(\bar{\xi}) + \sum_{i \in [k]} a_i \Delta(\tau_i)$ satisfies $\max(\mu') \in [\delta, \delta + uW]$. On the other hand, if a marking μ with $\max(\mu) \in [\delta, \delta + uW]$ exists, then $k \geq 1$, which implies that $\mathcal{P}$ is unbounded since $\alpha_1 \cdot \tau_1^i$ is a firing sequence for any $i \in \mathbb{N}$. Hence, we can decide the complement of the boundedness problem, and therefore the boundedness problem itself, (nondeterministically) in space polynomial in

$$\text{size}(\mathcal{P}) + n \operatorname{ld}(\delta + uW) + n \operatorname{ld}(u) + r$$
$$= \text{size}(\mathcal{P}) + n \operatorname{ld}(\max(\mu_0) + 2uW + 1) + n \operatorname{ld}(u) + r$$
$$\overset{P}{\leq} \text{size}(\mathcal{P}) + n \operatorname{ld}(u) + r$$

by guessing a marking μ with $\max(\mu) \in [\delta, \delta + uW]$ and checking if μ is reachable.

Covering Problem. Let μ^* be the marking for which we want to know if it can be covered. Assume that μ^* can be covered, and let $\mu \geq \mu^*$ be a reachable marking with its corresponding sequences $\xi, \bar{\xi}, \tau_i$ as of Definition 1. Let $M := \{\Delta(\tau_i) \mid i \in [k]\}$, and $\mu' := \mu_0 + \Delta(\bar{\xi}) + \sum_{d \in M} \max(\mu^*) \cdot d$. Marking μ' is reachable because we can construct a firing sequence leading to μ' by appropriately inserting, for each $i \in [k]$, a number of copies of τ_i into $\bar{\xi}$. Furthermore, if $(\mu_0 + \Delta(\bar{\xi}))(p) < \mu^*(p)$ for some place p, then $d(p) > 0$ for some $d \in M$. Therefore, μ' covers μ^*. Note that $\max(d) \in [0, uW]$ for each $d \in M$ and thus $|M| \leq (uW+1)^n$. By the simple observation $\sum_{i \in [k]} a_i \leq \prod_{i \in [k]} a'_i$ if $a_1, \ldots, a_k \in \mathbb{N}_0$ and $a'_i \geq \max\{a_i, 2\}$ for all $i \in [k]$, this implies

$$
\begin{aligned}
\max(\mu') &\leq \max(\mu_0) + \max(\Delta(\bar{\xi})) + \sum_{d \in M} \max(\mu^*) \cdot \max(d) \\
&\leq \max(\mu_0) + uW + |M| \cdot \max(\mu^*) \cdot \max\{\max(d) \mid d \in M\} \\
&\leq \max(\mu_0) + uW + (uW+1)^n \cdot \max(\mu^*) \cdot uW \\
&\leq (\max(\mu_0) + 2) \cdot 2uW \cdot (2uW)^n \cdot \max(\mu^*) \cdot uW =: d'.
\end{aligned}
$$

Hence, we can decide the covering problem (nondeterministically) in space polynomial in

$$
\begin{aligned}
&\text{size}(\mathcal{P}) + n \, \text{ld}(d') + n \, \text{ld}(u) + r \\
&= \text{size}(\mathcal{P}) + n \, \text{ld}((\max(\mu_0) + 2) \cdot 2uW \cdot (2uW)^n \cdot \\
&\qquad \cdot \max(\mu^*) \cdot uW) + n \, \text{ld}(u) + r \\
&\overset{P}{\leq} \text{size}(\mathcal{P}) + n \, \text{ld}(\max(\mu^*)) + n \, \text{ld}(u) + r \\
&\overset{P}{\leq} \text{size}(\mathcal{P}) + \text{size}(\mu^*) + n \, \text{ld}(u) + r
\end{aligned}
$$

by guessing a marking $\mu \geq \mu^*$ with $\max(\mu) \leq d'$ and checking if μ is reachable. $\qquad \square$

For each Petri net $\mathcal{P}$ of a simple structurally f-g-canonical class of Petri nets, we can use the canonical firing sequences to compute semilinear set representations of the reachability set $\mathcal{R}(\mathcal{P})$. To this end, we use the following strategy. We consider all possible relevant tuples of markings iteratively reached by parts of the backbones of the canonical sequences. Each tuple constitutes its own linear set, where the constant vector is the marking reached by the backbone, and the set of periods is the set of the displacements of all short positive loops enabled at some marking of the tuple.

Theorem 3. *Let C be a simple structurally f-g-canonical class of Petri nets, and $\mathcal{P} \in C$. Then, the SLSR*

$$
\mathcal{SL} = \bigodot_{(\mu_1, \ldots, \mu_{u_2}) \in M} \mathcal{L}\left(\mu_{u_2}, \bigcup_{i \in [0, u_2]} D_{\mu_i}\right),
$$

represents $\mathcal{R}(\mathcal{P})$ *and can be constructed in time*

$$p((\max(\mu_0) + 2u_1 W)^{u_2 n} \cdot 2^{p(\text{size}(\mathcal{P})) + n \, \text{ld}(u_3)} + r)$$

for some polynomial p, where

(a) $u_1 = f(n, m, W, \max(\mu_0))$, $u_2 = g(n, m, W, \max(\mu_0))$,
   $u_3 = f(n, m, W, \max(\mu_0) + 2u_1 W)$, *and r is the time needed to calculate* u_1,
   u_2, *and* u_3,
(b) $M = \{(\mu_1, \ldots, \mu_{u_2}) \mid \mu_{i-1} \to \mu_i \text{ and } \max(\mu_i) \leq \max(\mu_0) + u_1 W \text{ for all } i \in$
   $[u_2]\}$, *and*
(c) $D_\mu = \{\Delta(\tau) \mid \tau \text{ is a positive loop enabled at } \mu \text{ with } \max(\Delta(\tau)) \leq u_1 W\}$.

Proof. As before, we assume n, m, W, u_1, u_2, $u_3 > 0$ since otherwise μ_0 is the only reachable marking. Consider a reachable marking μ, and let ξ, $\bar{\xi}$, α_i, τ_i be its corresponding sequences as of Definition 1. Let $\alpha'_1, \ldots, \alpha'_{u'_2}$ with $u'_2 \leq u_2$ be the nonempty sequences of $\{\alpha_1, \ldots, \alpha_{k+1}\}$ such that $\alpha'_1 \cdots \alpha'_{u'_2} = \bar{\xi}$. Let μ_i, $i \in [0, u'_2]$, be defined by $\mu_0 \xrightarrow{\alpha'_1 \cdots \alpha'_i} \mu_i$, and $\mu_i := \mu_{i-1}$ for all $i \in [u'_2 + 1, u_2]$. Now, it is not hard to see that the properties of these sequences imply $(\mu_1, \ldots, \mu_{u_2}) \in M$ and, for all $i \in [k]$, there is a $j \in [0, u_2]$ with $\Delta(\tau_i) \in D_{\mu_j}$, i.e., $\mu \in \mathcal{L}(\mu_{u_2}, \bigcup_{i \in [0, u_2]} D_{\mu_{u_2}}) \subseteq \mathcal{SL}$. Therefore, $\mathcal{R}(\mathcal{P}) \subseteq \mathcal{SL}$. The other direction, namely $\mathcal{SL} \subseteq \mathcal{R}(\mathcal{P})$, is obvious.

In the following, we show the upper bound for the time needed to construct $\mathcal{SL}$. We first compute a reachability matrix $A \in \{0, 1\}^{d \times d}$ where $d := (\max(\mu_0) + 2u_1 W + 1)^n$ such that the entry corresponding to two markings μ, μ' with $\max(\mu)$, $\max(\mu') \leq \max(\mu_0) + 2u_1 W$ is 1 if and only if $\mu \to \mu'$. By Theorem 2 and the monotonicity of f, each entry can be determined in space polynomial in

$$\text{size}(\mathcal{P}) + \text{size}(\mu) + \text{size}(\mu') + n \, \text{ld}(u_3)$$
$$\overset{P}{\leq} \text{size}(\mathcal{P}) + n \, \text{ld}(\max(\mu_0) + 2u_1 W) + n \, \text{ld}(\max(\mu_0) + 2u_1 W) + n \, \text{ld}(u_3)$$
$$\overset{P}{\leq} \text{size}(\mathcal{P}) + n \, \text{ld}(u_3).$$

The whole matrix can be determined in time $p(d^2 \cdot 2^{p(\text{size}(\mathcal{P}) + n \, \text{ld}(u_3))})$ for some polynomial p.

Next, we construct all relevant sets D_{μ^*}. Since $|\bar{\xi}| \leq u_1$, we only have to consider the $(\max(\mu_0) + u_1 W + 1)^n$ different markings μ^* with $\max(\mu^*) \leq \max(\mu_0) + u_1 W$. Because $|\tau_i| \leq u_1$, we now check, for each such μ^* and all at most $(u_1 W + 1)^n$ different markings μ satisfying $\mu > \mu^*$ and $\max(\mu - \mu^*) \leq u_1 W$, if μ can be reached from μ^*. If this is the case for μ^* and μ, then we add $\mu - \mu^* > \mathbf{0}$ to D_{μ^*}. Using A, the total time to construct all sets is polynomial in the size of the matrix A, and thus is at most $p(d^2 \cdot 2^{p(\text{size}(\mathcal{P}) + n \, \text{ld}(u_3))})$ for some polynomial p.

We construct, for each $(\mu_1, \ldots, \mu_{u_2}) \in M$, the LSR $\mathcal{L}(\mu_{u_2}, \bigcup_{i \in [0, u_2]} D_{\mu_i})$. Now, we consider all $((\max(\mu_0) + u_1 W + 1)^n)^{u_2}$ possible tuples $(\mu_1, \ldots, \mu_{u_2})$ with $\max(\mu_i) \leq \max(\mu_0) + u_1 W$, $i \in [u_2]$, and check, using A, if $\mu_{i-1} \to \mu_i$ for all $i \in [u_2]$. If this is the case, then we construct the LSR mentioned above. The total time to compute u_1, u_2, u_3, to generate A, all sets D_{μ^*}, and all these LSRs is polynomial in

$$(\max(\mu_0) + u_1 W + 1)^{u_2 n} \cdot u_2 \cdot 2^{p_1(\text{size}(\mathcal{P}) + n \, \text{ld}(u_3))} \cdot d^2 2^{p_1(\text{size}(\mathcal{P}) + n \, \text{ld}(u_3))} + r$$

$$\overset{P}{\leq} (\max(\mu_0) + 2u_1 W)^{u_2 n} \cdot 2^{p_2(\text{size}(\mathcal{P})) + n \, \text{ld}(u_3)} + r$$

for two polynomials p_1, p_2.   □

Using this SLSR as a tool (which is not explicitly computed), we can also give an upper bound for the liveness problem in terms of f and g. The core of the proof is the observation that if the Petri net is not live, then there are a transition and a small marking serving as witnesses.

Theorem 4. *Let $\mathcal{C}$ be a simple structurally f-g-canonical class of Petri nets. Then, the liveness problem of $\mathcal{C}$ is decidable in space polynomial in*

$$\text{size}(\mathcal{P}) + n \, \text{ld}(f(n, m, W, \max(\mu_0) + f(n, m, W, \max(\mu_0))W)) + r,$$

where r is the space needed to compute

$$f(n, m, W, \max(\mu_0) + f(n, m, W, \max(\mu_0))W).$$

Proof. As before, we assume n, m, W, $u > 0$ since otherwise μ_0 is the only reachable marking, and the liveness property can be checked in polynomial time. Assume that $\mathcal{P} = (N, \mu_0) \in \mathcal{C}$ is not live. Then, there is a transition t and a reachable marking μ such that ξ and $\bar{\xi}$ are its corresponding sequences as of Definition 1, and no marking μ' reachable from μ enables t. If $\max(\mu) > \max(\mu_0) + uW$, then $\xi \neq \bar{\xi}$, and the marking ν reached by $\bar{\xi}$ satisfies $\nu < \mu$. Furthermore, for each marking ν' reachable from ν, there is a marking μ' reachable from μ such that $\nu' < \mu'$. Hence, ν is a smaller marking than μ that also witnesses that $\mathcal{P}$ is not live. Thus, if $\mathcal{P}$ is not live, then there is a small marking that witnesses that some transition t is not live.

We now show how we can check for a transition t and a marking μ with $\max(\mu) \leq \max(\mu_0) + uW$ if no marking reachable from μ enables t. Let $\mathcal{SL} = \bigodot_{i \in [\ell]} \mathcal{L}(\zeta_i, \Pi_i)$ be the SLSR for $\mathcal{R}(N, \mu)$ given in Theorem 3, and let $u' := f(n, m, W, \max(\mu)) \leq f(n, m, W, \max(\mu_0) + uW)$. If there is a marking μ' reachable from μ and enabling t, then there is a LSR $\mathcal{L}(\zeta, \Pi) := \mathcal{L}(\zeta_i, \Pi_i)$ for some $i \in [\ell]$ such that $\mu' \in \mathcal{L}(\zeta, \Pi)$, $\max(\zeta) \leq \max(\mu) + u'W$, and $\max(\pi) \leq u'W$ for all $\pi \in \Pi$. Because of $\mu' \in \mathcal{L}(\zeta, \Pi)$, if $\zeta(p) < F(p, t)$ for some place $p \in {}^\bullet t$, then there is a period $\pi \in \Pi$ with $\pi(p) \in [1, u'W]$. Hence, by appropriately combining the periods (for each place of ${}^\bullet t$ at most W periods), we find a marking $\mu'' \in \mathcal{L}(\zeta, \Pi)$ such that μ'' enables t, and

$$\max(\mu'') \leq \max(\zeta) + nW \cdot u'W \leq \max(\mu) + u'W + nu'W^2$$

$$\leq (\max(\mu_0) + uW) + 2nf(n, m, W, \max(\mu_0) + uW)W^2$$

$$\leq \max(\mu_0) + 3nf(n, m, W, \max(\mu_0) + uW)W^2 =: u''.$$

That means, we only need to check if no marking μ'' reachable from μ with $\max(\mu'') \leq u''$ enables t in order to ensure that no marking reachable from μ enables t.

Using these bounds, we can now show, how to decide the liveness problem. We iterate over all $t \in T$ and all markings μ with $\max(\mu) \leq \max(\mu_0) + uW$ and check if μ is reachable. For each such reachable marking μ, we test, by iterating over all μ'' with $\max(\mu'') \leq u''$, if at least one of these markings is reachable from μ and enables t. $\mathcal{P}$ is live if and only if all tests succeed. By Theorem 2, the amount of space needed by this algorithm is at most polynomial in

$$\text{size}(\mathcal{P}) + n\,\text{ld}(\max(\mu_0) + uW) + n\,\text{ld}(\max(\mu_0)$$
$$+ 3nf(n, m, W, \max(\mu_0) + uW)W^2) + n\,\text{ld}(f(n, m, W, \max(\mu_0) + uW)) + r$$
$$\overset{P}{\leq} \text{size}(\mathcal{P}) + n\,\text{ld}(f(n, m, W, \max(\mu_0))) + n\,\text{ld}(f(n, m, W, \max(\mu_0) + uW))$$
$$+ n\,\text{ld}(f(n, m, W, \max(\mu_0) + uW)) + r$$
$$\overset{P}{\leq} \text{size}(\mathcal{P}) + n\,\text{ld}(f(n, m, W, \max(\mu_0) + uW)) + r.$$

$\square$

For the equivalence problem, we first recall a result of Huynh.

Lemma 1 ([8], Lemma 4.1, also refer to [9]). *The equivalence problem of SLSRs, i. e., the following problem, is Π_2^P-complete: Given SLSRs $\mathcal{SL}_1$ and $\mathcal{SL}_2$, is $\mathcal{SL}_1 = \mathcal{SL}_2$?*

The following corollary is a direct consequence of it.

Corollary 1. *The containment problem of SLSRs, i. e., the following problem, is Π_2^P-complete: Given SLSRs $\mathcal{SL}_1$ and $\mathcal{SL}_2$, is $\mathcal{SL}_1 \subseteq \mathcal{SL}_2$?*

Proof. The containment problem can be reduced in polynomial time to the equivalence problem as follows. We combine the SLSRs $\mathcal{SL}_1$ and $\mathcal{SL}_2$ to a SLSR $\mathcal{SL}_1'$ of the set $\mathcal{SL}_1 \cup \mathcal{SL}_2$, and let $\mathcal{SL}_2' = \mathcal{SL}_2$. Then, $\mathcal{SL}_1 \subseteq \mathcal{SL}_2$ if and only if $\mathcal{SL}_1' = \mathcal{SL}_2'$.

For the other direction also a simple polynomial time reduction exists. Let k be the dimension of the vectors of $\mathcal{SL}_1'$ and $\mathcal{SL}_2'$, and let $\mathbf{0}_k$ denote the k-dimensional 0-vector. We obtain the SLSR $\mathcal{SL}_1$ of the set $(\mathcal{SL}_1' \times \mathbf{0}_k) \cup (\mathbf{0}_k \times \mathcal{SL}_2')$ by combining the SLSRs resulting from extending the vectors of the SLSRs $\mathcal{SL}_1'$ and $\mathcal{SL}_2'$ at the beginning and end by $\mathbf{0}_k$, respectively. In the same way, we obtain the SLSR $\mathcal{SL}_2$ of the set $(\mathcal{SL}_2' \times \mathbf{0}_k) \cup (\mathbf{0}_k \times \mathcal{SL}_1')$. Then, $\mathcal{SL}_1' = \mathcal{SL}_2'$ if and only if $\mathcal{SL}_1' \subseteq \mathcal{SL}_2'$ and $\mathcal{SL}_2' \subseteq \mathcal{SL}_1'$ if and only if $\mathcal{SL}_1 \subseteq \mathcal{SL}_2$. $\square$

The SLSRs of Theorem 3 can also be used to decide the equivalence and containment problems, which is a standard approach in Petri net theory.

Theorem 5. *Let $\mathcal{C}$ be a simple structurally f-g-canonical class of Petri nets. Then, for some polynomial p, the equivalence and containment problems of $\mathcal{C}$ are decidable in space*

$$p((K + 2u_1K)^{u_2n} \cdot 2^{p(s+n\,\text{ld}(u_3))} + r),$$

where

- s is the encoding size of the input,
- n is the total number of places of both nets,
- m is the total number of transitions,
- W is the maximum of all arc multiplicities of both nets,
- K is the largest number of tokens appearing at some place at the initial markings,
- $u_1 = f(n, m, W, K)$, $u_2 = g(n, m, W, K)$, $u_3 = f(n, m, W, K + 2u_1 W)$, and
- r is the time needed to calculate u_1, u_2, and u_3.

Proof. For the input Petri nets $\mathcal{P}_1$ and $\mathcal{P}_2$, we use Theorem 3 to compute the SLSRs $\mathcal{SL}_1$ and $\mathcal{SL}_2$ with $\boldsymbol{SL}_1 = \mathcal{R}(\mathcal{P}_1)$ and $\boldsymbol{SL}_2 = \mathcal{R}(\mathcal{P}_2)$. By Lemma 1 and Corollary 1, we can decide the containment and equivalence problems of SLSRs in space polynomial in the size of the SLSRs. Thus, the theorem follows.   □

4   Conservative Petri Nets

A Petri net is called *conservative* or, more specifically, *x-conservative* if $D^T x = 0$ for some $x \in \mathbb{N}^n$. Furthermore, a Petri net is 1-*conservative* if it is **1**-conservative. The defining property of an x-conservative Petri nets is that, for all reachable markings, the weighted (by x) sum of tokens is the same. This immediately implies that conservative Petri nets are bounded. Conservative Petri nets were introduced by Lien [12]. Jones et al. [10] showed (amongst other things) that the reachability and the containment problems of ordinary 1-conservative Petri nets are **PSPACE**-complete. Furthermore, they showed that the liveness problem of 1-conservative Petri nets is contained in **PSPACE**, but no lower bound was given.

In this chapter, we strengthen these results. Our results hold for all conservative Petri nets, including those with arbitrary arc multiplicities. The arguments used for the upper bounds are in essence the arguments used in [10], which are appropriately extended for dealing with nets that are not ordinary or 1-conservative. In addition to these generalized upper bounds, we also prove **PSPACE**-hardness (and thus **PSPACE**-completeness) for the liveness problem, as well as **PSPACE**-completeness for the RecLFS problem. As we will see, the property of being conservative leads to straight-forward arguments.

Obviously, a Petri net $\mathcal{P}$ is conservative if there is an $x \in \mathbb{Q}^n$ with $x \geq \mathbf{1}$ and $D^T x = 0$ since we can scale such a rational valued vector to an integer valued one. Using, for instance, Karmarkar's algorithm [11], we can find in polynomial time such a rational valued vector x (if it exists) which additionally satisfies $\max(x) \leq 2^{p(\mathrm{size}(\mathcal{P}))}$ for some polynomial p. (Hence, the recognition problem, which asks if a given Petri net $\mathcal{P}$ is conservative, can be decided in polynomial time.)

We remark that, instead of using Theorem 1, we could show directly that the class of conservative Petri nets is f-f-canonical for some appropriate function f, or show the complexity results without using our framework. For the same reason, however, it lends itself as a good example. Since we want to demonstrate our framework, we first show that the prerequisites of Theorem 1 are satisfied. Usually, this is the hard step when applying the framework (in [16], we showed this for generalized communication-free Petri nets).

Lemma 2. *There is a constant d such that, for each reachable marking μ of a conservative Petri net $\mathcal{P} = (P, T, F, \mu_0)$ with $n > 0$, $\max(\mu) \leq 2^{\mathrm{size}(\mathcal{P})^d}$ holds.*

Proof. Since $\mathcal{P}$ is conservative and $n > 0$, there is a constant c such that there is an $x \in \mathbb{Q}^n$ satisfying $x \geq 1$, $D^T x = 0$, and $\max(x) \leq 2^{\mathrm{size}(\mathcal{P})^c}$. Let $i \in [n]$ be an index such that $x_{[i]} = \max(x)$, and let Φ be a Parikh vector leading to μ. We observe

$$\max(\mu) \leq \mu^T x = (\mu_0 + \Delta(\Phi))^T x = (\mu_0^T + \Phi^T D^T)x = \mu_0^T x + \Phi^T (D^T x)$$
$$= \mu_0^T x \leq \max(\mu_0) \cdot e_k^T \cdot x \leq \max(\mu_0) \cdot \max(x) \leq 2^{\mathrm{size}(\mathcal{P})^d}$$

for some constant d, where e_k denotes the k-th standard unit vector. $\qquad\square$

Lemma 3. *There is a polynomial p such that, for each conservative Petri net $\mathcal{P}$ with $n > 0$ and each firing sequence σ of its wipe-extension $\widehat{\mathcal{P}}$ leading to the empty marking $\mathbf{0}$, there is a permutation φ of σ enabled in $\widehat{\mathcal{P}}$ with $\max(\mu_0, \varphi) \leq 2^{p(n+m+\mathrm{ld}\,W+\mathrm{ld}\,\max(\mu_0))}$.*

Proof. Let $\widehat{\mathcal{P}} = (P, \widehat{T}, \widehat{F}, \mu_0)$ be the wipe-extension of a conservative Petri net $\mathcal{P} = (P, T, F, \mu_0)$. Let μ' be some marking reached in $\widehat{\mathcal{P}}$ by some Parikh vector Φ', Φ be the projection of Φ' onto the transitions of the original Petri net $\mathcal{P}$, and μ be the marking reached by Φ in $\mathcal{P}$. (Note that Φ is indeed enabled since all transitions we discard only remove tokens from the net.) Then, by Lemma 2, we observe $\max(\mu') \leq \max(\mu) \leq 2^{\mathrm{size}(\mathcal{P})^d}$ for some constant d. $\qquad\square$

Lemma 4. *The class $\mathcal{C}$ of conservative Petri nets is simple structurally f-f-canonical, where $f(n, m, W, K) = 2^{p(n+m+\mathrm{ld}\,W+\mathrm{ld}\,K)}$ for some polynomial p.*

Proof. By Theorem 1 and Lemma 3, there is a polynomial p such that $\mathcal{C}$ is f-f-canonical for the function f defined by $f(n, m, W, K) = 2^{p(n,m,\,\mathrm{ld}\,W,\,\mathrm{ld}\,K)}$. As argued before, we can check in polynomial time if a Petri net is conservative. Hence, $\mathcal{C}$ is simple. Since the conservation property does not depend on the initial marking, $\mathcal{C}$ is structurally f-f-canonical. $\qquad\square$

Lemma 5. *The reachability, the covering, and the liveness problems of conservative Petri nets are in* **PSPACE**.

Proof. By Theorem 2, Lemma 4, and by the fact that r is polynomial in $\mathrm{size}(\mathcal{P})$, the reachability and the covering problems are decidable in space polynomial in

$$\mathrm{size}(\mathcal{P}) + \mathrm{size}(\mu) + n\,\mathrm{ld}\,f(n, m, W, \max(\mu_0)) + r$$
$$= \mathrm{size}(\mathcal{P}) + \mathrm{size}(\mu) + n \cdot p(n + m + \mathrm{ld}\,W + \mathrm{ld}\,\max(\mu_0)) + r$$
$$\overset{P}{\leq} \mathrm{size}(\mathcal{P}) + \mathrm{size}(\mu),$$

where p is the polynomial of Lemma 4. Similarly, Theorem 4 and Lemma 4 imply that the liveness problem is decidable in space polynomial in

$$\text{size}(\mathcal{P}) + n \operatorname{ld}(f(n, m, W, \max(\mu_0) + f(n, m, W, \max(\mu_0))W)) + r$$

$$= \text{size}(\mathcal{P}) + n \operatorname{ld}(2^{p(n+m+\operatorname{ld} W + \operatorname{ld}(\max(\mu_0) + 2^{p(n+m+\operatorname{ld} W + \operatorname{ld} \max(\mu_0))}W))})$$

$$\overset{P}{\leq} \text{size}(\mathcal{P}) + np'(n + m + \operatorname{ld} W + \operatorname{ld}(\max(\mu_0))) \overset{P}{\leq} \text{size}(\mathcal{P}),$$

where p is the polynomial of Lemma 4, and p' is some polynomial. □

We now show that the liveness problem is **PSPACE**-hard in the strong sense. We remark that a straightforward adaption of Hack's reduction [4] from the reachability problem to the liveness problem is not possible since it uses the zero-reachability problem as an intermediate step and, more importantly, it yields Petri nets that are not necessarily conservative. On the other hand, our approach is similar to that used by Jones et al. [10] for the reachability and containment problems of ordinary 1-conservative Petri nets, and to that used by Mayr and Weihmann [16] for generalized communication-free Petri nets and generalized S-systems/weighted state machines.

For languages $L \in$ **PSPACE**, we define a Turing machine in standard form deciding L.

Definition 2 (TM in standard form). *Let $L \in$ **PSPACE** be a language decided by a deterministic Turing machine $M = (Q, \Gamma, \Sigma, \delta, q_0, \square, F)$, where Q is a set of states, $\Gamma \supsetneq \Sigma$ is the tape alphabet, Σ (with $Q \cap \Sigma = \emptyset$) is the input alphabet, $\delta \subseteq (Q \setminus \{q_{acc}\} \times \Gamma) \times (Q \times \Gamma \times \{-1, 0, 1\})$ is the transition relation, $q_0 \in Q$ is the initial state, $\square \in \Gamma \setminus \Sigma$ is the blank symbol, and $F \in Q$ is a set of final states. Then, M is in standard form if $F = \{q_{acc}\}$, if it is a single-tape polynomial space TM, and if, on input $x \in \Sigma^*$, it exhibits the following behavior:*

- *at the beginning, the tape contains the word x in the first $|x|$ positions, and all other positions contain $\square$,*
- *M only uses the first $\ell_S = (|x| + 2)^{c_1}$ tape positions at each step of the computation for some constant $c_1 \in \mathbb{N}$,*
- *M halts after at most $\ell_T = 2^{(|x|+2)^{c_2}}$ steps for some constant $c_2 \in \mathbb{N}$,*
- *if M enters the state q_{acc}, then it immediately halts, all tape positions contain $\square$, and the head is over the first tape position.*

It is not hard to see that every language $L \in$ **PSPACE** has such a Turing machine. Let $L \in$ **PSPACE**, and M be a Turing machine in standard form deciding L. Using M, we will define a polynomial time reduction from L to the liveness problem. In the following, a transition $d \in \delta$ of M is called M-transition.

Definition 3 (Petri net $\mathcal{P}_{M,x}$). *Let $M = (Q, \Gamma, \Sigma, \delta, q_0, \square, q_{acc})$ be a Turing machine in standard form, and $x \in \Sigma^*$. Then, the Petri net $\mathcal{P}_{M,x} = (P, T, F, \mu_0)$ is defined in the following way:*

- *for each position $i \in [\ell_S]$, symbol $s \in \Gamma$, and state $q \in Q$ there are the places $p_{i,s}^{\Gamma}$ and $p_{i,q}^{Q}$,*

- *for each position $i \in [\ell_S]$ and M-transition $d = ((q, s), (q', s', y)) \in \delta$, there is a transition $t_{i,d}$ with $1 = F(p^\Gamma_{i,s}, t_{i,d}) = F(p^Q_{i,q}, t_{i,d}) = F(t_{i,d}, p^\Gamma_{i,s'}) = F(t_{i,d}, p^Q_{i+y,q'})$, and*
- *μ_0 contains exactly one token at p^Q_{1,q_0} and at each of the places $p^\Gamma_{i,x_{[i]}}$, $i \in [|x|]$, and $p^\Gamma_{i,\square}$, $i \in [|x| + 1, \ell_S]$, and all other places are empty.*

The place $p^\Gamma_{1,q_{acc}}$ is also denoted by p_{acc}.

Semantically, the places $p^\Gamma_{i,s}$ encode the contents of the tape, while the places $p^Q_{i,q}$ encode the position of the head and the state of M. The transitions of $\mathcal{P}_{M,x}$ are used to simulate the transitions of M.

Definition 4 (Configuration marking). *A marking μ of $\mathcal{P}_{M,x}$ corresponds to a configuration of a Turing machine $M = (Q, \Gamma, \Sigma, \delta, q_0, \square, q_{acc})$ in standard form, where only the first ℓ_S positions may be different from $\square$, these positions contain the string $y \in \Gamma^{\ell_S}$, M is in state q, and the head is over position i, if the following holds:*

- *$p^Q_{i,q}$ is marked,*
- *for each $j \in [\ell_S]$, $\mu(p^\Gamma_{j,y_{[j]}}) = 1$, and*
- *all other places are empty.*

A marking that corresponds to a configuration of M is a configuration marking. *The configuration corresponding to a configuration marking μ is denoted by $conf(\mu)$. The configuration marking corresponding to the unique accepting configuration of M is denoted by μ_{acc}.*

Note that, for each configuration C reachable by M on input x, there is a unique configuration marking corresponding to C. Moreover, the initial marking μ_0 of $\mathcal{P}_{M,x}$ is a configuration marking corresponding to the initial configuration of M.

Next, we show how firing sequences of $\mathcal{P}_{M,x}$ leading to configuration markings and computation paths of M on input x correspond to each other.

Lemma 6. *The following properties hold:*

- *(a) if a marking μ' is reachable from a configuration marking μ in $\mathcal{P}_{M,x}$, then μ' is a configuration marking,*
- *(b) if a transition sequence $\sigma = t_{i_1,d_1} \cdots t_{i_k,d_k}$ of $\mathcal{P}_{M,x}$ leads from a configuration marking μ to a configuration marking μ', then the sequence of M-transitions $d_1 \cdots d_k$ is a computation path of M and leads from $conf(\mu)$ to $conf(\mu')$, and*
- *(c) if a computation path $d_1 \cdots d_k$ of M leads from $conf(\mu)$ to $conf(\mu')$ and only uses the first ℓ_S tape positions, then there are $i_1, \ldots, i_k \in [\ell_S]$ such that $t_{i_1,d_1} \cdots t_{i_k,d_k}$ leads from μ to μ' in $\mathcal{P}_{M,x}$.*

Proof. Property (a) follows from the observation that if a transition of $\mathcal{P}_{M,x}$ is fired at some configuration marking, then the marking we obtain is also a configuration marking. Properties (b) and (c) are also shown easily: Assume that $t_{i,d}$ leads from a configuration marking μ to a configuration marking μ'. Then, we observe that executing d at $\mathrm{conf}(\mu)$ leads to $\mathrm{conf}(\mu')$. Consider an M-transition $d \in \delta$ that is executed at configuration $\mathrm{conf}(\mu)$, where the head of M is at position $i \in [\ell_S]$, yielding a configuration C, where the head is at position of $[\ell_S]$. Then, firing $t_{i,d}$ at μ yields a marking μ' with $C = \mathrm{conf}(\mu')$. We apply these arguments to all transitions of σ respectively all M-transitions of the computation path. $\qquad\square$

The correspondence of computation paths and firing sequences has a number of useful implications, which are collected in the next lemma.

Lemma 7. *There is a unique longest firing sequence σ of $\mathcal{P}_{M,x}$. This firing sequence σ satisfies $|\sigma| \le \ell_T$. Each firing sequence is a prefix of σ. Furthermore, the following are equivalent:*

- *M accepts x,*
- *μ_{acc} is reachable in $\mathcal{P}_{M,x}$,*
- *some marking μ with $\mu(p_{\mathrm{acc}}) \ge 1$ is reachable, and*
- *σ leads to μ_{acc}.*

Proof. Since M is deterministic and always terminates (in particular, it terminates in the unique accepting configuration if M accepts x), Lemma 6 implies that there is a unique longest firing sequence σ, and each firing sequence is a prefix of σ (i.e., $\mathcal{P}_{M,x}$ is a single-path Petri net). By this, by Lemma 6, and by the fact that M is in standard form, the rest of the lemma follows. $\qquad\square$

We can use the equivalences shown in the last lemma to finally obtain the desired lower bound for the liveness problem of conservative Petri nets.

Lemma 8. *The liveness problem of conservative Petri nets is* **PSPACE**-*hard in the strong sense, even if restricted to ordinary 1-conservative Petri nets.*

Proof. By Lemma 7, we can use p_{acc} as a control place, which can be marked if and only if it is eventually marked if and only if M accepts x. We obtain the ordinary 1-conservative Petri net $\mathcal{P} = (P', T', F', \mu_0)$ by modifying $\mathcal{P}_{M,x} = (P, T, F, \mu_0)$ in the following way. We add a new place p'_{acc} and two new transitions t, t' with $F'(p'_{\mathrm{acc}}, t) = F'(t, p_{\mathrm{acc}}) = 1$ and $F'(p_{\mathrm{acc}}, t') = F'(t', p'_{\mathrm{acc}}) = 1$. These transitions can transfer tokens freely between p_{acc} and p'_{acc}. Note that, once p_{acc} is marked for the first time, at least one of these new places remains marked. For each two places p, $p' \in P \setminus \{p_{\mathrm{acc}}, p'_{\mathrm{acc}}\}$, we add a transition t with $F'(p_{\mathrm{acc}}, t) = F'(p, t) = F'(t, p_{\mathrm{acc}}) = F'(t, p') = 1$. These transitions can be used to transfer tokens freely between the (original) places of P once p_{acc} is marked for the first time. (If necessary, we can transfer a token from p'_{acc} back to p_{acc} to enable these transitions.) Last, we add a transition t^* with $F'(p_{\mathrm{acc}}, t^*) = F'(p'_{\mathrm{acc}}, t^*) = F'(t^*, p_{\mathrm{acc}}) = F'(t^*, p^{\Gamma}_{1,\square}) = 1$. The transition t^* can be used to decrease the total number of tokens at p_{acc} and p'_{acc} to 1 if they together contain at least 2 tokens.

If M does not accept x, then none of the new transitions can ever fire. If M accepts x, then σ marks p_{acc}. As long as p_{acc} is marked, we can use the new transitions to freely transfer at least 2 tokens within the net. (Note that the net always contains at least 3 tokens since M is in standard form.) Since $\{p_{acc}, p'_{acc}\}$ is a trap, and therefore cannot be unmarked once it is marked, we observe that, for each transition $t \in T'$ and each marking μ reachable from μ_{acc} in $\mathcal{P}$, there is a marking μ' reachable from μ in $\mathcal{P}$ which enables t. Therefore, M accepts x if and only if $\mathcal{P}$ is live. $\square$

The proofs for **PSPACE**-hardness of the reachability and the covering problems of ordinary 1-conservative Petri nets given in [10] actually yield **PSPACE**-hardness *in the strong sense*. In total, we obtain the following result.

Theorem 6. *The reachability, the covering, and the liveness problems of conservative Petri nets are* **PSPACE***-complete in the strong sense, even if restricted to ordinary 1-conservative Petri nets.*

Proof. The theorem follows from (the proofs of) Theorem 3.1 and Corollary 3.2 of [10], and Lemmata 5 and 8. $\square$

We now consider the RecLFS problem.

Lemma 9. *The RecLFS-problem of general Petri nets using an (appropriate) unary encoding scheme is* **NP***-complete in the strong sense.*

Proof. **NP**-hardness in the strong sense has been shown by Watanabe et al. [18]. Membership in **NP** is implied by the fact that a nondeterministic Turing machine can guess the order in which the transitions of Φ can be fired. Each step also takes only polynomial time since each marking obtained when firing Φ has polynomial encoding size. $\square$

Corollary 2. *If* **NP** $\subsetneq$ **PSPACE***, then the RecLFS problem of general Petri nets is not* **PSPACE***-hard in the strong sense.*

Even though Corollary 2 implies that the RecLFS problem is probably not **PSPACE**-hard in the strong sense, we can, however, show that it is **PSPACE**-hard (in the weak sense) and subsequently **PSPACE**-complete.

Theorem 7. *The RecLFS problem is* **PSPACE***-complete, even if restricted to ordinary 1-conservative Petri nets.*

Proof. By Theorem 1 of [16], the RecLFS problem is in **PSPACE**. We now show the lower bound. We obtain the ordinary 1-conservative Petri net $\mathcal{P} = (P', T', F', \mu_0)$ by modifying $\mathcal{P}_{M,x} = (P, T, F, \mu_0)$ in the following way. First, we add a new place p^* and a new transition r_1 with $F'(p_{acc}, r_1) = F'(r_1, p^*) = 1$. Next, we add $n = |P|$ new places $p'_1, \ldots, p'_n$, each marked with $\ell_T \cdot |\delta|$ tokens, where ℓ_T is an upper bound on the running time of M on input x (see Definition 2). Last, we add a transition r_2 with $F'(p'_i, r_2) = F'(r_2, p) = 1$ for all $i \in [n]$ and $p \in P$, and $F'(p^*, r_2) = F'(r_2, p^*) = 1$. Consider the Parikh vector Φ with $\Phi(t) = \ell_T$ for all $t \in T$, $\Phi(r_1) = 1$, and $\Phi(r_2) = \ell_T \cdot |\delta|$.

Assume that M accepts x. By Lemma 7, $\mathcal{P}$ has a firing sequence σ of length at most ℓ_T leading to a marking at which p_{acc} is marked. Then, $\rho := \sigma \cdot r_1 \cdot r_2^{\ell_T \cdot |\delta|}$. $\prod_{t \in T} t^{(\ell_T - \Psi(\sigma)(t))}$ is a firing sequence of $\mathcal{P}$ with $\Psi(\rho) = \Phi$. If, on the other hand, M does not accept x, then, by Lemma 7, p_{acc} cannot be marked. Consequently, r_1 can never be fired which implies that Φ is not enabled. This reduction can be performed in polynomial time.   □

Last, we consider the containment and equivalence problems. For conservative Petri nets, Theorem 5 would not yield a good upper bound since it uses SLSRs as tool, which can have exponential size. Instead, we use a direct approach.

Theorem 8. *The containment problem and equivalence problem of conservative Petri nets are* **PSPACE**-*complete in the strong sense, even if restricted to ordinary 1-conservative Petri nets.*

Proof. We obtain the Petri net $\mathcal{P}_1 = (P_1, T_1, F_1, \mu_1)$ from $\mathcal{P}_{M,x} = (P, T, F, \mu_0)$ in the following way: We add $\ell_S + 1$ places $p_1^*, \ldots, p_{\ell_S+1}^*$, and a transition t_1^* with $F_1(p_i^*, t_1^*) = 1$, $i \in [\ell_S + 1]$ and $F_1(t_1^*, p) = 1$ for all p with $\mu_0(p) = 1$. The initial marking μ_1 of $\mathcal{P}_1$ has one token at each place p_i^*, $i \in [\ell_S + 1]$ and is empty at all other places. Transition t_1^* can be used to mark the places of P with μ_0. Now, we obtain $\mathcal{P}_2 = (P_1, T_1 \cup \{t_2^*\}, F_2, \mu_2)$ from $\mathcal{P}_1$ by adding a transition t_2^* with $F_2(p_i^*, t_1^*) = 1$ and $F_2(t_1^*, p) = 1$ for all p with $\mu_{acc}(p) = 1$. Transition t_2^* can be used to mark the places of P with μ_{acc}. Both $\mathcal{P}_1$ and $\mathcal{P}_2$ are ordinary 1-conservative Petri nets that can be constructed in time polynomial in $|x|$. The following are equivalent:

- M accepts x,
- μ_{acc} is reachable in $\mathcal{P}_{M,x}$,
- $\mathcal{R}(\mathcal{P}_2) \subseteq \mathcal{R}(\mathcal{P}_1)$, and
- $\mathcal{R}(\mathcal{P}_2) = \mathcal{R}(\mathcal{P}_1)$.

Hence, the lower bound of the theorem follows. For **PSPACE**-membership observe that if $\mathcal{R}(\mathcal{P}_1) \not\subseteq \mathcal{R}(\mathcal{P}_2)$ respectively $\mathcal{R}(\mathcal{P}_1) \neq \mathcal{R}(\mathcal{P}_2)$ holds, then, by Lemma 2, there is a polynomially sized reachable marking serving as a witness. Using Lemma 5, we can check in polynomial space if such a marking exists.   □

References

1. Cardoza, E., Lipton, R., Meyer, A.R.: Exponential space complete problems for Petri nets and commutative semigroups (preliminary report). In: Proceedings of the 8th ACM Symposium on Theory of Computing (STOC 1976), pp. 50–54. ACM (1976)
2. Esparza, J.: Petri nets, commutative context-free grammars, and basic parallel processes. Fundamenta Informaticae 31(1), 13–25 (1997)
3. Esparza, J., Nielsen, M.: Decibility issues for Petri nets - a survey. Journal of Information Processing and Cybernetics 30(3), 143–160 (1994)

4. Hack, M.: The recursive equivalence of the reachability problem and the liveness problem for Petri nets and vector addition systems. In: IEEE Conference Record of the 15th Annual Symposium on Switching and Automata Theory, pp. 156–164 (1974)
5. Howell, R.R., Jancar, P., Rosier, L.E.: Completeness results for single-path Petri nets. Information and Computation 106(2), 253–265 (1993)
6. Howell, R.R., Rosier, L.E.: Completeness results for conflict-free vector replacement systems. Journal of Computer and System Sciences 37(3), 349–366 (1988)
7. Howell, R.R., Rosier, L.E., Yen, H.C.: Normal and sinkless Petri nets. In: Csirik, J., Demetrovics, J., Gécseg, F. (eds.) Proceedings of the 1989 International Conference on Fundamentals of Computation Theory (FCT 1989). LNCS, vol. 380, pp. 234–243. Springer, Heidelberg (1989)
8. Huynh, D.T.: The complexity of semilinear sets. In: de Bakker, J., van Leeuwen, J. (eds.) ICALP 1980. LNCS, vol. 85, pp. 324–337. Springer, Heidelberg (1980)
9. Huynh, D.T.: A simple proof for the Σ_2^p upper bound of the inequivalence problem for semilinear sets. Elektronische Informationsverarbeitung und Kybernetik 22, 147–156 (1986)
10. Jones, N.D., Landweber, L.H., Lien, Y.E.: Complexity of some problems in Petri nets. Theoretical Computer Science 4(3), 277–299 (1977)
11. Karmarkar, N.: A new polynomial-time algorithm for linear programming. Combinatorica 4(4), 373–395 (1984)
12. Lien, Y.E.: A note on transition systems. Information Sciences 10(4), 347–362 (1976)
13. Lien, Y.E.: Termination properties of generalized Petri nets. SIAM Journal on Computing 5(2), 251–265 (1976)
14. Mayr, E.W.: An algorithm for the general Petri net reachability problem. SIAM Journal on Computing 13(3), 441–460 (1984)
15. Mayr, E.W., Meyer, A.R.: The complexity of the word problems for commutative semigroups and polynomial ideals. Advances in Mathematics 46(3), 305–329 (1982)
16. Mayr, E.W., Weihmann, J.: Completeness results for generalized communication-free Petri nets with arbitrary edge multiplicities. In: Abdulla, P.A., Potapov, I. (eds.) RP 2013. LNCS, vol. 8169, pp. 209–221. Springer, Heidelberg (2013)
17. Teruel, E., Silva, M.: Well-formedness of equal conflict systems. In: Valette, R. (ed.) ICATPN 1994. LNCS, vol. 815, pp. 491–510. Springer, Heidelberg (1994)
18. Watanabe, T., Mizobata, Y., Onaga, K.: Legal firing sequence and related problems of Petri nets. In: Proceedings of the 3rd International Workshop on Petri Nets and Performance Models (PNPM 1989), pp. 277–286 (1989)
19. Yen, H.C.: On reachability equivalence for BPP-nets. Theoretical Computer Science 179, 301–317 (1997)

On the Reversibility of Well-Behaved Weighted Choice-Free Systems

Thomas Hujsa[1,*], Jean-Marc Delosme[2], and Alix Munier-Kordon[1]

[1] Sorbonne Universités, UPMC Paris 06, UMR 7606, LIP6, F-75005, Paris, France
{Thomas.Hujsa,Alix.Munier}@lip6.fr
[2] Université d'Evry-Val-D'Essonne, IBISC, 91025, Evry, France
Jean-Marc.Delosme@ibisc.univ-evry.fr

Abstract. A Petri net is reversible if its initial marking is a home marking, a marking reachable from any reachable marking. Under the assumption of well-behavedness we investigate the property of reversibility for strongly connected weighted Choice-Free Petri nets, nets which structurally avoid conflicts. Several characterizations of liveness and reversibility as well as exponential methods for building live and home markings are available for these nets. We provide a new characterization of reversibility leading to the construction in polynomial time of an initial marking with a polynomial number of tokens that is live and reversible. We also introduce a polynomial time transformation of well-formed Choice-Free systems into well-formed T-systems and we deduce from it a polynomial time sufficient condition of liveness and reversibility for well-formed Choice-Free systems. We show that neither one of these two approaches subsumes the other.

Keywords: Reversibility, well-behavedness, polynomial conditions, decomposition, place-splitting transformation, weighted Petri nets, Choice-Free, Fork-Attribution, T-system.

1 Introduction

Weighted Choice-Free Petri nets constrain every place to have at most one output transition, hence structurally avoid conflicts. They extend the expressiveness of weighted T-systems, also known as generalized Event Graphs, which are equivalent to Synchronous Data Flow graphs (SDF)[1] and have been widely used to model embedded applications. Choice-Free Petri nets are called *output-nonbranching* in [2], where they are shown to be distributable.

Home markings can be reached from any reachable marking. Used as an initial data distribution of the system, they avoid a transient phase and define a reversible Petri net. In this context, all reachable markings remain reachable after any firing sequence. This reversibility property is often required in embedded applications that need a steady behavior. Moreover, the study of the reachability graph is consequently simplified.

---

* The work of this author is supported by Digiteo / Project Tatami.

G. Ciardo and E. Kindler (Eds.): PETRI NETS 2014, LNCS 8489, pp. 334–353, 2014.

Relationship with Well-Behavedness. Embedded systems have to keep all their functions active over time within bounded memory. In Petri nets, these requirements are formalized by the notions of liveness and boundedness, which, taken together, define well-behavedness. The objective is to build systems that are well-behaved and reversible. However, live systems are not necessarily reversible, while reversibility does not imply liveness [3]. In this paper, we focus on the reversibility property under the well-behavedness hypothesis. Since the well-formedness property, defining structural liveness and structural boundedness, is necessary for the well-behavedness of Choice-Free systems [4], we focus on systems that are well-formed.

Previous Results. All strongly connected well-behaved T-systems are known to be reversible [5]. Characterizations of liveness, well-behavedness and reversibility have been found for the class of Choice-Free systems [4], even though reversibility may not be deduced from well-behavedness for these systems. However, the existing reversibility condition is expressed in terms of the ability to fire a sequence whose size is exponential and does not lead trivially to a polynomial time algorithm for checking the reversibility or building a reversible marking of reasonable size. Live and reversible initial markings for Choice-Free systems are constructed in [4] by finding a solution of an integer linear program with an exponential number of constraints.

Home markings have also been studied in other subclasses of weighted Petri nets. For instance, in Workflow nets, reversibility in a variant of the system provides information on other behavioral properties [6]. The existence of home markings is stated for Equal-Conflict systems, which generalize Choice-Free systems [7], as well as the class of DSSP, which simulate Equal-Conflict systems [8]. However, the construction of home markings is not provided for these classes.

Another approach for studying the behavior consists in transforming the system while preserving some properties. Many transformation rules have been proposed, some of which can be found in [3,9,10,11]. However, they do not apply to the complete class of systems studied in this paper.

Contributions. We propose two new approaches for studying the reversibility of well-behaved Choice-Free systems.

First, extending a liveness characterization of [4], we show that the reversibility of a Choice-Free system can be expressed in terms of the reversibility of particular subsystems belonging to the Fork-Attribution class, where transitions have at most one input. This decomposition leads to the first live and reversible initial marking for Choice-Free systems that is constructed in polynomial time with a polynomial number of tokens, contrasting with previous exponential methods.

We focus then on well-formed Choice-Free systems, for which we provide a polynomial time transformation into a well-formed T-system by splitting places having several inputs while preserving the set of T-semiflows. Using a known polynomial time sufficient condition of liveness for well-formed T-systems, we obtain a polynomial time sufficient condition of liveness and reversibility for well-formed Choice-Free systems. We show that this condition neither implies the marking construction nor is induced by this marking. Thus both approaches are worthy of interest.

Organization of the Paper. In Section 2, we recall general definitions, notations and properties of Petri nets. Several structural and behavioral properties of Choice-Free systems are also detailed. In Section 3, we present the new characterization of reversibility and the construction of the polynomial live and home marking. We study then the particular case of T-systems. In Section 4, the place splitting transformation is detailed, as well as the new polynomial time sufficient condition of liveness and reversibility. Finally, the two conditions are compared.

2   Definitions, Notations and Properties

We first recall definitions and notations for weighted nets, markings, systems and firing sequences. Classical notions, such as liveness and boundedness, are formalized. We also consider particular subnets, subsystems and subsequences. We then present the special classes of nets considered in this paper, namely Choice-Free nets and some of their subclasses. Finally, we recall general results on the structure and behavior of Choice-Free nets.

2.1   Weighted and Ordinary Nets

A *(weighted) net* is a triple $N = (P, T, W)$ where:

- the sets P and T are finite and disjoint, T contains only transitions and P only places,
- $W : (P \times T) \cup (T \times P) \mapsto \mathbb{N}$ is a weight function.

$P \cup T$ is the set of the elements of the net.

An arc is present from a place p to a transition t (resp. a transition t to a place p) if $W(p, t) > 0$ (resp. $W(t, p) > 0$). An *ordinary* net is a net whose weight function W takes values in $\{0, 1\}$.

The *incidence matrix* of a net $N = (P, T, W)$ is a place-transition matrix C defined as

$$\forall p \in P \ \ \forall t \in T, \ \ C[p, t] = W(t, p) - W(p, t)$$

where the weight of any non-existing arc is 0.

The *pre-set* of the element x of $P \cup T$ is the set $\{w | W(w, x) > 0\}$, denoted by ${}^\bullet x$. By extension, for any subset E of P or T, ${}^\bullet E = \bigcup_{x \in E} {}^\bullet x$.

The *post-set* of the element x of $P \cup T$ is the set $\{y | W(x, y) > 0\}$, denoted by $x^\bullet$. Similarly, $E^\bullet = \bigcup_{x \in E} x^\bullet$.

We denote by max_p^N the maximum output weight of p in the net N and by gcd_p^N the greatest common divisor of all input and output weights of p in the net N. The simpler notations max_p and gcd_p are used when no confusion is possible.

A *source place* has at least one output transition and no input transition. A *join-transition* has at least two input places. A net is *well-connected* if it is connected and each place and transition has at least one input.

2.2 Markings, Systems and Firing Sequences

A *marking* M of a net N is a mapping $M : P \to \mathbb{N}$. We shall also denote by M the column vector whose components are the values $M(p)$ for $p \in P$. A *system* is a couple (N, M_0) where N is a net and M_0 its initial marking.

A marking M of a net N *enables* a transition $t \in T$ if $\forall p \in {}^{\bullet}t, M(p) \geq W(p, t)$. A marking M *enables* a place $p \in P$ if $M(p) \geq max_p$. The marking M' obtained from M by the firing of an enabled transition t, noted $M \xrightarrow{t} M'$, is defined by $\forall p \in P, M'(p) = M(p) - W(p, t) + W(t, p)$.

A *firing sequence* σ of length $n \geq 1$ on the set of transitions T is a mapping $\{1, \ldots, n\} \to T$. A sequence is *infinite* if its domain is countably infinite. A firing sequence $\sigma = t_1 t_2 \cdots t_n$ is *feasible* if the successive markings obtained, $M_0 \xrightarrow{t_1} M_1 \xrightarrow{t_2} M_2 \cdots \xrightarrow{t_n} M_n$, are such that M_{i-1} enables the transition t_i for any $i \in \{1, \cdots, n\}$. We note $M_0 \xrightarrow{\sigma} M_n$.

The *Parikh vector* $\vec{\sigma} : T \to \mathbb{N}$ associated with a finite sequence of transitions σ maps every transition t of T to the number of occurrences of t in σ.

A marking M' is said to be *reachable* from the marking M if there exists a feasible firing sequence σ such that $M \xrightarrow{\sigma} M'$. The set of markings reachable from M is denoted by $[M\rangle$.

A *home marking* is a marking that can be reached from any reachable marking. Formally, M is a home marking in the system (N, M_0) if $\forall M' \in [M_0\rangle, M \in [M'\rangle$. A system is *reversible* if its initial marking is a home marking.

2.3 Liveness and Boundedness

Liveness and boundedness are two basic properties ensuring that all transitions of a system $S = (N, M_0)$ can always be fired and that the overall number of tokens remains bounded. More formally,

- A system S is *live* if for every marking M in $[M_0\rangle$ and for every transition t, there exists a marking M' in $[M\rangle$ enabling t.
- S is *bounded* if there exists an integer k such that the number of tokens in each place never exceeds k. Formally, $\exists k \in \mathbb{N}\ \forall M \in [M_0\rangle\ \forall p \in P,\ M(p) \leq k$.
  S is *k-bounded* if, for any place $p \in P$, $k \geq \max\{M(p) | M \in [M_0\rangle\}$.
- A system S is *well-behaved* if it is live and bounded.

A marking M is live (resp. bounded) for a net N if the system (N, M) is live (resp. bounded). The structure of a net N may be studied to ensure the existence of an initial marking M_0 such that (N, M_0) is live and bounded:

- N is *structurally live* if a marking M_0 exists such that (N, M_0) is live.
- N is *structurally bounded* if the system (N, M_0) is bounded for each M_0.
- N is *well-formed* if it is structurally live and structurally bounded.

The algebraic properties of consistency and conservativeness are necessary conditions for well-formedness for all weighted Petri nets [12,13]. They are defined next in terms of the existence of particular annulers of the incidence matrix.

2.4 Semiflows, Consistency and Conservativeness

Semiflows are particular left or right annulers of an incidence matrix C that is supposed to be non-empty:

- A P-semiflow is a non-null vector $X \in \mathbb{N}^{|P|}$ such that ${}^{t}X \cdot C = 0$.
- A T-semiflow is a non-null vector $Y \in \mathbb{N}^{|T|}$ such that $C \cdot Y = 0$.

A P-semiflow is *minimal* if the greatest common divisor of its components is equal to 1 and its support is not a proper superset of the support of any other P-semiflow. The same definition applies to T-semiflows.

We denote by $\mathbb{1}^{n}$ the column vector of size n whose components are all equal to 1. The conservativeness and consistency properties are defined as follows using the incidence matrix C of a net N:

- N is *conservative* if a P-semiflow $X \in \mathbb{N}^{|P|}$ exists for C such that $X \geq \mathbb{1}^{|P|}$.
- N is *consistent* if a T-semiflow $Y \in \mathbb{N}^{|T|}$ exists for C such that $Y \geq \mathbb{1}^{|T|}$.

The net on Figure 1 is conservative and consistent.

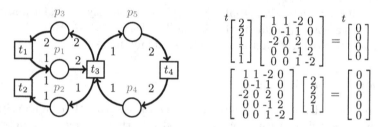

Fig. 1. This weighted net is conservative (the *left vector* $[2, 2, 1, 1, 1]$ is a P-semiflow and its components are ≥ 1) and consistent (the *right vector* ${}^{t}[2, 2, 2, 1]$ is a T-semiflow and its components are ≥ 1)

2.5 P-subnets, P-subsystems and Subsequences

The sequence σ' is a *subsequence* of the sequence σ if σ' is obtained from σ by removing some transitions of σ. The *restriction of σ to the set* $T' \subseteq T$ *of transitions* is the maximum subsequence of σ whose transitions belong to T'.

The net $N' = (P', T', W')$ is a *P-subnet* of $N = (P, T, W)$ if P' is a subset of P, $T' = {}^{\bullet}P' \cup P'^{\bullet}$ and W' is the restriction of W to P' and T'. Figure 2 shows two P-subnets of the net in Figure 1.

The system $S' = (N', M_0')$, with $N' = (P', T', W')$, is a *P-subsystem* of $S = (N, M_0)$ if N' is a P-subnet of N and its initial marking M_0' is restricted to P', i.e. $M_0' = M_0|_{P'}$.

2.6   Choice-Free Nets and Subclasses

$N = (P, T, W)$ is a (weighted) *Choice-Free net* if each place has at most one output transition, *i.e.* $\forall p \in P, |p^\bullet| \leq 1$. A *T-net* (Event Graph) is a Choice-Free net such that each place has at most one input transition, *i.e.* $\forall p \in P, |{}^\bullet p| \leq 1$. A *Fork-Attribution* net (or FA net) is a Choice-Free net in which transitions have at most one input place, *i.e.* $\forall t \in T, |{}^\bullet t| \leq 1$.

The nets presented in Figures 1 and 2 are Choice-Free. The net on the left hand side of Figure 2 is an FA net while the net on the right hand side is a circuit, hence a particular T-net and FA net.

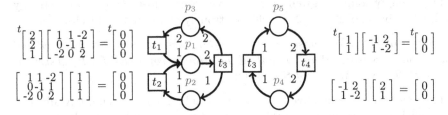

Fig. 2. Two FA P-subnets of the net of Figure 1. On the left, the P-subnet is defined by the set of places $\{p_1, p_2, p_3\}$. The net on the right is defined by the set of places $\{p_4, p_5\}$. Moreover, these two nets are conservative and consistent.

In this paper, we focus on well-formed Choice-Free nets. We recall next properties of Choice-Free systems that arise from their absence of conflicts and deal with well-formedness, liveness and firing sequences. The next proposition expresses a necessary and sufficient condition of well-formedness for this class and states its necessity for well-behavedness, which is not the case for all Petri nets.

Proposition 1 ([4]). *Suppose that N is a weighted and strongly connected Choice-Free net. The properties*

- *N is consistent and conservative*
- *N is well-formed*

are equivalent. Moreover, if a marking M_0 exists such that (N, M_0) is well-behaved, then N is well-formed.

Figure 1 shows a strongly connected, consistent and conservative, thus well-formed, Choice-Free net. Similarly, the two nets of Figure 2 are well-formed.

The existence of T-semiflows induces strong structural and behavioral properties. In the case of well-formed Choice-Free nets, they are detailed below.

Proposition 2 ([4]). *If $N = (P, T, W)$ is a well-formed and strongly connected Choice-Free net, then N has a unique minimal T-semiflow Y. Moreover, the support of Y is the whole set T.*

A decomposition theory has been developed for Choice-Free systems and larger classes [4,14], allowing to get insight into their structure and behavior by studying particular subsystems. The next results show the relevance of FA P-subsystems to the study of well-formedness and liveness in Choice-Free systems.

Proposition 3 ([4]). *Consider a strongly connected well-formed Choice-Free net N with unique minimal T-semiflow Y. If $N_* = (P_*, T_*, W_*)$ is a strongly connected FA P-subnet of N then N_* is well-formed, with a unique minimal T-semiflow Y_*, and $Y_{|T_*}$ is a multiple of Y_*. Moreover, N is covered by such FA P-subnets.*

The strongly connected well-formed Choice-Free net of Figure 1 is covered by the FA P-subnets of Figure 2, which are strongly connected and well-formed.

Proposition 4 ([4]). *Consider a Choice-Free system $S = (N, M_0)$ without source places. S is live if and only if all the strongly connected FA P-subsystems $S_* = ((P_*, T_*, W_*), M_0|_{P_*})$ of S are live.*

This characterization of liveness in terms of subsystems does not trivially lead to an efficient algorithm for checking liveness, as one may have to check an exponential number of subsystems.

A system is persistent if every reachable marking M that enables two transitions t_1 and t_2 enables the sequence $t_1 t_2$. Persistent systems encompass the structurally persistent Choice-Free systems and have a *confluent* language [4,15,16,17]. This property is also known as the *Church-Rosser* property in the context of rewriting systems. A constructive theorem of confluence for persistent systems exists [16], however, we only need the following one, illustrated in Figure 3.

Proposition 5 (Confluence ([4])). *Consider a Choice-Free system (N, M_0). If M_1 and M_2 are reachable markings such that $M_0 \xrightarrow{\sigma} M_1$ and $M_0 \xrightarrow{\tau} M_2$ then a marking M_3 exists such that $M_1 \xrightarrow{\alpha} M_3$ and $M_2 \xrightarrow{\beta} M_3$, where the feasible sequences α and β satisfy the following conditions for every transition t:*

$$\vec{\alpha}(t) = \max\{\vec{\sigma}(t), \vec{\tau}(t)\} - \vec{\sigma}(t)$$
$$\vec{\beta}(t) = \max\{\vec{\sigma}(t), \vec{\tau}(t)\} - \vec{\tau}(t).$$

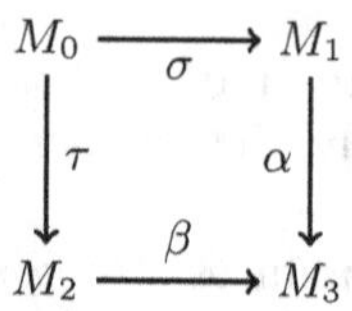

$$\begin{array}{ccc}
M_0 & \xrightarrow{\sigma} & M_1 \\
\downarrow{\scriptstyle\tau} & & \downarrow{\scriptstyle\alpha} \\
M_2 & \xrightarrow{\beta} & M_3
\end{array}$$

Fig. 3. If the sequences σ and τ are feasible in the Choice-Free system, then the feasible sequences α and β exist and reach the same marking M_3

3   Reversibility of Well-Behaved Choice-Free Systems

In Choice-Free systems, well-behavedness does not imply reversibility [4]. Under the well-behavedness hypothesis, we provide a new necessary and sufficient condition of reversibility that is expressed in terms of the reversibility of particular subsystems, namely strongly connected FA P-subsystems. This result extends the liveness condition of Proposition 4 for well-formed Choice-Free systems, improving our understanding of their behavior from the decomposition point of view. To prove this condition, we exploit a known characterization of reversibility as well as a property of the sequences that are feasible in P-subsystems. Moreover, this approach allows to construct, for these systems, a *polynomial*, meaning in polynomial time with a polynomial number of tokens, live and reversible initial marking, whereas the older characterization gives no direct solution to this problem. Finally, we compare our result to the liveness and reversibility of the T-system subclass, in which the interesting P-subnets are circuits.

3.1   A Known Necessary and Sufficient Condition of Reversibility

A characterization of reversibility for well-behaved Choice-Free systems, presented in [4], is recalled below. This statement relies on the feasibility of a sequence whose Parikh vector is equal to the minimal T-semiflow.

Proposition 6 ([4]). *Consider a well-behaved and strongly connected Choice-Free system $S = (N, M_0)$ with unique minimal T-semiflow Y. S is reversible if and only if a sequence σ_Y such that $\vec{\sigma}_Y = Y$ is feasible at M_0.*

This proposition is used in the sequel to prove the new reversibility condition.

3.2   Preliminary Result about Subsequences and P-subsystems

We present a general technical result that deals with the restriction of sequences to P-subsystems. Such subsequences have been used in [14].

Lemma 1. *Consider a system $S = (N, M_0)$, where $N = (P, T, W)$, together with one of its P-subsystems $S' = (N', M_{0|P'})$, where $N' = (P', T', W')$. For every feasible sequence σ in S, the subsequence $\sigma_{|T'}$ is feasible in S'. Moreover, if $M_0 \xrightarrow{\sigma} M$ in S and $M_{0|P'} \xrightarrow{\sigma_{|T'}} M'$ in S', then $M_{|P'} = M'$.*

Proof. We prove the claim by induction on the size of a feasible sequence of size k in S. If σ is empty, it is feasible in both systems and the marking is unchanged.

Hence, suppose that $\sigma = \sigma_1 t$ is feasible in S, where σ_1 has size $k-1$, and that the claim is true when the size of the sequence is strictly smaller than k. We note $M_0 \xrightarrow{\sigma_1} M_1 \xrightarrow{t} M_2$ in S. By the induction hypothesis, $\sigma_{1|T'}$ is feasible in S', we note $M_{0|P'} \xrightarrow{\sigma_1|_{T'}} M_1'$ in S', and for every place p in P', $M_1(p) = M_1'(p)$.

As S' is a P-subsystem of S, a transition belongs to T' if and only if it is an input or output of at least one place of P'.

If t is not in T' then $\sigma_{1\,|T'}$ equals $\sigma_{|T'}$, which is thus feasible in S'. Moreover, t does not modify the marking of places in P', thus $M'_1 = M_{2\,|P'}$.

Otherwise t belongs to T' and is enabled in (N, M_1). Moreover, $M_{1\,|P'} = M'_1$, implying that the input places of t that belong to P' are enabled in (N', M'_1), thus t is enabled in (N', M'_1). We note $M'_1 \xrightarrow{t} M'_2$. Finally, a place p in P' is an input or output of t in N if and only if it is one or the other in N' thus $M_{2\,|P'} = M'_2$. □

3.3   A New Necessary Condition of Reversibility

As mentioned earlier, we focus on strongly connected well-behaved Choice-Free systems. We present here the necessity part of our characterization of reversibility. For that purpose, we need the following lemma, deduced from [4].

Lemma 2 ([4]). *Consider a strongly connected and well-formed Choice-Free system $S = (N, M_0)$ with minimal T-semiflow Y. If there exists a positive integer k, $k \geq 1$, and a feasible sequence σ in S such that $\vec{\sigma} = k \cdot Y$, then there exists a feasible sequence σ_Y in S such that $\vec{\sigma}_Y = Y$.*

Now we are able to prove the necessary condition of reversibility.

Theorem 1. *Consider a strongly connected and well-behaved Choice-Free system $S = ((P, T, W), M_0)$. The reversibility of S implies the reversibility of each of its strongly connected FA P-subsystems.*

Proof. By Propositions 1 and 2, S is well-formed and has a unique minimal T-semiflow Y whose support is the whole set T. S is reversible, thus by Proposition 6, there exists a sequence σ_Y that is feasible in S and whose Parikh vector is equal to Y. Consider $S_* = ((P_*, T_*, W_*), M_{0\,|P_*})$ a strongly connected FA P-subsystem of S, with minimal T-semiflow Y_*. The sequence $\sigma_{Y\,|T_*}$ is feasible in S_* by Lemma 1. Moreover $\vec{\sigma}_{Y\,|T_*} = Y_{|T_*}$ and $Y_{|T_*}$ is a multiple of Y_* by Proposition 3. We deduce that $\vec{\sigma}_{Y\,|T_*}$ is a multiple of Y_*. Thus, by Lemma 2, there exists a sequence σ_{Y_*} feasible in S_* and with Parikh vector equal to Y_*. By Proposition 6, S_* is reversible. □

3.4   A New Characterization of Reversibility

We prove the sufficiency part of the characterization, stating that the non-reversibility of the whole system implies the existence of a non-reversible FA P-subsystem. For that purpose, we formalize below relations between T-semiflows and reversibility with the help of several definitions, and an intermediate characterization of reversibility that involves firing sequences. Then, using decomposition arguments, we prove the main characterization of reversibility.

Definition 1. *Consider a system $S = (N, M_0)$ having a T-semiflow Y. A sequence σ that is feasible in S is* transient relative to Y *if its Parikh vector is smaller but not equal to Y, that is $\vec{\sigma}(t) \leq Y(t)$ for every transition t and $\vec{\sigma}(t') < Y(t')$ for at least one transition t'. The firing of σ in S, leading to a marking M, induces a* transient system *denoted by the vector (N, M, σ, Y).*

In order to simplify our study of transient sequences and systems, we partition the places and transitions into *ready* and *frozen* ones, as specified below.

Definition 2. *Consider a transient system $S = (N, M, \sigma, Y)$. A transition t is ready in S if $\vec{\sigma}(t) < Y(t)$, otherwise the transition is frozen in S, in which case $\vec{\sigma}(t) = Y(t)$. A place is ready in S if it is an input of a transition that is ready in S, otherwise it is frozen in S.*

In a system that is transient relative to a T-semiflow Y, the firing of a ready transition reduces the number of steps to attain Y. However, ready transitions may not be enabled. We formalize next the notion of blocking systems, whose ready transitions cannot be fired.

Definition 3. *A transient system is* blocking *if it contains no enabled ready transition.*

Hence, we focus on strongly connected well-behaved Choice-Free systems, which are well-formed (Proposition 1) and have a unique minimal T-semiflow whose support contains all transitions (Proposition 2). Thus, the Parikh vector of any feasible sequence is smaller than some multiple of the minimal T-semiflow Y. If such a system $S = (N, M, \sigma, Y')$ is blocking then liveness induces the existence of an enabled frozen transition in S and Y' is the smallest multiple of Y that is greater than $\vec{\sigma}$. For these systems, the following characterization of reversibility is an alternative to Proposition 6 that involves blocking systems.

Theorem 2. *Consider a strongly connected Choice-Free system S that is well-behaved. S is reversible if and only if there exists no feasible sequence in S that leads to a blocking system.*

Proof. To prove that the system is reversible, it suffices to consider the empty sequence, which is transient relative to the unique minimal T-semiflow Y (Propositions 1 and 2). The corresponding transient system is not blocking, thus a ready transition is enabled. Firing only ready transitions, every reached marking enables a ready transition until a sequence whose Parikh vector equals Y is fired. By Proposition 6, the system is reversible.

If $S = (N, M_0)$ is well-behaved and reversible, there exists a feasible sequence σ_Y whose Parikh vector equals the minimal T-semiflow Y, such that $M_0 \xrightarrow{\sigma_Y} M_0$ (Proposition 6). Thus, for every $k \geq 1$, the sequence $\sigma_{kY} = (\sigma_Y)^k$ is feasible.

Consider a feasible sequence σ and the smallest integer k such that σ is transient relative to the T-semiflow $Y_k = k \cdot Y$ with $M_0 \xrightarrow{\sigma} M$. The confluence property (Proposition 5) states the existence of two feasible sequences α and β such that $M_0 \xrightarrow{\alpha} M_0$ and $M \xrightarrow{\beta} M_0$, satisfying, for every transition t,

$$\vec{\alpha}(t) = \max\{\vec{\sigma}_{kY}(t), \vec{\sigma}(t)\} - \vec{\sigma}_{kY}(t) = \vec{\sigma}_{kY}(t) - \vec{\sigma}_{kY}(t) = 0$$
$$\vec{\beta}(t) = \max\{\vec{\sigma}_{kY}(t), \vec{\sigma}(t)\} - \vec{\sigma}(t) = \vec{\sigma}_{kY}(t) - \vec{\sigma}(t).$$

The feasible sequence β completes the transient sequence σ up to the T-semiflow Y_k, i.e. $\vec{\sigma} + \vec{\beta} = k \cdot Y$ and we note $M_0 \xrightarrow{\sigma.\beta} M_0$. This particular use

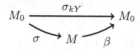

Fig. 4. If both sequences σ_{kY} and σ are feasible, then there exists a sequence β such that $\sigma.\beta$ is feasible and $\vec{\sigma}_{kY} = \vec{\sigma} + \vec{\beta}$

of confluence is illustrated in Figure 4. We deduce that the transient system (N, M, σ, Y_k) contains an enabled ready transition, hence it is not blocking. □

The following lemma shows the existence of a blocking subsystem.

Lemma 3. *Consider a transient Choice-Free system $S = (N, M, \sigma, Y)$ that is strongly connected. If S is blocking then it contains at least one non-empty strongly connected FA P-subnet $N_* = (P_*, T_*, W_*)$ such that the transient P-subsystem $(N_*, M\,|_{P_*}, \sigma\,|_{T_*}, Y\,|_{T_*})$ is blocking.*

Proof. We prove the claim by induction on the number n of join-transitions. If $n = 0$, S is an FA system and we are done. Otherwise, let t be a join-transition.

If t is ready, denote by p one of its non-enabled input places. Such a place exists since the whole system is blocking. Otherwise, t is frozen, and since S is strongly connected and blocking, thus transient, there exists in S an elementary path (*i.e.* that does not contain two occurrences of the same node) from a ready transition to t containing an input place p of t.

A new system S' is obtained by deleting all input places of t except p. Denote by R the reduced graph of S', *i.e.* the directed acyclic graph defined as follows: every node of R is the contraction of all the nodes of a maximal strongly connected component of S' into one point, while every arc (a, b) of S' such that a belongs to a node u in R and b belongs to a node v in R, $u \neq v$, infers in R the associated arc (u, v) with the same label (weight). Let G be a node of R with no input. Denoting by $N_G = (P_G, T_G, W_G)$ the subnet of S' corresponding to G, we show that $G = (N_G, M\,|_{P_G}, \sigma\,|_{T_G}, Y\,|_{T_G})$, which is strongly connected, is a non-empty blocking P-subsystem of S.

G Is a Non-empty P-subsystem of S. Since S has a T-semiflow, it contains at least one place and one transition. Moreover, S is strongly connected and the only inputs of nodes that have been deleted are inputs of the transition t, which has one input after the deletion. Thus, every node of S' has at least one input *i.e.* S' is well-connected. We deduce that G contains at least one place and one transition. For every place p of G in S', all inputs of p in S' belong to G since G has no input in R, while the unique output of p in S' belongs to G since G is strongly connected. Thus, G is a P-subsystem of S', which is a P-subsystem of S since only places were removed. Hence G is a non-empty P-subsystem of S.

G Is Blocking. Consider that S is obtained from $S_0 = (N, M_0)$ by firing σ. Since G is a non-empty P-subsystem of S, $Y|_{T_G}$ is a T-semiflow of G and $\sigma_{|T_G}$ is feasible in $G_0 = ((P_G, T_G, W_G), M_0|_{P_G})$ by Lemma 1. Moreover, for every transition t of T_G, $\vec{\sigma}|_{T_G}(t) = \vec{\sigma}(t)$, thus if t is ready in S, it is ready in G. We show first that G contains a ready transition.

Suppose that G contains only frozen transitions, then consider a frozen transition t_f in G. Since S is strongly connected, an elementary path c from a ready transition t_r to t_f exists in S. This path does not exist in S' since G has no input, thus c contains a deleted input place of t. We note $c = c_1\, t\, c_2\, t_f$. The elementary path $t\, c_2\, t_f$ exists in S' and belongs to G since G has no input in R. If t is ready, we have a contradiction. Otherwise t is frozen, and by the choice of its deleted input places, there exists an elementary path c_1' from a ready transition t_r' to t in S'. The path $t_r'\, c_1'\, t\, c_2$ belongs to G, which thus contains a ready transition, a contradiction.

We deduce that G contains at least one ready transition and $\sigma_{|T_G}$ is transient relative to $Y|_{T_G}$ in G_0. Moreover, all the transitions of G have the same inputs in G as in S'. Thus, if t belongs to G and is ready then its input place was chosen to be non-enabled, which is the case in G. The other ready transitions of S' are not enabled either, thus no ready transition of G is enabled and G is blocking.

Finally, G is a strongly connected blocking Choice-Free P-subsystem of S that contains strictly fewer join-transitions than S. Applying the induction hypothesis on G, a non-empty strongly connected and blocking FA P-subsystem $F = ((P_*, T_*, W_*), (M|_{P_G})|_{P_*}, (\sigma_{|T_G})|_{T_*}, (Y|_{T_G})|_{T_*})$ exists in G, thus exists in S with $(M|_{P_G})|_{P_*} = M|_{P_*}$, $(\sigma_{|T_G})|_{T_*} = \sigma_{|T_*}$ and $(Y|_{T_G})|_{T_*} = Y|_{T_*}$. $\qquad\square$

We are now able to prove the characterization of reversibility.

Theorem 3. *Consider a strongly connected and well-behaved Choice-Free system $S = ((P, T, W), M_0)$. S is reversible if and only if each of its strongly connected FA P-subsystems $S_* = ((P_*, T_*, W_*), M_0|_{P_*})$ is reversible.*

Proof. The necessity comes from Theorem 1. We prove the sufficiency next.

If S is empty or contains a unique place or transition, then the claim is true. Hence we suppose that S has a place and a transition. Suppose that S is not reversible, then by Theorem 2 a sequence σ is feasible in S such that $M_0 \xrightarrow{\sigma} M$, leading to the blocking system $S^b = ((P, T, W), M, \sigma, Y)$, where Y is a T-semiflow of S. Besides, Lemma 3 applies and S^b contains a non-empty strongly connected blocking FA P-subsystem $S_*^b = ((P_*, T_*, W_*), M|_{P_*}, \sigma_{|T_*}, Y|_{T_*})$, obtained by firing $\sigma_{|T_*}$ in $S_* = ((P_*, T_*, W_*), M_0|_{P_*})$. By Propositions 3 and 4, S_* is well-behaved. Applying Theorem 2, S_* is not reversible. $\qquad\square$

3.5 A Polynomial Live and Home Marking for Choice-Free Systems

We provide the first *polynomial* live and reversible initial marking for strongly connected well-formed Choice-Free systems, extending a polynomial live marking of [18] that was improved in [19]. To achieve this construction, we use the following polynomial markings for FA and Choice-Free systems.

The Set of Markings M_{FA} for FA Systems. Each place p of an FA system defines a marking M_p of M_{FA} satisfying $M_p(p) = max_p$ and for all other places p', $M_p(p') = max_{p'} - gcd_{p'}$.

The Marking M_{CF} for Choice-Free Systems. Consider a Choice-Free system having at least one join-transition. For all input places p of join-transitions, $M_{CF}(p) = max_p$ and for all other places p', $M_{CF}(p') = max_{p'} - gcd_{p'}$.

Their main behavioral properties are now recalled.

Theorem 4 ([19]). *Consider a strongly connected and well-formed Choice-Free net N. If N is not an FA, then (N, M_{CF}) is well-behaved. If N is an FA and M_* belongs to M_{FA}, then (N, M_*) is well-behaved and reversible. Moreover, in both cases, any larger initial marking also possesses these properties.*

We extend this theorem, showing the reversibility of the polynomial marking M_{CF} in well-behaved Choice-Free systems.

Theorem 5. *Consider a strongly connected and well-formed Choice-Free net N that is not an FA. The system $S = (N, M_{CF})$ is well-behaved and reversible.*

Proof. Every non-empty strongly connected FA P-subsystem $S_* = (N_*, M_*)$ of S contains at least one input of a join-transition, otherwise strong connectedness would imply the existence of a place p in S_* having an input that does not belong to S_*, contradicting the fact that S_* is a P-subsystem. Since M_* is the restriction of M_{CF} to the places of N_*, we deduce that a place p in S_* contains max_p tokens, while all other places p' of S_* are assigned at least $max_{p'} - gcd_{p'}$ tokens. Thus, M_* is greater than or equal to a marking of M_{FA} and by Theorem 4, S_* is live and reversible. Applying the characterization of Theorem 3, the Choice-Free system is live and reversible.   □

3.6   Comparison with the Special Case of Weighted T-systems

T-systems form a proper subclass of Choice-Free systems. When strongly connected and well-behaved, they are covered by well-behaved circuits [5]. A characterization of reversibility for these systems is recalled next.

Theorem 6 ([5]). *If a weighted strongly connected T-system is well-behaved, then it is reversible.*

Thus, under the well-behavedness hypothesis, the reversibility of a strongly connected T-system is equivalent to that of all its strongly connected circuit P-subsystems, constituting a particular case of Theorem 3.

In the general case of Choice-Free systems, well-behavedness of the whole system ensures that of all its FA P-subsystems, which may however not be reversible. This contrast is illustrated in Figure 5.

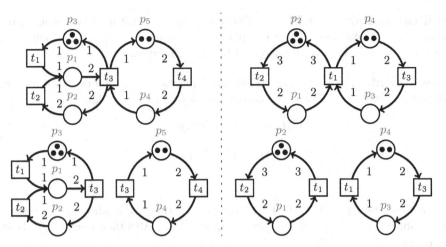

Fig. 5. On the left, the well-behaved Choice-Free system is not reversible and contains an FA P-subsystem that is well-behaved but not reversible (*bottom left*). On the right, the well-formed T-system is well-behaved and reversible, as well as all its circuit P-subsystems.

We presented two new necessary and sufficient conditions of reversibility for well-behaved strongly connected Choice-Free systems. For this class, the decomposition into FA P-subsystems induces polynomial markings that are reversible. However, these markings impose a distribution of the initial tokens over the entire system. In particular, no place is initially empty, which may cause difficulties in designing specific systems. In the next section, we develop another polynomial time sufficient condition of liveness and reversibility that provides more flexibility on the initial distribution of tokens.

4   The Place Splitting Transformation

In this section, we propose a polynomial time transformation of a strongly connected and well-formed Choice-Free system into a strongly connected and well-formed T-system with the same set of T-semiflows. We show that the liveness of this T-system is sufficient to ensure both liveness and reversibility of the initial Choice-Free system. We then derive an original polynomial time sufficient condition of liveness and reversibility for well-formed Choice-Free systems.

4.1   Definition of the Transformation

Let $S = ((P, T, W), M_0)$ be a strongly connected well-formed Choice-Free system. By Proposition 2, S has a unique minimal T-semiflow Y whose support is T. We denote by U the least common multiple of the components of Y. The system $S' = ((P', T, W'), M_0')$ has the same set of transitions and is obtained from S as follows.

Splitting of Particular Places. Every place p having at least two input transitions $t_1 \ldots t_k$ and an output t is replaced by k places $p_1 \ldots p_k$ in P' such that, for every $i \in 1 \ldots k$, p_i is an output of t_i and an input of t.

New Weights. For every place p split into k places $p_1 \ldots p_k$, for every $i \in 1 \ldots k$, all the weights surrounding the place p_i are determined as follows:

$$W'(t_i, p_i) = U \cdot W(t_i, p)$$

$$W'(p_i, t) = W'(t_i, p_i) \cdot \frac{Y(t_i)}{Y(t)} .$$

Since the support of Y is T, the division by $Y(t) \geq 1$ is allowed. Moreover, by definition of U, $\frac{U}{Y(t)} \in \mathbb{N}$, thus $W'(p_i, t) \in \mathbb{N}$. All other weights are kept identical.

New Marking. The initial marking M_0' is computed from the marking M_0 according to:

$$M_0'(p_i) = \left\lfloor \frac{M_0(p) \cdot U \cdot W(t_i, p) \cdot Y(t_i)}{gcd_{p_i} \cdot W(p, t) \cdot Y(t)} \right\rfloor \cdot gcd_{p_i} .$$

This transformation is illustrated in Figure 6.

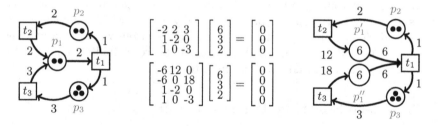

Fig. 6. The Choice-Free system on the left has the minimal T-semiflow $(6, 3, 2)$, thus $U = 6$. Applying the transformation, $W'(t_2, p_1') = 2 \cdot 6$, $W'(t_3, p_1'') = 3 \cdot 6$, $W'(p_1', t_1) = 3 \cdot 12/6$ and $W'(p_1'', t_1) = 2 \cdot 18/6$. The marking of p_2 and p_3 does not change. Since $gcd_{p_1'} = 6$, $W(t_2, p_1) = 2$, $gcd_{p_1''} = 6$ and $W(t_3, p_1) = 3$, we get $M_0'(p_1') = M_0'(p_1'') = 6$. We obtain the T-system on the right with the same minimal T-semiflow.

4.2   Properties of the Transformation

The transformation clearly preserves strong connectedness. As shown below, it also preserves the set of T-semiflows and well-formedness.

Theorem 7 (T-semiflow preservation). *Consider the well-formed strongly connected Choice-Free system S and the transformed T-system S'. Both systems have the same set of T-semiflows and S' is well-formed.*

Proof. S and S' have the same set of transitions T. The system S, being well-formed, has a unique minimal T-semiflow Y, whose support is T (Proposition 2). For every transition t_i, $Y(t) \cdot W'(p_i, t) = Y(t_i) \cdot W'(t_i, p_i)$, thus Y is a T-semiflow of S'. We deduce that S' is consistent and strongly connected, thus well-formed (Proposition 1) and it has a unique minimal T-semiflow with support T (Proposition 2). Since Y is a T-semiflow of S' and the gcd of its components is 1, there is no smaller T-semiflow in S', thus Y is the unique minimal T-semiflow of S'. As each T-semiflow is a multiple of Y, the set of T-semiflows is preserved.   □

This property is illustrated by Figure 6, where both systems are well-formed and have the same set of T-semiflows, including the unique minimal one.

The next property compares the number of initial tokens in both systems.

Theorem 8 (Marking bound property). *Consider a well-formed strongly connected Choice-Free system (N, M_0) and its transformation (N', M_0'). The following inequality is satisfied for each place p transformed into k places $p_1 \ldots p_k$:*

$$\sum_{i=1}^{k} M_0'(p_i) \leq M_0(p) \cdot U.$$

Proof. By definition of M_0', we obtain:

$$\sum_{i=1\ldots k} M_0'(p_i) = \sum_{i=1\ldots k} \left\lfloor \frac{M_0(p) \cdot U \cdot W(t_i, p) \cdot Y(t_i)}{gcd_{p_i} \cdot W(p, t) \cdot Y(t)} \right\rfloor \cdot gcd_{p_i}$$

$$\leq \sum_{i=1\ldots k} \frac{M_0(p) \cdot U \cdot W(t_i, p) \cdot Y(t_i)}{W(p, t) \cdot Y(t)}$$

$$\leq \frac{U \cdot M_0(p)}{W(p, t) \cdot Y(t)} \cdot \sum_{i=1\ldots k} W(t_i, p) \cdot Y(t_i)$$

Since $\sum_{i=1}^{k} W(t_i, p) \cdot Y(t_i) = W(p, t) \cdot Y(t)$, the claim is proved.   □

On Figure 6, $M_0'(p_1') + M_0'(p_1'') = 12$ while $M_0(p) \cdot U = 2 \cdot 6 = 12$.

The inclusion of the language of S' in the language of S is shown below.

Theorem 9 (Language inclusion). *Every sequence that is feasible in S' is feasible in S.*

Proof. We prove the claim by induction on the size of a sequence σ that is feasible in $S' = (N', M_0')$.

If σ is empty, then it is also feasible in $S = (N, M_0)$. Hence suppose that $\sigma = \sigma_1 t$ has size $k \geq 1$ and the property is true for σ_1, thus σ_1 is also feasible in S. We note $M_0 \xrightarrow{\sigma_1} M_1$ and $M_0' \xrightarrow{\sigma_1} M_1' \xrightarrow{t} M'$.

If no input of t has been modified by the transformation, then for each of its input places p, the weights surrounding p have not been modified and the corresponding transitions have been fired the same number of times, thus $M_1'(p) = M_1(p)$ and t is enabled by M_1 in S. Otherwise, the same argument applies to any non-modified input place of t, and for every input place p of t that has been transformed into places $p_1 \ldots p_k$, we show that if the places p_i, $i = 1 \ldots k$, are enabled by M_1' in S' then p is enabled by M_1 in S. It is equivalent to show that $M'(p_i) \geq 0, \forall i \in \{p_1, \ldots, p_k\}$, implies $M(p) \geq 0$ where $M_1 \xrightarrow{t} M$. For every such place p_i, $i \in \{1, \ldots, k\}$,

$$M_0'(p_i) + W'(t_i, p_i) \cdot \vec{\sigma}(t_i) - W'(p_i, t) \cdot \vec{\sigma}(t) \geq 0 \,.$$

From the definition of W', we get

$$M_0'(p_i) + U \cdot W(t_i, p) \cdot \vec{\sigma}(t_i) - U \cdot W(t_i, p) \cdot \frac{Y(t_i)}{Y(t)} \cdot \vec{\sigma}(t) \geq 0 \,.$$

By summing the preceding inequality over places $p_1 \ldots p_k$, we obtain

$$\sum_{i=1\ldots k} M_0'(p_i) + U \cdot \left(\sum_{i=1\ldots k} W(t_i, p) \cdot \vec{\sigma}(t_i) - (\sum_{i=1\ldots k} W(t_i, p) \cdot Y(t_i)) \cdot \frac{\vec{\sigma}(t)}{Y(t)} \right) \geq 0$$

Since $\sum_{i=1\ldots k} W(t_i, p) \cdot Y(t_i) = W(p, t) \cdot Y(t)$,

$$\sum_{i=1\ldots k} M_0'(p_i) + U \cdot \left(\sum_{i=1\ldots k} W(t_i, p) \cdot \vec{\sigma}(t_i) - W(p, t) \cdot \vec{\sigma}(t) \right) \geq 0$$

From the marking bound property (Theorem 8), it follows that

$$U \cdot \left(M_0(p) + \sum_{i=1\ldots k} W(t_i, p) \cdot \vec{\sigma}(t_i) - W(p, t) \cdot \vec{\sigma}(t) \right) \geq 0$$

thus $U \cdot \left(M_1(p) - W(p, t) \right) \geq 0$ and σ is feasible in S.   □

4.3   A Sufficient Condition of Liveness and Reversibility

We show that the transformation induces a sufficient condition of liveness and reversibility for strongly connected well-formed Choice-Free systems. For that purpose, we need the following characterization of liveness, given in [4].

Proposition 7 ([4]). *Consider a Choice-Free system $S = (N, M_0)$, its set of transitions T and the incidence matrix C of N. S is live if and only if there exist a reachable marking $M \in [M_0\rangle$ and a sequence σ that is feasible in (N, M) such that $\vec{\sigma} \geq \mathbb{1}^{|T|}$ and $C \cdot \vec{\sigma} \geq 0$.*

We are now able to prove the sufficient condition of liveness and reversibility.

Theorem 10. *Consider a strongly connected and well-formed Choice-Free system S. Denote by S' the T-system obtained by applying the transformation to S. If S' is live, then S is live and reversible.*

Proof. Both systems have the same unique minimal T-semiflow Y and S' is well-formed (T-semiflow preservation, Theorem 7). If S' is live, then it is reversible (Theorem 6) and a sequence σ_Y, with Parikh vector equal to the minimal T-semiflow Y of both systems, is feasible in S' (Proposition 6). By the language inclusion (Theorem 9), σ_Y in also feasible in S, which is consequently live (take $M = M_0$ and $\sigma = \sigma_Y$ in Proposition 7) and reversible (Proposition 6).   □

The Sufficient Condition Is Not Necessary. The liveness of the T-system is not necessary for the liveness and reversibility of the Choice-Free system, as highlighted by the counter-example on the left in Figure 7.

Comparison with the Polynomial Live and Reversible Markings. The example on the left in Figure 7 shows that the live and reversible markings of M_{FA} for FA systems are not always detected by the sufficient condition. The same holds for Choice-Free systems that are marked with M_{CF}, as pictured on the left when considering the dotted place p_4. Moreover, there exist markings that are live and reversible without being greater than or equal to some marking of M_{FA}, while detected by the sufficient condition, as pictured on the right in Figure 7. This is also the case for the marking M_{CF}, when the dotted place p_4 is added. Thus, the set of markings detected by one method neither is included in the other set nor includes it.

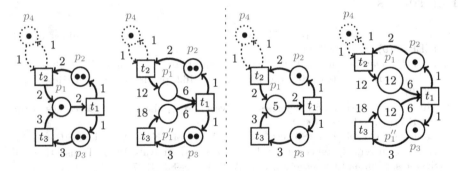

Fig. 7. On the left, the well-formed FA system (resp. Choice-Free, with the *dotted part*), marked with M_{FA} (resp. M_{CF}) hence live and reversible, is transformed into a non-live T-system. On the right, the initial marking of the FA (resp. Choice-Free) system is not greater than or equal to any in M_{FA} (resp. M_{CF}), since $max_{p_3} - gcd_{p_3} = 3 - 1 = 2$. However, the transformation leads to a well-behaved T-system, satisfying the sufficient condition, and the FA (resp. Choice-Free) system is live and reversible.

4.4   A Second Polynomial Time Sufficient Condition of Reversibility

The complexity of checking the liveness of a T-system is not known. However, a non trivial *sufficient* condition of liveness has been developed in [20] for well-formed T-systems, leading to a polynomial time algorithm whose complexity is $\mathcal{O}(\max\{|P|\cdot|T|, |P|\cdot\log(\min_{p\in P} max_p)\})$. By Theorem 10, this algorithm applies to the T-system S' issued from a well-formed Choice-Free system S to obtain a polynomial time sufficient condition of liveness and reversibility for S.

5   Conclusion

For the class of strongly connected, weighted and well-behaved Choice-Free systems, we provided a new characterization of reversibility in terms of the reversibility of particular FA P-subsystems, generalizing a known liveness condition. This decomposition leads to the first polynomial time construction of live and reversible initial markings with a polynomial number of tokens, whereas prior methods were exponential. We then presented another sufficient condition of liveness and reversibility based on a polynomial time transformation into a weighted T-system. Comparing these two sufficient conditions, the set of live and reversible markings detected by one is not included in the other. Moreover, using a known polynomial time sufficient condition of liveness for T-systems, we obtained a polynomial time sufficient condition of liveness and reversibility for well-formed Choice-Free systems. Perspectives encompass extensions of these results to other weighted classes as well as applications to model-checking and to the design of embedded systems.

References

1. Lee, E.A., Messerschmitt, D.G.: Synchronous Data Flow. Proceedings of the IEEE 75(9), 1235–1245 (1987)
2. Best, E., Darondeau, P.: Petri Net Distributability. In: Clarke, E., Virbitskaite, I., Voronkov, A. (eds.) PSI 2011. LNCS, vol. 7162, pp. 1–18. Springer, Heidelberg (2012)
3. Murata, T.: Petri Nets: Properties, Analysis and Applications. Proceedings of the IEEE 77(4), 541–580 (1989)
4. Teruel, E., Colom, J.M., Silva, M.: Choice-Free Petri Nets: A Model for Deterministic Concurrent Systems with Bulk Services and Arrivals. IEEE Transactions on Systems, Man and Cybernetics, Part A 27(1), 73–83 (1997)
5. Teruel, E., Chrzastowski-Wachtel, P., Colom, J.M., Silva, M.: On Weighted T-systems. In: Jensen, K. (ed.) ICATPN 1992. LNCS, vol. 616, pp. 348–367. Springer, Heidelberg (1992)
6. Barkaoui, K., Petrucci, L.: Structural Analysis of Workflow Nets with Shared Resources. In: van der Aalst, W.M.P., De Michelis, G., Ellis, C.A. (eds.) Proceedings of Workflow Management: Net-Based Concepts, Models, Techniques and Tools (WFM 1998). Computing Science Report, vol. 98/7, pp. 82–95 (1998)

7. Teruel, E., Silva, M.: Liveness and Home States in Equal Conflict Systems. In: Marsan, M.A. (ed.) ICATPN 1993. LNCS, vol. 691, pp. 415–432. Springer, Heidelberg (1993)

8. Recalde, L., Teruel, E., Silva, M.: Modeling and Analysis of Sequential Processes that Cooperate through Buffers. IEEE Transactions on Robotics and Automation 14(2), 267–277 (1998)

9. Berthelot, G., Lri-Iie: Checking Properties of Nets Using Transformations. In: Rozenberg, G. (ed.) APN 1985. LNCS, vol. 222, pp. 19–40. Springer, Heidelberg (1986)

10. Berthelot, G.: Transformations and Decompositions of Nets. In: Brauer, W., Reisig, W., Rozenberg, G. (eds.) APN 1986. LNCS, vol. 254, pp. 359–376. Springer, Heidelberg (1987)

11. Colom, J., Teruel, E., Silva, M., Haddad, S.: Structural Methods. In: Petri Nets for Systems Engineering, pp. 277–316. Springer, Heidelberg (2003)

12. Memmi, G., Roucairol, G.: Linear Algebra in Net Theory. In: Brauer, W. (ed.) Net Theory and Applications. LNCS, vol. 84, pp. 213–223. Springer, Heidelberg (1980)

13. Sifakis, J.: Structural Properties of Petri Nets. In: Winkowski, J. (ed.) MFCS 1978. LNCS, vol. 64, pp. 474–483. Springer, Heidelberg (1978)

14. Teruel, E., Silva, M.: Structure theory of Equal Conflict systems. Theoretical Computer Science 153(1&2), 271–300 (1996)

15. Keller, R.M.: A Fundamental Theorem of Asynchronous Parallel Computation. In: Feng, T.-Y. (ed.) Parallel Processing. LNCS, vol. 24, pp. 102–112. Springer, Heidelberg (1975)

16. Best, E., Darondeau, P.: Decomposition Theorems for Bounded Persistent Petri Nets. In: van Hee, K.M., Valk, R. (eds.) PETRI NETS 2008. LNCS, vol. 5062, pp. 33–51. Springer, Heidelberg (2008)

17. Lien, Y.E.: Termination Properties of Generalized Petri Nets. SIAM Journal on Computing 5(2), 251–265 (1976)

18. Delosme, J.M., Hujsa, T., Munier-Kordon, A.: Polynomial Sufficient Conditions of Well-behavedness for Weighted Join-Free and Choice-Free Systems. In: Proceedings of the 13th International Conference on Application of Concurrency to System Design (ACSD 2013), pp. 90–99 (2013)

19. Hujsa, T., Delosme, J.M., Munier-Kordon, A.: Polynomial Sufficient Conditions of Well-behavedness and Home Markings in Subclasses of Weighted Petri Nets. Transactions on Embedded Computing Systems (to appear, 2014)

20. Marchetti, O., Munier-Kordon, A.: A Sufficient Condition for the Liveness of Weighted Event Graphs. European Journal of Operational Research 197(2), 532–540 (2009)

(Stochastic) Model Checking in GreatSPN

Elvio Gilberto Amparore, Marco Beccuti, and Susanna Donatelli

Università di Torino, Dipartimento di Informatica, Italy
{amparore,beccuti,susi}@di.unito.it

Abstract. GreatSPN is a tool for the definition and solution of Generalized Stochastic Petri Nets (GSPN). This paper presents the model checking features that have been recently introduced in GreatSPN. Through a new (Java-based) graphical interface for the GSPN model definition, the user can now access model checking of three different logics: the classical branching temporal logic CTL, and two stochastic logics, CSL and its superset CSL^{TA}. This allows to integrate easily classical and probabilistic verification. A distinctive feature of the CTL model checker is the ability of generating counterexamples and witnesses. The CTL model checker employs symbolic data structures (decision diagrams) implemented in the Meddly library [6], developed Iowa State University, while the CSL^{TA} model checker uses advanced solution methods, recently published, for Markov Renewal Processes.

1 Objectives

Generalized Stochastic Petri Nets (GSPNs) [16] are an extension of the basic P/T nets with priorities and inhibitor arcs to include a stochastic (exponential) delay for transitions. GSPNs have been extensively studied in the past, and they have been used for representing the behavior of hardware and software systems, with relevant applications in the field of flexible manufacturing systems, business work-flows and biological systems, to cite a few. GSPN have established a bridge between classical formalisms for analysis of concurrency, like standard Petri nets, and classical formalisms for performance evaluation, like queueing networks and Markov chains. As such, the supporting tools have paid particular attention to the integration of qualitative analysis (for functional correctness) and quantitative analysis (for performance evaluation). More recently this duality has been well reflected in the advancement in model checking: of temporal logics (for qualitative verification) and of stochastic logics (for probabilistic verification). This paper describes the evolution of the GSPN tool GreatSPN [4][5] to deal with model checking of temporal and stochastic logics.

GreatSPN was first released by the University of Torino in the late 1980's. It was the first GSPN tool with a graphical interface, and the first tool which supported the extension of GSPN with colors. It has been used by several research groups in different universities and/or research centers. GreatSPN [4] implements several efficient analysis algorithms for GSPN and its colored extension, now standardized [8] as Stochastic Symmetric Net[1]: GSPN and SSN models can be analyzed through discrete event simulation [14], or through the generation of the underlying stochastic process (representing

---

[1] Previously known as Stochastic Well-formed Nets, or SWN.

G. Ciardo and E. Kindler (Eds.): PETRI NETS 2014, LNCS 8489, pp. 354–363, 2014.

the model behavior in time) and its solution with the computation of standard performance indices. GreatSPN also supports analysis of classical Petri net properties (like P- and T-invariants, check for liveness, absence of deadlocks, etc). One of the most characterizing aspects of GreatSPN is its advanced analysis techniques for SSN, based on the automatic exploitation of the symmetries of the model.

Being a "tool with a history" has some advantages, like having lots of material, examples and experience around it. But it has also several drawbacks: the software organization follows old standards, solvers that do not exploit the most recent results on efficient data structure, and the Graphical User Interface (GUI) is obsolete. Three years ago GreatSPN was upgraded [5] with the introduction of decision diagram (DD) data structures for state space generation, with an implementation which is based on the DD library Meddly [6], developed at Iowa State University. Being able to compute very large state spaces is important, but it can be only partially useful if no adequate analysis techniques are provided for checking various forms of safety and liveness property, as provided by CTL and LTL model checkers. Since GreatSPN is a tool oriented towards performance evaluation, it is important that the CTL/LTL support is complemented by a probabilistic model checker for stochastic logics. The currently available GreatSPN's GUI, implemented using Motif toolkit, is more than 15 years old. It is not easy to use for newcomers, since it does not meet the modern GUI standards, and it is not easily portable (due to the current limited availability of updated Open Motif libraries).

To cope with the outlined drawbacks in this paper we present an upgrade of Great-SPN which features a new (Java-based) GUI and a model checking facility for CTL (with counterexamples and witnesses), CSL, and CSL^{TA}. This makes GreatSPN an advanced state-of-the-art tool for the integrated analysis of qualitative and stochastic properties of GSPNs.

The structure of the paper follows the indication provided in the supplemental material of the call for papers: Section 2 reports the new functionalities of the tool, Section 3 outlines the architecture and the installation information, Section 4 is an introduction to the tool from a user point of view, while Section 5 compares the behavior of the tool against other two similar model checkers (SMART and MARCIE) and discusses future improvements.

2   Functionality

In this section we give an overview of GreatSPN's GUI and of the model checking functionalities.

GreatSPN's GUI. GreatSPN is now equipped with a new graphical user interface, designed and implemented to draw GSPN models. The interface is built in Java to enhance portability, and provides a number of new features. It has WYSIWYG editing capabilities, cut/copy/paste, full undo/redo support, interactive editing and token simulation, and other capabilities expected from a modern GUI application.

Figure 1 shows the canvas structure of the new GUI. Editing is based on an SDI approach with multiple nets opened at the same time, shown in the top-left corner. Currently, the editor supports a full language for non-colored GSPN, with immediate/exponential transitions, multiplicity on arcs, weights, named constants, N-server

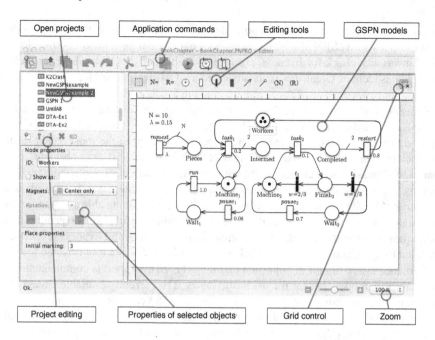

Fig. 1. Canvas structure of the new GreatSPN GUI

transitions, and so on. Models can be exported in the GreatSPN format (net/def files) which allows one to run the whole set of GreatSPN solvers through command line. Models are drawn with a vector-based rendered with LaTeX labels on objects and PDF printing, for publishing. An example is the GSPN of Figure 3 which has been drawn with the new GUI and exported in PDF format. In addition, the interface has an interactive token game simulation and an interactive visualization of P- and T-semiflows. Since some modeling capabilities are still missing (e.g. colors, result visualization), the old GUI is still provided in the GreatSPN package distribution.

CTL model checking. The CTL model checker of GreatSPN checks CTL formulae for Petri nets with priorities and inhibitor arcs. The model checker is implemented using the symbolic data structures (i.e. Multiway Decision Diagram - MDD, and Multi-Terminal MDD - MTMDD) provided by Meddly [6], an open-source library developed at Iowa State University. Meddly supplies two types of interfaces: a "simple" one, meant to hide from the library users a lot of implementation details, and an "expert" one, which requires a better knowledge of decision diagrams and of their realization inside Meddly. While model checking a CTL formula Φ for a GSPN model N of initial marking m_0, the first step is the computation of the set of reachable states (RS) of N: the states are generated and encoded in an MDD with a state space exploration methods based on the well-known saturation algorithm [10]. The MDD has one level per place, and the bounds of each place can be provided manually by the user or computed by the Great-SPN bounds analysis tool. The place ordering (i.e. the ordering of the MDD variables) can also be automatically computed with an ad-hoc heuristic based on P-invariants and clustering of places of common transition, or can be given in input by the user through an external file. If the set of P-semiflows does not cover all places, or if their computation is prohibitive, the user has to provide the bounds and the ordering by hands.

The model checker computes the satisfaction set (*Sat-set*) of a formula using rather standard symbolic algorithms on decision diagrams [13], and answers "true" if the initial marking is part of the *Sat-set*. The model checker implements the existentially quantified CTL operators, and translates universal operators using existential ones. The fixed-point operators *EF* and *EG* are implemented in two ways, with the classical fixed-point algorithm and using *constrained saturation* [10].

The quality of a model checker is not only its ability in analyzing very large state spaces, but also on how helpful it is in supporting the user in the verification process. It is for this reason that the model checker developed for GreatSPN includes a new symbolic algorithm that computes *tree-like counterexamples* [12] and witnesses: the algorithm, starting from the whole formula, recursively constructs the counterexamples for all its sub-formulae from the bottom up. For each sub-formula the Sat set of the states which satisfy the negation of the sub-formula is computed and stored in the MDD_0. Then, all the states reaching a state in the MDD_0 in i steps are encoded on the MDD_i, so that this set of MDDs can be efficiently visited to generate the shortest counterexample. To the best of our knowledge other model checkers of CTL for Petri nets do not include such a feature.

CSL^{TA} model checking. The CSL^{TA} model checker available in GreatSPN is taken from MC4CSL^{TA}, a probabilistic model checker for Markov chains [2] that has been developed in our research group. In CSL^{TA} properties have the form $P_{\leq\alpha}(A)$, where A is a 1-clock deterministic Timed Automaton (DTA), and the property holds in state s if the probability of all the CTMC paths, starting from s and accepted by A, is less than or equal to α. Since the acceptance automaton A allows the use of a clock, the acceptance is based on the actions and states of the paths, as well as the time at which events happen. In MC4CSL^{TA} the CTMC can be expressed in different formats, in particular those of PRISM and of MRMC [15], and, of course, that of GreatSPN. The tool implements both forward and backward analysis, which means, from a user point of view, to enquire whether state s satisfies a formula (forward analysis), or to request the computation of the whole Sat-set. The model checking of a CSL^{TA} formula requires the steady state solution of a Markov Renewal Process, as described in [3]. When the CSL^{TA} model checker evaluates CSL formulae, the algorithmic complexity automatically reduces to that of a CSL model checker [1].

3 Architecture

The architecture of the additional features introduced in the GreatSPN framework is depicted in Figure 2 where the framework components are presented by rectangles, the component invocations by solid arrows, and the models/data by dashed arrows. For the CTL model checking the new GreatSPN GUI is used to design GSPN models, which are then used in the solution processes calling the two programs: *struct* and **RGMEDD**.

The *struct* program generates the input needed for automatically computing the ordering and the bounds of the DD variables used to encode in MDD both the RS and the next state function. Indeed exploiting only the net structural information *struct* generates the net P-semiflows and its place bounds (i.e. upper/lower bound) storing them in the two files *.pinv* and *.bnd* respectively. Its execution is optional since bounds and ordering can be given in input as well.

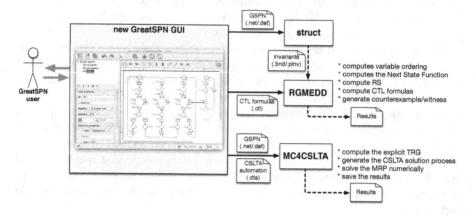

Fig. 2. Architecure of the new GreatSPN GUI for CTL

The **RGMEDD** program is responsible for CTL model checking and works in three steps: encoding of the next state function, RS generation and CTL verification. Encoding of the next state function uses a $2*N$ level MDD (if N is the number of places) while the initial marking is encoded in an N level MDD, reading the *.net* and *.def* files that describe the GSPN. The MDD variables' ordering and their bounds can be specified by the user or automatically derived exploiting the information stored in the file *.pinv* and *.bnd*. The generation of the RS of the net using the saturation algorithm applied on the above generated MDDs. This task is performed using the "simple" interface of Meddly which automatically handles the complex aspects of using DD like the node garbage collection and the operation cache. RS generation is launched by:

ord_rgMEDD "net_directory/net" [-B INTEGER] [-P/-F] [-h INTEGER]

where the first parameter specifies the net name and the optional parameters in square brackets are meant to specify an upper bound for all the MDD variables (*-B*), to enable the automatic generation of a variable ordering exploiting the P-semiflows (*-P*), to specify directly the variable ordering through the file *.place* (*-F*), and to fix the maximum cache dimensions in Bytes (*-h*).

CTL verification assumes the formulae are specified in a *.ctl* file. The full Sat-set is computed, and the output can be limited to true/false (with respect to the initial marking) or to the whole listing of the Sat-set. Optionally the shortest counterexample or a witness can be displayed, if applicable. To make the CTL operators more efficient, they are developed combining the high level MDD operators provided by the "simple" interface of Meddly with more specific ones directly implemented through the Meddly expert-level. Indeed, the Meddly expert-level interface allows the programmer to access to the advanced features of the library (like the setting of the storing policy associated

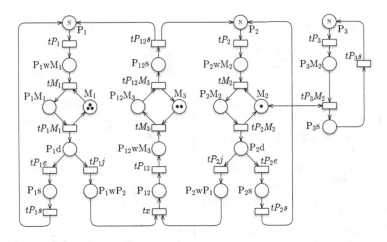

Fig. 3. The FMS model, drawn with the new GUI editor.

with the nodes or the directly access to the unique and computation tables). The CTL model checking can be executed by command-line by adding the option -*C* to the RS generation command. Two further options are possible: -*o* to store all the states belonging to the formula Sat set into a file and -*c* to enable the counterexample generation.

Installation instructions The GreatSPN tools and manuals are freely available for non-commercial use at `http://www.di.unito.it/~greatspn/index.html`, while the new GUI interface is available at `http://www.di.unito.it/~amparore/mc4cslta/editor.html`.

4 Use Case

This section presents a user point of view of the GreatSPN's model checking functionalities, through the use of the classical FMS net. The objective of a user in using our tool is to acquire confidence on the correct behavior of the FMS, by checking both qualitative and quantitative properties, and then use the model for the computation of performance indices of interest.

The FMS GSPN of Figure 3 has three types of parts, and at any time there are N of each in the system (marking of places P_i). The FMS has three types of machines: M_1, M_2, and M_3. The three machines of type M_1 process only parts of type $P1$, while Machine M_2 can either process a part of type $P2$ or of type $P3$, one at a time. Finished parts of type $P1$ and $P2$ can be also assembled together by the two machines of type M_3. The analysis work-flow illustrated above is done on the FMS model as follows.

The first step in the analysis work-flow is to draw the model and perform basic analysis. The model is drawn in the GUI, and the analysis starts with semiflows computation, which computes 6 P-semiflows and 4 T-semiflows that can be displayed in the GUI. The net being bounded, the RS can be computed. The CTL model checking session can then start. Properties peculiar of Petri nets should be checked first, like liveness of transitions, absence of deadlock, presence of a single home space (which ensures ergodicity

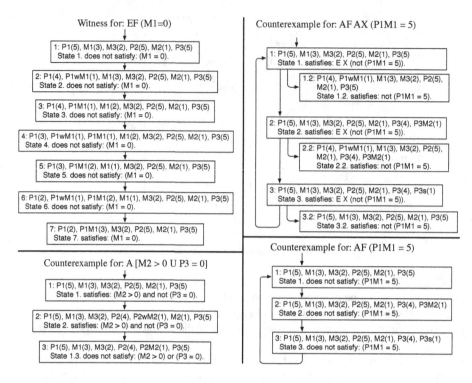

Fig. 4. CTL counterexamples and witnesses

on the underlying Markov chain), followed by the analysis of FMS-specific properties. For the first category we can check the property deadlock, which results in an empty Sat-set, since the system has no deadlock. We can check the liveness of a transition t through AG EF en(t): the property is true for $t = t_x$, which indicates that the synchronization of the parts to be worked by machine M_2 can always take place. For the second category we have a vast choice of properties. Figure 4 illustrates the result of the analysis for four formulae, resulting in a witness and in three counterexamples, for the net with $N = 5$. With formula EF $M_1 = 0$ we can check that all the machines of type M_1 are actually usable. The formula is true and a witness can be generated, which is a prefix of length 7, depicted in the top left of the figure. To study whether there is the need to always have a M_2 machine available for emptying P_3 we can check A $(M_2 > 0 \; U \; P_3 = 0)$, which does not hold and generates the very simple counterexample shown in the left bottom part of the figure: in the first two states $M2 > 0$ is true, but $P_3 = 0$ is not, while in the third state neither of the two is true, which falsifies the Until. But in CTL counterexamples can be more complex, with looping and branching structure, as shown by the two next examples. The formula AF($P_1 M_1 = 5$) is false (not all parts of type P_1 can be worked by machine M_1 at the same time). The counterexample takes the form of a loop of three states (bottom right of the figure) in which $P_1 M_1 = 5$ is always false, and the path can be considered as a witness of EG ($P_1 M_1 \neq 5$). Finally, the top-right of the figure shows a nested counterexample for the nested formula AF AX ($P_1 M_1 = 5$):

it is a loop of three states, and for each state there is a branching prefix of length 2 that falsifies $AX(P_1M_1 = 5)$. It is obvious that, by nesting formulas, arbitrary complex counterexamples or witnesses can be generated. The current implementation prints out the branching counterexamples/witnesses in a textually nested manner, following the same approach of the nuSMV[11] tool: states are indicated with a dotted notation, in which each dot corresponding to a level in the nesting, and loops are marked by the additional text "loop starts/ends here" properly aligned with respect to testing. The text reported in the boxes is exactly what comes out of the tool, and we have only added the arrows for better reading.

Finally we can integrate the analysis with stochastic model checking. Consider the formula E $[\Phi(3)$ U E $[$ $\Phi(2)$ U E $[\Phi(1)$ U $\Phi(0)]$ $]$ $]$, where $\Phi(k)$ is: (P2=N and P3=N and M1=k and M2=1 and M3=2), which is true in the initial marking and states that there are executions that use one after the other all the instances of M_1 without ever touching the other machines and the other parts.

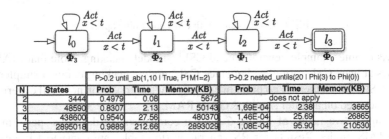

		P>0.2 until_ab(1,10 | True, P1M1=2)			P>0.2 nested_untils(20 | Phi(3) to Phi(0))		
N	States	Prob	Time	Memory(KB)	Prob	Time	Memory(KB)
2	3444	0.4979	0.08	5672	does not apply		
3	48590	0.8307	2.13	50143	1,69E-04	2.38	3665
4	438600	0.9540	27.56	480370	1,46E-04	25.69	26865
5	2895018	0.9889	212.66	2893029	1,08E-04	95.90	210530

Fig. 5. Reported results for the CSL^{TA} model checker

To check how probable this (potentially unique) behavior is in a real system we can verify its stochastic counter part. The FMS model is enriched with an exponential distribution of delays and we check the formula $P_{\leq\alpha}(A)$, where A is the DTA shown in Figure 5 that accepts all paths satisfying the nested CTL Until above, with an additional timing constraint ($t < \infty$). The same figures reports also the computed probabilities (if greater than 0.2 the property is satisfied) for different initial markings. Note that stochastic model checking is intrinsically more expensive than CTL. In the current implementation for CSL^{TA}, only relatively small CTMCs (around 10^6 states) can be checked.

5   Comparison

This section compares the CTL model checker of GreatSPN against that of other tools that can do also do CTL model checking for Petri nets, in particular SMART[9], MARCIE [17] and PNxDD follow a similar approach, being all based on various forms of DD. We have decided to consider here only SMART[9], which is strictly related to the Meddly library and MARCIE [17], which performed among the best tools at the latest Petri net model checking contest and to leave a thorough comparison to the next contest. We use SMART version 1.1 and Marcie version 20-gen-2014. The comparison is for state space generation and CTL model checking only, since only GreatSPN

FMS		RGMEDD				SMART 1.1				MARCIE (20 Gen 2014)			
N	|RS|	nodes	peak	time	mem(KB)	nodes	peak	time	mem(KB)	nodes	mem-dd	time	mem(KB)
5	2,89E+06	224	328	0.01	2760	224	306	0.06	4,376	224	1	0.05	115,680
10	2,50E+09	579	908	0.02	3008	579	781	0.10	4,416	579	1	0.06	117,532
20	6,03E+17	1739	2799	0.11	3908	1739	2331	0.17	4,944	1739	1	0.09	118,328
50	4,24E+22	8819	15241	1.12	7640	8819	11781	0.57	14,112	8819	1	0.20	125,188
100	2,70E+26	32619	56766	8.00	21972	32619	43531	2.40	72,200	32619	1	0.70	158,760
200	1,95E+30	125219	218731	60.80	91856	125219	167031	16.53	462,820	125219	2	3.77	392,520

FMS	AG (M1 = 0 -> P1wM1 < N)			EF [M1 = 0]			AF AX (P1M1 = N)			A [M1 > 0 U P1 = 0]		
N	RGMEDD	marcie	Smart	RGMEDD	marcie	Smart	RGMEDD	marcie	Smart	RGMEDD	marcie	Smart
5	0.001	0.04	0.071	0.001	0.04	0.015	0.001	0.04	0.029	0.001	0.04	0.069
10	0.014	0.04	0.199	0.008	0.05	0.024	0.004	0.05	0.054	0.005	0.04	0.113
20	0.047	0.06	0.264	0.025	0.08	0.038	0.011	0.06	0.130	0.019	0.07	0.355
50	0.563	0.22	0.534	0.238	0.36	0.143	0.096	0.22	0.861	0.844	0.28	4.375
100	3.834	0.97	1.107	1.637	1.72	0.698	0.587	0.94	6.234	2.634	1.38	50.712
200	27.632	6.76	2.896	11.599	9.70	4.417	4.094	8.64	45.265	15.844	13.52	608.382

Philosophers-PT-N

				RGMEDD					
				Reachability set				E [(Eat_1 = 0) U (Eat_2 = 1)]	E G (Eat_1 = 1)
N	|RS|	Places	Transitions	nodes	peak	time	mem(KB)	time	time
5	243	25	25	226	267	0.02	3,232	0.001	0.001
10	59049	50	50	242	288	0.02	3,616	0.001	0.001
20	3.48678e+09	100	100	642	745	0.04	5,224	0.003	0.004
50	7.17898e+23	250	250	4008	4258	0.16	10,216	0.025	0.094
100	5.15378e+47	500	500	15352	15848	0.51	19,924	0.088	0.039
200	2.65614e+95	1000	1000	20800	21808	2.34	38,848	0.168	0.270

Fig. 6. Experiments with FMS and Philosophers

supports counterexample generation and CSL^{TA} model checking. Note that MARCIE supports at least CSL formulas, but since CSL model checking is much simpler than that of CSL^{TA}, then there is no point in carrying out a comparison now. All experiments were conducted on an Intel i7 with 8 GB of RAM.

The upper two tables of Figure 6 show a comparison of the tools' performances on the FMS model. Results for RS generation (top table) are consistent in terms of number of states and even in the final number of DD nodes (although the DD types are not exactly the same), peak number of nodes is not shown for MARCIE since it is not reported by the standard tool execution. The tools perform rather similarly for up to $N = 20$ (about 10^{17} states) while for bigger state spaces MARCIE shows better performances. All tools use the same order of variables for sake of comparison. For model checking we have considered 4 different formulae, again for "not too big" models they all perform compute the Sat-set in very little time (always less than a minute but for a single case of Smart).

The lower table in Figure 6 shows the experimental results of GreatSPN on the *philosopher model*. Here, the number of places and transitions is not constant, but grows linearly with the number N of philosophers. This impacts the number of MDD levels. Again, the tool generates very large state spaces in very little time and memory.

GreatSPN is still under development. While the full graphical definitions of GSPNs and DTAs are already complete, we are still integrating the whole set of solvers available in the previous GUI. We also plan to work more on the graphical rendering of the counterexamples, possibly with a display of the simulation traces in the GUI. We are also exploring statistical model checking using Cosmos [7], to do CSL^{TA} model checking of very large stochastic systems using Monte Carlo simulations.

References

1. Amparore, E.G., Donatelli, S.: A Component-Based Solution Method for Non-ergodic Markov Regenerative Processes. In: Aldini, A., Bernardo, M., Bononi, L., Cortellessa, V. (eds.) EPEW 2010. LNCS, vol. 6342, pp. 236–251. Springer, Heidelberg (2010)
2. Amparore, E.G., Donatelli, S.: Improving and assessing the efficiency of the MC4CSL^{TA} model checker. In: Balsamo, M.S., Knottenbelt, W.J., Marin, A. (eds.) EPEW 2013. LNCS, vol. 8168, pp. 206–220. Springer, Heidelberg (2013)
3. Amparore, E.G., Donatelli, S.: A component-based solution for reducible Markov regenerative processes. Performance Evaluation 70(6), 400–422 (2013)
4. Baarir, S., Beccuti, M., Cerotti, D., De Pierro, M., Donatelli, S., Franceschinis, G.: The GreatSPN tool: recent enhancements. SIGMETRICS Perform. Eval. Rev. 36(4), 4–9 (2009)
5. Babar, J., Beccuti, M., Donatelli, S., Miner, A.: GreatSPN Enhanced with Decision Diagram Data Structures. In: Lilius, J., Penczek, W. (eds.) PETRI NETS 2010. LNCS, vol. 6128, pp. 308–317. Springer, Heidelberg (2010)
6. Babar, J., Miner, A.: Meddly: Multi-terminal and edge-valued decision diagram library. In: International Conference on Quantitative Evaluation of Systems, pp. 195–196. IEEE Computer Society, Los Alamitos (2010)
7. Ballarini, P., Djafri, H., Duflot, M., Haddad, S., Pekergin, N.: COSMOS: a statistical model checker for the hybrid automata stochastic logic. In: QEST 2011, pp. 143–144. IEEE Computer Society Press, Aachen (2011)
8. Chiola, G., Dutheillet, C., Franceschinis, G., Haddad, S.: Stochastic well-formed coloured nets for symmetric modelling applications. IEEE Trans. on Comp. 42(11), 1343–1360 (1993)
9. Ciardo, G., Jones III, R.L., Miner, A.S., Siminiceanu, R.I.: Logic and stochastic modeling with SMART. Perform. Eval. 63(6), 578–608 (2006)
10. Ciardo, G., Lüttgen, G., Siminiceanu, R.: Saturation: An efficient iteration strategy for symbolic state-space generation. In: Margaria, T., Yi, W. (eds.) TACAS 2001. LNCS, vol. 2031, pp. 328–342. Springer, Heidelberg (2001)
11. Cimatti, A., Clarke, E., Giunchiglia, E., Giunchiglia, F., Pistore, M., Roveri, M., Sebastiani, R., Tacchella, A.: NuSMV 2: An OpenSource Tool for Symbolic Model Checking. In: Brinksma, E., Larsen, K.G. (eds.) CAV 2002. LNCS, vol. 2404, pp. 359–364. Springer, Heidelberg (2002)
12. Clarke, E., Jha, S., Lu, Y., Veith, H.: Tree-like counterexamples in model checking. In: Proceedings of the 17th IEEE Symposium on Logic in Computer Science, pp. 19–29 (2002)
13. Emerson, E., Clarke, E.M.: Using branching time temporal logic to synthesize synchronization skeletons. Science of Computer Programming 2(3), 241–266 (1982)
14. Gaeta, R.: Efficient Discrete-Event Simulation of Colored Petri Nets. IEEE Trans. Softw. Eng. 22(9), 629–639 (1996)
15. Katoen, J.P., Zapreev, I.S., Hahn, E.M., Hermanns, H., Jansen, D.N.: The ins and outs of the probabilistic model checker MRMC. Performance Evaluation 68(2), 90–104 (2011)
16. Marsan, M.A., Balbo, G., Conte, G., Donatelli, S., Franceschinis, G.: Modeling with Generalized Stochastic Petri Nets. J. Wiley, New York (1995)
17. Schwarick, M., Heiner, M., Rohr, C.: MARCIE - Model Checking and Reachability Analysis Done EffiCIEntly. In: Proceedings of QEST 2011, pp. 91–100 (2011)

StrataGEM: A Generic Petri Net Verification Framework

Edmundo López Bóbeda, Maximilien Colange, and Didier Buchs

Centre Universitaire d'Informatique
Université de Genève
7 route de Drize, 1227 Carouge, Suisse

Abstract. In this paper we present the Strategy Generic Extensible Modelchecker (StrataGEM), a tool aimed at the analysis of Petri nets and other models of concurrency by means of symbolic model-checking techniques. StrataGEM marries the well know concepts of Term Rewriting (TR) to the efficiency of Decision Diagrams (DDs). TR systems are a great way to describe the semantics of a system, being readable and compact, but their direct implementation tends to be rather slow on large sets of terms. On the other hand, DDs have demonstrated their efficiency for model-checking, but translating a system semantics into efficient DDs operations is an expert's matter. StrataGEM describes the semantics of a system in terms of *strategies* over a TR system, and automatically translates these rules into operations on DD to handle the model-checking. The ultimate goal of StrataGEM is to become a verification framework for the different variants of Petri nets by separating the semantics of the model from the computation that performs model-checking.

1 Introduction

Decision Diagrams (DDs) have demonstrated their efficiency towards model-checking [1], especially for Globally Asynchronous Locally Synchronous (GALS) systems. However, they require a careful encoding of the operations at the DDs level. Most works in the area focus on a low-level encoding, which is a major obstacle for non-expert modelers.

High-level interfaces, easily understandable for the user not familiar with DDs, are desirable in order to ease and widen the use of DDs. With model-checking as goal, such an interface should provide a language for the description of the semantics of the systems to be evaluated, and an automatic translation of this semantics into DDs operations. It should also feature some predefined model-checking algorithms, along with opportunity to define new algorithms, *e.g.,* through the language used for the semantic description. This language should meet two criteria: be expressive enough to capture the largest possible class of systems, and be easy to read and write for a human being. This aim is similar to the principles used in successful SAT based model-checker such as bounded model-checker where there is a separation between the encoding of the problem in propositional logic and the SAT engines themselves.

G. Ciardo and E. Kindler (Eds.): PETRI NETS 2014, LNCS 8489, pp. 364–373, 2014.
© Springer International Publishing Switzerland 2014

StrataGEM is a prototype of such an interface, relying on Term Rewrite Systems (TRSs) as its language for semantic description, to achieve both expressiveness and readability. Term Rewriting (TR) rules are especially well-suited to describe local modifications, which suits asynchronous systems. Standard TR rules however suffer two drawbacks. First, GALS systems often feature various degrees of synchronization among local modifications; such synchronizations are not easy to express with standard TR rules. Second, model-checking algorithms often tweak the semantics of the system to increase performance, *e.g.*, by prioritizing concurrent transitions. Such operations are not easy to describe with standard TR rules either.

StrataGEM adresses these problems thanks to *TR strategies*. They enrich the language by allowing to combine standard TR rules in various ways. Thus, the semantics of a system is given in two steps: standard TR rules describe atomic semantic steps, and strategies using these atoms describe more elaborate transitions (such as synchronizations), or semantic tweaks for optimization [2,3].

Strategies also allow to describe model-checking algorithms, either built-in in the tool or designed by the user. Thus, semantics of systems and model-checking algorithms are treated uniformly, considerably easing the use of the tool.

As the use of TRS to describe the semantics of a system assumes to represent states of said system as terms, the natural choice for the underlying DDs is Σ Decision Diagrams (ΣDDs) [4]. Designed to represent efficiently large sets of terms, they come with basic efficient manipulation operations. In particular, they allow to apply a TR rule to a set of terms in one elementary step.

Thanks to its extensibility, StrataGEM is not only aimed at people wanting to model-check Petri nets, but also at developers of model-checkers, willing to implement their algorithms on top of ΣDD.

This paper is structured as follows: in Section 2 we informally present transition systems, based on TRS and strategies, as defined in StrataGEM. Section 3 presents the tool architecture and also introduces its basic usage. Section 4 presents an assesment of the tool, comparing it to another similar model-checking tool. The results are quite promising, the comparison with PNXDD indicating a trend towards a better asymptotic performance for StrataGEM.

2   StrataGEM Transition Systems

In this section, we informally present how to describe Transition System (TS) in StrataGEM. We first introduce the TRS and rewrite rules, that serve as basic bricks to describe local evolutions of the system. We then present the strategies that allow to combine these building blocks into elaborated semantics and algorithms. Their purpose is threefold: they describe the non-local transformations of the system, the model-checking algorithms, and the optimizations that can be done in these algorithms. Terms, that describe the states of the system, rewrite rules and strategies, that describe its semantics, are gathered to form a StrataGEM Transition System. To support our presentation, we use as running example the Kanban model, expressed as a Petri Net on Figure 1.

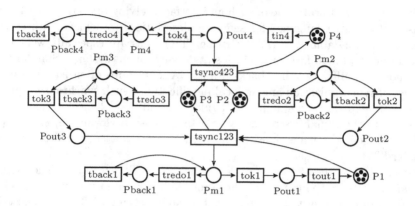

Fig. 1. Kanban Petri Net

2.1   Term Rewrite Systems

The first step is to define a signature: a set of function names used to build terms
that encode the states of the system. Several encodings with different signatures
may be possible. The construction of terms in StrataGEM follows the theory of
Order-Sorted Signatures [5], which we do not detail here.

Let us describe the signature used by StrataGEM for Petri nets. Non-negative
integers are encoded as terms being either `zero`, or `suc(t)` where `t` is an integer term. For clarity, in the following integer terms are often replaced by plain
integers.

For a given Petri net, a function name of arity 2 is defined for each of its places.
The first argument is the marking of the place (an integer term), and the second
argument is the subsequent list of places. The function name `empty` of arity 0 denotes the empty list. The state (marking) of a Petri net is then a term containing
all places exactly once with their respective number of tokens. Thus, in our running example, an initial state would start with `Pm4(0, P4(5, Pback (0, ...)))`,
indicating that places `Pm4` and `Pback` initially contain no token, whereas place `P4`
contains 5 tokens.

Basic local operations of the system are described in terms of rewrite rules,
and aggregated with strategies. A rewrite rule `l ⤳ r` states that if a term `t`
matches its left-hand side `l`, then it is replaced by its right-hand side `r`. Note
that both `l` and `r` may contain term variables. In the case of Petri nets, each arc
gives rise to a rewrite rule, a transition of the net is then described by a strategy
aggregating its adjacent arcs. For example, the arc removing a token from `Pm4`
(either to fire transition `tredo4` or `tok4`) is described by the rewrite rule `arc1 =`
`Pm4(suc($x), $p) ⤳ Pm4($x, $p)`, where values preceded by a dollar sign denote
variables. Similarly, an arc adding a token in the place `Pm4` (either from transition
`tback4` or `tin4`) is described by `arc2 = Pm($x, $p) ⤳ Pm4(suc($x), $p)`. Note
that StrataGEM only handles linear rewriting rules, *i.e.*, that do not contain
multiple occurrences of a variable in its left and right sides.

2.2   Term Rewriting Strategies

Expressing the Petri Nets transitions in terms of rewrite rules would be cumbersome, especially if the places modified by the transition are not close in the state vector. To cope with this problem we use Term Rewriting strategies [6,7], that are meant to control the application of rewrite rules. A TR rule might succeed and modify the term on which it is applied or fail, in which case the strategy returns nothing. A fail in a strategy can be seen as an exception that is raised.

Basic Strategies. The *simple strategy* wraps a standard rewrite rule as a strategy, and applies it at the *root* of a given term. Thus, a simple strategy is defined for each arc of the Petri Net, that embeds the arc rewrite rule described above.

Note that a simple strategy only applies its embedded rewrite rule at the top of a term. If the rule is applicable to a subterm, but not to the root, then the simple strategy fails. We denote the application of a strategy with square brackets. For example, arc1[Pm4(suc(0), empty)] = Pm4(0, empty). However, arc1[P4(suc(0), Pm4(suc(0), empty))] will fail, because the term where it can be applied is a *subterm* of the root term, and not the root term itself.

Such basic strategies are sufficient to express the semantics of Petri Nets arcs, and we present in the following how to combine them to express the semantics of a whole transition. StrataGEM allows a more generic setting for simple strategies. A simple strategy embeds an ordered list of rewrite rules, and applies only the first of the rules that is applicable. We do not use this feature in the paper, but it is quite useful when several rewrite rules are applicable to the same term. The ordered list describes a priority between rules to resolve any ambiguity. If no rule in the list is applicable at the root, then the simple strategy fails.

Simple strategies serve as atomic building blocks for the transition relation. To combine them, StrataGEM provides a set of basic strategies, mostly inspired from Tom strategy language [7]. The user may also define custom strategies.

We introduce three basic strategies, and then combine them to apply an arc rewrite rule at the appropriate, but not *a priori* known, depth. The first of these basic strategies, One(S,n), applies the strategy S to the n-th subterm of the root. This overcomes the limitation of simple strategies to apply only at the root of a term. The second strategy is the *choice strategy*, a simple conditional application of strategies: Choice(S1,S2)[t] tries to apply S1 to t. It returns S1[t] if this application succeeds, and S2[t] if S1 fails.

We now the third define a strategy *recursively*. It is for instance useful for the recursive propagation of a strategy on subterms, to apply it at an arbitrary depth. For instance, to apply an arc rewrite rule at the appropriate depth, we use the recursively defined strategy ApplyOnce(S) = Choice(S, One(ApplyOnce(S),2). ApplyOnce(S) thus tries to apply S at root level. If it fails, it tries to apply it on the second subterm. If this also fails, given the definition of our state terms, it means that it was applied on empty and legitimately fails. This strategy thus descends the subterm tree until it finds a subterm where it can be applied. Note that this does not require to know the depth where the strategy S should be applied: this application depth is discovered dynamically.

We have described how to apply an arc rewrite rule at the appropriate depth. We now describe how to encode the semantics of a Petri net transition. It is simply the synchronization of the rewrite rules for all the incident arcs. This synchronization is performed with the *sequence strategy*: Sequence(S1,S2) first applies S1, then S2. If one of its arguments fails when applied, the sequence strategy also fails. To improve readability, it is also possible to define a n-ary sequence strategy, that applies its arguments one after the other. Thus, if a transition t of a Petri net has iarc1, ..., iarcN as input arcs and oarc1, ..., oarcP, then its semantics is given by the strategy Sequence(iarc1, ..., iarcN, oarc1, ..., oarcP). This ensures that the input arcs rules are applied before the output arcs rules, thus ensuring the enabling precondition: if one input place does not contain enough tokens, the whole strategy fails.

Note that this encoding could be further improved by releasing constraints on the order the arc rewrite rules are evaluated, so as to avoid unnecessary walks along the term tree structure. The only constraint that should be retained is that the enabling precondition be retained. Another improvement would be the design of a strategy for a commutative sequence of strategies, that would determine dynamically the order in which the arc rewrite rules are applied.

Model-Checking Strategies. Strategies are not only meant to describe the transition relation of a system, but they can also describe how to explore the state space to check a property. We first extend the strategies to sets of terms: S[T] = { S[t] | t ∈ T , S does not fail on t }. The elements on which the strategy fails are removed from the resulting set. If the strategy fails on all terms in the set, then it fails on the set.

We define two more strategies to better handle sets of terms. The first one allows to gather the results of several strategies: Union(S1,S2)[T] = S1[T] ∪ S2[T]. The union fails if either S1 or S2 fails. As previously done for the sequence strategy, we use an n-ary union to ease readability. The order of its arguments is not relevant, since it is commutative.

Fixpoint applies a strategy to a set of terms until a fixpoint is reached: Fixpoint(S)[T] = S^n[T] where n is the smallest integer s.t. S^n[T] = S^{n+1}[T]. We use these strategies to encode the state space generation of a concurrent system, such as the Petri Net of Figure 1. Say that the concurrent system has N transitions, encoded as strategies T1, ..., TN. The strategy that generates the state space of such a system is: Fixpoint(Union(Identity, Choice(T1, Identity), ..., Choice(TN, Identity))). The Identity strategy rewrites a term to itself. Its presence in the union is necessary to keep states computed so far. Choice keeps strategies from failing, which would make the Union fail.

Optimizing Strategies. Most model-checking algorithms perform challenging computations, and it is in our best interest to perform them optimally. When using DDs, there are three main ways to improve the strategies:

– performing less operations;

- exploiting locality;
- exploiting subparts of the system that share similar behavior.

Consider for instance the operation ApplyOnce(arc1) defined above. We recall that arc1 = Pm4(suc($x), $p) ⇝ Pm4($x, $p). If Pm4 does not contain enough tokens, arc1 fails, and ApplyOnce(arc1) continues its descent of the subterm tree, eventually stopping at the end of the tree. But, by construction of our state terms, if arc1 fails at this very level, it will not apply at any other level. Hence the recursive descent of ApplyOnce(arc1) becomes useless. To avoid this unnecessary and costly descent, we can first check if the appropriate depth is reached, and apply arc1 only if true. In this case, the failure of arc1 is not pursued by a descent on the subsequent places. We introduce a conditional strategy: ITE(S1, S2, S3) [1] first applies S1, then it applies S2 if successful. If the application of S1 fails in the first place, it applies S3 to the input term. The trick here is to use a strategy that checks whether the good level is reached, without modifying the term. Let cPm4 be the rewrite rule Pm4($x, $p) ⇝ Pm4($x, $p). This rule acts as the identity only for terms whose root is Pm4, and fails on any other ones. Thus, ApplyOnceOpt(cPm4,arc1) = ITE(cPm4, arc1, One(ApplyOnceOpt(cPm4,arc1), 2)) performs the recursive descent only if Pm4 has not yet been reached, avoiding the aforementioned unnecessary steps.

Another optimization consists in exploiting locality: transitions that affect the same places can be gathered so as to be evaluated together, thus avoiding unnecessary upwards and downwards walks of the state term. StrataGEM introduces the notion of *clusters* of places, a subset of the places of the net adjacent to a common set of transitions. In the Kanban model, Pm2, Pback2 and Pout2 together with transitions tredo2, tback2 and tok2 form such a cluster. These transitions can be applied at the cluster level, rather than on the whole term. The state terms slightly change to handle this optimization: the places of a given cluster are encoded contiguously in the state vector, limits of clusters being highlighted with new function names in the term. The transitions of a cluster are applied on the corresponding subterm only, identified by said cluster limits.

Beside avoiding unnecessary walks of the terms to find the appropriate level of application, we also note that the evaluation of a fixpoint can also be pushed at the cluster level. This is very similar to the optimization for fixpoint evaluation on Decision Diagrams known as saturation [2,8].

But the materialization of clusters also allows for further optimization. By an appropriate hierarchy in the state term and renaming of the places, cluster subterms can share their representation in memory. Thanks to DDs unicity tables and caches, this allows to share the representation and semantics of clusters with similar behaviors. This may considerably speed up the computations if the input net presents a high level of similarity between its clusters.

Details about the strategies generated for this example model, both non-optimized and optimized, are presented in http://sourceforge.net/projects/stratagem-mc/files/ .

---

[1] This strategy also allows to define Choice(S1, S2) as ITE(S1, Fail, S2), and Sequence(S1, S2) as ITE(S1, S2, Fail).

Note that all these optimizations require to know (good) clusters for the input system. StrataGEM features a clustering algorithm, activated by default, that automatically detects clusters in the input net, and exploits them to use the above optimizations. The description of the clustering algorithm goes beyond the scope of this paper, but roughly speaking, it relies on a maximization of the ratio between the size of the cluster (the number of places it embeds) and its frontier (number of adjacent transitions). The automatic cluster detection is currently only available for Petri Nets, although similar algorithms could be designed for other input formats.

Sum Up We sum up in Table 1 the strategies available in StrataGEM. In this table, i and n are integers, S, S1, S2 and S3 denote strategies, t and t_1 through t_n denote Σ-terms, T a set of Σ-terms, and f is a symbol of arity n in Σ.

Table 1. The strategies available in StrataGEM

simple strategy	wraps a term-rewriting rule as a strategy
one	$\mathtt{One(S},i)\mathtt{[f(t_1,\ldots,\ t_n)]} = \mathtt{f(t_1,\ldots,\ S[t_i],\ldots,\ t_n)}$
choice	$\mathtt{Choice(S1,S2)[t]} = \begin{cases} \mathtt{S1[t]} & \text{if S1 is successful on } t \\ \mathtt{S2[t]} & \text{otherwise} \end{cases}$
sequence	$\mathtt{Sequence(S1,S2)[t]} = \begin{cases} \mathtt{S2[S1[t]]} & \text{if S1 is successful on } t \\ \text{fails} & \text{otherwise} \end{cases}$
if-then-else	$\mathtt{ITE(S1,S2,S3)[t]} = \begin{cases} \mathtt{S2[S1[t]]} & \text{if S1 is successful on } t \\ \mathtt{S3[t]]} & \text{otherwise} \end{cases}$
union	$\mathtt{Union(S1,S2)[T]} = \begin{cases} \mathtt{S1[T]} \cup \mathtt{S2[T]} & \text{if S1 and S2 do not fail on T} \\ \text{fails} & \text{otherwise} \end{cases}$
fixpoint	$\mathtt{Fixpoint(S)[T]} = \mathtt{S}^n\mathtt{[T]}$ where $n = \min_{i>0}(\mathtt{S}^i\mathtt{[T]} = \mathtt{S}^{i+1}\mathtt{[T]})$

3   Architecture

We shortly describe the architecture of the tool and its usage. StrataGEM can be used as a standalone command line tool or as a library. It is available at `http://sourceforge.net/projects/stratagem-mc/`, and we also provide a set of examples (including the Kanban model) at `https://sourceforge.net/projects/stratagem-mc/files/examples/`.

3.1   Architecture and Implementation

StrataGEM is written in Scala and comprises 3700 lines of code. It is packaged as a jar archive, as is common for Scala tools. The choice of Scala renders the tool platform-independent.

StrataGEM features three main parts, as shown on Figure 2. The core is the ΣDD implementation, with their relevant operations. It is extended by a layer implementing terms, rewrite rules, strategies and their combination to describe a transition system. The third part is the import, that translates a model expressed in a given modeling language to a StrataGEM transition system whose semantics is described with rewrite rules and strategies. So far, StrataGEM features an import of Petri nets expressed in PNML [9]. This import includes an automatic detection of the clusters of a Petri net, as described above.

It also features an import from the language GAL [10]. This language serves as an intermediate, and already features translators from various inputs, such as DVE language used in the BEEM benchmark [11], amd Timed Automata, increasing the number of input formats for StrataGEM.

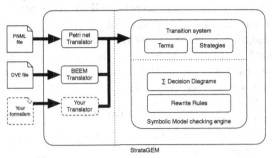

Fig. 2. Architecture of the StrataGEM

3.2 Standalone Tool

In its simplest form, StrataGEM currently computes the state space of the input model. Several levels of optimization are activated through the option -t, from the plain regular encoding described at the beginning of Section 2.2 to the use of hierarchized clusters as described at the end of Section 2.2.

The cluster detection, activated by default, is deactivated with an option. It can also be used alone, without computing the state space.

It is also possible to print the transition system with its rewrite rules and strategies generated for the input model by invoking `./stratagem analyzer -ts Kanban.pnml`.

Users also may add formalisms to StrataGEM. It only requires to translate the semantics of the input formalism into rewrite rules and strategies. The syntax of rewrite rules is quite straightforward and easy to use. All the strategies described in this paper are available to combine rewrite rules. It is also possible to define new strategies.

4 Benchmarks

We perform a quick experimental evaluation of our tool, to demonstrate the feasibility of our approach. Inspired by the Model Checking Contest @ Petri nets [12], we compare the performance of StrataGEM for the generation of the state space of some parametric Petri nets with the performance of PNXDD [13], a symbolic model-checker aimed at Petri nets. PNXDD also performs a cluster detection to produce hierarchized terms [14], and participated to the MCC since its first edition in 2011.

The compared tools present a lot of differences, so that the comparison of the raw data should be done very carefully. First of all, StrataGEM runs on the

Java virtual machine, that introduces an important time and memory overhead compared to PNXDD, written in C++. Moreover, PNXDD relies on a symbolic engine with years of maturity, highly optimized, whereas StrataGEM has no more than six months. The engine of PNXDD features many optimizations that are not at all present in StrataGEM. Also, StrataGEM was designed primarily as a demonstration prototype of the use of rewriting techniques on top of decision diagrams. Therefore, we choose to compare the *ratio* between the runtimes of both tools, so as to leverage these overheads. The evolution of the ratios among several instances of the same model gives us an indication of how this method scales compared to PNXDD.

We perform the comparison on three parametric models, expressed as Petri nets, used in the MCC 2013. The results are presented in Table 2. Besides the first, small, instances, models in the MCC are intended

Table 2. Runtime Comparison with clustering enabled

Model	Instance	PNXDD time (s)	StrataGEM time (s)	ratio P./S.
Eratosthenes	10	0.08	0.24	0.33
	20	0.11	0.79	0.14
	50	0.25	1.95	0.13
	100	1.14	6.48	0.18
	200	6.28	24.71	0.25
RailRoad	05	0.33	3.82	0.09
	10	103.90	83.06	1.25
SharedMemory	05	0.15	2.4	0.06
	10	1.08	3.55	0.30
	20	12.91	17.75	0.73

to be quite hard. That, and the current lack of fine-tuning of StrataGEM, limits the number of instances on which exploitable results can be obtained. An increase in the runtime ratio indicates that StrataGEM begins to close the gap with PNXDD. On the three models, we see that the ratio of runtime performance between StrataGEM and PNXDD evolves in favor of StrataGEM. The decrease of this ratio for the three first instances of the Eratosthenes model are anecdotic: the runtimes of PNXDD are close the time measurement errors on these instances. Furthermore, we are rather interested in the asymptotic behavior of this ratio. We also notice that StrataGEM ouperforms PNXDD on the last instance of the Railroad model, despite its aforementioned disadvantages.

These preliminary results are quite encouraging, and are a first validation of the use of rewriting systems on top of symbolic data structures. As we have said, there is room for improvement and optimization in the StrataGEM prototype. Tuning work is planned in the near future, so as to make StrataGEM participate at the MCC 2014, that will enable a better assessment of its performance.

5   Conclusion

We have presented StrataGEM, a prototype implementing a novel approach for the manipulation of DDs. The operations on DDs are represented using rewriting rules and strategies to combine them. We have shown how they can describe the semantics of a Petri net. Other languages, such as the BEEM language, is also supported as an experimental feature. This approach is intended to address the need for a clear and user-friendly interface for the efficient manipulation of such symbolic data structures. Our small assessment demonstrates that, despite its youth, our prototype has an acceptable performance. The room left for optimization and tuning promises quick improvements towards a participation in the next edition of the Model Checking Contest.

Beside this development work, future work includes the generalization of this approach to other formalisms. Algebraic Petri Nets seem to be a good middle-term target, and would demonstrate the flexibility of our approach.

References

1. Burch, J.R., Clarke, E.M., McMillan, K.L., Dill, D.L., Hwang, L.: Symbolic Model Checking: 10^{20} States and Beyond. Information and Computation 98(2), 142–170 (1992)
2. Ciardo, G., Marmorstein, R., Siminiceanu, R.: Saturation Unbound. In: Garavel, H., Hatcliff, J. (eds.) TACAS 2003. LNCS, vol. 2619, pp. 379–393. Springer, Heidelberg (2003)
3. Wolper, P., Godefroid, P.: Partial-Order Methods for Temporal Verification. In: Best, E. (ed.) CONCUR 1993. LNCS, vol. 715, pp. 233–246. Springer, Heidelberg (1993)
4. Buchs, D., Hostettler, S.: Sigma Decision Diagrams. In: Corradini, A. (ed.) TERMGRAPH 2009: Preliminary Proceedings of the 5th International Workshop on Computing with Terms and Graphs. Number TR-09-05 in TERMGRAPH Workshops, Università di Pisa, pp. 18–32 (2009)
5. Goguen, J.A., Meseguer, J.: Order-Sorted Algebra I: Equational Deduction for Multiple Inheritance, Overloading, Exceptions and Partial Operations. Theor. Comput. Sci. 105, 217–273 (1992)
6. Borovanský, P., Kirchner, C., Kirchner, H., Moreau, P.E., Vittek, M.: ELAN: A Logical Framework Based on Computational Systems. Electronic Notes in Theoretical Computer Science 4, 35–50 (1996)
7. Balland, E., Brauner, P., Kopetz, R., Moreau, P.-E., Reilles, A.: Tom: Piggybacking Rewriting on Java. In: Baader, F. (ed.) RTA 2007. LNCS, vol. 4533, pp. 36–47. Springer, Heidelberg (2007)
8. Hamez, A., Thierry-Mieg, Y., Kordon, F.: Hierarchical Set Decision Diagrams and Automatic Saturation. In: van Hee, K.M., Valk, R. (eds.) PETRI NETS 2008. LNCS, vol. 5062, pp. 211–230. Springer, Heidelberg (2008)
9. International Organization for Standardization: ISO/IEC. Software and Systems Engineering - High-Level Petri Nets, Part 1: Concepts, Definitions and Graphical Notation. International Standard ISO/IEC 15909 (December 2004)
10. MoVe Team: GAL, http://move.lip6.fr/software/DDD/gal.php
11. Pelánek, R.: BEEM: Benchmarks for Explicit Model Checkers. In: Bošnački, D., Edelkamp, S. (eds.) SPIN 2007. LNCS, vol. 4595, pp. 263–267. Springer, Heidelberg (2007)
12. Kordon, F., Buchs, D.: Model Checking Contest Page, http://mcc.lip6.fr/
13. MoVe Team: The PNXDD Home Page (2013), https://srcdev.lip6.fr/trac/research/NEOPPOD/wiki/pnxdd
14. Hong, S., Kordon, F., Paviot-Adet, E., Evangelista, S.: Computing a Hierarchical Static Order for Decision Diagram-Based Representation from P/T Nets. In: Jensen, K., Donatelli, S., Kleijn, J. (eds.) ToPNoC V. LNCS, vol. 6900, pp. 121–140. Springer, Heidelberg (2012)

A Steering Server for Collaborative Simulation of Quantitative Petri Nets

Mostafa Herajy[1] and Monika Heiner[2]

[1] Department of Mathematics and Computer Science, Faculty of Science,
Port Said University, 42521 - Port Said, Egypt
[2] Computer Science Institute, Brandenburg University of Technology
Postbox 10 13 44, 03013 Cottbus, Germany
http://www-dssz.informatik.tu-cottbus.de

Abstract. In this paper we present a Petri net simulation tool called Snoopy Steering and Simulation Server, S^4 for short, which works as a stand-alone extension of Snoopy. The server permits users to share and interactively steer quantitative Petri net models during a running simulation. Moreover, users can collaborate by controlling the execution of a model remotely from different machines (clients). S^4 is shipped with an Application Programming Interface (API) which enables user-defined extensions of the core functionalities. Stochastic, continuous and hybrid Petri nets are supported, both as low-level and coloured ones. S^4 is platform-independent and distributed free of charge for academic use.

Keywords: stochastic, continuous, hybrid Petri nets, computational steering, collaborative simulation.

1 Introduction

There exists a wide range of software tools that permit the modelling and execution of Petri nets. Most of them are concerned with facilitating the process of designing and editing a Petri net model and to make it as flexible and convenient as possible, but pay little attention to simulation features. However, improving the user support for running simulations is imperative in certain circumstances. As an example consider the simulation of quantitative Petri nets, such as continuous, stochastic, or hybrid Petri nets, which may become computationally very expensive. For instance, consider the spatial modelling of planar cell polarity in the drosophila wing via Petri nets [6]. This scalable model may contain about 1,000,000 places and 1,000,000 transitions, and the runtime may range from several hours to days or even weeks, particularly when stochastic simulation is involved. Therefore, such models call for sophisticated simulation environments with flexible features for model execution. Examples of such key features are: remote simulation on powerful machines, on-the-fly change of key simulation parameters, collaboration between peer users, or the exploration of one and the same model by different simulation engines.

G. Ciardo and E. Kindler (Eds.): PETRI NETS 2014, LNCS 8489, pp. 374–384, 2014.

High performance computers are usually hosted at central locations. Therefore, a software tool should allow users to run Petri net models remotely and control their execution via computer terminals. Moreover, such a feature is of great importance to facilitate the sharing of computational resources. For instance, computationally expensive simulations can run on powerful clusters, while the monitoring of the results can be done from a laptop.

Traditionally, a simulation is restarted from the very beginning when a new parameter set is required to be tested. However, for bigger models it consumes a lot of time to restart the simulation from scratch each time when we notice that the simulation goes in a wrong or undesirable direction. As an alternative method, key simulation parameters should be changeable on-the-fly, and the simulation should just continue execution with the new values for these key parameters [13]. By this way, users obtain more control over the model execution which permits to amend errors or play with the model, e.g. to explore the kinetic parameter space or try design alternatives.

Furthermore, it is useful to permit the collaboration between users with different backgrounds. Such interaction may promote the sharing of knowledge. Besides, changes done by one user should also be propagated to the others.

Nonetheless, in some application domains of Petri nets it is important to explore one and the same model definition using different simulation techniques. For instance, systems biology often suggests to simulate a quantitative Petri net using either the deterministic, stochastic or hybrid approach. This will render it possible to compare results of the different modelling paradigms in order to study which simulation method fits this type of model best.

In this paper we present a software tool called S^4 (Snoopy Steering and Simulation Server) that works as a stand-alone extension of Snoopy [20] and permits to distribute, collaborate, share, and interactively steer Petri nets during a running simulation. S^4 is completely written in C++ in a platform-independent manner. S^4 supports three main Petri net classes: stochastic [17], continuous [7], and hybrid Petri nets [11]. The theory behind S^4 can be found in [13], and a detailed technical documentation in [12]. S^4 was previously known as SSServer.

2 Functionality

In this section we list the main functionalities provided by S^4. Moreover, we discuss how it can communicate and interact with other software (including Snoopy) to read Petri net models. The different simulation algorithms which are supported by S^4 are also pinpointed.

2.1 Main Features

- **Remotely run and control a simulation.** Users can run their simulation at remote computers. This feature allows the access to machines with high computational power from a local computer. The simulation will run at a server machine while the visualization of the results is done at a different machine, serving as graphical user interface (GUI) client.

- **Execution of one model using different simulation algorithms.** Sometimes it is useful to study a model via different paradigms, i.e., stochastic, continuous, or hybrid. Using S^4, one and the same model definition can be executed with different simulation algorithms.
- **Managing different models concurrently with possibly different simulators.** Different models can be simultaneously executed at the server side. A separate simulator is assigned to each model and can be executed independently from other running models. Moreover, running models can be saved on the server side for future restore.
- **Defining different views to explore simulation results.** Views provide a quick means to explore simulation results from different perspectives. Each view is defined by a set of data curves and their associated attributes. Several different views can be defined for a model.
- **Exploring the running models on-the-fly.** By help of the steering graphical user interface (Steering GUI), users can easily navigate among different models. The list of running models at the server side can be refreshed if another user adds/deletes a model to/from the server.
- **Steering simulation parameters while a simulation is running.** The main goal of S^4 is to enable users to interact with their models during simulations. Users can change model parameters as well as the current marking and immediately monitor the system's response to such changes. This is a very useful tool since a user is allowed to ask "what-if" questions.
- **Controlling the simulation speed.** The simulation speed can be set to an appropriate level to facilitate the interaction with a running model during its execution. This feature is especially important if simulation parameters are allowed to be changed while the simulation is running.
- **Connecting to a simulation at any time from whatever place.** S^4 is flexible to let users connect/disconnect to/from running models without affecting their execution. Moreover, users can connect to running models from different places, for example from the office or from home.
- **Collaborating with other people while simulating a model.** More than one user is permitted to connect to the same models. Users can collaborate by executing and steering a running simulation.
- **Platform-independent implementation.** The core communication library is written in standard C++, thus it can run on different platforms, among them Windows, Mac OS X, and Linux. Clients and servers need not to run on the same platform.

2.2   Petri Net Model Definition

Before S^4 can be used to execute a simulation, a model needs to be defined. The model has to be specified in terms of quantitative Petri nets: places, transitions, arcs, kinetic parameters, transition rates (rate functions), and initial making, with the specific constraints depending on the net class, see [7,11,17] for details. S^4 accepts models that are defined by either of two ways: through Snoopy [9], or via an Application Programming Interface (API) [13].

Defining a model via Snoopy. Snoopy is a powerful tool to design and edit Petri nets. It supports many different Petri net classes. Thus, we sought to make use of Snoopy's capabilities as a way of conveniently defining a Petri net model, and afterwards the model is communicated to S^4. In a typical scenario, a user constructs a Petri net and then asks Snoopy to execute it in the steering mode. Snoopy then inquires the address of a running server on the local or a remote computer. Snoopy knows how to communicate with S^4 as they are compatible with each other.

Defining a model via API. Sometimes it may be more appropriate to define a Petri net model without using a graphical user interface. For instance, if the model is automatically generated from another specification, or if the model will be designed by other tools which are not close relatives of Snoopy. In these cases, S^4 permits the definition and communication of the Petri net using API calls [13]. Figure 1 gives an overview of the different classes supported by the API. A complete documentation as well as some examples can be found in [12].

2.3   Model Exploration

Once a Petri net model has been defined and sent to S^4, it can be further explored. The initial exploration process is meant to provide basic information about the model under study. This includes information about places, transitions, and the connections between these two node types. Model exploration can be done either on the server side or remotely through the graphical user interface.

2.4   Monitoring and Steering

During the execution of a Petri net model by help of S^4, users can remotely monitor the progress of the simulation results via Snoopy's GUI. Moreover, users can change key simulation parameters, and thus steer the simulation. In this case, they will immediately get a feedback according to their changes; see Section 4 for a typical user scenario. Figure 2 presents a screenshot of Snoopy's GUI. It is worth mentioning that it is not a prerequisite to submit a model in order to be able to monitor and steer it. One can also make use of an existing one, which has been previously submitted by another user.

2.5   Supported Petri Net Classes

S^4 supports the following Petri net classes.

- $\mathcal{GSPN}$ – Generalised stochastic Petri nets provide four transition types: stochastic, immediate, deterministic and scheduled transitions. In biological context, these transitions correspond to different reaction types. There are also five arc types: standard, read, inhibitory, equal and reset arcs.
- $\mathcal{CPN}$ – Continuous Petri nets are built from continuous places and transitions. Unlike $\mathcal{GSPN}$, $\mathcal{CPN}$'s places hold non-negative real numbers as net markings, and arcs can be weighted with non-negative real numbers.

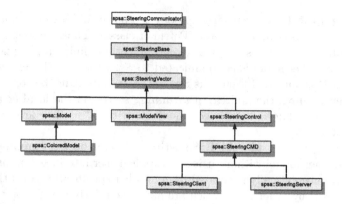

Fig. 1. Inheritance diagram of Snoopy's steering APIs (SPSA). The Snoopy steering API classes can be classified into four main functional categories: communication, data structures, control commands, and end point components.

- $\mathcal{GHPN}$ – Generalised hybrid Petri nets combine all features of $\mathcal{GSPN}$ and $\mathcal{CPN}$ into one net class. They permit the full interplay between the stochastic and continuous components.
- $\mathcal{GSPN}^{\mathcal{C}}$, $\mathcal{CPN}^{\mathcal{C}}$, $\mathcal{GHPN}^{\mathcal{C}}$ – In addition to the low-level Petri nets, S^4 reads the coloured counterparts; see [9] for more details re the relation between these Petri net classes.

2.6   Available Simulators

Petri net models submitted to S^4 can be simulated via a wide range of simulation techniques. These simulators can be classified into three main categories: deterministic, stochastic, and hybrid. Any simulation algorithm can be used to execute a model independently of the original net type. For instance, a net that has been originally designed as a continuous Petri net can be later simulated using the stochastic approach. However, an alert will be issued at the beginning of the simulation. Besides, S^4 permits the adaptation of external simulators, provided by the users, to produce the model dynamics. Furthermore, the simulation library is structured in such a way that it can be used independently of S^4.

Deterministic. One way to produce the model dynamics is to execute the model deterministically. This simulation approach involves the transformation of continuous Petri nets into a set of ordinary differential equations (ODEs) [7]. The set of ODEs are then solved numerically using an ODE solver. S^4 supports 14 different ODE solver types (seven solvers for stiff models and seven for solving non-stiff models) ranging from simple fixed step-size, explicit solvers (e.g., Runge Kutta) to variable step-size, variable order, implicit solvers (e.g., Backward differentiation formula). For the latter solver types we deploy the numerical integration library SUNDIAL CVODE [15].

Stochastic. Stochastic simulation applies a different approach to producing model dynamics. Unlike in the deterministic simulation, the fluctuation

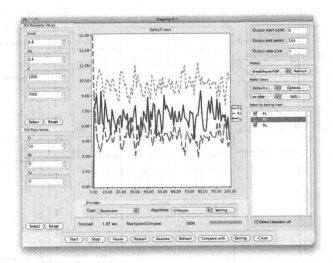

Fig. 2. Snoopy's steering GUI: steering panel (left), output panel (middle), control panel (bottom) and manipulation panel (right). The user can select a subset of the model parameters to change their values on-the-fly while the simulation is running. The simulation results can be viewed as a table, xy plot, or histogram plot; they can also be exported in csv or image format.

of tokens is captured when a model is simulated stochastically. Moreover, stochastic simulation provides a more convenient approach to permit the intervention of user changes during a model execution. The steering action can be immediately carried out during the individual firing of a stochastic transition instead of after each time step as it has to be done for deterministic simulations. S^4 currently supports one algorithm (the Gillespie stochastic simulation algorithm [8]) to simulate Petri nets stochastically; alternative algorithms are scheduled for further developments.

Hybrid. With the progress of modelling and simulation, it becomes crucial to handle systems involving some degree of complexity. Such models can often not be executed using exclusively either the deterministic or the stochastic paradigm. As an example consider the model in [14]. Thus, a hybrid method that combines both discrete and continuous places as well as stochastic and continuous transitions is required [11]. S^4 provides the ability to execute such a model via the hybrid approach applying either static or dynamic partitioning [10,11]. In the former, place types (discrete/continuous) and transition types (stochastic/continuous) are explicitly specified by the modeller, while in the latter, place as well as transition types are changed on-the-fly during the simulation based on some dynamically determined measures (e.g., the current values of the transition rates).

Other Simulators. For more flexible functionality, S^4 allows advanced users to adopt external solvers to produce the model dynamics. This feature is specifically useful if legacy code exists that has been maintained and debugged over a long time.

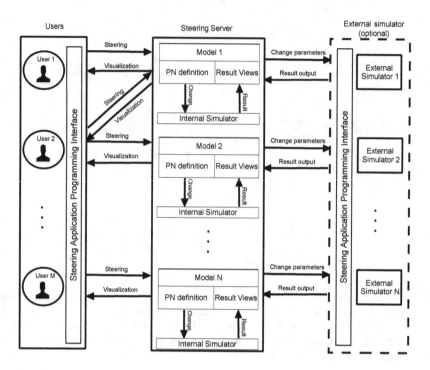

Fig. 3. The S^4 architecture. The core components are the models, which consist of the Petri net definition and the result views. Additionally, each model is associated with an internal simulator. S^4 can communicate with an external simulator or GUI client by an API library. Snoopy also adopts the API library to communicate with S^4.

3   Architecture

Figure 3 presents the different components of S^4. It consists of one or more models, internal simulators, and a set of clients. Moreover, S^4 can communicate with an external simulator as well as a GUI client through an API library. In the sequel, the different components of S^4 are briefly discussed.

3.1   Models

The basic building blocks inside S^4 are the models. Multiple models can reside in the server memory, and they can run simultaneously. When a new Petri net is submitted via the GUI or the API, a new model data structure is created. A model consists of two main components: the Petri net definition and the model result views.

The Petri net definition captures the main model components. It consists of all necessary information that are related to places, transitions, and arcs.

Result views are elegant tools to view the simulation results from different perspectives. They can be defined by a user and submitted to S^4 in order to be shared by other users connected to the same model. Each model can contain several, different views. Views are specified by selecting a set of places and/or transitions for which the progress shall to be monitored. Additional information, such as visualization methods and curve colours, can also be specified.

3.2 Internal Simulators

Each model is associated with an internal simulator to produce the model dynamics. Different simulators that are associated with different models can run simultaneously by creating an individual thread for each running simulation. The supported algorithms are sketched in Section 2.6.

3.3 Clients

S^4 stores the mandatory information about connected users in a special data structure called clients. Clients can be a GUI client or an external simulator. In the former, S^4 creates a separate thread and afterwards replies to the GUI requests, while in the latter it receives simulation results from a (probably remote) external simulator.

4 Typical Use Case

The main purpose of S^4 is to provide sophisticated user support to steer a running simulation. In general, it can be deployed for any application where a quantitative simulation of Petri nets is required. However, the particular application domain, for which S^4 has been developed, is systems and synthetic biology. As an example of models where monitoring and steering is important, we consider the modelling of circadian oscillation – a mechanism that is found in many organisms [5]. A $\mathcal{GHPN}$ model for this process is given in [11].

Figure 4 presents the final results of simulating this $\mathcal{GHPN}$ model using S^4. Without user intervention, the simulation will continue with the same values of the key parameters. However, using the computational steering capabilities of S^4, the user is able to change some key parameters while the simulation is in progress, e.g. to explore the parameter space, and the simulator will directly respond with the accordingly adjusted simulation results. Please refer to [10] and [13] for the detailed intermediate steering steps for this $\mathcal{GHPN}$ model.

5 Comparison

S^4 provides a number of dedicated functionalities that are not found in other software tools which utilize Petri nets for modelling and simulation. Thus, we compare S^4 with other tools that provide one or more similar functionalities. We use three tools for comparison purpose: CPN Assistant II, Cell Illustrator, and VCell. However, none of these tools does support the steering of key simulation parameters during model execution.

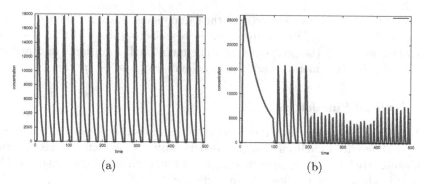

(a)   (b)

Fig. 4. Simulation results of the $\mathcal{GHPN}$ model for circadian oscillation. (a) The same key parameter values are used throughout the whole simulation time. (b) Different values are used during the running simulation, fed by the steering feature.

CPN Assistant II [16] is a simulation management tool for coloured Petri nets which were designed using CPN tools [2]. It supports users to prepare, run, and manage multiple simulations over a network. Although CPN Assistant II provides useful features to the users such as the execution of post-processing plug-ins, it does not enable them to collaborate with each other during the simulation. CPN tools do not explicitly support stochastic, continuous or hybrid Petri nets.

VCell [3] is a computational environment for modelling of cell biology. It is a distributed software tool where all models are stored on the server side. VCell permits users to collaborate in model construction, however, there is no collaboration supported during the simulation. VCell only supports the simulation of deterministic and stochastic models.

Another (commercialised) software that is known in the literature to model biological systems, is Cell Illustrator [19]. It is based on hybrid functional Petri nets [18]. Recently, Cell Illustrator has been extended to support the remote simulation of Petri net models. Nevertheless, it does not allow the adaptation of external simulators to execute model dynamics if the users are not satisfied with the simulator provided by the software. Furthermore, neither stochastic nor hybrid (deterministic – stochastic) simulation are offered.

6   Installation

S^4 is a platform-independent application. Installation packages for Windows, Mac OS, and some selected Linux distribution are available at http://www-dssz.informatik.tu-cottbus.de/snoopy.html. A complete documentation of the installation process as well as the hardware and software requirements are given in [12]. Moreover, a comprehensive user manual, quick start, and a product sheet can be found in [12]. Although the implementation of S^4 builds on several additional libraries (e.g., wxWidgets [4], BOOST [1], and SUNDIAL [15]), no additional dependencies are required in order to run it.

Acknowledgements. The authors would like to thank Christian Rohr for his valuable comments during the implementation of S^4. We would also like to acknowledge the work of Fei Liu for implementing coloured Petri nets in Snoopy.

References

1. Boost website, http://www.boost.org/ (accessed: January 14, 2014)
2. CPN tools website, http://cpntools.org/ (accessed: January 10, 2014)
3. Virtual cell website, http://vcell.org/ (accessed: January 10, 2014)
4. wxWidgets website, http://www.wxwidgets.org/ (accessed: January 15, 2014)
5. Barkai, N., Leibler, S.: Biological rhythms: circadian clocks limited by noise. Nature 403, 267–268 (2000)
6. Gao, Q., Gilbert, D., Heiner, M., Liu, F., Maccagnola, D., Tree, D.: Multiscale Modelling and Analysis of Planar Cell Polarity in the Drosophila Wing. IEEE/ACM Transactions on Computational Biology and Bioinformatics 10(2), 337–351 (2013)
7. Gilbert, D., Heiner, M.: From Petri nets to differential equations - an integrative approach for biochemical network analysis. In: Donatelli, S., Thiagarajan, P. (eds.) ICATPN 2006. LNCS, vol. 4024, pp. 181–200. Springer, Heidelberg (2006)
8. Gillespie, D.T.: Exact stochastic simulation of coupled chemical reactions. Journal of Physical Chemistry 81(25), 2340–2361 (1977)
9. Heiner, M., Herajy, M., Liu, F., Rohr, C., Schwarick, M.: Snoopy – A unifying Petri net tool. In: Haddad, S., Pomello, L. (eds.) PETRI NETS 2012. LNCS, vol. 7347, pp. 398–407. Springer, Heidelberg (2012)
10. Herajy, M.: Computational Steering of Multi-Scale Biochemical Networks. Ph.D. thesis, BTU Cottbus, Dep. of CS (January 2013)
11. Herajy, M., Heiner, M.: Hybrid representation and simulation of stiff biochemical networks. J. Nonlinear Analysis: Hybrid Systems 6(4), 942–959 (2012)
12. Herajy, M., Heiner, M.: Snoopy Computational Steering Framework – User Manual Version 1.0. Tech. Rep. 02-13, BTU Cottbus, Dept. of CS (July 2013)
13. Herajy, M., Heiner, M.: Petri net-based collaborative simulation and steering of biochemical reaction networks. Fundamenta Informatica (129), 49–67 (2014)
14. Herajy, M., Schwarick, M., Heiner, M.: Hybrid Petri Nets for Modelling the Eukaryotic Cell Cycle. In: Koutny, M., van der Aalst, W.M.P., Yakovlev, A. (eds.) ToPNoC VIII. LNCS, vol. 8100, pp. 123–141. Springer, Heidelberg (2013)
15. Hindmarsh, A., Brown, P., Grant, K., Lee, S., Serban, R., Shumaker, D., Woodward, C.: Sundials: Suite of nonlinear and differential/algebraic equation solvers. ACM Trans. Math. Softw. 31, 363–396 (2005)
16. Korečko, Š., Marcinčin, J., Slodičák, V.: CPN Assistant II: A tool for management of networked simulations. In: Haddad, S., Pomello, L. (eds.) PETRI NETS 2012. LNCS, vol. 7347, pp. 408–417. Springer, Heidelberg (2012)
17. Marwan, W., Rohr, C., Heiner, M.: Petri nets in Snoopy: A unifying framework for the graphical display, computational modelling, and simulation of bacterial regulatory networks. In: Methods in Molec. Biol., vol. 804, ch. 1, pp. 409–437 (2012)

18. Matsuno, H., Nagasaki, M., Miyano, S.: Hybrid Petri net based modeling for biological pathway simulation. Natural Computing 10(3), 1099–1120 (2011)
19. Nagasaki, M., Saito, A., Jeong, E., Li, C., Kojima, K., Ikeda, E., Miyano, S.: Cell Illustrator 4.0: a Computational Platform for Systems Biology. Silico Biology 10 (2010)
20. Rohr, C., Marwan, W., Heiner, M.: Snoopy - a unifying Petri net framework to investigate biomolecular networks. Bioinformatics 26(7), 974–975 (2010) (Advanced Access published February 7, 2010)

Kaira: Development Environment for MPI Applications

Stanislav Böhm, Marek Běhálek, Ondřej Meca, and Martin Šurkovský

Department of Computer Science
FEI VŠB Technical University of Ostrava
Ostrava, Czech Republic
{stanislav.bohm,marek.behalek,ondrej.meca,martin.surkovsky}@vsb.cz
http://verif.cs.vsb.cz/kaira/

Abstract. This tool paper presents Kaira (http://verif.cs.vsb.cz/kaira/) – a tool for simplifying development of parallel applications in the area of scientific and engineering computations for distributed memory systems. Our goal is to provide an environment in which a user can implement and experiment with his or her ideas in a short time; create a real running program; and verify its performance, scalability, and correctness. A unifying element in our approach is a visual programming language inspired by Colored Petri Nets that is used to define the parallel behavior, to show an inner state of a developed application back to the user, and for configurations of analyzes.

Keywords: MPI, C++, profiling, debugging, Coloured Petri Nets.

1 Introduction

This tool paper presents development environment Kaira. Our area of interest is programming of distributed memory applications for scientific and engineering computations. Our goal is to provide an environment in which a user can implement and experiment with his or her ideas in a short time; create a real running program; and verify its performance, scalability, and correctness. Kaira is an open source application and it is freely available at http://verif.cs.vsb.cz/kaira/. In this paper, we want to give an impression about what Kaira provides and how it can be used. The latest texts that explain features of Kaira more deeply are papers [1,2] and thesis [3].

2 Objectives

The industrial standard for programming applications in our area of interest is *Message Passing Interface* (MPI)[1]. Even though MPI is relatively simple to use, it represents a quite low-level interface. Hence development of applications directly in C++ with MPI can be laborious and time-consuming. Furthermore, the

---

[1] http://www.mpi-forum.org/

G. Ciardo and E. Kindler (Eds.): PETRI NETS 2014, LNCS 8489, pp. 385–394, 2014.
© Springer International Publishing Switzerland 2014

complexity of creating parallel applications lies also in other supportive activities like debugging and profiling. Even an experienced programmer of sequential applications can spend a lot of time learning a new set of complex tools. Therefore, for many non-experts in the area of parallel computing, it can be difficult to create, debug, and analyze their distributed applications.

The overall goal of our research is to reduce this complexity in programming of MPI applications. Our design goals are the following.

- *Prototyping* – The user should be able to create a working version of a developed application fast and in a form that allows experimenting, easy modifications, and performance evaluations.
- *Unification* – All activities during development should be controlled and presented in the same conceptual frame. Results from different analyzes should be easily comparable and reusable.
- *Real applications* – The primary output should be a real application that can be executed on a real parallel computer. The performance of the resulting application should be as close as possible to a manually created solution.
- *Integration* – Existing sequential codes should be easily reusable in the developed program. The integration should also work in the other way, i.e. the tool is able to create parallel libraries that can be called in any sequential application.

Hence for an experienced MPI programmer, our tool can serve as a prototyping tool with easily accessible features like profiling and performance analyzes. For a non-expert in this area, who just wants to occasionally use a supercomputer without a huge time investment, it represents a stand-alone development environment with a unified control over typical activities occurring during development.

3   Functionality

The key aspect of our tool is a usage of a visual program. In Kaira, the user specifies *communication* and *parallel aspects* in a visual way. However, the application is not completely programmed visually. Sequential parts of the developed application are written in C++ in a textual form and they are inserted into the visual program. The visual representation serves also as a natural unifying element for supportive activities – debugging, performance analysis, and verification. Kaira is developed as a stand-alone development environment and its functionality can be summarized as follows.

- *Program editing* – Kaira contains an editor for visual programs (Figure 1) together with a C++ editor that allows to edit codes in the visual program (Figure 2).
- *Program generating* – Kaira is able to generate a stand-alone MPI application from the visual program in fully automatic way. Such a generated program

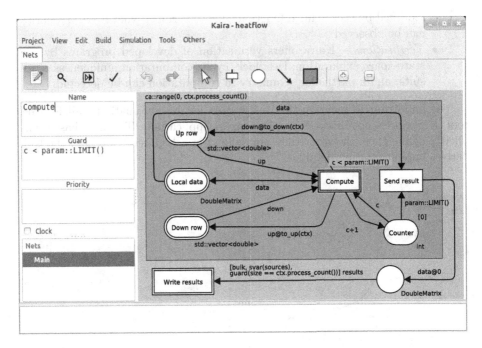

Fig. 1. A screenshot of a visual program (*heatflow* example from Kaira's distribution)

can be run directly on a cluster computer. For debugging purposes, multi-threaded and sequential versions of the application can be generated. Kaira also generates C++ libraries and modules for Octave[2].

– *Supportive activities* – Kaira provides the following basic features; their configurations and a presentation of results are unified through the visual representation of the program.

  • *Visual debugger* – It allows to control and show an inner state of an execution of the generated application in a simulated environment with an arbitrary number of processes. The state is shown in the similar way as "token game" in Petri nets tools, i.e. the inner state is shown in the form of labels over the original model (Figure 4).

  • *Tracing* – An application developed in Kaira can be generated in the tracing mode. Such application records its own run into a *tracelog*. When the application finishes its run, the tracelog can be loaded back into Kaira and used for the visual replay or for the graphical presentation of performance data.

  • *Online simulations* – Kaira provides performance predictions through online simulations with an analytical model of the communication layer. The communication model can be specified by a user-defined C++ function. Computation times of elements in the visual program can be also

---

[2] http://octave.org

modified by user-defined functions, hence various "what if ..." scenarios can be observed.

- *Verifications* – Kaira offers verification of developed programs by the state-space exploration. Deadlock, cyclic computation, uniqueness of results, and a particular symmetry in computation can be detected.

It is important to mention that our tool is *not* an automatic parallelization tool. Kaira does not discover parallelisms in applications. The user has to explicitly define them, however they are defined in a high-level way and the tool derives implementation details.

Fig. 2. Code editing in transition *Compute*

4   Architecture

The abstract computation model in Kaira is based on Coloured Petri Nets (CPNs) [4]. They naturally describe a distributed computation and also visually capture a distributed state of this computation. The implementation of the program visualization in Kaira is heavily inspired by CPN Tools[3]. Because of the specific needs of Kaira, we have modified and extended CPNs to be more suitable for parallel programming with MPI. In short, the most distinctive element is the usage of queues to store tokens instead of multisets. The detailed description of the visual language together with the formal definition of semantics can be found in [3].

As the language for sequential codes, C++ was chosen as one of major programming languages with a large variety of existing libraries.

Kaira itself is written in Python and C++. In the minimal installation it depends on $GTK+$[4] as the library for the graphical user interface, *Matplotlib*[5] for drawing charts and *GtkSourceView*[6] for the text-editing widget with syntax

---

[3] http://cpntools.org/

[4] http://www.gtk.org/

[5] http://matplotlib.org/

[6] https://projects.gnome.org/gtksourceview/

highlighting. The statespace analytical subsystem also depends on *sparsehash*[7] and *mhash*[8].

Kaira consists of three main parts:

- *Gui* – The most visible part from the user's perspective. It allows editing of nets and source codes, control of simulations, and showing of analyzes results.
- *PTP* (Project-To-Program) – It is the compiler that translates nets into a C++ code.
- *Libraries* – Kaira consists of six C++ libraries that are, if necessary, linked together with resulting programs.

5   Example of Usage

In this section, some Kaira's features will be demonstrated on example *Workers*. It solves a classic problem where a master node (process 0) divides jobs to working nodes (other processes). When a working node finishes an assigned job then it asks the master node for a new job. This process is repeated until all jobs are computed. In our example, a job is an interval of numbers and the task is to find prime numbers in this interval.

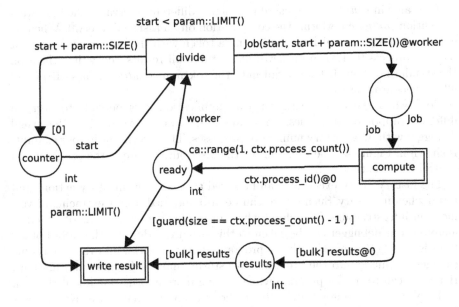

Fig. 3. The net for example *Workers*

To solve this problem in Kaira, the user captures the communication aspects and parallelization through the visual programing. The solution is depicted in

---

[7] http://code.google.com/p/sparsehash/
[8] http://mhash.sourceforge.net/

Figure 3. The basic notation is the same as for CPNs, hence circles (places) represent memory spaces and boxes (transitions) represent actions. Places have its types defined in lower right corner. In the upper right corner, there is an initial marking. This net is executed on each (MPI) process. The initial marking is evaluated only in the first process (process 0). The double bordered transition contains a C++ code that is executed whenever the transition is fired. An enriched C++ is used as an inscription language on arcs. The expression in the form `expr@target` means that created tokens (by evaluating `expr`) are sent to another process determined by evaluating `target`. It allows communication between (MPI) processes. The net has two parameters: LIMIT and SIZE. They are constants whose values are determined at the beginning of the program execution. The master node assigns intervals from 0 to LIMIT-1. The attribute SIZE defines the size of intervals assigned to workers. For the sake of simplicity, it is assumed that SIZE divides LIMIT. More information about the used notation can be found in [3].

Place *ready* holds process identifications (ranks) of idling workers; it is initialized by process ranks except 0. Place *counter* keeps a start of a next assigned interval. Transition *divide* takes a value from place *counter* (variable `start`) and a rank of an idling process (variable `worker`) and it sends a new interval to the worker.

The value in *counter* is increased to assign a different interval in the next step. Transition *compute* performs the computation on an assigned interval. When an execution of a job is finished, results and a token with the process rank are sent back to process 0. Transition *write result* takes all results and writes them on the standard output. It has to wait until the token in *counter* reaches LIMIT and all workers are ready.

Now, when the user creates such an application it is possible to perform different supportive activities. For example, it can be executed in the visual debugger with an arbitrary number of processes. The screenshot for our example is shown in Figure 4. The user can see the distributed state of the program and control its execution.

The history of the execution can be saved as a list of elementary actions and rerun when necessary. Such record can be also obtained from the tracing or verification infrastructure. Therefore, when an interesting situation is observed in analyzes, our debugger can be taken to this situation. Because the record of actions is loosely connected with the program, it remains relevant even when some changes are made into the program (like storing more debugging information). Hence we can rerun the program while gaining more information about the run.

To obtain more information about the run on real hardware, Kaira offers tracing features. For example in our case, we want to observe the behavior of transition *Compute*. The configuration is done through placing a label into the visual program (Figure 5). Additionally, traced data in the case of places can be specified by C++ functions. Various statistics from program trace can be obtained or simply exported for processing in other tools. The tracelog can be also replayed in the visual debugger.

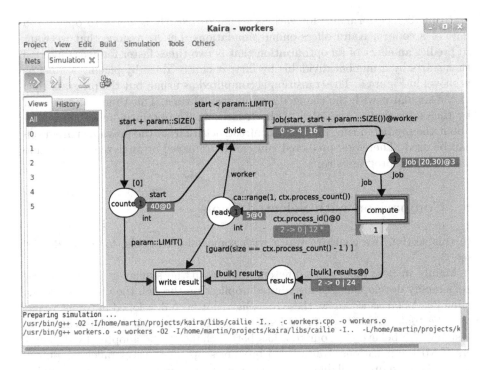

Fig. 4. A screenshot of a simulation of the program from Figure 3

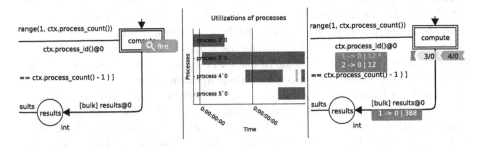

Fig. 5. Profiling in Kaira. Figures show a configuration what to measure, an utilization chart obtained from a tracelog, and a replay of a tracelog

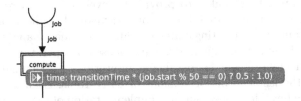

Fig. 6. A configuration for the online simulator

To predict performance for various scenarios like "It is worth to optimize a part of a code?", Kaira offers online simulations. Let us assume that we want to predict an effect of an optimization that is two times faster for every interval that starts by a number dividable by fifty. It can be done by placing a label as is shown in Figure 6. The transition is computed as usual, but the program runs in the simulator with the changed computational time. This time is determined by the expression in the label of the transition. To obtain more detailed data about the predicted run, the tracing infrastructure from the previous paragraph can be used. Therefore, predicted run can be replayed or analyzed in the same way as a real program's run.

6   Comparison with Selected Tools

In this section, we compare Kaira with some selected tools, for more details see [3].

Mainly in 90s, there were different tools with the similar goals like Kaira, i.e. simplify development of distributed application through the visual programming [5]. As far as we know, these tools have not been developed in recent years, and the tools themselves are no longer available or run on obsolete computer systems. We believe that our tool has better chance to be adopted by developers of MPI applications. Kaira has a broader scope and also parallel computers have become more available; therefore, more non-experts have the opportunity to create programs for them.

Because CPN Tools was a great inspiration for us, it is natural to compare it with Kaira. The fundamental differences that distinguish these two tools emerge from their different main goals. CPN Tools is a generic modeling tool; hence a large collection of problems that exceeds the scope of Kaira can be modeled and analyzed. But it would be difficult to use CPN Tools as a development environment, because it cannot create a stand-alone application or collect performance characteristics from a running application. Furthermore, where Kaira uses C++, CPN Tools uses Standard ML, hence an integration with many existing libraries would be more complicated. There is a possibility to combine CPN Tools with C/C++, but if we want to use CPN Tools similarly as we use Kaira, we would need to manually maintain two different versions of a developed program: an actual implementation for executions on real hardware and a second version for analysis. Furthermore, the user would have to make sure that these versions do the same thing. Our goal is to provide a development environment where analytical features are executed directly on a developed application.

Also, we did not reuse existing statespace and performance analytical features from CPN Tools. One reason is that we are focused on operating system Linux; it is the major environment for parallel computations. Unfortunately, it is not supported in the last two major versions of CPN Tools. Even more important reason, why we have developed our own implementation of these features, is that we plan to parallelize these features in the environment of distributed memory systems in the future. Our users should naturally have access to a computer with such architecture; therefore it can be utilized not only for the computation itself but also for analytical purposes. We are not aware of any tool that could be used in Kaira and simultaneously runs in MPI environment.

The usage of queues connects Kaira with stream programming [6]. Kaira is a more low-level tool than stream programming environments; Kaira uses a simple and explicit mapping of computations to MPI processes, in contrast to the sophisticated algorithms for scheduling and mapping of computations in stream environments. The approach that Kaira offers is less automatic and gives the user more control of resulting programs. This is important if we want to experiment with different kinds of algorithms.

From the perspective of MPI applications, there are many supportive tools. They are generic tools that can be used with any program and are often more mature and optimized in comparison to our implementation. But they are usually single-purpose tools with different terms, configurations, and ways of displaying results. In Kaira, we try to roof all activities by the semantics of Kaira and unified their usage under a single concept through the visual language.

As examples of such tools, we can name TotalView[9], Distributed Debugging Tool[10] as debuggers; Scalasca [7], TAU [8] as tracers; SimGrid [9] as a tool for performance prediction with online simulations; MPI-Spin [10] and ISP [11] as formal verification tools.

7 Installation

Kaira is an open-source software released under GPL[11]. It is freely available at http://verif.cs.vsb.cz/kaira/. To run it, the user needs Linux and several libraries that are commonly available in any Linux distribution. The install instructions are described at http://verif.cs.vsb.cz/kaira/docs/userguide. html.

8 Conclusion

This paper briefly introduces tool Kaira and its features after three years of development. In the current phase of the development, when version 1.0 was released, we want to promote our tool. Currently, our tool is not widely used. It is freely available, but we are not aware of other users beside people that are involved in Kaira development. Still, everything described in this paper is ready to use. We have verified ideas and functionality on various examples together with experimenting with resulting applications on Anselm – the supercomputer owned by IT4Innovations Center of Excellence[12].

---

[9] http://www.roguewave.com/
[10] http://www.allinea.com/products/ddt/
[11] http://www.gnu.org/licenses/gpl.html
[12] http://www.it4i.cz/

Acknowledgments. The work is partially supported by: GAČR P202/11/0340 and the European Regional Development Fund in the IT4Innovations Center of Excellence project (CZ.1.05/1.1.00/02.0070).

References

1. Böhm, S., Běhálek, M.: Usage of Petri nets for high performance computing. In: Proceedings of the 1st ACM SIGPLAN Workshop on Functional High-Performance Computing, FHPC 2012, pp. 37–48. ACM, New York (2012)
2. Böhm, S., Běhálek, M., Meca, O., Šurkovský, M.: Visual programming of MPI applications: Debugging and performance analysis. In: The 4th Workshop on Advances in Programming Language, WAPL (2013)
3. Böhm, S.: Unifying Framework for Development of Message-Passing Applications. PhD thesis, FEI VŠB-TUO Ostrava, 17. listopadu 15, Ostrava (November 2013), http://verif.cs.vsb.cz/sb/thesis.pdf
4. Jensen, K., Kristensen, L.M.: Coloured Petri Nets - Modelling and Validation of Concurrent Systems. Springer (2009)
5. Browne, J.C., Dongarra, J., Hyder, S.I., Moore, K., Newton, P.: Visual programming and parallel computing. Technical report, Knoxville, TN, USA (1994)
6. Stephens, R.: A survey of stream processing. Acta Informatica 34(7) (1997)
7. Geimer, M., Wolf, F., Wylie, B.J.N., Mohr, B.: A scalable tool architecture for diagnosing wait states in massively parallel applications. Parallel Comput. 35(7), 375–388 (2009)
8. Shende, S.S., Malony, A.D.: The TAU parallel performance system. Int. J. High Perform. Comput. Appl. 20(2), 287–311 (2006)
9. Casanova, H., Legrand, A., Quinson, M.: Simgrid: A generic framework for large-scale distributed experiments. In: Proceedings of the Tenth International Conference on Computer Modeling and Simulation, UKSIM 2008, pp. 126–131. IEEE Computer Society, Washington, DC (2008)
10. Siegel, S.F., Avrunin, G.S.: Verification of halting properties for MPI programs using nonblocking operations. In: Cappello, F., Herault, T., Dongarra, J. (eds.) PVM/MPI 2007. LNCS, vol. 4757, pp. 326–334. Springer, Heidelberg (2007)
11. Vakkalanka, S.S., Sharma, S., Gopalakrishnan, G., Kirby, R.M.: ISP: a tool for model checking MPI programs. In: Proceedings of the 13th ACM SIGPLAN Symposium on Principles and Practice of Parallel Programming, PPoPP 2008, pp. 285–286. ACM, New York (2008)

Erratum to: Complex Networks and Link Streams for the Empirical Analysis of Large Software

Matthieu Latapy[1,2] and Tiphaine Viard[1,2]

[1] Sorbonne Universités, UPMC Univ Paris 06, UMR 7606, LIP6, Paris, France
[2] CNRS, UMR 7606, LIP6, Paris, France
`FirstName.LastName@lip6.fr`

Erratum to:
Chapter 3 in: Gianfranco Ciardo Ekkart Kindler (Eds.)
Application and Theory of Petri Nets and Concurrency,
DOI: 10.1007/978-3-319-07734-5_3

The author list of this paper has been updated due to a name change.

The updated original online version for this chapter can be found at
10.1007/978-3-319-07734-5_3

G. Ciardo and E. Kindler (Eds.): PETRI NETS 2014, LNCS 8489, pp. E1, 2016.
© Springer International Publishing Switzerland 2016
DOI: 10.1007/978-3-319-07734-5_23

Author Index

Printed in the United States
By Bookmasters